TAMOTSU SHIBUTANI

Society
and
Personality

AN INTERACTIONIST APPROACH
TO SOCIAL PSYCHOLOGY

PRENTICE-HALL, INC
Englewood Cliffs, *N.J.*

this
book
is
for
Tomi

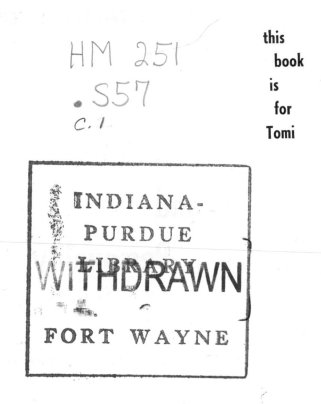

Current printing (last digit):
17 16 15 14 13 12 11 10 9

Library of Congress Catalog Card No.: 61–9218

Printed in the United States of America
82001-C

Preface

The serious study of
human nature reaches back into antiquity. Discussions of art, history,
literature, and philosophy almost invariably lead to certain basic
issues, the recurrent problems that confront men in their efforts to
get along with one another. How satisfying is success won at the
cost of personal integrity? Is brutality used in the attainment of
noble ends self-defeating? Which values bring men their most lasting gratifications? There are as yet no definitive answers to such
questions, and this has aroused considerable dissatisfaction in some
quarters. Perhaps impatience with the slow and inexact route of the
humanities accounts for the increasing interest in the scientific study
of human behavior.

The subject matter of social psychology is much like that of the
humanities, but its methods are more like those of the physical and
biological sciences. But the discipline is young, and the development
of demonstrated knowledge is still only a fond hope. The fact that
social psychologists have thus far failed to solve some of the oldest
problems confronting mankind should not discourage us from continuing the quest, however, for there is nothing inherent in human
conduct that renders it unsuitable for scientific study. Furthermore,
demonstrated knowledge does not develop in a vacuum; it evolves
gradually during a long period of exploration and speculation. It is
hoped that this book may play a part in the recruitment of more
explorers for the charting of this fascinating and important frontier.

In spite of the short history of the field, the research literature has
become so extensive that it is now impossible for any single person
to claim mastery of all of it. During the past fifty years thousands of
investigations—clinical, descriptive, and experimental—have been
carried out, and countless facts have been recorded about the typical
things men do under given circumstances. Since facts become significant only insofar as they are relevant to general principles, they
have been presented in connection with a set of interrelated gen-

eralizations. No attempt has been made to include a sample of all
the topics studied by those who call themselves social psychologists; materials have been selected on the basis of a theory of human
behavior. It is hoped that some kind of provisional order can thereby
be introduced into what may otherwise remain fragmentary and
unrelated.

In the development of this point of view I have drawn heavily
upon two great intellectual traditions: *pragmatism* and *psychoanalysis*. Of the pragmatists I am most indebted to John Dewey,
George H. Mead, Robert E. Park, and Edward Sapir; of the psychoanalysts, to Sigmund Freud, Karen Horney, and Harry S. Sullivan.
In spite of their apparent differences, these writers worked with a
remarkably consistent set of presuppositions. Since both schools
have been handicapped considerably by their extensive jargons, a
somewhat simplified vocabulary has been substituted. Terms such
as "libido," "significant symbol," "social act," and "superego" do not
appear in this book. In the quest for a common denominator each
concept has been defined behavioristically—in terms of the type of
activity, overt or covert, being designated. There are, of course,
several other prominent approaches to contemporary social psychology, each with many noteworthy contributions. Where relevant,
materials have been drawn from these sources, and alternative interpretations of data have been cited in footnotes and in many of
the recommended readings.

In a volume designed to introduce readers to a field of inquiry it
would be desirable to adhere to the accepted canons of science and
to limit coverage to theorems that are well established. To do this in
social psychology, however, would leave very little to discuss. Since
propositions are difficult to test unless they are formulated explicitly,
however, many generalizations have been stated in a form more
definite than is warranted by the evidence. Available data have
been introduced wherever relevant, but all too often the evidence is
inconclusive. Many of the studies cited are only illustrative, even
when they are experimental in design. Some of them are technically
defective, but they constitute the best materials on hand. It cannot
be emphasized too strongly, therefore, that the orientation presented
in this book is highly tentative.

There has been some controversy among social psychologists over
the proper training of future specialists in the field. Some advocate

training in mathematics and physics; others insist upon the study of biology; still others call for exposure to the humanities. Whatever else social psychologists must know, it appears obvious that the effective study of human behavior requires some familiarity with the intimate details of the lives of a variety of people. But many students have been so well protected that they know little of what goes on outside of middle class communities. One economical way of overcoming this handicap is the extensive reading of first person documents—autobiographies, letters, diaries, and the clinical records of psychiatrists. A short list of published documents, most of them readily available in college libraries, has been appended for this purpose. The items vary considerably in literary merit, but each provides a valuable record of human experience and throws light on at least one of the central problems taken up in the text.

In the course of writing this book I have become indebted to many people. My thinking has been influenced most by four sociologists with whom I have had the privilege of studying—Herbert Blumer, Everett C. Hughes, William I. Thomas, and Louis Wirth. Anyone who is familiar with their views will recognize at once the extent of my debt to them. All books are improved immeasurably by the work of conscientious editors, and I wish to thank Anselm Strauss and Guy E. Swanson for their careful and critical reading of the manuscript and Darrell Husted for his countless suggestions on style. Elaine MacDonald prepared the index, and Doris Kihara typed successive drafts of the manuscript. Most of all, I wish to acknowledge the sympathetic support of my wife; without it, this project could not have been completed at this time.

Contents

CONCLUSION

Introduction

1

The
systematic
study
of
human
behavior

During the latter part of the nineteenth century, extensive studies were carried out on the therapeutic uses of hypnotism. Many amazing feats were demonstrated for the scholars attracted to the two rival centers which developed in France, one in Paris under the famed psychiatrist Janet and the other in Nancy under Bernheim. On one occasion Dr. Bernheim instructed a subject that *after* he had been awakened from his hypnotic trance he would take the umbrella of a colleague, open it, and walk twice up and down the veranda to which the room opened. When awakened, the man picked up the umbrella as instructed. Although he did not open it, he did walk twice up and down the corridor. When asked to account for his peculiar conduct, he replied that he was "taking the air." Asked if he felt warm, he answered that he did not; however, he insisted that he made a prac-

3

tice of occasionally walking up and down "out here." When questioned about having an umbrella in his possession belonging to someone else, he was quite surprised. He had thought it was his own, and he hastily returned it to the rack.

To specialists the facts of post-hypnotic suggestion had been well known for a long time, but to a young Viennese physician named Sigmund Freud, who had witnessed such demonstrations during a visit to Nancy in 1899 and had translated two of Bernheim's books into German, this remarkable phenomenon provided the basis for a revolutionary insight. What struck Freud was the fact that a man could do things for reasons of which he himself was unaware, and having performed the deeds he could subsequently invent plausible explanations. When the man with the umbrella was questioned about his strange conduct, he attempted to justify what he was doing by providing respectable reasons. This was not deliberate deception, for he was a person of unquestioned integrity and was speaking in complete sincerity. In much the same manner other people are continually giving reasons for the things they do. When a student is asked why he is attending school, for example, he replies that he wants to broaden his intellectual horizons, to please his parents, to qualify for some desirable position, to maintain prestige in his community, or to be near his fiancee. Actually, there is considerable evidence that many students are not quite sure what they are doing in school. Although it had long been recognized that the explanations people give for their activities are not always reliable, Freud made this observation one of the cornerstones of a systematic theory of human behavior.

Men are continually trying to develop a better understanding of themselves and of their fellows by providing explanations for the things that they do, and social psychologists are only trying to construct tools that will permit the formulation of more reliable explanations. Like Freud, they are looking for a more impersonal way of accounting for human behavior, preferably one that is in line with the accepted canons of modern science. Their aim is to reduce the diverse things that men do to a limited set of *general principles*, principles that will account even for the fact that men continually explain their deeds—to themselves as well as to others. Furthermore, they seek maximum reliability by introducing greater precision into their formulations and by testing them through an examination of *evidence*—empirical data that have been collected in an orderly manner. The subject matter of social psychology is very old, but the procedures currently in use have only recently been instituted.

Scientific Knowledge and Common Sense

Although the fascination with which children behold the world apparently loses its edge with age, most people retain some measure of curiosity, and the quest for knowledge is one of mankind's stable interests. While we sometimes think of knowledge as something esoteric, the exigencies of daily life require our having some kind of working conception of what is happening in order to make intelligent decisions, to avoid unnecessary discomfort, and to attain all kinds of gratifications with minimal effort. Because of his specialized knowledge, a mechanic on vacation can drive his automobile over isolated areas without suffering the anxieties that plague the average motorist. The difference between the service rendered by a doctor who happens to be at the scene of an accident and the inept though well meaning efforts of other passers-by is one of knowledge. The effective pursuit of one's interests as well as the planning of a better life requires knowing something about the world and the creatures inhabiting it. Knowledge, then, is not something separate and standing by itself—only to be contemplated in intellectual exercises. It is intricately involved in the processes through which human life is sustained.

Most of the beliefs providing the basis for daily living consist of what is called "common sense." This term refers to our working conception of reality—the characteristics of various physical objects, of expected sequences of events, and of the traits called "human nature." A sensible person knows that he will not be greeted on the street by a dead man whose funeral he has just attended; he knows that men cannot walk through stone walls; and he would be quite shaken if the different parts of a friend's face became detached and rearranged. Although people who are psychotic may have such experiences, it is taken for granted that such events are impossible in the "real" world. Many popular beliefs have developed through countless experiences over many generations, and they survive because they are found useful in meeting the requirements of daily life. From day to day we are confronted by the necessity of making a variety of decisions, and for this most of us must depend a great deal upon common sense knowledge—even though it is usually inexact and sometimes completely groundless. For example, medical men have long known that leprosy is not nearly as contagious as tuberculosis or syphilis, but those who are unfamiliar with the scientific appraisal of the disease still dread and ostracize lepers.

Because of its fabulous achievements, men in our age tend to look upon science in awe; yet the difference between common sense and scientific knowledge is only one of degree. Scientific knowledge enjoys the great prestige that it does today precisely because it provides such highly effective instruments for adjustment. The development of the theory of microbes, for example, has made mandatory the institution of specific measures to insure antiseptic cleanliness, especially in surgery. In spite of the high death rate such procedures had previously been resisted by most doctors as unnecessary and wasteful; until such knowledge was established, the complications following surgery could not be traced to the unseen agents of infection. The more accurate the explanations, then, the more useful they are in forming judgments and in planning programs of action. Scientific knowledge represents a codification of the best that men have thus far been able to achieve, explicitly stated and tested through empirical evidence. But it is far from perfect and is subject to constant revision; indeed, progressively more reliable knowledge is continually developing. Scientific research may be regarded as a type of activity that has evolved gradually in the efforts of men to find more effective ways of coping with their difficulties.

Of course, many of the regularities in nature have been recognized intuitively long before scientists got around to formulating their principles. Cheese and wine were being made and meat and fish were being preserved through smoking before bacteriologists and chemists were able to explain the process. Soap was invented before the theory of ions, and the selective breeding of domesticated animals took place long before Mendel formulated his laws of genetics. Many other practical problems have been solved before men understood what they were doing. The demand for scientific knowledge, however, often arises in those areas in which common sense proves inadequate, as men attempt to improve upon practices hitherto resting upon popular beliefs.

Men have apparently always been curious about human behavior. This is not strange: the solution of some of the most mundane problems of daily life requires our knowing something about human beings. One is called upon to choose friends, to select a mate, to make decisions about a career, or to pass judgment upon an acquaintance who has violated a rule. Uneasiness in the presence of strangers arises from uncertainty. Men cannot act with confidence unless they can anticipate, within reasonable limits, what others are likely to do. One cannot even walk across a street without faith that the driver of an approaching automobile is not doing his best to strike down pedestrians.

Successful participation in society also requires a minimum understanding of oneself. Some may feel that they lack sufficient ability to do their work effectively. Others may feel guilty about hating their parents, their inability to control their tempers, or their excessive preoccupation with sex. Still others may be disturbed about their compulsive eating, smoking, masturbation, or daydreaming.

In handling such difficulties men generally rely upon popular beliefs. But common sense is sometimes wise and sometimes stupid, for no distinction is made between the accumulated wisdom of the ages and the current and local superstitions. Many Americans are convinced, for example, that beauty, charm, wealth, and an abundance of handsome suitors will make any young woman happy; yet successful actresses and heiresses with all these treasures are known to have committed suicide, insisting that they had "nothing to live for." Many parents believe that the happiness and success of their children depend upon their acquiring a home in a "nice" neighborhood, providing a separate room for each well stocked with toys, getting the best available medical care, and participating in various community activities. In spite of the sacrifices that are made in their behalf, however, the recipients of such "advantages" sometimes become criminals or are driven to insanity. Furthermore, many popular beliefs are contradictory. Francis Bacon once collected a number of generalizations about human behavior from fables, proverbs, and maxims and was able to find an antithesis for each one.

Thus, it is often claimed that "absence makes the heart grow fonder." This is plausible, but so is the contention: "out of sight; out of mind." These observations all suggest that something better than common sense is required.

Social scientists are finding themselves under increasing pressure to provide knowledge that is more reliable. The pressure is intensified by the fact that we are beset with practical problems of great magnitude. The incidence of mental disorders is frightening. With the increasing concentration of political power, the success of a single lunatic could conceivably spell ruin for millions. Advancing knowledge in the physical sciences has made war so destructive that for the first time in human history the extermination of the species has become a distinct possibility. The need for reliable knowledge about human behavior is now felt to be more urgent than ever, and in an age in which science is idolized it is not strange that men are in increasing numbers turning hopefully toward the application of the procedures that have proved so successful in other fields to the study of man. Although it may not be entirely justified by the results achieved thus far, there seems to be an increasing faith in the ability of social scientists to provide answers that constitute an improvement over common sense.

The efforts of students of human behavior to emulate the better established disciplines have had both desirable and misleading results. Problems have been selected with greater care, and there has been more precision in the formulation and testing of hypotheses. With increasing recognition of the importance of empirical verification far more emphasis has been placed upon the orderly collection and analysis of data. Serious efforts are being made to design experiments, however crude the initial results may be.

Unfortunately, however, there has also been a blind imitation of the external paraphernalia of the successful sciences, which in some instances may be hindering the development of verified knowledge. Unable to resist the lure of a technical vocabulary, social scientists have developed a forbidding jargon. Sometimes the specialized terms are essential for making distinctions not ordinarily made in popular discourse, but many of the terms are only synonyms for words in daily use. Impressed with the elaborate procedures used in other fields, social scientists have also developed complex techniques for indirect observation and measurement. In some cases these ingenious devices have facilitated the study of subject matter which had hitherto been difficult to observe, but all too often they have been used to investigate insignificant problems, resulting sometimes in an incredible expenditure of effort to confirm some trivial point. The most unfortunate consequence of concentrating so much attention upon technical elegance has been the limitation of inquiries to problems easily studied by the approved research techniques. Some have even refused to study admittedly important problems on the ground that procedures do not exist for the precise measurement of relevant data. As one critic has observed, the preoccupation with perfecting technical apparatus is much like concentrating all one's efforts upon polishing his glasses rather than putting them on in order to see.[1]

Unfortunately, merely copying the superficial characteristics of the older sciences does not automatically provide reliable knowledge. Some students of human behavior proclaim loudly that they are "scientists" and insist upon being accorded the privileges and respect commensurate with such a designation. But such claims appear to be premature. What is reliably known about human behavior is still elementary, and most generalizations have not yet been subjected to crucial tests. Even the best experimental evidence is crude, showing only gross relationships between loosely defined variables. Where clinical or observational data are used, there is usually no assurance of the representativeness of the sample being examined. There are many areas of human activity about which plausible hypotheses have not been formulated so that even educated guesses are lacking. In spite of extravagant claims from some quarters, there are as yet very few verified generalizations about human behavior.

The fact that the scientific study of human conduct is still in its infancy becomes painfully apparent when any effort is made to apply the generalizations currently entertained by social scientists to concrete problems. Child rearing practices based upon diverse theories of socialization provide an excellent illustration. Parents who believe in learning theory, with its emphasis upon reward and punishment, sometimes discipline their children sternly to prevent the formation of undesirable habits. On the other hand, those who

[1] Abraham H. Maslow, *Motivation and Personality* (New York: Harper & Bros., 1954), pp. 13–21. Cf. Franklin P. Kilpatrick, ed., *Human Behavior from the Transactional Point of View* (Hanover: Institute for Associated Research, 1952), pp. 195–212.

have accepted psychoanalytic theory emphasize the importance of breast feeding, lenient toilet training, and a permissive atmosphere in which frustration is minimized. There are indications, however, that neurotic parents frequently have neurotic children, regardless of what procedures they utilize. Another example is provided by the care of the mentally ill. In spite of the dedicated efforts of countless specialists in developing various techniques of chemical, surgical, and persuasive intervention, there is little evidence that patients actually recover from psychosis through such therapy. Indeed, there are an embarrassing number who apparently recover "spontaneously" without benefit of any systematically administered treatment. Those who must handle behavioral problems—like social workers, parole officers, teachers, administrators, and psychiatrists—find that they must often resort to "rule of thumb" judgments and do the best they can. Of course, they get some help from the books they read. In contrast to the knowledge furnished by physiologists to surgeons, however, much of what social scientists provide them proves to be too remote from the living creatures with whom they deal.

The systematic study of human behavior, at present, is in some respects much like mathematics before Euclid. There was certainly considerable mathematical knowledge at that time, as is revealed in the astonishing feats of Egyptian engineers in building the pyramids. But geometry consisted of a collection of isolated facts, useful empirical rules for surveying and construction. By introducing precision into definitions, relating the terms into propositions, and deducing propositions from one another, Euclid transformed this existing information into a systematic body of knowledge. Similarly, there is today much accumulated knowledge about human behavior, but it has not yet been adequately systematized.

To admit that the social sciences are not yet comparable to the better established fields certainly is not to imply that they are useless. From day to day pressing problems arise from the inability of men to get along with one another, and we cannot afford to declare a moratorium upon efforts at solution. Men must act on the basis of the best knowledge available, and some programs of action will of necessity take on a hit-or-miss character. By virtue of the fact that social scientists are specialists who focus their attention upon observing and reflecting upon human behavior, many of their judgments may prove more useful than those of laymen. Once the limitations of a young discipline are acknowledged and accepted, it can be of value. There is every reason to believe that social scientists will develop explanations that will successively replace popular beliefs and render comprehensible more and more sectors of human life.

All fields of inquiry have started with seemingly unpromising beginnings. The growth of scientific knowledge has been a cumulative movement, starting with common sense and becoming more reliable with the progressive elimination of errors. The pioneering efforts in any field of inquiry are bound to appear amateurish, for the investigator often starts with the language of daily discourse, asks ordinary questions, and comes out with answers that sound reasonable even to the untrained layman. The early discoveries in any discipline appear so obvious that some may wonder whether the study was worthwhile, but subsequent workers, building on the efforts of the pioneers, are able to produce knowledge that is less obvious and eventually move on to matters that could never have been guessed from a common sense outlook. At first the generalizations are inexact, but with successive improvements they become more reliable. In one field after another folklore has been displaced by scientific knowledge, and in the study of human behavior the movement is only now getting under way.

The Development of Social Psychology

Social psychology is but one of several disciplines specializing in the study of human behavior. It is not yet firmly established as a separate field of inquiry; in many universities, courses in this area have been the center of jurisdictional disputes between different departments. Much of the difficulty arises from the fact that the boundaries of the field are not clearly defined. While those who conceive of themselves as social psychologists generally show an interest in a more or less similar subject matter, there are many disagreements as to how these topics are to be studied. A perusal of the literature gives one the impression that there are almost as many conceptions of the field as there are social psychologists.

As is frequently the case during the early history of any field, there are several competing schools of thought, and the literature is filled with polemics. Among the dominant points of view are Gestalt psychology, learning theory, psychoanalysis, and the interactionist approach (sometimes referred to as "self theory" or as "role theory"); and each of these orientations is further subdivided into several branches. This diversity of outlook can be traced in part to the unusual history of the field. Social psychology is a discipline that is just now being shaped from the convergence of interests on the part of scholars trained in a variety of intellectual traditions—among them, anthropology, psychiatry, psychology, and sociology. Since those whose perspectives differ often arrive at dissimilar conclusions even when examining the same data, it is not surprising that these men have had so much difficulty in understanding one another. All too often those in each school, convinced of the correctness of its position, have tended to look upon the others as misguided souls who, if fortunate, might eventually see the light.

Psychologists have traditionally studied the uniformities in individual behavior. Theoretically this could include everything that men do, but interest has actually centered upon the study of perception, memory and thinking, learning, and personality development. Toward the latter part of the nineteenth century there was some interest in the problem of how individuals participating in groups affect one another's behavior, and studies of crowd phenomena, hypnotism, and suggestibility attracted considerable attention. But most psychologists retained a strong individualistic bias, viewing the human body as their basic unit of analysis. They argued that even when men are participating in groups, what they feel, think, and do can still be explained in terms of the principles of individual behavior. Some even went so far as to contend that groups really do not exist, that they consist of nothing more than a gathering of individuals. Although William McDougall's *Introduction to Social Psychology* was published as early as 1908, until quite recently the social context has been ignored by most psychologists.

In spite of the efforts of pioneers like Floyd Allport, F. C. Bartlett, Kurt Lewin, and Walther Moede to develop an experimental approach to social psychology, there was considerable skepticism until findings began to accumulate that could not be explained adequately in terms of what is presumably encapsuled within the skin. Sherif's study of autokinetic effect attracted considerable attention. In complete darkness a small, stationary light appears to move; it may seem to be in different places each time one looks at it, especially if he does not know the distance between himself and the source. The light cannot be localized because there is no point of reference in a dark room. In an experiment on perception under such circumstances subjects were asked to estimate the direction in which the light moved and the distance. When the subjects were performing alone, there was a tendency for each individual to set his own standard of judgment. But when the same persons observed the light in one another's company, the judgments tended to converge; those making their observations together tended to agree on direction and distance. Actually the light was always stationary. What this experiment revealed, then, was that what men perceive is not a direct copy of what is "out there" and that under some circumstances what is seen is strongly influenced by the reports of other people.[2]

A number of other studies have demonstrated further the extent to which the various perceptual and cognitive processes depend upon the behavior of other people, and in increasing numbers psychologists have been turning toward a more systematic consideration of the group affiliations of their subjects. In spite of the enthusiasm of many psychologists, however, this tendency has by no means won unanimous support. There are still some who express serious misgivings over the new interests of their colleagues.[3]

Sociologists have traditionally studied the regularities in the formation, maintenance, and dissolution of groups. Almost from the very beginning they have regarded social psychology as an integral part of their subject matter. Many of the pioneers—like Emile Durkheim, Georg Simmel, Gabriel Tarde, and Max Weber—conceived of groups as consisting of the interaction of human beings with one another. Hence, they could hardly avoid becoming concerned with the individual participants whose behavior made up the patterns of interaction that they were describing.

In the United States the development of social psychology among sociologists was a part of a more inclusive intellectual movement in

[2] Muzafer Sherif, "A Study of Some Social Factors in Perception," *Archives of Psychology*, XXVII (1935), no. 187.

[3] Cf. Gordon W. Allport, "The Historical Background of Modern Social Psychology," *Handbook of Social Psychology*, Gardner Lindzey, ed. (Cambridge: Addison-Wesley Publishing Co., 1954), Vol. I, pp. 3–56; and John Gillen, ed., *For a Science of Social Man* (New York: The Macmillan Co., 1954), pp. 160–256.

which some of the implications of Darwin's theory of evolution were amplified. Pragmatists like John Dewey, William James, George Mead, and Charles Peirce tried to work out a new way of looking at man and society. Instead of the study of substance, they emphasized the primacy of activity; rather than searching for the substances of which the human mind is composed, they looked upon perception and cognition as types of behavior. Instead of preoccupying themselves with the study of stable forms, they directed attention to the regular ways in which changes occur—genesis and development. They moved away from the analysis of the structure of persons and of social institutions to the analysis of processes—a study of *how things work* as living organisms, individually and collectively, come to terms with life conditions.[4] Social psychology assumed such great importance for a philosopher like Mead because he believed that the distinctive characteristics of man—the ability to think in abstractions, to form perceptual objects of themselves, and to engage in purposive and moral conduct—evolved as the human species adapted to the exigencies of living in groups. Thus, social psychology received an impetus from the efforts of a group of philosophers to pursue more comprehensive interests.

Considering the intellectual climate in which the field developed, it is not surprising that many of the early American sociologists were more receptive than the psychologists to studies of suggestibility. The social group was seen as consisting of interacting persons, and the various patterns of interaction were viewed as collective adjustments to life conditions. Crowd behavior, then, would become but one of many possible ways of meeting a crisis. Furthermore, they became vitally concerned with the problem of socialization: how do human infants, born helpless and undeveloped, acquire the capacity for participating in organized groups? For Charles H. Cooley, Robert E. Park, and W. I. Thomas the study of personality development became one of the major subfields of sociology.[5]

Anthropologists have traditionally been concerned with the description of cultures—especially the customs, the kinship systems,

[4] Cf. Horace M. Kallen, "Functionalism," *Encyclopedia of the Social Sciences,* Vol. VI, pp. 523–26; Edna Heidbreder, *Seven Psychologies* (New York: D. Appleton-Century Co., 1933), pp. 152–233; and Albion W. Small, *General Sociology* (Chicago: University of Chicago Press, 1905).

[5] Cf. Fay B. Karpf, *American Social Psychology* (New York: McGraw-Hill Book Co., 1932).

and the artifacts found in non-industrial societies. But not all anthropologists were content with mere description, and the psychological interpretation of these findings has long enjoyed a respected place in the field. Lucien Levy-Bruhl and W. H. R. Rivers were among the pioneers who attempted to explain esoteric practices in terms of general psychological principles. By 1920 Edward Sapir was asking whether culture consisted of anything more than the patterned behavior of the people in the groups under observation, and a decade later Margaret Mead published her comparative study of personality development in different cultures—thereby demonstrating the utility of ethnographic data for the analysis of problems of more general interest. More recently, the concern with cultural change has led to questions of how individuals learn a new culture, and the interest in different patterns of cultural integration has led to a search for corresponding patterns of personality integration. Whereas field workers once sought out isolated groups to describe their quaint customs and material culture, they now devote considerable time to collecting autobiographies, and many go forth armed with psychological tests. In return, the influence of anthropologists upon other social psychologists is revealed in the increasing appreciation of the range of variation to be found in behavior patterns.[6]

The primary concern of psychiatrists has been the treatment of people who are adjudged mentally ill, but effective therapeutic measures must be based upon reliable knowledge. In the absence of adequate formulations about human behavior from other sources they have had to rely upon their own research. In spite of the fact that psychiatrists become so intimately involved with their patients in their clinical work, for a long time there was little explicit recognition of the importance of social relationships. Like psychologists, they concentrated upon the study of the individual patient. Furthermore, perhaps because of their medical training, many were convinced that all disorders could eventually be traced to some kind of organic disturbance—brain damage, upset metabolism, or toxins in the blood. Although a wide variety of therapeutic procedures are still in use, an increasing number of psychiatrists now base at least part of their work on the doctrines of Freud, who broke with the

[6] Cf. Clyde Kluckhohn, "Culture and Behavior," Lindzey, op. cit., Vol. II, pp. 921–76; and A. L. Kroeber, ed., Anthropology Today (Chicago: University of Chicago Press, 1953), pp. 417–29, 597–667.

older preoccupation with rationality and focussed upon the study of unconscious emotional reactions. His techniques consisted largely of attempts to manipulate experiences through communication. Although Freud tried unsuccessfully to reduce his theories to physiological and chemical terms, many of his successors—among them, Alfred Adler, Norman Cameron, Karen Horney, Erich Fromm, and Harry S. Sullivan—frankly discuss personality disorders as products of disturbances in interpersonal relations. Actually, this is not a contradiction of Freud; Freud was very much concerned with such ties but did not incorporate his many insightful observations into his formal theory. Sullivan in particular, who was strongly influenced by Sapir, defined psychiatry as the study of interpersonal relations, and especially in the United States, where his views are gaining increasing acceptance, many psychiatrists are becoming social scientists.[7]

Until recently there has been surprisingly little communication among these specialists, even though they were all concerned with similar problems. Because of the unfortunate tendency of intellectual traditions to develop independently of one another, much of the work done in each field has remained largely unknown to outsiders. But with the increasing recognition of the fact that many of the situations confronting man today require knowledge far beyond the confines of a single field, the walls are beginning to crack. Psychologists and psychiatrists are departing from their traditional approach to study the relation of their subjects to other people, and sociologists and anthropologists are beginning to acknowledge the importance of personality differences. This means that whether one wishes to study personality formation, personal conflict, perception, reflective thought, voting, the exercise of authority, or sex practices, the individual is no longer viewed as an organism acting in isolation but as a participant in some kind of social context. Attention is centered upon events in which people are interacting with one another, and the fact of social interaction is taken specifically into account. This shift in emphasis is facilitating the establishment of common ground, although the controversies have not ended, neither within each field nor among those from different fields. But more

[7] Cf. Ruth L. Munroe, *Schools of Psychoanalytic Thought* (New York: The Dryden Press, 1955).

than ever before there is developing a recognition of common interests. This trend has been further implemented by institutional support for "interdisciplinary" studies involving specialists from many fields.[8]

This convergence of interests has been greatly facilitated by the widespread adoption in most of the social sciences of a *behavioristic* orientation, for this makes possible the reduction of data from diverse sources to a common denominator. This is not to suggest that everyone is becoming a follower of John Watson, who is erroneously credited with founding the movement among psychologists called "Behaviorism." Watson took an extreme position and thereby won notoriety, but his views represent but a single expression of a more pervasive tendency in American thought.[9] Social scientists are becoming more behavioristic in that they are studying men—individually and collectively—by focusing attention upon *what they do*. At first glance this appears to be a silly statement, but for a long time scholars attempted to study human beings primarily in terms of the products of their activities—their artifacts, literature, or legal documents. This does not mean that political scientists are no longer interested in laws and constitutions, but they are turning more and more to the analysis of what men do when engaging in political activities. Similarly, anthropologists are not giving up their archaeological explorations, but they are becoming more concerned with the behavior patterns that characterize the men who used these objects. Psychologists have by no means given up the study of thinking and other mental processes; these phenomena are conceived as forms of activity, largely linguistic in nature. Indeed, the "action frame of reference" is becoming so widely adopted that many now speak of the "behavioral sciences" rather than the "social sciences."

Social psychology is emerging as an independent discipline largely because of the reluctant recognition by those in different fields that their specialties could not satisfactorily meet certain problems. Psychologists found that they could not explain many of the observed facts of perception and cognition; sociologists could

---

[8] Cf. Leonard S. Cottrell and Ruth Gallagher, *Developments in Social Psychology: 1930–1940* (New York: Beacon House, 1941).

[9] Willard Harrell and Ross Harrison, "The Rise and Fall of Behaviorism," *Journal of General Psychology*, XVIII (1938), 367–421.

not fill in their account of the manner in which group structures are sustained and transformed; anthropologists found that some of their generalized descriptions of cultures seemed empty and lifeless unless the personal experiences of the participants were taken into account; and psychiatrists were forced to consider alternative theories of human behavior when therapeutic measures based upon other views proved inadequate. The inability to handle such difficulties led to an increasing recognition of what should have been obvious from the beginning, that men everywhere live in groups and that most of the things they do have something to do with the past, present, and future behavior of their associates. The fact that social psychology has had such a diversified origin means that it will probably be plagued by controversies for some time, but as communication becomes more effective the cross-fertilization will no doubt prove beneficial to all concerned.

The Social Matrix of Human Behavior

Since curiosity about human behavior is apparently as old as mankind itself, the question arises as to whether there is anything distinctive about social psychology. Astute observations about human nature can be found in proverbs, in folklore, in political ideologies, and in the religious beliefs of all peoples. Great works of literature are frequently said to contain "truths," which, upon examination, turn out to consist of insights about typical human reactions in recurrent situations. Ethical strictures are predicated upon the recognition of the common frailties of man, which are all too readily discernible in daily life. Social psychology introduces novelty into an ancient pastime by attempting to systematize this enterprise. Although the attempts thus far have been far from successful, a concerted effort is being made to transform the study of human conduct into a scientific discipline.

Scientific research is but one of several types of intellectual activity, and its central characteristic is that the criterion for the acceptability of generalizations is neither authority nor logical consistency but *empirical evidence*. Although some persons speak of "science" as if there were a single, well established method about which there is complete consensus, logicians and methodologists actually disagree upon almost every phase of research procedure. But most scientists start on the assumption that events in nature occur in an orderly manner, although there are controversies even on this point. Applied to the study of human conduct, this implies that the things men do are manifestations of regular processes, and that the task of social scientists is to isolate and describe these uniformities.

But are there such regularities in the deeds of men? Human conduct seems to be so infinitely variable that it is difficult to see any kind of order in it, and some scholars have expressed doubts over the possibility of formulating reliable generalizations about it. Part of the current difficulty is semantic. In the early history of any field common sense concepts are used, and it is only gradually that the confusing and irrelevant associations are eliminated so that more systematic inquiries can begin. For example, attempts are now being made to formulate generalizations about "juvenile deliquency," and the results are disappointing. But this term includes behavior as diverse as assault, theft, sexual promiscuity, or anything else condemned by law enforcement agencies. Since different people disapprove of different things, what is regarded as delinquent differs somewhat from person to person. Furthermore, one boy may steal a car for the thrill of riding a new vehicle; while another may do the same thing to show his friends that he is not a coward. A promiscuous girl may engage in sexual activity for her own enjoyment, from fear of not being able to hold a lover, as a symbol of romantic attachment, or from some compulsion that she cannot understand. It is unlikely that reliable generalizations can be formulated about acts that are superficially similar but basically different. Students of human behavior are just beginning to look beneath the apparent similarities which form the basis of many common sense concepts. In all probability men do act in an orderly manner, but most of these regularities are not yet discernible because of the faulty concepts being used.[10]

There are many standpoints from which human behavior might be studied, and social psychology constitutes but one of several possibilities. Behavior may be viewed as consisting of biochemical processes, as muscular contractions, or as manifestations of per-

[10] Cf. Alfred Schuetz, "Common Sense and Scientific Interpretation of Human Action," *Philosophy and Phenomenological Research*, XIV (1953), 1-38.

sonality structures. But a social psychologist sees men as participants in groups; it is his belief that many of the things men do take a certain form not so much from instincts as from the necessity of adjusting to their fellows. The central task of the social psychologist becomes that of ascertaining those things that are true of human beings by virtue of the fact that they live in association with one another. This is not to deny that men are animals nor that behavior is an organic process. Interest centers upon those particular properties of human behavior that would presumably be lacking if men were creatures that lived in isolation. Thus, social psychologists are *not* concerned with *all* of the things that men do; their attention is focussed only upon *those regularities in human behavior that arise out of the fact that men are participants in social groups.* As such, it becomes apparent that this emerging discipline is really not a subdivision of any of the fields from which it has developed. Its broad generalizations are basic to all of the social sciences.

There are a number of commonplace observations that can be cited to indicate the potentialities of such an approach. While participating in lynching mobs individuals do things which subsequently fill them with horror and disgust; indeed, some persons are so deeply ashamed of what they have done that they cannot even remember what happened, and a few are known to have committed suicide. A man reading pornographic literature when alone or with a group of male friends behaves quite differently from the way in which he would act if given access to the same materials in the presence of his mother, his wife, or his children. There are a number of things, not necessarily prohibited, that one would hesitate to do in the presence of another human being, such as, unabashed self-admiration before a mirror, picking his nose, or revealing certain parts of his body. Thus, the mere presence of another human being, even a complete stranger, sets up a lively interchange which definitely transforms the conduct of any socialized person. It is with this aspect of human conduct that we shall be concerned.

The crucial importance of the social context is shown in the apparent contradiction in the treatment of Negroes in a Midwestern city, as revealed in a study reported by Reitzes. It is frequently believed that the discriminatory treatment of any ethnic minority is based upon "prejudice," and since such attitudes are presumably a part of one's personality, a prejudiced man would be expected to act consistently in all situations. But Reitzes found that this was not the case. In the neighborhood he studied, where a large number of people were employed in two highly unionized plants, there was general acceptance of Negroes at work but vociferous objection to their moving into the area. In the neighborhood there was a property owners' association dedicated exclusively to keeping out Negroes. By contrast, the C.I.O. union had a policy of non-discrimination, and the management of both plants held similar views; hence, there were no segregated facilities. Approximately 150 of the employees of these plants living in this area were interviewed, and the data were evaluated in terms of the extent of personal involvement in the neighborhood, extent of involvement in union activities, and acceptance or rejection of Negroes at work and as neighbors. Of the 68 who rejected Negroes in the neighborhood only 11 rejected them at work; of the 66 who accepted Negroes at work only 10 were willing to have them live in the area. There was a high positive correlation between participation in the property owners' association and rejection of Negroes as neighbors, and a similarly high correlation between involvement in union activities and acceptance of Negroes as fellow workers. Individual reactions to Negroes varied, then, not with personal feelings about them but with the circumstances in which they were seen.[11]

The extent to which behavior depends upon the anticipated reactions of others is revealed in Gorden's study of members of a cooperative living group. He discovered some remarkable inconsistencies between privately expressed views about Soviet Russia and responses to the same questions in the presence of the other members. In the sessions in which each was questioned publicly there were many indications that group pressure was being felt; some subjects made attempts to get out of answering, and others spoke almost inaudibly. Each person had also been asked to estimate the position shared by the group, and in 13 out of 24 cases the openly avowed opinion approximated the views regarded as sanctioned in the group more closely than they did the private views that had been confessed earlier. Only three people took the same stand in both situations.[12]

[11] Dietrich C. Reitzes, "The Role of Organizational Structures," *Journal of Social Issues*, IX (1953), 37–44.
[12] Raymond L. Gorden, "Interaction between Attitude and the Definition of

In this book no attempt is made to cover all the topics investigated by scholars who conceive of themselves as social psychologists. Attention is focussed upon four problem areas: social control, motivation, interpersonal relations, and socialization. Furthermore, a single point of view is presented. For want of a better label, it may be called the *interactionist* approach to social psychology. It is a theoretical orientation that has been developed largely by sociologists, although in recent years notable contributions have been made by psychiatrists. It represents but one of many possible ways of looking at the things men do.

Although some have argued that scientific knowledge should be restricted to a description of the uniformities in nature, others have pointed out that generalizations not directly verifiable through observation often render the observed facts more meaningful. While there is a tendency to disdain theory as "empty speculation," theories are actually necessary for research. Speculation transcends direct experience because an effort is being made to explain, to unify, to underpin the chaos of experience and to reveal some kind of order. A theory binds diverse observations together into a coherent unit and provides a working orientation toward one's subject matter. No scientist can rely exclusively upon observations. Any investigator starts out with a set of assumptions about his subject matter, and the initial organization of his study depends upon these assumptions. Inquiry gets its direction from the formulation of a problem, and what is problematic is generally an observation that cannot be explained adequately in terms of existing theory. The initial hypothesis is also derived from theory, although this may be successively revised and replaced in the light of accumulating evidence. The tactics used in observation and measurement also rest upon premises about the salient characteristics of the subject matter.

What characterizes the interactionist approach is the contention that *human nature and the social order are products of communication*. From this standpoint, behavior is not regarded merely as a response to environmental stimuli, an expression of inner organic needs, nor a manifestation of cultural patterns. The importance of

the Situation in the Expression of Opinion," *American Sociological Review*, XVII (1952), 50–58. Cf. Bertram H. Raven, "Social Influence on Opinions and the Communication of Related Content," *Journal of Abnormal and Social Psychology*, LVIII (1959), 119–28.

sensory cues, organic drives, and culture is certainly recognized, but *the direction taken by a person's conduct is seen as something that is constructed in the reciprocal give and take of interdependent men who are adjusting to one another.* Furthermore, *a man's personality*—those distinctive behavior patterns that characterize a given individual—*is regarded as developing and being reaffirmed from day to day in his interaction with his associates.* Finally, *the culture of a group* is not viewed as something external that is imposed upon people, but as consisting of *models of appropriate conduct that emerge in communication and are continually reinforced as people jointly come to terms with life conditions.* If the motivation of behavior, the formation of personality, and the evolution of group structure all occur in social interaction, it follows logically that attention should be focussed upon the interchanges that go on among human beings as they come into contact with one another.

Whenever possible, the generalizations will be evaluated in terms of evidence from observational, clinical, and experimental studies. Much of this research has been done by men working with different theoretical orientations; hence, in many cases the findings are only tangential, but they constitute the only evidence that is available. Among the procedures that scientists in many fields have found useful both in the discovery and in the demonstration of uniformities in nature is the experiment. Since experimental work in social psychology is still relatively undeveloped, the results are often quite crude and inconclusive; nonetheless, preference will be given to such studies. In addition, particular attention will be directed toward some of the bizarre experiments ruthlessly performed by nature—such as, persons suffering of schizophrenia, hermaphrodites, drug addicts, multiple personalities, victims of Parkinson's disease, children who survive in isolation from other human beings, or those deprived of the capacity to see or hear. While such unfortunate cases are to be regretted, the records are useful, for much light is thrown upon problems of daily life when comparisons are made with such grotesque abnormalities. In them the accidental control of some crucial variable makes possible a testing of generalizations which would otherwise be difficult to verify.

There are many ways in which observed facts may be interpreted, and since the most common procedure will *not* be used, a word may be added about explanatory models.[13] In popular discourse events are usually explained in terms of "cause" and "effect" sequences. Thus, if a man commits suicide, the deed may be accounted for by pointing to a disagreeable incident in which he had been scorned by his business associates. The bad temper of an acquaintance is said to be the consequence of mistreatment as a child. A person is said to eat because of hunger, which results from the contractions of his stomach muscles, which in turn are preceded by secretions from his endocrine glands. An event is explained, then, by locating some antecedent occurrence which is cited as its "cause." But logicians of diverse persuasions have raised serious doubts as to whether any event can be explained merely by recalling another event that came before it. For example, if someone is killed in a shooting, is the "cause" of his death the cessation of vital functions from the lack of oxygen, the stopping of the pumping motion of his heart, the piercing of his heart by a bullet, the explosion of the powder that propelled the bullet, the blow of the firing pin on the bullet, the pulling of the trigger, the state of mind of the man who pulled the trigger, or the acts of the victim which had infuriated the murderer? It becomes apparent at once that any event that is singled out is being lifted from a complicated context. In any particular situation as soon as the antecedent events have been provided in sufficient fullness to make possible some kind of calculation of the consequences, they have become so multitudinous that they are unlikely ever to recur in that particular combination. As we shall see, this popular conception of "cause" and "effect" is essentially an anthropomorphic projection to the universe of the notion of responsible agency, an impression that emerges from uniquely human experiences.[14] No search will be made, then, for the "causes" of human behavior.

The explanatory model that will be used is one that is gaining increasing acceptance in many other fields. Field theory is widely used in chemistry and physics, and similar explanatory schemes have been developing in other disciplines—the "organismic" approach in biology, the Gestalt movement in psychology, prag-

[13] Cf. Ivan D. London, "The Role of the Model in Explanation," *Journal of Genetic Psychology*, LXXIV (1949), 165–76.

[14] Cf. Bertrand Russell, *Mysticism and Logic* (New York: Doubleday & Co., 1957), pp. 174–201; and John Dewey, *Logic: The Theory of Inquiry* (New York: Henry Holt & Co., 1938), pp. 442–62.

matism in philosophy, as well as the various "functional" orientations in the social sciences. Events are regarded as manifestations of functioning systems, one operating within another. The simplest illustration that can be given is the organization of the human body. A cell is a system within some kind of tissue, which is part of an organ, which in turn is part of a larger system—respiratory, circulatory, digestive, reproductive. None of these systems can function apart from the rest of the body; a heart in isolation does not have the same significance as a heart which is pumping within a living body. By operating as it does, each system contributes to the perpetuation of the larger unit of which it is a part. Attention is directed, then, to ascertaining the characteristics of the various systems. The constituent parts do not exist and operate by themselves; each has its distinctive properties only by virtue of its participation in a larger context. Furthermore, there is an organizing principle which gives each system a characteristic pattern; this makes the whole something more than a mere sum of its parts. Emphasis in this type of analysis is upon finding out how things work.[15] In this book an attempt will be made *to account for the things that men do in terms of the properties of five functional units—act, meaning, role, person, and group.*

The objective of this book is the presentation of a reasonably consistent point of view, one that is basically sociological but supported by available evidence from other fields. Pretentious claims cannot be made for the reliability of most of the generalizations, for they are not backed by conclusive evidence. At this stage in the development of the field, all theories are at best only tentative, and in presenting this position it is hoped that a few steps might be taken toward a somewhat better comprehension of the behavior of men.

Summary and Conclusion

The first task of life is to live, and to live successfully men must know something about themselves and the world in which they par-

[15] Cf. Morton Beckner, *The Biological Way of Thought* (New York: Columbia University Press, 1959), pp. 110–58; Paul Meadows, "Models, Systems, and Science," *American Sociological Review*, XXII (1957), 3–9; and Alfred N. Whitehead, *Science and the Modern World* (New York: The Macmillan Co., 1926).

ticipate. The reasons that men give for their own deeds are not adequate, for even when speaking in complete sincerity they too often give themselves the benefit of doubt. But if one is not to accept the explanations given by those who are acting, is it possible to develop a scheme for providing more reliable explanations of human behavior? Thus far most of the mutual adjustments of men have been based upon common sense notions, but the problems of our times have become so pressing that demands are growing for more reliable knowledge. Social psychology is but one of the many disciplines in which an attempt is being made to develop such knowledge.

But the field is still very young, and it is suffering from "growing pains." A considerable body of literature is being produced, but much of it is speculative; indeed, in some respects it is only a slight improvement over common sense. There are still a number of conflicting schools of thought, and some social psychologists spend much of their time in acrimonious debate. Although the accomplishments are thus far quite modest, there is reason for optimism. All fields of study begin with common sense observations, and refinements are introduced only gradually. The study of man as a participant in an organized society will probably improve in the same manner in the years to come.

The development of systematic knowledge of human behavior, perhaps the most ambitious of all scientific undertakings, is a serious challenge. Men are constantly pressing forward on many frontiers—to scale the highest mountain, to conquer a crippling disease, to fly faster than the speed of sound, to reach and colonize new planets. The exploration of uncharted frontiers of knowledge can be an adventure no less fascinating, with its moments of excitement and toil as well as triumph and disappointment. Thousands of dedicated men throughout the world are pushing ahead—accumulating facts, checking observations, developing and testing new theories. Success on this frontier could mean that countless thousands of men and women would be able to enjoy fuller, richer, more rewarding lives.

Suggested References

CANTRIL, HADLEY, *The "Why" of Man's Experience*. New York: The Macmillan Co., 1950. A pioneering effort to restate some of the traditional concerns in psychology from a contextualistic standpoint, with special emphasis upon the organization of perceptual experiences.

DEWEY, JOHN, *Logic: The Theory of Inquiry*, pp. 1–119, 442–512. New York: Henry Holt & Co., 1938. A discussion of scientific inquiry as an outgrowth of the efforts of men to solve practical problems, with special consideration of the difficulties facing students of human behavior.

KARPF, FAY B., *American Social Psychology*. New York: McGraw-Hill Book Co., 1932. An account of the development of social psychology as a subdivision of sociology. Although it is restricted to the early history of the field, it is a valuable reference.

LINDZEY, GARDNER, ed., *Handbook of Social Psychology*, Vols. I & II. Cambridge: Addison-Wesley Publishing Co., 1954. Though tending to overlook contributions by sociologists, the most comprehensive survey of the field as it is today, containing discussions of theoretical positions, research techniques, and areas of specialization.

LYND, ROBERT S., *Knowledge for What?* Princeton: Princeton University Press, 1939. A critical review of the social sciences, pointing to the difficulties arising from the failure to recognize the value-oriented character of research.

WIENER, PHILIP P., *Evolution and the Founders of Pragmatism*. Cambridge: Harvard University Press, 1949. A historical account of one of the intellectual circles in which pragmatism developed, with a summary of the contributions made in a variety of fields by its outstanding participants.

Suggested References

Part One

Social Control

2

The
structure
of
organized
groups

Although we are generally inclined to regard the state of nature as an unorganized jungle, all living creatures are actually participants in an intricate web of life. Plants draw carbon dioxide from the atmosphere, giving off oxygen; animals use the oxygen and return carbon dioxide to the atmosphere. Far more than we realize, all creatures in a given habitat are dependent upon one another for their very existence. Flatworms and algae are unable to complete their respective life cycles without each other; the flatworms live on the products of the photosynthesis of the algae, and the latter live on the nitrogenous waste matter of the flatworms. If the number of humble bees is reduced, so is the supply of red clover, for only these bees can reach the nectar to carry out the necessary fertilization. A surplus of insects in a given area brings in spiders and certain species of birds; when the food supply becomes insufficient, many of the invaders die. Each organism has a niche in the biotic community, and man, like all other living creatures, is inextricably involved.

What distinguishes human beings is their versatility. Being omnivorous, man can survive on a variety of diets. He can move about, making it easy to abandon unfavorable surroundings. Most important of all, he can alter and to some extent control his circumstances by growing his own food, domesticating animals, altering temperatures, and developing an exchange system for surplus goods. Even though man lacks the size, speed, and strength of many other animals, the species can dominate much of the earth. This dominance, no doubt a transitory phase in the history of our planet, apparently arises from a remarkable capacity for cooperation. It has been contended that a number of skills—linguistic communication, reflective thought, and self-discipline, for example—which have enabled the species to outstrip others in the struggle for existence are products of group life. This suggests that men are dependent upon one another to a far greater extent than other living creatures. If living together is indeed so important for survival, then a careful study of human groups is certainly in order.

The study of sociology begins with the recognition of the fundamental fact that everywhere and always human beings have lived in association with one another. All available evidence from history and archeology supports the belief that human beings, as we know the species, have never lived in isolation. The universality of collective life is not surprising, once we recognize that it is a matter of biological necessity; the human infant is born in such an undeveloped and helpless state that it cannot survive if left alone. Group life is inevitable, and the central interest in sociology lies in describing the regularities in the things that men do together as units.

The Group as a Functional Unit

If it can be agreed that the core of sociological inquiry centers around the analysis of groups, the first question that arises is: what is a social *group?* In daily discourse the term is used to refer to a fairly stable aggregate of individuals, and many social psychologists have adopted this common sense conception. Among human beings there is differential association; each person is associated with a limited number of others in varying degrees of intimacy. Each belongs to a variety of smaller groups—such as family, church congregation, school classes, and social clubs. Such groups are characterized by readily identifiable membership, clearly defined central activity, and the binding of the members to one another in well established relationships. There is no doubt that such aggregates are social groups, but a serious question may be raised as to whether this is the only type of collectivity with which we ought to be concerned.

Some of the difficulty in comprehending the sociological approach to human behavior arises from the fact that many students work with a static conception of the group. When attention is focussed only upon stable associations, emphasis is placed upon their membership and upon those characteristic attitudes that one develops by virtue of belonging. If someone is in a puritanical group, his views on sex are expected to be different from those who belong to more libertine groups. A businessman is expected to have conservative political views, just as a union man is believed more susceptible to radical notions. If a person belongs to groups with conflicting views, he is expected to suffer from inner conflicts; and if he leaves one group to join another, he is expected to develop new attitudes. Much research has been done from this standpoint and has unearthed valuable data. It is possible, however, that even more could be achieved by conceiving of groups in terms of *action* rather than in terms of structure.

Although sociologists are by no means in complete agreement on this matter, a number have advocated working with a dynamic conception of the group. A social group may be regarded as consisting of *men acting together as a unit*. So conceived, there are many kinds of human collectivities, ranging from casual street crowds to well organized corporations employing millions of men. But what is important is that these temporal and spatial aggregates of human beings have a capacity for common endeavor; this is what makes a social group something more than a mere aggregation of individuals. Thus, a group may be viewed as any collection of persons who are capable of consistent, coordinated action—action which is consciously or unconsciously directed toward some common objective, the achievement of which will bring gratifications of some kind to all the participants.[1] If we define groups as aggregates consisting of people who are cooperating in some common enterprise, this would

[1] Cf. Robert E. Park, *Society*, Everett C. Hughes *et al.*, eds. (Glencoe: The Free Press, 1955), pp. 13–21.

include both organized and unorganized aggregates, those which are stable as well as those which are transitory. With a slight shift in emphasis, then, we have a far more inclusive concept.

In working with a dynamic conception of the group, interest centers not so much upon membership as upon *participation* in collective activity. Individuals are viewed not so much as members of this or that organization, but rather as active participants in some kind of action. We are concerned not with the individual as a total organism, but with those aspects of his behavior that constitute his contributions to cooperative enterprises. For example, a star halfback is an essential part of a football team, but what he does in a game constitutes only a small part of his life, actually only a small part of his total activities on the day of the contest. He eats breakfast; he talks to his friends; he ogles an attractive girl on the streetcar; he apologizes to a man he has accidentally bumped. Each man's behavior may be viewed as constituting phases of a succession of larger transactions in which he is playing a part.

If the distinctive feature of a social group is the capacity of the participants for joint activity, this suggests that a fruitful point of departure for the study of groups is the analysis of *action* rather than *structure*. It should be noted, however, that these alternative conceptions are merely different ways of looking at people. One way is not necessarily right, nor the other wrong; each may be useful. Those working with a dynamic conception of the group place emphasis upon the study of *how society works* rather than upon how its parts are arranged. Such an approach, however, does not rule out the possibility of studying stable and well organized groups.

Group action may be regarded as something that is constructed out of the diverse efforts of independently motivated men moving together toward some shared objective. There is an astonishing variety of things that men can do together, but all transactions have two essential characteristics: *division of labor* and *flexible coordination*. Division of labor is an allocation of various tasks. In all group activities, different participants do different things, and their respective lines of action are integrated into a collective pattern. In any cooperative enterprise action that is initiated in the behavior of one person is completed in the behavior of others. In a football game the man who throws a pass does not have to run downfield to catch the ball, nor does a customer making payment for a purchase have to jump over the counter to get his change from the cash register. All group activities involve the behavior and experiences of a number of people, each with a somewhat different contribution to make. This means that the participants are interdependent; each person must do his share or the unit as a whole breaks down.

Flexible coordination is that high degree of adaptability which makes it possible to meet the peculiarities and changes that occur in each situation. Men who are involved in joint enterprises are not mere puppets responding to one another in a mechanical fashion; the general direction of coordinated action is built up in the successive give and take that occurs among the participants. Turning again to football, an excellent illustration of such flexibility is provided by the maneuvers of a defensive unit that has just intercepted a pass. Although pass interceptions are not uncommon, the disposition of the players on the field is never twice the same. Yet downfield blocking is quickly organized in which adjustments are made to unforeseen contingencies. If the man who has the ball is slow and clumsy, the blocking is different from what it would be for a dazzling broken field runner. If a large number of opposing tacklers are concentrated on one part of the field, adjustments are made to facilitate the runner's avoiding that sector. Each blocker must make his own judgments and decisions, but the acts fit together. The exigencies of each situation are taken into account as each man contributes in his own way to the achievement of a collective goal.

When groups are conceived in terms of concerted action, it is apparent that there are many kinds. Groups may range in size from two lovers in amorous embrace to millions of men and women mobilized for modern warfare. There may also be considerable variation in the distribution of the participants. They may be in close and constant contact, as in a clique; or they may be dispersed throughout the world, as would be the case for the representatives of a foreign office or the members of a professional society. The composition may vary along several lines. Participants may be relatively homogeneous, as in many elite groups, or heterogeneous, as in American political parties. Similarity of age, sex, ethnic identity, or any common interest may constitute the basis for association.

It is possible to differentiate between different groups not only in terms of such attributes as size, composition, and spatial distribution of the participants, but also in terms of the central cooperative task and the manner in which it is executed. Each transaction is characterized by an overall action pattern. Such patterns vary both in content and complexity—fighting duels, getting married, performing in symphony orchestras, playing bridge, evacuating danger zones, constructing highways, or electing presidents. The action required may involve locomotion, perception, communication, some form of manipulation, or a combination of several types of behavior.

It is important to remember that the action pattern characterizes the group as a whole. The configuration arises from the multitude of contributions made by the various participants. Each group has an "impersonal form" in that its history cannot be identified with the biography of any of the particular individuals in it. Joint enterprises exist only in the behavior of men, but they are distinct wholes for which human behavior is only a medium. A number of individuals collaborate in a task that none could accomplish alone. It is in this sense that social groups may be regarded as functional units; there are regularities in the development of cooperative activities which are distinct from regularities in the behavior of the participating individuals.[2]

It should also be noted that the action patterns do not "cause" the behavior of the participants; on the contrary, they become discernible in the coordinated activities of men. Just as the law of falling bodies does not compel objects to drop, these patterns only describe what happens.

Viewing joint enterprises as units, each with a beginning and an end, suggests that they also vary in temporal span. A casual street crowd attracted by a department store Santa Claus is hardly formed before dispersing. People come together momentarily, laugh and exchange a few comments, and then go their respective ways, never to meet again. Lynching mobs last somewhat longer, but they too are ephemeral, being dissolved as soon as the deed is accomplished. There are other transactions, like wars, that drag on and on. Well established activities, such as classroom recitations, have persisted over such a long period that the procedure is continued even when the personnel has been completely displaced a countless number of times. Some action patterns last for centuries.

[2] Cf. Charles H. Cooley, *Social Process* (New York: Charles Scribner's Sons, 1918), pp. 19–29.

Groups also differ in the degree of self-consciousness and deliberate effort that characterizes the participants. In secular as well as religious ceremonies, especially those which are very familiar, people act habitually, and some manage to make the appropriate contributions while almost asleep. This is true of all rituals. In virtually all other organized activities, however, most of the participants are more or less self-conscious. Each man seeks to advance his interests, but in doing so he takes into account the fact that others have their concerns as well. Hence, they try to anticipate one another's reactions. Especially in situations in which there are competing or conflicting interests, a high degree of self-consciousness characterizes most of the people involved. Each is careful to examine critically any move made by his opponent and at the same time plans his own strategy with care. In sharp contrast, there are other transactions, such as the cheering that goes on in the rooting sections during a hard fought athletic contest, in which self-awareness is minimized. The participants sometimes become so excited that they forget themselves and yell and scream in ways that would normally be inhibited. Thus, some forms of group action are carried out almost automatically; others are carried out through deliberate cooperation; others involve a give and take between parties seeking to manipulate one another; and still others involve a blind, impulsive explosion of tensions.

Some transactions occur just once or only a few times and are then forgotten, but others take place again and again. Whenever activities are repeated, especially by the same personnel, they tend to become stabilized. Repetition fixes the activities into the habits of the individuals. As people meet over and over to perform similar tasks together, they come to expect one another's cooperation. They also develop a sense of mutual identification and before long come to feel that they are bound by special obligations. Boundaries of group membership then become more clearly defined. When this has happened, the participants enter their common endeavors with set expectations; and, before long, procedures are instituted to bring those who deviate back into line. When action patterns become well established in this manner, the group may be said to have become formalized. This suggests, then, that groups vary considerably in their *degree of formalization*.

Thus, the *organized group* is only one of many kinds of human collectivities. It has a fairly stable and identifiable personnel. It lasts long enough so that the participants develop some notion of what they are doing, can recognize one another as collaborators, and have fixed expectations of one another. The action pattern is sufficiently formalized so that the direction of most efforts can be readily anticipated. This underscores the major advantage of utilizing a dynamic conception of the group. When social groups are defined in terms of concerted action, both stable and transitory units can be discussed within a common conceptual framework.

It becomes apparent, then, that there are an amazing variety of things that men do together. However groups may differ in other respects, in all of them the participants must take one another into account while pursuing their respective interests. Whatever a person contributes while partaking in any of these different types of transactions is of concern to the social psychologist.

Data for the study of groups are available in published accounts of almost every imaginable type of enterprise, but they are not equally reliable. Most of the systematic studies conducted by anthropologists and sociologists are confined to organized groups, depicting them in their community settings or analyzing some particular aspect of their organization. There is a more extensive literature on less formalized activities, but most of these have been prepared by historians, journalists, and eye-witnesses of exciting incidents. Although there are some notable exceptions, most of these studies are descriptive; attempts to formulate or test particular hypotheses about groups are not common.

For the systematic observation of groups several research techniques have been developed. For a long time anthropologists relied largely upon *informants,* gathering detailed accounts of the way things are done from a small number of well informed and articulate persons whose confidence they are able to win. Many sociologists have advocated *participant observation,* in which records are kept by someone who is a part of the group being studied. In actual practice the extent of active participation has ranged from the investigator's merely living in the community under scrutiny to a strong personal involvement in the group. In recent years specialists in both fields have developed a variety of *interview* procedures, directing pertinent questions to key persons who are likely to have the desired information. Among the difficulties that have confronted investigators using these techniques have been the problems of accuracy and representativeness. Assuming that all persons providing information are being honest, there is still no assurance that the private views of a single informant, a participant observer, or a handful of respondents will not color the account to the point where it becomes inaccurate.

There has been much concern over such difficulties, and observational techniques are continually being refined. To facilitate the study of large-scale enterprises and of entire communities involving hundreds, perhaps thousands, of people, various sampling procedures and survey techniques are being developed. Furthermore, to gather data on complex organizations the trend in recent years has been toward developing team research, with materials being collected by a number of strategically located observers. Techniques are also being developed for more detailed recording, especially in the study of smaller groups.[3] There are still many problems, some of them seemingly insurmountable, but increasingly more reliable data are becoming available.

The Problem of Social Control

Regarding groups as forms of joint action leads to one of the central problems in sociology, a problem which arises from the recognition of certain commonplace facts. In each group there is an action pattern that is discernible in the controlled and coordinated activities of the participants; this pattern gives the diverse movements the appearance of unity. At the same time, each individual participant is physically separated from the others. Although he may not always be as free as he believes, each man is capable of some measure of independent action. Each has a unique personality, and each has his own desires and aspirations. In most situations there is no physical or biological necessity for any individual to cooperate with the others, and it is possible for him to decline to do his share. Unless one is to postulate the existence of some kind of collective intellect, an approach that is almost universally rejected

---

[3] For further discussion of the various research techniques see William J. Goode and Paul K. Hatt, *Methods in Social Research* (New York: McGraw-Hill Book Co., 1952); and Claire Selltiz *et al., Research Methods in Social Relations* (New York: Henry Holt & Co., 1959).

by sociologists, it is very difficult to account for the coordination. How is it possible for independently motivated individuals to organize their respective lines of action in such a manner that their contributions fit together into a unit? How is joint activity possible among human beings?

There are a number of ways. The most general hypothesis concerning the execution of joint enterprises in diverse contexts centers on the concept of *consensus*. *The extent to which independently motivated men are able to coordinate their respective activities depends upon the degree of consensus that exists among them.* Consensus refers to some kind of mutual understanding, a sharing of perspectives. It is, however, neither an absolute nor a static agreement. It is not absolute in that it is unlikely that even the most intimate of associates would be able to share all their inner experiences, and it cannot be static in that each person's orientation toward his world is constantly undergoing some kind of transformation.[4] Before there can be mutual adjustment, however, each participant must know enough about the others to be able to anticipate, within reasonable limits, what they are likely to do.

In recurrent and well organized situations men are able to act together with relative ease because they share common understandings as to what each person is supposed to do. Cooperation is facilitated when men take the same things for granted. We are willing to wait in line in a grocery store on the assumption that we will be waited on when our turn comes up. We are willing to accept pieces of paper of little intrinsic value in return for our labors on the assumption that money can subsequently be exchanged for the goods and services that we desire. There are thousands of such shared assumptions, and society is possible because of the faith men place in the willingness of others to act on them. Consensus refers to the common assumptions underlying cooperative endeavors.

The daily routine in classrooms provides good examples of concerted action based upon consensus. In spite of the remarkable variety of interests and personalities represented, the exercises are generally carried out without mishap. Some students claim to be

[4] Cf. Mary P. Follett, *The New State* (New York: Longmans, Green & Co., 1923), pp. 19–78; and Louis Wirth, *Community Life and Social Policy*, E. W. Marvick and A. J. Reiss, eds. (Chicago: University of Chicago Press, 1956), pp. 192–205, 368–91.

taking a course in social psychology because of a theoretical interest in the subject matter; some, because they are worried about their personal problems and feel that they might find helpful solutions; some, because a professor advised them to take it; some, because their friends happen to be registered for it; some, because they have heard about the hilarious jokes told by the professor; and some, because it happens to come at a convenient hour. In spite of this diversity of intention, the enterprise goes on, for all of the participants share certain minimal understandings. There are common assumptions regarding the time and place of the meetings, the appropriate dress for these occasions, and the division of labor in which the professor has primary responsibility. It is generally understood that professors are likely to be upset if people are consistently late, argue too vehemently with them, or appear disrespectful; hence, most students make some effort to arrive on time and to suppress their tendencies toward aggression or falling asleep. Such common understandings may be referred to as group *norms*.

Since many students regard themselves as being in a competitive situation in which only the most deserving are rewarded with high grades, other norms arise which actually have little to do with education. There is much preoccupation with the equitable distribution of grades. It is felt that rewards should be proportionate to effort; hence, those who are too lazy to study should not receive high grades, unless they happen to be of exceptional brilliance. When students catch one another cheating during examinations, some protest on moral grounds. The most vehement objections, however, usually rest on the contention that the cheaters are gaining an unfair advantage over their classmates. Arguments by faculty members that the dishonest students are only hurting themselves appear quite unconvincing, even though few would dispute the claim that those who cheat do not learn and therefore fail to acquire an education. This points to the extent to which group norms may develop which vary from the officially stated ideals. In some situations formally announced objectives are reduced to little more than slogans.

W. I. Thomas long ago pointed out that what each man does depends upon his *definition of the situation.* He was emphasizing the fact that behavior is ordinarily not a response to environmental stimulation but constitutes a succession of adjustments to interpretations of what is going on. A man orients himself to the context in which he finds himself, ascertains his interests, and then proceeds as best he can to cope with the circumstances.[5] When there is consensus, the definitions of those involved in a common enterprise are very much alike, even though each individual has his unique standpoint. Although there is a division of labor, each participant has a working conception of the total transaction; hence, in his imagination he can experience vicariously the different contributions to be made by the others. When men share common understandings, then, they also have common expectations of one another. Since each has some notion of what the others are supposed to do, he can anticipate their acts and conduct himself in such a manner as to accomplish a reciprocating adjustment. Group activities of all kinds are greatly facilitated when the different participants develop a common definition of the situation.

The extent to which behavior can be organized in terms of group norms is revealed by the manner in which manifestations of emotional dispositions, generally thought to be quite spontaneous, are circumscribed in those standardized situations in which there are understandings as to how the participants are supposed to feel. This is most apparent in congenial gatherings, where everyone is expected to be gay, regardless of how he actually feels. If one has a headache, he cannot complain too loudly lest he be dismissed as a "wet blanket." In funerals everyone is supposed to be sad, even though some of the bereaved may be anticipating with glee the reading of the will. When professors make their efforts at arousing mirth in classrooms, the students are expected to be amused, and they generally cooperate. Conformity to such norms leads to the formation of a dominant mood that surrounds the collectivity like an atmosphere. Each participant contributes to this atmosphere to the extent that he displays the appropriate emotional reactions, and each is affected by such moods to the extent that they inhibit or facilitate his behavior.

Communication and transportation facilities are so highly developed in societies like ours that people from different backgrounds are brought together in common activities, providing opportunities for a general, though admittedly imprecise, test of the contention

---

[5] William I. Thomas and Florian Znaniecki, *The Polish Peasant in Europe and America* (New York: Alfred A. Knopf, 1927), Vol. II, pp. 1846–49; and Thomas, *Primitive Behavior* (New York: McGraw-Hill Book Co., 1937), p. 8.

that concerted action rests upon consensus. One of the most readily visible contexts for making pertinent observations is in the contact of different ethnic groups. In his study of the development of the "color line" in the Southern regions of the United States, Doyle shows that in the days of slavery, when the status of Negroes was fixed in custom and law, cooperation between persons of the two groups was reasonably efficient. While many Negroes were not pleased with the arrangement, there was little question of their responsibilities and their rights. During the reconstruction period following the Civil War, however, when these norms broke down, there was considerable tension, not so much from conflicting interests as from an inability to understand one another. People in both groups frequently felt offended in situations in which no offense was intended. Then, when the "Jim Crow" practices were reestablished, relationships once again became stable. Therefore, it is Doyle's contention that ill will and violence arise when a system of ethnic stratification either is in the process of formation or is breaking down—in situations in which people on both sides are not quite sure of what to expect from each other. Once a system of domination and exploitation is well established, coordinated activities proceed smoothly.[6] There is other evidence to support this view. From 1890 to 1940 inter-ethnic tension was estimated as being more intense in the Northern cities, where the status of Negroes was not clearly defined.[7] Similar manifestations of hostility were not apparent in the South until World War II, when many Negroes being drafted into military service indicated they were no longer willing to accept their subordinate status.[8] One implication of these observations is that many people, especially in subordinate groups, may publicly support norms that they privately reject. As long as they do so, coordination goes on with relative ease.

Some of the illustrations used thus far may suggest that group norms are explicitly defined, as are the prerogatives of a policeman

---

[6] Bertram W. Doyle, The Etiquette of Race Relations in the South (Chicago: University of Chicago Press, 1937). The author is not attempting to justify such exploitation; he is merely pointing to the importance of consensus even when it involves the suffering of many people.

[7] Cf. St. Clair Drake and Horace R. Cayton, Black Metropolis (New York: Harcourt, Brace & Co., 1945), pp. 58–76, 263–86; and Charles S. Johnson, Patterns of Negro Segregation (New York: Harper & Bros., 1943).

[8] Cf. Howard W. Odum, Race and Rumors of Race (Chapel Hill: University of North Carolina Press, 1943).

and the laws he is hired to enforce. This is often true; however, there are many instances in which the understandings are merely implied. Men interact constantly on the basis of unwritten rules, and frequently a sense of what is appropriate is only intuitively felt. There are some norms that are so deeply ingrained that people have difficulty in recognizing them when they are explicitly stated. A good example is linguistic behavior. Even children can use their mother tongue with reasonable facility. Yet as students, and later as adults, they have difficulty in learning the grammar of their own language, even though grammar is nothing more than a systematic statement of the norms of linguistic behavior, norms which persist only because people speak and write in regularized ways. Each person has a sense of what things should go together and what things should be kept apart, and he feels uncomfortable whenever there is any violation of his sense of propriety.

Indeed, the better established the norms are, the less likely it is that people will be aware of them. When there is a high degree of consensus, the assumptions are shared to such an extent that no one would even think of raising questions. What is important about any group, then, is what is taken for granted, what is silently and unconsciously presupposed. Precisely because so many important norms are not made explicit, it is often difficult for strangers to feel at home in any new group. An example is the plight of many European intellectuals who fled to America to escape Nazi persecution. Even before their arrival they had read extensively about their adopted land, and in many cases the refugee scholars knew more about American history, law, and regional customs than the natives. Yet they frequently found themselves perplexed by the strange reactions they encountered. Using the distinction that William James made famous, the scholars had a "knowledge of" American life, but they did not have an "acquaintance with" it. In spite of all they knew, they were unable to understand many simple things that any child reared in the United States could intuitively feel as the proper thing to do. Since such "obvious" matters are not stated explicitly, discussions of them cannot be found in books. One can develop familiarity with such norms only through long and intimate participation in the group.[9]

[9] Alfred Schuetz, "The Stranger: An Essay in Social Psychology," *American Journal of Sociology*, XLIX (1944), 499–507.

Most norms are so much a part of our lives that we do not become conscious of them until there is some violation or misunderstanding. When concerted action breaks down, those who violate norms attempt to justify their failure by calling attention to the special difficulties involved in meeting their obligations under the circumstances. At the same time, the others show their displeasure by emphasizing their expectations. This suggests that the sources of resentment and indignation can be particularly revealing of what the participants had been taking for granted. When a student addresses a professor in an insulting manner, both become acutely conscious of their respective rights. If a professor insists that students forget about grades and concentrate upon educating themselves, many complain that he is an "idealist." It is not that anyone disagrees with the virtues of his position; to those who have worked for grades throughout their lives it seems unnatural to work for anything else in school. Thus, when the unexpected occurs, we become aware of some of the assumptions underlying our cooperation with others.

Group norms are not merely ways of doing things; they are the correct ways. In familiar settings each participant has an intuitive sense of the appropriate procedure to be followed, and whenever anyone fails to conform there is an uncomfortable feeling that something is out of place. The totality of the norms upon which the various transactions in any collectivity rest may be referred to as the *culture* of that group. This concept is used in a number of different ways in the social sciences. Following Redfield, culture will be defined here as consisting of those *conventional understandings, manifested in act and artifact, which characterize particular groups.*[10] In speaking of understandings manifested in action, reference is made to those beliefs and assumptions which underlie consistent and recurrent behavior. In speaking of understandings manifested in artifact, reference is made to the fact that material objects are made and used in a particular manner and that their significance depends not upon their physical structure but upon the manner in which it is deemed proper to handle them. Any group that persists develops a distinctive set of norms, and the concept of culture will be used to refer to those particular understandings shared by persons in a specific group.

[10] Robert Redfield, *The Folk Culture of Yucatan* (Chicago: University of Chicago Press, 1941), p. 132.

Men who share a common cultural heritage are able to cooperate with comparative ease, for they approach one another with similar assumptions. Each person curtails the exclusive pursuit of his individual interests and makes adjustments to the expectations that he can readily impute to those about him. Flexible coordination among human beings, then, rests upon self-control.

Social Role as a Functional Unit

In the study of organized groups it is sometimes useful to isolate some of the constituent phases of recurrent transactions. Where the division of labor is clearly defined, the contributions expected of the various participants may be called *roles*. Although this concept has become central in sociology, it is used rather loosely.[11] For our purposes it will be sufficient to regard a *conventional role* as representing a prescribed pattern of behavior expected of a person in a given situation by virtue of his position in the transaction—such as a father in a family, a left-fielder in a baseball game, or a passenger in a bus. The concept refers to the way in which the group norms apply to each of the participants. Each person is able to locate himself in the cast of the drama of which he is a part and thereby develops a working conception of what he should do. Whenever one walks into a grocery store, by virtue of the fact that he is a customer, he has the privilege of examining objects that he contemplates buying, of asking for things he cannot find, of commenting upon the prices, but not of walking out without paying for what he desires. Similarly a person who becomes seriously ill is not only in an organic "condition" but also assumes a role; he is exempted from the performance of his usual duties, not held responsible for what has happened to him, and is treated with special consideration.[12] What each person does in well-defined situations is best understood, then, in terms of this concept, which refers to the part a man plays in a larger, organized enterprise. The kinds of things that one might do are largely circumscribed by his conception of his role.

Since the popular conception of group is static, it is not surprising

---

[11] Lionel J. Neiman and James W. Hughes, "The Problem of the Concept of Role: A Resurvey of the Literature," *Social Forces*, XXX (1951), 141–49.

[12] Cf. Talcott Parsons, "Illness and the Role of the Physician," *American Journal of Orthopsychiatry*, XXI (1951), 452–60.

that we are inclined to regard the component elements of groups as consisting of the individual members. But if groups are viewed in terms of joint activity, they are not composed of human beings taken as whole units but only of behavioral segments. Group action is made up of portions of the activities of several persons, of those particular contributions which in their combination make up the transaction. Each man plays a role; and role, not the individual, is the unit to be examined.

Since roles are always parts of larger, organized enterprises, they are necessarily related to other roles. As in a drama, all roles make sense only if there is a supporting cast. Therefore, roles cannot be identified in terms of a set pattern of expected behavior alone, but as a pattern of reciprocal claims and obligations. An *obligation* is what one feels bound to do by virtue of the part he is playing; there are certain things other people expect him to do. A mother is supposed to be concerned over the welfare of her child, whether she really cares or not. She need not be quite so worried about a neighbor's child, even though she may be very fond of him. A teacher has many obligations to his students: to treat them impartially, to make a reasonable effort to make the learning process stimulating, and not to exercise harsh and unnecessary restraints. A sick person has the responsibility of trying his best to get out of his role as soon as possible and to cooperate with the physician toward this end. What facilitates concerted action in all standardized situations is the fact that the conventional roles fit together in understood ways. Hence, as long as each participant lives up to his obligations, the coordination continues smoothly.

But each person who assumes a role also has claims upon the other participants. A *claim* consists of those things that others are expected to do for him, again by virtue of their relationship in the transaction. A customer has a claim on a clerk to treat him with courtesy; a man who greets an acquaintance on the street expects him to acknowledge the greeting, and he would feel insulted if it were not; a teacher has a claim upon his students to make a reasonable effort to learn. Because roles are interrelated, these expectations are necessarily reciprocating. What constitutes a claim for one partner is an obligation for the other.

Human beings go through life enacting a variety of roles, each appropriate for the situations in which they are involved. *Role-*

playing consists of living up to the obligations of the role that one assumes and insisting upon others' meeting his claims. Each person has some notion of what constitutes the appropriate lines of action both for himself and for others. For example, a student who feels sleepy in a classroom may be aware of the fact that the professor is so absorbed in his own remarks that he would not notice his taking a nap. Yet, insofar as he feels that students should not sleep in a classroom, he makes a diligent effort to remain awake. As the voice of the lecturer drones on and on, he goes through the ritual of taking notes, awakening with a start from time to time to notice the manner in which his handwriting wanders all over the page. He does his best to remain awake, largely in an effort to live up to his conception of his role. Furthermore, he expects some assistance from his classmates. He would feel betrayed if a neighbor did not nudge him back into consciousness when he is about to begin snoring.

When there is consensus, the participants are not only able to play their own roles but can also understand those being played by others, and this is what makes intricate adjustments possible. It is far easier for a man to cooperate when he has some comprehension of the parts of the enterprise that are being carried out by the others. Only when one has some appreciation of the intentions of others can he get a clear picture of how they might react to what he is doing or is about to do. An appreciation of the relationship among the various roles arises from each participant's projecting himself imaginatively into the standpoint of the others. A customer, for example, tries to imagine how his request is likely to sound to a clerk, and he speaks apologetically or demandingly. Thus, *role-taking* is an important part of role-playing. The two concepts are not to be confused. Role-playing refers to the organization of conduct in accordance with group norms; role-taking refers to imagining how one looks from another person's standpoint. It involves making inferences about the other person's inner experiences—pretending temporarily to be someone else and perhaps even sympathizing with him.[13] When the participants of a group are not able to anticipate one another's reactions in this manner, joint activity breaks down.

Much of the orderliness of daily life arises from the fact that each person plays a succession of conventional roles. Most of us are so

[13] Walter Coutu, "Role-Playing versus Role-Taking," *American Sociological Review*, XVI (1951), 180–87.

familiar with them that we rarely appreciate the extent to which the things we do are circumscribed. An excellent illustration is provided by the roles played by a nurse. Almost daily she comes into contact with strange men, and in the course of her duties she must undress them, bathe them, and sometimes even handle parts of the body that are regarded as highly private. She can perform these tasks without embarrassment either to herself or her patients—as long as she is wearing her uniform. When out of uniform, however, the same woman would not dream of doing these things. The uniform is the symbol for her special position, the external mark giving clear indication of the part a person is playing in a therapeutic agency. Without it, she is only a strange woman. In much the same manner—though less drastically—the expectations that each of us imputes to other people shift as we move from one role to the next.

Most people become conscious of the roles they are playing only under unusual circumstances. Their activities seem so "natural"; they do the proper things habitually and often cannot even conceive of behaving differently. They become acutely aware of their claims upon others especially in situations in which they are challenged. If an acquaintance deliberately fails to acknowledge a greeting, one becomes indignant at being snubbed. A mother becomes conscious of her prerogatives when her child refuses to obey and thereby challenges her authority. Automobile drivers become upset when others refuse to give them the right of way to which they feel entitled. The very fact that indignation is aroused under such circumstances implies that some unfulfilled obligation had been taken for granted.

New students on a university campus often feel lost, primarily because they are unable to define their new roles with sufficient clarity. What is lacking is a clear understanding of what is expected of them. While they may have received general instructions, they almost invariably find themselves confronted with problems that had not been covered. Under such circumstances they watch the others from the corners of their eyes, imitating them externally; they try their best to appear nonchalant and hope that the others do not notice their discomfort. It is in the learning process that one spells out to himself the specific tasks that are expected of him and what he can expect from his associates; in this way each newcomer to a group constructs his conceptions of the various roles.

Where concerted action is characterized by a high degree of formalization, the component roles are impersonal. The reciprocal claims and obligations remain the same regardless of who the particular performers may be. This point can be illustrated by looking once again at a football squad. Each team has a set of plays, which may be regarded as norms of group action. In each play there is a clearly defined role for each of the eleven players. The quarterback, for example, is expected to handle the ball in a particular way, and all his teammates act on the assumption that he will do his part. The personnel is interchangeable. Whether the man handling the ball is the star of the first team or someone from a reserve unit, the obligations remain the same. Of course, the players recognize individual differences in ability and make allowances; if a particular quarterback is a slow runner, the others will block in a manner designed to permit him more time to execute the required maneuver. Different individuals can play the role of automobile driver, host at a dinner party, or chairman of a club meeting. Their performances vary considerably in style, but appropriate patterns of behavior as well as attitudes to be manifested are prescribed for any and all persons who play a given role. The standardization of such expectations is what makes cooperation possible even among strangers.

Role-taking is also facilitated under such circumstances, for concern over the idiosyncratic reactions of other people can be minimized. The less formalized group enterprises are, the more important it becomes to take into account the anticipated responses of specific people; for when the patterns of social differentiation are not sufficiently standardized, it becomes possible for each person to pursue his private interests. As long as people know one another as individuals these personal interests can be taken into account in role-taking. Within a family, for example, each is sufficiently aware of the predilections of the others to know what to avoid. But similar cooperation among strangers would be difficult. Where a transaction is standardized, however, self-control is facilitated by the fact that each participant can form self-images by assuming a standpoint shared by all of the others—whether the group consists of performers in a symphony orchestra, contestants in a hockey match, or guests at a cocktail party. Because they share a common definition of the situation each participant can visualize the entire transaction and can locate himself within it; since conventional roles are related to each other in understood ways, he can see himself in relation to all the others. This enables him to regulate his movements and to integrate his contributions into the larger pattern. Men can co-operate in spite of diverse personalities as long as there is an inter-penetration of perspectives; then, they are able to see themselves and one another from a common standpoint.

Conventional roles are learned through participation in organized groups. Models of appropriate conduct differ from group to group. Steady coordination depends upon the extent to which the partici-pants share conceptions of one another's roles. Where this is not the case, there is bound to be misunderstanding and perhaps conflict. It is not surprising, therefore, that people with different cultural back-grounds often have considerable difficulty in cooperating. Even when each person acts in good faith he finds that his efforts do not mesh with those of others. Since he is acting conscientiously, he may become angered or suspicious at the failure of others to comply to what he regards as his legitimate claims upon them. Before long the various participants begin to impute malicious intent to one an-other, and unless they are able to clarify their differences through communication, concerted action breaks down. In highly diversified societies like ours such misunderstandings are commonplace.

Sociologists have gathered a considerable body of data on some of the typical difficulties arising from conflicting conceptions of roles in courtship and marriage. In dating, for example, a woman may define her role in terms of the idyllic love relations shown in many motion pictures. She may believe that true happiness is to be found only in marriage to one, and only one, person. She may also believe in love at first sight. She may feel that a suitor should undergo ordeals and brave dangers as a part of his courtship. But the man may conceive of his role purely in terms of seeking thrills and the possibilities of sexual exploitation. He may be concerned only with being able to boast to his friends of the number of seductions he has carried out. If so, the relationship is not likely to persist beyond one disastrous outing. Among immigrants and their American-born children conceptions of proper conduct in courtship and marriage may be even farther apart. Many immigrants conceive of marriage as a means of perpetuating and enhancing the prestige of their families; hence, the principals involved are viewed merely as agents of the group. Children educated in America, however, regard marriage as a way of seeking personal happiness and resent the well meaning efforts of their parents to arrange suitable matches for them. Countless quarrels and even suicides have occurred in virtually all ethnic minorities over this issue.[14]

A test of the assertion that continued cooperation rests upon shared conceptions of one another's roles is to be found in a study of marriage by Jacobson. Since each partner brings into the union a working conception of the proper roles for the husband and for the wife, it is reasonable to assume that success or failure would be related to the compatibility of such expectations. To test the hypothesis that divorced couples would exhibit greater disparity in their conceptions of appropriate conduct than married couples, Jacobson constructed a scale on which to measure each person's views on each of the roles. A scoring procedure was instituted in which a low score would be indicative of a view favoring male domination and a high score a view favoring equality for women. He then interviewed 100 divorced couples and 100 married couples, questioning each person in the absence of the present or former spouse. Although there was considerable variation in each category, the divorced male had the lowest average score; then came the married male; then, the married female; and finally, the divorced female. The difference between the average scores of the divorced couples was more than four times as great as the difference between the scores of married couples. All 100 of the divorced women had scores higher than those of their ex-husbands, but among those who were still married one-fourth of the women actually scored lower than their husbands. In this sample, those who failed to keep their marriages intact had far greater differences in their conceptions of familial roles than those who have thus far succeeded.[15]

Just as group activities differ in degree of formalization, so do their component roles. Some roles are very clearly defined. For example, in a military organization there is no doubt about the line

[14] The pioneering inquiry in this field was reported in Thomas and Znaniecki, *op. cit.*, Vol. II, pp. 1134–70, 1800–21. Their findings have been confirmed in a number of more recent studies.

[15] Alver H. Jacobson, "Conflict of Attitude toward the Roles of the Husband and Wife in Marriage," *American Sociological Review*, XVII (1952), 146–50. Cf. Clifford Kirkpatrick, "The Measurement of Ethical Inconsistency in Marriage," *International Journal of Ethics*, XLVI (1936), 444–60.

of authority, the manner in which orders are to be given, nor the way in which they are to be obeyed. There is so little room for improvisation that personality differences become almost irrelevant. But in a changing society there are many roles that are only vaguely defined; the claims and obligations of those who are more or less related to one another are not firmly established, and much depends upon the personal views of those who happen to be involved. In a recent study in New England on the position of superintendent of schools, a remarkable lack of agreement was found concerning the obligations and appropriate conduct of those holding this office. Members of school boards and superintendents each tended to assign considerably more responsibility to their own respective tasks.[16]

Another example of the difficulties that arise from a low level of consensus over roles is reported by Hulett in his study of the polygamous Mormon family, based upon retrospective accounts of children who grew up in them. From 1852 to 1890 polygamy was espoused openly by the Mormons, although some of the men who had several wives apparently were not convinced that the practice was justified. Through vigorous proselyting, the sect had drawn the bulk of its adult members from the outside world; hence, there were many who conceived of their marital roles in terms of standards generally accepted elsewhere. A man was expected to have sexual interests in only one woman and to enjoy uninterrupted association with her for life. Thus, although polygamy was practiced, monogamous expectations prevailed. There were many quarrels among the various wives and among the children of different wives, and sometimes there was open competition for favors and for inheritance rights. But the Mormons did not develop special procedures for dealing with such difficulties, placing the responsibility for settling disputes upon the individual husbands. Some men withdrew from the conflicts, either through physical isolation or by developing ailments like migraine headaches or rheumatism. Other men insisted upon remaining unaware of the conflicts, blotting them out of their consciousness. Some even resorted to separating their wives from

[16] Neal Gross, Ward S. Mason and Alexander W. McEachern, *Explorations in Role Analysis* (New York: John Wiley & Sons, 1958), pp. 95–163. Cf. James C. Brown, "An Experiment in Role-Taking," *American Sociological Review*, XVII (1952), 587–97; and Alvin Zander et al., *Role Relations in the Mental Health Professions* (Ann Arbor: Research Center for Group Dynamics, 1957).

one another, sometimes using the pretext of possible prosecution by federal authorities, even though they lived in isolated rural areas inhabited only by Mormons.[17]

Concerted action is facilitated by the fact that the participants play conventional roles. As long as they are agreed about the claims and obligations that constitute their respective parts reciprocal role-taking and self-control are relatively easy. They can make adjustments to one another even when confronted by unexpected events. The extent to which cooperation can proceed smoothly, then, depends upon the clarity with which roles are defined and the extent to which such definitions are shared.

Some social psychologists have spoken of behavior as being "determined" by roles, as if the latter existed independently of human conduct and forced men into some mold. Roles, however, exist only in the behavior of men, and the patterns become discernible only in their regularized interaction. Roles are models of conduct which constitute the desired contribution of those participating in group activity. But even in stable societies men are not automatons, blindly acting out conventional roles.[18] The very fact that deviation is possible indicates that such models do not "cause" behavior.

Sanctions and Legitimate Authority

When those who participate in joint enterprises become involved in sustained association, they form an organized group. When transactions are repeated over and over by the same persons, the action pattern becomes fixed. The component roles become clearly defined and related to each other in understood ways. Responsibility for various tasks becomes fixed as common understandings become well established. Once formed, such groups tend to perpetuate themselves, for the participants continue to do what they believe to be expected of them even when they no longer have any personal desire or interest in doing so. Especially in changing societies, people may support one another in activities that relatively few actually care to continue.

[17] J. E. Hulett, "The Social Role of the Mormon Polygamous Male," *American Sociological Review*, VIII (1943), 279–87.

[18] Cf. Bronislaw Malinowski, *Crime and Custom in Savage Society* (London: Routledge & Kegan Paul, 1926), pp. 9–16.

Many organized groups appear to have been instituted for some purpose, and this has led some sociologists to explain collective activities in terms of such ends. It is sometimes contended, for example, that the family exists for the purpose of procreation, that armies exist for the purpose of carrying out national policy, and that schools exist for the purpose of educating the young. But this is misleading. Although some voluntary associations are established to accomplish certain avowed objectives, in most groups a central interest is not at first clearly formulated. On the contrary, in most cases the common interest is one of the products of joint activity. People may come together to pursue a variety of personal interests, but once they are together new aims develop in the course of their interaction with one another. Even though many of the more stable associations appear to have been instituted for some purpose, most groups are shaped by trial and error; they grow up through groping and striving and only gradually attain some measure of clarity and coherence in avowed purpose. While some associations, especially those which have developed an ideology or rationale, can be understood teleologically, most of them have taken their form after countless adjustments and readjustments. There are not many men who propose by declaring, "I wish you to be the mother of my children," even though procreation may become an objective after the marriage has taken place. Hence, group norms and roles may be regarded as products of collective adjustments to life conditions. As such, they are subject to further transformations as life conditions continue to change.[19]

Since people who are in sustained association do many things together, the various norms usually become interrelated to form a system. Certain types of norms are generally found in stable groups. There is some plan for dividing responsibility, and there are more or less standardized ways in which the central activity is carried out. These often include understandings concerning such matters as order of performance, spatial arrangements, and appropriate use of language. Some things are valued more highly than others, and there are often shared understandings concerning what is good and what is bad, what is beautiful and what is ugly, what is desired and what

[19] Cf. Morris Ginsberg, "Association," *Encyclopedia of the Social Sciences,* Vol. II, pp. 284–86; Park, *loc. cit.;* and Florian Znaniecki, *Social Actions* (New York: Farrar & Rinehart, 1936).

is to be avoided. In most groups there is also a status hierarchy; the various roles are evaluated in terms of their relative importance, and there are rules about the deference with which those in various positions are to be addressed. Groups usually have procedures for inducting new participants and teaching them their culture. Standards are set for membership, and there are often complex methods of training and indoctrination. This is readily apparent in military organizations and in the various professions. Whenever a group is in constant contact with other groups, there generally develops a set of provisions for improving or maintaining its position in relation to the outsiders. Thus, well organized professions usually have a code of ethics regulating relationships with the clientele as well as with rival or related professions. In many groups there are norms concerning the departure of participants, voluntarily or through expulsion. The network of such conventional understandings, in their totality, may be referred to as the *social structure* of a group.

Social structure provides a framework within which joint action can be carried on with minimum difficulty. It should be noted, however, that conventional norms do not determine behavior. Norms are only models, understandings concerning the proper behavior of persons assuming various roles. The rules merely permit some moves and forbid others; they do not dictate the line of action. In most situations there is considerable variation in the extent to which conformity is expected. In some instances, such as the norms concerning sex relations among unmarried college students, a certain degree of deviation is expected. Indeed, in some circles those who conform too rigidly to puritanical standards may even be suspected of hypocrisy. Frequently there are alternative ways of acting which are not regarded as reprehensible, and under extenuating circumstances one may violate most norms without severe repercussions. Since all conventional norms are subject to violation, every organized group provides for enforcement, especially of those standards which are regarded as important for continued survival. Norms concerning the enforcement of other norms are referred to as *social sanctions*. In all organized groups there are procedures through which the conduct of erring individuals is brought back into line with accepted usage.

Social sanctions may be either positive or negative. There are a number of ways in which people can show their approval of those who conform to expectations, especially under circumstances in which such conformity involves personal discomfort. Such persons are given special considerations, showered with praise and encouragement, or bestowed with honors. In general, however, sociologists have paid more attention to negative sanctions, the instruments through which disapproval is shown to those who fail to conform. These procedures vary considerably; those who deviate from group standards may face a sneer of contempt, open denunciation, formal expulsion from the group, or even death.

Social sanctions also vary in degree of formalization. In most stable associations there are highly formal procedures, such as ceremonies for honoring those whose services are believed to have contributed to the well-being of the membership and for the degradation or expulsion of those whose activities have been deemed harmful. In our society, for example, there are courts of law and means of judging criminals which are so complex that only specialists can understand them. Some sociologists attach great importance to such highly formalized sanctions and have even defined the organized group as one in which the social structure is protected and reinforced through formal sanctions. Such norms are without doubt deterrents to deviant behavior, but for most people the less formal sanctions, the spontaneous displays of approval or disapproval, prove more effective. Those who are about to violate some rule are often stopped short by the show of displeasure on the part of others. Ridicule and gossip are especially effective. In some cases deviant parties may be ostracized informally, even when they continue to retain membership in the group. Among the most effective of the informal sanctions is the deprivation of reciprocal services, the refusal of others to honor the claims of the violator's role. Since roles consist of reciprocating claims and obligations, they cannot be maintained without the cooperation of others in complementary roles. When a person speaks to a colleague, he ordinarily has a minimal claim upon him to respond in some way. Others may, however, refuse to live up to their obligation to be polite as a way of indicating their disapproval.[20]

One illustration of the extent to which behavior may be circum-

[20] A. R. Radcliffe-Brown, "Social Sanctions," *Encyclopedia of the Social Sciences,* Vol. XIII, pp. 531–34. Cf. Richard T. Morris, "A Typology of Norms," *American Sociological Review,* XXI (1956), 610–13.

scribed by stringent prohibitions is the taboo. The violation of a taboo is often regarded as the defilement of some sacred object or relationship, and it is assumed that the violator automatically will be punished, perhaps by supernatural forces. In Polynesia animals which are regarded as sacred are neither molested nor eaten even when the people are facing starvation. In other societies there are taboos restricting contact with menstruating women. Among the Crow Indians a man's relationships with his wife's mother and grandmothers are strictly regulated; they may neither speak nor look at one another. In rural India, where the caste system is still observed, contact with certain categories of people is forbidden, and one who has accidentally been "defiled" is required to undergo a purification ceremony. Even in our secular society there are taboos against the consumption of certain foods and against incest. What is significant about taboos is the reaction of those who have inadvertently violated the norm. Just as a Crow Indian who had accidentally eaten forbidden food might blame his illness thirty years later upon this unintentional transgression, the very thought of incest to someone in our society is often so repulsive as to make him ill.[21]

In a sense each person is an agent of his group in that the customary practices are continually reinforced through his nods of approval and frowns of disapproval. In all organized groups, however, there are some persons who are vested with the special responsibility of coercing recalcitrant members to conform. If they are personally incapable of coping with the situation there are generally other arrangements to support them. Mothers, for example, may ask their husbands to discipline unruly children. When the right to enforce group norms is supported by consensus, the person is said to have *legitimate authority*, and such authority may rest upon law, tradition, or personal loyalty. Authority is legal when the common understandings are explicitly stated and codified in law, and are backed by formal regulatory institutions, such as police officers, courts of law, and prisons. Authority is traditional when the common understandings concerning the enforcement of norms are so well established in popular beliefs that they are taken for granted. Except in unusual cases of brutality, no one challenges the

[21] Cf. Robert H. Lowie, *Social Organization* (New York: Rinehart & Co., 1948), p. 163.

right of a mother to discipline her child. Authority may also be legitimized by personal ties. Obedience and conformity may arise from admiration and respect for a particular person. A family may be held together during a trying crisis largely through the affection of all members for the mother; an infantry squad under fire may perform valiantly on the basis of a shared faith in the platoon leader; an adolescent gang may become similarly disciplined through regard for the gang leader. In such instances, authority does not rest upon conventions but upon a common estimate of the qualities of someone in a position of leadership. In each group there are shared understandings as to who has the primary responsibility for enforcing the norms, but the basis for selecting such persons may differ.[22]

The behavior of anyone participating in social groups is circumscribed. It is subject to *social control*. This concept is frequently misunderstood because of the popular connotation of the word "control." Ordinarily we think of "control" in terms of the exercise of power to direct, restrain, regulate, or otherwise dominate the behavior of persons or the course of events. This is physical control, and though it is an important aspect of human society, it is only a small part of the picture. Men may be said to be subject to social control in that they are ordinarily not free to do as they please. By virtue of participating in a succession of collective enterprises, often highly organized, each person is continually confronted with the necessity of making adjustments to the demands of others. In the process of making such adjustments, he must inhibit and redirect some of his impulses. The things that a man might do in most situations are almost unlimited; but his behavior is restricted to a few acceptable alternatives. These channels are generally not dictated by biological or physical necessity, but by a sense of obligation that participants in cooperative ventures have toward one another.

Of the hundreds of acts that most persons perform in the course of a day, the vast majority are carried out in accordance with the requirements of their conventional roles. In most instances the possibility of violating norms is not even considered. Most men have an intuitive sense of what is appropriate and simply meet their obliga-

[22] Cf. Max Weber, *The Theory of Social and Economic Organization*, trans. A. M. Henderson and Talcott Parsons (New York: Oxford University Press, 1947), pp. 124–32, 324–63.

tions. Social sanctions become necessary only when newcomers are being instructed or in crisis situations in which unusual temptations arise. Even under these circumstances, however, the sanctions are effective only when there is consensus concerning the appropriateness of their application and the authority of those empowered to enforce them. Social control refers to keeping behavior within the bounds of group expectations, and in the last analysis this rests upon consensus.

One implication of the sociological approach to the study of human behavior is that men are always participants in joint enterprises of one sort or other and that all individualistic explanations of the things men do are necessarily incomplete. Men are rarely isolated and acting purely as independent agents. Respiration is essentially an involuntary organic process, but even that is subject to social control. Men deliberately check their panting if they do not wish to appear cowardly or weak, or they may sigh to indicate hopelessness. Even passive acquiescence and failure to act are social to the extent that such hesitation arises from the anticipated reactions of other people. Each person is involved in many transactions to which he may contribute and thereby modify but only in his capacity as a participant in them. This means that what a man does cannot be explained exclusively in terms of his personality traits, his attitudes, or his motives. People frequently do things they do not want to do. Human behavior is something that is constructed in the course of interaction with other people, and the direction it takes depends upon the inclinations of others as well as those of the actor.

In speaking of social control, then, reference is being made to the fact that men interact with one another in regularized ways as they cooperate to accomplish collective goals. In organized groups the activities of the participants are curtailed by the conventional roles that they play. But such control is not restricted to formalized settings. Participants in lynching mobs are not free to do as they wish; a man who is not in sympathy with the prevailing mood may be torn to pieces if he tries to assert his opposition. Even those who are physically alone often take into account what the reactions of other people are likely to be if they should find out about what he is doing. *Social control refers to the fact that human behavior is organized in response to expectations that are imputed to other people.* This does not necessarily involve coercion; various constraints are placed upon the things men do by virtue of their participation in groups.

Summary and Conclusion

Sociology is the study of groups. There are many kinds of groups, and one inclusive way of conceiving of them is in terms of concerted action. All joint enterprises involve some kind of social differentiation and an integration of the various contributions, and such coordination is facilitated when there is consensus. Even in familiar situations, however, concerted action takes place under constantly changing circumstances, and every detail of a cooperative venture cannot possibly be anticipated. Hence, it becomes necessary for the participants continually to make adjustments to one another. This process is greatly facilitated when they are playing conventional roles, for collective goals may then be realized as each lives up to his obligations. Since norms are subject to violation, there are other norms to enforce some measure of conformity, but these sanctions are effective only insofar as they too enjoy consensus.

From birth to death each human being is a participant in a variety of groups, and neither he nor anything he does or experiences can be understood when separated from the fact of such participation. As John Donne so eloquently expressed it, "No man is an island, entire of itself." Human conduct is continually subject to social control. What one does often depends more upon the demands he imputes to other people than it does upon his own preferences. The manner in which a person works his way through the maze of obligations by which he is surrounded and carves out a career constitutes the subject matter of social psychology.

Suggested References

COYLE, GRACE L., *Social Process in Organized Groups*. New York: Richard R. Smith, 1930. A much neglected treatise on the formation and maintenance of social structure in voluntary associations, including discussions of many problems largely ignored in more recent sociology.

GROSS, NEAL, WARD S. MASON, and ALEXANDER W. MCEACHERN, *Explorations in Role Analysis*. New York: John Wiley & Sons, 1958. A

62 SOCIAL CONTROL

study of the position of the superintendent of schools in various New England communities, based upon interviews with superintendents and with various categories of people with whom they deal.

Hughes, Everett C., "Social Institutions," in *Principles of Sociology*, Alfred M. Lee, ed., Part V. New York: Barnes & Noble, 1955. An introduction to the study of the structure of organized groups with an excellent treatment of the manner in which individual lives are patterned through participation in such transactions.

MacIver, Robert M., *The Web of Government*, Parts I & II. New York: The Macmillan Co., 1947. An eminent sociologist's account of legal authority and of the types of popular beliefs upon which it rests.

Park, Robert E. and Ernest W. Burgess, *Introduction to the Science of Sociology*, pp. 24–57, 161–67, 198–209, 785–99. Chicago: University of Chicago Press, 1924. A pioneering work in which the conceptual scheme developed in this book was first presented—a volume still worthy of serious study.

Parsons, Talcott, *The Social System*, Chaps. I–V, VII, X. Glencoe: Free Press, 1951. A recent attempt to outline a scheme for the study of organized groups, containing suggestive categories for the analysis of conventional roles.

3

Self-conscious
participation
in
groups

Human beings are not the
only creatures who live in groups, but concerted action among men
is marked by a higher degree of flexibility. Chimpanzees, for example, live in groups and cooperate in a variety of tasks. When
confronted by strange situations, they sometimes display considerable ingenuity in meeting them. But the range of their cooperation
as well as the complexity of the problems they are able to solve is
quite limited. The "social insects"—ants, bees, termites, and wasps—
live in highly organized communities. There is a complex division of
labor, and specialists engage in such diverse tasks as breeding, child-
rearing, constructing housing, cultivating food, fighting enemies,
and foraging. But these activities are carried on almost automatically; indeed, on the basis of archaeological evidence some entomolo-
gists have estimated that the structure of certain ant communities
has not changed significantly in more than 50 million years. What
characterizes human beings is a remarkable capacity to improvise in
meeting changes in life conditions, to do things differently, to develop new patterns of cooperation. How is this possible?

It has been contended that flexible coordination is achieved as each participant acts independently, taking the contributions and expectations of his associates into account, but making his own decisions as he goes along. Before going into an analysis of this process, however, it will be necessary to introduce a number of concepts for the designation of various adjustment tendencies found in man.

The Act as a Functional Unit

For purposes of analysis the things that men do may be broken down into functional units which *begin with a condition of disequilibrium within the organism and end with the restoration of equilibrium.* This unit will be called an *act.* Acts vary considerably in complexity, ranging from a simple motion like brushing off a fly to a complicated series, such as asking someone for a date. Many activities—going to a movie, for instance—consist of a succession of related acts which fit together into still larger units. Since all acts involve the intricate coordination of thousands of neuro-muscular movements, many psychologists have proposed concentrating attention upon these physiological units. Other psychologists have argued, however, that such reductionism is not fruitful and that acts have properties that can be described irrespective of the muscular, glandular, or neural processes that make them possible. For example, even the most sensitive equipment now available cannot reveal all of the neuro-muscular movements involved in telling a story, but there are many features of story telling as a form of behavior that can be studied without this information.[1] What is important is that acts and systems of related acts have a structure, and all of the component phases—perceptual cues, neuro-muscular sets, subjective experiences, motor responses—take on significance only in terms of this organization. In spite of the wide range of phenomena involved, acts have certain common properties, and this greatly facilitates the study of human conduct.

When a man who feels insulted assaults his tormenter, we are able to observe the fact that he lashes out and then make inferences

[1] Edward C. Tolman, *Purposive Behavior in Animals and Men* (New York: The Century Co., 1932), pp. 3–23. Following this critique Tolman goes on to develop a point of view quite different from what is presented here.

concerning what his feelings must have been. The overt movements—the blows struck—do not "make sense" without some consideration of these inferred inner experiences. When the violent physical movements are taken in isolation, they are quite meaningless. Why should one organism suddenly swing at another? This suggests that each act has a history and that one must know something of this history before he can understand what a man does. Unfortunately, the earlier phases of all acts are not directly accessible to observation. What a man feels is not directly visible to others. Yet the blows become understandable only when they are seen within the larger context, as the final phases of an act initiated in the tension of a man fuming over an insult. To facilitate the study of such activity George Mead proposed the differentiation of four phases of the act: impulse, perception, manipulation, and consummation.[2] It should be emphasized that Mead did not believe that all acts necessarily went through this sequence. He was merely suggesting analytic categories which would be useful in studying the organization of behavior.

The *impulse* phase of the act may be regarded as the condition of disequilibrium that first sets an organism into motion. Whenever there is some maladjustment, there is a subjective experience of discomfort, and behavior may be regarded as an effort to eliminate this difficulty. One is activated, then, by some disturbance that disrupts equilibrium, and activity is likely to continue until the equilibrium is once more restored. If so much of human behavior appears to have a striving, goal-oriented character, this is because it consists of a succession of movements toward the reduction of tension.

There are many kinds of impulses. Most obvious are the periodic deficits arising out of the normal functioning of the organism—hunger pangs, sexual excitement, the need for oxygen and elimination of waste. There may be external disturbances, such as loud noises that interfere with one's sleep or work. Of greatest interest to social psychologists, however, are the numerous discomforts arising out of actual or potential disruptions in social relationships. Men are disturbed by a sense of guilt about not being able to meet an obligation; they experience anxiety over the possibility of not being able to please someone; they become upset when they cannot see the

<hr/>

[2] George H. Mead, *The Philosophy of the Act*, Charles W. Morris, ed. (Chicago: University of Chicago Press, 1938), pp. 3–25.

significance of a wink. Some persons are greatly disturbed if they are seated at a dinner table in a position which they do not regard as commensurate with their status. Men become uncomfortable from observing the suffering or embarrassment of someone else or from noting the success of a rival. In these and many other ways physical discomforts arise even in the absence of physical stimulation. What is important is that all these disturbances, whatever the source, upset the organism and initiate a line of action.

A word of caution should be added. The term "impulse" suggests some kind of force that pushes the organism in a given direction, and this is misleading. The concept refers to a condition of discomfort, which may be eliminated through a wide variety of movements, depending upon the circumstances. To be sure, there are limitations in the range of behavior through which given impulses may be consummated, but no particular course of action is dictated. A hungry man will continue to be uncomfortable until some kind of food enters his digestive tract and chemical processes in his stomach eliminate the hunger pangs. But there are an amazing number of digestible objects and techniques of consumption. Similarly, a frightened man is disposed to flee until he is able to view his position as secure, but this may be accomplished in a variety of procedures— by attacking the source of danger, by running away, by getting assistance, or by deluding oneself that the dangerous object has vanished. Thus, human behavior is highly flexible. Indeed, most impulses lead initially to random activity and a selective sensitivity to certain aspects of the environment. An impulse, then, is only a generalized disposition to act.

In speaking of *perception* as a phase of the act, reference is being made to the manner in which various aspects of the environment become involved in the organization of behavior. In the light of available evidence, it appears that *all perception is selective*. This is especially true of a man's conscious awareness of his surroundings.[3] Once an organism has been set into motion it becomes sensitized to those particular features of its environment which seem to be necessary for the elimination of its discomfort. Attention becomes

---

[3] For a critical survey of the experimental studies of perception see Charles E. Osgood, *Method and Theory in Experimental Psychology* (New York: Oxford University Press, 1953), pp. 261–97. Further discussions of perception and consciousness will be found in chapters IV and IX.

focussed. For example, in the heat of a closely contested athletic contest injured players are sometimes unaware of the fact that they have been hurt; they do not experience pain until someone calls their attention to the fact that they are badly bruised or bleeding. As we shall see, men may respond to various stimuli without conscious awareness, but there is reason to believe that even subliminal perception is selective. This means that men approach their surroundings by picking out what is relevant to activity that is already under way. They are acutely sensitized to some things and apparently blinded to others.

Furthermore, perception is not a mechanical recording of sensations, for objects are perceived largely in terms of their potential utility in completing action that is under way. Those who are involved in a heated argument become especially sensitive to the weak points of the opponent that may be used in effective rebuttal, but once the differences have been settled the other person's remarks are accepted more at face value. A man who is sexually aroused sees women as potential partners and evaluates them largely in terms of secondary sexual characteristics. After he has been gratified, however, he may see the same persons in terms of qualities other than limited physical and psychological attributes. As anyone who has participated in a cake-eating contest knows, what appears in the beginning as a tempting morsel gradually loses its appeal as one approaches satiation. This does not mean that the real world is so unstable; physical objects have relatively constant properties, but the manner in which they are experienced depends upon the condition of the organism and the direction of its activity.

These observations imply a conception of environment which differs considerably from common sense usage. Ordinarily we think of the environment as something that is "out there" and impinging upon us. To be sure it is there, but what we experience is not a "carbon copy" of what actually constitutes our surroundings. The effective environment is something that is *constructed* in the succession of interchanges which constitute the life process. Men are not passive creatures at the mercy of external stimulation; to a remarkable extent they create the world in which they live and act.

Behavior consists of a succession of adjustments. In the course of constructing their acts men take note of various aspects of their surroundings and control their movements by taking these features into account. The manner in which one goes about asking for a favor depends upon the reactions elicited by the initial overtures. Flexibility arises from the sequence of adjustments to the developing exigencies of the situation. John Dewey pointed to this characteristic of human behavior before the turn of the century, noting that what is ordinarily called a "stimulus" is a stimulus only because it affords an opportunity for carrying through action that has already been initiated. What is perceived serves as a fulcrum for the redirection of already initiated activity so that movements can continue toward a goal. Stimulus and response do not have separate existences, one "causing" the other; both are phases of a larger coordinated act and play parts in maintaining and reconstituting that coordination. Stimuli, therefore, do not initiate activity; they are pivots for redirection, and their significance can be seen only in this larger context. Dewey's speculations were borne out during World War II in experimental studies on tracking targets, as in machine gun fire. A rather obvious fact was noted: the gunner's observation of the difference between the target and the point where his bullets were striking served as the basis for adjustments to decrease that difference. The stimuli involved could hardly be regarded as the starting points of activity.[4]

Manipulation as a phase of the act involves actually coming into contact with relevant aspects of the environment and doing what needs to be done in order to restore equilibrium. This may involve seizing, handling, locomotion to or from an object, or any other form of movement. A man who has been insulted may strike his adversary, or he may turn around and walk away to avoid further possibilities of conflict. Manipulation, then, may consist of transformations either in the organism or in its environment, or both. As life conditions change, new forms of activity may be organized; and if such changes crystallize into habits, the organism may be said to have learned something. But adjustment is not necessarily a passive surrender to external circumstances; men frequently cope with their environment by changing it and establishing conditions under which they can subsequently pursue other interests more effectively.

Consummation as the final phase of the act involves the restora-

[4] John Dewey, "The Reflex Arc Concept in Psychology," *Psychological Review*, III (1896), 357–70; and Charles W. Slack, "Feedback Theory and the Reflex Arc Concept," *Ibid.*, LXII (1955), 263–67.

tion of equilibrium. The discomfort that originally initiated action is eliminated, and the organism has successfuly come to terms with its environment. Consummation may consist of such resting places as the reduction of some conflict, the dissipation of some incipient disorganization, or the construction of some new form of behavior that facilitates adjustment. This brings the organism once more to rest, and the subjective experience that usually accompanies such tension reduction is generally called "pleasure." But it is not always easy to ascertain when consummation has occurred. It is obvious in the case of a hungry man who eats until he is satisfied, but the discomforts which arise from a slurring remark may lead to a succession of acts over such a long period of time that a number of intervening acts take place. Sometimes a man may become so preoccupied with other matters that he may simply forget about the slur. Or there may be occasions on which men engage in substitute activities through which they become physically exhausted. Thus, tension reduction can occur in a variety of ways; what is important is that striving and endeavor come to a halt.

Not all human behavior is instrumental; some things are apparently done for the sheer pleasure of doing them. But many acts are goal-oriented. The goal is the elimination of discomfort and the restoration of equilibrium, and there are a wide variety of movements and objects that may be utilized to this end. That behavior usually has this instrumental character is shown by its persistence. If obstacles are met, they are by-passed or overcome, and the organism keeps moving in the same general direction. Most of the things men do have this striving quality; effort persists until the goal is reached and some other activity takes its place. The cessation of movements occurs ony when there has been a reduction of tension.

Human behavior also has a cumulative character. It may be regarded as consisting of a series of adjustments to constantly changing conditions. It is rarely a fixed response; more generally it is something that is constructed. Even the simple act of reaching for a pencil is not an automatic reflex; it consists of a complex succession of movements in which the position of the arm is successively guided and controlled by a sequence of perceptual cues of the diminishing distance between the hand and the pencil. If something should get in the way, adjustments are made. The variability of human behavior is to be accounted for by the fact that most acts are constructed on the spot, and the exigencies of the particular situation are taken into account. Thus, each act has a career; it is built up in a succession of responses. The component parts may consist of habits, reflexes, defense mechanisms, or images; they are all coordinated into a unit.

Human behavior is so complex that an adequate analysis is difficult no matter what kind of conceptual scheme is used. There is nothing sacred about any particular scheme. They are only analytic tools, and the only justification for the adoption of one rather than another is utility. One advantage in using the act as a functional unit is that it facilitates the description and explanation of the variability and flexibility that characterizes human conduct. Another is that it emphasizes the activity of living organisms, bringing in environmental stimuli only when they become involved in such action. The major advantage is that the scheme is inclusive. It does not deny the importance of inner strivings or external stimulation, but places such phenomena within the broader context of the organization of the act. It becomes possible to incorporate all observations into a single comprehensive framework.

Blockage and Secondary Adjustments

Of the thousands of acts that any person performs in the course of a single day the vast majority are consummated without difficulty. Indeed, most acts proceed so smoothly that they are performed with little awareness. Each morning we engage in a long succession of highly complex movements—dressing, brushing our teeth, washing our faces, combing our hair—and much of this ritual can be performed when we are still half asleep or while thinking of something else. Most routine activities are of this nature. But acts are sometimes interrupted, and it is the secondary adjustments that take place when such interferences occur that give human beings some of their distinctive characteristics. When gratification is delayed, the situation becomes temporarily indeterminate, action becomes tentative as the future is uncertain, and some form of exploration becomes necessary. It is under such circumstances that men become emotionally upset and consciously aware of themselves. Blockage of action already under way is the occasion for phenomena such as thinking, feeling, consciousness, and volition.

Blockage refers to any interference with an already initiated line of action, and such interruptions may arise in a number of ways. Some unexpected event may occur. A physical obstacle may suddenly loom forth, or someone may object or ask an embarrassing question. Alternatives may arise which require conscious choice; the necessity of picking a necktie of the appropriate color may temporarily interrupt the act of dressing. One may suddenly realize that he is incapable of performing the act, especially after an unsuccessful attempt. This requires a reevaluation of the situation and the formulation of a new plan of action. Of particular interest to social psychologists are the inner conflicts which arise from opposing tendencies within the organism itself. A man may be strongly tempted to violate some conventional norm and then suddenly be assailed by pangs of guilt. In all societies there are shared understandings that certain impulses "should" be curbed or at least be kept under reasonable control, for the free and unrestricted expression of sexual desires, hostility, greed, or contempt would soon lead to serious disruptions. Therefore, deferred gratifications of one sort or other are inevitable in all organized groups.

All blockages are somewhat disconcerting, although there is much variation in intensity. Sometimes there is considerable shock, and sometimes only slight uneasiness. In any event the initial reaction is organic and involuntary; behavior becomes emotional. In popular discourse *emotion* is regarded as an element or condition that "causes" wild and irrational behavior, but it may more properly be regarded as an attribute of behavior under stress. Although psychologists are by no means agreed concerning the nature of emotions, there is increasing consensus that emotional reactions occur when goal-oriented activity has been interrupted or delayed. Research by physiologists reveals that in spite of the variability of emotional behavior there are apparently only a few biological processes involved, innervated through the sympathetic division of the autonomic nervous system. The changes that take place—acceleration of the heart, constriction of blood vessels, inhibition of stomach contractions, raising of the hair, increased liberation of sugar from the liver, secretion of sweat, changes in the rate and depth of respiration—have been studied in great detail. Cannon, one of the pioneers of such research, has proposed the hypothesis that these changes are emergency reactions, the automatic mobilization of an organism for the extraordinary effort needed to overcome interference.[5]

When such biological changes occur, there are attendant transformations of subjective experience, generally called "feeling" or "affect." Although men can usually differentiate between experiences of disgust, fear, anger, depression, or elation, for a long time attempts by physiologists to isolate concomitant patterns were not successful. Cannon showed that most of the organic changes could be accounted for in terms of the increased secretion of adrenalin, but the discovery in 1948 of a second hormone, secreted by the adrenal medula, suggests the possibility of differentiating between reactions directed outward and those directed inward.[6] These findings are not yet conclusive, and what is now generally known suggests that the distinctions that are ordinarily made between the various affective experiences may depend more upon the character of the goal, the nature of the blocking agency, and the felt urgency for consummation. Since emotional reactions occur when goal-oriented activity is blocked, there is generally some kind of direction involved. A frightened man is inclined to flee, just as an angry man is mobilized to attack. Men who are upset are usually disposed toward specific kinds of action, for emotional reactions are always part of an act moving toward completion.

What is called "feeling" is apparently an experience that occurs when there is some incongruence between the neuro-muscular mobilization and the actual overt activity that takes place. Once a line of action has been initiated the entire organism is organized to carry through, and interference results in a discrepancy between the set and actual movement. For example, one feels sorrow when there is a readiness to cry. He feels less sorry when he starts to cry, and crying that is violent enough often eliminates the feeling. Similarly, one feels angry when there is a readiness to strike and afraid when

[5] Walter B. Cannon, "James-Lange Theory of Emotion: A Critical Examination and an Alternative Theory," *American Journal of Psychology,* XXXIX (1927), 106–24; and *Bodily Changes in Pain, Hunger, Fear and Rage* (New York: D. Appleton-Century Co., 1929).

[6] Cf. Daniel H. Funkenstein, Milton Greenblatt, and Harry C. Solomon, "Nor-Epinephrene-Like and Epinephrine-Like Substances in Psychotic and Psychoneurotic Patients," *American Journal of Psychiatry,* CVIII (1952), 652–62.

there is a readiness to run away, but such feelings are absent when he is actually swinging or running. Lust arises in situations where one cannot consummate sexual impulses at once. These observations suggest that feelings are subjective concomitants of motor attitudes that have been blocked, and in a series of experiments Bull attempted to isolate the conflicting tendencies involved in the more typical affective experiences. Her data show that disgust is experienced when nauseous visceral reactions conflict with avertive skeletal reactions; fear, when avertive skeletal movements coexist with a postural fixing of attention; and anger, when forward moving impulses to attack clash with secondary reactions of restraint.[7] Although the evidence is by no means conclusive, there are data to support the contention that behavior becomes emotional when there is blockage and that feeling is the subjective experience that one has during this intermediary phase in mobilization for action. Feelings arise when action is temporarily held up, and they are dissipated when the act is actually consummated.

Emotional reactions are involuntary and biologically integrated, but many of them occur within socially defined contexts. Consider, for example, the circumstances under which people become embarrassed. Men in military service are not particularly disturbed about using profanity among their comrades, but the inadvertent use of the same words elsewhere may lead to paralyzing embarassment. Nudity would be the source of some embarrassment in a classroom, but one thinks nothing of it in a gymnasium shower room. Food taboos also provide illustrations. Most Americans refuse to eat snake meat, horse meat, eel, octopus, and many other items that scientists certify as dietetically nourishing. During an infrequent visit to an exotic restaurant, if one were told that the delicious morsel he had just swallowed was eel, he might vomit. Even if he did not, he would experience a strong sense of repugnance. The reaction is biological, but the interference arises from the definition of the situation.

Another reaction to the blockage of on-going activity is the formation of *images*. Impulses that are not immediately consummated

[7] Nina Bull, *The Attitude Theory of Emotion* (New York: Nervous and Mental Disease Monographs, 1951). Cf. John Dewey, "The Theory of Emotion," *Psychological Review*, I (1894), 553–69, and II (1895), 13–32; and Frédéric Paulhan, *The Laws of Feeling*, C. K. Ogden, trans. (New York: Harcourt, Brace & Co., 1930), pp. 13–34.

are usually transformed into imagery. Whenever one is intent upon doing something and cannot accomplish his objective, the act is completed in his imagination. Thus, a hungry man imagines himself eating, and a student who is working hard in preparation for an examination imagines himself receiving just rewards. The fact that man has developed the capacity for imagination makes it possible for him to construct and manipulate his effective environment with comparative ease. One imagines wrongs perpetrated by others and becomes angry; then, he can imagine successful vengeance and be placated. Such images may be regarded as acts that fail to issue in overt behavior; they are incipient movements that are innervated but not actually carried out.

Although it is commonly believed that images are mysterious experiences floating about in an equally mysterious mind, there is considerable evidence to support the view that images actually consist of incipient neuro-muscular movements in the parts of the body that would be in motion if the imagined acts were actually carried out. In an effort to measure the movements occurring simultaneously with the subjective experience of various images Jacobson set up a complicated device to measure electrically the contraction of various muscular tissues. Then, while the subjects were lying relaxed in a dark room, he asked them to imagine performing various acts. When a subject was imagining lifting a weight, the galvanometer signal took large swings, indicating movements in the biceps region. When he imagined lifting his leg, however, there was no signal for the arm. When a subject imagined throwing a ball three times, three swings were recorded, even though no overt movement was visible. When an amputee who had lost his left arm as a child claimed he could imagine doing things with the missing arm, he was subjected to careful testing. The measuring device indicated that when he imagined such activity there were contractions in the stump of his left arm and in the corresponding muscles of his right arm. When subjects were told to imagine seeing their right arm bend, it was found that there were contractions both in the muscles of the right arm and of the eyeballs as well.[8] This suggests that whenever one imagines or remembers doing something, there are contractions in

[8] Edmund Jacobson, "Electrophysiology of Mental Activities," *American Journal of Psychology*, XLIV (1932), 677–94. Cf. Margaret F. Washburn, *Movement and Mental Imagery* (Boston: Houghton Mifflin Co., 1916); and Osgood, *op. cit.*, pp. 648–55.

some of the muscle fibers that would ordinarily be involved in actually carrying out the acts.

There is considerable evidence, both from daily observations and from experimental studies, that the greater the discomfort, the more men become preoccupied with images of gratification. It is common knowledge that hungry men show great interest in food, and several studies have been made of variations in imagery with increasing intensity of hunger. Sanford administered word-association and projective tests to subjects at different intervals from their last meal, ranging from a few hours to 24 hours of fasting. The latter exercise consisted of the Thematic Apperception Test, in which subjects are asked to interpret ambiguous pictures, thereby inadvertently revealing some of their private interests. As expected, he found that the frequency of food-associated responses increased proportionately with the time elapsed since last eating. McClelland and Atkinson made a similar study with some technical refinements in procedure and came out with substantially the same results. They showed their subjects blank sides, telling them that they were being tested on the acuity of their subliminal perception, and they also found that the frequency of food-related responses increased with the number of hours of deprivation.[9] Thus, with increasing tension both perception and imagery become increasingly focussed upon potential objects of gratification.

There is apparently a circular process in which the imagery reinforces the initial impulse, thereby adding to the discomfort and making action more imperative. Continued blockage may lead to obsession. A sexually aroused man who imagines being with a voluptuous woman becomes more uncomfortable than he was before and may become completely preoccupied with erotic objects. When he finds relief, however, his perspective suddenly reverts to its previous state. The studies on semi-starvation carried out with a group of conscientious objectors during World War II are revealing. After several days of continued hunger, food became the principal topic of conversation, reading, and daydreams. The men developed special interests in cookbooks and menus, collected recipes, and even purchased kitchen utensils for which they had no immediate

---

[9] R. Nevitt Sanford, "The Effect of Abstinence from Food upon Imaginal Processes," *Journal of Psychology*, II (1936), 129–36, and III (1937), 145–59; and David C. McClelland and John W. Atkinson, "The Projective Expression of Needs," *ibid.*, XXV (1948), 205–22.

use. Many expressed surprise at the frequency with which food appeared in motion pictures, and one man was so impressed with the importance of food that he decided to devote his life to its production.[10] Thus, under conditions of sustained deprivation men become preoccupied with possibilities of consummation, and under extreme stress some may even suffer hallucinations.

One of John Dewey's principal contributions was his insistence that *thinking* occurs only when there has been some kind of blockage. When activity is proceeding smoothly, there is no occasion to think. Thinking is a form of behavior that occurs when one is confronted with an indeterminate situation, and it facilitates the completion of interrupted action. When the original line of activity is disrupted, one experiences a number of images, each representing a possible way of meeting the situation. A man who finds that a bridge has been washed out considers several alternatives—finding a log to put across a narrow point of the river, looking for a boat in the vicinity, going back to the last house for help, looking for a shallow spot to ford the stream, undressing and swimming across, or sitting down and waiting for the water level to recede. Each image constitutes a plan of action, a possible route to consummation. Thinking may be regarded as a form of problem-solving that occurs through the manipulation of images.

Reflective thought consists of the comparison, evaluation, and eventual selection of one of the images. There is an imaginative rehearsal in which the probable consequences of each of the alternatives are contemplated. Each image arouses impulses which may facilitate or inhibit further consideration. For example, the man at the river imagines swimming across and then recalls that he almost drowned the last time he was in a river; he recoils in horror. He may consider stealing a boat, but the possibility of incarceration inhibits further consideration of this alternative. Men have the opportunity of trying out various possibilities in their imagination before making a choice. The capacity to think makes it possible for them to pre-test various programs before making commitments in overt action. The trial and error through which most other living creatures make their adjustments takes place largely in the imagination, and defective plans are rejected without the risk of injury or embarrassment. Thus,

[10] Ancel B. Keys *et al.*, *The Biology of Human Starvation* (Minneapolis: University of Minnesota Press, 1950), Vol. II, pp. 833–39.

thinking is a form of problem-solving behavior which facilitates overcoming blockages and thereby contributes to the eventual consummation of the act. Thinking arises out of specific needs and frustrations, and when it is successful, it leads to some measure of control. It is therefore an instrument of adjustment.[11]

Once a selection is made there is a redirection of activity, and further efforts are made to consummate the act. The guiding image thus provides a program for the remainder of the act. Once an objective is identified, there is further refinement in selective responsiveness to the environment. Irrelevant movements are eliminated, and efforts become more concentrated. A visualized goal helps coordinate movements and makes possible some measure of conscious control. Under such circumstances voluntary behavior is experienced as having a purpose; it is felt to have direction in that it is moving toward a goal in terms of a plan. This helps to account for the widespread practice of explaining behavior in terms of "motives," which are regarded as constituting the "causes" of conduct. What are popularly called "motives" are in most cases intentions, images of a successfully completed act. Such subjectively avowed intentions are often the only part of an act of which the actor is aware which might plausibly be interpreted as grounds for what is done. Furthermore, men are usually aware of their choice of goals. Hence, it is not strange that they believe they can understand their own behavior and that of others in these terms. But the fact that men believe that they are doing something because they intend to do so does not mean that such deeds are actually instigated by such imagery. In this book the concept of *motive* will refer to the consciously avowed objectives which provide direction, unity, and organization to a succession of movements. The term will be used in a manner that differs from the prevailing usage among psychologists.

Motives as avowed intentions are not to be confused with impulses, the discomforts that set the organism into motion. Motives constitute aims, not the "push" behind deeds. Motives are not present at the beginning of an act but arise only *after* there has been some interference. Their appearance facilitates the completion of already on-going action. Furthermore, the goals sought by men are

[11] John Dewey, *How We Think* (New York: D. C. Heath & Co., 1910). For a critical review of alternative theories of thinking as problem-solving and an evaluation of current research see Osgood, *op. cit.*, pp. 603–37.

rarely the naked gratification of biological impulses; indeed, many of them require years of cultivation, such as, the appreciation and enjoyment of strong cheeses, alcoholic beverages, complex techniques of sex play, or chamber music. In many discussions of motivation, even by professional psychologists, a clear distinction is not made between the condition of discomfort felt at the time equilibrium is disturbed and the variety of goals which develop in one's imagination after activity is under way.[12]

Effective thinking depends upon past experience, realistic evaluation of images, and logical ability. The skill with which any person can meet a perplexing situation depends upon the quality of the images he can bring to bear on the problem. The more experience one has had with similar situations in the past, the greater the likelihood that he will be able to act successfully. A city dweller lost in the jungles is not as likely to find his way out as the illiterate natives who live in neighboring areas. The capacity for meeting difficulties effectively also depends upon the ability to evaluate alternatives with a realistic estimate of probable consequences. Hence, a person who is relatively dispassionate is more likely to succeed than one who sees alternatives largely in terms of his personal desires. Finally, the ability to discern clearly the relations between means and ends is also important. The rules of clear thinking, sometimes called "logic," may be viewed as safeguards to assure the maximal yields under given conditions. Intelligence, then, may be regarded as the ability to solve present problems on the basis of past experiences in terms of possible future consequences.

The manner in which emotional reactions affect thinking depends upon their intensity. Mild excitement greatly facilitates the entire process of reflective thought. Stratton has emphasized the differences between such moderate excitement and the more violent, disorganizing explosions, such as intense fear and rage. He points out that in many unusual situations an anticipatory set is established. The receptive system is keyed up, and attention becomes alert and focussed. Hence, there is greater selectivity and acuity in perception. The process of reflection is facilitated by the increased

[12] Cf. Kenneth Burke, *Permanence and Change* (Los Altos: Hermes Publications, 1954), pp. 19–36; Hans Gerth and C. Wright Mills, *Character and Social Structure* (New York: Harcourt, Brace & Co., 1953), pp. 112–29; and Weber, *op. cit.*, pp. 93–96.

capacity for concentration upon the task at hand by the elimination of competing interests. Furthermore, motor coordination is enhanced. There is greater refinement in movement, more strength, and a readiness for instant action.[13] This suggests that the "emergency" hypothesis of Cannon applies more accurately to moderate excitement than to the more intense reactions that he studied.

Frustration and Compensatory Reactions

On many occasions secondary adjustments fail. The barrier is too formidable, or one simply does not have the capacity to overcome the interference. Under such circumstances the discomfort and tension mount, and there is an increasing sense of urgency for doing something that sometimes approaches desperation. When confronted with such *frustration*, men use a set of typical strategies, and one of the lasting contributions of psychoanalysis lies in the isolation and description of the regularities in behavior that takes place under these circumstances. Terms like "regression," "rationalization," and "sublimation" have now become common household expressions. They refer to various forms of substitute gratifications; when the original impulse cannot be satisfied directly, it is still possible for the organism temporarily to be brought to rest through alternative routes. Freud showed how a variety of objects and behavior patterns could be substituted for each other and how some measure of relief is afforded by a replacement which becomes symbolic of the originally intended act.

Psychoanalysts have attempted to explain the regularity with which such reactions occur in terms of the tendency of living organisms to seek and to maintain a constant level of excitation. When an organism is mobilized to act, there must be some kind of discharge. Freud sometimes spoke of the organism as an economic unit, a closed system of production and consumption. What is produced must be consumed through some form of activity. Hence, if blockages prove too formidable, there arises a compelling necessity for some kind of substitute activity. Such behavior has direction, but

[13] George M. Stratton, "Excitement as an Undifferentiated Emotion," *Feelings and Emotions: A Wittenberg Symposium*, Martin L. Reymert, ed. (Worcester: Clark University Press, 1928), pp. 215–21.

the goal is tension reduction of some sort and not necessarily the consummation of the original act.[14] K. S. Lashley once characterized this conceptual scheme as a theory of "psychohydraulics" in which repressed tendencies are regarded as liquids under pressure, exerting an outward stress which is equal at all points.

Reactions to frustration apparently take two general directions: *aggression* or *withdrawal*. It is a matter of common sense observation that one way of adjusting to a frustrating situation is to lash out at the source of the difficulty, and this has been formalized by social psychologists into the "frustration-aggression hypothesis." It states that whenever the activity of an organism is blocked by some obstacle, the organism engages in aggressive action toward the obstacle or some suitable substitute. If a man who is hurrying to answer a telephone in the next room trips over a chair, he may vent his anger by kicking the chair. Sometimes, the aggression is not directed toward the obstructing agent, but may be displaced upon oneself. Thus, the same man may blame himself for his clumsiness and even kick himself. In other instances the aggression may be directed against some substitute object which may happen to be available. A person who has been humiliated by an adversary too strong to attack may kick a stray dog he encounters on his way home. Similarly, a man who has had an irksome day at work may find his wife's remarks unusually irritating and may suddenly explode with a vicious reply. Even the most casual reflection over one's own experiences points to the general truth of the hypothesis—under limited circumstances. The major difficulty with it is that frustration does not always result in aggression. This leads to the crucial but still inadequately answered question: what are the conditions under which frustation evokes aggression? There is considerable evidence to support the hypothesis in a general way, but it still requires refinement.[15]

[14] Sigmund Freud, "Instincts and Their Vicissitudes," *Collected Papers,* Joan Riviere, trans. (London: Hogarth Press, 1925), Vol. IV, pp. 60–83; and Otto Fenichel, *The Psychoanalytic Theory of Neurosis* (New York: W. W. Norton & Co., 1945), pp. 11–22.

[15] The clearest formulation can be found in John Dollard *et al., Frustration and Aggression* (New Haven: Yale University Press, 1939); subsequent revisions and other studies can be found in Theodore Newcomb and Eugene Hartley, eds., *Readings in Social Psychology* (New York: Henry Holt & Co., 1947), pp. 257–96.

The second general class of adjustment to frustrating situations is withdrawal, which is usually accompanied by some kind of compensation. The withdrawal may be physical, as in a strategic retreat in the face of superior opposition, or it may be psychological, such as persuading oneself that he must have been mistaken. It may also be conscious or unconscious. When it is conscious, it is called *suppression*. Thus, a woman who finds herself erotically attracted to the husband of her best friend usually rejects her impulses. She tells herself that no decent person would stoop so low as to exploit the opportunities arising in such friendship, that it is beneath her dignity. She thereby suppresses the impulse and resigns herself to fate. But the suppression of an impulse is not its annihilation, and it may be pursued on some subsequent occasion should the situation change. There are cases in which tendencies which are socially condemned are pursued in private. There are a number of rather common gratifications that most men would be reluctant to seek in the presence of others, such as masturbation. Such practices are often harmful, for even if a person is never caught, he evaluates himself in terms of group standards and feels ashamed. He may even develop guilt feelings and a sense of inferiority, for even a depraved person must be able to justify his activity to himself.

When the conflict between opposing tendencies is acute, the withdrawal is often unconscious, and this is called *repression*. Very painful experiences are pushed out of the realm of awareness and forgotten. But the fact that a person is not aware of an impulse does not mean that it has been extinguished, and it was Freud's belief that such tendencies remain active and would force themselves into awareness unless they are actively resisted. Since they press constantly toward realization, considerable effort is required to prevent their reappearance in consciousness. It is the various ways in which such repressed impulses appear in disguised form that has in large part engaged the attention of psychoanalysts. Freud showed how forbidden envy, desire, or hostility can be inadvertently expressed in seemingly innocent jokes, through the slip of the tongue, or in symbolic form in dreams. People sometimes enjoy gossip that they do not actually believe, for they get indirect satisfaction from attacking the reputation of those whom they privately dislike. It is difficult to hold them personally accountable for the accuracy of the reports, for they are merely passing on something of interest that they happened to hear. Those who feel sexually deprived may gain vicarious enjoyment from reading about the illicit activities of others, for they themselves cannot be condemned for the misdeeds of others. Thus, many of the frustrations of daily life are redirected into disguised channels, making it possible for men to drain off some of their tensions innocuously and still maintain their respectability.

Another possibility is *sublimation.* A blocked impulse may be coordinated with other interests in the construction of some new line of activity, one that is sanctioned in one's group. Frequent reference is made to the manner in which repressed erotic tendencies may be partially gratified through participation in artistic activity or the manner in which hostile impulses may be released in competitive sports. But there are many other patterns of sublimation. A person in some underprivileged group—a child growing up in poverty, an outcast, or someone in an ethnic minority—may be deeply pained upon being slighted or snubbed. His initial reaction may be a violent hatred of all those in positions of privilege and authority, but his aggressions may subsequently become converted into an abiding conviction that all social injustice must be remedied. He may devote his entire life to carrying his convictions through to execution and perhaps even succeed in pushing through some reforms. In this manner, therefore, a person may indirectly satisfy his frustrated impulses and at the same time win social approval and even acclaim.

Should embarrassing inconsistencies arise from the pursuit of such substitute gratifications, they can usually be explained away. Freud was especially impressed by the ability of men to utilize their intellectual equipment for the justification of acts that they performed for reasons they did not know. He referred to this technique as *rationalization.* A person who fails in some competitive enterprise may assuage his hurt feelings by discounting the value of the object he was seeking; thus, a man who did not win the affection of a beautiful woman suddenly discovers some negative attributes and says that she was not worth the effort to begin with. This is commonly called a "sour grapes" rationalization. Or the object may be over-evaluated; a rejected suitor may declare that the girl was simply "out of his class." This concept has enjoyed widespread use, and a word of caution should be injected. Men are constantly verbalizing about the things they do. Whenever an explanation sounds plausible, we are inclined to accept it as the "reason" for one's conduct. If it seems suspicious, however, we dismiss it as a "rationalization." This suggests that the designation of explanations as "rationalizations" depends upon the frame of reference of the person making the judgment. Interest at this point centers not upon the identification of the "real" bases of human behavior but upon the fact that men are able to maintain a reasonably coherent conception of themselves in spite of the fact that some of their activities may seem incongruent.

One of the most common reactions to frustration is *fantasy*, in which images are used as substitutes for gratification. A young woman who is dissatisfied with the men she actually knows and dates can daydream of being courted by a handsome screen idol; a boy of limited athletic prowess can enjoy a fantasy of participating in the World Series; a man who has just lost a heated argument can chuckle to himself upon imagining his adversary's falling into an open manhole. Fantasy differs from reflective thought; in thinking images are used as instruments through which a delayed act is eventually consummated, but in fantasy the image is the substitute for the consummation itself. The image is consummatory rather than instrumental.

Fantasy has a unique property that sets it off from most other forms of human behavior: it is not necessary for the dreamer to take into account the possibility of unexpected or undesirable responses on the part of others. In real life there are certain conditions to which adjustments must be made, but in fantasy the difficulties that block the attainment of goals can be conveniently brushed aside. A student dreaming of graduating *summa cum laude* can ignore his intellectual shortcomings, just as a crippled boy who dreams of his glory on the gridiron can ignore his physical condition. This feature of fantasy—the ability of the actor to control all of the essential conditions of action—makes it an effective technique for completing otherwise difficult or impossible acts. Many daydreams deal with the remotely possible rather than the probable, and even the dreamer himself usually recognizes the unlikelihood of such dreams coming true. Although the practice is sometimes condemned as abnormal, it is apparently universal. It becomes pathological only when the dreamer can no longer distinguish between his dream world and the world of consensus.

Some daydreams enable men to crystallize their aspirations, and in this respect they resemble the instrumental imagery of reflective thought. When a young pre-medical student dreams of performing great services in the midst of an epidemic, his goals are brought into sharper focus. Impulses are reinforced and cultivated, and he may become less concerned with competing interests. Through such vicarious participation a person may actually come to appreciate better what he would have to face.

Although individuals vary considerably in this regard, most day-dreams are apparently compensatory. They are means of padding some forlorn hope, tempering a feeling of inferiority, or mitigating some actual hurt. Those who are irked by their slow progress toward their life goals dream of fabulous success; restless people dream of adventure, domestic felicity, or of debaucheries; those who have doubts about their personal worth enjoy "conquering hero" dreams in which they become the source of awe and devotion because of their irresistible charm and incredible combination of skills. Children who have been slighted and adults who feel they have been unfairly treated sometimes have "suffering hero" dreams in which they incur serious injury or die a magnificent death after performing some heroic deed. A punished child may dream of being killed while saving the life of a younger child who lives next door, thereby forcing those who had mistreated him to feel guilty. They get great satisfaction from imagining the lamentations of those who now realize their error. Similarly, underprivileged people dreaming of success place emphasis upon the added prestige arising from the widespread recognition of the great odds against which they battled. By and large, then, daydreams are cathartic; the vicarious completion of acts in the imagination gives a temporary satisfaction which permits other activities to go on. Fantasies are often like sedatives; they pacify the dreamer and make life more bearable. Indeed, it is fortunate that men are equipped with such a convenient safety valve.

Attempts have been made to test the hypothesis that fantasy permits some measure of tension-reduction. Feshback, who wanted to see whether aggressive impulses are actually minimized when angry people have an opportunity to express their hostilities in fantasy, divided his subjects into three groups. One group was deliberately insulted and immediately thereafter asked to take the

Thematic Apperception Test, thereby having an outlet for giving vent to their feelings. A second group was similarly abused and then kept so busy with other tasks that there was no opportunity for musing of any kind. A third group was administered the test without being harangued. After these exercises an effort was made to ascertain the extent of aggression directed against the tormenter through a variety of observations. In general the results confirmed the hypothesis. A comparison of the two groups taking the TAT showed that those who had been insulted revealed considerably more aggression in their fantasy than the others. There was a negative correlation between the amount of aggression shown in fantasy and the actual hostility subsequently directed against the tormenter. Finally, a comparison of the two groups that had been abused revealed that those who had taken the TAT were less hostile toward their tormenter after the exercises than the people who had been kept busy.[16] This suggests that there would probably be far more overt conflict among human beings were it not for the possibility of temporary relief through the imagination.

If a man is still frustrated even after such compensatory adjustments, his emotional reaction may become so overwhelming that his behavior becomes disorganized. It is a matter of common observation that people who are very upset are unable to act effectively. At the termination of an intense love affair, after failing an important examination, or when contesting a crucial point in a championship game, some persons "crack up." There is considerable experimental and clinical evidence that anger or fear, when it surpasses a certain degree of intensity, disturbs vegetative preparedness and paralyzes voluntary conduct.[17] There are, of course, personality differences in the threshold of disorganization; different people have different "breaking points." Some manage to control themselves even in the face of grave dangers; while others become hysterical at the slightest provocation.

Emotional behavior varies considerably in intensity, and disorganization is found only when there is extreme tension. When

[16] Seymour Feshback, "The Drive-Reducing Function of Fantasy Behavior," *Journal of Abnormal and Social Psychology*, L (1955), 3–11.

[17] Cf. Lewis M. Hurxthal and Natalija Musulin, *Clinical Endocrinology* (Philadelphia: J. B. Lippincott Co., 1953), Vol. II, pp. 1357–62, 1365–69; and Hans Selye, *The Stress of Life* (New York: McGraw-Hill Book Co., 1956).

there is excessive innervation and visceral activity, disturbances occur in perception, motor coordination, and thinking. As the perceptual process disintegrates there are unrealistic accentuations and erratic fixations. Indeed, students of legal psychology have long contended that testimony concerning events witnessed under great stress is unreliable.[18] The motor processes are jammed, and there is a loss of coordination. A terrified man "freezes," and an angry boxer may "lose his head" thereby exposing himself to a severe beating. Under such circumstances conscious reflection becomes extremely difficult. Because thinking involves the manipulation of images, which are incipient neuro-muscular movements, any condition that interferes with muscular contractions will also disrupt directed thought. When taking examinations under pressure students sometimes "black out," being unable to recall even the most commonplace materials. As emotional reactions increase in intensity, more muscular systems become involved in attempted adjustments, and thinking becomes progressively more difficult as incompatible motor systems are innervated.[19] Thus, whether emotions facilitate or impede adjustment depends upon their intensity.

Yelling, sobbing, laughing, or aimless physical movement sometimes characterizes the behavior of people who are acutely upset. Sometimes there is *regression* to a pattern that had been formed earlier in life. There are a large number of behavior patterns that become well integrated in infancy or childhood which are subsequently replaced. Crying when in trouble, for example, is common for children, but most adults outgrow this practice. But later in life, when confronted with some unbearable situation, one may revert to behavior patterns that had previously proved satisfactory. In emotional outbursts some people cry like babies, and grown men are known to call out for their mother when helplessly trapped in dangerous situations. In intense excitement, men may prattle, lose control of their bladder, assume a fetal posture, or even bark like dogs. Such behavior has been observed repeatedly on battlefields, in disasters, and in religious revivals. A number of systematic studies

[18] Leo Postman and Jerome S. Bruner, "Perception under Stress," *Psychological Review*, LV (1948), 314–23. Cf. Hugo Munsterberg, *On the Witness Stand* (New York: The McClure Co., 1908); and L. William Stern, "The Psychology of Testimony," *Journal of Abnormal and Social Psychology*, XXXIV (1939), 3–20.

[19] Cf. Margaret F. Washburn, "Emotion and Thought: A Motor Theory of Their Relations," in Reymert, *op. cit.*, pp. 104–15.

have been made on regressive behavior, but the results are unfortunately inconclusive largely because of the diverse usages of the concept.[20]

When frustrations are recurrent, a variety of physical disorders may develop. Considerable interest has centered upon the formation of various psychosomatic symptoms, such as, headaches, stuttering, ulcers, muscular pains, skin diseases, and a variety of allergies like asthma and hay fever. Although the evidence is not conclusive, there are indications that in many cases such disturbances are reactions to chronic tensions.[21]

Each person develops characteristic ways of coping with frustrating situations. A defensive strategy that proves adequate on one occasion may be used repeatedly in similar and analogous situations until it become fixed in one's personality. Unusually painful experiences may leave scars, for some men continue to defend themselves even in situations that do not require it, and the defensive stance itself becomes crystallized. Some people characteristically withdraw whenever they meet any kind of opposition and retreat into a world of daydreams. Some people live in private worlds to such an extent that they are almost incapable of viewing objects from an impersonal standpoint, thereby increasing the probability of further conflicts and misunderstandings. When tension reduction is incomplete in some dramatic event, guilt and remorse may arise, forming the basis for neurotic symptoms. Thus, each person is characterized by a peculiar combination of techniques for coping with difficulties, and these may be regarded as forms of *adaptation*. In contrast with the concept of adjustment, which refers to an organism's coming to terms with the exigencies of specific situations, adaptation refers to the more stable solutions—well organized ways of coping with typical problems which become crystallized through a succession of adjustments.

Self-Control and Concerted Action

It has been noted that concerted action among human beings is

[20] Robert R. Sears, *Survey of Objective Studies of Psychoanalytic Concepts* (New York: Social Science Research Council, 1943), pp. 76–104.

[21] Cf. Flanders Dunbar, *Mind and Body: Psychosomatic Medicine* (New York: Random House, 1955).

not automatic, but highly flexible. Although there is a network of conventional norms in all recurrent contexts, each historical situation is unique. Nothing happens twice in exactly the same manner; even in ritualistic observances accidents occur. Unexpected events take place, but men are versatile and devise ingenious ways of meeting such difficulties. Such flexible coordination is possible because *each participant acts independently,* making adjustments to his associates as they move together toward a common goal. Social structures provide the general framework within which cooperative activities go on, but they do not determine the contribution of any particular person. In each case the man exercises judgment and acts according to his own estimate of the situation.

Each person is capable of violating group norms. It is precisely because such deviations are possible that the fixing of responsibility is such a widespread practice. Unless each person had some choice, there would not be any point in talking about his personal responsibility. The existence of such a notion implies that the offender could have acted differently had he chosen to do so.

But if each person acts separately, how does cooperation occur? It was George Mead's contention that mutual adjustments among independently acting men are greatly facilitated by their ability to form perceptual objects of themselves through role-taking. A portion of the perceptual field of each participant becomes differentiated into what he experiences as himself; each person is able to form a *self-image.* This enables each party to examine whatever he is about to do from the standpoint of the others involved in the situation. In the previously used example of the intercepted pass, each football player is able to see himself in relation to all of the other athletes on the field. If a blocker notes that he is the only man on his team between the ball carrier and two potential tacklers, he must gird himself for a difficult task. He is able to fix his own responsibility because he can imagine how he appears to the others, and it is generally understood that a blocker in such a situation should attempt to immobilize both opponents. Personal responsibility in each situation is fixed, then, by the actor's imagining what the others expect of him. The separate lines of action of the various participants fit together in a reciprocating fashion because each can take the roles of the others, form a self-image from their presumed standpoint, and make adjustments to the intentions and expectations imputed to them.[22]

Contrary to common sense belief men are not always aware of themselves as distinct units; indeed, the extent to which they are self-conscious varies remarkably. There are times when self-consciousness is acute. A person unaccustomed to public speaking who is called upon to address a large group may become so preoccupied with himself that he forgets what he had planned to say. A young man being introduced to a strikingly beautiful woman may be so concerned over the impression that he is making that he stumbles clumsily over the furniture. A person applying for a job may become tongue-tied from paying undue attention to himself. On the other hand, there are circumstances in which self-consciousness disappears almost completely. When one is absorbed in an exciting motion picture or novel, he is unaware of anything but the development of the plot. His vicarious participation is so complete that he becomes aware of himself only when the drama is over or when something unusual happens to disrupt his concentration. Similarly, when relaxing on a beach with his face covered, one can hear the roar of waves and occasional voices of yelling children; his experience is such that he feels as if he blends into the landscape. There is no awareness of oneself as a distinct object, set off from everything else. Some religious mystics have even attempted to cultivate a special capacity for having this kind of experience. Most of the time men range somewhere between these extremes. The extent to which they are conscious of themselves varies from situation to situation, and this suggests that there may be identifiable conditions under which self-images are formed.

The formation of self-images is especially noticeable in those situations in which a person is participating in some kind of joint enterprise in which his own gratifications depend upon the cooperation of others. There are many forms of activity in which success calls for such reciprocation; on a primitive level, reproduction is possible only with the cooperation of some party of the opposite sex, and the survival and well-being of the human infant requires the care of elders. Since organisms are sensitive to anything likely to

[22] George H. Mead, *The Philosophy of the Present*, Arthur E. Murphy, ed. (Chicago: Open Court Publishing Co., 1932), pp. 176–95.

affect the consummation of an on-going act, any person who must depend upon the cooperation of others becomes responsive to their views. He must be careful to conduct himself in a manner designed not to alienate them. He cannot afford to do anything that would lead others to hesitate, withdraw their support, or oppose his efforts. Whenever men are interdependent, they must concern themselves with the kind of impression they are making upon one another. The formation of self-images, then, is an extension of the adjustive tendencies found in all living creatures. It is well developed in human beings because men always live in association with one another.

Images emerge when there is some kind of interference in activity, and this general principle holds true for self-images. One becomes conscious of himself when there is some strain, opposition, or struggle. A person does not notice his own breathing until his respiration becomes difficult. Self-consciousness is enhanced in situations in which action has been interrupted by some uncertainty concerning the reactions of the other participants. When purchasing a newspaper at the corner stand there is little self-awareness because the exchange is carried out in a routine manner. But where there is the possibility of alternative responses, as in the case of a client who might accept, decline, delay, become insulted, or laugh upon being asked to conclude a transaction, there is much concern over the kind of impression that is being made. Acute self-consciousness occurs in situations in which a person is completely at the mercy of others, as in the case of a man who has belched loudly at a formal dinner party. A man becomes aware of himself as a distinct object, then, in the kind of situations in which he is in some manner dependent upon others, when he is a participant in some joint enterprise in which his success requires the assistance of others and when there is a possibility that such cooperation may not be forthcoming.

It may be objected that people are sometimes self-conscious even when they are all alone. When returning home from a party one may suddenly realize that he had made a stupid blunder, and he may blush in embarrassment while sitting by himself in a street car. He is physically alone, but others are present in his imagination. He imagines what the other people who were present must be thinking and rehearses what he might say upon encountering them on the next day. Thus, he is still performing in a social context.

Mead argued that human beings are able to control themselves because of their capacity to act toward themselves in much the same manner as they act toward other people and as others act toward them. Thus, a person can berate himself, praise himself, make excuses to himself, or indulge himself—just as he can do these things to others. One can become the object of his own activities. Similarly, each can act toward himself just as others act toward him. In well defined situations he can anticipate what others are likely to do and react to himself in the same manner. Anyone who does something that is generally disapproved can expect a scolding, and men often scold themselves for their own misdeeds even before being detected by others. The mistreatment of a helpless old lady is likely to arouse aggressive reactions on the part of witnesses, and a person who even considers such a possibility often feels guilty. As Freud pointed out, guilt feelings may be regarded as a form of self-punishment. Thus, a man becomes conscious of himself as a distinct unit through role-taking; he responds to his own activity as if he were someone else. He responds covertly to his own behavior in the same way in which he expects others to respond overtly. The capacity to form self-images, then, makes self-criticism and self-control possible.

Self-control is impossible without self-images. Unless one can form a perceptual object of himself and visualize what he is about to do, he cannot possibly respond to it. Once a person has formed a self-image there is an imaginative rehearsal in which the possible reactions of others can be evaluated. Because he can appreciate the point of view of the other participants he can anticipate what each of them is likely to do in response to his actions. Such anticipation makes possible the inhibition of some alternatives and the facilitation of others, thus making it more likely to elicit the desired reactions. A blocker attempting to take out an opposing tackler can appreciate the intention of his opponent to break through. If moving to his left gives him his best opportunity, he may deliberately feint to throw his adversary off balance and then hit him from the desired direction. Because a man can respond vicariously to his own forthcoming behavior he can manipulate himself and others to exercise some measure of control over the situation.

Self-consciousness provides protection against impulsive behavior. An infatuated young man may be sorely tempted to seize the girl and to smother her with kisses, but he can readily imagine how repulsive such conduct would appear both to her and to the others who may be present. He can also anticipate her chagrin as well as the dismay of those who rush to her rescue. Since the self-image he forms is displeasing, he recoils from it and redirects his attention elsewhere. Self-consciousness is therefore a way of isolating people from one another and of making their conduct more conventional. With the introduction of deliberate planning activity becomes less spontaneous, but the mutual adjustment of persons with diverse interests proceeds much more smoothly.

Self-control refers to behavior that is redirected in the light of the manner in which it is imagined to appear from the standpoint of other people who are involved in a cooperative task. Once a person defines a situation and locates himself within it in terms of a conventional role, he becomes cognizant of expected patterns of behavior both for himself and for the other participants. Men are continually inhibiting themselves out of consideration for others. People who dislike alcohol become "social drinkers" rather than disappoint a tactless host, and they refrain from speaking sharply lest they inadvertently offend someone. Self-control, then, is a recurrent form of behavior, a complex process whereby a person responds to images of himself and thereby channels his conduct. In this sense, a man's self-image may be regarded as a part of his effective environment, for he responds to himself just as he takes other objects into account.

The capacity for self-control apparently gives man many of his unique attributes. Mead believed that man's ability to form a perceptual object of himself constituted one of the major differences between human beings and other living creatures. Other animals can respond directly to one another; human beings can also do this, but in addition they can respond to what they experience as their own activities. Other animals presumably have a variety of experiences, but probably not self-consciousness. They can hear, see, smell, and feel, but they probably do not have knowledge of themselves as distinct objects. Only man is aware of the fact that it is he himself that has these experiences.

This discussion suggests that social control rests largely upon self-control. Human society is an on-going process in which each participant is continually checking his own behavior in response to real or anticipated reactions of other people. Coordination is possible because each person controls himself from within, and it is self-consciousness that makes such voluntary conduct possible. Concerted action depends upon the voluntary contributions of the individual participants, but since each person forms a self-image from the standpoint of the perspective shared in the group, such self-criticism serves to integrate the contributions of each into an organized social pattern. But there are vast differences in the manner in which conventional roles are enacted. Some make their contributions with considerable reluctance; others, with a sense of duty; others, with sadistic glee. This suggests that some of the people who perform adequately would actually prefer to be doing something else. This leads to the question of the "real" man who stands behind such a "front."

Summary and Conclusion

The study of human behavior can be greatly facilitated by breaking down the multitude of things that men do into functional units called acts, which begin with a condition of disequilibrium and are terminated with the restoration of equilibrium. Activity may be initiated by any discomfort, and impulses are consummated through the perception and manipulation of relevant features of the environment. Should habitual patterns of activity fail, secondary adjustments occur. The delayed act is then brought to completion through reflective thought, involving an imaginative rehearsal of alternative routes to gratification, and through the extra effort made possible by emotional mobilization. If these adjustments prove inadequate, there is frustration, and there are a variety of techniques through which tension reduction is sought even though the original impulse cannot be consummated. Should even the substitute gratifications prove unsatisfactory, there is disorganization, an emotional explosion in which behavior becomes highly ineffective. Thus, activity persists until tension has somehow been relieved. Any conceptual scheme for the study of human behavior must provide for the analysis of such range and flexibility.

One important premise is that the activities of men may be viewed fruitfully in terms of adjustment tendencies inherent in all living creatures. The things that men do may be regarded as consisting of the successive adjustments of living organisms to constantly changing conditions. The life of any person is a continuous process of interchange between an ever developing organism and an ever changing environment. Therefore, none of the component acts making up this on-going process can be accounted for in terms of any single antecedent event—environmental stimuli or internal motives—which can be labelled as its "cause." The understanding of what men do requires nothing less than the study of the life process itself, and the student of social psychology is concerned with those distinctive properties of human life which emerge by virtue of group participation.

Since men who live in association with one another are interdependent, each must concern himself with the manner in which his conduct will affect the others. One of the peculiarities of human beings is the capacity to form self-images, which enables each person to evaluate what he is about to do before committing himself in overt action. Acts that are likely to elicit adverse reactions may therefore be inhibited and redirected. When all participants engage in such self-control, concerted action proceeds smoothly.

Suggested References

BARTLETT, FREDERICK C., *Remembering*. Cambridge: Cambridge University Press, 1932. A series of experimental studies on perception and memory, showing the importance of the social framework within which experiences are organized.

BULL, NINA, *The Attitude Theory of Emotion*. New York: Nervous & Mental Diseases Monographs, 1951. A provocative theory of emotion as the product of conflicting tendencies, supported by data from the author's experiments as well as other evidence.

DEWEY, JOHN, *Human Nature and Conduct*. New York: The Modern Library, 1930. A classic treatise on the place of impulse, habit, and reflective thought in the organization of human behavior.

GOLDSTEIN, KURT, *The Organism*, pp. 67–121, 157–226, 291–397. New York: American Book Co., 1939. A critique of mechanical explanations of behavior in the light of evidence from biological research and the formulation of a conceptual scheme from the Gestalt standpoint.

HEBB, DONALD O., *The Organization of Behavior*. New York: John Wiley & Sons, 1949. A discussion of selected psychological problems in the light of recent research in neurophysiology, containing at many points remarkable confirmations of earlier speculations by Dewey.

VARENDONCK, J., *The Psychology of Daydreams*. London: George Allen & Unwin, 1921. A pioneering study of autistic thinking based upon introspective data, attempting to account for imagination in terms of adjustment tendencies inherent in living organisms.

4

The
cultural
matrix
of
role-playing

A glance at the steno-
graphic pool in any large organization will reveal at once the amazing variety of standards by which Americans live. Some of the
women take their work very seriously. They are punctual, are careful in their performance, worry at night over errors they have made,
practice shorthand in their spare time, and aspire for advancement
to supervisory positions. Others make some effort to keep pace, falling behind from time to time. They do not really mind their work
but forget about it as soon as they leave the office. Still others regard their job as a nuisance that unfortunately must be tolerated in
order to earn a living. They are easily distracted, spend much time
in the washroom, and make an effort only when watched. During
coffee breaks some are preoccupied with marriage; they speculate
about the personal lives of the various men on the staff, wonder
whom they could meet by joining the company bowling team, discuss their dates avidly, and gossip about the love affairs of those in
the office. Others are fashion conscious; they are immaculately

groomed, discuss the various dresses on sale at nearby stores, and observe with scorn those who do not bother to wear girdles. Although there is usually a friendly tolerance of such diverse interests, it is not surprising that the women periodically become suspicious of one another's intentions. Those who work hard are suspected of having ulterior motives, perhaps special privileges denied to others, and they are called by uncomplimentary epithets. Sometimes they are viewed with compassion as unfortunate creatures incapable of appreciating the better things in life. The concientious workers in turn look upon the others with disdain as shirkers who have no sense of responsibility. They wonder why women who are "clothes horses" or "man crazy" do not choose occupations in which they could pursue their interests more directly.

This illustration reveals differences not only in interests but in the assumptions with which the various women are approaching their work. It is difficult to understand what any person does without some notion of her definition of the situation, and the manner in which she defines a given situation depends upon her presuppositions. A woman who regards her job as a stopgap arrangement—a convenient way to send her husband through school—is not likely to see a challenging task in the same light as one who takes great pride in her ability as a stenographer. This suggests that many of the tensions in modern societies arise from the fact that people who are in daily contact do not experience their environment in the same manner.

This brings up questions of fundamental importance. What is the character of the environment in which human beings live and act? How can the experiences of different persons become shared? What are some of the circumstances under which the establishment of consensus becomes especially difficult?

Meaning as a Functional Unit

Much of current social psychology is devoted to the study of attitudes, habits, sentiments, motivated behavior patterns, concept formation, fixations, stereotypes, object cathexes, and similar topics. All these terms refer in one way or other to a relatively stable orientation on the part of some individual toward some aspect of his environment. It may be contended that someone has a favorable attitude toward redheads, or that red hair has some particular significance for him, or that for him persons with such hair are "cathected" in a particular way. Such expressions all point to a consistent organization in the behavior of a given person whenever he comes into contact with some object or class of objects. Since the various words all refer to these sustained relationships, matters could be simplified by the adoption of a single term to designate this functional unit. Rather than using one of the better known concepts and thereby becoming entangled in doctrinal quarrels, the more neutral term *meaning* is proposed. Although this concept has had a stormy career among philosophers, it is only rarely used as a technical term in social psychology. It has the additional advantage of being in accord with common sense usage.

The effective environment in which men live and act is made up of all kinds of meanings—meanings of physical objects, of people, of colors, of emotional reactions, of images, of various types of activity. Since meanings are generally believed to depend upon the characteristics of the objects themselves, those who have somewhat different backgrounds of experience often get into arguments over what things "really" are. A rancher whose holdings are so extensive that he must rely upon horses to do his work views these animals quite differently from a city dweller who rarely sees a horse except in motion pictures. Some people use books primarily for decorative purposes, and others use them only as paperweights; such persons are frequently condemned by those who actually read books as not appreciating their "real" significance. It is often assumed that such variations in "interpretation" arise from differences in the capacity of people to appreciate the inherent properties of objects.

Meanings, however, can be identified more fruitfully from a behavioristic standpoint—in terms of what people *do* with objects. This is particularly noticeable in the early definitions of children, who refer to a table as an object "to put something on," a chair as something to "sit on," or an automobile as something "to ride." This suggests not only that we initially learn meanings through action but also that *meanings are primarily a property of behavior and only secondarily a property of objects.* Seen in this light it is not strange that the same object can mean different things to different people. One need only note the differences in the meaning of the identical dog to its owner, to the operator of a pet shop, to an employee of the city pound, and to the postman to get some appreciation of the extent to which the meaning of an object with identical attributes can vary. A cross has a very special meaning for Christians; but there are many parts of the world in which it would be meaningless, for there are no organized ways of acting toward it. The significance of any object arises, then, from the manner in which it is used. Charles Peirce once declared that there was no distinction of meaning so fine as to consist of anything more than a possible difference in practice.[1] The physical properties of objects are important only in that they place limitations upon what men can do with them.

That meanings are primarily properties of behavior is demonstrated by the variability of sensations and by experiments in distorted perception. If meanings depend upon the attributes of objects, they should change whenever an object is perceived as being different. But this is not the case. Everything in the perceptual world is continually undergoing change, and nothing is ever experienced twice in the same way. Our experiences with even the most familiar object, like a wristwatch, differ in each instance as we see it from different angles, in different light, and in varying states of anxiety over time. In spite of this variation in what is actually seen, however, activities involving the wristwatch remain quite regular. Particularly instructive in this connection are the early experiments conducted by Stratton on the inversion of retinal images. For several days the psychologist wore special glasses through which he saw everything upside down. He notes over and over that he continued to act as he had done habitually in the past, repeatedly finding himself moving in seemingly inappropriate ways, i.e., in opposite directions. This suggests that he was not responding to stimuli emanating from the objects he handled; he was approaching them in ways that had become crystallized through past experience. Although after several days he became more accustomed to his inverted world, he found his conception of his surroundings to be more stable than he had anticipated.[2]

[1] Charles S. Peirce, *Chance, Love and Logic*, Morris R. Cohen, ed. (New York: Harcourt, Brace & Co., 1923), p. 44.

[2] George M. Stratton, "Some Preliminary Experiments on Vision without Inversion of the Retinal Image," *Psychological Review*, III (1806), 611–17;

That meanings cannot be the property of objects is further demonstrated by the existence of meaningful fictions. In every culture there are objects like Santa Claus, negative numbers, ghosts, and "races" of men characterized by certain psychological traits which can easily be shown not to exist. Such fictions are often useful, and they are sometimes supported by men who know that the beliefs which sustain them are false. As long as men act as if such things exist, these objects will remain meaningful.[3]

Although meanings can best be identified in behavioristic terms, they cannot be isolated merely by pointing to any specific thing that a man may do. Meanings are *generalized* orientations which cannot be specified in terms of what a man does in a particular time and place, for his reactions vary from situation to situation. Depending upon the circumstances under which one is confronted by a cross, he may kneel down before it, gaze at it, scoff at it, or turn away from it in shame. Recognizing that particular acts depend upon the exigencies of the situation, some psychologists have attempted to locate common elements in the reactions occurring under dissimilar circumstances, but their efforts have not been successful. What apparently makes possible the recognition of what objects mean to people is the fact that the various responses fit together into a *pattern;* there is a configuration that gives unity to the diverse movements. Meanings become discernible not so much in terms of what is common in what a man does under different circumstances but in terms of organization.

The different responses in various situations gain unity from the fact that the object is characterized *as if* it had certain stable properties. Thus, the meaning becomes discernible in spite of the diversity in behavior because all acts are predicated upon a consistent set of assumptions concerning the attributes of the object. As a result of past experience each person has a working conception of what an object is like, and this enables him to anticipate the kinds of experiences he would have upon meeting it under various circumstances. Because he can anticipate what is likely to happen in each case, he is prepared to act in particular ways. When a man sees an

---

and "Vision without Inversion of the Retinal Image," *ibid.,* IV (1897), 341–60, 463–81.

[3] Cf. Hans Vaihinger, *The Philosophy of "As If,"* C. K. Ogden, trans. (New York: Harcourt, Brace & Co., 1925).

automobile bearing down upon him, he does one thing; when his own car gets dirty, he does another; and when he has to get somewhere in a hurry, he does still something else. But all these acts rest on the assumption that automobiles have certain constant characteristics. It is through observing such combinations of responses that we make inferences as to what an object must mean to each person. In the same way, we are able to detect differences in meanings between individuals by observing contrasting combinations of reactions. If a man spends all his spare time polishing his car, is highly sensitive to advertisements on the care of automobiles, proves reluctant to drive it over bad roads, and beams in obvious pride whenever others admire its appearance, we conclude that his car does not mean the same thing to him as the vehicle of another man who does not notice a dent on his fender for over six months. Thus, each person develops stable orientations toward various objects. Depending upon the nature of his orientation, different acts become appropriate under different circumstances. But in spite of the diversity of reactions the relationship between a given person and an object remains relatively constant.

Of particular importance to human beings are the meanings of *categories*, the meanings of classes of objects and events. The necessity for classification arises from the fact that the environment in which we live is far too complex for us to take into account the unique qualities of each object we encounter. If men had to examine each object they were handling, they would be stopping constantly. Hence, objects and events are grouped into categories and are approached as if all the specific instances had the same characteristics. Once a category is defined, we can anticipate a certain kind of experiences in dealing with any concrete case. There are millions of horses in the world, and each one is unique; however, we place them together into a class and act toward any horse in a standardized manner. We know nothing of the idiosyncrasies of a particular horse we may encounter, but we are able to guide our conduct in terms of fixed expectations about horses in general. We take it for granted that horses can run faster than men, that they cannot fly, and that they will make no attempt to eat us. Hence, we would not be disposed to run away in fright, as might be the case were we confronted by a tiger. The particular tiger might actually be quite tame and much safer than most horses, but we would probably act in terms of our general characterization of tigers as ferocious and dangerous. Once any category is defined in terms of a set of properties, our expectations become fixed, and we are prepared to act in appropriate ways. It follows, then, that categorization involves much more than mere classification; each category is a meaning, a pattern of organized dispositions to act.

Categories are formed by ignoring differences in particulars and responding selectively to those properties which are relevant to carrying out an act. The capacity of men to construct and use such abstract meanings greatly facilitates the process of adjustment. Because men are able to perceive concrete events as instances of a general class, they can prepare themselves to act even when utilizing objects they have never seen before. Upon entering a classroom for the first time a student is able to approach a chair and to sit down without having to examine it to see whether or not it will support his weight. He may never have seen this particular chair before, but he is able to act appropriately because he can assume that it is much like any other chair. This means that men are able to face an ever changing world as if it were stable, orderly, and to a large extent predictable. Needless to say, this greatly simplifies the task of living.

One of the dimensions along which meanings vary is in their degree of complexity. Some meanings are relatively simple in that there are only a limited set of responses available, and others are highly complex in that an extensive variety of reactions might occur, depending upon the context in which the object is encountered. Whether meanings are simple or complex, however, does not depend upon the properties of the object, but upon the past experiences of the persons involved. For example, a housefly is a relatively simple object for most people; it is regarded as a nuisance, to be chased away and killed whenever possible. But to an entomologist specializing in the study of flies it is far from simple; indeed, there are literally thousands of things that he might do with reference to it.

Meanings also vary in the extent of their stability. Most meanings are relatively stable. Repeated experiences with similar objects tend to be sufficiently consistent to reinforce a stable set of assumptions concerning their characteristics. This does not mean, of course, that meanings do not change; they can usually be altered through contradictory experiences. A man who is firmly convinced that all snails are filthy and poisonous objects may change his mind after a trip to a French or Chinese restaurant, and a mother who is certain of the unworthiness of her son-in-law may be pleasantly surprised as she gets to know him better. There are some meanings, however, which are rigidly established and do not change even in the face of negative evidence. Such inflexible meanings, which will be called *fixations*, have been of special interest to psychiatrists, who suspect that they are defensive measures. Certain objects or events—hair color, darkened rooms, snakes, competitive situations—arouse fixed reactions which the person himself cannot understand. A man may develop a fear of cats, stiffening and shivering with every possibility of contact. No matter how frequently he tells himself that it is silly to be afraid of such a harmless object, he cannot help himself. In time he may learn to mask his overt reactions more skillfully, but inwardly he continues to react as if cats were dangerous.[4]

Meanings also differ in the extent to which men are consciously aware of them. In most instances men are more or less conscious of their orientations toward various objects, which may be characterized in imagination and in some cases even explicitly described in linguistic terms. Consciousness is especially acute when meanings are being learned; however, once they are well established, the responses become habitual, and a number of complex maneuvers can be executed with little awareness. For example, a person who is just learning to drive an automobile is very conscious of the various movements required to operate the vehicle, but once he has become a skilled driver, he can perform almost automatically with little awareness of what he is doing. But such meanings can be recalled to consciousness if necessary, as would be the case if the driver had to instruct someone else. As Freud pointed out, however, there are some meanings which are repressed; the person remains unconscious of them even when they are apparent to others. Thus, a woman may treat her brother as a dangerous rival and be completely unaware of her orientation. Her feelings would be too painful for her to admit them to herself, but the relationship becomes discernible in

[4] Cf. Sigmund Freud, *The Problem of Anxiety*, Henry A. Bunker, trans. (New York: W. W. Norton & Co., 1936); and Maurice N. Richter, "The Conceptual Mechanism of Stereotyping," *American Sociological Review*, XXI (1956), 568–71.

her behavior, which is remarkably consistent. When he is successful in his courtship, she forgets to congratulate him and becomes seriously ill on the day of his wedding; she accidentally loses things she knows to be of great value to him; she inadvertently exposes him to danger and then does nothing to defend him, being unable to perceive any reason for concern. Consciously she may speak of her love, but with every safe opportunity she engages in some kind of aggression. Should a psychiatrist call her attention to such matters, she would be shocked. But the fact that she denies in all sincerity the existence of any malice does not alter the fact that she is oriented to act toward her brother with disguised hostility.

Meanings range in clarity from rather vague, fragmentary impressions to clearly organized patterns. An example of a clearly identified meaning is the semantic ideal of science, a concept which is defined operationally. The operations through which the identification of such a concept is achieved consist of the procedures that the scientist undergoes in order to ascertain its meaning. A chemist can define sodium as an element that will register at a certain weight, and he can indicate the transformations that will occur if it is mixed with other elements under stated conditions. These are forms of behavior directed toward particles of sodium, and the pattern constitutes the meaning of the concept. When the most significant operations can be explicitly stated so that they can be repeated by others, the meaning has attained a clarity that is rare in daily life. But most meanings are far less clear, for people generally are not confronted with the necessity for precision that faces scientists. One may supplicate before a cross when he wants something badly, or adore it in a moment of ecstasy; but if someone should ask him what a cross meant, he would have difficulty in replying. If it were suggested that it symbolized the power and justice of God, he might agree, but without being quite sure of what these words represent. Similarly, one may feel uneasy in the presence of certain people. A person may find that he likes something without knowing why, or he may suddenly lash out at some comment with a ferocity that surprises himself as well as others. Such acts are predicated upon meanings which are only intuitively felt.[5]

[5] Cf. Kenneth Burke, *The Philosophy of Literary Form* (Baton Rouge: Louisiana State University Press, 1941), pp. 138–67; and Percy W. Bridgman,

There are relatively few objects that are emotionally neutral, like doorknobs which can be handled over and over without arousing feelings of any kind. Most objects elicit some kind of emotional reaction, and for each person there are some objects that have deep affective significance. Psychiatrists have pointed out that some meanings are so constructed as to elicit psychosomatic reactions such as sneezing, stomach aches, allergies, or even temporary blindness. This suggests that meanings vary considerably in the manner in which objects are evaluated and that the estimates of each object may differ considerably from person to person. Valuations may be viewed behavioristically as preferences—what one covets, wishes to avoid, or seeks to destroy. An object may be said to have *value* when one has a special interest in it.[6]

Objects are evaluated in terms of past experience. Through experience, direct or vicarious, expectations become fixed, and judgments are made in terms of what is anticipated. In general, whatever is regarded as a source of gratification is positively valued, and whatever is viewed as a source of frustration or pain is negatively valued. The general orientation toward a desirable object—a beautiful home, a position of prestige, a happy child—is to acquire and preserve it. If one possesses such objects, he looks after their well being; if he does not, he covets them. Objects which have been sources of pain are defined as dangerous, and the general tendency is to escape them. If they are sources of repeated or chronic frustration, they may become hated objects, which one seeks to destroy. Although they are not viewed as dangerous, disgusting objects are avoided. Contact is experienced as debasing and degrading, and intensity of disgust increases with degree of intimacy. This is true whether the object is the waste product of some animal, food that is taboo, or a person in some pariah group. Thus, not only physical objects but people as well are evaluated in these ways.

The specific emotional reactions aroused by such objects differ from situation to situation, depending upon the circumstances, but the general patterns of approach, hostility, and avoidance are readily discernible. When an attractive object is in one's possession,

"Some General Principles of Operational Analysis," *Psychological Review*, LII (1954), 246–49, 281–84.

6 Cf. Ralph B. Perry, *General Theory of Values* (New York: Longmans, Green & Co., 1926), pp. 115–212, 306–68, 400–519.

his pleasure is difficult to conceal, just as jealousy is difficult to hide when it is in the possession of a rival. When such an object is missing, one is stricken with anxiety: and when it is found again, he feels relieved. When a dangerous object is present, one subjectively experiences fear and takes up a defensive stance. If he has any choice on the matter, he tries to avoid it. If he must approach it, he does so with caution, seeking whatever aid and protection he can. When it is gone, he becomes relaxed. Objects which are viewed as ugly and repugnant sometimes evoke tendencies to vomit. Various neutral objects may also acquire this quality through contact; thus, most people will not eat from a container of stool or sputum, even after it has been cleaned. If something thought to be disgusting is touched inadvertently, there is often a lingering feeling of dirtiness.[7] As in the case of any meaning, the measure of the value a person attaches to an object is not what he says about its preciousness but the care he devotes to obtaining and using the means without which it cannot be attained.

Although supporting evidence is by no means conclusive, it has been contended that objects which consistently elicit strong emotional responses are those in which the meaning is made up of conflicting impulses. Especially when there is opposition between the organic mobilization to act and socially sanctioned conduct, impulses that are frequently aroused are regularly inhibited. An object may be felt to be dangerous, but for all but small children there are conventional norms discouraging the open display of apprehension. There may be a strong impulse to escape, but one does not dare run away unless others also recognize a clear necessity for doing so. Or one may be sexually attracted to someone who is taboo. If so, upon each contact impulses are aroused which are checked immediately by strong feelings of guilt. Difficulties may also arise from constant association with people regarded as base objects made unavoidable by the character of one's work. In such cases, blockage and conflict are built into the meaning of the object. Feelings of anger, fear, or disgust are repeatedly experienced, for inhibiting tendencies are aroused by anticipating the social consequences of consummating one's initial inclinations. The most poignant discomforts arise when one is ambivalent.[8]

[7] Cf. Andrus Angyal, "Disgust and Related Aversions," *Journal of Abnormal and Social Psychology*, XXXVI (1941), 393–412.

[8] Cf. Sigmund Freud, *Group Psychology and the Analysis of the Ego*, James

Some social scientists have insisted that the study of values has no place in their work. This objection arises largely from confusing the fact that human beings act toward values with the danger of a scientist's being blinded by value judgments. To make the study of human behavior approximate the canons of science, propositions must be judged on the basis of empirical evidence and not on the basis of the personal preferences of the scientist. One can agree with this contention and still recognize the fact that human beings are constantly evaluating the various meanings they construct, sharpening their interests, and making choices in an effort to pursue some values and to avoid others. Desires and aversions are activities which are observable. Hence, propositions about valuations are not themselves value judgments; they are statements about regularities in the things men do and can be checked through evidence.[9] Valuation is a form of behavior which is much too important to be ignored by social psychologists.

Precisely because social psychologists have long been aware of the importance of stable orientations that people develop toward various aspects of their environment, numerous attempts have been made to study them empirically. The most common procedure has been the use of scales for the measurement of attitudes. Thurstone, one of the pioneers in this field, constructed a scale to indicate the extent to which a person is for or against some object by asking them what they would do or how they would feel if confronted by it under a variety of circumstances. Taking these symbolic representations of responses in different situations toward a common object, he devised a technique for computing a quantitative score for each person. Other scales, like those developed by Bogardus and Likert, rest on the same rationale. Guttman was more concerned with the intensity of such orientations and attempted to develop a scale to measure this feature.[10] Much valuable data have been gath-

---

Strachey, trans. (New York: Liveright Publishing Co., 1949), pp. 18–19, 55–56, 60–70; and Bull, *op. cit.*

[9] John Dewey, "Theory of Valuation," *International Encyclopedia of Unified Science*, Otto Neurath, ed. (Chicago: University of Chicago Press, 1939), Vol. II, No. 4.

[10] For a review of earlier techniques and results see Gardner Murphy, Lois B. Murphy, and Theodore M. Newcomb, *Experimental Social Psychology* (New York: Harper & Bros., 1937), pp. 889–1046; more recent procedures are described in Samuel A. Stouffer *et al.*, *Measurement and Prediction* (Princeton: Princeton University Press, 1950). For a critical evaluation of such studies see

ered, and the scales have proved useful in many experimental studies; however, one serious objection can be raised to these currently accepted practices. The scores on all scales are computed by adding or subtracting quantitative values assigned to the responses indicated for each situation. However, meanings are discernible in the *configuration* of responses, and such patterns cannot be described through the summation of component elements. Many years ago Faris suggested that one might study attitudes more fruitfully by asking individuals for their characterizations of the object in question, but until recently his suggestion has been ignored. Promising starts are now being made in this direction, especially by Osgood and his colleagues.[11]

The Social Validation of Meanings

Meanings, once they have been formed, tend to be self-sustaining. Even though new events are continually taking place, each man is able to conceive of his world as being reasonably stable. Although nothing ever happens twice in the same manner, men are able to ignore differences in particulars, to classify objects and events into categories, and to characterize each class in terms of given attributes. They are prepared to act in understood ways, and their environment remains meaningful as long as everything happens in accordance with their expectations. The relative stability of the orientation of men toward their world is assured by the very character of human perception.

Men attempt to cope with their environment through perception. Although it is generally assumed that what is experienced is a mirror-like reflection of what is "out there" in reality, all perception is selective. Perception is also *cumulative* and *constructive*. It is not so much a reaction to stimuli but a serial process in which men note and respond to cues to which they are already sensitized, form hypotheses about the characteristics of the object with which they

---

Quinn McNemar, "Opinion-Attitude Methodology," *Psychological Bulletin,* XLIII (1946), 289–374.

[11] Ellsworth Faris, *The Nature of Human Nature* (New York: McGraw-Hill Book Co., 1937), pp. 127–43. Cf. Charles E. Osgood, George J. Suci, and Percy H. Tannenbaum, *The Measurement of Meaning* (Urbana: University of Illinois Press, 1957).

are confronted, and then confirm these expectations by making further observations.

In general, then, men do not react passively to what happens; they approach their environment through a succession of hypotheses. These expectations, which are derived from the meanings of various objects, are indications of the kinds of experiences one would have if his assumptions about this aspect of the world are correct. When dealing with a familiar object each person has a working conception of its attributes, and the various stimuli are selected and organized into cues which serve as the basis for inference. For a man who is going for a walk toward evening, a hazy blue in the sky is not simply a color but a cue indicative of how much time he has left to return without difficulties. A hungry man does not react to a mere mass of soft fibres but sees food which can bring him pleasure as he devours it. What men are inclined to see in any situation depends upon what they anticipate, and what they anticipate depends upon the meanings with which they have entered the situation.

Once such hypotheses have been projected, men become acutely sensitized to those cues which will enable them to test their expectations. The perceptual field is organized to maximize the possibilities of noting cues that are relevant to the hypotheses and to minimize reacting to cues that are not. Thus, perceiving is never just receiving; there is always discrimination and selection. A person walking alone at night by a graveyard or through a dark alley is especially alert to sounds indicative of the presence of an assassin. It is taken for granted that assault and robbery could occur under such circumstances, and the possibility that such a criminal may be lurking in wait is a hypothesis that is seriously entertained. All this suggests that the manner in which anyone perceives his environment depends upon the meanings that various objects have for him as well as upon what he is doing.[12]

Since meanings are products of past experience, people from different cultural backgrounds should perceive identical situations in somewhat different ways. Those with different meanings will project different hypotheses; hence, they will be responsive to different cues

[12] Cf. Leo Postman, "Toward a General Theory of Cognition," in *Social Psychology at the Crossroads*, John H. Rohrer and Muzafer Sherif, eds. (New York: Harper & Bros., 1951), pp. 242–72; and Mead, *The Philosophy of the Act, op. cit.*, pp. 103–73.

and construct different perceptual objects. This was demonstrated by Bagby in an ingenious experiment comparing Mexican and American subjects. He set up ten pairs of slides to be viewed through a stereoscope. On one side he mounted a picture of an object that would be familiar to most Mexicans—such as a bull-fighter, a dark haired girl, and a peon—and on the other side a similar picture of an object with which most Americans would be acquainted—such as a baseball player, a blonde girl, and a farmer. The corresponding photographs resembled one another in form, contour of the major mass, texture, and the distribution of light and shadows. In some cases the subjects saw a mixture of the two pictures, and in other cases they saw the two superimposed; and there were even instances in which they saw only the picture that was culturally strange. In the vast majority of cases, however, the Americans saw only what was already familiar to them, and the Mexicans likewise saw only the scenes placed in their own culture. This study thus supports the contention that the selection and interpretation of cues depend upon one's expectations, which in turn are learned while participating in an organized society.[13]

Further evidence of the extent to which perception depends upon meanings, especially upon values, is provided by an experiment by Bruner and Goodman. A group of children from prosperous families and another group drawn from the slums were asked to indicate the size of various coins. All children overestimated size, but the amount of overestimation increased regularly with the monetary value of the coins and not with their actual size. Thus, a dime is smaller than a penny but is worth more, and the deviation between actual and judged size for the dime was greater than that for the penny. Furthermore, it was found that the poor children, who are presumably much more preoccupied with money, overestimated the size of coins considerably more than the rich ones. In addition, the exaggerated appraisal became relatively greater as the value of the coins increased. Several attempts have been made to repeat this study, sometimes with refinements in technique, and the findings have not always been consistent. In no case, however, have the data

[13] James W. Bagby, "A Cross-Cultural Study of Perceptual Predominance in Binocular Rivalry," *Journal of Abnormal and Social Psychology*, LIV (1957), 331–34.

supported the view that perception is a direct response to stimulation.[14]

Special problems arise in the perception of human beings—unique individuals as well as categories of people. During the latter part of the nineteenth century the German philosopher Dilthey, in support of his argument for the development of special methods in the social sciences, contended that the observation of human beings is fundamentally different from the observation of physical objects in that in the former the observer could enter into the life of the object through sympathetic introspection. In this way *personifications*, what human beings mean to one another, differ from all other meanings. The perception of another as a living creature involves projecting to the object a capacity for making choices, which may include acting contrary to what appears to be in their best interests. This variability in conduct makes the anticipation of human activities more difficult; indeed, without some appreciation of the inner experiences of the other person it is almost impossible to anticipate effectively what he is likely to do. This means that the hypotheses used in the perception of people usually include an imputation of motives. Such inferences generally rest upon a partial identification with the other, imagining how the observer himself would feel if he were the other person. Thus, the perception of people requires some measure of role-taking.

But the inner experiences of other people cannot be observed directly. One can only make inferences on the basis of observations of overt behavior, and this presents many difficulties. People differ considerably in the manner in which they reveal their feelings, and most adults have a repertoire of diversionary gestures to facilitate concealment. Furthermore, the same external movements can sometimes be interpreted in several different ways, all of them plausible.[15]

[14] Jerome S. Bruner and Cecile C. Goodman, "Value and Need as Organizing Factors in Perception," *ibid.*, XLII (1947), 33–44. Cf. Launor F. Carter and Kermit Schooler, "Value, Need, and Other Factors in Perception," *Psychological Review*, LVI (1949), 200–07; and Wayne R. Ashley, Robert S. Harper, and Dale L. Runyon, "The Perceived Size of Coins in Normal and Hypnotically Induced Economic States," *American Journal of Psychology*, LXIV (1951), 564–72.

[15] Patrick Gardner (ed.), *Theories of History* (Glencoe: Free Press, 1959) pp. 213–23. Cf. H. A. Hodges, *Wilhelm Dilthey: An Introduction* (London: Rout-

Should a companion yawn in the midst of a conversation, this may be interpreted as an indication of restlessness and boredom. This may result in special efforts to enliven the discussion, especially if it is not known that the person had been up most of the night before wating at the airport for a visiting relative. Under the circumstances it is amazing that the perception of people is as reliable as it generally proves to be.

While we are able to characterize those we know personally in terms of their distinctive traits, most of our contacts, especially in urban communities, are with strangers. Strangers are usually perceived as instances of some category. Human beings may be classified in many ways, but the most commonly used categories are the various stereotypes found in all communities. A *stereotype* is a popular concept, designating a rough grouping of people in terms of some easily noted mark, supported by widespread beliefs concerning their attributes. Such abstractions are formed by combining the accentuated forms of conduct on the part of some of the people so classified. People in ethnic minorities are often approached as if they were all alike. Negroes are often characterized as lazy, ignorant, unreliable, having a good sense of rhythm, prone to fight with razors, and having strong preferences for chicken and watermelon. Jews are frequently regarded as crafty, aggressive, and constantly preoccupied with money. Other common stereotypes include the woman driver, who can be counted on to do the wrong thing, and the spinster, with her sublimated interest in sex, predilection for cats, and vulnerability to attentive males. Although college graduates should know better, many of them go through life thinking of professors as kindly, stoop-shouldered gentlemen, badly in need of a haircut, absent-mindedly conversing in an esoteric vocabulary, often with a foreign accent. Such categories are perpetuated in spite of the numerous inaccuracies because some of the features in terms of which they are lumped together are sometimes acknowledged by the people themselves. Those who are stereotyped often consist of people who identify themselves as being of a kind. Even when such beliefs are completely unjustified, they may serve as the basis for invidious distinctions, for they provide definite hypotheses with

ledge & Kegan Paul, 1944), pp. 11–35; and Charles H. Cooley, *Sociological Theory and Social Research* (New York: Henry Holt & Co., 1930), pp. 289–309.

which to approach people about whom nothing else is known [16]

The category into which a person is placed is a matter of considerable importance, for the motives that can be plausibly imputed to him depend upon it. If those in a given category are assumed to have certain characteristics, they are expected to act in a particular way, and others become sensitized to cues indicative of such conduct. If a person is labelled as a "good" woman, it is assumed that she has no sex interests outside of marriage; if she should make gestures which appear to have erotic overtones, they are dismissed as irrelevant. In contrast, a woman who is reputed to be "bad" may have difficulty in persuading others that she is not making seductive overtures. Studies of political campaigns show that partisans tend to perceive the stand taken by candidates of their own party as being like their own, whether in fact this is the case or not. Similarly, the position of the opponent is seen as unfavorable. Therefore, once a speaker is classified as representing the opposition party, nothing that he says seems to matter. If there are no particular items to which objections can be made, his sincerity is questioned. When listening to speakers of one's own party, however, only the best motives are imputed.[17] Thus, the kind of hypotheses that can be projected to people depends upon the manner in which they are classified and the evaluation placed upon the category. Much of the tension characterizing modern society becomes more understandable once we get an appreciation of some of the weird assumptions with which people approach one another.

If men perceive familiar objects of all kinds by projecting expectations and then becoming sensitized to cues relevant to them, the question arises as to whether their respective worlds are not entirely in the imagination. After all, each man does construct his working conception of his surroundings, even creating fictional meanings having no counterpart in reality. They can never be directly aware of the real world as such, only of the nervous im-

[16] Walter Lippmann, Public Opinion (New York: Harcourt, Brace & Co., 1922), pp. 79–156. Cf. Louis Wirth, The Ghetto (Chicago: University of Chicago Press, 1928), pp. 63–95; and Paul F. Secord, "Stereotyping and Favorableness in the Perception of Negro Faces," Journal of Abnormal and Social Psychology, LIX (1959), 309–14.

[17] Bernard Berelson, Paul F. Lazarsfeld, and William N. McPhee, Voting: A Study of Opinion Formation in a Presidential Campaign (Chicago: University of Chicago Press, 1954), pp. 215–33.

pulses emanating from their organs of sensitivity. How, then, can the correspondence between what is perceived and what is "out there" be explained? To the extent that the hypotheses constitute the basis for behavior, most of them must be reasonably accurate if they are to remain effective foundations for adjustment. This suggests that all hypotheses are subject to repeated confirmations of some kind.

The most common form of confirmation is reality testing. Meanings constitute generalized relationships between a living organism and an object. Because an object is assumed to have certain properties it is approached with fixed expectations, and the relationship can be sustained only as long as these expectations are fulfilled. Men would not continue to regard a tiger as a dangerous object if each tiger they met smiled and licked their hands, nor would they regard a speeding automobile as something to be avoided if the vehicles splintered upon coming into contact with human bodies. Our beliefs about the human species would become untenable if people did not cry when sad, laugh when happy, or scream when in contact with something hot. It is the actual occurrence of what one had anticipated that reinforces meanings and gives men confidence in their perspectives. Whenever expectations are not confirmed, as in a mirage, it is said that the experience was "only in the mind," and further efforts are made to construct better hypotheses. Thus, man's outlook may be shaped through his interests and socially defined categories, but its validity depends at least in part upon the characteristics of the real world. It is in this sense that perception is seriated; it consists of a succession of trials. Man learns by acting, by testing his beliefs in practice.

There are many instances, however, in which direct reality testing does not occur. Under such circumstances meanings are sometimes confirmed through their consistency with other beliefs. When one is not certain that he has heard a word correctly, he checks the general context in which it is used to see whether or not it belongs there. In the now famous broadcast by Orson Welles on October 30, 1938, many listeners who were not sure whether or not a real invasion from Mars was being reported checked with other sources. Some switched to other stations to see whether they were also reporting the "news," and others looked up the radio program in the newspaper. Cantril found in his study of the incident that the participants in the mass panic that resulted from the broadcast consisted of people who did not make such checks or did so unsuccessfully. Thus, confirmation of expectations is facilitated by supporting hypotheses and inhibited by contradictory ones.[18]

Confirmation may also arise from consensus. Whenever one is uncertain about what he has perceived, he turns to others to see whether they have had the same experience. How is one to be certain that he is not dreaming? How does one differentiate between hallucination and reality? It is largely through a comparison of experiences with others. If others agree that something has happened, however unexpected it may have been, one has greater confidence in his own sensations. Furthermore, confirmation comes not only from such explicit communication but also from the observation of deeds. When confronted by a horrifying scene a person also notes the shock on the faces of others around him, and if for any reason they do not appear as upset as he feels they should be, he re-examines the situation. When one overhears an uncouth remark but sees that no one else appears to be offended, he concludes that he did not hear correctly. Thus, people do not always "trust their eyes and ears"; they need direct and indirect assurances from other people in whom they have confidence. Even when one feels positive about his own experience, if all others insist that he is mistaken, he may begin to raise questions about his sanity. In the last analysis, then, consensus may prove to be the crucial criterion of reliability. In our highly technical society there are many scientific hypotheses which laymen cannot test for themselves. Often they are inconsistent with popularly accepted beliefs, and yet the scientific account of the world is often accepted as true.

Sometimes, even in the face of contradictions from all other sources, people may cling to their own hypotheses through inner convictions, especially if they are congruent with their emotional dispositions.[19] A pious man may infer the existence of God from observing the overwhelming beauty of some scene, reasoning that it could not possibly have been created by any power but God. Or

[18] Hadley Cantril, Hazel Gaudet and Herta Herzog, *The Invasion from Mars* (Princeton: Princeton University Press, 1947), pp. 91–95. Cf. Leo Postman and Jerome S. Bruner, "Hypothesis and the Principle of Closure," *Journal of Psychology*, XXXIII (1952), 113–24.

[19] Jerome S. Bruner, Jacqueline J. Goodnow, and George A. Austin, *A Study of Thinking* (New York: John Wiley & Sons, 1956), pp. 17–21.

a man with paranoid tendencies may perceive with absolute certitude voices plotting his destruction. To others the barely audible sounds may have no particular structure, but he is able to project his own aggressive hypothesis. It appears that the more consistent a particular hypothesis is with one's interests, the fewer cues are necessary for its confirmation. There are vast differences between people in their ability to retain their perspectives in the face of contradictions from others.

In general, whenever expectations are not confirmed, activity is temporarily disrupted while new alternatives are considered. In the face of such incongruence continued dependence upon challenged hypotheses occurs only under unusual conditions. In ambiguous situations greater reliance is placed upon suspected hypotheses, especially when sufficient sensory cues are not available. To a terrified child walking by a graveyard on a very dark night the slight rustling of leaves may confirm his suspicion that an ogre is about to pounce upon him, for he cannot see well enough to make further tests of this impression. It is to be noted that the cues in Bagby's experiment were similarly ambiguous. The strength of a hypothesis also depends upon the frequency of past confirmations. Those who have never heard a wall talk take it for granted that this is impossible. Should one hear articulated sounds emanating from a wall, he is likely to search for a concealed person or loudspeaker. Should he fail to locate such a plausible source, he would probably conclude that he is losing his mind before accepting the judgment that the wall had actually talked.[20]

Thus, meanings are constantly reaffirmed in action. Since most deeds are performed by men in their capacity as participants in some kind of collective enterprise, virtually all meanings are subject to some measure of social control. Most meanings are social in that what any man is likely to do with reference to a given object is largely circumscribed by group norms concerning its appropriate use. Especially in the evaluation of objects there are accepted criteria for ascertaining what is wise or unwise, economical or extravagant, effective or futile. On the basis of such understandings certain modes of conduct are adjudged silly, dangerous, or sensible. Meanings are patterns of potential activity, and the responses that

[20] Cf. Postman, op. cit.; for experimental evidence see Leo Postman, Jerome S. Bruner and Richard D. Walk, "The Perception of Error," British Journal of Psychology, XLII (1951), 1–10.

might be elicited in various situations are limited by social considerations.

Of course, not all meanings are shared in this manner. They differ in the extent to which they enjoy consensus, ranging from purely *private* meanings which are peculiar to a given individual to those which are highly *conventional*, like scientific concepts that are operationally defined. A meaning is conventional when most of the people in a given culture share common beliefs concerning the properties of an object and when there are group norms about its use. There is usually a range of sanctioned variation in behavior, but the bounds of appropriate conduct are limited by custom. Thus, an automobile may be treated in a variety of ways, but should a person enshrine one or use it to live in, others are bound to raise questions about his sanity. Or in the case of a common object like a chair, a carpenter knows how to make one; a furniture dealer knows how to get it and what to do with it; and other people use it for purposes of sitting. All of these acts are predicated upon common assumptions concerning the attributes of chairs. Conventional meanings, then, are patterns of accepted behavior which have been crystallized from the standpoint shared in a group. By virtue of the fact that each person has a unique background of experience, however, he develops special ways of acting toward many conventionally defined objects and thereby forms distinctive meanings of his own. Such meanings are private, not in that they are inaccessible to others but in that the organization of behavioral tendencies is idiosyncratic.

In the case of meanings that enjoy a high degree of consensus the anticipated reactions of other people are a part of the expectations with which one approaches the object. A person anticipates tacit approval when conforming to customary usage, praise if he acts correctly even at considerable sacrifice, and condemnation or some other kind of negative sanction when he does not act properly. Such expectations are a part of his orientation toward the object. As an illustration let us take the case of a man suffering from a severe cold who discovers just as his nose begins to run that he has misplaced his handkerchief. If an American flag hanging nearby were the only piece of cloth available, it is very unlikely that he would use it, even though its physical properties might be admirably suited for such a purpose. Indeed, it probably would not even occur to him that the flag might be suitable for blowing his nose, and even if it did, he would reject the possibility at once. He can easily anticipate the shock and dismay, if not the outrage, of others were they to observe him committing such a sacrilege. Thus, the American flag has a conventional meaning as a symbol, and this special meaning precludes many acts which are physically possible. Most of the hypotheses through which familiar objects are perceived include such reactions on the part of others. Many of the things that men do are social, then, not only in that they constitute responses to other people but also in that *the anticipated responses of other people are incorporated into the actual organization of conduct.*

These observations suggest that *man's conception of reality is largely a social process.* This is not to imply that there is no real world "out there" but that what men know about it is a product of group participation. Men approach their world through expectations learned as participants in organized groups, hypotheses which may even be reaffirmed without reality testing. Thus, man's conception of his environment is something that is constructed. Each person learns to participate in this world by having his behavioral tendencies corrected and by having the appropriate acts appreciated, until finally he learns to behave as others expect him to behave. Although categories are revised or replaced from time to time and inaccurate beliefs are successfully corrected, at any given time most meanings are essentially what people in a given universe of discourse agree that they are. What people generally call "reality" is a working orientation over which there is a high degree of consensus.

The Symbolic Organization of Experience

Behavior consists of adjustments to changing life conditions, but the environment to which men adjust is essentially a substitute environment. Men do not live in the world of immediate sensory impressions, for their effective environment has spatial and temporal extension. What a man does depends upon his definition of the situation. Much that is actually present is ignored; one simply does not notice many features of the world around him. Definitions also include much that is not physically present. A man who has just missed a bus need not run after it; he is reasonably certain that another will come along in time, even though he cannot see it. In making decisions he may worry about the probable reactions of his mother, who has been dead for several years. One talks meaningfully about foreign countries he has never visited, and he bases many decisions upon considerations of which one knows only indirectly through reading. Furthermore, men avoid doing all sorts of things in anticipation of future consequences, events that have not yet occurred. Thus, the world in which men live and act includes the present, past, and future; it includes the remembered and the expected, the potential as well as the actual. The definition of the situation is a reconstruction from sensory experiences; it arises from selecting what is pertinent and bringing to bear upon it memories of other events thought to be relevant.

The manner in which a person consistently defines a succession of situations depends upon his organized perspective. A perspective is an ordered view of one's world, what is taken for granted about various physical objects, events, and human nature. The environment in which men live is a unity of order, not merely an aggregate of things. The substitute world consists of a set of meanings, and behavior is predicated upon all kinds of understandings about the attributes of various categories of objects. Perceptual cues arouse hypotheses about the characteristics of an object, many of which cannot actually be seen. For example, an attractive woman often draws appreciative whistles. The sensory clues consist of light waves reflected by her movements, the color of her hair, or her facial expressions. The whistles are not reactions to these sensations, but to the hypotheses elicited about the object. The response is to what is imagined about coming into contact with such a human being. Thus, the world is organized in terms of the assumptions men make about various objects and classes of objects, and this organization is more imposed upon sensory data than elicited from them.

Sensory data are organized into conceptions not only of things and their qualities but also of the order of things in spatial coexistence and of the order of things in time.[21] Men do not walk through walls, and one can see more accurately in bright light than in the dark. There are assumptions about appropriate sequences. If a spectator at a baseball game were to see a ball flying toward center field before the bat is swung, he would be quite upset. A

---

[21] Cf. Ernst Cassirer, *The Philosophy of Symbolic Forms*, Ralph Manheim, trans. (New Haven: Yale University Press, 1957), Vol. III, pp. 107-90.

perspective, then, consists of premises concerning what is plausible and what is possible. What is called "knowledge" is not simply a collection of things with which we are familiar; it is an orientation toward a real or imaginary order of the possible—a scheme of space and time, of relations between objects, an order governed by rules. It is on the basis of this order and within its rules that men act. Without it life would be chaotic; even doubts and questions are possible only within an unquestioned frame of reference. As Riezler puts it, one's perspective is an outline scheme, which, running ahead of experience, defines and guides it.[22] By assuming such regularity, even when they know that events are not absolutely predictable, men are able to pursue their interests with reasonable assurance that the world of tomorrow will be much the same as it is today.

The construction of perspectives is greatly facilitated by the capacity of men to use symbols, especially linguistic symbols. The world is presented in sensory experience as a kaleidoscopic flux of impressions, which are organized in terms of the categories that each person learns in his group. Nothing ever happens twice in exactly the same manner; yet men are able to adjust to each occurrence with some assurance that things will happen much as they had in the past. Because men can break up their experiences, classify them into units, and use words to refer to these segments, it becomes possible to give organization to the inchoate sequences of sensation. By abstracting out of historical reality they can hold a segment of the totality constant, relive it in memory, and compare it with similar occurrences in the past. Most experiences are thus classified.

Human life takes on some of its distinctive characteristics because men have the ability to use symbols to refer to meanings. But what is a *symbol?* Roughly speaking, a symbol is anything that stands for something else. A flag is a symbol for a nation. The piece of colored cloth often evokes patriotic sentiments and plays an important part in the mobilization of millions of men for war. Seeing someone treat the flag with disrespect can arouse the most violent emotional reactions, for men often regard the piece of cloth as if it were the

[22] Kurt Riezler, *Man: Mutable and Immutable* (Chicago: Henry Regnery Co., 1951), pp. 62–72. Cf. Alfred R. Lindesmith and Anselm Strauss, *Social Psychology* (New York: The Dryden Press, 1956), pp. 46–80; and Alfred Schuetz, "Choosing among Projects of Action," *Philosophy and Phenomenological Research*, XII (1951), 165–69.

nation with which they identify themselves. Hence, the discourtesy is experienced as a personal insult. In our society a kiss is widely accepted as a symbol of affection; therefore, the willingness of a girl to kiss on a first date is taken as an indication of her desire to continue the association. Most important are the linguistic symbols, the combinations of articulated sounds as well as written marks which are used to represent almost all meanings. A symbol, then, is any object, mode of conduct, or word toward which men act as if it were something else. Whatever the symbol stands for constitutes its meaning.

Although there are some exceptions, in most cases the connection between a symbol and the meaning it represents is arbitrary; the meanings designated are generally a matter of convention. Therefore, the meaning of a symbol cannot be derived from an examination of the symbol itself. There is nothing intrinsic in a piece of colored cloth that would necessitate or even suggest its standing for a nation, and to a person unfamiliar with the practice even the most exhaustive study of the cloth would not lead to its meaning. A wink may be an indication of knowing something that others do not know or in some contexts may be an invitation to seduction, but there is nothing in the shutting of the eyelids which points to either meaning. The wearing of "duckbill" haircuts is symbolic of membership in certain juvenile groups, just as the refusal to wear lipstick may be indicative of belonging to certain religious cults; again the connection rests upon consensus. Nowhere is this principle better illustrated than in linguistic symbols. The various sound combinations that make up our words are of themselves of little significance, but within each universe of discourse there are a number of common understandings as to what is represented by each word.

The actual significance of a symbol, then, is out of all proportion to the apparent triviality of meaning suggested by its intrinsic properties, for men perceive symbols and then act toward the meanings they represent. Soldiers risk their lives on battlefields to save a flag from falling into the hands of the enemy; the cloth in itself is of little value, but what it stands for is of great importance. Similarly, the sounds used in human speech are commonplace; almost anyone can articulate most of them with relative ease. Under some circumstances, however, these symbols can move men to engage in holy wars, to undertake dangerous pilgrimages, to participate in brutal lynchings, or to lay down their lives in the heroic defense of a hopeless cause. In such behavior there is an imputation of significance which goes far beyond what is inherent in the symbol itself.

The capacity to form abstractions and to refer to them by symbols frees human beings from the dictates of their immediate environment. Only infants, other animals, and some psychotic patients are confined to the world of the "here and now." Others are not directly dependent upon their sensory experiences, for they live in a substitute world.

If perspectives are organized in terms of linguistic symbols, it follows that people who speak different languages should experience their respective worlds in somewhat different ways. One's capacity to comprehend and manipulate his world is circumscribed by the linguistic symbols available to him. The theory of the symbolic transformation of human experience has been entertained by philosophers, anthropologists, and philologists for over a century, and it has been stated most clearly in recent times by Sapir and Whorf.[23] A language, once formed, has a self-contained organization somewhat like mathematics, and it previsages possible experience in accordance with accepted formal limitations. Since meanings are not so much discovered in experience as imposed upon it, perception is limited by each language; men put what they perceive into preexisting linguistic categories. Differences in vocabulary, then, affect the content of thought; in some groups it is possible to make detailed distinctions between colors, and in others elaborate refinements can be made in the delineation of human sentiments. Whorf contended that not only the content but the structure of thinking also depends upon language, that certain kinds of temporal relationships, for example, cannot be expressed in some languages because of the peculiarities of their grammar. Thus, language, by limiting the meanings that can be designated and manipulated, provides the matrix within which action and thought take place.

Both Sapir and Whorf were unimpressed with the differences among the various Indo-European languages and turned their attention to the various American Indian tongues. To show that different

[23] Edward Sapir, *Selected Writings in Language, Culture, and Personality,* David Mandelbaum, ed. (Berkeley: University of California Press, 1949), pp. 160–66; Benjamin L. Whorf, *Language, Thought, and Reality* (New York: John Wiley & Co., 1956), pp. 134–59, 207–19. A critical assessment of this approach can be found in *Language in Culture,* Harry Hoijer, ed. (Chicago: University of Chicago Press, 1954).

peoples dissected nature in diverse ways they pointed to contrasts in grammar and to presumably corresponding distinctions in world view. While such studies illustrate that language and outlook vary from group to group, they do not necessarily demonstrate the hypothesized relationship between these two aspects of culture. Therefore, attempts have been made to introduce greater control over the variables. Two experiments by Carroll and Casagrande are instructive. When reference is being made to "breaking" in the language of the Hopi Indians, distinctions are made which are not ordinarily noted in English. One verb is used when there is a single fission; and another, when the object is shattered into many pieces. Three sets of line drawings were prepared in which such differences might be detected by those sensitized to them. Hopi-speaking and English-speaking subjects were expected to classify them in different combinations, and the results roughly supported the hypothesis. Another experiment was conducted among the Navaho Indians. When verbs designating "handling" are used in Navaho, the speaker must indicate the shape or some other essential attribute of the object being manipulated; hence, Navaho-speaking subjects would be expected to show greater sensitivity to form. Ten pairs of objects which varied in shape, size, and color were prepared, and three groups of subjects were asked to classify them. The results showed that the Navaho-speaking children tended to classify by shape rather than by size or color more often than the English-speaking Navaho children. However, the performance of the third group, American children living in Boston, resembled that of the Navaho-speaking subjects. When comparisons were made by age, however, the Navaho-speaking children outstripped the others in sensitivity to form at a very young age, although the differences were minimized with increasing age.[24] While the results are inconclusive, most of the data support the hypothesis.

There are sources other than cross-cultural studies from which relevant data may be drawn. Although memory is generally regarded as a neurological process, there are grounds for believing that it rests at least in part upon linguistic devices. Dates and calendars organize the distribution of events over time, and one can

[24] John B. Carroll and Joseph B. Casagrande, "The Function of Language Classifications in Behavior," in *Readings in Social Psychology*, Eleanor E. Maccoby, Theodore M. Newcomb, and Eugene L. Hartley, eds. (New York: Henry Holt & Co., 1958), pp. 18–31.

readily imagine how difficult it would be to disentangle past occurrences without such a symbolic framework. Similarly, how could
anyone recall the color of his childhood home if he had no vocabulary for designating colors? Most people are unable to remember
complex dances even of their own culture, but students of the dance
are able to recreate hundreds of intricate routines from all over the
world. The difference is that choreographers have a special system
of symbols for recording in detail every movement of the human
body, even the flick of a finger. Among social psychologists concerned with memory Halbwachs emphasized the importance of the
social context. He contended that a person who had been assimilated into a new group with a markedly different perspective would
have difficulty in holding on to his old memories, for he would have
to adopt a different scheme of designation. Furthermore, the remembered events would be seen in a new light.[25] A good example is
a person who has learned psychoanalytic theory. He sees his past
life from a new standpoint, and what had previously seemed trivial
now appears to have been of crucial importance. Furthermore, what
is recalled is couched in a new vocabulary, such as, "oral fixation"
and the "failure to resolve the Oedipal situation."

The experiences of handicapped persons, such as the deaf and
blind, are especially instructive. Although deprived of the sense of
sight and hearing from infancy, Helen Keller wrote a number of
books in which she described vivid colors and made references to
beautiful music. When questioned about this, Miss Keller replied
that she could comprehend the meaning of such words from analogy. She indicated that she could think, reason, and draw inferences as if she had five senses. Furthermore, she noted that her
dreams were apparently not too different from those of other people,
that she dreamed of speaking to others and of hearing their replies.
It is a safe assumption that her outlook corresponded not so much
to the sensory world of other people but to their symbolic environment. Anyone familiar with her writings knows that she does indeed participate quite effectively in this common milieu. She
pointed out further that other people are constantly talking about
things they have never seen nor heard. The bulk of the world's
knowledge is made up of objects that have been experienced only

[25] Maurice Halbwachs, *Les cadres sociaux de la mémoire* (Paris: Felix Alcan,
1925), pp. 113–54.

vicariously. Historical events, for example, cannot possibly be experienced directly; they can be relived only in the imagination. Thus, perspectives are more a product of communication than of direct experience.[26]

The use of concepts in science points both to the validity and limitations of the hypothesis of Sapir and Whorf. Scientific knowledge represents the ultimate development in our time of the symbolic organization of human experience. The objective of scientific research is to cut through the phenomenal diversity of things as they appear in daily experience and to get at generic processes. To explain something one shows that it is an instance of a general class and delineates the properties of the class. Scientific concepts sometimes destroy the world as we know it. Diamonds become a form of carbon, and other familiar objects become molecules of one sort or other. Scientific knowledge develops as the language of common sense is successively replaced by concepts which categorize objects in terms of invariably associated properties rather than superficial similarities in appearance. Some concepts refer to phenomena that can be identified only by those with highly specialized training and are completely strange to the layman. In spite of the efficiency of highly abstract and accurate knowledge of this nature, however, science also has its limitations. Sharply defined classifications are necessary for scientific research, but in real life the different modes of existence shade off into each other. The clarity with which the concepts are defined is what makes the verification of scientific generalizations possible, but this very sharpness leads to a loss of reference to the many unique features that are found in actual life. Many meanings cannot be clearly designated by linguistic symbols, but they are nonetheless important in life.

Although linguistic symbols are by far the most important, other symbols are also used to organize experience. Sequences of musical notes, color combinations, and various movements all represent meanings. Perhaps most important for maintaining a stable conception of any society are the various status symbols, which continually reinforce assumptions concerning the appropriate arrangement of people. A variety of marks—such as clothing, badges, uniforms, physical features, or ritualistic observances—serve to indicate each

[26] Helen Keller, *The World I Live In* (New York: The Century Co., 1908), pp. 84–112, 134–82.

person's standing in a community. There are a number of acts that are primarily symbolic. The ritual of shaking hands is an indication of good will and of a willingness to enter some joint endeavor on a more or less equal basis. In the South many are reluctant to shake hands with Negroes; it is not that they believe that Negroes are dirty and that they would risk infection by clasping hands. The act in itself is unimportant, but it stands for an acknowledgment of social equality. Negroes are sensitive about this ritual for the same reason, not because of an overwhelming desire to touch white hands. Smoking, rowdyism, and even sexual promiscuity may be practiced not for enjoyment but as symbols of defiance against conventional norms. Thus, men do many things they do not particularly care for in order to let others know just where they stand. Such acts contribute to the preservation of an orderly perspective in that a given arrangement of people is reaffirmed.

One cannot understand what is happening around him unless he can categorize his experiences and place them within a larger frame of reference. Without appropriate symbols this is extremely difficult, and adjustment takes on a hit or miss character. The uneducated often cannot comprehend many things that educated people find quite simple, and scientists can understand many things that puzzle even well read laymen. Doctors can diagnose disorders that their patients cannot recognize even when they themselves are suffering from the symptoms; most patients do not have the vocabulary to sensitize them to the various transformations in body conditions. Effective action rests upon clear understanding, and the clarity of one's conception of his world rests upon the adequacy of his stock of symbols. Much depends, then, upon the adequacy of the symbols available in a group for delineating significant categories of experience.

Role-taking and self-control, which make coordinated action possible, are greatly facilitated by the fact that men live in a common symbolic environment. Such shared perspectives constitute the culture of each group. Since the norms that make up these perspectives constitute the premises of action, it is not surprising that men who share a common culture are characterized by common modes of action. All cultures are products of communication. Perspectives are organized in terms of symbols, and those who can communicate with these symbols come to share one another's views. Hence, they form a common outlook which serves as the basis for concerted action.

Differential Association and Pluralism

Ordinarily when one speaks of a community he is concerned with people who identify themselves as belonging together by virtue of occupying a common habitat. To some extent community sentiment in this sense still exists; it is manifested in the pride displayed when a local boy achieves eminence or in the shame felt when some spectacular crime is committed in the area. But such feelings are being superseded by other bases of identification. Prior to the development of the media of mass communication—newspapers, books, magazines, radio, television, and motion pictures—social interaction was limited largely to those who occupied a common territory. Since the people in each community took the same things for granted, they could understand one another, while finding strangers odd and uncouth. This difference further reinforced their isolation and sense of solidarity. Each culture had a territorial base, and anthropologists could speak meaningfully of "culture areas" in pointing to fundamental similarities in the cultures of adjacent peoples.

But common perspectives arise not from physical contiguity but from communication. In recent times the development of efficient communication and easy transportation has made it possible for people who are geographically dispersed to interact with one another. *Those who participate in the same communication channels develop a common outlook,* and what complicates the picture is the fact that these networks are often territorially overlapping. Furthermore, there is segmentalized participation in several different channels by each individual. Since communication networks are no longer coterminous with territorial boundaries, culture areas overlap and have lost their ecological foundations. What is remarkable about our society is the diversity of perspectives among people who live together. Next door neighbors may be complete strangers. Even in common parlance there is a recognition of these variations in outlook, and we speak of people living in different social worlds—the world of science, the world of sports, or the world of fashion.

This leads to an important question: what are *communication channels?* Almost all human beings can receive and transmit information, but except under unusual circumstances men who are within one another's range do not enter readily into communicative transactions. In all groups there is differential contact and association. Each person is selectively sensitized to certain sources of information and pays little heed to others. In a stratified society, for example, those in elite groups generally ignore the gossip of their subordinates, and in military units enlisted men rarely speak freely to their officers. In virtually all groups certain kinds of information are kept secret from some segments of the population, especially the young. Among those who do interact the confidence with which messages are received depends upon the credibility attributed to the source, and in each community there are conventional norms defining the reliability of various sources. In discussions of the weather a meteorologist or perhaps a farmer is regarded as a competent source. People read carefully the instructions provided by manufacturers for the proper use of their products, but they do not necessarily accept the statements of the National Association of Manufacturers on political issues.[27] Communication channels, then, are not merely points of contact; they are products of the social control of communicative behavior. They arise from shared understandings concerning who is to speak to whom on what subject with what degree of confidence. Such barriers to free interchange are a part of the structure of organized groups, and they break down temporarily only in crisis situations.

Formal communication channels are an integral part of all organized groups. Every bureaucracy—military, commercial, governmental, or educational—has its regular channels. Certain officials are responsible for getting and disseminating information through understood routes of transmission, and efforts to circumvent these channels often lead to difficulties, even when they are successful. Although emphasis is placed upon writing in the formal communication that occurs in modern industrial societies, it should be emphasized that conventionally established channels need not involve

[27] Cf. Carl I. Hovland, Irving L. Janis, and Harold H. Kelley, *Communication and Persuasion* (New Haven: Yale University Press, 1953), pp. 19–55; Elihu Katz and Paul F. Lazarsfeld, *Personal Influence* (Glencoe: Free Press, 1955); and Herbert F. Lionberger, "The Relation of Informal Social Groups to the Diffusion of Farm Information in a Northeast Missouri Farm Community," *Rural Sociology*, XIX (1954), 233–43.

written records. In areas in which the literacy rate is low, there is no alternative to oral transmission. For example, Stycos describes an isolated Greek village in which the people learn of the outside world largely from newspapers dropped at irregular intervals by the driver of a bus that passes nearby. The newspapers are read aloud at the local tavern either by the village priest or the schoolteacher. These men are also expected to evaluate the news, to explain whatever the people do not understand, and to provide advice on how to meet the situation.[28] Much of the formal communication in our society is also oral; in military units, for example, many orders are simply barked out by sergeants.

No matter how elaborate the formal channels of communication, they are almost always supplemented by auxiliary networks—the "grapevines." The local barber shop, the latrines of military units, the drinking fountains in business offices, and the faculty clubs in universities become focal points of contact. An examination of the grievance procedures in a large factory may reveal that union stewards are not always the men through whom complaints reach the management. There are numerous ways of "cutting the red tape." Accidental points of contact assume unusual importance; a foreman who is engaged to the manager's secretary or the private who had been a classmate of the battalion sergeant major become key sources of news. Thus, informal communication channels are built up around social relationships that are formed on a personal basis, and the confidence placed in such sources rests upon the reputation of the participants for honesty and reliability. Such channels are usually supplementary, for when information from the "grapevine" is contradicted by an official announcement, it is usually dismissed as a "rumor." Under some circumstances, however, such illicit news may actually supersede formal announcements, especially when there is reason to believe that something is being held back.[29]

Since shared perspectives are products of communication, each channel gives rise to a distinctive culture. Modern mass societies are made up of a bewildering array of social worlds—the underworld,

[28] J. Mayone Stycos, "Patterns of Communication in a Rural Greek Village," *Public Opinion Quarterly*, XVI (1952), 59–70.

[29] Cf. Raymond A. Bauer and David B. Gleicher, "Word-of-Mouth Communication in the Soviet Union," *ibid.*, XVII (1953), 297–310; and Oscar E. Millard, *Underground News* (New York: R. M. McBride & Co., 1938).

the world of high finance, the world of the theater, the world of horse racing, the world of Protestant missionaries. Although some people speak glibly of an "American culture," actually there are a large number of overlapping perspectives in the United States. This diversity is reflected in American literature—in the twilight world of Ring Lardner, the disappearing Irish-Americans of James T. Farrell, the small Midwestern town of Sinclair Lewis, the impoverished rural South of Erskine Caldwell, the modern urban slum of Nelson Algren, and the proper Bostonians of John P. Marquand. Each social world is a universe of regularized mutual response. Each is an arena in which there is a structure which permits the anticipation of the responses of others, an arena in which one may pursue his interests with reasonable confidence. *Each social world, then, is a culture area, the boundaries of which are set neither by territory nor by formal group membership, but by the limits of effective communication.*

Of all social worlds probably the greatest sense of mutual identification and solidarity is to be found in the various subcommunities. Among the more obvious of these is the underworld with its complex system of stratification. There are the professional thieves and gunmen, the racketeers who operate under the protection of corrupt officials, the various types of "grifters" who depend upon fraud rather than violence, and the "hustlers," a category of marginal people such as retail dope peddlers, prostitutes and procurers, and the distributors of counterfeit currency. While there are some differences among these categories, those in the underworld have standards of conduct which set them apart from outsiders. People in ethnic minorities, if there are enough of them in a given area, generally form a colony. They identify themselves as being alike by virtue of common ancestry, real or imaginary. Their culture often includes many of the values of the old world, although such colonies are usually not replicas of "home." The social elite in almost all communities set themselves apart from the others. In Europe of the recent past there was the *grande monde* of the titled aristocracy and the wealthy with its special code of honor. Even in our democratic society families in the social register usually separate themselves from ordinary people, just as privileged Communist officials maintain distance from their other comrades. Some religious cults, especially in their early days, also establish isolated communities.

They are regarded with suspicion by outsiders, and they regard themselves as the only ones who know the road to salvation. They care little about the views of people in the outside world, whose souls are lost in any event.[30] One mark of a community, according to MacIver, is that one's entire life may be lived within it, and many people in these social worlds do confine themselves largely to contacts with others within. Outsiders seem strange; often they do not really seem to be human.

Frequently such sub-communities are also geographically segregated, thus bolstering their separation from the outside, while special channels like the "grapevine" or the foreign language press facilitate the establishment of contacts within. Sometimes, as in the case of ethnic minorities or the underworld, segregation is enforced by the hostility of outsiders. Such groups are usually found in or adjacent to slum areas, where rents are cheap and where no one cares too much about the respectability of his neighbors. In other instances, such as the social elite and some religious cults, segregation arises from a desire for separation. The wealthy often live in suburbs where others cannot afford to live, and cultists search for inconspicuous places where they can practice their ways without interference. Segregation, however it may arise, is of fundamental importance, for it multiplies intimate contacts within and reinforces the barriers against the outside. People who conceive of themselves as being of a kind associate primarily with those with whom they identify; contacts with outsiders are ephemeral and categorical.[31]

A second type of social world consists of networks of interrelated voluntary associations—such as the world of organized labor, the world of the opera, the world of the steel industry, the various religious denominations, the fraternal organizations, and each of the professions. The participants in most cases are geographically dispersed and are bound by their involvement in common activities and membership in related groups. They are served by periodicals like *Variety, The C. I. O. News,* the *Wall Street Journal,* the *American*

[30] There have been a number of sociological studies of such communities; among them are E. Digby Baltzell, *Philadelphia Gentleman* (Glencoe: Free Press, 1957); Paul G. Cressey, *The Taxi-Dance Hall* (Chicago: University of Chicago Press, 1932); Drake and Cayton, *op. cit.;* John R. Seeley, R. Alexander Sim, and Elizabeth W. Looseley, *Crestwood Heights* (New York: Basic Books, Inc., 1956); and Pauline V. Young, *Pilgrims of Russian Town* (Chicago: University of Chicago Press, 1932).

[31] Cf. Wirth, *The Ghetto, op. cit.*

Legion Magazine, the *Harvester World*, the publications of alumni associations, and a number of highly specialized journals, each of which provides access to an arena that is strange to non-readers. Churches often have their own magazines and mimeographed bulletins, which sometimes flatly contradict what is printed in the media of mass communication concerning some controversial issue. In the various fraternal and religious organizations participation is segmentalized, and total commitment is usually found only among the paid officials; on the other hand, in the world of corporation executives and in the academic world many participants devote a large portion of their lives to their work. Among the better organized of these worlds are the professions. Since a long period of training is usually required for admission, once a person has been initiated, he rarely leaves; indeed, he develops a sense of pride in his calling. Professional groups often have standards of conduct more stringent than what is required by law; therefore, they have procedures for punishing their own violators. The common values are upheld by a special system of social control—professional ethics.[32]

Finally, there are the loosely connected universes of special interest—such as the world of ice hockey, the world of the stamp collector, the world of women's fashions, the world of hunting and fishing, and the world of each radio or television serial. Most of the participants move in and out of these arenas. Since they are drawn together only periodically by the limited interest they have in common, there are many degrees of involvement, ranging from the fanatically devoted to the casually interested. Because of the ease of participation these worlds are usually quite extensive, often involving millions of people and providing possibilities of commercial exploitation. The latest developments in sports, in women's fashions, and in the various entertainment fields are carried in the media of mass communication, readily available for anyone sufficiently interested to read. Those who want more are served by periodicals like *Field and Stream, Sports Illustrated, Hotrods, Popular Photography,* and *Seventeen.* Although these arenas are only loosely organized, the participants nonetheless develop common standards of conduct, especially if their interests are strong and sustained. Fashion-conscious women can identify one another easily, and their

[32] William J. Goode, "Community within a Community: The Professions," *American Sociological Review*, XXII (1957), 194–200.

reciprocating appraisals are often in terms of criteria different from those applied to other women. Enthusiastic fishermen also have definite standards—to give the game a fighting chance, to use relatively light tackle, to get enjoyment from the skill required in landing the quarry rather than from merely catching something to eat. They are often contemptuous of people who use worms when fishing for mountain trout. The world of the fisherman is sufficiently organized so that complete strangers meeting at some resort have no difficulty in going over their technical problems.

Since there are a wide variety of communication channels, differing in stability, range, and effectiveness, social worlds vary in composition, in size, and in the territorial distribution of their participants. Some, like local cults, are small and concentrated; others, like the world of sports, are vast, and the participants are dispersed. Some, like many ethnic minorities, have a relatively homogeneous population; others are utterly mixed. Social worlds differ in the extent and clarity of their boundaries; each is circumscribed by some kind of horizon, but this may be wide or narrow, clear or vague. Although some men regard their own perspectives as absolute, the fact that these arenas are not coterminous with the entire universe is often recognized; those in the underworld, for example, are well aware of the fact that outsiders do not share their values. Social worlds also differ in their exclusiveness and in the extent to which they demand the loyalty of their participants. Some require special qualifications for initiation; one cannot become a corporation executive, a socialite, or a racketeer simply by announcing his intention, but anyone can become a baseball fan. Some worlds are open only to those who dedicate themselves completely; one cannot be a part-time nun. A priest or a soldier has but one supreme loyalty; everything else is secondary to his duty. But there are other worlds in which most of the participants are only occasional spectators. Loyalty to the St. Louis *Cardinals*, for example, does not require wagering on the weaker team in a World Series.

Within each social world there develops a special universe of discourse; experiences are categorized in particular ways, and a special set of symbols is used to refer to such meanings. The argot of soldiers, prostitutes, and drug addicts as well as the dialects used in ethnic minorities differ from the standard tongue. Jazz fans who speak of "cats" are not concerned with feline creatures, nor are they displaying any interest in geometry in discussing "squares." Baseball fans know that a "rhubarb" is not a vegetable, and gamblers know that a "soft play" refers to a stupid bet. The vocabulary of any group, to the extent that it differs from the general vocabulary, is an excellent index of its interests and preoccupations. The symbols that are unique refer to the special distinctions that are necessary to carry out the activities that characterize the group. Soldiers and drug addicts have experiences peculiar to them, and they develop special terms to represent these categories. The development of such distinct languages creates further barriers from outsiders, for others are sometimes completely baffled by what is being said. Each social world is a scheme of life—a way of acting, talking, thinking. It is an arena within which special meanings are shared, where one who is a part of it feels "at home."

In each social world there is a characteristic set of activities, and there are norms to guide them. Thieves do not steal from fellow thieves, although they do rob racketeers; gamblers pay their gambling debts, even though they may still owe their relatives. Elite groups often develop a code of honor—a set of special obligations to which only the members are held. The failure of outsiders to live up to such norms is regarded as additional evidence that they are not deserving of admission.

In each social world there develops a somewhat different historical orientation, selectively emphasizing past events of particular interest. Such common memories are built up and reinforced in constant association. To those who are not steeped in naval history and tradition many customs appear silly. What is the point in saluting when boarding or leaving a ship? Why the insistence upon using words like "port," "starboard," "bow," or "ladder" when there are perfectly good words in the general vocabulary which are far more familiar? Admirals look with nostalgia to the glorious days of the battleships, and the reluctance of some to accept the realities of the atomic age must be seen in this light. The values of people in each social world become comprehensible when they are viewed within such historical contexts.

In a pluralistic society it is difficult to appreciate the aspirations of any person without knowing something about the social world in which he seeks to carve out his career. Something of the dreams of a people are epitomized in their heroes, and there are different heroes in each arena. Scientists who have international reputations among their fellow specialists are unknown to most baseball fans. Many who have never heard of Albert Einstein can recall to a remarkable extent the details of the great performances of idols like Babe Ruth and Carl Hubbell. In each social world there is a different prestige ladder, and there are also typical career lines. Doctors, circus acrobats, hold-up specialists, ballerinas, and gossip columnists—all serve their apprenticeships after some kind of training. Upward mobility and success in each case is measured in terms of the values shared within that particular arena, and outsiders are not likely to understand why the person undergoes such sacrifices to succeed in something that they regard as quite trivial or even senseless. What is highly esteemed in one social world is of no consequence in another.

Each man forms a conception of himself by locating himself in the various arenas in which he plays a role. Most social worlds have names, and people are able to identify themselves as participants. There are understandings concerning the composition of the world— who is included in the "we" and who is left out. In short, there is some kind of consciousness of kind. Those who belong assume obligations for maintaining the traditions of the group and hold themselves responsible; people in the theater feel that the "show must go on." They expect from one another considerations that they do not impute to outsiders, and they are also acutely aware of the special claims that others within the circle have upon them. In a class society, for example, a nobleman answers the distress call of another nobleman, even though his own servant may suffer thereby. People in each social world have some notion of the kind of creatures they claim to be as well as what outsiders regard them to be. In each arena there are prevalent ideas about the nature of the universe and of man's place therein, and it is in these terms that a man defines himself.

Human conduct becomes understandable only when the observer has some appreciation of the actor's audience and the general frame of reference he is using to orient himself toward his world. Such perspectives are shaped through participation in groups, and what makes things so complicated in modern mass societies is the ease with which each person can participate in a wide variety of groups. Hence, the identical situation may be defined differently by people with contrasting perspectives. As paradoxical as it may seem, many of the difficulties in establishing consensus arise from the development of overly efficient channels of communication.

Summary and Conclusion

The Greek philosopher Protagoras is said to have proclaimed that man is the measure of all things, and this observation seems to be borne out by current research. The effective environment in which men live may be viewed as consisting of meanings, ordered ways of acting which have evolved through past experience and are constantly reaffirmed in new experience. Although we ordinarily think of meanings as the property of the various objects with which we come into contact, they are actually characteristic ways of approaching various aspects of the environment. The meaning of anything is an organized orientation that can be identified as a configuration of behavioral tendencies, all predicated upon the assumption that the object has certain characteristics. Thus, familiar objects are perceived in terms of expectations, and each person's conception of these objects is reinforced as these hypotheses are confirmed. What is significant about human beings is that both the expectations and the confirmations usually include the reactions of other people.

Human beings actually live simultaneously in two environments— the natural environment, which consists of all the things that are actually present, and a symbolic environment. Viruses are a part of the natural environment of all men, and they affect life processes whether their victims know about them or not. But viruses are not a part of the symbolic environment of many peoples; and when one of their number dies, his demise is explained in other terms—the anger of evil spirits, the violation of some taboo, or weakness of the blood. The symbolic environment is not a mere reproduction of the external world; by virtue of their capacity for using symbols men are able to reconstruct their surroundings. Fleeting sensations that blend almost imperceptibly into one another are categorized and labelled so that they can be recalled for comparison. Even though nothing ever happens twice in exactly the same manner, each man is able to form an orderly outlook, and those who utilize the same symbols are able to develop a common orientation. Since they approach their respective worlds with similar expectations, they can understand and reinforce one another. Men live, then, in a substitute environment, one that is largely a product of communication.

Although social psychologists generally write from the standpoint of a disinterested observer, as if they were among the proverbial men from Mars, they cannot, of course, escape the fact that they are human beings living in an organized society. The concepts used, to the extent that they differ from the general vocabulary, refer to special distinctions not ordinarily made in daily discourse. Each theoretical scheme, then, is a symbolic environment, a special way of looking at human conduct which, it is hoped, will prove more effective than the common sense view. There would be no point in studying social psychology unless its mastery made possible the comprehension of many phenomena which otherwise would remain strange.

Suggested References

BRIDGMAN, PERCY W., *The Intelligent Individual and Society*, pp. 1–174. New York: The Macmillan Co., 1938. An eminent physicist's discussion of the difficulties involved in using operational definitions in the study of human behavior.

HALLOWELL, A. IRVING, *Culture and Experience*, Parts I–III. Philadelphia: University of Pennsylvania Press, 1955. A series of sophisticated studies of the subtle ways in which human experiences are organized in terms of conventional norms.

LANGER, SUSANNE K., *Philosophy in a New Key*. New York: Penguin Books, Inc., 1948. A treatise on the transformation of human life through man's capacity to use symbols, based upon materials drawn from many areas of specialization.

MANNHEIM, KARL, *Ideology and Utopia*, Louis Wirth and Edward Shils, trans. New York: Harcourt, Brace & Co., 1936. A classic in the sociology of knowledge, presenting hypotheses on the manner in which knowledge is related to social groups and their prevailing interests.

PEPPER, STEPHEN C., *The Sources of Value*. Berkeley: University of California Press, 1958. A comprehensive study of how men derive and experience values, with a hypothesis on the manner in which they arrive at decisions.

WHORF, BENJAMIN L., *Language, Thought, and Reality,* John B. Carroll, ed. pp. 57–159, 207–70. New York: John Wiley & Sons, 1956. The selected writings of a distinguished philologist, with particular emphasis upon the organization of experience through linguistic symbols.

5

Communication
and
social
control

In carnivals and in night
clubs many have gaped in disbelief at the performance of "mind
readers" whose feats include such astounding deeds as reading the
date from a wedding ring held by a confederate standing more than
50 feet away. Since the "mind reader" is often blindfolded, this can
hardly be accounted for in terms of abnormal visual acuity, and
since the ring is taken from the finger of a woman selected at random from the audience, often someone who is well known in the
local community, there is little suspicion of its having been prearranged. Men marvel at such skills and speculate as to how the
trick is done. But in daily life each person accomplishes feats only
slightly less astonishing, for basically all communication involves a
similar series of interchanges and inferences. Indeed, if men did not
have this capacity, human society as we know it would not be possible.

Society exists only in concerted action, and if men who are capable of independent action are to act together as a unit, each must
somehow be able to anticipate what his associates are likely to do.
Without some appreciation of the intentions of others, cooperation

is difficult; but how is such appreciation to be achieved? Direct "mind reading" is apparently impossible; hence, men must settle for the best available substitute—the reading of external gestures which are indicative of inner experiences. Men communicate by making inferences on the basis of gestures. In spite of the numerous possibilities of error, concerted action rests upon this process. Without it cooperation of the kind that characterizes human society is impossible; communication is the touchstone of society.

Consensus as Mutual Role-Taking

The common sense way of looking at communication is mechanical; individual organisms are viewed as influencing each other through interstimulation. When two people are said to be communicating we think of one person's emitting signals, usually vocally, these sound waves then striking the sense organs of a second party, who then interprets the message. Thus, an "idea" in the mind of one person is transmitted to the mind of the second. Much of the research on communication by social scientists has been predicated upon the same working conception, nicely summarized in Lasswell's famous formula: who says what in which channel to whom with what effect? Hence, the study of communication is generally broken down into the analysis of source, content, channel, target, and effect.[1] Much useful information has been accumulated through this procedure, but the conception is misleading. To be sure, such a mechanical interchange does take place, but this constitutes but a small part of the communicative process. There is another way of looking at communication. Exchanges of all kinds take place among those who are engaging in any form of concerted action, and from the interactionist standpoint the various things that people do and say are examined not as isolated entities but as parts of a larger unit of activity.

The product of communication is not merely the modification of the listener's attitude or behavior through the stimulation, but the

[1] Harold D. Lasswell, "The Structure and Function of Communication in Society," in *Mass Communications,* Wilbur Schramm, ed. (Urbana: University of Illinois Press, 1949), pp. 102–15. For a representative selection of current research in this field see Bernard Berelson and Morris Janowitz, eds., *Reader in Public Opinion and Communication* (Glencoe: The Free Press, 1953).

establishment of some measure of consensus. Consensus is the sharing of perspectives among those cooperating in joint action; it is an on-going process, a sharing that is built up, sustained, and further developed through a continuing interchange of gestures. The communicative process is rarely a single instance of stimulation and response, such as the reaction to a scream of terror, but a sequence of exchanges within a larger context. Consensus is rarely complete even for purposes of a relatively simple enterprise. It is partial; there are almost invariably areas of uncertainty, and it is about these that most of the interchanges take place. With each gesture the uncertainties are successively minimized or eliminated, enabling each person to contribute his share and to enjoy greater confidence in the responses of others. In most situations, then, communication is a continuous process. Men who are acting together try to develop and maintain mutual orientations to facilitate the coordination of their respective efforts, and the interplay must continue until the task is accomplished. The concept of *communication* refers to that interchange of gestures through which consensus is developed, sustained, or broken.

Coordination requires that each participant be able to anticipate the movements of the others, and it is for this purpose that men who are cooperating watch one another. But in most cases a man's reactions cannot be predicted merely from a familiarity with the surrounding conditions, for a wide variety of acts may arise under similar circumstances. Human beings are able to make choices, and from time to time they act contrary to what is acknowledged to be in their best interests. Much depends upon the meanings of the key objects in the situation, and these vary with the background of the particular persons involved. Hence, a knowledge of the external circumstances is not enough; anticipating what another human being is likely to do requires getting "inside" of him—to his subjective experiences, his particular definition of the situation and his conception of his own place within it. Put in another way, the behavior of another person can be anticipated only through effective role-taking.

Consensus is established through reciprocal role-taking. When there is consensus, there is an interpenetration of perspectives which enables the participants in concerted action to have some appreciation of the point of view of the others; hence, it becomes possible to make allowances, to take into account special difficulties or advantages, to appreciate the way in which the peculiar exigencies must seem to a given person. There is intersubjectivity in that the participants are oriented to one another's plans of action. By appreciating the other's definition, one can make inferences about their interests and thereby impute motives. With an appreciation of the direction in which the other is moving, it becomes possible to make adjustments to them.

Consensus refers to the temporary sharing of a common definition of the situation by persons of diverse backgrounds. Since they face a common situation together, they are able to anticipate things together. The extent to which the participants in common activities can suffer together is revealed in a study by Renold and his associates of the decrease in the level of circulating eosinophil under conditions of physical duress. Blood samples were taken at various intervals from members of the Harvard crew, the coxswain, and the coach both during their preparation for the race with Yale and during the crucial contest. Although there were individual variations, a characteristic pattern was found for the oarsmen both in practice and in the match. But during the race, which turned out to be very close, both the coxswain and the coach also developed a pattern similar to that of the oarsmen, even though their overt muscular activity was in no way comparable to that of the men who were rowing.[2] Such data support Jacobson's contentions about the muscular basis of imagery and also indicate the extent to which men involved in joint enterprises live within one another's minds.

Successful role-taking requires developing an appreciation of someone else's subjective experience. But this is not accessible to direct observation, for the only experiences that anyone can have are his own. We must make inferences about what others are probably experiencing on the basis of the best available evidence—whatever can be seen or heard of their external behavior. Since no one can read the mind of another, inferences are made by reading his *gestures*. When carrying on a conversation with someone we listen carefully to his voice, though we may find it rasping and irritating, for this is one of the few ways in which we can get any basis for

[2] Albert E. Renold *et al.*, "Reaction of the Adrenal Cortex to Physical and Emotional Stress in College Oarsmen," *New England Journal of Medicine*, CCXLIV (1951), 754–57.

forming judgments about his intentions. We also watch his face intently, even though it is not handsome and we get no aesthetic enjoyment from seeing it, for this is another source of valuable hints.

A gesture is any perceptible sound or movement which serves as an indicator of inner experiences. A gesture cannot be identified in terms of any particular type of action; any act can become a gesture when another party responds to it and uses it as a basis for judgment. Thus, a gesture is always a phase of a larger transaction, a part of a cooperative act. A man who sticks out his tongue behind his rival's back is not communicating, however satisfying such an expressive movement may be; it becomes a gesture only if the other man happens to see it reflected in a mirror. A lone man yelling on a desert island may verbalize his inclinations admirably, but unless his remarks reach a responsive ear, they do not constitute gestures. Movements and sounds become gestures only in a social context, when they serve to give indications of the intentions of the man who makes them, thereby providing others with some basis for responding in a reciprocal manner.

Although we ordinarily think of communication in linguistic terms and are concerned primarily with phonemes, words, and sentences, there are a wide variety of acts that may serve as gestures. To be sure, the most versatile and reliable communication occurs through vocal gestures—the articulation of sounds in the vocal musculature. Along with the articulation of words there are other effective gestures, such as, the scream of a terrified woman, laughing on the part of someone who is delighted, or the singing of love songs. But all of the organs of sensitivity are involved in communication. Inferences about inner experiences can rest upon physical contact, as in striking blows, kissing, rubbing noses, pushing one another, placing an arm on another's shoulder, holding hands, or sometimes by the mere fact of proximity. A variety of motions that are only seen may become gestures. Changes in the facial musculature are often indicative of feelings, and there are a number of conventional body movements, such as thumbing a ride or holding one's nose. Although we rarely think of communication through smell, perfumes are sometimes used deliberately to convey an impression. Any act can become a gesture, then, if it serves to coordinate the contributions of people who are acting together as a unit.

Furthermore, the meaning of a gesture is not inherent in its structure. What a given gesture may stand for varies to a remarkable extent, depending upon the context in which it occurs. A policeman's placing his hand upon a man's shoulder does not represent the same intent as the same act on the part of a friend. A loud scream from a woman walking alone in a dark alley does not mean the same thing as a similar vocal gesture produced in the midst of a boisterous party. Even the meanings of words vary somewhat in different social contexts.

Role-taking is a complex process involving the perception of gestures, vicarious identification with another person, and the projection upon him of one's own behavioral tendencies. Some measure of temporary identification with the other person is essential in all communication, for it is only by placing oneself imaginatively in the position of another that one can guess his inner feelings. Remembering his own humiliations, bereavements, and triumphs, one can sympathize with others in analogous circumstances. Thus, the inferences that are made about the inner experiences of others constitute the projection of one's own implicit acts. Upon hearing another person speak one can participate in his stream of thought. Men are able to appreciate one another's acts through co-performance.[3]

This suggests that the ability of a man to participate effectively in concerted action depends upon his capacity to become several people in his imagination. The extent to which this remarkable capacity is developed in some people is demonstrated in Harriman's experiments on the dissociation of personality through hypnosis. When subjects were asked while in a hypnotic trance to become someone other than themselves, they often assumed the roles of specific people they knew. One woman, for example, played the role of an acquaintance of whom she was very envious. When subjects were asked to show a "good" or "bad" side of themselves, already organized behavior patterns emerged, often patterned after the conduct of approved or disapproved people they knew.[4] The roles enacted by other people apparently exist in organized form in each person's neuro-muscular make-up.

[3] Cf. Alfred Schuetz, "Scheler's Theory of Inter-Subjectivity and the General Thesis of the Alter Ego," *Philosophy and Phenomenological Research*, II (1942), 323–47; and Richard H. Williams, "The Method of Understanding as Applied to the Problem of Suffering," *Journal of Abnormal and Social Psychology*, XXXV (1940), 367–85.

[4] Philip L. Harriman, "A New Approach to Multiple Personality," *American Journal of Orthopsychiatry*, XIII (1943), 638–43.

The manner in which gestures are interpreted may depend more upon the perspective of the perceiver than it does upon the person who produces them. There are many instances in which a number of alternative motives seem equally plausible. For example, the rudeness of a guest at a cocktail party may constitute a way of indicating boredom with the conversation, a compulsion to attack people who appear insincere, or a deliberate effort to avoid being invited to similar affairs in the future. The inference that is made depends upon the assumptions about interpersonal relations held by the person making the judgment.

Differences in cultural background and personal experience set definite limitations upon what each person can comprehend in the behavior of others. In the South, for example, Negro men have been abused for "leering" at white women at whom they were merely glancing from curiosity. Because of the absurd belief that Negroes have overdeveloped sexual propensities such motives can be imputed plausibly in some circles on the basis of gestures which are meaningless for Negroes. In the same way many persons who have never cultivated a taste for classical music are convinced that it can never be anything more than an instrument for snobbery, for they cannot imagine anyone actually enjoying it. Similar limitations arise from a lack of personal experience. Can a person whose parents are both alive appreciate fully the feelings of a friend crying over the loss of his mother? How can a healthy doctor understand the grimaces of a patient complaining of a chronic disorder? A person can understand evil motives on the part of others only if he himself is capable, under similar circumstances, of the same kind of performance. Those who have known only affectionate family ties are completely dumbfounded upon hearing someone express contempt for his parents. He searches for other cues that might provide a more plausible explanation, for to him it is inconceivable that anyone could feel that way about his own parents.

The extent to which the interpretation of gestures depends upon the perspective of the perceiver is even more clearly demonstrated in the case of psychotherapy. There are a variety of acts—such as compulsive hand washing, tics, twitches, the avoidance of certain colors, the intense dislike of older women—which are either meaningless or just "odd" to most people. To a psychiatrist, however, they serve as the basis for inferences concerning a number of unconscious tendencies. Thus, the patient unintentionally communicates with the psychiatrist, revealing behavioral dispositions of which he himself had no awareness. The psychiatrist is able to read these gestures only because of his specialized training.

But those engaged in psychotherapy are also human beings who differ considerably among themselves in personality. Hence, it would be reasonable to expect differences among them in the interpretation of gestures. The personal problems of a therapist are apparently related to the manner in which his client's problems are evaluated, for the therapist himself is sensitized to certain kinds of gestures and blind to others. In one study Weingarten rated some advanced trainees in clinical psychology on the basis of materials in their autobiographies. She then compared the ratings made by these student therapists of projective materials collected from their patients. Although many of her correlation coefficients were low, they were consistent and positive, supporting the hypothesis that each therapist was more responsive to indications of the same kinds of difficulties that he himself had encountered in the past.[5]

It is through a succession of interchanges of this character that consensus is built up and sustained. Each person deliberately or unintentionally reveals some of his intentions through a variety of gestures, which serve as the bases of judgments on the part of others who are involved in a common undertaking with him. It should be remembered, furthermore, that role-taking is rarely confined to a single act of perception and judgment. Upon making an inference about the probable orientation of another person one becomes further sensitized to subsequent gestures that will either confirm or challenge this judgment. If a man believed to be frightened conducts himself casually even when the situation is seemingly deteriorating even further, one has to revise his original estimate. On the other hand, if he appears hypersensitive and becomes extremely cautious, the judgment is reaffirmed. It is in this manner—through constant testing, revision, and confirmation—that men are able to anticipate the way in which their associates are likely to act. Communication is usually a continuing process.

Since the effectiveness of communication depends upon the capacity of the participants in concerted action to assume one another's roles, there is considerable variation in the degree of con-

[5] Erica M. Weingarten, "A Study of Selective Perception in Clinical Judgment," *Journal of Personality*, XVII (1949), 369–406.

sensus that may be achieved. Many undertakings are carried out with a high measure of concurrence concerning the plan of action, but the attainment of such accord is more difficult than commonly believed. The difficulty in arriving at mutual understanding even in matters clearly defined in law is revealed daily in the slaughter that occurs on American highways. It is of particular interest to note that safety experts estimate that nine out of ten pedestrians killed in traffic accidents are non-drivers. People who do not drive are apparently unable to appreciate the difficulties that drivers face in seeing pedestrians in the dark or in rain, especially as they are turning corners or preoccupied with other traffic. Furthermore, successful role-taking may be unilateral, as in the case of a confidence man who appreciates the standpoint of his victim but merely uses his understanding to his personal advantage.[6] There are many instances in which men think that they are agreed until they are suddenly shocked as someone does the unexpected. It is under such circumstances that communication assumes greatest importance, for men who understand one another adequately have no need for further conferences.

Even when men do understand one another, they may still disagree concerning the desired program of action. Whether or not those sharing a common outlook agree depends upon their respective interests rather than their capacity for role-taking. It is under such circumstances that communication takes on a manipulatory character, as men attempt to influence one another by deliberately producing gestures likely to create desired impressions. Because of the skill with which most people read gestures, each person develops a variety of protective measures to guard his privacy against the intrusion of ever peering eyes. Nor are these efforts confined to deliberate deception for selfish ends; a man with a headache may do his best not to show how miserable he is so that he will not spoil the fun of others. Because such diversionary gestures are so common men learn to make allowances for pretending, and sometimes social interaction consists largely of mutual manipulation and guessing. There are, of course, many situations in which

[6] Cf. Ralph H. Turner, "Role-Taking, Role Standpoint, and Reference Group Behavior," *American Journal of Sociology*, LXI (1956), 316–28; and Max Scheler, *The Nature of Sympathy*, Peter Heath, trans. (New Haven: Yale University Press, 1954), pp. 8–36.

those who are disagreed engage in open argument, attempting to persuade others of the merits of their respective positions. Although attention is frequently focussed upon such deliberate efforts to influence other people, actually much of the communication that occurs among human beings is not of this nature.

Thus, although we ordinarily regard communication as a device for the transmission of "ideas" from person to person, it is primarily a mode of activity which facilitates the reciprocal adjustment of the conduct of others with that of the speaker. Various movements and sounds become communicative when they are used in the context of mutual assistance and direction. The heart of communicative activity, therefore, is not the expression of antecedent thoughts and feelings, but the establishment of cooperation in an activity which involves partners, in which the behavior of each participant is modified and to some extent regulated by the fact of partnership.[7] Communication is that exchange that procures the cooperative assistance of others, making possible coordinated action of great complexity.

The Conventional Aspect of Communication

Consensus is built up primarily through *symbolic communication,* interaction that occurs through an elaborate set of conventional symbols which stand for shared meanings. The most important form of symbolic communication is *language,* a system of phonetic and written symbolism. Each conventional meaning—each of the numerous categories of experiences, events, or situations differentiated in a group—is designated by some kind of symbol. To make indications to one another it then becomes unnecessary for men to perform the many acts which make up the meanings which constitute the culture of their group; they simply utter the sounds which stand for them. Since sounds can be combined and manipulated with infinitely greater ease than the complex behavioral systems which they represent, the extent to which concerted action is facilitated by the development of linguistic skills is readily comprehensible.

Available evidence indicates that human beings are the only creatures that have a highly developed language, and ethnologists

[7] Cf. John Dewey, *Experience and Nature* (Chicago: Open Court Publishing Co., 1926), pp. 166–207.

assure us that every human group, no matter how simple the material culture, has a complex language. Although we are sometimes inclined to assume that "primitive" peoples have simple tongues because they are illiterate, research in linguistics reveals that some of the unwritten languages are among the most complicated ever developed. Needless to say, the manner in which experiences are categorized differs from group to group, and the linguistic symbols which stand for these categories and the manner in which they are ordered into sentences also differ. But everywhere speech is the most important medium through which human cooperation is achieved; it is the easiest way in which the diverse activities of men are coordinated for the attainment of common ends. Linguistic communication, then, is the form of human behavior that makes other forms of concerted action possible.

Speaking his native tongue seems so natural that one seldom realizes that it constitutes *behavior that is subject to social control.* Indeed, speech is ordinarily not even regarded as a form of behavior, even though it is obvious that a man who is talking is doing something. But the sounds that make up a language are not primarily expressive or communicative; they are modes of behavior—like locomotion, seizing, or crunching. Furthermore, vocal activity is circumscribed by a variety of group norms—norms concerning the manner in which sounds are to be uttered, the proper order of articulation, and the meaning to be represented by each combination of sounds. These conventional understandings are so well established that they are simply taken for granted. The articulation of words is fixed in habit to such an extent that most adults are not conscious of what they are doing as they speak. They do not find it necessary to plan the production of each syllable, and the fact that execution is automatic makes speech seem easy and spontaneous. Only when one observes the difficulties encountered by a child or an immigrant trying to learn a language does he get some realization of the enormous difficulties involved in the organization of appropriate linguistic conduct.

There is an amazing variety of sounds that can be produced in the human vocal organs, but in each group vocal behavior is restricted in understood ways. Speech is not a mere expressive flow of sounds; it is broken into identifiable units. Sounds actually blend into each other, but in each language there are various combinations which make up conventional units—words. The vocal gestures which constitute a language are standardized, and each word stands for at least one conventional meaning. Each word, therefore, is a symbol. When people who speak the same language come together, trial and error attempts at mutual adjustment can be cut to a minimum, for they can use these symbols with reasonable assurance that most of their remarks will be interpreted as intended. Thus, of the enormous range of sounds that men are capable of producing there are a limited number of combinations that are actually articulated in each group. Of course, there are individual variations and preferences, but everyone must learn to approximate the standard patterns or risk being misunderstood.

Upon hearing words men usually respond to the meanings they represent rather than to the sounds as such. Since this substitution occurs so readily they generally fail to recognize the fact that the assignment of sounds to meanings is arbitrary. Arguments over the "real" meaning of words are futile, for there is no necessary connection between a vocal gesture and the meaning it symbolizes. It has already been indicated that most symbols imply meanings which cannot be derived directly from an examination of the symbols themselves, and the most careful analysis of words will not reveal their "true" meanings. The relationship between a word and what it represents is a matter of convention. Furthermore, the absence of a necessary tie between the symbol and its referent is a matter of great importance. If men were restricted to natural signs—substitutes which have a connection of some kind with the objects for which they stand, such as smoke to represent fire or feigning blows to indicate hostility—the number of categories to which reference could be made would be quite limited. But they are able to behave linguistically much like the mathematician who says, "Let x equal . . . ," and then substitutes whatever he wishes. Therefore, human speech and thought are freed from the limitations imposed by the physical characteristics of gestures. As long as there is consensus over what is being signified, effective communication is possible.

Although languages consist for the most part of such arbitrary symbols, an astute student of linguistics has suggested that some of these gestures may at one time have been a part of the meaningful behavior that they now symbolize. Sapir points out that whenever a man is acting, his movements are not limited to the primary organs performing the task; the entire organism is mobilized. If for any reason the central organs are inhibited, the energy mobilized for the execution of the act may be released through some other part of the body. A person confronted with danger but unable to run away may scream in terror. The more socialized the person, the more likely it is that he will inhibit many of his impulses and redirect them along more acceptable routes. Sticking out one's tongue at someone may be physically ineffective, but it is symbolically gratifying in that it does help to relieve tension as a substitute for striking. In the same manner the articulation of sounds may become an alternative channel for releasing impulses that otherwise would require far more complicated bodily movements. For most adults these conventional patterns are well established; however, especially in moments of intense excitement, the accepted forms of linguistic usage sometimes fall away, and people make a whole series of involuntary sounds which are highly expressive. In great sorrow there is uncontrollable sobbing, and in intense fear men have been observed barking like dogs. Thus, while the assignment of sounds in a fully developed language is arbitrary, it is possible that speech may have evolved through the formalization of expressive movements, which have lost whatever original connections there may have been. The spontaneous ejaculations and adjustments may have become refined and conventional through repeated use.[8]

What makes vocal gestures particularly useful as instruments for communication is the versatility of the vocal organs and the ease with which men are able to perceive their own gestures. Speech is peculiarly suited for communication because of the almost infinite combinations of sounds that can be articulated through a limited set of muscles, thus making possible the production of symbols for a vast number of meanings. Vocal gestures are also important because the speaker can hear his own remarks in much the same manner as his listeners. Since he is then more likely to appreciate his own gestures from the standpoint of another person, this greatly facilitates role-taking and the establishment of consensus.[9]

[8] Edward Sapir, "Language as a Form of Human Behavior," English Journal, XVI (1927), 421–33.

[9] Cf. George H. Mead, Mind, Self and Society, Charles W. Morris, ed., (Chicago: University of Chicago Press, 1934), pp. 61–68.

Along with the conventional understandings concerning the manner in which words are to be articulated there are norms regarding the circumstances under which various remarks may be uttered. Even professors who make frequent use of slang expressions in their lectures carefully avoid certain words that they dare not employ in any classroom exercise. Of course, both professors and students know what these words mean, and they may serve quite admirably for the purposes at hand, but all parties are aware of the fact that such usage would lead to immediate difficulties with administrative officers. It is said that expressions such as "light meat" and "dark meat" became accepted ways of referring to various parts of the anatomy of cooked fowl during a puritanical age in the recent past when women were highly offended by such uncouth words as "breast" and "leg." Thus, while many persons speak quite informally and violate some of the norms of linguistic conduct, most people remain well within the bounds of adventurous safety.

Conspicuous deviations from the norms of linguistic usage are punished through negative social sanctions in much the same manner as violations of other customary procedures. Men lose respect for those who do not have what is regarded as an adequate command of their native tongue, just as they often hold in esteem a person who can manipulate such symbols with unusual skill. The mispronunciation of words is a rather common offense, and while it does not elicit harsh punishment, the offender is often subjected to ridicule. People who speak pidgin English may at first be thought to be entertaining as they ask of the whereabouts of a friend with such colorful expressions as, "Where he went?" Even though the meaning may be perfectly clear, it is not too long before such verbalizations lead to snickering and the feeling that the speaker is not quite civilized. Sometimes, when a well educated man uses grammatically incorrect sentences, he may be regarded in open contempt. Swearing in polite company can result in one's being ostracized. In general, the use of language in unconventional ways leaves the listener with a feeling that something is out of place, and such infractions usually lead to the same reactions as other forms of deviant behavior.[10]

Although emphasis has thus far been placed upon verbal inter-

[10] Cf. Erving Goffman, "Alienation from Interaction," *Human Relations,* X (1957), 47–60.

change, symbolic communication also occurs through a number of other gestures. In every group extensive use is made of a variety of vocal gestures other than words. These sounds are not part of the formal language, but they nonetheless stand for conventional meanings. For example, Americans sigh to indicate boredom, snort in scorn, cough or "ahem" to attract attention, or hiccough to refer to intoxication. Laughter usually indicates amusement, but when it is done in a forced manner it signifies boredom. Such gestures appear so natural that they are sometimes confused with instinctive expressive movements; one realizes how conventional they are only when cross-cultural comparisons are made. Among Americans hissing is a rude way of indicating disapproval; among the Basuto performers are applauded through hissing, and in Japan the same sound made through inhaling is a way of showing polite deference. In some parts of Africa laughter is used to indicate surprise, wonder, and even embarrassment and discomfiture; it is not necessarily a sign of amusement. What is sometimes called "black laughter" appears uncanny to many Europeans only because the latter make the mistake of supposing that the same gestures have identical meanings everywhere. Americans make a practice of whistling at attractive women, but foreign visitors so greeted often do not know whether to feel complimented, insulted, or endangered. It is not unusual for travellers to offend their host inadvertently through gestures which are completely misinterpreted. In some countries in Asia a guest is expected to belch after a meal to indicate that he is highly pleased; the same gesture in an American home is not likely to lead to further invitations. In spite of the spontaneous manner in which they are used such gestures are learned while participating in particular groups.

Among the most important of the gestures representing conventional meanings are facial expressions. Like the vocal organs the muscles of the face are capable of rendering a large number of finely differentiated movements, and this versatility enables men to communicate quite effectively by manipulating their facial musculature. Although many of the changes in countenance are innate expressive movements, many others are deliberately produced gestures. One may wink, blink his eyes in surprise, or wrinkle his brows to indicate puzzlement. The smile is a symbol of friendliness and agreement. Indeed, in recent years the use of the smile has become so standardized in our society that some people stand before mirrors for hours to practice it. The extent to which such gestures are subject to social control is revealed when people from different cultures come together. The Chinese show displeasure by widening their eyes, and some wonder why it is that so many Westerners are constantly angry. A wink is almost meaningless outside of Western culture; other people wonder why a person keeps closing one eye and may even offer assistance in removing the irritant that is believed to be bothering him. Travellers and immigrants frequently complain that all the natives look alike, never showing anything on their faces. The natives can detect a wide variety of changes in facial appearance among themselves, but an outsider is able to read only the spontaneous expressive movements. Experimental studies by psychologists also tend to confirm the contention that while there is considerable accuracy in judging facial expressions within a given group, outside one's own culture many of the gestures are not even noticed.[11]

There are also a wide variety of bodily movements which serve as conventional symbols. An American may drum a surface with his fingers in a deliberate effort to indicate impatience, bite his nails to signify playfully either shyness or remorse, or pull at his beard or chin as a good natured affectation of wisdom. An excellent illustration is provided by the antics of the third base coach of a well organized baseball team. Especially when there are runners on the bases, he rubs his nose, claps his hands, jumps up and down, swings his hands or clasps them together, adjusts his hat, or pats his shoulders. Both the base-runners and the batter glance at him repeatedly, for he gives the signal for the batter either to attempt to hit the ball or to let it go by. When a "hit and run" play is on, the various persons involved learn of it from reading the coach's gestures. The arbitrary character of the connection between these movements and the meanings they represent is obvious. Since the coach is in full view of the opposing players who are trying to "steal" the signs in order to anticipate the next play, he produces a number of diversionary gestures. Yet he manages to communicate with members of his own team while leaving his opponents guessing.

[11] Cf. Delwin Dusenbury and Franklin H. Knower, "Experimental Studies of the Symbolism of Action and Voice," *Quarterly Journal of Speech*, XXIV (1938), 424–35.

Again cross-cultural comparisons reveal the extent to which such gestures are customary. In our society spitting upon someone is a symbol of contempt; among the Masai it signifies affection and benediction; while the spitting of an American Indian medicine man upon his patient is only one of the kindly offices of a doctor. Urination upon another person is regarded as an even graver insult, but in some groups in Africa it is a part of the transfer of power from the medicine man in various initiation and curing rituals. Americans stand up in the presence of superiors, but Fijians and Tongans sit down to show deference. In Sicily men show defiance by flicking their thumbnails on their front teeth. The American hand gesture for "go away" would summon a waiter in a restaurant in Buenos Aires, for there it means "come here," but the American motion for "come here" is the gesture for waving "good bye" in many parts of Southern Europe. Stroking the chin in Italy means that one is so bored that he is starting to grow a beard, but a loquacious American tourist is not likely to catch the hint.[12]

In an effort to ascertain the extent to which bodily gestures are standardized in different cultures, Efron made a comparative study of Jewish immigrants from Lithuania and Poland, immigrants from Southern Italy, and the American educated children in both groups. Collecting his data through extensive observations, sketches, and motion pictures, he devised a complex procedure for coding each movement. He found that the two immigrant groups could be distinguished quite easily, for each was characterized by a traditional pattern of gesticulation. Upon examining the data on the younger generation, however, he found that neither of the traditional patterns appeared. In general, there was less gesticulation accompanying their speech, and the gestures used in the two groups resembled one another much more than they did either of the parental groups.[13] In all probability neither the parents nor the children realized the extent to which the second generation had become assimilated to American life.

Symbolic communication can occur through any gesture that can be produced voluntarily, as long as there is consensus over the

[12] Cf. Weston Labarre, "The Cultural Basis of Emotions and Gestures," *Journal of Personality*, XVI (1947), 49–68; and John B. Carroll, "The Analysis of Verbal Behavior," *Psychological Review*, LI (1944), 102–19.

[13] David Efron, *Gesture and Environment* (New York: King's Crown Press, 1941).

meanings to be represented by the various sounds and bodily movements. Among the natives of the Canary Islands communication takes place through a system of whistles as well as through words; in some parts of Africa messages are exchanged through drum beats; and most military units have their bugle calls. The blind communicate through braille, and the deaf mutes depend upon hand and finger gestures. The hula dance of Polynesia tells stories to those who know what the various movements mean, and automobile drivers indicate their intentions to turn by directional lights. In fact, men could communicate by wriggling their ears were it not for the fact that most people cannot exercise sufficient control over these muscles. Symbolic communication is characterized, then, by the voluntary production of gestures and the assignment of meanings to them by common assent.

The behavior involved in symbolic communication varies considerably in degree of formalization. Because non-linguistic gestures are less standardized there is a greater likelihood of misunderstanding. The production of facial and bodily gestures is not taught in the same manner as the enunciation of words; most people become intuitively familiar with them after a long period of participation in group activities. The difficulties involved in communicating through gestures that are not explicitly defined is particularly noticeable in music, where various rhythms and tonal qualities are intended to represent moods and acts. For many Americans tunes like Rodgers and Hammerstein's *Oh, What a Beautiful Morning* "naturally" indicate joy, and many would also agree that Alfred Newman's *Cry of the City* is symbolic of the romance of urban life. But to many others such interpretations seem entirely gratuitous. In his biography of César Franck, D'Indy insists that the sections in the *Beatitudes* depicting human perversity constituted the weakest parts of the master's compositions because Franck, who was a very pious man, was unable to conceive of evil. To someone thoroughly familiar with the symbolism of the Franckian school such a statement may be meaningful, but to others there seems to be too much room for conjecture. Although music is international in that people of different nationalities undeniably enjoy one another's works, an appreciation of the intent of a composer is possible only for those who can read his gestures with some assurance.

Symbolic communication is a conventional form of social interaction that has apparently developed from less formal types of interchange to facilitate coordinated action. Successful cooperation requires mutual orientation to one another's intentions on the part of the participants, and gestures are used as instruments for attaining such consensus. As the use of gestures becomes increasingly subject to social control, they are transformed into more effective instruments, making possible even more complex coordination as well as refinements. With increasing formalization the gestures become less personal; individual variations in their production become less important. As long as they are recognizable, they can stand for conventional meanings; hence, even complete strangers are able to interact through a formal language. In speaking of symbolic communication, then, reference is being made to a system of gestural interchanges which is subject to some measure of social control.

One of the major contributions of behavioristic psychology to contemporary social thought is the insistence that consciousness is a form of behavior and that thinking consists largely of linguistic communication.[14] Although this matter is still controversial, everyone has had the experience of talking to himself when attempting to solve a complex problem. A man who makes a conscious interpretation of something is explaining it to himself, at least in part by manipulating the linguistic symbols he has learned as a participant in a social group. Such communicative activity is generally not audible to others, but the process is remarkably similar to what happens in gestural interchanges between people. Furthermore, this procedure facilitates the formation of consensus. A person engaging in role-taking is interpreting the gestures of another; if both he and the party whose role is being taken categorize their experiences in a similar fashion and use identical symbols to refer to each category, the problem of arriving at a common definition of the situation is greatly simplified.

The Personal Aspect of Communication

Because of the unquestioned importance of symbolic communication there is a tendency to ignore the personal aspect of social

[14] Cf. Harrell and Harrison, *op. cit.* This hypothesis is elaborated, and some of the evidence supporting it is examined in Chapter IX.

interaction. While carrying on a conversation, however, each person is actually doing two rather distinct things. On the one hand, each speaker uses words as symbols for the categories to which he wishes to make reference; on the other hand, he gives some hint of his own attitude toward whatever it is that he is saying. What he intends to say is indicated by the *content* of his remarks; what he personally feels about the whole matter is revealed in the *style* of his speech. Thus, it becomes important to distinguish between *what* a man says and *how* he says it. The fact that almost any word or phrase can be made to take on a wide variety of meanings indicates that in all linguistic behavior there are intertwined identifiable patterns of two kinds, although they are never to be separated except in abstraction.

Except in cases in which the participants are very upset, communication is carried on in accordance with customary usage; what each man says in a given situation is largely circumscribed by the conventional role he is playing. He is expected to maintain the amenities, to address those of higher status with appropriate deference, and to refrain from hurting the feelings of others. But personal preferences, which are not always consistent with conventional obligations, are revealed through all kinds of *expressive movements* of which he himself is usually unaware. Expressive movements are largely involuntary and always accompany the deliberately organized acts. It might be more accurate to speak of the expressive component of behavior. The more intense one's effort, the greater his tension, the greater is the likelihood that the expressive component of his behavior will be noticeable. Behavior that is intentionally constructed is goal-oriented and instrumental; expressive movements are not. They are simply the external manifestations of the state of an organism—the smile and sprightly walk of a healthy man, the benevolent mien of the kind and affectionate, and the slumping posture and hopeless expression of one who is depressed.[15]

Speech is always compounded with expressive movements which are ordinarily left out of account in formal designations of linguistic processes. Since the face is generally exposed to naked view, men who are involved in a joint undertaking often examine one another's

[15] Maslow, *op. cit.*, pp. 179–98. Cf. Gordon W. Allport and Philip E. Vernon, *Studies in Expressive Movement* (New York: The Macmillan Co., 1933); Herbert Blumer, "Social Attitudes and Non-symbolic Interaction," *Journal of Educational Sociology*, IX (1936), 515–23; and Werner Wolff, *The Expression of Personality* (New York: Harper & Bros., 1943).

faces in search for fine nuances of constantly changing feelings. The look in a man's eyes, the changing position of his lips, jaws, or eyebrows, as well as the color and moistness of the skin all serve as the basis for judgments. The quality of one's voice is also important. If it is high in pitch, shrill, loud, or tremulous, it is often regarded as indicative of anxiety. Sudden spurts or outbursts of words, the lack of pauses, the snapping of words, overtalkativeness, forced or inappropriate laughter, and rapid and shallow breathing are also regarded as symptoms of tension. Other features of speech to which men are sensitized include the rhythmic alteration between high and low pitch, sudden variations of speed, sighs, and the constant interruption of others.[16] A strained posture, forced motions, twitches, tremors, as well as the overall rhythm and vigor of muscular movements also provide clues to inner experiences. Most gestures are both instrumental and expressive.

Expressive movements are instinctive reactions and are not to be confused with conventional facial and bodily gestures. Feelings are the subjective counterparts of emotional behavior, the organic mobilization that occurs when there is blockage in on-going action, and expressive movements are the external manifestations of these internal transformations. Tears, grimaces, and the various involuntary sounds are not in themselves "expressions" of feelings that exist prior to them; they are constituent parts of larger organic patterns. Such movements are not only involuntary but difficult to control. Because most adults are aware of the fact that others read their expressive movements, efforts are made to conceal one's feelings through suppression or exaggeration. Men learn to force a smile when insulted, to feign anger when teased, and not to cry when in pain. Although skillful actors may exercise a remarkable measure of control, when feelings are intense, even they are not successful. Especially revealing in this respect is Klineberg's study of the gestures described in Chinese literature. He found that the expressive movements of the Chinese were identical with those of Americans; there were reports of trembling, hair standing on end, cold sweat, immobility, uncontrolled urination, and the flushing of the face. But many other gestures were described which would be strange to most Americans—such as, stretching out the tongue in surprise,

[16] Cf. Jurgen Ruesch and A. Rodney Prestwood, "Anxiety: Its Initiation, Communication and Interpersonal Management," *Archives of Neurology and Psychiatry,* LXII (1949), 527–50.

opening the eyes in anger, scratching one's ears and cheeks in happiness, and clapping one's hands in worry or disappointment. These gestures are conventional and learned through long participation in Chinese society.[17] Although they are formed in much the same manner as expressive movements, they are not so indicative of individuality.

Although expressive movements are instinctive, they differ in subtle ways from person to person. Therefore, they can be interpreted with reasonable accuracy only by those who know a person well. Hebb found that even in the case of the greater apes the external manifestations in terms of which judgments could be made about emotional dispositions were highly individualized. Caretakers who knew given animals well could judge them with considerable accuracy and could enter their cages with confidence, even though they did not always know just what it was that made them so sure that it was safe. New men, however, sometimes found themselves in dangerous situations, for in spite of the care with which they observed the chimpanzees they made mistakes and found themselves under attack. A careful study of the various forms of expression revealed that only by getting to know particular animals could one make judgments with accuracy.[18] The extent to which such gestures can vary among human beings is shown in Bonner's experimental study of changes in speech patterns under conditions of stress. She found that when they were uneasy or frightened, most of the subjects showed increased pitch, rhythm, and accentuation. But there were cases that showed a decrease in some of these attributes. All subjects registered some kind of change in their vocal behavior, but the character of the change was different in each case.[19] In this age of mass advertising and charm schools some persons develop a dazzling smile which they can turn on and off like a faucet. Strangers are often unable to tell whether or not such persons are sincere, but their intimate friends are able to detect their preferences quite accurately. Close associates are able to differentiate

[17] Otto Klineberg, "Emotional Expression in Chinese Literature," *Journal of Abnormal and Social Psychology*, XXXIII (1938), 517–20.

[18] D. O. Hebb, "Emotion in Man and Animal: An Analysis of the Intuitive Processes of Recognition," *Psychological Review*, LIII (1946), 88–106.

[19] Miriam R. Bonner, "Changes in the Speech Pattern under Emotional Tension," *American Journal of Psychology*, LVI (1943), 262–73.

between a habitual response pattern and a spontaneous indication of glee.

People differ considerably in the ease with which they reveal their private inclinations. Some people develop an inscrutable façade, and it is extremely difficult to tell just where they stand; others disclose their feelings quite easily. Since expressive movements are the external manifestations of emotional reactions, they are most readily discernible among those who are acutely or chronically upset, and studies of the speech patterns of psychotic patients are instructive. In a comparative study of different types of disorders Lorenz found that those who were diagnosed as manic spoke in such a manner that the disposition of the speaker was more apparent than the message ostensibly being communicated. Not only in expressive movements but also in the choice of words such persons revealed their personal anxieties and desires. They contrasted sharply with depressed patients whose listless voice, lax articulation, and sparing use of pitch and accent made it difficult to detect individual differences.[20] To a lesser degree each person develops a characteristic style of participating in communicative transactions.

Although expressive movements are produced involuntarily and often without awareness, the gestures may be consciously interpreted by others. A frightened person may not be aware of his restlessness, but the fact that he does not know what he is doing does not prevent someone else from making observations and forming inferences about him. Psychiatrists frequently watch the manner in which their patients speak, sometimes paying more attention to the style than to the content of verbalizations. In most cases, however, the detection of feelings is not a conscious process. There has been considerable controversy among psychologists about the perception and interpretation of expressive movements. Some insist that the observer imputes feelings that have in the past been associated with given gestures; some insist that the observer projects his own feelings to others; and some insist that the meaning of expressive

[20] Maria Lorenz, "Expressive Behavior and Language Patterns," *Psychiatry*, XVIII (1955), 353–66. Cf. Stanley Newman and Vera G. Mather, "Analysis of Spoken Language of Patients with Affective Disorders," *American Journal of Psychiatry*, XCIV (1938), 913–42; and Charles E. Osgood and Evelyn G. Walker, "Motivation and Language Behavior," *Journal of Abnormal and Social Psychology*, LIX (1959), 58–69.

movements is grasped directly from the other person's appearance.[21] In any event the detection of affective states is usually intuitive; judgments are made on grounds that the observer cannot make explicit. One just "feels" that another person is frightened, happy, or depressed, but he is unable to specify just what it is that makes him so certain that this is the case. Thus, information pertaining to the condition of the speaker is frequently transmitted without the awareness of either participant.

Even creatures incapable of making conscious interpretations respond to emotional reactions. An infant who has not yet learned a language can often differentiate between genuine and feigned anger. A child who usually pays little heed to the half-hearted scoldings of his mother suddenly becomes extraordinarily well behaved when she is really upset, even when she says nothing. Domesticated animals can also detect human feelings. Mules can apparently distinguish between men who are afraid of them and those who are not, and they are reported to be considerably less cooperative when in the company of the former. Apparently dogs also recognize the difference between jest and irritation, and they generally know when to get out of the way. Feeble-minded persons as well as psychotic patients who have lost their ability to use a language are similarly responsive to emotional behavior. Although there is no evidence that such reactions result from the reading of expressive movements, the observed facts support the contention that one need not be capable of symbolic communication to detect the personal dispositions of others. Such recognition is apparently a primitive adjustive process that is well developed in many mammals.[22]

Expressive movements generally reinforce symbolic communication, for speakers usually feel much as they claim they do. This is nicely demonstrated in a study by Krim in which the gestures of six subjects being interviewed by a social worker were observed from behind a one way mirror. Although there were some discrepancies, it was found that the personal feelings inferred by the concealed observer from the expressive movements alone corresponded quite closely with the record of the symbolic interchange kept by the

---

[21] Cf. Rudolf Arnheim, "The Gestalt Theory of Expression," *Psychological Review*, LVI (1949), 156–71.

[22] Cf. Murphy, Murphy, and Newcomb, *op. cit.*, pp. 138–54, 231–37.

interviewer.[23] But this need not necessarily be the case. Because most men are aware of the possibility that the denotative and expressive aspects of speech may not correspond they sometimes interpret statements in a sense that is completely at variance with their supposed meaning. As Emerson once wrote, "When the eyes say one thing and the tongue another, a practiced man relies on the language of the first." Insincerity is often detected by ignoring the deliberately produced diversionary gestures, and expressive movements apparently play an important part in "giving a man away." Often such judgments are intuitive; one cannot specify why he should be convinced that someone is lying. Although the observer may not reveal that fraud has been detected, in making adjustments the inferred orientation is taken into account. Under some circumstances, then, the conversation of expressive movements supersedes symbolic communication.

It has been suggested that attraction to and repulsion from various persons, especially before there has been an opportunity to get to know them, constitute reactions to expressive movements. Upon meeting someone men often form "first impressions"; one likes or dislikes the person without having any tangible basis for the judgment. Since greetings are largely ritualistic, there is little in the symbolic interchange that could justify the impression, and Simmel has proposed the hypothesis that such impressions rest upon facial expressions indicative of inner dispositions.[24] The same may be true in erotic attraction. When someone of the opposite sex strikes one as being voluptuous, in many cases there is nothing in particular about the person that can be cited as the source of excitement. It is often contended that beauty is the primary basis for attraction, but there are handsome men and beautiful women who are regarded as "cold." It is also believed that the display of portions of the body customarily covered by clothing is exciting, but as most medical men and artists can testify, erotic impulses are not necessarily aroused even by nudity. Although there is a wide range of individual variation in this regard, it is conceivable that many people are excited not

[23] Alaine Krim, "A Study in Non-Verbal Communications: Expressive Movements during Interviews," Smith College Studies in Social Work, XXIV (1953), 41–80.

[24] Georg Simmel, "Sociology of the Senses: Visual Interaction," in Robert E. Park and Ernest W. Burgess, Introduction to the Science of Sociology (Chicago: University of Chicago Press, 1924), pp. 356–61.

so much by physical attributes as they are by expressive movements—the pitch and resonance of the voice, the rhythm of bodily motions, modes of staring or smiling—which are indicative of personal inclinations. As one Hollywood actress who has portrayed the "bad woman" in numerous pictures is quoted as saying, "You don't have to undress to be sexy. Sex is in your manner. Your eyes do the talking."

The hypothesis that personal orientations are revealed largely through expressive movements can be tested by examining cases in which such gestures cannot be formed or perceived. Among the symptoms of Parkinson's disease are the freezing of facial expressions into a mask-like mien and the inability to produce pitch modulations in speech. Since the cognitive processes are not affected, however, it is possible for these patients to speak, and facts can be communicated quite readily. But hospital personnel working with them frequently report feeling insecure; although messages can be understood, there is no way of ascertaining the person's individual preferences. These patients may be contrasted with those afflicted with *aphasia*—a group of disorders, often following brain injury, in which the victims suffer some kind of impairment in their ability to use linguistic symbols. Even when symbolic communication is difficult if not impossible, it is easier to establish personal relationships with a victim of aphasia than it is to form similar ties with someone suffering of Parkinson's disease.[25] Further support for the hypothesis comes from comparing the relative efficiency of the various media of mass communication. The print media are in most cases least effective. The importance of these subtle gestures is also revealed in the preference people show for discussing matters of which they are ashamed where it is dark and in their reluctance to settle important questions where lighting is inadequate. Where the private view of the other party is important, men try to gain access to his expressive movements.

Human beings are delicately attuned to one another's expressive movements, for these involuntary gestures reveal each individual's actual inclinations rather than the façade that he feels obliged to maintain. But why is it so important to know where a person really

[25] George Frankl, "Language and Affective Contact," *The Nervous Child*, II (1943), 251-62.

stands? In standardized situations a man plays conventional roles and conforms to group expectations, but in the long run his consistent behavior is a manifestation of his personality. His choice of roles, the selections he makes in situations permitting alternatives, and the enthusiasm with which he performs various duties all depend upon what he actually prefers. Furthermore, in enterprises marked by a low degree of formalization what a participant does depends largely upon his unique interests. Knowledge of a particular person is important, then, in that it facilitates role-taking and the anticipation of what he is likely to do. Thus, people almost automatically evaluate the attitudes of those about them, and they are relaxed or cautious, depending upon the dispositions imputed to them. In general, when men learn to detect each other's feelings, they can get along with considerably less friction. Each person says what he feels obliged to say, but if others take into account the actual feelings that are being disguised or concealed and make allowances for them, cooperation proceeds more smoothly. A person who is resentful may not openly disclose his discomfort, but he will be relieved nonetheless if others make it easier for him to depart from the scene gracefully. Externally, everyone goes on playing conventional roles, but minor adjustments can be made to facilitate the reduction of tensions.

People differ considerably in their ability to appreciate the affective orientations of others. This capacity to enter vicariously into the mind of another person, sympathize with him, and to take his feelings into account in dealing with him has been designated as *empathy.* Empathy is not the same as role-taking. A thief can take the role of his victim, and a person who is unsympathetic has little difficulty in understanding the symbolic communication of another party. Some are intuitively responsive to any display of feelings on the part of others and immediately identify with them; they "feel with" the other person, and they inhibit themselves, controlling their own interests out of consideration for the other. Such persons are sometimes characterized as having "warmth." The fact that there are wide differences among people in this respect is recognized, and attempts have been made to develop a scale providing a quantitative index of this capacity.[26] It is probable that this attribute does

[26] Leonard S. Cottrell and Rosalind F. Dymond, "The Empathic Responses:

not vary on a unidimensional scale; what is involved is no doubt far more complex. Since each person has a limited set of experiences that he can plausibly impute to others, the kinds of personifications with whom each can identify are probably limited. So little is known about this process, however, that the construction of the scale may be regarded as an important step forward.

These observations suggest that communicative activities can be fully appreciated only in the social contexts in which they occur. The analysis of symbols, a very useful way of studying certain aspects of communication, always gives incomplete results. While there is considerable consensus concerning the meanings represented by many gestures, the various connotations can be ascertained only in a given situation. A statement in real life is never detached from the context in which it is uttered, for each verbalization reveals the momentary feelings of a particular person. Furthermore, it is necessary to take into account the silent participants in the common activity, for their mere presence often makes a difference in what is or is not said. The proper unit for the study of communication, then, is the social situation in which it takes place.[27]

Communication varies both in degree of formalization and in extent of personal involvement. Some instances are highly impersonal and factual; the objective reporting of facts is impersonal in that the idiosyncrasies of the reporter make little difference in what is reported. On the other hand, there are instances that are highly personal; much of what is communicated depends upon the personality of the speaker. When participating in common enterprises men make major adjustments to one another on the basis of definitions that become shared through symbolic communication, but the refinements depend upon the more spontaneous interchanges among them.

A Neglected Field for Research," *Psychiatry*, XII (1949), 355–59. Cf. Jan Ehrenwald, "Patterns of Neurotic Interaction," *American Journal of Psychotherapy*, VII (1953), 24–40; and H. L. Raush and E. S. Bordin, "Warmth in Personality Development and in Psychotherapy," *Psychiatry*, XX (1957), 351–63.

[27] Cf. Bronislaw Malinowski, "The Problem of Meaning in Primitive Languages," in C. K. Ogden and I. A. Richards, *The Meaning of Meaning* (New York: Harcourt, Brace & Co., 1946), pp. 296–336.

Society as a Communicative Process

John Dewey popularized the notion that society exists in and through communication, and most students of human behavior now agree upon its importance. In some cases, however, the acceptance of this contention is much like the recitation of a slogan. It is obvious that unless people understand one another it would be difficult for them to cooperate, but apparently few appreciate the full implications of Dewey's position. In a sense, he was saying that society *is* communication. The reality to be observed in the study of social groups is the interaction among people, and the regularities discernible in these interchanges constitute social structure.

Sapir notes that although society may appear to be a series of stable structures, it actually consists of a vast array of partial and complete understandings, which are sustained and creatively reaffirmed from day to day in a number of particular acts of a communicative nature.[28] What he is saying is that group patterns are discernible only as long as people conform to the expectations they have of one another. In daily life men are continually bolstering and supporting one another's perspectives in their conversation of gestures. Participants in group activities approach one another with expectations learned through past experiences in similar contexts; as long as each person acts as he is supposed to act, others can adjust to him in the usual manner, and the expectations themselves are reinforced. If someone does not conform, coordination breaks down. By responding in the expected manner other people are continually lending their support to what each person is doing. Each person, by carrying out the expectations of the group, as a by-product of his own adjustment gives added confirmation to social structure. Without any awareness of what he is doing, he unintentionally lends his support to the constantly developing group patterns. Social structure consists of a continued flow of coordinated activity in which the participants provide one another with mutual support.

Consensus does not mean agreement in the sense that men have harmonious interests. Even in conflict antagonists support one another's expectations by responding to aggressive gestures in the

[28] Sapir, *Selected Writings, op. cit.*, p. 104.

anticipated manner. Whenever a man becomes indignant upon being insulted, he is supporting the perspective of his opponent by conforming to this expectation. What would happen if the offended party does not become angry? What would happen if he merely "turns the other cheek" and smiles sympathetically? One's initial reaction is that he did not hear correctly, and the insult is repeated. If he still continues to smile, one may conclude that he is insane. If everyone smiles, the aggressor may conclude that something is wrong with himself. His orientation toward the world becomes seriously shaken, and he retreats to find out just what is happening. It is in this sense that each person is an agent of social control. Merely by responding to other people's gestures in the manner that is expected in his group each person is contributing his share toward sustaining its structure.

Thus, each man's orientation toward his world is reinforced daily through the constant support he receives from other people. Perspectives are always hypothetical, and they are reinforced each time an anticipated event actually takes place. The meanings of various objects are supported in the regularized reactions of others; social norms are reaffirmed through the conformity of others; and a man's conception of himself is similarly supported by the consistent responses of the people he knows. Whenever his expectations are confirmed, one has a sense of assurance and can continue acting with confidence. Each person's conception of the world, then, is constantly being buttressed through communication.

This general theory can be put to a crude test by seeing what happens in cases in which there is interruption of communication. If society is indeed a communicative process, any interference with communication should result in a corresponding breakdown of cooperation. Conventional meanings, which make up the symbolic environment that is shared in a group, consist of approved ways of acting toward objects which are nurtured in a social matrix. Hence, if for any reason a person withdraws from a group, he runs the risk of losing contact with its conception of reality. When one is isolated from others, his hypotheses become more difficult to test, and meanings lose the support they otherwise would enjoy. Isolated people of necessity act more in terms of private meanings, which may be internally consistent with one another but senseless to other people. Although the evidence is far from conclusive, there seems to be a general relationship between isolation from others and the de-

terioration of conventional behavior patterns. The inability to understand others often leads to more difficulties, and one may retreat
even further until in the end all channels of communication are cut
off—as in insanity. Rigidity of meaning in the face of contradictory
gestures is likely only when a person becomes insensitive to those
about him.

If "reality" is a social process, it follows that any person who is cut
off from social contacts would encounter considerable difficulty in
participating in concerted action. A large body of literature is available containing accounts of the experiences of men who have
voluntarily isolated themselves for considerable periods of time
—philosophers, religious mystics, eccentrics, hermits, or scholars
engaged in secret research—and of men who have been forced to
remain isolated—members of religious orders requiring extended
seclusion, prisoners in solitary confinement, shepherds in remote
mountains, explorers who are lost, or shipwrecked men left adrift in
the ocean. These records show with remarkable consistency such
phenomena as hallucinations, attempts at suicide, impairment of
ability to get along with people, the development of apathy sometimes bordering on mere vegetative existence, and psychotic breakdowns. Of particular interest is the report of many isolated persons
of the deterioration of previously well established habits, such as,
the etiquette of eating and habits of personal cleanliness and groom-
ing. Some conventional meanings do deteriorate. However, the evidence is not conclusive, for the records also show that many men
survive long periods of solitude without ill effects.[29]

Although severe disorders of personality have long been the
object of intensive study, psychiatrists are still baffled, and there are
disagreements on almost every topic under investigation. Among the
few points on which there seems to be some consensus is that people
are to be designated as "psychotic" if they are "out of touch with
reality." For psychiatrists who work on the naïve assumption that
whatever they themselves experience constitutes reality the task of
identifying delusions is easy; anything that differs from their personal experience is unreal. Many psychiatrists, however, recognize
that the matter is not so simple. If reality is viewed as a social

[29] Park and Burgess, op. cit., pp. 226–77; Maurice H. Small, "On Some
Psychical Relations of Society and Solitude," Pedagogical Seminary, VII (1900),
39–53; and Negley K. Teeters and John D. Shearer, The Prison at Philadelphia:
Cherry Hill (New York: Columbia University Press, 1957).

process, a person is psychotic if he is not able to share the same conception of the world as "normal" people. A man is adjudged psychotic if he does not participate in the world over which there is consensus. The outlook of most psychiatrists is "realistic" in that they share the same perspective as most other people, and their patients live in an "unreal" world in that their orientations contain many unconventional meanings. There is evidence that many patients themselves recognize this fact, and under some circumstances efforts are made to translate their private meanings for the benefit of those who do not understand. Special interest centers upon one type of psychosis, called schizophrenia. *Schizophrenia* is a general term used rather loosely to refer to a variety of personality disorders characterized by such symptoms as inability to respond in accordance with group expectations, inappropriate emotional reactions, peculiar modes of thought which seem illogical, impairment in the capacity for self-control, and in many instances deterioration of well established habits. Since dozens, perhaps hundreds, of different disorders may be included in this blanket category, generalizations are difficult to form or to test. It should be understood, therefore, that anything that is said about schizophrenia is highly tentative.

It has been observed frequently that most schizophrenic patients are withdrawn. They do not mingle freely with other people, apparently preferring to be alone. Communication with others appears to require extraordinary effort, and there seems to be a strong predilection for replacing the overt acts that would be required in playing conventional roles with imaginative episodes. They often sit alone, sometimes talking to themselves, living in a dream world. But retrospective accounts provided by former patients, substantiated by the testimony of others present in the situations described, indicate that what is sometimes mistaken for a catatonic stupor is simply a refusal or inability to make an overt response. Patients believed by nurses and attendants to have lost contact with reality altogether subsequently demonstrate that they were actually well aware of what was happening but gave no overt indication of this.[30] It is often contended that such persons live in a shell, isolated from others. A schizophrenic patient represents a case of a person in

[30] Cf. Maxwell Boverman "A Factor in 'Spontaneous' Recovery," *Bulletin of the Menninger Clinic*, XIX (1955), 129–34; and Marguerite Sechehaye, ed., *Autobiography of a Schizophrenic Girl* (New York: Grune & Stratton, 1951), pp. 3–106.

serious trouble with no one to whom he can talk with confidence. Such inability to communicate meaningfully with people who are physically present may constitute the most extreme form of social isolation.

There seems to be considerable consensus among psychiatrists that many of the difficulties encountered by those adjudged schizophrenic arise from their use of private symbols. Some patients use neologisms. One might remark, for example, that "the ahesses are the styahns of myahm." Others use bizarre gestures. One might turn his head to the right, tilt it upward, close his eyes, and rub his right fist against his neck to designate "God the Father." Conventional symbols are sometimes used to represent special meanings. One might refer to his private alphabet as the "printed talon." In some cases the patient may recognize the fact that others cannot understand him, differentiating between "schizy talk" and "straight talk" and occasionally granting "straight talk" to his doctor as a gift. Those who are in sustained, intimate contact with a given patient may in time learn many of these distinct meanings; if so, they may be able to communicate with him. But to others it is extremely difficult, for it is much like talking to a man who speaks in a foreign tongue. Even the remarks that are made in conventional symbols often appear inappropriate, for the listener cannot be sure of the context in which they are being made. Each patient apparently builds up a private world with meanings that are not subject to social validation. Experiences are categorized and interpreted in unique ways. Thus, a patient may become terrified at something that others hardly notice, for the object has a special meaning for him. Most of these people are not participants in any world over which there is consensus. In severe cases there is a loss of the ability even to use a private language, and the patients become mute and unresponsive. In time they come to resemble desocialized animals.[31]

The deterioration of previously well established behavior patterns is common in schizophrenia. A patient may become unable to defecate or urinate without soiling himself. Sometimes a patient may even forget how to eat, necessitating his being fed like an infant. This primitivation of behavior is often regarded as a form of regression,

[31] Cf. Donald L. Burnham, "Some Problems in Communication with Schizophrenic Patients," *Journal of the American Psychoanalytic Association,* III (1955), 67–81; and Jacob S. Kasanin, ed., *Language and Thought in Schizophrenia* (Berkeley: University of California Press, 1951).

although psychiatrists are by no means agreed on this point. The meanings of even the most familiar objects may become so disorganized that everything appears strange. Retrospective accounts indicate that the patients have the most bizarre experiences. People sometimes appear to be metallic and lifeless, like robots, and even members of one's own family may not be recognized. If one sees a human face in several pieces, with the different parts revolving around one another, it is not surprising that he becomes terrified. As conventional meanings are abandoned, private meanings apparently assume greater importance. It then becomes increasingly more difficult for fellow inmates, technicians, nurses, or doctors to communicate with him. In extreme cases a patient may be reduced to a vegetative existence. There are vast differences among patients in the extent to which conventional patterns disintegrate, and it is of interest to note that the extent of regression may be related to the degree of isolation.[32]

To test the hypothesis that concerted action is based upon effective communication, Slotkin conducted a simple experiment in a mental institution among patients whose vocal behavior was heavily interspersed with private symbols. For a period of approximately seven weeks 15 patients were brought into the same room each day. The experimenter made no effort to interfere with whatever the patients wished to do and made a record of all socially oriented activity that took place. In general, the patients simply sat in the room until they were told to leave. They said nothing to each other and seemingly paid no attention to anyone else, although there is evidence that they were well aware of what was happening in the room. Sometimes the patients responded to one another's expressive movements. When someone began to laugh, perhaps for no ostensible reason, others would join in; indications of fear were similarly contagious. When one person began to talk loudly, others also raised their voices. But much of this speech activity was not communicative. Each patient was vocalizing while participating in a private world of fantasy, and the remarks were not addressed to

[32] Cf. Silvano Arieti, *Interpretation of Schizophrenia* (New York: Robert Brunner, 1955), pp. 183–318; Norman Cameron, *The Psychology of Behavior Disorders* (Boston: Houghton Mifflin Co., 1947), pp. 388–494; and Harry S. Sullivan, *Clinical Studies in Psychiatry*, Helen S. Perry *et al.*, eds. (New York: W. W. Norton & Co., 1956), pp. 3–190.

anyone in the room. Sometimes those sitting nearby would refrain from talking while another person was speaking, but when their turns came it was apparent from their remarks that no reply was being made to what had been said before. Each patient just talked without addressing his remarks to anyone in particular.

Although the same patients saw each other almost daily for a long period, the only concerted action that took place was of the most rudimentary sort. From time to time one of the patients attempted to utilize another for his own purposes, but such efforts almost invariably failed, for the other would soon withdraw or become angry. No stable relationships were established, for no patient would approach another in an effort to make any kind of arrangement for cooperative activity. No social hierarchy developed; it was apparent, however, that most patients had some conception of differences in status, for they spoke to members of the hospital staff whenever they wanted something. Games requiring cooperation, such as cards or checkers, would occasionally get under way, but they were disorganized affairs and always ended in failure. Each inmate had his own rules and his individual version of how the game should be played, and since they could not communicate effectively, there would soon be accusations of cheating. The only pattern that became established was the seating arrangement; each patient usually went to the same seat each day. Since they apparently respected one another's rights to given seats, it might be said that some sort of structure developed. But this was the only cooperation recorded in a period of almost two months.[33]

The importance of mutual support becomes especially apparent in crisis situations. When sudden changes in life conditions disrupt established social relationships and conventional norms prove inadequate, there is a transition period during which people are not certain of what to expect of one another. They do not know what to do, nor do they know what others expect of them. Under such circumstances men become highly sensitized to one another. They constantly ask one another of their opinions; they compare experiences; they make suggestions but do not insist upon their being carried out. Those who act do so with caution, proceeding in a trial and error

[33] James S. Slotkin, "The Nature and Effects of Social Interaction in Schizophrenia," *Journal of Abnormal and Social Psychology*, XXXVII (1942), 345–68.

manner. They watch one another carefully for any hint of new, developing patterns of activity. Several observers have noted that loneliness becomes intolerable in such emergencies. People want to be with others, even with those they do not particularly like. Being unsure of themselves, they seem to crave some kind of reassurance from other human beings. Such observations underscore the contention that social structures are constantly developing as men come to terms with continually changing life conditions. They make their adjustments together, and they construct new schemes of cooperation through communication.

Whenever two or more human beings come together, they interact. That interchange molds the individuals concerned—makes, unmakes, and remakes them without end; it also composes individuals into relationships, perhaps after decomposing other relationships. This reciprocating give and take is the social process. Society consists of the recurrent adjustment and cooperation of associated persons through which action patterns of all kinds are formed, sustained, modified, evaded, or contravened. Sometimes the coordinated activities become highly organized, but there are also transient forms of interaction. All this suggests that human society might best be regarded as an on-going process, a *becoming* rather than a *being*. Society might be viewed most fruitfully as a succession of events, a flow of gestural interchanges among people.

Summary and Conclusion

The mark of society, that which differentiates a social group from a mere aggregate of individuals, is the capacity of the participants to engage in concerted action. In recurrent situations joint enterprises are built up in the reciprocating adjustments of the participants, and such coordination is greatly facilitated by the formation of consensus. But consensus is not static. The world is always changing, and each act in itself constitutes a modification of the situation, however slight the change may be. If perspectives are to remain useful, they also must change. Hence, the outlook of each participant is constantly undergoing transformation, and indications of these changes are given in a variety of gestures. Common understandings arise in and are continually reinforced in a succession of communicative transactions. The gestures involved may be produced intentionally or be the by-products of something else a man is doing, and they may be carefully interpreted or only intuitively noted. But it is through communication, deliberate or accidental, that the participants are able to check one another's intentions. As they interact with one another, their conceptions of the roles they are playing and of their relations with those in reciprocating roles are confirmed, altered, or replaced. In this sense society can be said to exist only in the give and take among human beings.

Some social scientists speak of behavior as being "determined" by culture or by social structure. Although these expressions may serve the purpose of emphasizing the importance of behavior that is learned in contrast to what is instinctive, such mechanical explanations are deceptive. Some write as if the various group patterns have an existence independent of human beings, as if they can be studied in their historical development and geographic distribution apart from people. Some even write as if these patterns constitute an agency coercing individuals into a mold. To point to the obvious, concepts such as "culture" and "social structure" are abstractions; abstractions only describe what men do in generalized terms and do not force anyone to do anything. Sociologists and anthropologists have abstracted somewhat fictive patterns from the visible realities of everyday life, and some have become so preoccupied with these models that they have often lost sight of the individuals whose activities make the patterns discernible to begin with. It is the fact that men interact in a regularized manner that enables an observer to construct these abstractions; to turn around and to declare that the models "cause" behavior involves a logical error—the fallacy of misplaced concreteness. Group patterns are discernible in coordinated action, and such coordination is possible only because certain modes of conduct enjoy mutual support. Concepts referring to these patterns are useful, as long as they are not transformed into mysterious "forces" that push people about.

Suggested References

DEWEY, JOHN, *Experience and Nature*, Ch. V. Chicago: Open Court Publishing Co., 1926. A classic presentation of a behavioristic view of communication as the interchange of gestures through which cooperation is achieved.

MALINOWSKI, BRONISLAW, *Coral Gardens and Their Magic*, Vol. II, Part IV. New York: American Book Co., 1935. An ethnographer's discussion of the place of linguistic behavior in the cultural life of the Trobriand Islanders, with special attention to the difficulties involved in recording unwritten languages.

MORRIS, CHARLES W., *Signs, Language and Behavior*. New York: Prentice-Hall, Inc., 1946. An attempt to develop a conceptual scheme for the systematic study of all symbolic behavior, drawing materials from linguistics, aesthetics, logic, and psychiatry as well as the social sciences.

RUESCH, JURGEN, *Disturbed Communication*. New York: W. W. Norton & Co., 1957. An analysis of the various sources of breakdowns in communication, with extensive suggestions of categories with which psychiatrists might assess conventional and expressive gestures.

SAPIR, EDWARD, *Selected Writings in Language, Culture and Personality,* David G. Mandelbaum, ed., pp. 7–166, 308–31, 357–72, 533–59, 564– 68. Berkeley: University of California Press, 1949. Essays by a foremost authority in linguistics, presenting a behavioristic account of language and culture, and an insightful account of society as a communicative process.

SCHELER, MAX, *The Nature of Sympathy*, Peter Heath, trans., Parts I & III. New Haven: Yale University Press, 1954. A treatise by a phenomenologist on the manner in which men are able to achieve knowledge of the minds of others, containing many distinctions not ordinarily made in American social psychology.

Part Two

Motivation

6

Consciousness
and
voluntary
conduct

In American communities each case of homicide sets into operation a complex procedure for ascertaining how it happened. Even after a confession that leaves little doubt over the identity of the murderer, many duties still remain for a number of public officials—representatives of the district attorney's office, the police, and the coroner's office—and for the defense attorney. Everyone who had been involved in the affair is questioned in the search for corroborating evidence. Piece by piece the items of information are put together in an effort to reconstruct the course of events leading to the crime. Homicide is neither new nor unusual to these people. Then why do they go to so much trouble? Implicit in this complex procedure is the assumption that each overt act, however similar it may be to other familiar acts, has a unique history. Therefore, it cannot be understood except in the context of its peculiar development.

In attempting to reconstruct the offense, investigators become concerned with how the murderer committed the crime, and why he did it. In doing so, they raise the same questions as a social psychologist who is concerned with motivation. But their answers are rarely given in terms of "drives," instincts, or other inner urges. They compile a record of the complex sequence of events leading to the fatal transaction; they take note of unrelated incidents that throw light upon the personalities of those involved; they take account of various extenuating circumstances and chance occurrences. In many cases they find that there is no simple "reason" for what happened. The problem of motivation is one of bewildering complexity, and although social psychologists are generally agreed on its importance, there is little accord on how it should be approached.

The Problem of Motivation

Probably the most common way of accounting for what a man does is by citing an antecedent event which is regarded as its "cause," using this term in the most naïve sense. The antecedent event is blamed or credited for what happened, as if it were a responsible agent. This practice is widespread among laymen and social psychologists alike. If a thief steals a diamond bracelet, it is contended that he was attracted by its glitter or that he anticipated presenting it to a woman in return for sexual favors. The instigation is sometimes regarded as external to the organism—the beauty of the jewel, perhaps, or the voluptuous attributes of the woman—and sometimes internal—for instance, the glandular secretions underlying sexual excitement. This means that human behavior is generally explained either as a response to environmental stimuli or in terms of "needs," which are viewed as forms of internal stimulation. At first blush such analytic schemes seem reasonable enough, but closer examination reveals glaring deficiencies.

The difficulty with explanations in terms of single antecedent events is that they fail to account for the range and flexibility of human behavior. A man who is sexually aroused may engage in a wide variety of activities. He may ingratiate himself before a woman from whom he seeks favors; he may excite himself further by reading pornographic literature; he may commit a crime; or he may go to a gymnasium to divert his attention and work off some of his tensions. Pointing to a single "need" like sex is hardly an adequate explanation of the choice made from several possible alternatives. Furthermore, much of human behavior is goal-oriented and remarkably flexible. It is rarely automatic and stereotyped; a given set of stimuli, internal or external, is not necessarily followed by a fixed overt reaction. Indeed, much of what any man does depends upon the requirements of the particular circumstances in which he finds himself. The course of action followed by a thief, for example, depends upon the changing situation—the restful slumber of the watchman, the noise suddenly erupting from a party in the apartment above the store, or the chance appearance of a passerby. Purposive behavior persists in spite of temporary inconveniences and barriers, but what is actually done depends upon the exigencies of the moment.

Some psychologists have looked upon the problem of motivation as that of accounting for activity on the part of an organism, as if it were inert unless stimulated. But all living creatures are active. The challenge is to account for the *patterning, timing, and direction of behavior*, especially for persistent movement toward a goal.[1] Of the hundreds of things that a man might conceivably do in a given situation, why does he pursue one course of action rather than another? As social psychologists, we are not concerned with the direction of all human activity; our interest is limited to the conduct of a person who is participating in some kind of joint undertaking.

In experimental studies on learning, psychologists—by observing the degree of pain a rat is willing to undergo to reach gratification—have not only isolated certain basic "drives," like sex and hunger, but have also measured their intensity. There can be little doubt that human beings are also aroused periodically by such organic deficits, and these findings are certainly not irrelevant to the study of man. But any attempt to explain *all* human behavior in these terms is bound to fail, for such inner dispositions assume overriding importance only under quite limited circumstances—in cases of extreme deprivation. A man who is half starved may lunge desperately for food, ignoring all other considerations. Lust may also became intensified to the point where nothing else matters. But, ordinarily, what characterizes man is the ability to delay immediate gratification, especially when there is a likelihood of adverse reactions on the part of other people. Men have foresight; they are capable of planning

---

[1] Cf. Donald O. Hebb, *The Organization of Behavior* (New York: John Wiley & Sons, 1949), pp. 171–73; and David C. McClelland *et al.*, *The Achievement Motive* (New York: Appleton-Century-Crofts, 1953), pp. 6–96.

their activities. Any scheme to account for motivation in human beings must not only include a place for such organic deficits, which are admittedly important as starting points of acts, but must also account for the manner in which such impulses are inhibited and redirected. The explanatory model must make possible the inclusion of conscious intent.

Psychoanalysts have emphasized the crucial importance of "unconscious motives." There seems to be little question that men become oriented toward a variety of objects which have special meanings for them and that they are often unaware of what they are doing. Many of the meanings that make up each person's world are unconscious, and they give rise to impulses that he does not understand, impulses that may eventuate in behavior that does not make sense to anyone. Such activity is goal-oriented in that tension reduction does not occur until certain ends are achieved. A man feels strangely relieved after accidentally kicking a colleague that he admires, or a child's asthmatic symptoms disappear as soon as he is separated from his mother, whom he professes to love. Freud found it necessary to postulate unconscious dispositions to account for the regularity with which so many acts contradict sincere beliefs. There is ample evidence that such dispositions exist and that they are important, but they constitute only one part of human life. It is not surprising that psychiatrists emphasize such impulses, for they apparently lie at the root of many personality disorders. Their importance is not to be underestimated; however, it would be a mistake to explain *all* human conduct exclusively in these terms.

Another way in which human conduct gains direction is in terms of the consciously avowed intentions of the actor. The goal, often an image of consummation, plays an important part in the execution of an act, for it helps to coordinate the diverse movements into a unit. When a man knows what he wants to do, he can eliminate irrelevant movements and concentrate his efforts. Of course, one's purpose is not always clear, and he may raise questions about his intentions. Sometimes it is only an inference based upon observed behavior. It is in this sense that Weber used the term "motive"—to refer to what appears to the actor himself and to an observer as adequate grounds for the conduct in question. Purpose is an instrument which is employed to make behavior intelligible both to ourselves and to others.[2] Far from being the "causes" of behavior, what are ordinarily called "motives" are linguistic designations of intentions.

Popular beliefs concerning the adequate grounds for various acts differ from group to group. In each culture the things that men do are classified somewhat differently, and there are common understandings concerning the plausible reason for each category of activity. This means that in each group there is a distinct vocabulary of motives. In the United States today, individualistic, hedonistic, and pecuniary motives are generally regarded as the plausible springs of action, and it is difficult for most of us to realize that such intentions have not always been accepted elsewhere. If someone declares that he did something in order to make money or to have a good time, his statement is usually accepted as true, even by those who disapprove of what he did. But there is a tendency to question the sincerity of those who avow religious motives. During the Middle Ages a monk who found a sick woman at the monastery gates, violated the rules of his order by taking her inside, and then nursed her back to health could insist that he was only carrying out God's will; his explanation would probably have been accepted by many people. Today, however, it would be suspected that the monk was actually struck by the woman's beauty, but being pious, he repressed and sublimated his erotic impulses, thereby deceiving himself into believing that he was an instrument of divine purpose. The second explanation may sound more plausible to us, but what assurance is there that the motives to which we are accustomed are any more authentic than those used in another universe of discourse? Are we not being ethnocentric in insisting that our vocabularly of motives is universal? The motives that may be inferred with plausibility are matters of conventional usage in each social group.[3]

But the question invariably arises: are avowed intentions the "real" motives? Of course, there is sometimes a difference between publicly avowed and privately confessed explanations of one's behavior, but what of the latter? To avoid begging the question the query can be put in another way: are the reasons that men give for what they do adequate explanations of their conduct? Since many of

[2] Weber, *op. cit.*, pp. 98–99. Cf. Prescott Lecky, *Self-Consistency: A Theory of Personality* (New York: Island Press, 1951), pp. 103–4.
[3] C. Wright Mills, "Situated Actions and Vocabularies of Motive," *American Sociological Review*, V (1940), 904–13.

the things that men do are involuntary and unconscious, the answer is obviously in the negative. But the fact remains that many persistent efforts are directed toward announced objectives, and this should not be ignored in the construction of a theory of motivation. There are shared assumptions in each culture concerning the reasons for various categories of activity, and once a person locates what he is about to do within such a framework, his sensitivities and selections are circumscribed by group expectations. Psychiatrists sometimes dismiss avowed intentions as "rationalizations" and contrast them with the "real" motives. Do they actually have evidence of the authentic "causes" of behavior, or are they observing their subjects with a different vocabulary of motives?

In making avowals and imputations of motives, people who share a common cultural heritage are likely to achieve consensus, even though their explanations of what they are doing may seem inadequate to social psychologists. A young man may insist that the only reason he wants to become a doctor is to serve humanity. A psychoanalyst may challenge the adequacy of such an interpretation; but concerted action rests upon mutual understanding, and those who are satisfied with the young man's account will cooperate with him. As long as men share the same vocabulary of motives, they can engage in concerted action. When strangers interact, tensions frequently arise from their inability to define one another's conduct in similar terms.

Social psychologists are confronted with the task of ascertaining how goal-oriented behavior is carried out by people who are participating in joint transactions. There is no question that such participants are periodically upset by organic deficits, but such impulses may be consummated in a number of different ways. Especially in situations in which immediate consummation might arouse negative reactions on the part of others they tend to be inhibited and redirected. Furthermore, each participant enters the situation with a number of unconscious meanings that sometimes elicit embarrassing impulses. This may prove quite bothersome, for concerted action may break down if any of the participants do things that are odd and unexpected. In the main, however, it is conscious volition that plays an important part in cooperative activity. The participants make choices while keeping an eye upon others about them. They are not only aware of their own desires but also make inferences about the probable intentions of their associates. This constant appraisal—of oneself as well as the others—is greatly facilitated by the fact that men are able to classify and symbolize their activities and the grounds upon which they presumably rest. Flexible coordination rests largely upon the self-control of the participants; therefore, attention will be directed primarily toward the study of voluntary conduct.

Consciousness as Inner Communication

It is not surprising that a phenomenon of such great importance as thinking would be the object of widespread philosophical and popular speculation. In the Western intellectual tradition there has been a tendency to separate the mind from the body; mind has often been conceived as something without substance and contrasted with the body with its obvious physical attributes. It has often been regarded as something operating independently of the body in which it resides, something which on occasion struggles against the instincts for control over behavior. During the past century many attempts have been made to resolve this dichotomy by locating the mind in the nervous system, in the brain, or in some other part of the body. Among the many views on the nature of the human mind is the position of psychologists of behavioristic persuasion, who insist that consciousness and thinking are forms of activity. It is apparent that a man who is thinking is doing something, but there is the question of just what it is that he is doing. It has been contended that *consciousness is a form of communication*, that a man who is conscious of something is making indications to himself in much the same manner in which he might call it to the attention of someone else. Conscious awareness involves making indications to oneself, and reflective thought consists of the manipulation of such designations in the course of solving some problem. The human mind is regarded not so much as a substance but as a form of behavior—largely sub-vocal linguistic behavior.

Conscious awareness is a communicative process which differs from mere perception. Men can perceive without consciousness, for strictly speaking perception refers to any kind of discriminating responsiveness on the part of a living organism. Men respond to all kinds of sensory cues without being aware of them. This is referred to as *subliminal perception*. In the performance of habitual tasks, for example, such as brushing one's teeth, few people ever miss the brush when squeezing toothpaste upon it even though they may not be paying much attention to what they are doing. Nor do they fail to hit their mouths with the properly prepared brush. Experienced drivers operate their automobiles through a succession of complex movements, such as shifting gears, steering, stepping on the accelerator or on the brakes. Such coordination implies perception; yet, except under unusual circumstances there is no awareness of these movements. Conscious attention, then, is not only more selective than perception but involves communication. A man becomes aware of something only when he points it out to himself.

As implausible as this notion may sound at first, the fact that men perceive without consciousness has been demonstrated in a number of ingenious experiments. McCleary and Lazarus set up a device for showing that men are capable of discriminating among sensory cues even when they are not able to distinguish them consciously. Their subjects were repeatedly exposed to a number of five letter nonsense syllables; half of the items were always accompanied by an electric shock. Using an instrument to measure the galvanic skin responses (GSR), one of the automatic defenses against shocks, they flashed the items in random order upon a screen at speeds much too fast for recognition. When the subjects were asked to identify the items, they could only guess and made many mistakes, but the GSR registered consistently for the shock-associated items. Thus, differential responses were recorded even when the items were moving too rapidly to be recognized.[4] Experimental studies of hypnosis also reveal the extent to which conscious awareness can be controlled through linguistic communication. In studies on anaesthesia induced through hypnosis, it was demonstrated that many subjects could be subjected to considerable pain without awareness. As they were being burned or stuck with pins, they insisted that they felt no pain. Careful measurements revealed, however, that the automatic emergency reactions were taking place; there were changes in the pulse rate, respiration, and GSR. But the conventional reactions to pain—

[4] Robert A. McCleary and Richard S. Lazarus, "Autonomic Discrimination without Awareness," *Journal of Personality*, XVIII (1949), 171–79. Cf. N. F. Dixon, "The Effect of Subliminal Stimulation upon Autonomic and Verbal Behavior," *Journal of Abnormal and Social Psychology*, LVII (1958), 29–36.

grimaces, verbal reports, and consciousness—could be abolished through the command of the hypnotist.[5] Thus, the body reacts defensively to painful stimuli, but there is no awareness of the response. Men perceive all kinds of cues, but they become conscious of them only when they make indications to themselves.

Consciousness covers a wide range of experiences, and regarding it as a form of communication suggests some of the dimensions along which variations occur. Among other things the clarity of any experience would vary with its communicability. There are many things that one can explain quite explicitly in terms of the linguistic symbols at his command, and these matters are clearly understood. There are other things that one can only feel intuitively. He makes judgments which rest upon grounds of which he is only vaguely aware. Even when his orientation is definitely structured, he may not have the words to describe it adequately. If so, he cannot account for what he does either to himself or to other people. For each person there are some well established behavior patterns that can be observed by others, especially by psychiatrists, of which he himself has no awareness at all. These are meanings about which he is unable to communicate. There are considerable differences among people in the extent to which they can verbalize their experiences. To some extent this depends upon the adequacy of one's vocabulary, but there are other barriers to communication.

Unified, directed action arises through foresight. Coordinated effort arises from the fact that the latter phases of the act—images of the state of consummation—can provide organization for the earlier phases. This entire process is facilitated by the use of linguistic symbols. Reflective thought is one of the secondary adjustments following the blockage of on-going action, one which enables men to compare alternative routes and to pretest them in their imagination before committing themselves to overt action. The process of comparison and selection is greatly simplified when symbols can be substituted for meanings and images, for it is much easier to manipulate words. Some images are usually involved in reflective thought, but men can think without them, as in the solving of a mathematical problem. While thinking can take place without linguistic symbols, the capacity of men to make such substitutions has

[5] Clark L. Hull, *Hypnosis and Suggestibility* (New York: Appleton-Century-Crofts, Inc., 1933), pp. 250–70.

so extended the range and complexity of the problems handled that human life has taken on new characteristics.

A man who is thinking does much the same thing he would if talking to someone else, except that there is no one else present to listen to what he says. Only he himself benefits from his remarks. There are two other differences; internal communication is characterized by inaudibility and brevity. In general, thinking is carried on in silence, although there are exceptions which highlight the similarity of the processes involved. When one is confronted with a problem of considerable difficulty, he mutters to himself and goes over each step aloud as he struggles toward a solution. He may even write down the argument, as he might if he were explaining the difficulties to someone else. Among people who are just learning a new language and among children much of what would constitute thinking is expressed aloud. But for most adults in most situations thinking cannot be heard. Furthermore, in adults internal communication is abbreviated. The designations that men make to themselves are much shorter than those they would make on the same topic to someone else because it is not necessary for a person to tell himself what he already knows. Basic assumptions as well as many transitional remarks and subsidiary arguments can be omitted; they are simply taken for granted.[6]

Thinking is private in the sense that others do not have access to one's thoughts, but it is social in that it is carried on in terms of conventional symbols which stand for meanings over which there is a high degree of consensus. On the whole, men think in terms of the same symbols they use to communicate with others. Of course, there are sensations that cannot be designated with words; men can visualize and hear images of all kinds. But it is the use of linguistic symbols that makes possible the organization and manipulation of such experiences. For example, a boy who is daydreaming of his days of glory on the gridiron or in the World Series describes his fantastic exploits in the very words used by radio or television announcers, not only using the technical vocabulary of these sports but also imitating the intonation of the voice customarily used when describing the accolades of the crowd. In his daydreams the boy is controlling his visual and auditory imagery by manipulating symbols. Since symbolic communication is conventional, it follows that

[6] Cf. L. S. Vigotsky, "Thought and Speech," *Psychiatry*, II (1939), 29–52.

consciousness and thought constitute an importation of the social process.

Because thinking takes place so naturally and spontaneously, we do not appreciate the extent to which it depends upon customary usage. The common understanding shared in a group necessarily become involved in the thinking of all men other than those who are psychotic. As in the communication that occurs between persons, the expectations imputed to the audience place limitations upon what the speaker can say with plausibility. Even when one is talking to himself, he must say things that "make sense." The human mind may be regarded as the internalization of the speech process, which is organized largely in terms of conventional norms.[7] This suggests that the operation of the various mental processes is to some extent circumscribed by the culture of the group in which a person is participating.

Although some philosophers believe that logic is something that is inherent in the relationship of things in nature, others contend that the process of logical reasoning develops through participation in social groups. Logic is born of necessity, the necessity of influencing and convincing other people in an argument. Whenever others express doubt, efforts are made at verification; ideas and their presentation are tested. Rationality involves an appreciation of the relations of means to ends. Logic consists of nothing more than the rules for ascertaining the appropriate procedures for arriving at rational conclusions—a systematization of the rules that make thinking a more effective instrument of adjustment. One cannot persuade others unless he reasons in a sound manner; indeed, he cannot even persuade himself unless he can meet these standards. Logical procedures are shaped by the rebuffs and approvals received from one's audience as he seeks to justify his reasoning. Conscious thought is usually rational precisely because it is social.[8]

Since the contention that mentality consists of sub-vocal linguistic behavior is at odds with the common sense view, an examination of the evidence is in order. A number of attempts have been made by

[7] Mead, *Mind, Self, and Society, op. cit.,* pp. 186–92.

[8] Cf. C. Wright Mills, "Language, Logic, and Culture," *American Sociological Review,* IV (1939), 670–80; and Jean Piaget, *Judgment and Reasoning in the Child,* Marjorie Warden, trans. (New York: Harcourt, Brace & Co., 1928), pp. 199–256.

physiologists to measure movements in the speech musculature as subjects engaged in a variety of intellectual activities. Although most of these studies, including the previously cited experiments of Jacobson, revealed swift contractions in the muscles of the lips and tongue, the evidence was vague until Max hit upon an ingenious solution. Since the finger and arm muscles are the locus of the gestural communication of the deaf, electrodes were placed upon these muscles to see whether incipient movements occur when deaf people are thinking. The control group consisted of persons with normal hearing. Abstract thought problems elicited manual action-currents in 84 per cent of the deaf as compared with only 31 per cent of the control group; no overt movements were visible in either. When the deaf subjects were asleep, the onset of dreams could be detected in many instances by the appearance of large action-currents in the arm and finger muscles, although such responses were generally not accompanied by overt movements. Max also found that simple arithmetic problems were answered immediately without the accompaniment of action-currents and that the more intelligent and better educated people tended to register fewer electromyographic responses in the course of solving problems.[9] This suggests that thinking may be more abbreviated for those who do not have to work out each step. The more a man knows and the more intelligent he is, the less he has to tell himself. Although the evidence is still not conclusive, it is sufficient to indicate that the behavioristic view is not without foundation.

These findings are consistent with evidence from other sources. The extent to which thinking is linguistic is especially apparent to those who are bilingual and to those with special language problems. Many immigrants go through life thinking in the tongue they learned as children. Even after 40 or 50 years of residence in their adopted land they find it necessary to think in one language and then to translate their conclusions into the other. There are clinical records indicating that blind people think in braille. Freeman and Williams report the case of a woman who had been blind since 13 who reported having hallucinations—sometimes visual and sometimes in braille. Although the hallucinations disappeared after brain

[9] Louis W. Max, "Experimental Study of the Motor Theory of Consciousness," *Journal of Comparative and Physiological Psychology*, XXIV (1937), 301–44.

surgery, the patient reported that her thoughts continued to flash before her in braille.[10]

It is popularly believed that thinking takes place in the head, and there is now little doubt that the brain and the nervous system are conspicuously involved in the various mental processes. However, when Hebb reviewed the clinical reports on brain injuries and on brain surgery, some seemingly contradictory evidence emerged. He found many cases in which intelligence, as measured by the ability to do I.Q. tests, is not significantly diminished even when large parts of the brain had been cut away. Other skills may be affected, but the ability to use words and to solve problems is not. He concluded that there is little direct evidence of intellectual defect from cerebral damage, *except* when there is damage to that part of the brain controlling speech. Then, impairment in thinking is definitely noticeable.[11]

Since damage to the areas of the brain controlling speech seems to be of such exceptional importance, evidence from studies of aphasia may be examined in more detail. The term aphasia is used somewhat loosely to refer to a variety of disorders, generally involving brain injury, in which there is some impairment in the ability to use linguistic symbols. Extensive studies were conducted by Head, who devised a series of ingenious tests for measuring the mental capacity of such patients. One of his findings was that victims of aphasia are unable to imagine something that is not physically present; they are restricted to the here and now, to their immediate environment. A patient aiming at a basket with a ball of paper is able to make hits with considerable skill until the basket is placed behind a screen where he can no longer see it; he is then unable to guess the location of the target. He cannot strike an imaginary match, nor can he hit an imaginary nail with an imaginary hammer, although he is able to perform both tasks when actually handling these objects. A patient can draw from a model immediately before him, but not from memory. A British Army officer who had worked with elephants for many years in India was unable to reproduce one

---

[10] Walter Freeman and Jonathan M. Williams, "Hallucinations in Braille," *Archives of Neurology and Psychiatry*, LXX (1953), 630–34.

[11] Donald O. Hebb, "The Effect of Early and Late Brain Injury upon Test Scores," *Proceedings of the American Philosophical Society*, LXXXV (1942), 275–92; and "Man's Frontal Lobes: A Critical Review," *Archives of Neurology and Psychiatry*, LIV (1945), 10–24.

from memory; after his recovery, however, he had no difficulty at all.[12] It appears, then, that persons who are unable to manipulate linguistic symbols cannot form assumptions about anything that is not immediately present. Since foresight and planning—so essential in reflective thought—are impossible without imagination, the difficulties confronting victims of aphasia become understandable.

Many kinds and degrees of impairment are included in aphasia, but much of the literature deals with patients who are still able to communicate to some extent with their doctors. After many years of inquiry, Goldstein concluded that the major difficulties in aphasia arise not so much from a lack of words but from the inability to categorize experience. Even those who can still use words are unable to use them as symbols for categories. Being unable to form abstractions, they are limited to responding to each concrete object with which they are confronted; the patient is reduced to a succession of specific adjustments, much like other animals and infants. Goldstein devised a number of tests—tasks requiring the formation of abstractions and reference to them by symbols—and the performances of his subjects confirm his view. Victims of aphasia have great difficulty in classifying objects in terms of simple criteria, such as brightness or size. Even when they succeed, they are unable to repeat their performance.[13] Although the evidence is not conclusive, it is reasonably consistent and strongly suggests that many of the routine acts that most men take for granted depend upon their capacity to use linguistic symbols.

Since the thinking of mental patients diagnosed as schizophrenic is often quite different from that of other people, efforts have been made to study their linguistic behavior. Some psychiatrists, like Vigotsky, have contended that those suffering from schizophrenia, like the victims of aphasia, are unable to form categories; but the evidence is not clear on this point. Hanfmann and Kasanin devised a test to examine the ability of schizophrenic patients to form concepts. Using twenty-two wooden blocks—in five colors, six shapes, two heights, and two sizes—they asked their subjects to divide them

[12] Henry Head, *Aphasia and Kindred Disorders of Speech* (New York: The Macmillan Co., 1926), Vol. I, pp. 349–80; Vol. II, pp. 513–32.

[13] Kurt Goldstein, "The Problem of the Meaning of Words Based upon Observations of Aphasic Patients," *Journal of Psychology*, II (1937), 301–16; and *Human Nature in the Light of Psychopathology* (Cambridge: Harvard University Press, 1940), pp. 69–84.

into four groups, thereby disclosing a hidden principle of classification. The test was given to sixty-two patients, fifty college graduates,
forty-five hospital attendants, and twenty-four patients with damaged brain tissue. There was considerable variation in the performances, ranging from the complete inability to grasp any
principle to the pursuit of an orderly procedure until the problem
was solved. The performance of those with schizophrenia was in
general poorer than that of the others; when education was held
constant, however, the better educated in each group made higher
scores. But eleven subjects classified as schizophrenic ranked among
the highest for their respective educational levels.[14] In view of the
fact that so many different disorders are included under the term
"schizophrenia," it is not surprising that the results are so inconclusive. There seems to be little doubt, however, that many persons
so diagnosed have difficulty in forming and using categories.

In many cases of schizophrenia there is apparently an impairment in the ability to reason logically—just what would be expected
of those who are isolated from human society. Cameron presented
his patients with a series of incomplete sentences ending with "because" and asked to have them concluded. The subjects revealed a
marked inability to discern conventionally accepted means-ends
relationships. The wind blows "because it's time to blow." When
asked what makes it blow, a patient replied that it was "the air."
When queried about the air, he spoke of "the sky." When asked how
the sky makes it blow, he went on, "Because it's high in the air."
There is only a cluster of more or less related events, and most people
would regard this line of reasoning as absurd. But what is regarded as a plausible "casual" relationship is often a sequence of
events regarded as "realistic" in some group. It rests upon a set of
assumptions concerning the attributes of various objects and their
relationships to one another, and these premises constitute the culture of the group. Since these patients have withdrawn from the
world of consensus, it is not strange that they should fail to comply
with conventional norms. If logic is sharpened in proving points to
others, it is a matter of no concern to many patients. They are un-

[14] Eugenia Hanfmann and Jacob Kasanin, *Conceptual Thinking in Schizo-
phrenia* (New York: Nervous and Mental Disease Monographs, 1942). Cf. L. S.
Vigotsky, "Thought in Schizophrenia," *Archives of Neurology and Psychiatry,*
XXXI (1934). 1063–77.

able to take a listener's point of view and can see no necessity for even trying. Whiteman repeated Cameron's study using matched samples of psychotic and normal subjects, and while his findings are less conclusive, they tend to confirm the original findings.[15] Although the evidence is not entirely adequate, it does provide some support for the hypothesis that logic is developed and sustained in social interaction.

Thus, men get some of their distinctive characteristics from the fact that they can think. Because they can communicate with themselves they are able to project themselves out of the immediate situations in which they are involved. The ability of a person to inhibit his impulses and to hold himself overtly in a state of suspension while he responds to a succession of images and symbolic representations is what constitutes his inner life—his mentality. The fact that he can make designations to himself about activity that is still under way makes possible a measure of control that would otherwise be impossible. Because he is not at the mercy of his immediate environment he can consider alternatives in his imagination and address himself to goals that are far beyond. It is in this manner that conduct becomes voluntary.

Self-Control as a Serial Process

From time to time a community is shocked by a seemingly incomprehensible event. An heiress who is believed to have "everything"—beauty, a number of handsome suitors, a magnificent home, permissive parents, a new sportscar, remarkable aptitude in each of her various interests—suddenly commits suicide. Or a man may suddenly go beserk and kill the delivery boy and the mailman; when questioned by the police, he insists that they had been conspiring with his wife to get rid of him—a charge that completely dumbfounds her. Such conduct is difficult to explain in terms of organic deficits; indeed, these illustrations point to the importance of the

---

[15] Norman Cameron, "Reasoning, Regression, and Communication in Schizophrenics," *Psychological Monographs*, L (1938), #221; and "Schizophrenic Thinking in a Problem-Solving Situation," *Journal of Mental Science*, LXXXV (1939), 1012–35. Cf. Martin Whiteman, "The Performance of Schizophrenics on Social Concepts," *Journal of Abnormal and Social Psychology*, XLIX (1954), 266–71.

definition of the situation. What a man does, then, is not so much a response to the natural environment as to his interpretation of a part of it.

The manner in which the concept of the "definition of the situation" is frequently used conveys the notion that such interpretations are static affairs to which a single response is made. This is misleading. To point to the obvious, the scene on which men act is constantly undergoing change. Each new event that is relevant to what one is doing has to be labelled and placed. Thus, each person's perceptual field is continually being transformed. To understand what any person does, then, the observer must get some picture of how particular definitions develop. How did the heiress come to regard her situation as "hopeless"? How did the temporarily crazed man develop the beliefs which enabled him to interpret various sensory cues in a manner that confirmed and reinforced his suspicions? *Voluntary conduct is constructive and creative; it is something that is built up in a succession of adjustments to an ever changing perceptual field.*

Since most acts take place within a social context, the manner in which voluntary conduct develops rests upon the self-images one forms from the standpoint imputed to others involved in the enterprise. Since a person can react to each of his self-images as others might, he is able to anticipate the moves they are likely to make and to adjust to them in advance. This does not mean that men always comply with group expectations; they only take them into account. One may very well appreciate the views of people he dislikes and then deliberately go out of his way to spite them. In most cases of concerted action, however, all participants engage in such imaginative rehearsals from a common perspective, and their respective contributions fit together in a reciprocating manner. All this indicates that the process of self-control is a highly complex form of behavior. It involves (1) taking the role of an audience, (2) forming a succession of self-images, and (3) readjusting one's plans in accordance with the anticipated reactions of others.

Men cannot always control their impulses. It is a rare person who is able to comply readily with the request of his dentist to "relax" just as a drill is lowered upon a sensitive tooth. But many impulses are successfully inhibited and do not eventuate in overt behavior. A person may not be able to do too much about the "beast" in himself, but he can make life more bearable for his associates by acting as if it did not exist. Men frequently suffer intense deprivations in refusing to do things that they desire—to satisfy their sexual curiosity, to lash out at their rivals, to advance themselves by cheating. Such possibilities are sometimes within reach, but many deem such conduct as being beneath their dignity. Thus, external demeanor is purchased at the price of frustration. The difference between inner experiences and overt behavior gives some indication of the effectiveness of self-control. Indeed, the fact that such differences exist is so widely recognized that most people learn not to take all the acts of others at face value. They learn to observe people carefully, especially when their vital interests are at stake and when the usual inhibitions may be weakened; under such circumstances some may forget their obligations to others and act in terms of their personal preferences.

Consciousness and volition are found only in delayed acts, and interrupted acts are often marked by an inner struggle between contradictory tendencies. Impulses that are not immediately consummated evoke images; and although some images reinforce already existing discomforts, others arouse inhibitory responses. A hungry man may want to steal some food, but he imagines being incarcerated and recoils from this possibility. Similarly, a man who is sexually excited may want to seize a beautiful woman but withdraws upon recognizing the probable consequences of such conduct. The fear of condemnation by friends and relatives instigates inhibitory impulses. Self-control is a process in which one impulse arises to block another.

The impulses of a particular human being constitute his spontaneous reactions to the situations in which he finds himself. Since the meanings of the key objects making up the environment vary from person to person, different individuals are likely to define the same situation in somewhat different ways. What constitutes a terrifying experience for one person may strike another as an event involving only minor risks. Even when the definitions are similar, the impulses aroused in the various participants may be quite different. For example, of the millions of people who watch a television comercial for some alcoholic beverage, each reacts somewhat differently. One man, who is fond of drinking, may suddenly feel thirsty and get up for a bottle; a second person, an ardent advocate of prohibition, may become outraged and resolve to dispatch a protest to the F.C.C.; a third person, and executive in a rival firm, may scrutinize the presentation and reconsider the plans for his own promotional campaign; elsewhere, a child observing the same program may find something in the announcer's gestures comical and laugh uproariously. Each person, by virtue of the fact that he enters the situation with a unique background of experience, reacts in a distinctive manner; impulses may be regarded as manifestations of one's personality. Whenever these spontaneous reactions are inconsistent with group norms, however, they tend to be inhibited and redirected along conventional channels, thereby reducing the observable differences among people. Even though men cooperate by conforming to conventional norms they retain their individuality, for their inner experiences remain unique.

The fact that inner struggles take place suggests that there is an internal audience that reacts to the succession of impulses. Because each person has acquired the perspective shared in his group, he can define and evaluate what he would like to do from this collective standpoint. Thus, a man is able to submit his plan of action to self-criticism before commitment to overt action. The contemplation of an act that is roundly condemned in the group prompts negative reactions. Unfair tactics are condemned in most groups, and a person who thinks of taking advantage of someone experiences shame; he condemns himself just as the others would if they only knew of his thoughts. If a contemplated deed is so foul that he cannot stand being identified with it, he may even project his plan upon others, accuse them of having loathsome motives, and then demand retributions. Although it is difficult to forecast a given man's impulses, his overt conduct can generally be anticipated with reasonable accuracy, for he is likely to conform with group standards. Thus, *self-control is essentially social control.* Each man tries to maintain his self-respect in his own eyes, but he sees himself from the standpoint of his group.

The development of voluntary conduct is a serial process in which a person responds to a succession of self-images. A man who is famished is sensitized to anything that is likely to eliminate his hunger pangs. Should he see fruits on trees on a farm surrounded by a wire fence, his initial reaction may be that of jumping over the fence and picking some. He imagines himself eating the fruits, and the delectable flavor reinforces his impulse. Then he notices a sign: "Danger! High tension wire!" His line of action is checked, as he visualizes himself grasping a wire and being fried crisp. He is frightened by this image and pulls back; he shudders as he contemplates what might have happened had he not noticed the sign in time. If he is still hungry upon recovering, a succession of other images may be aroused—going under the fence, asking the caretaker to throw him some fruit, complaining to the police about the dangerous fence. The alternatives considered depend upon the memories the man brings into the situation from experiences in similar contexts in the past. Conduct is built up as he responds in turn to each image. The planning and direction of overt behavior become possible because men are able to respond to themselves in their imagination; they can chart their course in such imaginative rehearsals by pre-testing various plans of action.[16]

Self-control is greatly facilitated when this inner rehearsal can take place symbolically. When symbols are used to represent the various impulses, categories of experience, group norms, and other considerations that enter into the organization of an act, the entire procedure is greatly simplified, for symbols are so much easier to manipulate. The struggle between personal preference and moral obligation may then take on a conversational character. Instead of merely feeling that something would be desirable a person can tell himself that a particular position is rewarding and that he should work for it. Instead of being uncomfortable about wanting something that is prohibited he can tell himself that he ought to be ashamed. A man in a quandary often carries on conversations with himself concerning the relative merits of contradictory lines of action. Such dialectical interchanges are more readily observable in children who have not yet internalized the process. A child reaches for some forbidden object and then says, using the intonation of his mother's voice and her gestures, "No, no! Don't touch!" He draws back in response and then reaches again, only to repeat the admonition and to retreat. The child proceeds in the same manner as an adult; the only difference is that he has not yet learned to make his remarks to himself inaudible to others. He forms a self-image

---

[16] Cf. George H. Mead, "The Social Self," *Journal of Philosophy*, X (1913), 374–80; also his *Mind, Self, and Society, op. cit.*, pp. 173–78, 186–200, 209–22.

by taking the role of his elders and then responds to it. Commands like "don't touch" constitute the symbolic representation of group norms. In adults the same communicative process is carried on internally and is very much abbreviated.

Such inner communication becomes especially important when concerted action is interrupted by unexpected events. The situation must be redefined, and this is done by manipulating symbols. It is precisely in situations in which something unusual has taken place, when there is a temporary lapse in mutual understanding, that attempts are made to reestablish consensus through the imputation of motives. When a mother looks after her child, no one asks why; but when a woman neglects her offspring, questions about her motives arise. When a beautiful woman marries a homely man beneath her station in life, eyebrows are raised. The implication is that something abnormal has happened, and a search begins for some ulterior motive. Furthermore, inquiries about motives occur only in situations in which there is some possibility of choosing among alternatives. If there is only one road between two towns, no one asks why a traveller took it. Questions about motives come up in situations in which activity has been temporarily suspended, where there is some uncertainty as to what is happening. Each person appreciates the fact that the others are acting voluntarily and that there is a possibility that they will not live up to their obligations. But cooperation requires that each party be able to anticipate the direction in which his associates are moving, and this often involves making inferences about their inner experiences. It is under such circumstances that questions emerge concerning motives.[17]

Mutual adjustments are made through the avowal and imputation of motives. When a male student approaches a coed and starts talking about the weather, she forms several hypotheses—he is trying to arrange for a date; he is unimaginative and can think of nothing else to discuss; he is a student of meteorology who is actually concerned about the weather. Each hypothesis involves expectations of subsequent actions, and she becomes sensitized to those aspects of his conduct that would provide further clues concerning his intentions. When he seizes the first opportunity to ask what she is doing that evening, this largely confirms one of her suspicions. She imputes

[17] Mills, "Situated Actions and Vocabularies of Motive," *op. cit.*

a motive and responds accordingly. Thus, concerted action is built up as the participants adjust successively to one another's intentions. The attribution of motives is a form of behavior that makes possible the continuation of coordination that has been blocked temporarily by doubt and uncertainty. By making inferences concerning the intentions of the other person, one gains a better understanding of what he is doing, can anticipate his future acts, and can prepare to respond to these expected events.

Motives are convenient ways of symbolizing intent, fictions that facilitate social intercourse. The attribution of motives enables each person to understand his own conduct as well as that of others. He avows certain purposes, and this enables him to place his activities into a meaningful context. Others simultaneously impute intentions to him; and, to the extent that the motives which are inferred and those that are acknowledged happen to coincide, cooperation proceeds smoothly. When the parties are playing conventional roles, the task of motive attribution is greatly simplified, for there are only a limited number of alternatives that are regarded as plausible for each role. A threatening gesture by a parent may be interpreted as an attempt to enforce discipline, an effort to pad his wounded pride, or as a quest for personal vengeance, but it would not "make sense" to view it as an expression of religious ecstasy.

Individuals vary considerably in the manner in which they deal with inconvenient impulses. Each person develops distinctive ways of handling and controlling dispositions that are not socially approved. Whenever there is a conflict between impulses and conventional norms, there are several possible ways of resolving the difficulty. One is to inhibit the impulse and to control oneself in accordance with customary usage; another is to attempt to change part of the environment so that the impulse can be consummated more easily; and a third is to indulge oneself by giving in to the impulse. Most people follow each of these alternatives at different times, depending upon the circumstances, but there are considerable differences among them in the solution most frequently used. Thus, the characteristic way in which impulses are handled becomes a significant dimension of a man's personality.

Some people cope with their inner conflicts by denying that the impulses exist. They suppress inclinations that are embarrassing and uncomfortable, and when the conflict becomes too intense, they push them out of awareness. Such persons show self-control to an amazing degree. By denying one's desires as unreal or unimportant they render themselves more manageable. Such persons also tend to be withdrawn and relatively self-sufficient. This type of adaptation stresses the perceptual phase of the act. It involves detachment and restraint as perceptual experiences are manipulated. The organism is not totally committed.

Some people adjust to such conflicts by attempting to manipulate the inconvenient objects. If they find that they hate someone whom they are supposed to like, they may alter the relationship and thereby eliminate the incongruence. An attempt is made to reconstruct the world in the service of their desires. This type of adaptation emphasizes the manipulatory phase of the act. The actor seeks to dominate the scene; he acts upon the object and initiates changes in it.

There are also people who characteristically come to terms with their world by indulging their impulses and giving vent to their feelings. They restrain themselves as long as the pressure is not too great, but when confronted by any serious conflict, they simply let themselves go. If they dislike someone, they move aggressively against him. If they fall in love with someone, they show their affection, even when it is not prudent to do so. This type of adaptation stresses the consummatory phase of the act. The organism is receptive, permitting an object to act upon it as its impulses are fulfilled. It is essentially a passive orientation, and one becomes dependent upon his environment—and other people.[18]

Voluntary conduct is a complex process involving a succession of adjustments to an ever changing perceptual field. The organization of that field is something that arises in an imaginative rehearsal in which the actor manipulates perceptual objects, images (including self-images), and a variety of symbols. Many of the component adjustments are instinctive or unconscious, but many phases of this continuous process of coming to terms with one's world are deliberately controlled. Although people differ considerably in the extent and manner in which they control themselves, for all but a few the anticipated reactions of others constitute a significant part of their effective environment.

[18] Cf. Charles W. Morris, *Paths of Life* (New York: George Braziller, 1956), pp. 13–113; see also his *Varieties of Human Value, op. cit.*, pp. 192–93.

Impairment and Cultivation of Control

Self-control, then, is a complex form of behavior, which depends upon the capacity of a person to get "outside" of himself, to form self-images from the standpoint of others, and to adjust to their anticipated moves. The procedure rests upon the ability of a person to perceive and to think, and any deterioration of perceptual or cognitive processes will seriously undermine his ability to act voluntarily. Defective perception—from fatigue, preoccupation with other objects, or organic disturbances—can interfere with the process. Role-taking remains at a rudimentary level unless one can construct categories and refer to them with linguistic symbols, and those who are unable to use a language have difficulties. In addition, the cognitive processes depend upon the smooth operation of the neuro-muscular transactions underlying the formation of images and the manipulation of symbols, and any impairment of these movements seriously affects a man's ability to inhibit troublesome impulses. A breakdown may occur anywhere in this complex procedure, and a study of the circumstances under which difficulties arise is instructive.

Even a relatively simple act such as reaching for a book lying on a table is difficult to execute unless one is able to see what he is doing. Experiments on tracing targets, such as the previously cited study by Slack, show that the perception of one's own activity is essential for effective control. Similar evidence comes from studies of deafness. Kline and his associates made a comparative study of people who were organically deaf, those rendered temporarily deaf through hypnosis, and those who were awake and able to hear. Using a device enabling the subject to hear himself a fourth of a second after he had spoken, they observed the consequences of such delayed speech feedback. Those who were really deaf manifested no changes in their speech patterns, but the others encountered numerous difficulties. The speech of the subjects who were awake was marked by accentuation, slurring, and stammering. To a lesser extent this was also true of those who were hypnotically deaf. This reveals that even in activities as deeply ingrained as talking control rests upon being able to hear oneself; it also confirms the hypothesis that hypnotic anaesthesia involves an artificial restriction of consciousness and that the person actually responds to sensory cues.[19] In another experiment Hebb and his associates placed cotton wool soaked with petrolatum into the ears of their subjects for a period of three days and found that all of them spoke too loudly or too softly. These people could hear what they were saying, but they had no clue as to the loudness of their voice; hence, they could not control volume.[20] Thus, the execution of even the simplest of acts rests upon the ability to perceive oneself; coordination arises from adjusting successively to what one experiences himself as doing.

It is a well known fact that intoxicated men have difficulty in controlling themselves. They feel more free to say and do as they please, for their usual inhibitions are relaxed. There is less self-consciousness and less preoccupation with one's own affairs, and social contacts are established with greater ease. The social distance customarily maintained between people through various formalities is overcome, and inebriated men sometimes reveal their most intimate secrets to complete strangers. The relaxation of inhibitions is also revealed in the high degree of suggestibility that characterizes those who are drunk. Critical judgment requires a comparison of images; without the ability to reason and to inhibit socially proscribed alternatives, however, one's conduct develops along the lines of least resistance. Intoxicated men act more in line with their personal inclinations, especially when they are supported by encouragement from others. By dulling the operation of the neuromuscular systems underlying reflective thought, the consumption of alcohol impairs self-control.[21] Even more spectacular transformations have been attained by the use of sodium amytal, sometimes called the "truth serum." This amazing drug has been used by psychiatrists and by the police to counteract inhibitions against talking about matters a person would otherwise conceal.

Some drugs interfere with sensory capacities to such an extent that it becomes extremely difficult, if not impossible, for a person to maintain a meaningful orientation toward his world. Studies with

[19] Milton V. Kline, Henry Guze, and Arthur D. Haggerty, "An Experimental Study of the Nature of Hypnotic Deafness," *Journal of Clinical and Experimental Hypnosis*, II (1954), 145–56.

[20] D. O. Hebb, E. S. Heath, and E. A. Stuart, "Experimental Deafness," *Canadian Journal of Psychology*, VIII (1954), 152–56.

[21] Cf. Ernest H. Starling, *The Action of Alcohol on Man* (New York: Longmans, Green & Co., 1923), p. 77.

mescalin and lysergic acid show that the intoxicated subjects, while conscious and able to report their experiences with some difficulty, saw their surroundings in a manner quite different from anything they had even imagined through their socially ordered perspectives. They apparently had difficulty in using conventional categories; since they were unable to make assumptions about objects not directly experienced, their perceptual field was reduced to their immediate environment. The world as they saw it was continually changing, but there was complete indifference to such matters as the passage of time—a social concept. Huxley reported that he no longer looked upon furniture in terms of utility but only in the light of aesthetic form. Many of the subjects reported difficulties in differentiating between themselves as distinct units and their environment; they were unable to form clear self-images.[22] Under the circumstances it is not surprising that those who are under the influence of such drugs have great difficulty in participating in concerted action.

The most common source of interference with self-control is excessive excitement and tension. Typing errors often become cumulative, especially if one is disturbed by the first one; he makes more and more mistakes as he becomes progressively more disgusted with himself. A participant in an important conference may become so anxious over the outcome that he is unable to give an effective presentation of his case; he thereby contributes substantially to the very failure he feared. Under conditions of extreme stress a person may lose his ability to control himself altogether. A man who is burdened with great grief tries to hold back his tears as long as he can and then gives way to uninhibited sobbing. He has little awareness of himself and simply cries and thrashes about until his tensions are somewhat reduced. In intense anger, enthusiasm, or fear some people have spasms, foam at the mouth, or lose control of their bladder and anal orifice. Self-images are usually not involved in such responses, and a person remembers little of what he did while he was "not himself." He is often surprised to see his soiled clothing and apprehensively makes inquiries about what happened.

[22] Cf. Aldous Huxley, *The Doors of Perception* (New York: Harper & Bros., 1954); Max Rinkel, H. Jackson de Schon, Robert W. Hyde, and Harry C. Solomon, "Experimental Schizophrenia-Like Symptoms," *American Journal of Psychiatry*, CVIII (1952), 572–78; and Robert S. de Ropp, *Drugs and the Mind* (New York: St. Martin's Press, 1957), pp. 167–201.

Some of the most shocking deeds committed by human beings occur under conditions of collective excitement—in lynching mobs, in riots, in revival meetings, or in mass panics. The emotional reactions of the participants are apparently intensified as they reinforce each other's feelings by responding sympathetically to one another's expressive movements. Finally, unable to stand the tension any longer, they burst forth in impulsive activity. Many students of crowd phenomena have noted that the participants often lose their sense of personal identity. They become so preoccupied with one another and with the central object of attention—some hated object or source of ecstasy—that they lose awareness of themselves as distinct units. They lose their critical ability, become highly suggestible, and are readily persuaded by agitators who can give fitting expression to their aroused feelings. They may then engage in violent activities that would otherwise be inhibited.[23] Sometimes, in the midst of a closely contested athletic event, the most conventional people on a campus scream incredibly vicious insults from the stands.

What is particularly revealing are the typical reactions of people upon recovering from such temporary breakdowns. A man who "lost his head" is invariably ashamed of himself. Those who flee in panic usually run until they are physically exhausted and then hide. The flood of explanations with which they afterward approach their friends indicates that they feel compelled to provide some kind of justification for their conduct. Participants in mobs are also embarrassed as soon as their excitement has abated. Sometimes they hide for days. Men who realize that they have been drunk are also embarrassed. As the influence of alcohol wears off or after tensions have been released one's usual perspective is restored. There follows a retrospective evaluation of whatever is remembered, and the self-image formed becomes a source of discomfort. Whenever possible, restitutions are made.

Since self-control is so facilitated through symbolic communication, those who are unable to use a language can be expected to encounter difficulties. The planning of voluntary conduct requires that a person detach himself in his imagination from the rest of his

[23] Cf. Herbert Blumer, "Collective Behavior," in *Principles of Sociology*, Alfred M. Lee, ed. (New York: Barnes & Noble, Inc., 1955), pp. 174–85; and Gustave Le Bon, *The Crowd* (London: T. Fisher Unwin, 1896).

experience, and this calls for the use of symbols. Of particular interest is the mirror test devised by Head to study victims of aphasia. As the doctor placed each of his hands on various parts of his body, he instructed the patients to do the same thing. When both stood before a mirror, the patients had little difficulty, for all they had to do was to imitate the doctor. But when the doctor sat facing them, the patients became confused and were unable to perform even simple tasks, such as touching the right shoulder with the left hand.[24] When facing someone it becomes necessary to make a transposition; one must imagine himself in the position of the other and indicate to himself which hand had been moved to what part of the body. Simple imitation is not enough. Thus, even at this very rudimentary level role-taking is difficult, if not impossible, for those who are unable to use a language. Seen in this light, the inability of these patients to participate effectively in organized groups is understandable.

Many patients classified as schizophrenic are characterized by even more serious deterioration of self-control. In the chronic wards of mental hospitals some patients masturbate openly; women sometimes change their sanitary napkins in full view of others; and men walk about without making any effort to conceal an erection. Some spit and then play with their phlegm; others pick their noses and eat the mucus; and still others defecate and play in their feces. There are many bald references to sex and to perverted acts; vulgarity and cursing as well as homicidal and grandiose expressions are commonplace. It is believed that such conduct is not so much a manifestation of excessive sexuality as it is a relaxation of customary controls over sexual impulses. Although many victims of schizophrenia suffer some impairment in their ability to use linguistic symbols and are therefore unable to communicate effectively with themselves, there are probably other sources of difficulties. Since so many different personality syndromes are placed in this category, generalizations are difficult; but it is true that severely regressed patients usually have difficulties in using a conventional language.

Another revealing phenomenon is hypnotism, in which one man's conduct is controlled to a remarkable extent by another person with

[24] Head, *op. cit.*, Vol. I, pp. 356–59. Cf. Kurt Goldstein and Martin Scheerer, "Abstract and Concrete Behavior," *Psychological Monographs*, LIII (1941), #239, 1–31; and Lindesmith and Strauss, *op. cit.*, pp. 143–52.

whom he is in rapport. Rapport is apparently a form of selective sensitivity in which the subject's attention is almost exclusively centered upon the commands of the hypnotist. Although many phases of this process are still not understood, hypnotism seems to consist of the symbolic manipulation of imagery and experience. Through the medium of words the hypnotist defines situations and suggests how the subject is to act, in much the same manner that a person might make indications to himself. Indeed, in a succession of ingenious experiments Hull showed that the processes of auto-suggestion and hypnotic suggestion are basically alike.[25] Thus, hypnotism may be regarded as the establishment of an unusual social relationship in which the linguistic control over one's perception, cognition, and overt conduct is partially relinquished to someone else. But self-control is not surrendered altogether, for most people will not do in a hypnotic trance what they strongly oppose when they are awake. When ordered to do something of which they disapprove, they may decline the suggestion, have an attack of hysteria, or awaken from the trance. Suggestions are effective, then, only when they are consistent with the subject's dispositions and within the bounds of his standards. Seemingly contradictory evidence has appeared in some experiments, but a careful examination of the data shows that people can be persuaded to do things contrary to their usual standards of conduct only if the situation is first redefined so that they believe they are doing something that is not objectionable. A person may carry off someone else's wallet after being persuaded that it is actually his own, but he will not commit a theft while in a trance if he believes stealing to be morally wrong.[26]

There are marked personality differences in the ability to maintain self-control. When a person is confronted with intense deprivation, he can continue to meet his conventional obligations only by remaining self-conscious and by inhibiting compelling dispositions

[25] Hull, op. cit., pp. 41–63. Cf. Lawrence S. Kubie and Sydney Margolin, "The Process of Hypnotism and the Nature of the Hypnotic State," American Journal of Psychiatry, C (1944), 611–22.

[26] Albert Moll, Hypnotism, A. F. Hopkirk, trans. (London: Walter Scott Publications, 1890), pp. 171–72; M. N. Erickson, "An Experimental Investigation of the Possible Anti-Social Uses of Hypnosis," Psychiatry, II (1939), 391–414; and M. Brenman, "Experiments in the Hypnotic Production of Anti-Social and Self-Injurious Behavior," ibid., V (1942), 49–61.

to act in proscribed ways. There is considerable variation in the ability to withstand such pressure. Some people become upset so easily that their associates refer to them as being "hysterical." Among professional athletes men who can retain self-control even under extreme duress win special recognition. The "money player" or the "old pro" is one whose performance is reliable, perhaps even more effective, when under fire. Others are said to "choke up" as they make inexcusable errors at crucial junctures of important contests. Being hypnotized represents, in a sense, a partial surrender of self-control. Some people habitually focus so much attention upon themselves that they cannot be hypnotized; others fall into a trance almost at once. There are also differences among people in the characteristic manner in which they behave when self-control breaks down. Some act in a stereotyped manner; others act impulsively; and still others become highly suggestible, following the lead of anyone who happens to be present.

Since so much can be lost through the impairment of self-control, deliberate efforts of all kinds are made to bolster it. Some people encounter such difficulty in inhibiting mildly troublesome impulses that they resort to self-deception to achieve their aims. Those who desire to lose weight but are unable to remain on a strict diet sometimes take drugs to kill their appetite, thereby minimizing the temptation to eat. Similarly, some spendthrifts deliberately carry limited amounts of money with them; they may even keep their funds in a savings account rather than a checking account to make withdrawals more inconvenient. Such planning apparently makes resistance easier when irksome impulses arise. Programs for reinforcing self-control may also be quite formal. In stratified communities elite groups sometimes develop a special code of honor. From the time they are children those in the privileged classes are inculcated with the notion that they are superior human beings and therefore are not to succumb to "common" impulses. They come to conceive of themselves as the selected few whose duty it is to uphold the moral standards of the entire community. Noblesse oblige consists of special responsibilities that are constantly reinforced, not only by members of the elite group but also by the servants and teachers who serve them.

Most attempts to cultivate self-control consist of procedures designed to minimize emotional reactions. Athletes, businessmen, and soldiers are taught that they are far more likely to succeed if they relax.[27] Paradoxically, a number of complex tasks that require precision in timing and muscular coordination—such as, ballet dancing, boxing, playing chamber music, rifle marksmanship, and speed typing—require so much concentration on the task itself that they can be performed most effectively when self-images do not emerge. Concern with oneself in the midst of a performance sometimes raises doubts, and anxieties over one's reputation interfere with concentration. In training for such performances the technical aspects of the task are perfected to the point where the movements can be carried out automatically, and then a relaxed attitude is cultivated. Although the acts themselves may be enacted with a minimum of self-consciousness, the capacity to perform in this manner has to be cultivated deliberately over a long period of time.

An extreme case of refined self-control is found in Zen Buddhism, which is an integral part of Japanese archery, calligraphy, flower arrangement, swordsmanship, and tea ceremony—all of them arts requiring a high degree of concentration. The necessary technical skills are developed through constant repetition until the performances become automatic; at the same time students are taught to minimize their self-consciousness and to concentrate entirely upon the task itself. What is aimed for is freedom from disturbances from within, from worries and considerations of pride. To facilitate the development of this state of mind in each performance a number of preparatory ceremonies, which appear meaningless to outsiders, are taught along with the art itself. Once a man has succeeded in developing this capacity, he can perform by "yielding" to nature; he feels as if his bodily movements are being guided by some external agency, since he himself is presumably not giving the directions.[28]

Voluntary conduct is constructed in a serial process in which a person responds in turn to a succession of definitions—including what he experiences as himself. This entire procedure is greatly simplified by the substitution of linguistic symbols, which makes possible the planning and execution of far more complex activities. When there is interference with any of the component parts of this

[27] Cf. Joseph A. Kennedy, *Relax and Live* (New York: Prentice-Hall, Inc., 1953).

[28] Cf. Eugen Herrigel, *Zen in the Art of Archery*, R. F. C. Hull, trans. (New York: Pantheon Books, 1953).

complicated process—from emotional upset, intoxication, suggestibility, or inability to manipulate symbols—difficulties immediately
arise. Deliberate attempts to cultivate self-control consist largely of
attempts to minimize or counteract such possibilities. Some programs include extreme measures, such as cultivating the suppression
of self-images, but this takes place only after they have been used to
establish the desired habits.

Summary and Conclusion

Human behavior consists of a succession of adjustments to continually evolving interpretations of situations. Consciousness is to be
distinguished from mere perception; a man who is conscious of
something is communicating, usually to himself, although on occasion others may also hear what he is saying. Thinking consists of
an imaginative rehearsal of possible ways of meeting an unsual
situation. When linguistic symbols are substituted for images, the
manipulation of alternatives is so simplified that feats of great complexity become possible. It is the ability to use symbols that releases
man from the humdrum existence of most living creatures. The
great achievements in art, literature, philosophy, and science would
be impossible without ordered imagination. But this very gift also
enables men to cringe in fear before the ghosts of dead ancestors,
and it makes possible many mental disorders. Since the capacity for
symbolic communication arises through participation in organized
groups, it is not surprising that consciousness and reflective thought
are forms of behavior that are subject to social control. Voluntary
activity takes shape, then, in a communicative process involving the
manipulation of symbols which represent oneself and other features
of the environment.

Concerted action in stable situations depends upon each participant maintaining his personal reserve and controlling himself in
terms of group expectations. The more self-conscious a man is, the
more preoccupied he is with his self-images and the less spontaneous are his deeds. He acts properly by inhibiting impulses that
are forbidden or discouraged. Few self-respecting men would engage in extreme forms of crowd behavior unless thoroughly provoked, and many need alcohol before they can even "let their hair

down" in informal gatherings. But there can be too much self-consciousness. There are some tasks that can be accomplished only with the greatest concentration, and errors are minimized by deliberately checking self-consciousness.

Consciousness and reflective thought are instruments of adjustment. Some philosophers have contended that logic and scientific method are nothing more than refinements of behavior that is typical in emergencies, when difficulties emerge as activities are blocked. They point out that scientific study follows much the same procedure as a person's solving a practical problem, only with considerable formalization of method. Scientific inquiry begins with an indeterminate situation and ends with the temporary resolution of the problem. The rules of logic that are used emerge in the efforts of men to control such inquiry to maximize the benefits.

Suggested References

ALEXANDER, F. MATTHIAS, *The Uses of the Self.* New York: E. P. Dutton & Co., 1932. A discussion of typical difficulties encountered in the conscious control of physical movements, followed by proposals for overcoming them by learning to test sensory impressions and to inhibit reflexes.

GERTH, HANS and C. WRIGHT MILLS, *Character and Social Structure,* pp. 37–129. New York: Harcourt, Brace & Co., 1953. The presentation of a conceptual scheme to account for the goal-oriented activities of men as participants in organized groups, with emphasis upon motives, self-images, and audiences.

KASANIN, JACOB S., ed., *Language and Thought in Schizophrenia.* Berkeley: University of California Press, 1944. A collection of provocative papers on concept formation, the manipulation of linguistic symbols, and logic among victims of schizophrenia.

MORRIS, CHARLES W., *Six Theories of Mind.* Chicago: University of Chicago Press, 1932. An analysis and critical assessment of six recurrent theories of the nature of the human mind, permitting a comparison of the approach developed in this chapter with alternative views.

PERLS, FREDERICK S., RALPH F. HEFFERLINE, and PAUL GOODMAN, *Gestalt Therapy.* New York: Julian Press, 1951. A series of exercises to facilitate a person's locating and organizing experiences of himself within his perceptual field, with suggestions for the manipulation of these experiences in psychotherapy.

SNYGG, DONALD and ARTHUR W. COMBS, *Individual Psychology*, Chaps. II–VI. New York: Harper & Bros., 1949. A discussion from the Gestalt standpoint of the manner in which a man's experience of himself enters into the development of his conduct.

7

The
structure
of
personal
identity

Among the *Exemplary Novels* of Miguel de Cervantes is a fascinating tale of a man, temporarily deranged, who believed that he was made of glass. Whenever people approached him, he screamed and implored them to keep their distance lest they shatter him. He always walked in the middle of the street, glancing apprehensively at the rooftops for loose tiles that might fall upon him. On one occasion, when a wasp stung him on the neck, he did not dare strike it nor shake it off for fear of breaking himself. He refused to eat anything as hard as meat or fish and insisted upon sleeping only in beds of straw. Since glass is not only thinner than the skin but also transparent, he claimed that the peculiar construction of his body enabled his soul to see things more clearly, and he offered to assist those facing perplexing problems. Before long he became famous for his astonishingly astute observations. People followed him everywhere, seeking his advice. Whenever mischievous boys threw stones at him, he cried so loudly and desperately that adults came running to his assistance, and finally a wealthy patron hired a bodyguard to follow him about and to protect him against hoodlums.

Not many people outside of mental hospitals believe that they are made of glass, but there are persons who regard themselves as being somewhat fragile. Those who believe that they are unusually susceptible to colds, heat rashes, blisters, or freckles go out of their way to avoid exposure. Those who believe that their angelic children might become contaminated by contact with the filthy urchins who live in poorer neighborhoods take special care to see that their youngsters play exclusively with others of their own kind. All this suggests that much of what men do voluntarily depends upon what they conceive of themselves to be; Cervantes was merely pointing to an exaggerated instance of a common process.

It has already been noted that acts are inhibited or facilitated on the basis of self-images. Self-images vary from situation to situation, but each man also has a stable sense of personal identity. What he is willing or unwilling to do depends upon the kind of human being he thinks he is. Most persons, if lost and hungry in a strange city, would balk at searching garbage cans for food; they would rather remain hungry than do something that they regard as being beneath their dignity. A man who considers himself "no good," however, will certainly not resist temptations with the same determination as someone who is convinced that he is a decent person. An adequate theory of motivation, then, requires getting at the manner in which a man identifies himself.[1]

Personal Identity and Social Status

Self-images are specific and differ from one context to another; one visualizes himself as playing a game, talking to his friends, reciting in a classroom, or whatever else he may be doing. In spite of the variety of things that one does he experiences all of these deeds as being performed by the same person. Even though self-images are constantly changing and never twice exactly the same, one has no difficulty in recognizing himself. Each can identify himself as a

[1] Cf. Nelson N. Foote, "Identification as the Basis for a Theory of Motivation," *American Sociological Review*, XVI (1951), 14–21.

particular human being, characterized by a distinctive set of attributes; he regards himself as an individual of a unique sort. Each person, then, has a relatively stable *self-conception*. He knows that there are other people somewhat like him, especially if he thinks of himself as being "just average," but he also assumes that there is no one else who is exactly like him—who looks and acts the same, and has the same background. In our society it is taken for granted that there never has been anyone else like him in the past, and never will be in the future.

Very few people ever have occasion to ask themselves who they are. Each takes his personal identity so much for granted that he does not realize the extent to which his life is structured by the working conception he forms of himself. The things that a man does voluntarily, and in some cases even involuntarily, depend upon the assumptions he makes about the kind of person he is and about the way in which he fits into the scheme of things in his world. This becomes apparent under unusual circumstances—in an odd dream, in amnesia, or in temporary dissociation under hypnosis—when once familiar behavior patterns appear strange, incongruent, and out of place. A man is able to act with reasonable consistency in a wide variety of situations because of the relative stability of his self-conception.

Thus, flexible coordination rests upon the capacity of men to form self-images, and considerable regularity is introduced into the life of each person by virtue of a stable self-conception. Some psychologists have been reluctant to study these phenomena, frequently on the ground that they are too elusive to be examined objectively. To be sure, the study of what a person experiences as himself is difficult, but it is paradoxical that these scholars in their capacity as investigators should ignore such phenomena, when in their daily lives they are never so foolish. If a psychologist were confronted by a powerful drunk who insisted that he could "lick anybody in the house," he probably would not challenge the contention by claiming that self-images cannot be measured with precision. Should he go home and find his wife in the arms of a strange man who insisted he was her husband, it is unlikely that he would shrug his shoulders and say that personal identity has never been demonstrated to be important. Many of the difficulties in the study of these phenomena begin when a search is made for some physical object located somewhere in the body, when the concepts of self-image and self-conception both refer to complex forms of *behavior*. Each person can imagine what he has done, what he is doing, what he is able to do, or what he proposes to do and can respond to his own imagination. These concepts refer, then, not to some part of the human body but to uniformities in behavior.

Even casual observation reveals that all human beings, with the possible exception of infants and some patients in psychotic wards, have some kind of working orientation toward themselves. The personal world of every individual is centered around himself. In making judgments and decisions, in speaking of space and time, he uses himself as the central point of reference. This is true not only of egotistical persons, but of everyone, even the most considerate and unselfish. Each is able to recognize his own aspirations, disappointments, and fears, and can differentiate between these and similar experiences on the part of other people. Strictly speaking, a person can only experience his own sensations, but there is a bipolarization of this experience into what is acknowledged as one's own and what is imputed to the outside world. In spite of the complexity of the processes involved, most adults have little difficulty in making this distinction, although from time to time one may become a bit confused.

Each person regards himself as a separate entity, and this belief is reinforced by the fact that the human body can readily be set off as an organic unit. Actually, the boundaries of the organism are not as clearly demarcated as we believe. Is the air in our lungs or the food in our digestive tract a part of us or merely passing through? Physiologists contend that virtually every cell in a human body is replaced within ten years or less. The relationship between any living organism and its environment is one of continual interaction. But the fact that men regard themselves as independent entities greatly facilitates organized social life. Concerted action is possible because each participant is able to control himself. Self-control involves the formation of a perceptual object of oneself and imputing to this object certain responsibilities. This entire procedure is greatly facilitated when men conceive of themselves as separate, independent entities. The fact that bodies are separate units, even if the boundaries are blurred, makes the isolation and pinpointing of responsibilities possible.

A man's sense of identity also arises from the continuity of his experiences in time. There are memories of the past that cannot be escaped, and there are reasonable aspirations for the future. Secret inner thoughts enjoy continuity along with those which are shared. The consistency of all such experiences enables each person to integrate them into a unit, a whole which is also treated as a distinct entity by other people. This sense of continuity is broken only under very unusual circumstances; in most cases it is cut off only with death.

The feeling of being a distinct object also arises from one's sense of personal autonomy. Each person believes that he is able to exercise some measure of control over his own destiny. He is capable of making decisions and of selecting among alternative lines of action. It is this widespread belief that provides the basis for the philosophical doctrine of "free will" and for the concept of moral responsibility. Since men are assumed to be capable of making choices, they are held accountable for their deeds. It should be noted, however, that they usually refuse to accept responsibility for conduct which occurred while they were "not themselves"—such as what they did under the influence of alcohol or drugs, in a condition of severe strain or shock, in a hypnotic trance, or in the power of some "evil spirit." The argument is that it would be unfair for anyone to be blamed for acts over which he did not have full control. This suggests that the limits of a man's conception of himself are often set by the area over which he feels he can exercise control.[2]

Self-conceptions are reinforced by recurrent social relationships. By virtue of who he is, one is related to each person he knows and to various categories of people in understood ways. A woman expects her husband to treat her with special consideration and occasionally to make intimate disclosures to her, but she would be disturbed if he granted similar privileges to other women. Imagine how shaken anyone would be if he were to enter his home only to find his parents staring blankly at him as if he were a complete stranger. In a series of experiments on inducing dissociation of personality through hypnosis, Harriman found it necessary to tell his subjects that the hypnotist was a "man who lives down the street"

[2] Cf. Thomas D. Eliot, "The Use of Psychoanalytic Classification in Analysis of Social Behavior: Identification," *Journal of Abnormal and Social Psychology,* XXII (1927), 67–81.

to account for his presence in the room. Whenever a subject successfully transformed his identity, he was no longer able to define his relationship to the experimenter and became puzzled.[3] It is through being recognized as a particular human being that each individual gains status within a community.

In all communities there is some kind of differentiation of the participants into ranks. Although the concept of *social status* has been utilized in a variety of ways, it may be used here to refer to a person's standing in a community, identifiable in terms of the rights, duties, privileges, and immunities that he enjoys by virtue of his position.[4] Status is a social process; one can have status only in relation to others who recognize his place and approach him in an understood way. Status, no matter how lowly, is important, for without it one becomes an outsider without claims upon anyone. For example, custodians are often held in low esteem in American communities, but when they are in the buildings in their charge they can expel intruders and can get the police to enforce their prerogatives. Having status, then, enables a person to anticipate the manner in which he will be treated.

Even in democratic communities, human beings are ordered into positions of relative superiority and inferiority. There are many criteria for evaluation, such as occupation of the head of the household, size of income, lineage and ethnic identity, or level of intellectual attainment. In the United States, people are placed largely in terms of vocation and income; other criteria prevail elsewhere. Since such positions are placed in a rough hierarchy, each can be identified in terms of the prestige and influence the incumbents enjoy as well as the deference with which they are addressed. It should be noted that a person is often approached in a given manner by virtue of the position he occupies, quite apart from his personal qualities; many Army officers are addressed with respect even by enlisted men who look upon them in contempt. One's standing in a community, then, is largely a matter of accepted social usage.

Some systems of social differentiation are stable, but in the modern world many are undergoing change. In relatively stable

[3] Harriman, *op. cit.*, p. 640.
[4] Cf. Max Weber, *Essays in Sociology*, Hans H. Gerth and C. Wright Mills, trans. (New York: Oxford University Press, 1946), pp. 186–94.

communities, status is not only clearly defined but can be acquired only through inheritance or through well-established sequences of training and achievement. One cannot become a warrior simply by picking up a spear. Furthermore, characteristic patterns of conduct that are expected of incumbents are also clearly defined. Warriors are expected to display courage, and those who desire such status must learn to inhibit their impulses to flee in the face of danger. A singer aspiring to become a prima donna must undergo incredibly strenuous training; should she succeed, she is expected to be temperamental and to comport herself in regal fashion. Doctors undergo a prescribed program of training, pass standardized examinations, and fall into already delineated specialties; once established, they must observe a code of professional ethics and are expected to behave in a dignified manner. Somewhat more flexible career lines can be found for those who desire to become writers, professional athletes, senators, or racketeers. In a changing society there is less consensus over the rights and duties of those in various positions, and the avenues of advancement are not so clearly marked.[5]

The concept of social status, which refers to a person's standing in a community, is not to be confused with the concept of conventional role, which refers to a participant's contribution to an organized enterprise.[6] Status, once it is established, remains relatively constant; it can be enhanced, but slowly, and lowered only through degrading performances. But each man in the course of a single day plays many different roles. To be sure, there are a limited set of interrelated roles played only by those who occupy a given position. For example, a man who is practicing medicine in an American city plays fairly well-defined roles in a number of standardized transactions—examining patients, giving instructions to nurses, consulting with colleagues, checking reports with laboratory technicians, urging hospital administrators to purchase new equipment, or referring patients to other doctors. Outside of these established contexts the expectations become less clear; indeed, the further he moves from situations involving medical care, the less clear his obligations be-

[5] Cf. Everett C. Hughes, *Men and Their Work* (Glencoe: Free Press, 1958), pp. 102–15. Typical difficulties faced by people in such situations will be discussed in Chapter XVII.

[6] Cf. Albert Pierce, "On the Concepts of Role and Status," *Sociologus,* VI (1956), 29–34; and Robert K. Merton, *Social Theory and Social Structure* (Glencoe: Free Press, 1957), pp. 368–84.

come. But a doctor, by virtue of the high estimate placed upon his services to a community, enjoys considerable prestige; even when he is at an informal gathering he is expected to maintain the general demeanor considered proper for professional men. The role a person is called upon to play and the manner in which he is expected to perform may rest in part upon his status, but these concepts refer to different aspects of human behavior.

Personal identification is the basis of organized social life, for it is only when a person can be identified and placed in his niche that his responsibilities can be fixed. Whenever strangers meet, the first thing that they do is to ascertain one another's identity and status. This is essential, for there is no other way of knowing what to anticipate. Personal identity, then, constitutes one's only tie with the rest of society; each person has status in a community only in so far as he can identify himself as a specific human being who belongs in a particular place.

Furthermore, by virtue of his identity each person is also related in understood ways to various physical objects. This is what is meant by property. There is no necessary physical or biological connection between a man and the various things he owns. He can destroy or give away his belongings only because conventional norms permit owners relative freedom of action concerning their chattel. But a man can exercise his property rights only when he can identify himself as a specific human being. If men were not able to identify themselves and one another with consistency, our entire social and economic system would be in jeopardy.

The crucial importance of personal identity is demonstrated by an unusual form of dissociation popularly called amnesia. There are apparently many forms of amnesia, but the cases that attract attention are those in which a person finds himself walking about in a daze and approaches a police officer to report that he has forgotten who he is. There is a loss of memory, but in most instances the victims have not forgotten everything. They are usually able to perform a number of complex tasks, such as feeding and dressing themselves and speaking with conventional linguistic symbols to psychiatrists. Furthermore, those who approach police officers presumably remember that it is the duty of men in such uniforms to aid those in distress. There is a selective forgetting in which the victim is unable to recall only those items that would disclose his identity—his name, his place of residence, his place of employment, and his friends.[7] A person suffering from amnesia is a stranger. Since he has no ties with anyone, he has no claims on anyone other than those of any human being. He has no home to which to return, no firm in which he can count on steady employment, no one with whom he can relax; his life does not fit into any organized routine, for without personal identity there is no community in which he has definite status.

Because each man can conceive of himself in a consistent manner he can locate himself within the patterned activities of the groups in which he participates. As others respond to him in the manner that he regards as appropriate, this reinforces his sense of identity and enables him to continue to meet his obligations as he sees them. Concerted action then takes on a routine character, even when made up of voluntary contributions.

The Organic Basis of Self-Conceptions

What is there to look for when attempting to ascertain the manner in which a man identifies himself? It is commonly believed that a person's conception of himself is nothing more than a replication of what he actually is; indeed a search is sometimes made for some "essence" or "core" located within his body. But self-conceptions may extend far beyond the confines of the organism. In each person there is a bipolarization of experience into what is regarded as being a part of himself and what is regarded as being outside of him, but there is no necessary spatial or temporal coincidence between the boundaries of his conception of himself and the actual limits of his body.[8] *Each man locates himself as an object within his symbolic environment.* It is important to get at what a man believes himself

[7] Cf. Milton Abeles and Paul Schilder, "Psychogenic Loss of Personal Identity: Amnesia," *Archives of Neurology and Psychiatry*, XXXIV (1935), 587–604; and L. F. Beck, "Hypnotic Identification of an Amnesia Victim," *British Journal of Medical Psychology*, XVI (1937), 36–42. An account of some of the problems confronting a man who does not know who he is can be found in Shepherd I. Franz, *Persons One and Three* (New York: McGraw-Hill Book Co., 1933).

[8] Cf. Kurt Koffka, *Principles of Gestalt Psychology* (New York: Harcourt, Brace & Co., 1935), pp. 319–21.

to be, for much of what he does depends upon these beliefs and the prerogatives that follow logically from such a definition.

But there is much confusion between the body, what a man regards to be his physical attributes, and his self-conception. Since each human being is an organic unit, there are undeniable connections between his body and his sense of identity. All experiences are organic processes within the body, and they are all terminated with death. All somatic experiences are somehow related to one's conception of himself, and there is continuity in his life to the extent that he can organize them into some kind of unit. Thus, one's body becomes the nexus of the various experiences that enable him to identify himself as a person of a particular sort.

Furthermore, behavior itself consists of the movements of a particular organism; hence, responsibility for action is placed upon a specific body. When the police are searching for a criminal, they focus attention upon the attributes of his body. The identification of criminals presupposes the more general question: how can a particular human being be set off from all others? In 1882, the French anthropologist Bertillon advocated the use of anthropometric techniques for this purpose, and since that time efforts have been made to identify offenders in terms of their distinguishing features—body measurements, scars or other peculiar marks, moles, birthmarks, tatooing, teeth, and fingerprints. If these prove insufficient, attention is directed to characteristic modes of behavior—habits, voice, gait, handwriting, preferences in companions, or special accomplishments. In these ways detectives attempt to establish an association between a given human body and an offense. This is a refinement of what goes on in daily life.

Although a man's conception of himself is undeniably associated with his body, it is not a direct reflection of what he is or what he does. Self-conceptions, like the rest of the symbolic environment, are constructed through selective perception and imagination. No man can possibly experience everything that occurs in his entire body; he is selectively responsive to different cues at different times, depending upon what he is doing. Psychiatrists point out that men are not always willing to acknowledge all of their own behavioral tendencies, that their hateful impulses are often projected to other people.

Furthermore, as in the case of other meanings, a man perceives himself in terms of the linguistic categories and premises of his culture. If he lives in a society in which ghosts and spirits are taken seriously, he may believe that his dreams constitute the adventures of his soul, which departs from his body at night. In our society we assume a necessary connection between a unified set of experiences and a given body; as natural as this may appear to us, this presupposition is by no means universal. Self-conceptions, then, are constructed while participating in social groups.

Since the manner in which a person is treated depends in part upon certain features of his body, one's physical attributes provide an important foundation for the formation of self-conceptions. Noticeable deformities sometimes become the basis for invidious distinctions. In communities that are stratified on an ethnic basis, skin color and other characteristics indicative of ancestry become symbols of considerable importance, for they often set limitations to career lines. Most people are sensitive about their appearance, and Americans are probably more concerned about their "looks" than others. Some attach such great importance to their faces and bodies that plastic surgeons and health studios have made fortunes making minor alterations. Each man develops a working conception of himself as a physical object, and this becomes the basis for other beliefs about himself. Although physical attributes are more readily discernible than other characteristics, it should be noted that the manner in which each person regards his body also develops through selective perception.

Although a man's body and his conception of himself are related in various ways, the fact that they are separate and different can be demonstrated with evidence drawn from a variety of sources. For one thing, most child psychologists agree that an infant has no self-conception, although there is no question of the existence of its body; such personifications develop gradually as the growing child participates in organized groups. The distinction is shown even more clearly in clinical records of certain unusual cases. Studies of "phantom limbs" show that amputees are able to conceive of themselves as still having the limbs that they have lost. Studies of mescalin intoxication reveal that the usual demarcation between oneself and the rest of the world melts away, leaving one feeling that he is blending into his surroundings. Those who develop multiple personalities have two or more self-conceptions but only one body.[9] The development of self-conceptions, once under way, apparently goes on independently of the growth of the body.

The relative independence of self-conceptions of the body is revealed especially in *ego-involvements,* the establishment of identifications whereby objects that are clearly outside the body are experienced as part of oneself. The boundaries of what a man treats as himself are highly variable, and all kinds of objects may come to be regarded as connected with him. A person who has just purchased a new automobile winces when a fender is dented, as if he himself had been injured. A man may spend much of his life building a farm foot by foot from the wilderness. If it is temporarily confiscated, damaged by locusts, or ravaged in war, he works desperately to get it back into order. If it is lost beyond restoration, he mourns its loss as if a part of him had died. A mother who sees her child misbehave in public is likely to feel quite ashamed. Because of her identification with the child she reacts as if she herself had been detected doing something offensive.

In forming self-conceptions, men place themselves into conventional categories—among them, age-group, sex, occupation, ethnic group, and social class. Whenever a category with which one has identified himself is affected, he reacts as though he were personally involved. A woman becomes intensely conscious of the fact that she is a woman when she sees someone of her sex treated condescendingly; she may become infuriated even though nothing has been done against her. An American travelling abroad becomes highly conscious of his nationality when he sees a drunken compatriot making a nuisance of himself. As he sees the natives staring contemptuously and muttering "Yankee, go home!" he feels ashamed. Even though he himself has not misbehaved, he feels obligated to apologize for the conduct of the stranger. A Negro swells with pride when a Negro prizefighter wins the heavyweight championship of the world; indeed, people in all ethnic minorities gain considerable gratification from the achievements of others with whom they identify. Men also establish identifications with the communities in

---

[9] Cf. Erich Guttmann, "Artificial Psychoses Produced by Mescalin," *Journal of Mental Science,* LXXXII (1936), 211; and Paul Schilder, *The Image and Appearance of the Human Body* (New York: International Universities Press, 1950), pp. 63–70. The problem of dissociation is treated further in Chapter XIII.

which they live. Southerners are particularly sensitive to remarks about dirty and illiterate "hill billies." Ego-involvements of all kinds become most apparent when one's self-esteem is at stake. When such identifications exist, men react as if they themselves are directly involved.

Self-conceptions also have a temporal dimension, for men tend to see themselves in terms of some kind of career line including the past and the future. Acts are integrated into larger units. Because men live in a temporal perspective and are able to survey their acts retrospectively and prospectively, they can organize and plan a series of acts that cover a long period of time. Various subsidiary movements are preparatory for or subordinated to the pattern as a whole. A man's life has the character of a succession of episodes and adventures, and these are integrated into a general scheme of life— a career.[10] To understand anyone, one must know something of his history, and reasonable aspirations for the future definitely affect present conduct. Each person makes sacrifices—such as suffering through courses he does not care for in school—in order to achieve something in the future that he regards as worthwhile. A man who hopes to become a priest may control his temptations in a way that another person with less lofty aspirations may not. It is in terms of such a time span that each person views himself, and it is only in that light that his conduct becomes comprehensible.

The manner in which self-conceptions extend far beyond the body is revealed clearly in the fact that people become concerned over events that took place before their birth or those that may occur after their death. Men identify with their ancestors and their glorious history; insults against their progenitors are avenged, even though the ancestors, being dead, could not possibly be offended. Some people make elaborate preparations for what will happen after they are dead. Since one presumably has no sensations after his demise, it would seem that he should not be concerned with what happens. In some social worlds, however, men make incredible sacrifices, denying themselves all kinds of pleasure within their reach, in order to save enough money to pay for their own funeral. Similarly, many of the great achievements of individuals as well as some of their most trying difficulties arise from the concern they develop over their progeny, with whom they can readily identify because of the similarity of physical attributes as well as the sense

[10] Cf. Park, *op. cit.*, pp. 274–76.

of biological continuity. Some people work without rest to build gigantic industrial empires to provide income for their descendants. Much of the difficulty in inter-ethnic contacts arises from concern over the characteristics of the man one's great-granddaughter might marry; some people are so horrified at the prospect of having descendants with mixed physical features that they fight with desperation against the peaceful intermingling of groups.

The testimony of people who believe that they are about to die is particularly revealing. Those who have been condemned to the gallows or have contracted an incurable disease know that they will soon cease to exist as biological organisms. What are the kinds of things that they think about under such circumstances? Frequently, people recall their careers, and the extent to which they are contented depends upon their aspirations and standards. They ask whether they would live differently if given another chance. They recall their regrets, their sources of joy, and the tasks that must be left undone. Even those who are not religious sometimes wonder about the possibility of a life after death and about reincarnation. Many are not afraid of death as the extinction of flesh, but they are often concerned with other matters. They wonder about the things that they can leave behind—a monument, memories, progeny, a worthy achievement—something of value which is connected with themselves. Such questions presuppose an object that can be identified as a unit and labelled by a name, something that is separate from the body which is about to dissolve.[11]

Since careers are constructed within a symbolic environment, the manner in which people locate themselves in time differs from culture to culture. In Western society there is a tendency to orient one's life toward the future; people concern themselves with building up their business, performing deeds to be remembered by posterity, and may even regard their children as extensions of themselves, a legacy being left to the future. But in China, prior to the Communist revolution, the orientation was more to the past. Since one's attributes are derived from his predecessors, ancestors were worshipped. Having descendants, then, was viewed as an assurance of

[11] Cf. Mary Austin, *Experiences Facing Death* (London: Rider & Co., 1931); Percy Black, "Reflections before the Gallows," *Journal of Abnormal and Social Psychology*, XLVIII (1953), 303–10; and Helmut Gollwitzer, Kathe Kuhn, and Reinhold Schneider, eds., *Dying We Live*, Reinhard C. Kuhn, trans. (New York: Pantheon Books, 1956).

one's own future. Among the Aivilik Eskimos each person is viewed as a manifestation of his *tungnik*, something akin to a soul which has a career through eternity. A *tungnik* is believed to be able to leave the body, especially at night, and to engage in a number of adventures. When a man dies, the *tungnik* becomes permanently separated from his body. Subsequently, however, it enters the body of a newly born child upon the invitation of members of the family. The child is named for the person whose body had presumably been the home of the *tungnik* in its earlier life and is thereafter addressed by the kinship term assigned to his predecessor. As he grows up, the child is expected to live up to the reputation enjoyed by his namesake. Two children born at approximately the same time and given the same illustrious name may be required to compete to demonstrate who is *really* the man. Although some merely look upon their predecessors as namesakes, others make every effort to live up to their obligations. To those who believe, the death of the body is not seen as the ultimate end of life; thus, at least outwardly, death is met with calm resignation. Similarly, among devout Hindus personal identity extends infinitely into both the past and the future as the soul undergoes continuous reincarnation; each person has all eternity rather than a single lifetime to work out his fate.[12]

Thus, each person identifies himself as a distinct unit developing over a period of time, and his aspirations and satisfactions rest upon this personification. Many of the seemingly puzzling things that men do become easier to understand upon grasping the relationship between self-conceptions and the body. Although a man's body constitutes the basis of the manner in which he personifies himself, his sense of identity is actually constructed separately within his symbolic environment. The body is the source of all his experiences, and acknowledged physical attributes enter significantly into the formation of his conception of himself. But once such personifications are constructed, they develop somewhat independently, being extended through imagination and restricted through the repression of painful and degrading experiences. Many of the distinctive characteristics of human conduct arise from the fact that men are not simply gratifying instinctive organic deficits but are also attempting

[12] Edmund S. Carpenter, "Eternal Life and Self-Definition among the Aivilik Eskimos," *American Journal of Psychiatry*, CX (1954), 840–43; and Marian W. Smith, "Different Cultural Concepts of Past, Present, and Future: A Study of Ego Extension," *Psychiatry*, XV (1952), 395–400.

to fulfil or enhance their self-conceptions. Lofty ideals, lasting hatreds, plans of vengeance, and anxieties over social status—all become possible only because men are dissatisfied with what they recognize as themselves.

The contrasting significance of one's body and his sense of identity is clearly distinguished by Ferenc Molnar in his famous play, *The Guardsman*. After six months of a somewhat stormy marriage, a well established Hungarian actor suspects that his actress wife is becoming restless for an extra-marital affair. To test her fidelity he disguises himself as a dashing Austrian army officer and attempts to seduce her. Much of the play deals with his double reaction—his elation and his sorrow—as she alternately resists or gives in to his pleading. He is proud of his accomplishments as an actor, but the more he succeeds as an artist, the more pained he is as a husband. But why should such a contradiction exist, since the wife is involved with only one body? Should something akin to the episodes invented by the imaginative playwright occur in real life, the participants would become equally disturbed. If a person learns, for example, that someone else who had been mistaken for him has been assaulted, he becomes upset even though his own body remains unscathed. Identification, then, is a matter of crucial importance in human life.

Self-Conceptions as Personifications

If it is so important to get at the manner in which a man personifies himself in order to understand what he does, we are confronted with the problem of studying self-conceptions empirically. If they develop more or less independently of the body, what are they? Do they lack physical substance, like the soul? Do they consist of the pictures that men have of themselves? One promising approach consists of regarding a man's conception of himself as constituting what he means to himself and viewing such personifications behavioristically, as in the case of other meanings. A self-conception is neither the organism nor a picture of it, but the regularized manner in which a person acts with reference to himself. Thus, *a self-conception is a way of behaving*—like talking, coughing, running, or thinking. All these activities presuppose a living organism, but none is to be identified with it.

Meanings are behavioral systems, the manner in which one is organized to act with reference to some object. Meanings are primarily the property of behavior and only secondarily the property of the objects involved, but in the case of self-conceptions the same person is both the subject and object of his own activities. This is what makes such personifications a distinct kind of meaning. Since the same organism is the actor as well as its object, any change in one's inclination to act constitutes a transformation in the subject, who immediately perceives himself as a changing object. A self-conception may be regarded as a stable relationship between a man as an active agent and what he consistently experiences as himself. A particular person's conception of himself becomes discernible in the characteristic ways in which he is disposed to act toward himself.

Each person develops distinctive ways of approaching himself. Men are capable of acting toward themselves just as they act toward others and as others act toward them, and self-conceptions can be detected by noting the consistent manner in which a person is oriented to act with reference to himself. Just as some people are aggressive and suspicious in their encounters with others, so one may be hostile and punitive toward himself, being constantly harassed by feelings of guilt about acts and thoughts that others would regard as justified. Such persons often feel compelled to atone for their sins, much to the dismay of their associates. Just as some people are compliant and constantly giving in to the demands of others, one may submit to his own impulses and engage constantly in self-indulgence. He may berate himself for lacking "will power," but he continues to surrender to every whim and fancy. Some people find intimacy in social relationships uncomfortable and always maintain a polite distance from others; in the same way it is even possible for a person to remain a relative stranger to himself. He rarely relaxes his guard long enough to look closely at what he is doing. Some people place great emphasis upon conformity with conventional norms and are unable to make allowances for extenuating circumstances. They may be equally rigid in forcing themselves always to do what is correct. The characteristic manner in which each person controls his impulses depends upon such persistent styles of acting toward whatever he identifies as himself.

A man's self-conception, then, is *what he means to himself*. Like other meanings, a self-conception cannot be identified in terms of any particular response, for what a man is inclined to do depends upon the exigencies of the particular situations in which he is involved. Meaning becomes discernible in the *pattern* of response, for the diverse reactions are all predicated upon the same presuppositions concerning the stable properties of the object—oneself. In each situation a man forms a somewhat different self-image and reacts to it according to the requirements of that particular context, but consistencies in his behavior become noticeable because all of the responses are predicated upon the same assumptions about the kind of human being he is. He acts *as if* he were a certain type of person, marked by a given set of characteristics. He acts on the basis of premises concerning his physical appearance, his social status, and his idiosyncrasies. If a man thinks that he is weak but handsome, he avoids situations that are likely to prove challenging but approaches with confidence occasions in which women are likely to admire him. Another person with considerable physical courage may withdraw from the second type of context for fear of humiliation. The unity of each man's personification of himself comes from the organization of particular responses; there is a regular pattern, and the various dispositions fit together into a system. What holds one's experiences together and provides a sense of identity is not substance, but a coordinated structure of activities.[13]

Self-conceptions, once they are fixed in habit, tend to be self-sustaining. Since all perception is selective, each person is sensitized to those cues which tend to support his expectations. If a person regards himself as powerful, he expects others to give way and notes with satisfaction their withdrawal, even though some may have moved without even seeing him. He accepts challenges that others would gladly avoid, and with each success the personification is further reinforced. Conversely, a person who conceives of himself as a weakling is sensitive to becoming tired. Everyone tires, but some see the symptoms as indications of impending exhaustion. Only when caught unexpectedly in some desperate situation does

[13] Cf. Risieri Frondizi, *The Nature of the Self* (New Haven: Yale University Press, 1953), pp. 145-57, 173-88.

he exert himself; he may then be surprised to find out how hardy he really is. Thus, one's personification of himself is not a direct copy of reality. The assumptions one makes about himself need not be accurate; if they are consistent, his behavior will also be reasonably consistent. The selection of alternative lines of action, then, have their basis in the individual's personal organization, and the objective situation merely provides the occasions for making choices. A person's conception of himself, like other meanings, is a functional unit and tends to operate as a separate system. Through selective perception men note only those features of their own conduct and of the responses of others that tend to support their already developed predispositions, and they often do not notice those cues which tend to contradict their assumptions. Of course, most self-conceptions continue to develop, but drastic changes occur only under rather unusual circumstances.

Each man's conception of himself is necessarily unique, for each person begins with different physical attributes and has a unique background of experience. In spite of this extensive diversity in content, however, there are a number of regularities in the ways in which people act toward themselves, and it is possible to generalize. Although there are a number of dimensions along which variations may be noted, there are five in particular that are of special interest to social psychologists: degree of integration, extent of conscious awareness, degree of stability, evaluation, and the extent to which the personification enjoys consensus.

One of the most important dimensions along which self-conceptions vary is in their degree of integration. Individuals differ considerably in the extent to which their conduct is organized into a consistent scheme. Except for those who live in small, highly integrated communities each person in our society leads a more or less segmented life. His status in each of the social worlds in which he participates is different, and in each context he is expected to act somewhat differently. Common examples are the man who is feared at his office but is docile at home, especially in the presence of his wife, or the athlete who is known for his ferocious exploits on the playing field but is quite malleable in the hands of his fiancée. Such persons form different self-images in each context, but they usually have no difficulty in integrating these experiences into a single personification: the efficient tycoon who is misunderstood at home or the athlete who is a gentleman. Some measure of fragmentation seems inevitable in a pluralistic society, and perhaps no one ever fuses all his reactions to himself into a single, unambiguous, coherent whole. But there is considerable variation in the extent to which people can integrate their activities. On one extreme is the unusually well-integrated person whose component roles are so ordered toward a consistent set of values that he is unable to act out of character. He is unable to learn anything that does not fit into the already existing scheme and is frequently an unhappy misfit. His life is marked by a singleness of purpose, and his acts fit into a unitary pattern throughout his career. Whatever does not fit is rationalized to appear consistent, at least in his own eyes. Most people are more or less flexible and make the necessary adjustments as they move from one context to the next. On the other extreme is the dissociated person in whom the component roles not only fail to become integrated into a common framework, but whose personality is split so that he almost seems like a completely different person in each context. There is a lack of internal consistency, and at times the person himself may be troubled about it. Not only is there a lack of unity, but each segment may be crystallized as a unit of its own. In severe cases there may even be amnesia for the roles not being played, and serious questions of personal identity may arise. In a sense, such a man leads several different lives.

Another dimension along which self-conceptions vary is in degree of consciousness. With the possible exception of some persons who are psychotic, everyone is more or less aware of his reactions to himself; but there is considerable variation in the ease with which this occurs. Meanings need not be conscious; consciousness of meaning consists of inner communication about a relationship that is already there. What a man actually points out to himself about his own conduct, then, constitutes only a small part of the actual presuppositions in terms of which he approaches himself. Many things are just taken for granted. For all persons there are also a number of characteristic ways of acting that can be noticed only with great difficulty. A young man who is "going steady" with a girl he does not particularly like may be afraid to break off the relationship for fear that no other girl would reciprocate his affections. In rare moments of painful self-appraisal he may recognize this, but at all other times he does not think about it. A person in an ethnic minority may characteristically withdraw from situations requiring contacts with outsiders on the assumption that he will be treated as an inferior. Such consistent behavior may be acknowledged with reluctance when it is called to his attention, but ordinarily he is not conscious of it. There are still other behavior patterns of which the actor is unconscious. Like many other painful dispositions they are repressed. A person is not only unaware of the fact that he consistently treats himself in a particular way but is unable to see it no matter how clearly it may be demonstrated to him by a psychiatrist. Thus, a man may punish himself constantly. He never gives himself the benefit of the doubt and continually imposes challenges upon himself by undertaking impossible enterprises. Consciously, he may have a high opinion of himself and may even appear conceited, and it is only after a serious breakdown and a long period of therapy that he comes to recognize the fact that he continually throws up barriers against himself.

As unlikely as this contention may sound at first, there is experimental evidence that human beings can act in particular ways toward themselves without being aware of it. Huntley took photographs of his subjects in silhouette, had them write their own versions of a fairy tale, and took specimens of their handwriting and of their manual gestures. After six months the same persons were asked to evaluate the records, without knowing that their own had been included. The material was presented in such a manner that there was increasing likelihood of the subjects' recognizing their own performances, and sooner or later most of them were able to locate themselves. Huntley found that the self-judgments were initially highly partisan; each person consistently rated himself more favorably than he rated others, even *before* identity was established. The data showed that the judgments were most favorable when there was partial recognition, when the subject suspected that it might be himself but was not yet certain. Once the material was definitely established as one's own performance, however, a sense of modesty seemed to prevail and the estimates became less partisan.[14] Thus, differential responses to what is identified as oneself can occur even without conscious recognition.

[14] C. W. Huntley, "Judgments of Self Based upon Records of Expressive Behavior," *Journal of Abnormal and Social Psychology*, XXXV (1940), 398–427. Cf. Wolff, *op. cit.*, pp. 61–189.

People differ considerably in their ability to recognize their short-comings. Some are quite candid in admitting their faults; others, however, are apparently unable to do so. They turn away from frank appraisals of their activities. They are commonly regarded as people who have little "insight" into themselves, and in a real sense they may become strangers to themselves. Indeed, there are some persons whose conscious estimates and remarks are often a direct contradiction of what they actually do, and psychoanalysts have suggested that their voluntary conduct constitutes a "reaction formation" against the impulses that they find too painful to admit to themselves. There are administrators who go to great lengths to create the impression that their organization is "democratic" but who are continually manipulating people and forcing them to conform through indirect pressures. Some people insist that they have no personal ambitions, and yet almost everything they do is designed to advance them into positions of eminence, even at the expense of others. Such persons are usually not dishonest. They actually believe what they say but are unable to see irregularities in their own behavior that are obvious even to the more unsophisticated of the people who are in constant association with them. Thus, Polonius' advice that one should always be true to himself is extremely difficult for some people to follow.

Consciousness consists of a person's making designations to himself. Since there are stylistic differences in communicative behavior, the question may be raised as to whether there are similar stylistic variations in the manner in which people become aware of themselves. Self-conceptions are constructed from the experiences that a person has of himself, and self-awareness can be reached in a number of ways. In a study of speech and expressive movements among psychotic patients, Lorenz suggests that the manner in which a person becomes sensitized to various aspects of himself depends in part upon his affective orientation toward his surroundings. An analysis of the speech patterns of "hysterical" patients reveals a clear expression of emotional dispositions but only secondary concern over factual details. Such patients apparently experience themselves directly, that is, without the mediation of symbols. Those who are classified as "obsessive-compulsive" speak in a flat and colorless manner, and they seem to view themselves as if placing some foreign object under scrutiny. Those classified as "manic" appear to experience themselves through indirect reference, and those labelled as "paranoid" seem to regard themselves as the passive recipients of action.[15] Since inquiries of this kind are just now getting under way, no definitive conclusions can be reached, but the leads are promising.

There is also considerable variation in the extent to which self-conceptions are flexible. All meanings tend to be more or less persistent, but most people are not inaccessible to influence. Thus, consistent failure to achieve their goals or the insistence of others that they are being unreasonable leads most people to reappraise themselves. To some extent the career of all persons consists of a succession of imperceptible transformations in self-conceptions. In addition there are occasional crises in which redefinitions occur that result in significant modifications of behavior patterns. But people do differ considerably in their ability to change. Some are so uncertain of what kind of people they are, of what they should believe, of what constitutes their rights, that they shift readily to meet the demands of whatever situation in which they find themselves. On the other extreme are people who are so rigid that they cannot change even in the face of contradictory evidence. If necessary, they may conform externally, but they continue to regard themselves in the same light as before.[16] Most people are somewhere between these extremes, revising their self-conceptions when necessary but retaining reasonable consistency.

Since all objects with which one is in sustained contact are sooner or later evaluated, it is not surprising that each man places some kind of estimate upon himself. For most persons what is personified as oneself becomes an object of considerable value, and its preservation and enhancement come to be included among the basic necessities of life. But there are some who disparage themselves. The manner in which a person evaluates himself may be referred to as his *level of self-esteem*. Although self-esteem is usually regarded as an attribute that varies on a unidimensional scale, this is a gross oversimplification of the process of evaluation. However, in the absence of more definitive knowledge, it is best to keep the treatment relatively simple. Most people apparently have neither a very high nor a very low level of self-esteem. They have their moments of doubt

[15] Lorenz, *op. cit.*

[16] Cf. T. W. Adorno, *et al., The Authoritarian Personality* (New York: Harper & Bros., 1950), pp. 461–64.

and insecurity as well as their moments of triumph in the flush of success. But there are some persons who are constantly tormented by an acute sense of inferiority, sometimes so acute that they become immobilized. If a man does not regard himself as sufficiently worthwhile, there would be little point in his making any effort to achieve lofty aspirations; hence, he may be reduced to a life of self-indulgence. At the other extreme are those who appear to be entirely contented with themselves. They are confident that anything that they elect to do is satisfactory. They voice no doubt of their worth and seem to be under the impression that others agree with their exalted self-appraisal.

As in the case of all other meanings, there is considerable variation in the extent to which self-conceptions are supported by the views of other people. Absolute consensus is impossible, since men are not even aware of many of their own modes of approaching themselves. The extremes range from the high degree of consensus that develops about a man whose position in a community is well-defined and who performs his roles effectively, as in the case of a beloved and respected priest in a Catholic community, to the virtual absence of support, as in the case of a man in a mental hospital who insists that he is really Jesus Christ. The latter personification is a private meaning. Usually there is considerable agreement about some matters and dissension over others. If a woman asserts that she is of the female sex and should be accorded the privileges reserved for that category of human beings, there would be few who would dispute her claims. However, there may be considerable disagreement over her insistence that she is so considerate a person that she always places the welfare of her children before her own. Most people entertain at least a few beliefs about themselves that are not shared by others who know them, but there is usually a sufficiently large area of agreement so that the smooth coordination of joint activities is possible.

Each person, then, takes a number of things for granted about himself, and these assumptions—whether he is aware of them or not—are organized into a system. It is this unit that makes possible the consistency in his voluntary conduct. Because of this consistency people who know one another have little difficulty in anticipating each other's responses, and this is what makes smoothly coordinated enterprises possible. A man's conception of himself is a behavior pattern that plays an important part in the construction of many other complex forms of activity.

As in the case of other meanings, self-conceptions are represented by symbols, and the most important of these symbols is a person's name. Procedures for naming people differ from culture to culture, but the symbol by which a person identifies himself is so closely associated to his conception of himself that most people, unlike Juliet musing on the balcony over her lover's name, tend to confuse it with its referent. Although a name is only a symbol, people respond to its use as if they were directly involved. When his name is mispronounced, forgotten, or confused with that of someone else, one feels offended. The importance of the name is revealed in the plight of some illegitimate children in our society, who become confused about their identity simply because there is some question concerning their names. Studies of name-changing reveal that the alterations are usually not too drastic. Even criminals, who need anonymity to avoid detection, do not move too far away in changing their names. There seems to be a conflict between the desire to avoid recognition by the police and the fear of losing their sense of identity altogether. Foreign names may be Anglicized somewhat, but in general, ethnic origin is not completely obliterated. The same initials are retained in a large number of cases, and there is even a remarkable coincidence in the length of the syllables.[17]

Some of the seemingly odd things that men do become understandable once it is recognized that a person's face and some of his more obvious physical characteristics also serve as symbols for his conception of himself. The face constitutes an excellent symbol not only because it is so readily visible but also because it contains features that are highly individualized. Its very uniqueness makes it an easy basis for reference. Whenever one does something of distinction and wants to commemorate the occasion, he has a photograph taken in which the face is prominently featured. Even when a young woman wins a beauty contest on the basis of the remarkable quality of her legs and torso, she would be disturbed if her face were not included in the picture appearing in the newspapers on the following day. Captured criminals hide their faces when the newsreel men arrive. Thus, parts of the body which play an important part in

[17] A. A. Hartman, "Criminal Aliases: A Psychological Study," *Journal of Psychology*, XXXII (1951), 49–56.

the formation of self-conceptions may also become symbols for them.

With the increasing recognition of the importance of self-conceptions in the organization of behavior, there have been a number of research techniques proposed for their isolation and measurement. Among the most thoughtful is the groundbreaking work of Sheerer, who constructed a scale to differentiate between people in terms of criteria such as their choice of standards of conduct, whether they see themselves or others as responsible for what they do, the manner in which they evaluate themselves and other people, and various aspects of their philosophy of life. Attempts have been made to simplify Sheerer's scale, and a variety of other self-rating inventories have been developed.[18] Another device, which is widely used in clinical psychology, involves the sorting of cards containing descriptions of personal traits, and prominent among the procedures for their analyses is the Q-technique.[19] Procedures have also been developed for the rating of clinical interviews, and a number of standard projective tests can be scored for self reference. The TAT appears to be especially well suited for this purpose.[20] The essential difficulty is that a man's conception of himself cannot be observed directly; it is something that must be inferred from behavior in a wide variety of contexts. It is only in this way that it becomes possible to get at the presuppositions upon which a number of different acts are consistently predicated. That there is a structure of this kind can often be grasped intuitively, but to describe it accurately is difficult. Furthermore, one cannot rely entirely upon verbalizations, even when the subject is cooperative and honest, for the person himself is often unaware of the manner in which he approaches himself. Since so much attention is being directed toward this

[18] Elizabeth T. Sheerer, "An Analysis of the Relationship between Acceptance of and Respect for Self and Acceptance of and Respect for Others," *Journal of Consulting Psychology*, XIII (1949), 169–75. Cf. John J. Brownfain, "Stability of the Self-Concept as a Dimension of Personality," *Journal of Abnormal and Social Psychology*, XLVII (1952), 597–606; James F. T. Bugental and Seymour L. Zelen, "Investigations into the Self-Concept," *Journal of Personality*, XVIII (1950), 483–98; Llewellyn Gross, "The Construction and Partial Standardization of a Scale for Measuring Self-Insight," *Journal of Social Psychology*, XXVIII (1948), 219–36; and Manford H. Kuhn and Thomas S. McPartland, "An Empirical Investigation of Self-Attitudes," *American Sociological Review*, XIX (1954), 68–76.

[19] William Stephenson, *The Study of Behavior* (Chicago: University of Chicago Press, 1953).

[20] Adorno, *et al., op. cit.*, pp. 405–41, 489–600.

problem, it is reasonable to expect the development of more effective tools in the near future.

The Social Matrix of Identification

Each man forms a conception of himself on the basis of two sets of sensory cues. The first set consists of those things that he can experience directly—the visible movements of his limbs, his speech, the internal muscular strains, the pleasures and pains that accompany these movements. Since these subjective experiences are accessible to that person alone, each knows many things about himself that others could not possibly know. But all such experiences are not attributed to oneself; many are projected to other people. This suggests that tactile, thermal, painful, and other sensations can be organized into a unit only after one is able to identify himself as a distinct entity. The second set of cues—the consistent responses of other people—plays an important part in the construction of such a unit.

Self-conceptions, like most other meanings, are formed and creatively reaffirmed from day to day in the interaction of people with one another. Each person develops some notion of the kind of creature he must be from the regularity with which he is addressed by others with whom he is in sustained association. Each man's notion of his physical appearance, of what he is expected to do, and of the deference he commands arises through participating in organized groups. This is what led Cooley to describe a man's sense of personal identity as a "looking glass self." One's conception of himself is essentially a reflection of his attributes as they are mirrored in the society of which he is a part. He constructs the personification from the reactions imputed to other people. If one is consistently treated as if he were peculiar, he comes to conceive of himself as odd and different.[21] All men are highly sensitized to the reactions of other people to whatever they are doing; they are responsive to any cue that might be indicative of their orientations. In an inadequately defined situation, when one does not know what to expect, he feels uncomfortable. Thus, self-conceptions develop in social interaction.

G. H. Mead contended that each person forms a conception of

[21] Charles H. Cooley, *Human Nature and the Social Order* (New York: Charles Scribner's Sons, 1922), pp. 183–85.

himself by evaluating his subjective experiences from a collective standpoint. If so, what a man regards himself to be should be a reflection of what he *believes* others think of him, which is not necessarily what they actually do think. Miyamoto and Dornbusch set up an experiment to put this contention to a test. They divided 195 people into 10 groups and asked each subject (a) to rate himself, (b) to rate each of the other members of the experimental group, (c) to estimate how other members of the group would rate him, and (d) to estimate how people in general would rate him on four characteristics: intelligence, self-confidence, physical attractiveness, and likableness. They found that the average ratings of a person by others (b) as well as the average ratings imputed to others (c) were high for those with high self-ratings (a). What is of special interest, however, is that the ratings imputed to others (c) were closer to the self-ratings (a) than the actual ratings by the others (b). Another finding was that the generalized ratings (d) approximated the self-ratings (a) more closely than did the ratings imputed to the experimental group (c). Although the measuring instruments are crude, as is the case in the early phases of any inquiry, the findings consistently support Mead's theory. The manner in which a man evaluates himself corresponds most closely to what he believes people in general think of him and then to what he believes those in the temporary group in which he is participating think of him. What the latter actually do think of him turns out to be somewhat different.[22]

Mead contended further that men are able to form definite objects of themselves primarily through symbolic communication. All sensations blend into one another, and one can bipolarize his perceptual field only when he can break his experiences into units. The manipulation of such units in the imagination is greatly facilitated by the substitution of linguistic symbols. This suggests that the manner in which a man personifies himself is largely limited by the symbols that are available to him for describing and ordering his experiences. In our society we are restricted by such categories as personality traits, aptitudes, motives, and physical appearance. Much of the difficulty in describing self-conceptions arises from the fact that many nuances of human experience cannot be discriminated and

[22] S. Frank Miyamoto and Sanford Dornbusch, "A Test of Interactionist Hypotheses of Self-Conception," *American Journal of Sociology*, LXI (1956), 399–403. Cf. Mead, *Mind, Self, and Society, op. cit.*, pp. 144–64.

designated adequately in these terms. Self-conceptions arise, then, through a reconstruction of experiences in terms of the linguistic categories available in one's group.

This proposition can be tested in part by examining the fate of men unable to use symbols and cases in which symbolic manipulation takes on an unusual character. Studies of men suffering from aphasia show that such persons have great difficulty in detaching themselves as distinct units from the rest of their world; and retrospective accounts of persons who have recovered from schizophrenia also reveal that when the ability to use symbols is lost, the boundary between them and their environment also becomes blurred or lost.[23] Studies of hypnosis reveal that the manner in which the subject experiences his own body can be transformed through linguistic commands. Participants in experiments on hypnotic age regression find that various parts of the body are felt to have changed in size and that they see themselves as children. When a subject in this state is ordered to push his father aside, however, he finds that he must alter parts of his body image in order to comply, for the task requires more strength. The body is then suddenly experienced as being larger.[24] Thus, what is experienced as oneself is not only organized through linguistic symbols but can even be manipulated through them.

Since a man's conception of himself is a part of his symbolic environment, it is constructed not only in terms of the linguistic categories but also in terms of whatever else is taken for granted in the group. Just as people have different beliefs about the nature of the universe, they have different beliefs about man. Since self-conceptions may extend beyond the body, the boundaries differ somewhat from culture to culture. It is reported that the Wintu Indians of California do not conceive of themselves as strictly delimited and clearly defined but as concentrations that fade and give way to other objects. Assumptions concerning human nature and motivation also provide a framework within which each man locates himself. In our society it is generally assumed that most men are hedonistic and self-centered, and even altruism is justified as enlightened self-interest; but there are religious groups in which such a view is regarded as unrealistic. Such beliefs are especially important because

[23] Goldstein and Scheerer, *op. cit.*; and Sechehaye, *op. cit.*
[24] Edith Klemperer, "Changes of the Body Image in Hypnoanalysis," *Journal of Clinical and Experimental Hypnosis*, II (1954), 157–62.

so many other things that men do depend upon them.[25]

In those social worlds in which a status system is well established the development of self-conceptions is greatly facilitated, for those who occupy the various interrelated positions can indicate to themselves the kinds of behavior patterns and personal traits that are regarded as appropriate. A doctor or priest is expected to remain behind in an infested city, even when all others are encouraged to leave. A soldier must stand and fight while everyone else flees. A man's honor is the model he maintains as one in a given position, and the demands he makes upon himself are reinforced by the expectations of others. This phenomenon is most clearly revealed in pathetic cases of the *nouveau riche*, who are so anxious to comply with the demands of their new station in life that they sometimes make themselves appear ridiculous through the external imitation of behavior patterns they do not understand. When Coates and Pellegrin interviewed 59 top executives and 50 first line supervisors in a variety of bureaucratic organizations, they found that most of the executives conceived of themselves in the manner in which their category is popularly characterized. They described themselves as having drive and a strong desire for achievement, a sympathetic view of authority, decisiveness, the ability to organize, and a realistic orientation. The supervisors also attributed the same traits to their superiors and acknowledged the bases upon which the executives claimed ascendancy.[26] When a man places himself in a well-defined category, his behavior is thereby circumscribed, but it becomes easier for him to identify himself as a particular kind of human being.

Each person is involved in a web of social relationships, and group structure may be viewed as consisting of the regularized responses of other people. Men approach one another with hypotheses about themselves. By virtue of the fact that he is who he is, a person expects others to treat him in a given way; if the anticipated re-

[25] Dorothy Lee, *Freedom and Culture* (Englewood Cliffs, N.J.: Prentice-Hall, Inc., 1959), pp. 131–40. Cf. A. Irving Hallowell, *Culture and Experience* (Philadelphia: University of Pennsylvania Press, 1955), pp. 75–110; David C. McClelland, J. F. Sturr, R. H. Knapp, and H. W. Wendt, "Obligations to Self and Society in the United States and Germany," *Journal of Abnormal and Social Psychology*, LVI (1958), 245–55; and Mills, "Situated Actions and Vocabularies of Motive," *op. cit.*

[26] Charles H. Coates and Roland J. Pellegrin, "Executives and Supervisors: Contrasting Self-Conceptions and Conceptions of Each Other," *American Sociological Review*, XXII (1957), 217–20.

sponses actually take place, his hypotheses are confirmed, and this reinforces his conception of himself. When a Negro living in a segregated community enters a forbidden area, he anticipates hostile reactions from at least some of the people he meets. If he is greeted warmly, he is puzzled and may even become suspicious. Similarly, when a man approaches a strange woman to ask for directions, he must be prepared for the possibility of a cold rebuff. On the other hand, when he kisses his wife affectionately, he anticipates some kind of reciprocation. Thus, each person's sense of identity is constantly being tested in social interaction and repeatedly reaffirmed as other people live up to expectations. Furthermore, the more frequently and consistently such confirmations are forthcoming, the more he can take his assumptions about himself for granted and approach familiar situations with confidence.

Thus, a man's conception of himself is crystallized through consistent treatment by the people with whom he is in sustained contact. A variety of observations support this contention. If a person is treated as a subordinate, he often comes to regard himself as an inferior object, and his conduct may take on many childlike qualities. For example, in many military units officers complain that their men are completely dependent and incapable of assuming any responsibility; it should be noted that in most armies enlisted men from the time of their induction are treated as if they were totally incapable of initiative or intelligent judgment. Similarly, administrators in some colleges in which students are under constant observation and supervision, as if they were juvenile delinquents, are surprised that the honor system and responsible self-government do not work. During the Inquisition and other periods in which alleged religious heretics were hunted down and persecuted, some of the accused actually confessed to being witches and to having practiced sorcery. They became genuinely convinced of their guilt and concurred with the death sentence imposed by the courts. In an effort to atone for their evil deeds they even implicated some of their friends, who were equally innocent. It should come as no surprise, therefore, that in more recent times political prisoners who have been confronted by equally ridiculous charges have confessed voluntarily. Since some of these men have stood by their confessions even when an opportunity arose to recant, it must be concluded that they were actually convinced of their guilt. Some students of "brain washing" techniques have suggested that such men redefined themselves in response to the consistent treatment they received from all those with whom they came into contact following their arrest. Even fellow prisoners apparently participated in transforming the perspectives of the accused.[27]

The relationship between self-conceptions and social status is revealed in the sensitivity of some people about status symbols. Those who have anxieties over rank are especially careful about the symbols of their position. Graduate students are often more careful about their dress than professors. Interns drape their stethoscopes out of their blouses so that they will not be mistaken for laboratory assistants or technicians; well-established doctors are more careless about such matters. In our society status rests largely upon the kind of work done by the head of the household. When a travelling salesman insists that he is in "promotional work," when a Y. M. C. A. secretary calls himself a "group worker," or when a janitor insists that he is a "custodian," such hedging over labels suggests that the people are sensitive about the manner in which they are being evaluated by virtue of their occupation.[28]

Whenever a man's status changes, he must learn several new roles; the responses of other people, his own behavior patterns, and his conception of himself all undergo some modification. An excellent illustration is provided in the imaginative novel by Laura Hobson, *Gentleman's Agreement*, in which a Gentile writer informs his associates that he is Jewish and is amazed to find how differently he is treated. Although he has had Jewish friends all his life, he comes to understand for the first time what it is like to be identified as a Jew. When a man acquires a new job, especially if it is ranked much higher than the one he had held before, he must at first consciously inform himself of his new responsibilities and prerogatives. He may initially be taken aback at the deference with which others address him; before long, however, he becomes accustomed to it. After playing the new roles for some time, he finds that his natural behavior has changed. In the course of performing the new tasks new ways of addressing himself have crystallized. The difference between those who acquire a changed status and those who do not is revealed in

[27] Cf. Robert J. Lifton, "Thought Reform of Western Civilians in Chinese Communist Prisons," *Psychiatry*, XIX (1956), 173–95; and Charles Mackay, *Extraordinary Popular Delusions and the Madness of Crowds* (Boston: L. C. Page & Co., 1932), pp. 462–564.

[28] Cf. Hughes, *op. cit.*, pp. 42–55.

Blau's study of age identification on the part of elderly people in Elmira, New York. When 468 people—all sixty years of age or older—were asked to characterize themselves, 60 per cent described themselves as "middle aged," and 38 per cent said they were "elderly" or "old." Further analysis showed that those who maintained unbroken contacts with others their own age tended to regard themselves as younger; since their associates did not consider them old, they did not conceive of themselves as old. But those who had retired usually did think of themselves as old. Retirement disrupts relations with fellow workers; it is a social pattern in which one acknowledges that he is no longer fit to work, and the agreement of others is implied. When a person accepts the status of "retired," he alters his conduct and personifies himself as having reached the final phase of his life.[29]

The transformation is even more marked when a man becomes assimilated into a new group with a drastically different culture. He must learn a new set of symbols, and in time he develops a new perspective. He not only has a different position in a new social world, but he looks upon and evaluates himself from a different standpoint. Furthermore, his new associates respond differently to him. This process is most readily discernible among immigrants and among converts to religious or political cults, and to a lesser extent the same thing happens to many freshmen upon entering college. They encounter norms and values quite different from those of their home community, and they learn that college students are judged in terms of somewhat different standards. To the extent that one becomes absorbed in campus life his conception of himself is somewhat altered.

In the course of his career each person plays a number of conventional roles, and especially in pluralistic societies like ours he may even play incongruent roles. To some extent, then, each person acts somewhat differently in each situation. But if he forms different self-images in each context in which different demands are made upon him, how can he form a single self-conception? With few exceptions each person is able to identify himself as a specific human being, marked by a given name and a relatively stable set of characteristics. This arises in part from the continuity of his ex-

[29] Zena S. Blau, "Changes in Status and Age Identification," *American Sociological Review*, XXI (1956), 198–203.

periences and in part from the fact that he views himself from a perspective that transcends all the particular standpoints of the various groups in which he becomes involved. Most men have a more or less integrated outlook toward their surroundings, a perspective which incorporates the various meanings learned in the numerous contexts in which they have participated. This outlook becomes more and more inclusive as one participates in an increasing number of groups. Estimates of oneself from the standpoint of those at home, in school, in the neighborhood, and at work gradually become integrated into a single unit. A man is able to form and hold on to a consistent personification in spite of the diversity of his activities because he keeps looking at himself from a highly generalized standpoint.

It has already been noted that self-conceptions vary in their degree of integration. Although other variables are apparently involved, the extent to which a person's conception of himself is integrated depends in part upon the integration of the social system in which he participates. Self-conceptions are meanings into which the anticipated responses of other people are incorporated. In a pluralistic society those who are encountered in different social worlds behave differently; the hypotheses regarding oneself that are projected also vary. To the extent that the society in which one lives is stable and well-organized, the pursuit of a clearly defined career is greatly facilitated. But when participating in societies in which the component group norms are not mutually consistent, it becomes progressively more difficult for any man to integrate his various self-images into a single unit. When the differences are too great, a man may suffer from inner conflicts, and at times the pain may become so acute that he may suffer dissociation.

When sociologists claim that human beings have no identity apart from the social groups in which they participate, they are not suggesting that a person is only the subjective counterpart of a social system. Each man has his private experiences, sees his world in his own distinctive way, and develops a unique personality. But his sensations would not be highly differentiated nor could they be held constant without the linguistic symbols that he learns as a member of some society. Furthermore, the social structure of the groups in which he becomes involved enables him to define and locate himself. It is through the regularity in the responses of other people that he establishes his sense of identity, and his conception of himself is buttressed and reinforced by the continuation of these expected reactions.

Summary and Conclusion

In recent years more and more students of human behavior have come to recognize the importance of personal identity, for what a man does or does not do depends in large measure upon his conception of himself. Each individual is tied to a pattern of communal life by the manner in which he is identified. By virtue of being who he is, he assumes status in a group. He can locate himself and is recognized by others, and his relationship to each of the others is thereby defined. Far from being creatures of impulse, men generally inhibit their organic dispositions in order to live up to the standards of conduct that they set for themselves. They are constantly responding to what they believe themselves to be.

At first glance one might think of a man's conception of himself as something arising out of his body or what he experiences of it. More careful analysis reveals, however, that a person reacts to a variety of objects far beyond the boundaries of his body as if they were a part of himself. A personification depends upon the attributes of the organism, but it is not to be identified with it. In speaking of self-conceptions reference is being made, not to some substance encapsuled within the skin, but to a complex form of behavior—the regularized ways in which a man is organized to act toward himself. Self-conceptions, then, are meanings that take shape in the course of participating in cooperative activities. Voluntary conduct is not so much a manifestation of what a man "really" is but rests upon the beliefs he develops about himself—on the basis of the consistent manner in which he is treated by his associates.

Many of the distinctive features of human behavior arise from the fact that men orient themselves within a symbolic environment and strive to come to terms with what they believe themselves to be. Men give their lives willingly for a variety of worthy causes; they deny themselves many joys in order to build gigantic political or industrial empires; they build up social barriers to protect their progeny against miscegenation; they plot vengeance for a wrong suffered long ago by their ancestors; they create monuments in their own honor; they push their children to "make a name" for themselves; lovers commit suicide when they are denied the right to marry; artists paint happily for "posterity," serenely indifferent to the fact that their contemporaries regard them as mad. Although men take these activities for granted as a part of human life, no other animal is known to engage in such conduct. It is unlikely that any creature without self-conceptions would do any of these things. Human behavior consists of a succession of adjustments to life conditions, but each man must come to terms with himself as well as with other features of his world. To understand what men do we must know something about what each person means to himself.

Suggested References

ANGYAL, ANDRUS, *Foundations for a Science of Personality*. New York: Commonwealth Fund, 1941. The development of a theory of personal growth from the Gestalt standpoint, with special emphasis upon the location of oneself within a symbolic environment.

FISHER, SEYMOUR and SIDNEY E. CLEVELAND, *Body Image and Personality*. Princeton: D. van Nostrand Co., 1958. An assessment of research literature, followed by original studies on the manner in which a man's conception of his physical attributes is related to various forms of behavior.

JAMES, WILLIAM, *The Principles of Psychology*, Vol. I, pp. 291–401. New York: Henry Holt & Co., 1890. A classic statement on the nature of self-consciousness and the source of many of the concepts and hypotheses prominent in current research on the subject.

MEAD, GEORGE H., *Mind, Self, and Society*, Charles W. Morris, ed., pp. 135–273. Chicago: University of Chicago Press, 1934. A provocative discussion by an eminent philosopher of the formation of self-conceptions and the capacity for self-control through participation in organized groups.

SHERIF, MUZAFER and HADLEY CANTRIL, *The Psychology of Ego-Involvements*. New York: John Wiley & Sons, 1947. A critical review of the literature on the extension of self-conceptions beyond the boundaries of the body, with a valuable discussion of the growth, transformation, and breakdown of such identifications.

STRAUSS, ANSELM L., *Mirrors and Masks: The Search for Identity*. Glencoe: Free Press, 1959. A discussion of the manner in which a person's sense of identity is sustained or transformed in social interaction, with particular emphasis on the importance of symbols.

8

Social
status
in
reference
groups

Some of the behavior patterns that are found frequently among those who are successful in business and in the professions often baffle people outside their respective social worlds. Many find it difficult to understand why businessmen of considerable wealth go to such lengths to avoid paying income taxes—in some cases even giving away more money than they would have had to surrender to the Treasury Department. Many of these people are not moved by avarice; indeed, some are quite generous. Furthermore, many of them admit that they do not really need the money about which they carry on their annual struggle with the government. With the introduction of the principle of mass production into so many areas of American life—governmental agencies, hospitals, publishing firms, and universities—an increasing number of professional people are becoming employees of large corporations rather than individual practitioners. As such, they find themselves facing problems similar to those which have confronted industrial workers for some time. But most attempts to protect and further their interests through unions have failed. Union organizers as well as those who are sympathetic with the labor movement have often had difficulty in understanding why nurses, engineers, and those in other professions cannot be organized effectively, especially since the latter readily agree that they are underpaid and sometimes even exploited. Such conduct on the part of otherwise intelligent men is so incomprehensible that some observers have concluded that these people must be callous, greedy, or shortsighted.

Among the charges often levelled against them is that they are lacking in "social conscience." But the businessmen and professional people themselves are often puzzled by such charges, and they are certainly not filled with remorse or feelings of guilt. As far as they are concerned, they are acting quite properly, doing the only decent and intelligent thing, and their associates agree. Among themselves businessmen discuss avidly the various tactics used to win additional exemptions and express bitterness of the dangers of "creeping socialism." In various professional circles men shake their heads over the inability of union enthusiasts to understand that they could not participate in a strike, and they reaffirm what they regard to be the obligation of those in their calling to continue providing essential services even under adverse circumstances. These illustrations suggest that people who live in the same community not only experience their environment differently but also perform for somewhat different audiences. Any study of motivation, then, must take this fact into account.

Reference Groups as Perspectives

Each person acts on the basis of his definition of the situation. He categorizes the transaction in which he is involved, locates himself within it, and thereby decides upon his obligations. The consistency with which he defines a succession of situations arises from the fact that he generally uses the same perspective, one that he shares with his associates. Once he has adopted a particular point of view it becomes his working conception of the world, and he brings this frame of reference to bear upon each situation he encounters, whether or not anyone else from the group is actually on the scene. Since people with diverse orientations are selectively responsive to different aspects of their natural environment, identical events may be seen in divergent ways. A prostitute and a social worker walking down the same street in a slum area often have remarkably contrasting experiences. The leering men they pass, the drunk sleeping on a doorstep, the drug addict purchasing a "fix"—all are seen differently. But their respective outlooks differ no more than those of a traffic officer and of a motorist stopped for excessive speeding. The offender is irked by the delay; much like a naughty child who has been caught misbehaving, he sulks. If the officer speaks curtly, the motorist is resentful of what he regards to be an unnecessary display of authority. It does not occur to him that only a half hour ago the same officer may have helped load the body of a dead child upon an ambulance, the victim of an accident involving two speeding automobiles. The diversity of interpretations often arises from the fact that key objects, though designated by the same symbols, assume different meanings for different people. It is not surprising, therefore, that immigrants and tourists almost invariably misinterpret much of what they see.

There have been a number of experimental studies demonstrating the manner in which the definition of identical situations varies with perspectives. Among them is one concerning the spectators of a crucial football game between Princeton and Dartmouth on November 23, 1951. It was a fiercely contested match in which a large number of penalties were called. In the second quarter a Princeton star who had been prominently mentioned for All-America honors had to leave the game with a broken nose and a concussion, and in the following period a Dartmouth player was carried off the field with a broken leg. Immediately after the contest there were charges in the press of "dirty" football. A week later undergraduate students in both universities were given a questionnaire concerning the game. All Princeton students described the game as "rough and dirty"; of the Dartmouth students a tenth thought it was "clean and fair," a third judged it as "rough and fair," and the remainder acknowledged that it was "rough and dirty." Of the Princeton spectators nine-tenths insisted that the Dartmouth players had started the foul tactics; but of the Dartmouth observers only a third held their own team guilty, and the rest blamed both sides. When the students were shown a motion picture of the game and asked to note and to evaluate infractions of the rules, the Princeton students detected twice as many violations and rated them as being more flagrant.[1] All of these students were either in the same stadium or were exposed to the same motion picture, but what they saw differed to a remarkable extent.

Divergent meanings can sometimes be reconciled by comparing assumptions, but misunderstandings become less amenable to clarification when differences exist over such fundamental categories as *time*. At first glance nothing appears as simple as the concept of time; it just passes on inexorably in increments like hours or days. But the passage of time is of different significance in different cultures. Precision in keeping time, for example, is relatively unimportant for a peasant, for he begins works soon after dawn and continues until sundown. He harvests his crops when they are ready and rests when weather conditions are such that he cannot work. In a peasant community that is becoming industrialized, however, keeping time takes on a new meaning, for men work by the clock. In some areas the owning of a wrist watch has become a status symbol among those desiring to be in line with the latest trends. At the other extreme are those who work for the railroads, among whom almost everything is measured in terms of accuracy in timing.[2] Such contrasts in the unstated premises about the passage of time sometimes lead people to conclude that others are indolent or unnecessarily aggressive.

Differences in the meaning of categories such as success can lead to serious misunderstandings, for the manner in which men organize their careers depends upon such conceptions. In the United States a high value is generally placed upon success. It is taken for granted that each individual will strive to improve his station in life, and those who do not succeed are often regarded as indigent. But there are many different conceptions of the kinds of goals that are regarded as worth pursuing. In some social worlds men in competitive situations are expected to exert themselves to the utmost to win; victory is all important, and considerations of decency and fair play are viewed as luxuries for "idealists." In intercollegiate athletics, for

---

[1] Albert H. Hastorf and Hadley Cantril, "They Saw a Game: A Case Study," *Journal of Abnormal and Social Psychology*, XLIX (1954), 129–34.

[2] Cf. W. Fred Cottrell, *The Railroader* (Stanford: Stanford University Press, 1940); and Hallowell, *op. cit.*, pp. 216–35.

example, it has been reported that some athletes have been injected with amphetamine and similar stimulants by their coaches to make possible performances far beyond their normal capacity. Those who are familiar with the unreasonable pressures placed upon coaches and athletes view this practice with regret but with understanding. But many others are horrified, wondering what there could be about winning a contest that would justify risking the health of young men. Similarly, in some universities men doing research sacrifice themselves and their families, devoting themselves to their work 365 days a year; some of their colleagues wonder, however, whether anything such men may accomplish could really be worth the unbalanced lives they lead.[3] In some business circles the deception and exploitation of competitors and customers is regarded as perfectly natural; others wonder whether success built upon the misfortunes of other people can really be satisfying, and they condemn those who struggle so feverishly as being "power mad." Assumptions such as these provide the basis for deciding what goals are really worth seeking in life and the manner in which one is to go about pursuing his aspirations.

Many serious misunderstandings arise from differences in certain crucial values, especially in criteria of modesty, cleanliness, and sexual conduct. There are vast differences in standards of modesty. In some social worlds the exposure of the nude body, belching, and flatulence are simply accepted as a natural part of human life; in others such behavior is regarded as unforgivable and is concealed at all cost. The emphasis upon personal cleanliness ranges from high standards of sanitation to the retention of an outward appearance of neatness to a vague awareness of the problem. One person may be amused at those who are constantly washing themselves, while the latter wonder how their associate can possibly stand his own stench. There are norms in all groups concerning what constitutes proper sex conduct; this is true even in groups that are thought by outsiders to be without standards.[4] But there is remarkable variability in these norms, ranging from the open acceptance of sexual excitement as a part of human nature to the puritanical denial of

---

[3] Cf. Alvin W. Gouldner, "Cosmopolitans and Locals: Toward an Analysis of Latent Social Roles," *Administrative Science Quarterly*, II (1957–58), 281–306, 444–80.

[4] William F. Whyte, "Slum Sex Code," *American Journal of Sociology*, XLIX (1943), 24–31.

sexuality. Practices that are condemned as sinful perversions in one circle are accepted as the normal part of life in another. Since each group takes it for granted that its own ways are right and natural, people are easily convinced that outsiders are either lewd or unduly inhibited. In Polynesia the sexual techniques generally accepted by most Americans and Europeans are regarded as comical, and those who have been employed by planters, traders, or officials often entertain their friends by imitating these copulatory procedures in caricature.[5] Because understandings about sex are so deeply ingrained, people generally feel that there is something filthy or unnatural about the practices condemned in their group.

People with diverse cultural backgrounds often have different conceptions of human nature. In each universe of discourse explanations of the things men do are circumscribed by the available vocabulary of motives. There are a limited set of recognized intentions, approved and disapproved, which are thought to depict the natural inclinations of man. There are a limited number of words that are used to label these dispositions, and a motive that cannot be designated obviously cannot be imputed or avowed. Furthermore, in each social world there are shared assumptions as to the kinds of intentions that develop in each standardized context. In our society it does little good for a murderer to insist that his hand had been guided by the spirit of an ancestor for whom he had been named; he is more likely to receive a sympathetic hearing by claiming that he was the victim of a mysterious "inner urge" that he could not understand.

As one compares the perspectives that are shared in diverse social worlds, it becomes apparent that what differs are the premises underlying action. Identical situations are perceived differently because those starting out with unlike assumptions project contrasting hypotheses and are selectively responsive to different sensory cues. What makes the clarification of these divergences so difficult is that the differences are about matters that are taken for granted, matters on which alternatives are not considered. Beliefs concerning the importance of punctuality, cleanliness, or success, convictions about the proper contact between the sexes, as well as assumptions about the nature of love—all these meanings are intertwined with thousands

[5] Bronislaw Malinowski, *The Sexual Life of Savages* (New York: Halcyon House, 1941), pp. 337–39.

of others into an organized scheme. A successful challenge to any basic assumption can lead to searching questions about all the others. To challenge such fundamental beliefs is to challenge a man's orientation toward life. If he takes it seriously, he may be left dazed and bewildered, not knowing what is true and what is false.

Since perception is selective, those with one perspective often develop what Veblen called a "trained incapacity" to appreciate even the most elementary features of another culture. Active participants in the National Association of Manufacturers and various labor leaders are continually enraged by one another's pronouncements. Both find it difficult to comprehend how any decent human being could possibly take the stand assumed by the other. Indeed, much of the acrimony and self-righteous indignation that characterizes politics the world over arises from the fact that the adversaries work with such diverse assumptions that they cannot understand one another. The point can be illustrated even more readily by citing the vitriolic polemics to be found among social psychologists trained in different intellectual traditions. Many psychiatrists are trained in medical schools, and a medical education often fortifies doctors against all explanations of behavior that are not biological; to many of them the writings of psychologists and sociologists contain nothing but speculative nonsense. Many psychologists are appalled when sociologists insist that a knowledge of social structure is essential for an understanding of human behavior. They are convinced that a group consists of nothing more than an aggregate of individuals; there is nothing to study other than the personalities of the component individuals. Anthropologists and sociologists see the things that men do as manifestations of cultural or social systems in operation, and while they may acknowledge that there are individual differences in performance, they work as if such variations did not matter. They are shocked upon hearing psychologists and psychiatrists explaining behavior in terms of personality structure without reference to the social milieu. Most of these specialists find it much easier to talk to uninitiated laymen than to specialists trained in rival fields. After interdisciplinary conferences each departs filled with regrets about the "blind spots" of the others which prevent their seeing things that are so obvious.

The contention that men think, feel, and see things from the standpoint peculiar to the group in which they participate is an old one which has been repeatedly emphasized by anthropologists and students of the sociology of knowledge. But what makes this hypothesis so important for the study of modern mass societies is the fact that people may assume the perspectives of groups in which they are *not* recognized members, sometimes of groups in which they have never participated directly, and sometimes of groups that do not exist at all. For example, those seeking to raise their status are more responsive to the opinions of people in the social set to which they aspire than to the views shared in the circle to which they belong. Members of ethnic minorities who are becoming assimilated examine themselves from the standpoint of the dominant group; they often develop strong feelings of inferiority and condemn others in the minority for failing to live up to these outside norms. Servants and slaves sometimes accept the standards of their masters, and adolescent boys in slum areas sometimes adopt the code of the underworld, as they learn of it from motion pictures. There are many people, then, who try to live up to the standards of social worlds of which they learn from vicarious participation—through observation or through the various media of mass communication.

Furthermore, in societies characterized by cultural pluralism each person may acquire several perspectives, for he can participate simultaneously in a number of social worlds. Because cultures are products of communication a person develops a somewhat different perspective from each communication channel to which he is regularly exposed. Because of the ease with which one can gain access to a variety of channels, he leads a somewhat segmented life, engaging in turn in a succession of quite unrelated activities. Furthermore, the particular aggregate of social worlds of which one partakes differs from individual to individual; this is what led Simmel to declare that each person stands at that point at which the unique combination of social circles of which he is a part intersects.[6] This geometric analogy is a happy one, for it enables us to conceive of the almost endless permutations as well as the varying degrees of involvement in each circle. To understand any particular person, then, one must get a picture of his unique outlook. Since this is the product of his past experiences, real and vicarious, no two people are likely to have an identical outlook.

[6] Georg Simmel, *Conflict and the Web of Group-Affiliations*, trans. Kurt H. Wolff and Reinhard Bendix (Glencoe: The Free Press, 1955), pp. 127-95.

Since a given situation may be defined from so many different points of view, to understand what a man does an observer must get at the assumptions with which he begins. One of the most important things to know about a person is what he takes for granted. To take his role and to anticipate what he is likely to do it is necessary to identify the perspective he is using, the social world in which he is participating in a given act. The concept of *reference group* may be used to designate *that group, real or imaginary, whose standpoint is being used as the frame of reference by the actor.* This provides some notion of the meanings he is projecting upon the scene. Not only can different persons approach the same situation from diverse standpoints, but the same person in different transactions may utilize different perspectives. On a hockey field he has one orientation, and in a classroom he is participating in an entirely different social world. Each man acts, then, for some kind of *audience,* and it is important to know what this audience is and what kinds of expectations are imputed to it.

The reference group supports the values in terms of which a person estimates his own conduct; therefore, his line of activity depends upon the real or anticipated reactions of the other people for whom he is performing. There is a selective sensitivity to others; men are not equally responsive to the opinions of everyone present. Hardened criminals are well aware of the disapproval of most people but are not especially upset. Furthermore, the audience that counts need not consist of people whom one knows personally; frequently reference groups are quite large, and one can have direct contacts only with a few representatives. For example, those in ethnic minorities are usually highly responsive to the demands of others with whom they identify on the basis of common ancestry, but in most cases each knows on a personal basis only a small percentage of those who make up the category. In studying the behavior of human beings it is necessary to get "inside" the actor, to see the situation from his point of view, and the concept of reference group is useful for this purpose.

There are as many reference groups for each person as there are communication channels in which he participates, and individuals differ considerably in their range of participation. Each lives in an environment of which he is the center, and the dimensions of his effective surroundings are defined by the direction and distance from which news comes to him. Each time a man enters a new communication channel—subscribes to a new periodical, joins a new circle of friends, purchases a television set, or begins to listen regularly to some radio program—he is introduced into a new social world. People who communicate develop an appreciation of one another's tastes, interests, and outlook upon life; and as one acquires new standards of conduct, he adds more people to his audience. Each man's outlook is both shaped and limited by the communication networks in which he becomes involved.

A reference group, then, is any identifiable group whose supposed perspective is used by the actor as a frame of reference in the organization of his perceptual field. Men are usually most responsive to the views imputed to those with whom they are in direct and constant association, but reference groups may also be imaginary, as in the case of artists who are "born ahead of their time," scientists who work for "humanity," or philanthropists who give for "posterity." Such persons estimate their endeavors from a postulated standpoint imputed to people who have not yet been born. They sometimes undergo incredible sacrifices in anticipation of being appreciated by some future audience that presumably would be more sensible than the people who are now living. They are not concerned with immediate rewards and work slavishly for people who may actually never come into existence. There are others who live for a distant past, idealizing some period in history, longing for the "good old days" and constantly criticizing current events from a standpoint imputed to people long since dead—as in the case of the Southerner pining for the days of the Confederacy. There are some people who create a paradise in the next world—Valhalla, Heaven, or the "happy hunting grounds"—and forego pleasures in their present life on the assumption that they will be rewarded after death. An interesting problem is that of ascertaining how perspectives imputed to such imaginary audiences are constructed. One can learn about the typical ways in which people in the "Greek world" presumably lived, acted, and thought by reading history and studying archaeology, but what of the audiences that will not be born for another thousand years? The fact that there is no material basis for such reference groups does not make them any less important.

There are some categories of people with which men occasionally identify which are so amorphous that they may almost be regarded as imaginary groups. Two examples of vaguely defined audiences that play an important part in our society are public opinion and social class. Politicians, administrators, labor leaders, advertising men, and even dictators are constantly concerned with what they call "public opinion." Sometimes even the man of the street may refrain from doing something on the ground that "people won't like it." But who are these "people"? How does one go about ascertaining what it is that the "people" want? Although surveys and polls give some indications, there is no way of knowing for certain until after mass reactions are aroused. Public opinion is the source of so much concern precisely because a miscalulation of what people will tolerate can lead to disastrous consequences—embarrassing demonstrations, the loss of an election, demands for changes that threaten those in privileged positions, or a spectacular drop in the sales of some product. But most of the time those who are concerned with public opinion can only guess, and their conjectures are usually based upon very limited contacts. The same is true of social class. In a study of social stratification in England, where class lines are more clearly drawn than they are in the United States, Bott found that people are class-conscious and do act in terms of their understanding of their class position. But their conception of class structure is often vague and develops from the ways in which the various individuals personally experience prestige and power in their daily lives. Most people are conscious of class differences, but their conception of the system varies with their experiences. Bott concluded that a social class is a constructed reference group—an audience to which people project their own respective expectations and of which they do not in fact possess accurate knowledge.[7]

Actually, men become acutely aware of the existence of divergent standpoints primarily when they are caught in situations in which conflicting demands are made upon them. While they avoid making difficult decisions whenever possible, these contradictions sometimes force one to choose between two social worlds. Such inner conflicts are essentially struggles between alternative ways of defining a given situation, the options arising from each of two or more perspectives that might be brought to bear upon it. Examples of such

[7] Elizabeth Bott, "The Concept of Class as a Reference Group," *Human Relations*, VII (1954), 259–85. Cf. Kurt Riezler, "What is Public Opinion?" *Social Research*, XI (1944), 397–427.

dilemmas were provided by William James: "As a man I pity you, but as an official I must show you no mercy; as a politician I regard him as an ally, but as a moralist I loathe him." In playing roles in different social worlds, contrasting expectations are imputed to competing audiences, and sometimes these differences cannot be compromised. The problem is that of selecting the standpoint from which the situation is to be defined. It is in contexts in which alternative definitions are demanded that problems of loyalty arise.

There are individual differences in the flexibility with which one shifts from one reference group to another. There are some people who have a dominant perspective and insist upon defining virtually all situations from this standpoint. Such persons are sometimes reluctant even to acknowledge the existence of other viewpoints and insist that everyone who disagrees with them is wrong. Most people have a limited number of perspectives and are aware of the existence of others, and though they may feel uncomfortable in the company of people whose views are too different, they can tolerate some diversity. Still others change with the wind so that even their close associates are not certain of where they stand. Some can compartmentalize their experiences into units; others apparently find it difficult to do so.

Consistency in Voluntary Conduct

The demands that are made upon any given person vary from situation to situation; yet in most instances he acts with sufficient consistency so that his close associates are able to anticipate fairly well what he is likely to do. No two situations are ever the same, and yet there are recurrent features which give his conduct a distinctive quality. It is the fact that each man acts with reasonable regularity in a variety of settings that facilitates recognizing him as a specific human being. These persistent behavior patterns are in part a manifestation of his peculiar somatic make-up and of those spontaneous inclinations that constitute his personality. But much of the consistency that is found in overt, voluntary conduct arises from the fact that each person maintains a reasonably stable conception of himself.

Although self-conceptions are formed through participation in organized groups, once a man's sense of identity has crystallized, he can define a succession of situations independently of others. Most men act properly even when no one else is present to check up on them; they do not need the constant presence of others to reinforce their understanding of what is right and what is wrong. Thus, a person who conceives of himself as a decent, law-abiding citizen would resist temptations to steal even when opportunities arise; he regards theft as being beneath his dignity. Of course, a professional thief would not be so inhibited, for he defines the same situation quite differently. For him the object constitutes legitimate booty; furthermore, if a highly valued object is successfully stolen, his prestige among fellow thieves would be enhanced. The thief has a different self-conception and performs for a different audience; he is constantly sensitized to possibilities of taking things that do not belong to him, even when he is alone. Once a man has formed a relatively stable self-conception, then, he can act with reasonable consistency even without pressures from others.

In each situation in which there is some possibility of making a choice the alternatives are pretested from the standpoint one has acquired through group participation. Just as a decent person would object to someone else's hypocrisy as being morally wrong, he would also object to similar conduct on his own part. Generally, the possibility of doing something that is prohibited is not even considered. Should one be tempted, however, he immediately feels guilty. Guilt involves a judgment of oneself from the standpoint of his reference group. Even the most private of experiences is appraised from a collective standpoint. Most men are reasonably honest of their own accord, not from fear of detection. Consistency in voluntary conduct arises in part, then, from the fact that projected lines of action are habitually examined from the same standpoint.

But part of the consistency arises from the relative stability of each man's orientation toward himself. Many people, however puzzled they may be, are reluctant to raise questions at a large public meeting; they are afraid of being ridiculed by others. Such a self-image rests on the assumption that one is not too intelligent. But a person who admires and has confidence in himself may go ahead even in the face of open taunts by others, certain that they would appreciate his query once they saw his point. The manner in which one is inclined to respond to himself is one of the cornerstones of his personality and is carried over from one context to another. If one is accustomed to subordination and is inclined toward self-abasement, he would not only not ask questions but would probably hesitate to ask a girl for a date even when she hints broadly at her availability. Nor would he fight back if shoved out of line in a crowded store. Thus, the exclusion, suppression, or dissociation of impulses that are incongruent with an individual's preferred self-conception provides another basis for consistency in overt conduct.

Each person attempts to guide his conduct in a deliberate effort to maintain an acceptable view of himself. Whenever a man does something about which he has misgivings, he tries to justify the action to himself. Why is it necessary to justify? He wants to be able to conceive of himself as reasonably decent in spite of what he has done. Most men continually fight temptations. Why? One frequently gives up things that he really wants and does things that he does not care to do; he tempers his greed—all in an effort to maintain some measure of self-respect. Behavior among human beings, like that of other living organisms, consists of a succession of adjustments to life conditions. But in the case of man each perceives his surroundings as well as himself from the standpoint of the group in which he is participating; he takes into account certain expectations that can be reasonably imputed to others. Furthermore, each person makes many sacrifices to live up to his estimate of himself; thus adjustment includes coming to terms with oneself. Men generally live up to group standards because these are the criteria that they set for themselves.

Serious personality disorders may arise among those who are unable to regard themselves in an acceptable manner. There are accounts of "squealers" in the underworld who lose their sanity or commit suicide, even when there is little danger of retaliation. Crimes that would otherwise never be solved are sometimes cleared up when the offender unexpectedly confesses. Almost invariably such persons profess a sense of relief after a long period of inner turmoil. They could no longer go on keeping the secret, deceiving those around them into thinking that they were something that they are not. This principle is well illustrated in cases of persons who engage in sexual perversions of one kind or other. Although it is generally agreed by medical authorities that most of the practices so labelled are not organically harmful unless carried on in excess, such parties frequently develop strong feelings of guilt and of inferiority. How can a man respect himself as long as he is engaging in a form of behavior that he himself regards as disgraceful? Even though no other human being may know about activities carried on in private, because each person views himself from a perspective shared with others he cannot work out a satisfactory relationship with himself.

The contention that persistent patterns of voluntary conduct often rest more upon the manner in which a man personifies himself than upon his somatic make-up is supported by observations from several sources, although the evidence is not entirely satisfactory. There is a widespread though mistaken belief that the behavioral and intellectual characteristics that are popularly attributed to each ethnic group are biologically inherited; they are frequently regarded as inexorable, and people who identify themselves as belonging in such groups often believe that these traits are a part of them by virtue of their ancestry. There are many Negroes in the United states who are so fair and have so many other Caucasoid features that they could easily "pass" into the general population. But as long as such persons conceive of themselves as Negroes, they live up to the obligations of the minority group, even when most strangers do not make invidious distinctions. They may have more European than African ancestors; but they are classified as they are only because of the conventional practice of designating anyone with a single Negro ancestor as "black." Biologically they are not Negroid, but they feel guilty whenever they take advantage of "mistaken" identity. Similarly, when a person who had always conceived of himself as "white" discovers that he is of "mixed" ancestry—that his parents had "passed" or that one of his forebears had been indiscreet—he becomes quite upset over his Negro "blood" and sometimes even feels obligated to act differently. Such inner conflicts rest not upon genetics but upon false beliefs about inheritance.[8]

Of particular interest is the study by Ellis of the erotic interests of persons whose sex is difficult to ascertain. Although all persons have the rudiments of the organs of the opposite sex, there are a small number, called hermaphrodites, in whom the organs of both sexes are developed to an unusual degree. There are still others,

[8] Cf. Georgene Seward, ed., *Clinical Studies in Culture Conflict* (New York: Ronald Press Co., 1958).

called pseudohermaphrodites, who can be classified biologically as male or female in terms of the development of their gonads but who nonetheless possess the external genitalia of both sexes. If the growth of erotic interests depends upon the secretion of hormones, it would follow that the choice of love objects should rest upon somatic structure, regardless of how the person may be reared by his parents. An extensive review of the medical literature reveals, however, that of those who were brought up as male 87 per cent established heterosexual attachments to women; the remainder apparently were not concerned with erotic objects. Of those reared as female 73 per cent were attracted by men, 11 percent were attracted by women, 7 per cent were bisexual, and 9 per cent apparently did not develop sexual interests. The evidence is overwhelming that regardless of the development of the gonads those whose genital organs make clearcut classification difficult assume the roles of the sex in which they are reared by their parents. Those who are brought up as boys learn to think in masculine terms, to acquire characteristically male interests and skills, and to select women as erotic objects.[9]

The relationship between behavior patterns and self-conceptions is also revealed in studies, made by Reckless and his associates, of sixth grade boys who live in the area which has the highest delinquency rate in Columbus, Ohio. Teachers were asked to select the boys they regarded as most likely to acquire police records in the future and those they viewed as most likely to stay out of trouble. In all, 125 boys were nominated as "good" and 108 as "bad." The subjects were then given four tests, and the contrast was remarkable. Among those rated as "good" there was a strong sense of responsibility. The boys viewed themselves as law-abiding and obedient, did not believe they would get into trouble, and had a well-developed sense of right and wrong. They indicated that they liked school and that their home life was satisfactory. On the whole their friends thought much as they did, and most of the parents questioned were reasonably pleased with their sons. Although only a few of these boys had ever run afoul of the law, of the 108 nominated as "bad," 23 per cent were already known to the police. Boys in this category made little effort to avoid trouble, regarded themselves as dis-

[9] Albert Ellis, "The Sexual Psychology of Human Hermaphrodites," *Psychosomatic Medicine*, VII (1945), 108–25.

obedient, and made no secret of the fact that they did not get along at home. Many of the parents indicated that they did not approve of the companions of their sons and confessed that they frequently did not know where the boys went or what they were doing.[10] What will happen to these boys remains to be seen, but it is apparent that their self-conceptions are already crystallizing and that their behavior in several contexts—at home, at school, and in the eyes of public officials—is quite consistent.

Since symbols are so frequently confused with the meanings they represent, it is not surprising that some persons feel obligated to live up to behavior patterns suggested by their name. Some symbols are used in a variety of contexts, representing somewhat different meanings in each, and they may develop connotations separate from any particular referent. Many personal names have such connotations. In the United States, for example, boys named Chauncey, Horace, Aloysius, Percy, or Cuthbert are expected to be somewhat effeminate. A girl who is nicknamed "Ginger" may feel constrained to appear gay and energetic even when she does not actually feel that way. A partial test of this contention is provided in a study by Jahoda of the naming of boys among the Ashanti in West Africa. It is commonly believed among these people that the kind of personality a man develops depends upon the day of the week on which he was born. Since children are also named by the day of their birth, there should be some relationship between names and behavior patterns. Most of the names are of little significance, but two are of special interest. Boys born on Monday are named Kwadwo and are supposed to be quiet, retiring, and peaceful. Those born on Wednesday are named Kwaku and expected to be quick-tempered, aggressive, and troublesome. That juvenile delinquents are born on Wednesday is a traditional belief; it is said that "a Kwaku would naturally be wild." A check of the police records from 1948 to 1951 revealed that the incidence of delinquency is very low for boys born on Monday. Although the figures are not as high as expected for those born on Wednesday when all forms of delinquency are considered together, they are unusually high when corrected to include

[10] Walter C. Reckless et al., "Self Concept as an Insulator against Delinquency," *American Sociological Review*, XXI (1956), 744–46; and "The Self Component in Potential Delinquency and Potential non-Delinquency," *ibid.*, XXII (1957), 566–70.

only crimes of violence and offenses against persons.[11] These data suggest, then, that names may symbolize models of conduct and that some persons make an effort to live up to such expectations.

The relationship between self-conceptions and voluntary conduct is thrown into sharp relief in the lives of people who find themselves in a drastically different culture. When a man migrates to a foreign country, when one joins an esoteric religious or political cult, when one is unusually successful and enhances his status at a rapid pace, or when one moves from a small town to a huge metropolis, all kinds of demands are made upon him which are at first entirely strange. Some people change, so much so that their old friends have difficulty in recognizing them, but others remain much as they have always been. Some immigrants are known to live in their adopted country for over 50 years without altering their behavior patterns, other than making a few concessions on matters that are required by law. This is particularly true of immigrants who do not intend to stay and who regard the new country merely as a source of income. Such persons apparently never cease to regard themselves from the standpoint of their community of origin.[12] The same is true of most missionaries, anthropologists, and traders who leave their homes primarily to do a job. On the other hand, those who migrate with the intention of making new lives as part of another nation attempt to alter their self-conceptions. They sometimes give up practices they had treasured in the past in order to conform more closely to the customs of the new country. In neither case do drastic changes occur in the organic make-up of the person; whether or not new behavior patterns emerge depends upon the extent to which self-conceptions are transformed.

There are other contexts in which patterns of conduct are altered following a change in self-conceptions. A man who had doubts about his ability may be cast inadvertently into the role of a leader; he is amazed and delighted to see that others follow him and may reevaluate himself to the point of assuming increasing responsibility. Another person suffering from an acute sense of inferiority may win the hand of a beautiful girl and win eminence in his work; once he

[11] G. Jahoda, "A Note on Ashanti Names and Their Relation to Personality," *British Journal of Psychology*, XLV (1954), 192–95.

[12] Cf. Paul C. P. Siu, "The Sojourner," *American Journal of Sociology*, LVIII (1952), 34–44.

becomes accustomed to being addressed with deference, he may alter some of his habits. A juvenile delinquent becomes the father of a baby girl and for the first time considers the possibility of others like himself preying upon his daughter; he reevaluates his own activities, develops a new outlook, and thereafter develops a different orientation toward women in general. Cases of more spectacular transformations are reported in a study of the Chuckchee shaman, some of whom persuade themselves that they are of the opposite sex. When a young man is transformed into a "soft man" in response to a call of the "spirits," he initially impersonates a woman only in the manner of braiding and arranging the hair. Then he adopts female dress. Finally, he leaves off all the pursuits and manners of men and takes up those of women. He throws away his rifle and lance, the lasso of the reindeer herdsman, and the harpoon of the seal-hunter and takes to the needle and the skin-scraper. He learns their use quickly because the "spirits" are helping him. Even his speech changes from the male to female mode. His body does not change in its outward appearance, but he loses his strength, speed, and endurance and acquires instead the conventional helplessness of a woman. He loses his courage and fighting spirit; he becomes shy of strangers and fond of small talk and of nursing small children. In the end he becomes a woman with the body of a man.[13]

In an attempt to test this relationship more systematically, Benjamins asked a group of high school students to rank themselves in mental aptitude and four other characteristics and then administered an intelligence test. He then announced false reports on their performance and asked them to reevaluate themselves; after that he administered an alternative form of the same intelligence test. He also asked questions in an effort to ascertain which subjects had accepted the false scores and which were defiant and retained their old estimate of their ability. On the basis of the data on changes in self-rating he attempted to predict for each student whether the performance in the second test would be better or worse than the first attempt and was able to anticipate the changes correctly in 74 per cent of the cases.[14] Even in the case of a minor alteration in overt

[13] Vladimir G. Bogoraz, "The Chuckchee," *Memoirs of the American Museum of Natural History*, XI (1907), 448–57.

[14] James Benjamins, "Changes in Performance in Relation to Influences upon Self-Conceptualization," *Journal of Abnormal and Social Psychology*, XLV (1950), 473–80.

behavior following a single incident, the transformations reflect changes in what the person means to himself.

Even the emergence of new behavior patterns seemingly resulting from brain surgery turn out upon examination to involve a transformation of self-conceptions. Pre-frontal lobotomy, one of the most controversial therapeutic measures currently in use, consists of the surgical interruption of the neural pathways linking the thalamus to parts of the frontal lobes. The operation has been roundly condemned because failure sometimes transforms a psychotic patient into a helpless "vegetable." When the surgery is successful, however, patients sometimes experience relief from severe tensions; their delusions disappear; and intractable pain may be abated. But in many cases the patients also become tactless, irresponsible, and engage in boisterous laughter; these traits have developed so frequently that the combination has been called the "lobotomy syndrome." Furthermore, after recovery the patients seem to lack ambition and become unconcerned over possibilities of failure. Several observers have noted that one of the most profound changes takes place in the patient's conception of himself. There is apparently little or no temporal extension; those who have recovered from these operations seem to live in the "perpetual present." Some even deny having had the operation and insist that they have not changed. Many do not appear to be interested in themselves as distinct persons; they seem to be detached from themselves. Therefore, it has been suggested that the relief experienced arises from the fact that the patient has been cut off from his tortured self-conception of the past and thereby finds the present more acceptable. To test this hypothesis Robinson attempted to measure differences in the sense of self-continuity in lobotomized patients in comparison with a control group of persons who recovered from similar mental disorders without the operation. In general her findings confirm the hypothesis; indeed, she found that the more radical the surgery, the greater the reduction of the sense of continuity.[15]

Studies of plastic surgery are also enlightening. The appearance of one's body, and especially of the face, is important not only because it constitutes a stable basis of reference but also because it is

[15] Mary F. Robinson and Walter Freeman, *Psychosurgery and the Self* (New York: Grune & Stratton, 1954).

one of the foundations of the level of self-esteem. Those who have conspicuous deformities are ridiculed, called unflattering nicknames, and sometimes even mistreated as deviants. In many cases they conceive of themselves as freaks, for everywhere they go they are treated differently from others. They become preoccupied with their deformity, and they go about expecting negative responses—surprise, pity, curiosity, repulsion, but seldom acceptance on the same basis as other people. It is believed that some juvenile delinquents develop resentment and bitterness because of ugliness or some physical defect that they cannot accept. In a society that places as high a premium upon outward appearance as ours, this seems quite plausible. After plastic surgery and the successful removal of the deformity, remarkable changes in behavior patterns sometimes occur. What these people first notice is the change in the reactions of others; they are no longer stared at in dismay. Soon they become less withdrawn, less frightened of people. They also develop new joys, such as dressing up, when heretofore they had been uninterested in clothing. In some cases the transformations are so drastic that they seem like entirely different persons. But there are other cases in which relatively few changes take place, even when the surgery has been successful. Although the evidence is not clearcut, the hypothesis may be proposed that successful plastic surgery does not result in a transformation of behavior patterns unless there is a corresponding change in self-conceptions.[16]

Each person is capable of some measure of independent action, and this makes possible reasonable consistency in his behavior in spite of the fact that his environment is constantly changing. In spite of the variations in the demands which are made upon him he can act consistently as long as his self-conception remains relatively stable. By living up to the obligations that he assumes by virtue of the manner in which he identifies himself each person acts in a characteristic way in a variety of contexts. Of course, autonomous behavior is sometimes challenged by others, and individuals differ considerably in the extent to which they can continue to act as they believe they should even in the face of opposition.

[16] Frances C. MacGregor, et al., Facial Deformities and Plastic Surgery (Springfield: Charles C. Thomas, 1953). Cf. Adolph A. Apton, Your Mind and Appearance (New York: Citadel Press, 1951); and Maxwell Maltz, Doctor Pygmalion (New York: Thomas Y. Crowell Co., 1953).

The Preservation of Social Status

Most of the meanings that serve as the basis for cooperative activities enjoy some measure of consensus, and this is true of self-conceptions. Although a man's conception of himself is not a replication of what he actually is, neither is it a mere figment of his imagination. Like, other meanings, these personifications are subject to reality testing, becoming progressively more adequate through the corrective responses of other people.

Each person is inextricably involved in a complex web of social relationships, and his position within a social system constitutes his status. He locates himself within the larger community; he places himself into a category, assumes the responsibilities of that position, and expects others to respect his rights. Thus, *much of the behavior of man consists of acting in a manner designed to preserve or enhance his social status.* No matter how lowly a man's position in society, there are obligations that he must meet and rights that he can demand. The duties in terms of which a given position is defined come to be regarded as personal responsibilities, and one feels a sense of personal obligation to fulfil these requirements.

There are many people who make great sacrifices to live up to what they regard to be the responsibilities of their station in life. There are women, for example, who do not particularly care for children but feel that it is the duty of all married people to have them, especially if they have the income and education to provide a "good" home. For centuries, until the practice was abolished by the British, widows in India were expected to join their dead husbands on the funeral pyre. Though a woman may have hated her husband, this was her duty. This sense of responsibility is especially noticeable among those in well-established elite groups, who are taught from childhood that they must sacrifice some of their personal desires to live up to the requirements of their privileged position. Aristocrats as well as proper Bostonians must sometimes forego their passionate infatuations, suppress their vulgar tastes, control their anger in public, treat their subordinates with consideration, attend social affairs that they find deadly, and contribute generously to charitable causes—all to impress others of their superiority. *Noblesse oblige* in a more temperate form is found even in communities that are not so rigidly stratified. A study by Brown of differential participation in various voluntary associations in a rural community revealed that the better educated and the professional, business, and white collar workers in higher income brackets were more active than the others. These people were actually no more eager to participate, but many of them regarded it as their obligation to do so. Furthermore, the other people also expected such persons to take an active part in directing the affairs of their community.[17]

Since status is a social process, a given individual's position in a community can be ascertained only in terms of a network of well-defined relationships between himself and those occupying other positions. By virtue of who he is and the standing he is acknowledged to have, a person is related to certain other people in understood ways. It follows that the preservation of status consists of conducting oneself in such a manner as to insure the continuation of relationships that already exist, of being able to expect the same kind of treatment in the future that he has enjoyed in the past. Those attempting to enhance their status are seeking even more favorable responses. It is in this sense that sociologists speak of society as consisting of a network of reciprocal claims and obligations.[18]

Even those who fail to live up to their obligations go to considerable trouble to avoid unfavorable reactions, and Sullivan has emphasized that the type of discomfort called "anxiety" is aroused when there is a danger of losing the support of other people.[19] Blackmailing is a profitable enterprise precisely because a person who has been engaged secretly in some proscribed activity is willing to pay large sums of money, or make other sacrifices, in order to maintain his standing in his community. Assuming that the respect he is usually accorded would not be forthcoming were his offense generally known, the culprit takes steps to guarantee the continued flow of desired responses. Even when an offender is confronted or being censured, he tries to protect himself from the negative reactions that he feels he deserves. A person who has been caught doing something

---

[17] Emory J. Brown, "The Self as Related to Formal Participation in Three Pennsylvania Rural Communities," *Rural Sociology*, XVIII (1953), 313–20.

[18] Cf. Erving Goffman, "The Nature of Deference and Demeanor," *American Anthropologist*, LVIII (1956), 473–502.

[19] Harry S. Sullivan, "The Meaning of Anxiety in Psychiatry and in Life," *Psychiatry*, XI (1948), 1–13; and *The Interpersonal Theory of Psychiatry*, ed. H. S. Perry and M. L. Gawel (New York: W. W. Norton & Co., 1953), pp. 8–12, 113–14, 300–304.

of which he is deeply ashamed hides his face. Even when it is obvious that the stares of others are unavoidable, he does his best to avoid the eyes of those he knows and respects. He infers that they disapprove of his conduct, and this is painful enough without having his inference confirmed by the glare in their eyes. For human beings, then, self-preservation includes keeping up one's reputation in the eyes of others.

Although all men make sacrifices to protect their status, only a few are responsive to the expectations of everyone else. For each person there are a limited number of others whose views are deemed important. Each man performs for some kind of an audience; and it is important to ascertain in every instance *whose* reactions are taken into account, especially in modern industrial societies in which so many social worlds emerge because of the ease with which communication channels can be established. Those in an elite group are not concerned if "peasants" disagree with them. Members of ethnic minorities sometimes violate their group standards until someone else with whom they identify on the basis of common ancestry appears on the scene; then, they suddenly feel the pressure to conform. People are selectively responsive primarily to the reactions of those who are included in their reference group, for they seek to maintain their position largely in their eyes. Self-conceptions are constantly subjected to reality testing, and the confirming responses of others provide the necessary support. These personifications must be reinforced by someone, but not necessarily by everyone.

The status ladder in each social world is different, and what makes human behavior so difficult to understand in pluralistic societies like ours is the fact that there are so many reference groups and such a diversity of career lines. A great scientist, internationally esteemed in his field of specialization, is likely to go unnoticed at a cocktail party given in the honor of a fashion designer. A stamp collector may acquire a copy of every stamp ever issued in a given country, but his achievement would be appreciated only by other philatelists. Thus, a man who reaches the pinnacle of success in one social world is not even recognized in another. The arena within which an individual has status and within which he seeks to carve out a worthwhile career is bounded by the limits of effective communication.

The kinds of achievements sought by the inordinately ambitious can be understood only within such delimited cultural contexts. Men in each social world aspire toward goals that outsiders have difficulty in comprehending. They prepare themselves for years and give up comforts that are readily within their reach in order to achieve aims that others do not find worthwhile. Some men want to run a mile in less than four minutes; others long to climb to the summit of Mount Everest; others aspire to hit more than sixty home runs in a single season; others covet a beautiful figure to be pictured on magazine covers; others dream of becoming the first man to reach the moon; and others wish to become the most dreaded gangster in the land. All such persons are dedicated to tasks that they regard as worthwhile, but even their friends sometimes have difficulty in taking their roles. Should such a person succeed, however, he knows that the participants in his social world appreciate his efforts; should he fail, he admires others who did not, in a way that those who have not tried would never understand.

The symbols of achievement that people seek and sometimes flaunt also differ from group to group. In some circles attendance at the opening night of the opera, dressed in the latest Paris creation, is important; and those who cannot stand the music eagerly look forward to the event. In other groups labels on clothing are indicators of success, but there are many people who do not even know that their clothing bears such inscriptions. In some younger sets the number of dates a girl can have with boys of desirable social standing is of crucial importance; the personal characteristics of the people dated become secondary. The ownership of a German camera, a Swiss watch, an English bicycle, or an American fountain pen is of importance among upwardly mobile people in areas just undergoing industrialization. Such objects may be purchased even by those who have no occasion to use them, merely to indicate that they are keeping up with the times. Among nurses invidious distinctions are sometimes made on the basis of the reputation of the school in which one has been trained. Each school is symbolized by a distinctive cap, and those who have graduated from highly rated institutions wear their headgear with pride. To those who are outside these social worlds such symbols are meaningless. Many wonder why anyone would take the trouble to purchase useless objects, wear uncomfortable clothing, or put up with disagreeable people. Most patients cannot tell one nurse's cap from another, and the various types of haircuts among boys who live in slum areas are usually of significance to no one but those who wear them and to their friends.

Men are primarily responsive to the judgments of those who constitute their reference groups. One gains a sense of personal identity by locating himself within a meaningful social world, and he seeks recognition within this web of social relationships. He becomes concerned with the expectations and responses of those who share his outlook; will these people approve and support him or be angered and repulsed by his acts? In the reaffirmation of self-conceptions it is the responses of those with whom one identifies that count. Each person seeks recognition in *his* world; he tries to maintain an acceptable conception of himself in the eyes of those for whose opinions he cares. This world comprises everything that is immediately familiar. The Polish peasant at the turn of the century, for example, lived in a world bounded by the *okolika*—the area within which an individual is known well enough to be the subject of gossip, should he misbehave.[20] In modern mass societies, of course, many reference groups are extended in space and time and may include large numbers of total strangers.

This does not mean that men are completely insensitive to people outside their reference groups, but there seems to be a graduated scale of responsiveness. To some extent the mere presence of another human being, even a complete stranger, makes a difference. Furthermore, in most enterprises there are several categories of people who may become involved and whose possible reactions must be taken into account. There are, of course, the direct participants. But in addition there is often a public, consisting of people who may be affected by the consequences of the activity and are sufficiently concerned with the outcome to direct attention to it. Such on-lookers sometimes intercede, if the course of events moves in directions that they deem undesirable.[21] People in underprivileged groups are usually quite sensitive to the reactions of those in positions of power, for a single act that creates an unfavorable im-

[20] Robert E. Park and Herbert A. Miller, *Old World Traits Transplanted* (New York: Harper & Bros., 1921), p. 145.
[21] Cf. John Dewey, *The Public and Its Problems* (New York: Henry Holt & Co., 1927).

pression may reflect adversely upon the entire group. Since the fate of people in some minorities is tied together, each becomes aware of the fact that the other members of the group are watching him to be sure that he does not in any way invite trouble.

Since most people in pluralistic societies participate simultaneously in more than one reference group, the picture becomes more complicated. Each individual has a somewhat different position in each social world. A man who is the grand master of a lodge may be insignificant in his place of employment. Similarly, the captain of a football team may be viewed with contempt in other circles. Life therefore tends to become compartmentalized, and role-playing goes on in a succession of organized contexts. As his line of activity takes shape, each person is in turn sensitive to the other participants with whom he is cooperating at the time. There is a successive displacement of audiences.

This suggests further difficulties that are encountered in the analysis of human behavior, especially in modern industrial societies. A given pattern of conduct may develop its structure in a variety of contexts and have different meanings for different actors. Thus, deeds that are phenomenally similar may turn out to be generically quite different. We may take as examples cases of excessive smoking and the wearing of long, "ducktail" haircuts. A person may smoke for the enjoyable sensation and the feeling that he gets much needed stimulation; he may smoke to utilize one of the symbols of defiance in his reference group; or he may find smoking compulsive and impossible to stop. A young man may wear his hair in a particular way because he believes it enhances his best physical features; on the other hand, it may be one of the identification symbols of his gang. To understand what any man does it is essential to see the world as he experiences it. Only then can one appreciate the alternatives and pressures confronting him.

The contention that people do many of the things that they do in an effort to maintain or enhance their status within a delimited context can be tested to some extent by observing changes in their behavior either when their status within a reference group is modified or when reference groups are displaced. Especially when a man disowns one group and joins another that claims his total loyalty— as in joining a religious or political cult—he becomes a participant in a different social world, views his conduct from a different perspective, and forms a conception of himself from a new standpoint. His overt behavior may be altered so drastically that even his parents and childhood friends find it difficult to recognize him.

Each person acts for some kind of audience. He tries to maintain or enhance his status in some kind of reference group, and his voluntary conduct is difficult to understand without identifying this group. Each views his surroundings from a distinct frame of reference, usually a unique combination of reference groups; therefore, his definition of a situation may differ considerably from that of another man standing next to him. Each has to feel that he is doing something worthwhile, but what is regarded as having merit varies with the standards of judgment that he uses. The unit may be his gang or coterie of intimate friends; it may constitute the community in which he lives; it may include the whole world; or it may conceivably include all humanity, stretching out over thousands of years and including "posterity." Thus, much of his voluntary conduct depends upon his conception of his social status, as seen from the standpoint of his audience.

The Internalization of Social Control

Each normal adult may be regarded as a society in miniature. His personal outlook in large measure coincides with the perspectives of others in his reference group; hence, he views himself and what he is about to do from this common standpoint. Men set much the same standards of conduct for themselves that they set for others with whom they associate. Thus, self-control is essentially social control in that each individual restrains himself by evaluating his projected line of action in terms of the group norms that he has incorporated as his own.

Unlike many other living creatures, man is relatively free of his immediate environment. Because of his imagination he is not a slave to external stimulation; he is able to construct a substitute world which is extended in time and space. Each person has a unique orientation toward his surroundings, but it is organized largely in terms of the linguistic symbols he learns in his group. He perceives most objects in terms of social categories and cannot comprehend sensory cues that fall outside the premises of his reference group. Even his feelings are classified and labelled, in spite of the fact that emotional reactions are often difficult to differentiate from each other. Memory and foresight are private in that other people do not have access to them, but these cognitive processes take place largely in terms of public symbols. Of course, there are individual differences in the extent to which one's outlook is socialized; those who are psychotic live in a world which is quite unique.

The social process consists of the coordinated activities of a multitude of self-regulating persons who share a common conception of reality. Self-control may be viewed as the internalization of this larger process, the appearance in the experience of each participant of that part of the social structure in which he is participating—his conventional role. The act of controlling oneself is itself a part of the on-going social current; for as each individual adjusts in advance to the situation in which he is involved and reacts upon it, he makes more complex forms of cooperation possible. Precisely because each participant has incorporated into his own perspective the expectations of the others he is able to anticipate their responses and adjust to them in advance. The carrying out of such reactions to self-images on the part of all participants in a joint undertaking is what constitutes human society.[22]

Since the freedom of individuals to develop their distinctive interests without the interference of authorities is a cherished value in the United States, any mention of "control" quite understandably arouses anxieties. When sociologists speak of social control, however, they are in no way opposing freedom. Indeed, the opposite of social control is not freedom, but anarchy. Freedom is always linked with responsibility. Men can be free to the extent that each accepts the responsibility of maintaining minimum standards of equitable association. What are called "rights" are socially sanctioned alternatives from which properly qualified persons can make selections without undue pressure. If each man pursued his selfish interests without restraint, there would be little cooperation, and before long each community would become a jungle. Each person checks his impulses in conformity with group norms, and it is precisely because there is an organized society that he has the opportunities he enjoys to make selections.

Although society is often viewed as a restraining agency and sometimes even as a villain responsible for mental disorders, the

[22] Mead, *Mind, Self, and Society, op. cit.,* pp. 178–92.

more socialized a man becomes the more possible it is for him to exercise choice. Any impulse that is not controlled in some way— whether it be an appetite for knowledge, prestige, power, sex, or wealth—tends to become a tyrant. To the extent that an individual becomes enslaved by any of his impulses, he loses his freedom. Without restraints of some kind he has no occasions for making selections. Those who constantly indulge themselves often feel helpless—as if they were victims of some external force.

As paradoxical as this may sound, a man feels most free when his inner discipline is best developed. He then believes that he is the responsible agent, that he is making up his own mind, that he is doing what he wants to do.[23] Once an individual has incorporated the values shared in his group they no longer appear to him as limitations against which he is opposed, although in some instances this may be the case. The socially approved alternatives are usually the only images that are evoked. In general, men act in accordance with group norms, not from a fear of punishment but from an intuitive sense of what is right.

In some *avant-garde* circles it becomes fashionable from time to time to assail the "conformity" of the middle classes, insisting that creativity can occur only under circumstances in which individualism is encouraged. Although it is true that highly original men often have difficulty in winning acceptance of their innovations, much of the complaining is done by people seeking status in a special reference group. People who take great pride in being "uncommon" generally do not realize the extent to which they themselves are living up to the expectations of their associates. The regularity with which such persons appear in open-toed sandals, dress with a studied informality, express interest in esoteric foods, strain to remain *au courant* in literature and art, are preoccupied with psychiatry, and express hostility against organized religion suggests that the assault on "conformity" is itself a case of conformity. Everyone—from the most extreme individualist to the most extreme conformist—finds himself in situations in which he must comply with group norms as well as those in which he must depend upon his own resources.

[23] Cf. Emile Durkheim, *Sociology and Philosophy*, D. F. Pocock, trans. (Glencoe: Free Press, 1953).

Summary and Conclusion

In the drama of life, as in the theater, everyone performs for some kind of audience. In a small community the observers are easy enough to find; but in our complex, pluralistic society the people in whose eyes a person seeks to preserve and enhance his status are not so apparent. Much depends upon the communication channels in which he regularly participates. Voluntary conduct gets its direction from the efforts of men to form a conception of themselves as decent human beings; they try not to do things of which they would be ashamed. They seek confirmation for such personifications from those whose views they deem important, reinforcement that consists of their continuing to be treated in an acceptable manner. In dealing with the problem of motivation, then, it becomes necessary to take into account the fact that men must cope with themselves as well as with their environment. The comprehension of what a man does requires a record of (1) his definition of the situation, (2) the kind of creature he believes himself to be, and (3) the audience before which he tries to maintain his self-respect.

But standards of conduct, as well as the categories in terms of which behavior is explained, vary from group to group; and misunderstandings are bound to arise in communities in which people with different reference groups come together and interact. The reluctance of so many professional people to participate more actively in unions arises in part from their conception of their calling. A profession is not just a way of earning a living; it is a way of rendering a vital service to the community. Professional men usually do not see their interests as being opposed to those of management, and where there are recognized differences it is often assumed that these can be resolved through rational discussion. Within the world of business, men win prestige by maximizing their profits. Whether or not they actually need the money is a secondary consideration; it may subsequently be given away. Reluctance to pay taxes is only a part of a complex ideology in which any inconvenient governmental regulation is assailed as a step toward socialism. Outsiders who are unaware of the distinctive values shared within such reference groups may misinterpret the deeds of men who are acting in good faith, doing their best to cope with the world as they see it.

280   MOTIVATION

Suggested References

COHEN, ALBERT K., *Delinquent Boys: The Culture of the Gang.* Glencoe: Free Press, 1955. An attempt to account for juvenile delinquency in terms of the formation of reference groups of adolescents whose standards of conduct differ from those of middle class families.

DURKHEIM, EMILE, *Sociology and Philosophy*, D. F. Pocock, trans. Glencoe: Free Press, 1953. Essays by an eminent sociologist arguing that there is no real opposition between an individual and the society in which he lives, since personal inclinations constitute manifestations of group patterns.

GOFFMAN, ERVING, *The Presentation of Self in Everyday Life.* New York: Doubleday & Co., 1959. An insightful discussion of the various techniques that are used to project and maintain desired self-conceptions and of the customary procedures that facilitate such practices.

LYND, HELEN M., *On Shame and the Search for Identity.* New York: Harcourt, Brace & Co., 1958. A study of shame as the starting point for an analysis of the manner in which men identify themselves, with critical comments on the adequacy of current approaches to social psychology.

MACGREGOR, FRANCES C., THEODORA M. ABEL, ALBERT BRYT, EDITH LAUER, and SERENA WEISSMANN, *Facial Deformities and Plastic Surgery.* Springfield: Charles C. Thomas, 1953. Studies of changes in self-conceptions and behavior patterns following plastic surgery, including cases in which new and unexpected difficulties developed.

MERTON, ROBERT K., *Social Theory and Social Structure*, pp. 225–386, 439–508. Glencoe: Free Press, 1957. A critical assessment of the literature on reference groups and in the sociology of knowledge, with an attempt to point out areas requiring further research.

9

Personal
autonomy
and
social
control

The widespread practice of leaving "tips" has been called a form of taxation that no legislature would dare impose. Since at one time it implied condescension, a largesse thrown to a serf by a master, it has been condemned as being out of place in a democratic society. Labor leaders like Samuel Gompers have charged that accepting a tip is like taking a bribe for services which should have been rendered cheerfully and paid for with decent wages. But employers who have raised wages and abolished tipping have found their signs against the practice flagrantly violated. Customers also complain, but the practice has continued to grow. Not only waiters, bellhops, and taxicab drivers, but parking-lot attendants, furniture movers, men installing television sets, butchers, and even hospital attendants have also come to expect tips as a matter of course. Considering the widespread resentment that is aroused by this practice, how is this growth to be explained? The rationale that it insures better service is unconvincing, for tips are not given until after the service has been rendered, and it frequently occurs in situations in which the customer is unlikely ever to enter the establishment again. There is no law requiring a man to leave a tip. In many cases he will not profit from it, and in some cases it may even involve some personal sacrifice. Yet, he feels that he should leave a tip, and nearly always does. This is a good example of what is meant by social control.

Although there are some people who claim to be subject to the will of God or directed by the spirits of their ancestors, only a few Americans regard themselves as passive agents molded from without. Indeed, the presumed capacity for independent action has not only become embedded in the philosophical doctrine of "free will" but has even been incorporated into political institutions guaranteeing the rights of individuals, under stated circumstances, to make their own decisions. In some states a man married while intoxicated may sue for an annulment on the grounds that he did not exerci.e free choice. No matter how heinous the crime being investigated, lie detector tests can be used by the police only with the consent of those being interrogated. The use of mechanical devices that may lead a person inadvertently to reveal inner experiences that he desires to conceal is regarded as an invasion of privacy. Personal autonomy is highly treasured, and the possibility of losing such control arouses fear and resentment. The opposition to the "brain washing" techniques allegedly used by the Chinese Communists arises in part from horror at the thought of a human being becoming a puppet. Most people feel ill at ease even at the thought of being hypnotized; they are apprehensive lest they be forced or tricked into doing something that is contrary to their interests.

The fact that men feel a sense of responsibility and are willing to be held accountable for their deeds indicates that they believe that they can control themselves. Even in totalitarian states each person takes it for granted that he exercises some measure of autonomy, even though the range of choices may be limited. Regardless of their religious, political, or philosophical views, in daily life men act as if they were separate entities with control over their own activities. But the fact that men are under the impression that they are free to do as they wish does not necessarily mean that this is actually the case. In point of fact, their activities are circumscribed by a variety of social obligations—as in the case of leaving tips. This does not mean, however, that men are mere automatons stamped with the imprint of society, nothing more than individual aspects of organized wholes. Each person is capable of some measure of independent action. Unfortunately the question of the relative importance of the individual and the group has been the source of acrimonious debate among social psychologists. Rather than argue the merits of the alternative approaches, attention may be directed toward ascertaining the conditions under which each position is more fruitful. Under what circumstances does the normative framework of groups set drastic limitations upon what the participating individuals can do? Under what circumstances may men express their personal inclinations so that the course of events depends largely upon who happens to be present and what kind of people they are?

The Person as a Functional Unit

At one time or other almost everyone has raised questions concerning what he "really" is. Am I doing the kind of work for which I am suited? Am I married to a person who matches me? Am I living in a place that is congenial to my nature? We sometimes raise similar questions about other people we know. Such queries imply that each individual has some kind of inherent nature—something that makes him different from all others. Behind the conventional façade that everyone maintains there is presumably a distinct human being, one marked by a definite set of characteristics.

Although the things that men do are inextricably involved in a social matrix, it is useful in the study of many events to view each of the participants as a unit. Each person does retain some measure of independence, for he is not just a robot meekly obeying the dictates of society. If each individual were nothing more than the reflection of the culture of his group, then all the members of each group should be alike; this is obviously not the case. The person and the social group may best be regarded as separate functional units. The death of a man does not necessarily result in the termination of a social pattern, nor does the disintegration of a group necessarily mean the death of all its participants. A social group is a system of coordinated action, aspects of which are made up of the contributions of various persons; and each person is a separate system consisting of the various meanings that make up his personality. All men live in association with other men, acting and reacting upon one another, but in some respects each man is by himself. As Aldous Huxley noted, martyrs may go hand in hand into the arena, but each one is crucified alone.

In speaking of the person as a unit there is a natural inclination to think of the human body. To be sure, there is an organic unit, generally believed to be enclosed within the skin, which is relatively easy to identify. However, interest here does not center upon organisms, but upon units of activity. Each person is to be identified in terms of *his characteristic tendencies to act,* by his *personality.* Thus, a ventriloquist like Edgar Bergen can speak meaningfully of Charlie McCarthy as having a personality, for anyone familiar with the antics of this wooden dummy can readily recognize a typical set of interests and behavior patterns. The unusual cases of multiple personality, such as the one depicted in *The Three Faces of Eve,* are instructive; there is only a single organism which in turn assumes different, often contrasting, ways of approaching the world.[1] Furthermore, when a close friend loses his temper and starts throwing things about, we make excuses for his hysterical outburst by declaring that "he is not himself today." No one is suggesting that he has acquired a new body, only that he is, so to speak, temporarily "out of character." He is not acting in a manner that is typical of him.

Furthermore, each person is unique; there is no one else that is exactly like him. He is, as a person, irreplaceable and unrepeatable. Some social psychologists have asked whether anything so unique can be studied in terms of abstract concepts and whether generalizations can ever be formed. But individuality does not imply that the person cannot be analyzed; it implies only that each man possesses certain properties which are not duplicated elsewhere in this particular way. A man's personality is a synthetic and emergent property with a structure and composition which, because of its complexity and variety, is not likely ever to recur. Everything in nature is unique, but this has not prevented the development of scientific knowledge in other fields.

There is considerable consistency in a given person's conduct in a wide variety of contexts, for each man is marked by a characteristic bent. The behavior of a friend can be predicted with considerable

[1] Corbett H. Thigpen and Hervey M. Cleckley, *The Three Faces of Eve* (New York: McGraw-Hill Book Co., 1957).

accuracy, not because we know exactly what he will do but because we can anticipate the general direction in which he is likely to move whenever it is unnecessary for him to inhibit and redirect his impulses. Some people can approach dangerous tasks with equanimity, but others become so hysterical that they upset everyone else. Some consistently blame others for everything that goes wrong, but others typically examine their own deeds for mistakes they may have made. Each person, then, is not a chance combination of elements but *an organized system of meanings*. Since meanings tend to be self-sustaining, each person is constantly striving to move in certain directions. Although most of the meanings that make up a person's orientation toward his world are conventional, they are not necessarily alike. Meanings are products of experience, and insofar as each person's background is different, it is inevitable that his outlook will be unique.

Our actual experiences with many objects are direct, and what is immediately experienced cannot be communicated to others in all its detail. Each man's experience is necessarily unique, for it is inevitably imbedded in the distinct background of that person. All linguistic symbols refer to categories, and unless something can be described explicitly through symbols it cannot be accurately communicated. Thus, knowledge that is shared is largely categorized. In order to abstract out the common properties designated by a symbol one must remove himself from direct perception, ignoring those features of his experience which are not part of the conventional meaning. But there is much in life that cannot easily be categorized. A beautiful sunset may be experienced in terms of its sweeping grandeur and take on a meaning that cannot be stated in symbolic terms. One might describe his experience of a flower in terms of exquisite coloring and fragrance, but such terms are only vague descriptions. Poets of necessity use metaphors and analogies. To some extent, each man lives in a private world in that the peculiar qualities of his experiences are probably not repeated, at least not with the nuances with which he is familiar.[2]

Even when dealing with conventional meanings over which there is a high degree of consensus there are individual variations in approach. For example, most Americans know enough about baseball

[2] Cf. David Smillie, "Truth and Reality from Two Points of View," in *The Self: Explorations in Personal Growth,* Clark Moustakas, ed. (New York: Harper & Bros., 1956), pp. 98–108; and Nicolas Berdyaev, *Solitude and Society,* George Reavey, trans. (London: The Centenary Press, 1938), pp. 110–11.

to be able to recognize the game when they see it, but there are vast differences in its significance. For some it is an exciting spectacle to be observed; for others it is a contest between highly skilled artists and technicians; for others it is a source of prestige and monetary gain; and for other people it is a game that they enjoy playing with their friends. There are people who react strongly against those who drive a Cadillac or against a particular style of clothing. A man who is deeply ashamed of the fact that he was at one time very snobbish may become upset upon noting any trace of an affectation by anyone. These observations suggest that stylistic variations sometimes arise from differences in personal evaluations of common objects. In most cases the differences are not so great as to impede concerted action.

One fruitful source of illustrations of the range of individual variations in conventional meanings is the area of sex symbolism and erotic attraction. Except in unusual instances in which people are under so much tension as to be responsive to anyone of the opposite sex there are definite preferences. Erotic attraction is selective, and different people are excited by different attributes. A man may be aroused upon seeing a woman with curly black hair, a crooked smile, breasts of a certain contour, a particular rhythm in walking, or perhaps even by certain odors. Although most men probably cannot isolate the precise qualities which excite them, many such aphrodisiacs are widely recognized, defined, and subject to considerable discussion. Indeed, the swivel in the feminine walk is actually taught in schools for models and aspiring actresses. Some men find this standardized walking gait exciting; others regard it as graceful; others view it as offensive or disgusting; and still others find it comical. It is not strange, therefore, that different men are attracted to different women.

In addition to such stylistic variations, however, there are apparently a number of meanings which are purely idiosyncratic. Psychiatrists have been especially concerned with such private meanings, since they are often the sources of disturbances in interpersonal relations. They believe that there are many meanings, which involve seemingly irrational guilt or fear, which are organized during infancy, perhaps when the child is confronted by some strange and incomprehensible object or event. Later in life when there is a repetition of this situation or something reminiscent of it, the horrifying experience recurs, and the person has an unaccountable impulse to flee or to scream in terror. Some psychiatrists have also contended that personal problems such as excessive eating, the inflicting of injury upon oneself, cruelty to defenseless animals and persons, or the stealing of things one does not need can frequently be traced to such unusual meanings. Boss reports the case of a wealthy woman who had intense orgasms while engaging in petty theft. After each social gathering at her home she would slip into the kitchen to steal the tips left by her guests for the maids. She would clutch the coins and feverishly dig her nails into them; in a few seconds the excitement would be over, enabling her to regain her composure and to sneak undetected out of the kitchen. A number of cases have been reported of men who remain impotent unless they come into contact with any of a variety of objects not usually associated with erotic activity, such as leather shoes, fur wraps, gloves, or feces. For such men, ordinary contact with female genitals is not only unexciting but may even be repulsive. Fetishes, as such objects are called, are private meanings, meanings which are not shared with others. It has been suggested that in such meanings may lie the key to strange infatuations and marriages that astonish everyone who knows the pair; it is possible that the man in question finds beautiful hands irresistible and is relatively unresponsive to other attributes.[3]

The fact that many meanings do not enjoy consensus, however, does not imply that one's activity is not subject to social control. Impulses elicited by private meanings are inhibited in public, for each person is aware of the fact that others will regard him as a bit "queer" if he were to indulge himself. If a man screamed in terror whenever he saw a green hat, he would soon be confined in an asylum. He learns, therefore, to suppress his fear; indeed, he may even try to socialize the unique meaning by inventing plausible reasons why green hats make people feel uncomfortable and should be abolished.

Each person is oriented toward a distinct set of values, meanings of special significance to him. The consistency discernible in his conduct does not arise from the repetition of movements, for overt

[3] Medard Boss, *Meaning and Content of Sexual Perversions*, Liese L. Abell, trans. (New York: Grune & Stratton, 1949), pp. 39–55, 61–71. Cf. Vernon W. Grant, "A Fetishistic Theory of Amorous Fixation," *Journal of Social Psychology*, XXX (1949), 17–37.

acts are adjustments to the exigencies of particular situations. In each instance he has to do something a bit different, even when the situations are conventionally defined. Consistency arises from the stability of goals. A person remains "in character" not because his separate movements are recurrent but because most of his acts constitute efforts to maintain the same set of values. For example, a person who places a high value on success not only works hard and makes great sacrifices in an effort to get ahead, but he also admires other people who have been successful even when he dislikes them personally and tends to view with contempt those who are not willing to work. The distinctive patterns of thought and action in terms of which one person is marked off from another depend upon what each regards as important.[4]

Behavior may be regarded as the effort of a person to maintain his unity and integrity. Acts are initiated when there is some disturbance in equilibrium, but what upsets equilibrium differs considerably from one person to another. Attempts to explain human behavior in terms of universal impulses, such as sex or hunger, are not likely to prove fruitful; different people react very differently in identical situations. Each becomes especially sensitized to different aspects of a situation. Some people seem to be on a perpetual quest for a marriage partner; others, for possibilities of attaining power, for opportunities of making money, for ways of getting out of physical exertion, or for adulation. Different people have different predilections and aversions—toward fraudulent enterprises, the arbitrary exercise of authority, acts of snobbery, or aggressive people. There are different standards for acceptance and rejection; some, for example, may judge men primarily in terms of their social standing in the community, their physical appearance, or their personal attributes. People are sensitized to different features of their environment, and it is the consistency in selection that gives to each person the appearance of a style of life.

Of particular interest to social psychologists are the spontaneous ways in which each person relates himself to other people. Each has a characteristic way of approaching human beings in general, certain categories of people, and particular persons he knows as individuals. Some persons are docile and tend to comply readily with the

---

[4] Cf. Lecky, *op. cit.*, ch. V.

demands of others; some tend to withdraw, doing whatever they must to meet their obligations and then returning to their solitude; some are aggressive and attempt to dominate every scene. Careful observation will reveal that for each person there is also a typical pattern for approaching various categories of people. Some are sensitive to status; they approach all authority figures in the same way, with deference or perhaps rebellion. If they find themselves in positions of authority, they treat their subordinates in the same way—with understanding, condescension, or contempt. Some persons make a sharp distinction between the sexes; there are men who feel uncomfortable in the presence of any woman. In some cases all older women may be approached in one way and all younger women in another. For most people, specific individuals who are known intimately are approached in a consistent manner, for such individuals are perceived as unique objects.

Such orientations, once they are established, are of great importance, for they may hinder or facilitate cooperation. There are a number of ways of approaching other people which render participation in most groups less difficult. One may approach others in a self-effacing manner. He may be shy and modest, submitting easily to duty and obeying the commands of others. He becomes anxious about the approval of others, and feeling guilty upon offending, he is quick to condemn himself. Or one may render himself dependent upon others. He may regard others with respect and admiration, and being sensitive to their needs, he conforms trustingly to their wishes. In difficult situations he turns to them for help and leans on those who provide it. Another way of approaching others is by being agreeable, willingly contributing his share at all times. He may be affectionate and friendly, striving to please and constantly seeking reciprocal friendliness from others. Still another way of approaching others is by being helpful, being quick to give and taking over responsibilities and burdens in trying circumstances. He sympathizes readily with others and is easily aroused to pity. Almost everyone uses each of these patterns in approaching some people in certain kinds of situations, but there are some who are characteristically oriented toward most people in one or another of these ways. If so, he develops patterns of deference, dependency, cooperation, or helpfulness which become discernible in a wide variety of contexts.

There are also a number of ways of approaching other people which tend to hinder cooperation. One may view people with distrust. He may take pride in his "realism," being skeptical of their good will and wary of friendly overtures. He may be so suspicious of others that he seldom takes them at their word. If he meets with difficulties, he is bitter and rebellious, complaining loudly of being rejected by others. Or one may approach others sadistically, being punitive, sarcastic, and unkind. He may see the world as a jungle in which others are continually looking for opportunities for exploitation; hence, he is aggressive in defending whatever he regards as his prerogatives. Another way of approaching people is by perceiving them in terms of utility. A man may be concerned almost exclusively with his personal interests, constantly competing with others in an effort to assert himself. He tends to withhold cooperation unless there is a probability of return, and he does not hesitate to use others for his own purposes. Still another way of approaching others is by striving constantly to control them. One may be ambitious, trying to dominate all those with whom he comes into contact. He compulsively seeks power and respect. Although everyone approaches some people under some circumstances in each of these ways, any of these patterns may also become dominant in a given person, giving him a style for approaching people in general.[5] If so, the very presence of such a person can be the source of discord and can seriously disrupt any collective enterprise, no matter how well organized it may be.

Such spontaneous modes of approaching other people depend upon the personifications that are constructed. The manner in which one is prepared to act toward another human being depends upon the kinds of motives that can be plausibly imputed to him. Thus, one who is convinced that all men are selfish by nature is always ready to defend himself; another person who is convinced of the essential goodness of man meets each disappointment with a determination to correct his own mistakes. Reactions to specific individuals as well as categories of people depend upon the manner in which such personifications are *evaluated*. Human beings who are regarded as sources of great joy become coveted objects which are sought and cherished. Those who are thought to be sources of con-

[5] Cf. Timothy Leary, *Interpersonal Diagnosis of Personality* (New York: Ronald Press Co., 1957), pp. 3–87, 265–350.

stant frustration become objects of annoyance and are either avoided or attacked. Those who are viewed as sources of pain and danger are avoided. All dangerous objects provoke reactions of fear, and one experiences the impulse to flee. Those who can be manipulated easily without concern for their interests come to be regarded as inferior and harmless. As long as they remain in their subordinate position, they are tolerated and may even be prized. However, too intimate contact with such base objects sometimes arouses a sense of revulsion, and should such people seek to improve their lot, such "pretensions" may arouse aggressive impulses. This suggests that the manner in which each person is oriented toward other people depends upon what they mean to him.

The manner in which one participates in groups also depends upon the manner in which he is oriented toward himself. Each man forms some kind of personification of himself as well as of other people and places an estimate upon it. This evaluation is a crucial dimension of his personality, for much of what a man does or does not do depends upon his reaction to what he experiences as himself. If he regards himself as a desirable object, he acts with confidence. He assumes that other people appreciate him, brushes aside indications of doubt, and meets various challenges openly. On the other hand, a man who regards himself as an inferior object tends to avoid situations in which his performances are put to a test. He is unable to conceive of himself as worthy of the respect of others; if someone should treat him with deference, he becomes suspicious of ulterior motives. If a person regards himself as a dangerous object, he may voluntarily withdraw from situations in which he feels he might do harm, especially to those whom he loves. In many situations the manner in which the various participants relate themselves to one another depends upon the relative estimates each places upon himself in comparison to the others. A man may feel inferior to one person and superior to another; he may believe himself desired by one person and know that he is detested by another. Each makes his contributions to common enterprises accordingly.

Each man develops a unique personality by coming to terms with the particular environment in which he must make his way. The characteristic ways of coping with the world, which mark him off as a distinct person, rest upon the manner in which he evaluates various objects—physical and human. Each person has a unique configuration of interests which he strives to achieve as best he can whenever the opportunities present themselves. His constant pursuit of the same set of values is what gives him the appearance of consistency in spite of the variability of his conduct. In view of the fact that people are temperamentally different from the time of their birth and subsequently encounter the most amazing variety of experiences, it is not surprising that an extensive range of individual differences exist. What is amazing is that people who are so different still manage somehow to act together in groups.

The assessment of personality has been found to be a task of incredible difficulty, and although a number of procedures have been developed, thus far none has proved entirely satisfactory. There are a wide variety of "paper and pencil" tests in which subjects are asked questions concerning their ambitions, anxieties, reactions in common situations, and estimates of various objects. The responses are then evaluated from the standpoint of some theory, and each person's performance is usually described by some quantitative index. Among the most widely used of these tests is the elaborate Minnesota Multiphasic Personality Inventory (MMPI). Another common procedure is the use of rating scales for the evaluation of data from clinical interviews and from observers' records, sometimes prepared from behind one-way mirrors. The conduct of a person in a variety of circumstances is judged in terms of such categories as whether his aggression is directed outward or toward himself, whether he assumes leadership or waits for others to make decisions, and whether he prefers the company of older people or of those his own age. In recent years increasing use has been made of a number of projective tests in which subjects are asked to express themselves when confronted with ambiguous perceptual cues. In addition to the TAT there are tests in which responses are elicited from ink blots, incomplete sentences, pictures of clouds, and photographs of faces. The advantage of this technique is that the subject is often caught off guard, for the psychologist is not looking for the reactions most men deliberately conceal. In the Rorschach test, for example, the analyst is more concerned with the style of one's response to various ink blots than he is with the content.[6] Many of

[6] John E. Bell, *Projective Techniques* (New York: Longmans, Green & Co., 1948). Cf. U. S. Office of Strategic Services, *The Assessment of Men* (New York: Rinehart & Co., 1948); and Adorno, *et al., op. cit.,* Parts I–III.

the observational and analytic procedures are quite ingenious, and in spite of their shortcomings they have proved useful for various purposes. In addition, new techniques are continually being developed.

Patterns of Unconscious Behavior

There has been considerable controversy over the question of unconscious behavior, some insisting that men are often unaware of the most important things they do and others being equally adamant that any talk of "unconscious" or "subconscious" processes is fraudulent. The controversy has been heightened by the rise to eminence of psychoanalysis. Since most men are under the impression that they exercise fairly efficient control over themselves, they believe that except for momentary lapses they know perfectly well what they are doing. But there is considerable evidence that this view is unjustified. By definition, *any behavior about which the actor is not communicating with himself is unconscious.* Men are actually unaware of most of the things that they do, for consciousness is highly selective. Since tendencies of which one has no awareness are not likely to be inhibited and redirected, unconscious behavior patterns tend to persist. It is not surprising, therefore, that students of personality have focussed so much attention upon them. Apparently there are several types of unconscious behavior.[7]

The reading of expressive movements from the faces of other people is for the most part unconscious. One gets the impression that someone is frightened, jealous, or not telling the truth, but he cannot specify the sensory cues that lead to such inferences. The judgment rests upon something that has been perceived, but there is no awareness of it. All kinds of subtle nuances, distinctions of the utmost nicety, are discerned and acted upon. This suggests that in every group thousands of meanings are built up for which there are no linguistic symbols. Since there is no way in which they can be designated, distinctions can be intuitively felt but cannot be communicated—either to others or to oneself.

Unconscious behavior patterns may arise from purposely over-

[7] Cf. James G. Miller, *Unconsciousness* (New York: John Wiley & Sons, 1942).

looking something that is painful. Such deliberate suppression is a complex process in which one initially tells himself that something he suspects is really not there. He directs his attention elsewhere so that he does not notice what may be rather obvious to others. The momentary glee that one experiences upon noticing the discomfort or embarrassment of a very successful friend is quickly denied. A man who feels a sudden erotic attraction to someone who is taboo—his mother, his sister, his daughter, or the wife of his best friend—scolds himself that it is sinful even to think of such a possibility. This kind of magic—pretending that something is not there by refusing to look at it—is not by any means confined to childhood. At first a person closes his eyes and denies what is undesirable or unpleasant, but as he becomes accustomed to this orientation, he may actually forget the painful cues and consistently act as if they did not exist. Thus, each man becomes accustomed to looking upon a number of attractive women around him as being sexually neutral and upon his good friends as being incapable of hateful actions.

But many unconscious behavior patterns are not preceded by such deliberate suppression. A man who is very vain does not notice the contemptuous gestures of others, or he dismisses the unavoidable cues as indications of jealousy. Everyone else who is present may realize that he has been insulted, but he goes on unperturbed. An administrator who is deeply involved in his work and is especially proud of the superior performance of a unit he has built up is unable to see the rifts and factions within his staff, even when no one else is under any illusions about them. Should the difficulties be called to his attention, he may even become suspicious of the motives of those who are trying to help him avoid a serious crisis. Many of the cruelties inflicted by men upon one another are unintentional. Sullivan cites a case in which fairly safe inferences may be drawn concerning unconscious inclinations. A man who strongly resented a close associate without knowing it became ill or weary in his presence. Whenever the other person was humiliated, however, his illness was miraculously and unaccountably cured. There was no deliberate malice. The person vehemently denied that the state of his health was in any way related to his friend, but there was so much consistency that the psychiatrist could not help but wonder.[8]

[8] Harry S. Sullivan, "Psychiatry: Introduction to the Study of Interpersonal Relations," in *A Study of Interpersonal Relations*, Patrick Mullahy, ed. (New York: Hermitage Press, 1949), p. 103.

Sometimes one may be forced by some crisis to re-examine over-looked cues; if so, such reappraisals invariably involve severe agony. All perception is selective, but in some instances selectivity is accentuated to the point where a person is blinded to what is rather obvious to others.

An example of the complexity of the activities that can take place without consciousness is provided by somnambulism. Sleepwalkers perform a variety of dangerous tasks requiring minute coordination. A person may get out of bed and drive his automobile for many miles before awakening suddenly to find himself on a strange highway. Or he may be aroused from his slumber by the screams of horrified spectators watching him tiptoe along a ledge. The fine neuromuscular coordination is predicated upon precise perception, but there is no awareness until he wakes up to ask himself: "What am I doing here?" Although there is no generally accepted explanation of somnabulism, many psychiatrists contend that impulses that the actor is unable to face gain symbolic gratification in such episodes.

Freud was especially interested in unconscious behavior and expressed the belief that it involved something more than the mere lack of attention. When an experience is repressed, barriers are set up against awareness, barriers which can be broken down only under rather unusual circumstances. It is for this reason that calling such matters to a person's attention makes little difference; he continues to deny what is apparent to others, even when he is looking directly at it. In addition, he is unaware of the fact of resistance so that he is unable to indicate to himself that there is something he does not wish to see. In spite of the most conscientious efforts to comprehend his own conduct, an intelligent adult is often rendered incapable of seeing connections obvious enough even for a child to recognize. What makes these unconscious impulses so important is that the discomforts persist. Pressures toward the reduction of tension continue, and the fact that a person is not aware of what he is doing only complicates matters. When his peculiar conduct is challenged, it becomes necessary for him to justify what he is doing—to himself as well as to others. Whatever rationalizations he may develop only add to the confusion.[9]

Freud's views were immediately challenged. It was contended

[9] Cf. Freud, "Repression," *Collected Papers, op. cit.,* Vol. IV, pp. 84–97.

that it would be impossible to demonstrate the existence of behavioral tendencies if the person himself could not recognize them even when making a sincere effort. But experimental studies support Freud's position. Unfortunately, many of the experiments purporting to deal with repression are actually tests of selective responsiveness to pleasant and unpleasant stimulation, and they do not deal with unconscious processes as Freud conceived of them. But Rosenstock developed a test of repression by having his subjects read sentences describing aggressive or erotic inclinations toward their parents—such as, hoping that one's mother would die because of the manner in which she mistreated the subject, being jealous of one's parents' being in bed together, and wanting to sleep with the parent of the opposite sex. There were an equal number of neutral sentences for controls. The materials were shown in a dark room on a device on which the degree of illumination could be controlled, thereby making it possible to vary the ease of perception. Each subject was asked to write down what he saw. It was found that the sentences dealing with matters ordinarily repressed in our society proved more difficult to see, requiring much brighter illumination before they could be recognized. Furthermore, errors in recording these sentences occurred with more frequency than was the case in the neutral sentences.[10]

Freud believed that the development of such unconscious meanings constitutes a way of coming to terms with painful aspects of one's surroundings—trying to do what one is inclined to do while maintaining his safety and self-respect. Aggressive tendencies, attempts at sexual exploitation, or the enjoyment of the misfortunes of others would invite retaliation, and each person builds up defenses against such punitive reactions. Most important of all, since men examine their desires from the moral standpoint shared in the group in which they participate, strong feelings of guilt arise whenever such dispositions are experienced. Any awareness of such shameful inclinations evokes impulses of self-punishment, which are often more harsh than the negative sanctions imposed by other people. Thus, another person caught in an embarrassing situation

[10] Irwin M. Rosenstock, "Perceptual Aspects of Repression," *Journal of Abnormal and Social Psychology*, XLVI (1951), 304–15. Cf. Ruth A. Bobbitt, "The Repression Hypothesis Studied in a Situation of Hypnotically Induced Conflict," *ibid.*, LVI (1958), 204–12; Sears, *op. cit.*, pp. 105–20; and Irwin Smalheiser, "Repression in the Laboratory," *Complex*, VI (1951), 47–55.

comes to assume a somewhat different meaning. He is no longer the object of unmitigated mirth, as he might be to an unsocialized spectator; indeed, most adults become sympathetically embarrassed themselves. If they are not, they make adept use of diversionary gestures to give the impression that they are. The very existence of impulses that tend to evoke painful experiences, such as guilt feelings, is denied.

Freud insisted that unconscious meanings have special properties that make them fundamentally different from other meanings. Since a man can hardly respond to his impulses unless he is aware of them and can identify them as his own, unconscious tendencies are not subject to checking through deliberate inhibition. Once crystallized, such dispositions cannot be examined from the perspective of one's reference group; in brief, *unconscious behavior is not subject to social control*. While unconscious meanings may be formed as reactions to group norms, once they are established such fixations become compulsive. For this reason they are more reliable indicators of personality.

There is considerable body of clinical evidence to indicate that unconscious behavior is not necessarily logical. Association by contiguity or external resemblances often replaces the notion of a necessary relationship. Psychoanalytic concepts like displacement, condensation, and symbolization all refer to substitutions and transformations in terms of vague similarities in superficial traits or incidental attributes rather than necessary connections. Conscious thinking in the Western intellectual tradition rests upon the principle of contradiction—that an object cannot be "A" and "not-A" at the same time. But there is apparently no such rule in unconscious behavior, and blatant inconsistencies exist side by side. Spatial relations are sometimes distorted to the point where they seem impossible and are described as "bizarre." Conscious thinking also rests upon common understandings concerning plausible time sequences, but unconscious behavior is not necessarily predicated upon such a conventional order; in fact, there may be no conception at all of the passage of time. Thus, Freud contended that unconscious behavior is not logical. Since it is more cathartic than instrumental, it is not oriented toward the solution of problems in the real world.

The fact that a person denies the existence of certain forbidden dispositions does not mean that they become extinct. The spon-

taneous reactions persist and continue to press toward consummation. Since the open pursuit of prohibited interests would lead
almost at once to serious difficulties, they are often gratified in disguised form. This provides some measure of relief and at the same
time protects both the person and his self-respect. Freud pointed to
a number of common substitutes, such as slips of the tongue, jokes,
unintentional forgetting, and other relatively innocuous "accidents."
But he emphasized the symbolic gratification of such impulses, especially in dreams, in which the reduction of tension takes place
through some associated activity but where the connection between
the symbols and their referents is not always clear. Instead of entertaining fantasies of seducing some forbidden love object a person
may dream of a fire or of climbing up a ladder, otherwise meaningless dreams that frequently represent erotic passions. Or a woman
who has strong exhibitionist tendencies but who is ashamed of her
personal appearance may turn her house into the showplace that she
is not. Her home is not planned for daily living. She does not
tolerate any disorder, and she continually nags her husband and
children, who are treated more like interlopers than people who
belong there. The house is not really a place in which to live com-
fortably but a symbol of the lovely woman she longs to be—an
object to be placed on display and to be admired. Hence, her greatest satisfaction comes from the raves of her visitors and the envy of
her friends.

If such substitute activities are to be viewed as the disguised consummation of prohibited impulses, a cross-cultural comparison of
typical dreams may prove instructive, for different things are forbidden in different groups. Many of the dreams reported by European and American psychiatrists deal directly or symbolically with
illicit sex relations, and these may be compared with the dreams of
people in societies characterized by different sex mores. Of particular interest is Powdermaker's account of life in Lesu, a village on the
east coast of New Ireland. Marriage and divorce are easy in Lesu,
and extramarital affairs are accepted. In some cases a lover simply
pays the woman's husband for special privileges. But there are strict
taboos against incest, and the rule of exogamy is sternly enforced.
A person may not marry or have sex relations with anyone in his
own clan. Since there are only two clans in the village, for each
person half the people of the opposite sex are out of bounds. The

violation of this norm is punishable by death, and those who break it sometimes commit suicide. If they do not, they are killed by their own relatives. Under the circumstances, it is of interest to note that dreams of incestuous relationships are quite common; a man dreams of seducing his sister or some other woman in his clan. Such dreams were admitted to the ethnographer only with great reluctance and with obvious shame.[11] Since there is no way of measuring the relative frequency of such dreams in Lesu and in our society, such evidence cannot be accepted as conclusive, but the data are consistent with Freud's theory.

Psychoanalytic therapy rests upon the assumption that once a person becomes aware of the existence of such impulses, it will be possible to bring them under some measure of control. If so, behavior becomes subject to social control. It should be emphasized, however, that such consciousness and control can be established only with great difficulty. Upon learning that neatness is one of the traits in terms of which Freud identified an "anal character," a person who is not fully developed, people in some intellectual circles deliberately go out of their way to be sloppy—to demonstrate to their friends that they are not hampered by such compulsions. But such studied informality consists merely of altering a habit. Rooting out compulsive cleanliness in the sense in which Freud spoke of it is a matter of considerable difficulty.

There are a variety of things that men do without making indications to themselves, and ignoring such behavior leaves us with a very incomplete picture of human beings. The contrast between deliberate conduct and the unconscious modes of behavior suggests that the latter are more spontaneous and that rationality is an emergent property of man. Starting as creatures of impulses restricted only by the limitations imposed by environment and organic structure, human beings gradually developed the capacity for logical reasoning and self-control as instruments of adjustment. These instruments developed as men participated in groups and learned to share common perspectives with one another—assumptions about the attributes of things, sequences of events, frequent associations, and necessary connections. When for any reason a person does not participate in the world over which there is consensus, his behavior is again trans-

[11] Hortense Powdermaker, *Life in Lesu* (New York: W. W. Norton & Co., 1933), pp. 266–71.

formed. When there is no self-consciousness, there can be no self-control; hence, such behavior can no longer be inhibited in the light of group expectations. It is not strange that human unconscious behavior often resembles that of other animals.

The Personal Equation in Groups

In 1795 it was discovered at the Royal Observatory at Greenwich that there was a slight difference between the records of two observers timing the passage of stars across the meridian, and in 1822 a German astronomer showed that such individual differences were to be found in all observers. Such variations in recording time, recognized as an important source of error, have been referred to as the "personal equation." The term may be used more broadly here to refer to individual variations in the performance of any standardized task. No two people can act in exactly the same way, even if they wanted to be alike, and such differences are obvious in the enactment of conventional roles. The person and the social group are two distinct functional units. Under what conditions does the line of action depend upon group structure, and under what conditions can it be regarded as a manifestation of the personal qualities of the participating individuals? Put in another way, when do things go on as usual, regardless of who is present, and when does the presence of particular people significantly alter the course of events?

One way to get at this problem is to compare five roughly delineated types of situations in which the extent of personal intervention in the course of action varies. The greatest opportunities for individual influence arise in *crisis situations*. A situation may be regarded as critical whenever the conventional norms prove inadequate as guides for meeting the exigencies that arise. Crisis situations vary in magnitude and intensity, ranging from catastrophes such as earthquakes, disasters at sea, wars, and depressions to minor disturbances such as the unexpected appearance of a movie idol on a college campus. When the routine of daily life is broken, the established norms are temporarily suspended, and it becomes necessary for those who are present to improvise some mode of cooperation; therefore, all crises have one feature in common: people are receptive to new lines of action. When there is no conventional way of meeting the situation satisfactorily, those who are involved are thrown back on their own resources, and what happens depends upon the special interests and the idiosyncrasies of the more persuasive individuals who happen to be present. Since they are no longer bound by conventional norms, men express their personal views, which sometimes include interests that would otherwise be concealed from others. Crisis situations, then, provide opportunities for individual expression. But just as unusual opportunities arise for some, a crisis can also be the occasion for the downfall of those who had previously depended too much upon their social position.

Whenever the settled ways of life are disrupted, the course of events depends largely upon the personalities of those who happen to be present. The leadership that develops is decisive in meeting such emergencies. If a highly respected person becomes hysterical, the entire group may panic, and a disaster may be compounded. The appearance of a man with imagination and exceptional talent can facilitate coping with a dangerous situation, and an entire group may be handicapped by a person who compulsively seeks adoration and insists upon pointing to his contributions. A single stubborn man who reacts with rigidity whenever his pride is injured may render adjustments unnecessarily difficult, for new behavior patterns that may be deemed desirable by others cannot easily be instituted. Some persons may take advantage of such opportunities and attempt to dominate others whom they had secretly despised, and if they happen to be devoid of the particular aptitudes required, their mere presence can spell disaster. The values of those who assume command, those who can persuade others to follow them and to implement their decisions, provide the direction in which a group moves in such inadequately defined situations.

Although we tend to think of a leader as someone with special traits—such as courage, strength, intelligence, and the ability to inspire—it should be remembered that leadership is essentially a social process. A leader is a man who has followers. No matter how brilliant a person may be, no matter how engaging his personality, he is not likely to alter the course of history unless others will abdicate some of their prerogatives. Different kinds of men tend to dominate different types of situations. Under some circumstances almost anyone can get a hearing, even a man who is ordinarily shunned in the community. In a lynching mob, for example, the successful agitator is the man who most accurately reflects the aroused feelings of those present. In conflict situations fighters and tacticians are needed, and when the task to be accomplished is complicated, men with special skills in organization are called. Since those who emerge as leaders are the men who are able to carry out the interests of their followers, historians and philosophers have long debated the question of whether heroes are the product of their times or the producers of historical events. Do great men make history, or are they merely those who chanced upon the scene when opportunity arose? It appears that some have become heroes upon being thrown into a situation in which their distinctive abilities happened to be required; on the other hand, there are apparently other men who have produced the crises in which they excelled.[12]

The repetition of disruptions leads to the development of organized ways of dealing with them. Recurrent floods, the outbreak of wars and the dangers of enemy raids, unpredictable but disastrous shifts in the stock market, and the uncertainty of the moves of opponents in athletic contests often result in the establishment of special roles, such as, the director of disaster crews, the foreign minister and the chief of military units, the expert on financial exchanges, and the team captain. The second type of situation is one in which quick decisions are required but within an organized setting. Those who occupy key offices are vested with the responsibility of deciding what is to be done. In such situations the outcome rests largely upon the personal characteristics of the formally designated leaders, for they often exercise a considerable range of choice. The personality quirks of a single powerful official in an organization like the Atomic Energy Commission could conceivably alter the course of human history, perhaps even leading to the extermination of the species. But such persons are seldom free to do whatever they wish; their efforts are usually circumscribed by a number of regulations and conventions. Furthermore, those who occupy such offices are aware of the fact that their work is being evaluated, not in comparison with people in general but with others who have held the office in the past. They judge themselves and are judged in terms of special standards, and to this extent their behavior is curtailed. The past heroes serve as models, and specific expectations are formed.[13]

[12] Cf. Sidney Hook, *The Hero in History* (Boston: Beacon Press, 1955).
[13] Cf. Hughes, *op. cit.*, pp. 56–67.

The third type of situation is the most common—routine activities in recurrent contexts in which men interact with one another on the basis of conventional norms. In such situations the participants have an option, choosing from several acceptable ways of performing, for most conventional roles are not so rigidly defined that the line of action is prescribed in every detail. Slight deviations are tolerated. Although there may be some complaints and some variations may arouse scorn, no serious negative sanctions are invoked. In a simple transaction in a grocery store, for example, both the customer and the clerk must meet certain minimum obligations to each other, but each can temper his contribution. The two may engage in an animated conversation about matters unrelated to the customer's purchases, or the interchange may be cold and formal. What each person contributes can constitute a niggardly performance or a wholehearted and generous donation. Depending upon the personal inclinations of the individual participants, then, conventional roles may be enacted in a variety of ways.

Furthermore, except for the few people who are born kings or witch doctors, there are opportunities for choosing from among a wide variety of conventional roles. Especially in modern industrial societies, each individual enjoys considerable freedom in the selection of a career. At the very least, a man can avoid roles that require his doing things he cannot stand. Many of the difficulties in adjusting to occupational roles arise more from a lack of knowledge of what is expected than from a lack of opportunities. Even when the possibilities for upward mobility are somewhat curtailed, those with a lust for power find ways of dominating others. On the other hand, men of known ability sometimes refuse promotions; officers in infantry companies in combat zones sometimes have difficulty in finding enough sergeants. Even in conventional contexts, therefore, there are many opportunities for expressing personal preferences.

The fourth type of situation is one which is becoming increasingly common in modern industrial societies—the bureaucracies of large-scale organizations. Bureaucracies, whether they are of business enterprises, government, military organizations, or universities, are organized in much the same manner. There is a formally designated division of labor with an explicit set of regulations defining the responsibilities of each unit. There are formal communication channels, and the lines of authority are clearly defined. The assignment of personnel to the various roles takes place largely in terms of technical qualifications which are often ascertained through impersonal procedures, such as formal examinations. A deliberate effort is made to cultivate impersonal relationships, and this practice is often justified by the idea that familiarity breeds contempt. The range of choice open to the various participants is highly curtailed. Every event that requires decision is categorized, and the solution to a problem involves placing it into a category and selecting one of the fixed alternatives. Applications of all kinds from outsiders, for example, are accepted or rejected on the basis of a limited set of grounds.[14] To be successful in such organizations one must inhibit himself and fit his personality into the needs of the unit. Even in bureaucracies, however, personality does make a difference. A unit in charge of a timid man, who is efficient but lacking in imagination, is not likely to perform in the same manner as one under a bold man who countermands orders from above when he believes them to be wrong. But the second type of administrator is not likely to survive. Thus, while possibilities of personal choice do exist, they are quite limited.

The fifth type of situation is the performance of group rituals in which the component acts are so clearly prescribed that there are no alternatives left for the participants. Role-playing in a ritual is much like playing a part on the stage, for the lines are already specified. It is almost automatic, requiring only minor adjustments. When two men are introduced to one another, they shake hands and say, "How do you do?" The question is not answered. In a wedding ceremony when one is asked by the clergyman whether or not he wishes to take someone as his spouse, he is not being asked a question for which he can improvise an answer. A queen participating in a royal occasion has no choice; she smiles and does what she must, even if she happens to have a splitting headache. The only deviations tolerated are unavoidable accidents. But even in such rituals individuality is revealed in differences in style. As in theatrical productions each actor plays his part in his own distinctive way, bringing in his unique interpretation of the role. Style is something that cannot be controlled. Soldiers may be ordered to march "smartly," but there is a difference between genuinely enthusiastic cooperation and outward conformity to escape punishment. In rituals, then, par-

14 Cf. Merton, op. cit., pp. 195–206.

ticipants have little choice in what to do, but they still differ in the quality of their performances.

In comparing the five types of situations it becomes apparent that as the degree of formalization of the group increases, the range of choice is narrowed, for the participants are constrained by more clearly defined expectations on the part of their colleagues. Placing the situations on a continuum we find at one pole the rituals in which individual differences are revealed only in style. Ceremonies are much the same regardless of who performs; therefore, what happens depends largely upon group structure. At the other pole of the continuum is the crisis situation. Group norms are temporarily suspended, and anyone who can get a hearing is able to exercise disproportionate influence. But this does not mean that there is no social control; on the contrary, those who become leaders in such emergencies are men who are able to incorporate into their proposals the prevailing interests. Nonetheless, what happens depends largely upon the personalities of those who are present. These observations may be summarized in a somewhat more formal statement: *in any cooperative undertaking the extent to which an individual participant is able to pursue his personal interest without retribution is inversely related to the degree of its formalization.* When it is reduced to behavioristic terms, the statement is a tautology, but it is useful in pointing to the futility of arguing over the relative importance of the individual and the group.

What is distinctive about each man is not always observable in his overt conduct, for what he does in playing conventional roles is largely standardized. How, then, is one's personality to be detected? It is to be found in the spontaneous inclinations to act, the inner dispositions many of which are inhibited and not revealed to other people. For example, in a group of soldiers being severely chastised by an officer for some infraction of regulations each will stand at attention and say, "Yes, sir." Overtly their behavior is quite similar. Covertly, however, one man may feel an urge to break down and cry; another may find it difficult to suppress an impulse to assault the lieutenant; another may wish he could crawl into a hole to hide; and another may experience a strong inclination to argue back and to point out that the violation was unavoidable. The impulses elicited in a given situation vary from person to person; and it is these inner dispositions, which frequently do not eventuate in overt behavior, that are indicative of what kind of human being each man is. Personality may be regarded as consisting of potentialities for action. It is not so much what men actually do; it is the direction in which they would strive, were it possible for them to do so.

If overt behavior is not a direct manifestation of personality, why is it so important for social psychologists to study it? Furthermore, why are laymen so concerned with ascertaining the kind of person a new acquaintance "really" is? It is important for men to know something about the personalities of those with whom they come into contact because each person strives to attain his values whenever the opportunities present themselves. Men generally conform to group norms, but they do not have to do so. When the possibility of being caught is removed, some people knowingly violate rules and may even gain additional enjoyment from the fact of trespassing. In situations in which norms are absent, individuals frequently act in accordance with their personal values. For example, a daring young woman may be extremely careful in her place of employment where she cannot afford to take chances, but when driving her automobile she may frighten her passengers half out of their wits. Similarly, a very ambitious man who conceives of himself as honest may inadvertently take advantage of an opportunity to advance himself at the expense of his colleagues, not even noticing that he had done something unfair. Thus, consciously and unconsciously men strive to realize those potentialities represented by their basic values.

As a person shifts from one conventional role to another, his overt behavior patterns change, but his personality remains much the same. Furthermore, a man's personality is sufficiently stable so that one has little difficulty in recognizing as an adult a person that he knew as a child. It is not only the similarity in his external appearance that makes this possible but also the fact that he still approaches his world in much the same manner as he always had in the past. A person who was timid and shy as a poverty stricken child is likely to be much the same as a successful financier forty years later, although he may develop diversionary gestures for hiding his fear of people. He may even become outwardly genial and sometimes domineering, but his inner disposition upon meeting people is likely to be the same—to withdraw. If as a youth he tended to blame others for all his misfortunes but was restrained from expressing his views aloud, as a successful adult he might not hesitate to accuse others openly whenever things go wrong. This does not mean, of course, that one's personality is necessarily fixed for all time. It emerges through adaptation, the crystallization of the succession of adjustments to life conditions; it is a way of coming to terms with the particular world in which one finds himself. In some respects it is like a protective armor against external dangers and repressed impulses.[15] It is relatively stable over long periods of time, and this comparative stability makes it a valuable indicator of probable conduct in a variety of circumstances.

The expression of one's individuality—the preservation of those distinctive habits of thought and action which characterize a man and mark him off from all others—may itself become a value. But there are considerable differences among people in the extent to which they pursue this value. Some feel extremely resentful whenever they are treated without regard for their unique qualities. They comply when they must, but they feel restless and chafe under the restraints. They complain bitterly of being only a serial number in the army, a cog in the gigantic productive system of a factory, or just another student in the impersonal atmosphere of a large university. In "exclusive" stores, sales personnel learn the names of all their customers in order to "personalize" their service, thus inducing their clientele to continue paying an additional charge for being treated as individuals. On the other hand, there are people who make every effort to hide their inner dispositions, conforming readily to group norms. In military service they may have many other complaints, but they are not particularly disturbed about being "lost" in an impersonal mass of soldiers. They prefer to be just "average" and not to carry any unnecessary responsibilities. Those who are different attract attention to themselves, and some fear the spotlight to the point of inhibiting their other desires. Some people are so compliant that they are not even sure of what they want and constantly ask others what they should do. Such personality differences may account for the fact that some people are quite content to work in a bureaucracy while others are constantly seeking the excitement of rapidly changing frontiers.

[15] Cf. Wilhelm Reich, *Character Analysis*, Theodore P. Wolfe, trans. (New York: Orgone Institute Press, 1949), pp. 143–57.

Personality Differences in Autonomy

The pursuit of personal interests in the face of disapproval usually invites retaliation of some kind, and in some cases it can be disastrous. Therefore, most people conform to conventional norms most of the time. In a changing society, however, people occasionally find themselves in situations in which there are discrepancies between inner standards of conduct and the expectations of their associates. Under such circumstances individuals differ considerably in the extent to which they retain their independence. Some are able to do what they regard to be proper in the face of heated opposition. But how is this possible? Voluntary conduct rests upon self-conceptions, and these personifications are meanings that are subject to reality testing and revision. They must be reaffirmed from time to time by the confirming responses of other people.

By the time they reach adulthood most people have formed relatively stable self-conceptions. They believe that they know themselves fairly well; they are more or less aware of their strengths, limitations, and special aptitudes. But others do not necessarily see a person as he visualizes himself, for he is selectively sensitized to different aspects of his conduct. Even in something seemingly as obvious as one's appearance there is no direct correspondence between what others see and what one imagines himself to be. Most people are quite surprised when they first see motion pictures of themselves. Why should anyone be surprised? In the pictures one sees himself more as others see him, and in most cases this is somewhat different from the self-image he had entertained. Sometimes when a person is doing something intently, perhaps attempting to be jovial at a party, he may suddenly notice himself in a mirror hanging on the wall and be shocked. The shock suggests that he had been working on the assumption that he looked quite different and that the accidental glance at the mirror has brought on the sudden realization that he was not acting as he had thought. While there is a rough correspondence between one's conception of himself and what others regard him to be, the two are by no means the same.

In a study of the detection of anxiety, Ruesch and Prestwood asked a group of psychiatrists to make tape recordings of interviews with their patients. Then the psychiatrists were asked to evaluate all of the interviews, including their own performances, and to arrive at some estimate of the anxiety manifested in such transactions. Each therapist was asked to form both a participant-gained and an observer-gained impression of himself, of his patient, and of the interchanges that went on between them. Since psychiatrists are human beings, it is not surprising that each was quite surprised to find out how much anxiety he himself displayed. Indeed, at first each therapist tended to overestimate the anxieties of his patient and to underestimate his own, in comparison with the scoring by his associates on the panel. With repeated listening, however, each doctor became more accustomed to listening to himself; the defensive reactions were gradually relaxed, and each became more able to view his own conduct from a more detached standpoint. In time each psychiatrist's estimate of his own performance tended to approximate the judgment of his colleagues.[16] Thus, even psychiatrists, whose work requires considerable self-insight and almost incredible self-control, have relatively fixed self-conceptions and form self-images that are not quite the same as the perceptual objects that others form of them.

Once self-conceptions are formed, they tend to sustain themselves. Even casual observations reveal that most men are not mere captives of the definitions of other people. They sometimes repudiate the evaluations that others place upon them and demand to be treated as they "really" are. When a person places a higher estimate upon himself than others do, he feels that they are being unfair and that they do not fully appreciate his potentialities. He makes special efforts to demonstrate that he is actually different from what they believe. On the other hand, some people feel that they have been over-evaluated. They feel that they are being addressed with a deference they do not deserve and protest against the attention they receive, not merely from modesty but from a feeling that they are not what others regard them to be. They may even suffer acute anxieties lest others demand that they live up to these unreasonable expectations. Thus, human beings do not accept passively the assessment of their society; they can and do repudiate the judgments of others.

Even when the treatment accorded a man by his associates rests upon a personification that he does not avow, he is frequently able

[16] Ruesch and Prestwood, "Anxiety: Its Initiation, Communication and Interpersonal Management," *op. cit.*

to maintain his conception of himself through selective perception. Because personifications are constructed from selected cues, the continuation of some measure of disparity is possible. Each person is especially responsive to those particular gestures that tend to reinforce what he already believes about himself. A woman who conceives of herself as very beautiful expects some hostility from other women; should someone express distaste over her choice of clothing, she dismisses it as an indication of jealousy. Some persons with a low level of self-esteem approach others with hesitation, and even the slightest disagreement on the part of someone else is interpreted as a rebuff and further proof of his worthlessness. Some people in unpopular minorities go about with a "chip on the shoulder" attitude. When asked to wait for a few moments in a restaurant, they may leave in a huff, loudly protesting discrimination, when in fact there is no table of the appropriate size available at the time. All self-conceptions—other than those of some of the people who are psychotic—enjoy some measure of support, even though the sustaining gestures may not always represent the same meanings to other people.

In situations in which there is disagreement between group norms and what a man regards as his legitimate prerogatives there is considerable variation in the manner in which the difference is resolved, ranging from unquestioning compliance to rigid autonomy. Although most people retain some degree of independence, they differ considerably in their willingness to conform. At one extreme is the person who complies with most of the demands imposed upon him and is left with little individuality. He goes with the wind, doing whatever is required of him in each context by whoever happens to be present. On the other extreme there are persons who do not comply at all; indeed, some may even be negativistic, getting special delight out of shocking people. To the extent that reality is a social process, such persons may even get out of touch with the world over which there is consensus. Those in psychotic wards who conceive of themselves as Napoleon are highly autonomous; they live in their private worlds, ignoring completely the contradictory views of others. Most people, of course, are somewhere between these extremes. They differ considerably in the extent to which they can be self-sufficient, but most people are capable of independent judgment, even though they may lack courage and comply outwardly. Thus, one of the dimensions along which men vary is in the *degree of personal autonomy* that they characteristically retain.[17]

A person is closer to the autonomy pole of the continuum to the extent that he is able to retain his inner standards of conduct even in the face of inadequate confirmation from other people with whom he is in direct contact. He is more independent in that he does what he believes to be proper, irrespective of what the others around him may feel. One illustration of such a person is the college student who can maintain the moral standards he learned at home even when most of his campus friends are quite lax. They may taunt him, calling him a "saint," but he is able to tread the narrow path, maintaining his self-respect if not the regard of his companions. Such persons are generally not easily swayed about anything. Bold, forthright action depends upon the readiness to disagree, to sacrifice, to assume risks, and to tolerate frustrations; not everyone is willing to pay this price.

Since a high premium is placed upon "self-reliance" in our society, it is sometimes assumed by social psychologists and psychiatrists that such autonomy is always desirable. Several writers, especially those attempting to construct models of the "normal" person, speak of autonomous behavior as an ideal. But this value judgment has had some unfortunate consequences in that it has blinded many investigators to the fact that the extent to which people can be flexible is variable and that those on *both* ends of the continuum would probably be adjudged insane. Even those who are somewhat less rigidly independent get into serious difficulties. One study of soldiers who were absent without leave during World War II showed that the culprits differed from those who remained on duty only in one important respect. They did not identify themselves with any military organization and were therefore not concerned with the views of their fellow servicemen. They continued to look upon themselves from a civilian perspective; it becomes understandable, then, that army life appeared even more unbearable to them. Being insensitive to the opinions of other soldiers, they apparently did not think of desertion as a particularly serious offense.[18] Thus, thinking for one-

[17] Although it is placed in a somewhat different context, a perceptive discussion of the problem of autonomy can be found in David Riesman, *The Lonely Crowd* (New Haven: Yale University Press, 1950).

[18] Martin H. Stein, "Neurosis and Group Motivation," *American Journal of Psychiatry*, CII (1946), 658–65.

self does not necessarily result in satisfactory adjustment. This value judgment should be avoided, and attention should be focussed upon finding fruitful ways of describing people and showing the manner in which the variables are interrelated.

It has been observed that in general people who are characterized by a high degree of autonomy also tend to maintain polite distance between themselves and others.[19] Furthermore, they are frequently more self-conscious and quite deliberate about what they do. Self-consciousness is a way of protecting oneself from impulsiveness; it facilitates the inhibition of natural reactions. Behavior thus becomes less spontaneous but is always proper. This is not to suggest that such persons are necessarily unfriendly. They are, however, harder to "get close to"; they do not establish rapport easily, nor are they immediately responsive to the feelings of others. They are usually more cautious in dealing with people, perhaps because of difficulties in interpersonal relations in the past, and they tend to keep others at an arm's length. The farther apart people remain, the less personal are their obligations to one another. Autonomous persons also tend to be less excitable than others; in fact, sometimes, especially in crisis situations, they may even seem "cold" and calculating. This is to be expected, for excitement interferes with effective self-control.

When people retain their independence in the face of opposition by those immediately around them, they may enjoy the wholehearted support of imaginary personifications. This does not necessarily mean that they interact vicariously with people who do not exist; in many cases they are performing for an audience which is not represented on the scene. A soldier on duty overseas may refuse to carouse with his comrades and reinforce his decision by daydreaming of his sweetheart or wife at home. Similarly a girl confronted by "fast" company may visualize her mother's approval as she declines enticing invitations. Sometimes, however, the personifications may be fabricated. A prolific reader who lives in a small town may find that everyone else in the community regards him as "queer"; he can go on by daydreaming of a succession of episodes involving people who appreciate his interests. An architect with daring designs may persuade himself that he was born ahead of his time and enjoy fantasies of being vindicated in the distant future. Thus, one can maintain his conception of himself even in the ab-

[19] Cf. Maslow, *op. cit.*, pp. 228–30; and M. H. Small, *op. cit.*, 26–34.

sence of reinforcing gestures from those around him by constructing a supporting cast in his imagination. Some people enjoy life in their make-believe world so much that they lose interest in the world over which there is consensus. In extreme cases involving severe deprivations one may cling so desperately to the imaginary world that he may lose the ability to differentiate between the two. Then, he can go on as if the people around him do not even exist, and he becomes psychotic.

A person is closer to the compliance pole of the continuum to the extent that he submits to the demands of the people who are immediately present, even when their expectations conflict with his inner standards. He is unable to tolerate disagreement or disapproval, and he may rationalize his conduct by declaring: "When in Rome, do as the Romans do." To some extent this type of variability becomes almost necessary in a pluralistic society, but people differ considerably in the extent to which they are willing to act contrary to their standards of conduct. There are, of course, many situations in which outward conformity is required, but many people chafe and become restless. But there are others who do not even notice the restraints. Some people are apparently able to take the roles only of those they can see before them, like the driver who sanctimoniously stops a long column of automobiles to accommodate a single pedestrian, completely oblivious to the inconvenience to all the drivers who are jammed up behind him. Some persons are so compliant, so anxious over immediate approval, that they themselves are not quite sure of what they want. They are constantly asking others what they should do, being reluctant to make decisions of any kind. Their behavior is marked by no overt manifestations of irritation or hostility; some are continually apologizing and humbling themselves before others. They are so anxious to please that they act more in accordance with desires imputed to others than they do with their own interests. They are constantly preoccupied with the views of others, and in extreme cases they may actually feel that their conduct is being controlled from the outside. Should anything go wrong, therefore, they disclaim personal responsibility; they refuse to accept the blame, insisting that they were only complying with the wishes of others. Such persons are sometimes characterized as "passive-dependent" personalities, for they enter readily into dependency relationships and sometimes cling with desperation to people who have nothing but contempt for them.

Clinical observations as well as experimental studies reveal that people who are extremely compliant tend to be very sociable and able to establish rapport easily. They are characterized by a high degree of empathy, the ability to recognize and respond sympathetically to the unique reactions of each person. They are often poor story tellers and have difficulty in explaining things; they identify so readily with others that they assume their listeners know everything they do, and they do not bother to explain each step. Dymond gave a battery of tests—intelligence, Rorschach, TAT, and self-analysis—to the subjects who made extreme scores in her empathy scale. She found that those who made high scores in empathy were outgoing, optimistic, warm, emotional, and have a strong interest in other people. They were also highly flexible. In contrast, she found that those who made low scores were rigid, introverted, subject to outbursts, self-centered and demanding, and inclined to stress an intellectual and abstract approach to life.[20] Thus, everyone is able to engage in some kind of role-taking, but there are differences in their ability to identify with others. Some are able to "feel with" other people, but others are detached and can see people only as a spectator who is not involved in their affairs.

Thus, people differ considerably in the extent to which they are responsive to one another. Some persons are more "inner-directed" in that they tend to be self-sufficient and to act more in terms of their own conceptions of proper conduct. They are also more insensitive to the feelings of others and can break off relationships, should a conflict ensue. Others are more "other-directed" in that they tend to submit more readily to the expectations of other people. They are sometimes so easily influenced that they might be regarded as suggestible. These superficial observations suggest the general hypothesis that *the extent to which men are autonomous or compliant depends in part upon the degree of social distance characteristically maintained from other people.* Each person typically maintains some kind of distance from others. Some build walls around themselves, and although they may seem to be reasonable and

[20] Rosalind F. Dymond, "Personality and Empathy," *Journal of Consulting Psychology*, XIV (1950), 343–50. Cf. Richard S. Crutchfield, "Conformity and Character," *American Psychologist*, X (1955), 191–98.

friendly, it is almost impossible to get to know them on intimate terms. This does not mean, of course, that they are physically isolated. They may be surrounded by people but still live in a private world of the imagination. But others readily establish warm and intimate contacts with anyone who is responsive to them. The more a person is withdrawn and reserved, the more he is able to act on his own; the closer one is to others, the more he feels compelled to conform to their views.

Thus, the ability to live up to one's personal obligations as he sees them is related to the extent to which he is sensitive to the views of people around him. But the relationship is not quite so simple. Somehow a person's level of self-esteem also enters the picture. In a study of autonomous conduct among college students, Couch found that those who are more securely anchored in some acceptable social group are less concerned with the views of their fellow subjects in the experiment, and in another study Janis found that persons characterized as "passive-dependent" lack self-confidence and are frequently plagued by a sense of inadequacy.[21] It has been suggested that such persons may be products of overprotection by excessively indulgent parents. But there is also evidence that those who are extremely independent, in spite of their outward appearance of self-confidence, may also have a low level of self-esteem. Those who appear self-possessed and even haughty are often afraid of people. It is quite possible, then, that persons on both poles of the continuum place a low evaluation upon themselves.

The hypothesis on social distance may be tested in a preliminary way by examining extreme cases, such as the isolation of those who are psychotic. Of particular interest are those designated as paranoid. There is no agreement among psychiatrists concerning paranoid disorders, but some consensus exists concerning certain minimum features of the syndrome. A person who is paranoid apparently lives in a pseudo-community, a community populated by a number of imaginary personifications. People he actually knows may be endowed with attributes that they themselves would hardly recognize. Such a patient is often characterized by delusions of grandeur; he conceives of himself as a person of superlative ability

[21] Carl J. Couch, "Self-Attitudes and Degree of Agreement with Immediate Others," *American Journal of Sociology*, LXIII (1958), 491–96; and Irving L. Janis, "Personality Correlates of Susceptibility to Persuasion," *Journal of Personality*, XXII (1954), 504–18.

who is unfortunately misunderstood and unappreciated. Sometimes personages of some importance, such as motion picture stars, are thought to fall in love with him. To a man who conceives of himself as a genius there would be nothing implausible about being loved by a beautiful actress. There is also a tendency to project his own aggressive dispositions upon others; since they are personified as being hostile, he is constantly suspicious of their motives. He imputes vile intentions to people he dislikes and becomes so angered in his imaginary interaction with them that he may in desperation resort to violence. In his enlightening discussion of the disorder Cameron compares a person who has become a paranoid to a woman who has just purchased a hat that is a bit ahead of the latest fashions. At first she hesitates to wear it, wondering if others will laugh at her. Finally, she ventures forth on the street and notes that the first man she encounters is smiling as he passes her. Convinced that he had been amused by her hat, she retreats indoors to change; actually the man was smiling to himself about a practical joke he had pulled on a friend the night before and had not even noticed her. In the same manner, when a man who is psychotic sees people laughing, he may conclude that they are laughing at him. If he sees someone standing at a street corner waiting for a date, his suspicion that an agent of his enemies is stalking him is confirmed. The difference between the woman and the patient is that the woman can talk things over with her friends; backed by their reassurances she can again venture forth with her new hat, this time without mishap. However, the person who is psychotic cannot communicate. He isolates himself by rejecting everyone who questions his delusions. Isolation makes reality testing impossible; his self-conception remains the same, for all contradictory evidence is dismissed.[22] Perhaps as a result of past disturbances in interpersonal relations those who are paranoid have withdrawn from the society of men. Hence, they cannot correct their self-conceptions and must act autonomously.

Other phenomena that throw light on the question of personal autonomy include what has been called the "psychopathic personality" and the "bum" on "skid row." Actually there is considerable

---

[22] Norman Cameron, "The Development of Paranoic Thinking," *Psychological Review*, L (1943), 219–33; "The Paranoid Pseudo-Community," *American Journal of Sociology*, XLIX (1943), 32–38; and "The Paranoid Pseudo-Community Revisited," *ibid.*, LXV (1959), 52–58.

disagreement among psychiatrists as to what is being designated by the label "psychopathic." More and more, however, the term is being used to refer to depraved criminals who seem to lack a "conscience." They are able to commit brutal crimes from which most other criminals would recoil. Afterwards there is apparently no feeling of guilt, and many express no regrets over what they have done. Such persons can violate the strongest of taboos without remorse. They cannot be said to be incapable of role-taking, for the successful execution of the crime requires some ability to anticipate the moves of the victim. They can observe the victim in a detached manner, sometimes with remarkable insight, but without sympathetic identification. They coldly maintain their isolation and do what they set out to do. Such criminals represent extreme cases of insensitivity to other people, and their conduct is unquestionably "inner-directed."[23] A somewhat less shocking type of independent men are those who live alone in the slums. In a study of petty offenders—those repeatedly arrested for being drunk, for loitering, or for vagrancy— Deutscher found that most of these men are also alienated from people. Their one common characteristic is their isolation, and even those who drink together and are frequently incarcerated together are not friends. They only know each other.[24]

Men who are involved in situations in which there is a conflict between group norms and their personal standards of conduct may act on their own for different reasons. One person may stand up against community opinion because he has confidence in his own judgment and is convinced that all others are mistaken; another may do the same thing because he is generally negativistic and characteristically hostile; and a third person may do the same thing because he is rigidly isolated from other people and not concerned with their reactions. One can only tell by observing the same person in innumerable contexts. There are, of course, cultural differences in the evaluation placed upon independent action. In some societies conformity is constantly encouraged; in others, emphasis is placed upon self-reliance and personal honor. In spite of these variations, how-

[23] Cf. Harrison G. Gough, "A Sociological Theory of Psychopathy," *ibid.*, LIII (1948), 359–66; and Paul W. Preu, "The Concept of Psychopathic Personality," *Personality and Behavior Disorders*, John M. Hunt, ed. (New York: Ronald Press Co., 1944), Vol. II, pp. 922–37.

[24] Irwin Deutscher, "The Petty Offender: A Sociological Alien," *Journal of Criminal Law, Criminology, and Police Science*, XLIV (1954), 592–95.

ever, everyone, with the possible exception of those who are psychotic, is to some extent responsive to the judgments of others.

Summary and Conclusion

Each person, although thoroughly socialized, is an autonomous unit. No one is a robot automatically acting out cultural patterns; there is always some room for variation and originality as well as the possibility of outright revolt. Each person is characterized by a distinct set of behavioral tendencies, and much of the consistency in his inclinations to act arises from the fact that he is oriented toward a unique set of values. Many of these meanings are behavioral systems of which he is unconscious, but the fact that he cannot communicate with himself about them does not make them a less important part of his personality. This suggests, however, that it may be futile to search for universal motives, for each person is oriented toward his world in his own unique way.

In the study of motivation the problem consists of accounting for the direction taken by a person's conduct. The spontaneous inclinations that characterize a given individual provide an adequate explanation only under limited circumstances, for these impulses are so often inhibited and redirected. Each person is a functional unit seeking to preserve its integrity, but the extent to which he is free to do as he desires is inversely related to the degree of formalization of the group transaction in which he is implicated. In rituals there is not much opportunity for individual expression, but the personal equation is considerable in crisis situations. Human behavior may be viewed as a phase of the coordinated action of associated persons. Each participant has a personality, the product of his unique history. Group structures exist only in the behavior of cooperating men, but each has a history which is independent of any particular person, the pattern having been sustained in the behavior of other men long before the current performers appeared on the scene. To understand what happens in any situation, then, it is necessary to know something about the regularities in the functioning both of groups and of persons.

It is ironic that the term "personality" has come to designate the spontaneous tendencies that characterize a particular individual. In

Greek the term "persona" referred to the mask used by actors to conceal their individuality. It represented the role being performed in the play. But the concept now refers to what stands behind the mask, what one would do if given the opportunity. As long as such occasions do not arise, however, each person continues to wear a mask of respectability—whatever this may be from the standpoint of his reference group.

Suggested References

ADORNO, T. W., ELSE FRENKEL-BRUNSWIK, DANIEL J. LEVINSON, and R. NEVITT SANFORD, *The Authoritarian Personality*, Part I–III. New York: Harper & Bros., 1950. A comprehensive study of a single type of person, providing detailed demonstrations of several of the advanced techniques currently used in personality research.

ALLPORT, GORDON W., *Personality: A Psychological Interpretation*. New York: Henry Holt & Co., 1937. A standard reference work, treating personality as a unique configuration of traits and emphasizing the importance of stylistic variations.

CAMERON, NORMAN and ANN MAGARET, *Behavior Pathology*, Ch. II, IV, VII, XIII–XVII. Boston: Houghton Mifflin Co., 1951. A discussion of various neurotic and psychotic symptoms as adjustments to the demands of the social environment, with an excellent treatment of paranoid disorders.

FREUD, SIGMUND, *The Basic Writings of Sigmund Freud*, A. A. Brill, trans. Books I, II, IV. New York: Random House, 1938. Classic treatises on the manner in which unconscious impulses appear in disguised form in dreams, jokes, slips of the tongue, unintentional mistakes, and the forgetting of familiar materials.

LECKY, PRESCOTT, *Self-Consistency: A Theory of Personality*, Ch. V–IX. New York: Island Press, 1951. The posthumously published lectures of a brilliant psychologist, who viewed individuality as the product of one's being oriented toward a unique set of values.

THOMAS, WILLIAM I., and FLORIAN ZNANIECKI, *The Polish Peasant in Europe and America*, Vol. II, Part IV. New York: Alfred A. Knopf, 1927. A sociological classic, illustrating with the life record of an immigrant the manner in which a man's life gains consistency by becoming oriented toward a distinct set of values.

Part Three

Interpersonal Relations

10

Sentiments
and
interpersonal
roles

It has frequently been contended that literary men present a more convincing depiction of human life than social psychologists. Scholars who study human behavior appear somehow to fail to come to grips with some of the very attributes that make men human. Even in the best of their studies, something seems to be missing. Novelists and playwrights are preoccupied largely with love, friendship, infatuation, hero worship, hatred, jealousy, resentment, vengeance, and other sentiments. The central theme in so many literary works centers upon the various affective ties binding the characters together, their development and transformation, and the joys, sorrows, and poignant conflicts which arise from them. Although these phenomena are unquestionably a central part of the drama of life, social psychologists have until quite recently avoided their study.

But there can be little doubt that an important part of the immediate world of each person consists of other human beings, each of them unique and each making a distinct set of demands. Every individual is surrounded by a number of personifications, some of them imaginary, and he must learn to deal with those with whom his lot has been cast.

More than 200 years ago a group of philosophers in Scotland—among them Adam Ferguson, David Hume, and Adam Smith—insisted that it was the various sentiments which were shaped and nurtured in intimate associations that distinguished men from other animals. In spite of the great influence of these writers over their contemporaries and in spite of the development of this notion in the romanticist movement of the following century, until very recently this contention has been ignored by social scientists. Notable exceptions, such as Cooley and McDougall, were like cries in the wilderness. During the past few decades, however, there has been a convergence of interest in the study of intimate contacts. Psychiatrists, who have always been concerned with the manner in which men are related to one another, have been spurred on by Sullivan, who insisted that personality development was necessarily a part of a network of interpersonal relations. Moreno pioneered attempts to devise procedures for describing and measuring such networks, and with his associates he has developed a variety of sociometric techniques. A number of psychologists, noting that the perception of human beings is a somewhat more complex process than the perception of inanimate objects, have established this as a special area of inquiry. In addition, the rise of the current interest in small groups as well as the increasing popularity of existentialism have directed even more attention to these phenomena.[1] In spite of the still undeveloped state of knowledge in this field, the subject is one of utmost importance.

The Problem of Interpersonal Relations

In virtually all group transactions the participants interact simultaneously in two capacities: as role-players and as unique human beings. When playing conventional roles, men are acting as units in a social structure. There is consensus over the contributions to be

[1] Cf. Jerome S. Bruner and Renato Tagiuri, "The Perception of People," in Lindzey, *op. cit.*, Vol. II, pp. 634–54; Gladys Bryson, *Man and Society* (Princeton: Princeton University Press, 1945); and Edward A. Shils, "The Study of the Primary Group," in *The Policy Sciences*, Daniel Lerner and Harold D. Lasswell, eds. (Stanford: Stanford University Press, 1951), pp. 44–69.

made by each role-player, and the conduct of each participant is circumscribed by expectations that are derived from cultural norms. Each person categorizes himself and the others, recalls the appropriate models of conduct he has learned through past participation in similar settings, and then meets his obligations. Concerted action then proceeds in a prearranged manner.

When they are involved in such enterprises, however, men also interact with one another as living creatures—as unique persons. What the reactions of each of them will be depends upon the distinctive attributes of those who happen to come into contact. No two human beings are alike; even when they are playing the same conventional role, the performance of each person is different, in style if in no other way. Hence, the pattern of reciprocal attraction or repulsion is in each instance different. The initial reactions may range from love at first sight to an immediate loathing of the other person. Some kind of estimate is made, for it is very unlikely that two or more people could interact and remain indifferent. If the contact is sustained, the participants may become friends or rivals; they may or may not become dependent upon one another; they may become resentful, grateful, or jealous. What is important is that the manner in which each person reacts to his associates sets up a second framework of claims and obligations. *The pattern of interpersonal relations that develops among those who engage in joint action constitutes another matrix that places further limitations upon what each person may or may not do.*

Even in the most ephemeral transactions some kind of interpersonal response apparently takes place. It is doubtful if two people can meet without some emotional reaction, however slight, taking place between them. When men and women of reproductive age come together, for example, there is often a reciprocal evaluation in erotic terms. If the meeting is between strangers who are well mannered, it is unlikely that either party will do anything to reveal his inner experiences. Comments about some particularly attractive person of the opposite sex are usually reserved for one's intimate friends. Sometimes people are unaware of their response. Those who are happily married or engaged to be married may even deny being attracted by someone else, but the vehemence of such denials sometimes belies a stronger attraction than they would care to admit— even to themselves. In most passing contacts, however, such reactions are matters of little concern to either party and are soon forgotten.

When people continue to associate with one another for some time, however, more stable orientations emerge. One person may become extremely fond of a second and develop a blinding resentment toward a third. Such sentiments may be viewed as persistent ways in which one individual approaches another, steady dispositions that remain fairly stable from situation to situation. Although the term *interpersonal relations* has been utilized in a number of ways in psychiatry and in social psychology, it will be used here to refer to the mutual orientations that develop and crystallize among individuals who are in sustained contact. The character of the relationship will depend in each case upon the personality traits of those involved.

Just as one expects special consideration from his close friends and would be reluctant to ask a favor of those he dislikes, each party in a network of interpersonal relations finds himself bound by a set of special claims and obligations. Each man plays a role, but such *interpersonal roles* are not to be confused with conventional roles. Although both types of roles can be identified in terms of shared expectations, there are important differences. Conventional roles are standardized and impersonal; the rights and duties remain the same regardless of who plays the part. Although no two men play the same conventional role in the same manner, the model of ideal conduct remains the same. But the claims and obligations that make up an interpersonal role depend entirely upon the personal characteristics of the participants. Ties are established on the basis of their unique sensitivities and preferences. Unlike conventional roles, which are often units within well-established career lines, most interpersonal roles are not taught explicitly. Each person develops his own ways of treating partners, enemies, or heroes by adjusting to the demands made upon him by the particular individuals with whom he comes into contact.

Although no two networks of interpersonal relations are alike, there are a number of recurrent contexts in which men come together, and those with similar personalities respond alike to the same kind of treatment. Hence, it is not surprising that typical patterns of interpersonal relations become discernible in diverse cultural settings and that typical interpersonal roles can be named and recognized. Men become associated with one another while engaging in a wide variety of collaborative tasks, and among the numerous interpersonal roles that emerge in such contexts—depending in each instance upon the personality traits represented among the participants—are the colleague, the partner, the client, the lover, the love object, the provider, and the shirker. People also become involved with one another while competing for like interests, and among the interpersonal roles that arise in this context are the rival, the enemy, the conspirator, and the ally. Should another person attempt to mediate differences, he becomes the arbiter. Another recurrent context is one involving the exercise of power, where one party is dominated by another. If such domination is supported by consensus, it constitutes legitimate authority, and those who enjoy ascendancy assume the role of the authority figure. But the actual capacity to direct the conduct of others is not always in the hands of those whose conventional role is vested with authority; a child who knows how to use temper tantrums, for example, may rule his harassed parents. Among the interpersonal roles that emerge in contexts marked by a disparate distribution of power are the leader, the follower, the hero, the stooge, and the protector. Although customary procedures often develop in each group as to how some of these roles should be played, they remain analytically distinct from conventional roles in that each person assumes his role by virtue of his personal attributes.

The formation of interpersonal relations occurs independently of customary procedures; hence, a variety of interpersonal relations may develop in the same conventional setting. In each organized group there are common understandings as to how the participants are supposed to feel about one another. In a family, for example, the relationship between mothers and sons is conventionally defined. Mothers have a number of responsibilities for looking after the welfare of their children, and sons are expected to accept parental discipline. But within this cultural framework the manner in which any particular mother and son actually approach one another varies considerably. Mothers are supposed to love their sons, and most of them do; however, there are differences in the quality of their love. Furthermore, cases of mothers who hate or are jealous of their sons are not unusual. Some sons adore their mothers and are completely subservient to them, but others are defiant and in constant rebellion.

Some sons are sexually attracted to their mothers; others are so repelled as to want to avoid them at all times. Some mothers exploit their sons, just as some sons dominate their mothers. Three sons of the same mother may each be oriented toward her in a different way, and in spite of all her efforts at impartiality she may find that she consistently favors one over the others. Similarly, a husband and wife may be infatuated with one another; they may be rivals for the affection of their only child; they may seek constantly to use one another; or they may cling desperately to each other in spite of their animosities for fear of being single again. The kinds of sentiments that are supposed to develop frequently do arise, but there are many cases in which people find it difficult to feel as they should, however conscientiously they may try. Overtly they conform to group norms, but inwardly each knows that the appearances being maintained are only a façade. Thus, even when playing the same conventional roles different people become related to one another in different ways—ranging from orientations that are accepted to those that are proscribed.

The independence of interpersonal roles from conventional roles is further revealed in the fact that similar interpersonal relations can be found in different conventional settings. The appropriate conventional roles for classrooms and for places of work are quite different; yet remarkable similarities appear in the ties that develop between a teacher and her students and between an employer and his employees. An employer may suppress all individuality, treating his workers as an extension of his own efforts; although many of his workers rebel and quit, others obediently turn to him for all decisions. In the same manner a teacher may attempt to control her students with an iron hand, dealing with them as instruments for carrying on efficient pedagogical exercises in a fastidiously maintained classroom. Some students become highly resentful and even contemptuous, but others become very devoted to her and find comfort in having everything decided for them. Some offices are marked by jovial camaraderie, and even the office boy calls his employer by his first name. Similarly, some classrooms are characterized by an atmosphere of gaiety, and the teacher who is liked as an understanding friend is not addressed with conventional deference. An employer may be in love with his stenographer, and the bookkeeper, who is also in love with her, may resent him as a rival. In the same manner a teacher may have a pet student whom she favors, and the student's close friends may compete with her for his affection. These observations suggest that any kind of interpersonal relationship can develop in any conventionally ordered situation.

The distinction stands out quite clearly when the claims and obligations that make up the conventional role clash with those which constitute the interpersonal role. Difficulties arise, for example, when friendships are formed between people who are supposed to maintain their distance. Although some people choose their intimate associates on the basis of propriety or potential utility, whether one spontaneously likes or dislikes another depends upon the compatibility of their respective personalities. One enjoys the company of people with similar personal values whose idiosyncrasies elicit sympathetic responses, but such individuals are not always of the appropriate social status. The problem becomes even more pressing in the choice of love objects. In spite of all the customary barriers "falling in love" does not always occur within approved boundaries, especially when erotic attraction is involved. A person suddenly becomes infatuated and sometimes even has difficulty in justifying the compelling attraction to himself. Some of the most poignant conflicts faced by men arise when they find themselves drawn toward someone with whom contact is forbidden—an enemy in time of war, a person of a different social class or a despised ethnic minority, or a member of their own family. The same kind of inner struggle arises when members of a respectable family develop an intense dislike for one another. Two brothers who become jealous rivals for the hand of the same girl may still be bound by their common affection for their parents. Furthermore, they play conventional roles that require their showing some consideration toward one another. Attempts are often made to conceal such incongruities, but they do manifest themselves, especially in crisis situations when the customary standards of conduct become less enforceable.

The fact of independent variation is further supported by the observation of similar interpersonal relations throughout the world, in spite of the diversity of culture. In all societies some individuals dominate others by virtue of their remarkable personal attributes, although the traits that inspire awe may vary considerably. Men and women everywhere become infatuated with one another, although such ties do not necessarily constitute the basis for marriage. In all societies heroes are acclaimed and admired, and sibling rivalries for the affection of elders erupt and are suppressed. The moral code calling for the establishment of appropriate sentiments in each cultural setting differs from group to group, but the violation of such codes occurs everywhere.

Thus, while participating in concerted action men simultaneously interact in terms of two sets of gestures. As they interact in their capacity as performers of conventional roles, they use conventional symbols, saying and doing those things that are deemed proper. These gestures are subject to social control. At the same time, however, the unique personal orientation of each actor is manifested in the style of his performance as well as in what he does in inadequately defined situations in which he can exercise some choice. The detection of personality traits in turn elicits reciprocating responses, which are often unconscious. If a man feels that his colleague's contributions are something less than wholehearted and sincere, he may become resentful, perhaps disappointed, or even disdainful—depending upon his own characteristic reaction to shirkers. He may experience impulses to strike, to caress, to express concern, or to scream in rage at some of his associates. Although such dispositions are usually inhibited, they are frequently manifested in a variety of expressive movements that are noted by the other participants. Among those who are involved in a common enterprise, then, there is a continuous interchange of gestures in terms of which mutual adjustments are made. Part of this interchange is deliberate and largely symbolic; the rest is more spontaneous and direct.

These two forms of interaction blend almost imperceptibly into each other. The distinction being made is analytical, for the two processes actually go on simultaneously. But the distinction is an important one, and the failure to make it can lead to considerable confusion. The difference is not always taken into account, for example, in studies of leadership. There are people who assume positions of responsibility by virtue of inheritance or some other conventional arrangement. They are addressed with deference, at least in public, but some of them are not respected as individuals. Such personages may be contrasted with the "natural leaders" who emerge in crisis situations—in spontaneous rebellions or in infantry combat. Such charismatic leaders are followed by virtue of their unusual personal qualities and are not easily replaced; whereas those who attain high positions by virtue of institutional arrangements can usually be replaced without much difficulty.[2] Similarly, misunderstandings may arise when anthropologists who study patriarchal, authoritarian societies describe the countless customs in which male dominance is manifested without taking individual differences into account. When the distinction between conventional and interpersonal roles is not made, readers get the impression that all men in a country like Japan dominate the women with whom they are in sustained contact. The fact that the Japanese make such frequent reference to the *"kaka-denka"* suggests, however, that there are probably as many "hen-pecked" husbands in Japan as elsewhere. Although it may not be apparent to those who observe only the conventionally submissive conduct of Japanese women, especially in the presence of strangers, what happens in a particular family depends upon the personalities of its members.[3] It is for this reason that some ethnographers have advocated the collection of life histories, which are especially valuable in revealing differences between the outward compliance with group norms and what happens in private life.

Our interest, then, centers upon the more lasting ties that are formed among unique individuals. Whenever people are in sustained association with one another, they enter into highly personalized relationships which impose special claims and obligations upon them that are independent of their respective conventional roles. When a person likes someone, he feels constrained to be considerate, to overlook shortcomings, and to rush to his assistance when needed. But he feels no particular obligation to do such things for someone he dislikes; indeed, he may feel much better if he goes out of his way to spite him. To the extent that such tendencies become established the network of interpersonal relations may be regarded as another agency of social control. The task confronting social psychologists is the construction of an adequate conceptual scheme for the study of these phenomena.

[2] Cf. David G. Mandelbaum, *Soldier Groups and Negro Soldiers* (Berkeley: University of California Press, 1952), pp. 15–39; and Fritz Redl, "Group Emotional Leadership," *Psychiatry*, V (1942), 573–96.

[3] Cf. Oscar Lewis, "Husbands and Wives in a Mexican Village," *American Anthropologist*, LI (1949), 602–10.

Sentiments as Behavioral Systems

The basic unit of analysis for the study of interpersonal relations is the *sentiment*. In common parlance we sometimes think of love, hatred, jealousy, pride, or resentment as "feelings" which arise from time to time "inside" of someone. The vocabulary of common sense is often vague, and such terms are used to refer both to transitory subjective states as well as to sustained orientations toward particular human beings. It is in the latter sense that the terms will be used here. When a man says that he is in love with a woman, he is referring to a relationship that is comprehensive and relatively enduring. It is much more than a momentary experience; it is an orientation that persists in a wide variety of transactions. Behavioristically, a sentiment may be viewed as what one person *means* to another. It is to be recalled that a meaning is not some vague "idea" floating about in the head, but a complex form of behavior—an organized disposition to act in a circumscribed manner toward an object. A sentiment is one type of meaning—an organized disposition to act toward a personification upon which some kind of value is placed. To hate someone is to be prepared to act in an aggressive or defensive manner toward him.

What is a sentiment as a form of behavior? As in the case of all other meanings, sentiments are not to be identified in terms of any particular line of action, but through a *pattern* of response. Among the most fruitful formulations is that of the British psychologist Shand, who pointed out at the turn of the century that sentiments are organized systems. He described some of the basic patterns by citing four emotional reactions that are regularly aroused under specified circumstances. He noted that when a man is in love with a woman, he experiences joy in her presence, sorrow in her prolonged absence, fear when there is danger of losing her, and anger if she is attacked. He then observed that when one hates someone, the same reactions are evoked under the opposite conditions. Since actual responses depend upon the exigencies of the situation in which one is involved, they vary considerably. But sentiments are behavioral systems which become discernible in the configuration of responses toward a given person. Until very recently Shand's work has been virtually ignored in the United States, but in Europe it elicited considerable interest.[4]

Thus, sentiments may be defined behavioristically not so much in terms of any particular act but through their organization. The various movements are directed toward a goal, but diverse means are selected to achieve it, depending upon the circumstances. In hatred, for example, the end is the immobilization or destruction of an opponent, and a man who hates becomes sensitized both to danger and to opportunities for attack. In the presence of his foe aggressive motor tendencies are mobilized; he is visualized in the worst possible light, and a number of justifications for the hostility emerge. Imagery, perceptual sensitivity, and motor processes are all selectively oriented to move in a general direction. Consistency arises not in recurrent movements, but in their structure. Sentiments are ways in which people approach, avoid, protect, and otherwise organize themselves to act with reference to one another. As such they rest upon inferences concerning the characteristics of the other person. As in the case of other meanings, each component act is predicated upon the assumption that the other person is a human being of a particular sort. The various situational responses rest upon certain consistent properties that are imputed to the object.

Furthermore, sentiments involve an evaluation of personifications. Some kind of estimate is placed upon any object that is regarded as a source of agreeable or disagreeable experiences; a man evaluates his associates on the basis of the way in which they affect him. If a person is the source of some sort of gratification, he becomes a desirable object and is liked; if he is the source of frustration, he becomes an irritating or even a dangerous object and is disliked. It appears that Freud was thinking along similar lines when he spoke of "object cathexes."

It is through the pattern of responses that people are able to detect sentiments even when they are not acknowledged. For example, how can one tell that his sister is in love in the face of her repeated denials? Is it not an inference that is made after observing her choices and expressive movements in various situations? When she accidentally bumps into the boy, she blushes. She glows when-

[4] Alexander F. Shand, *The Foundations of Character* (London: Macmillan & Co., 1920), pp. 35–38. Cf. William McDougall, *An Introduction to Social Psychology* (Boston: John W. Luce & Co., 1918), pp. 125–63; and Alexander H. Leighton, *My Name is Legion* (New York: Basic Books, 1959), pp. 226–75, 395–420.

ever he speaks cordially to her, and her eyes follow him about the room. When another boy tries to gain her attention, he is virtually ignored. When another girl monopolizes his attention, she becomes irritable. The value that a person places upon any object is not what is said about its preciousness but the care that is devoted to obtaining it and to protecting its integrity.

As Adam Smith pointed out so long ago, the distinctive mark of sentiments, in contrast to other meanings, is that they rest upon empathy. There is some measure of sympathetic identification with another person, the recognition of the other as a human being—a creature who is able to make choices, to suffer agonies, to enjoy gratifications, to have hopes and dreams, and in general to react in much the same manner that one himself might react under similar circumstances. As Buber put it, to recognize another person as a "you" rather than an "it" implies a conception of him as being endowed with qualities much like one's own.[5] Thus, sentiments are predicated upon an imputation of attributes that one sees in himself.

Seeing another person as a "you" implies a recognition of his individuality and the fact that he is striving toward a distinctive set of interests. He is seen as a unique creature, and a sentiment rests upon one's knowledge of the dispositions that characterize a particular individual—his personality. One is resentful toward one man who takes advantage of his position of authority, if a sadistic delight can be imputed to him. But another person who acts in much the same manner may be regarded with compassion, if it is assumed that he just cannot help himself. Thus, sentiments rest upon one's ability to take the role of a specific person, to identify with him, and to define situations from his unique standpoint. Since people differ considerably in their capacity for empathy, there are personality differences in the ability to form sentiments.

When empathy is absent, even human beings are treated as if they were physical objects. Many of the social contacts that take place in a large city are devoid of sentiments. When one comes into contact with strangers, especially if they happen to be of a different social class or ethnic group, he interacts with them more as things than as people. The most callous disregard for others occurs even among those who mean well simply because they do not identify themselves with most of the people with whom they deal. Bus

[5] Martin Buber, *I and Thou*, Ronald G. Smith, trans. (New York: Charles Scribner's Sons, 1958).

drivers, for example, are often addressed as appendages on the steering wheel. The distinction between treating someone as a "you" and as an "it" has been made even for the sexual embrace, presumably one of the most personal of the many forms of social interaction. Through the ages men who have patronized prostitutes have complained that something was "missing" in their amorous escapades. In order to hold their clientele the women learn to act as if they were excited, but in their frank confessions they reveal that they are indifferent to their customers, if not contemptuous of them. They are merely things—a source of money. In contrast, many prostitutes are able to establish relationships with their lovers that are psychologically gratifying, even though the interchanges are physically like those with their patrons.[6] What is important, then, is not so much the biological fact that a given organism is of the category *homo sapiens* but the projection to it of those qualities which facilitate establishing some kind of sympathetic identification. This suggests that there are a number of conventional roles—such as, that of a hangman or of a soldier in combat—which can be performed more efficiently when sentiments are absent.

Since no two people are alike, there are probably an infinite number of sentiments. Like other meanings, sentiments vary along several dimensions, and one of the ways in which they differ is in the extent to which their component tendencies are internally consistent.[7] Examples of almost rigid consistency can be found in orientations toward idealized personifications, as in infatuations and cases of hero worship. A person is placed upon a pedestal and revered, and all inconsistent impulses are suppressed or repressed. At the other extreme are cases in which two or more dissociated personifications are constructed of the same individual, with each personification being evaluated so differently that the various acts predicated upon them turn out to be contradictory. Most sentiments apparently fall somewhere between these poles; as Freud points out, the manner in which most people are oriented toward those with whom they are in intimate contact tends to be ambivalent. Just as a child sees his mother at times as a "good mother" and at other times

---

[6] Cf. C. H. Rolph, ed., *Women of the Streets* (London: Secker & Warburg, 1955), pp. 85–88; and Harold Greenwald, *The Call Girl* (New York: Ballantine Books, 1958).

[7] For a thoughtful discussion of a different set of dimensions see Vera V. French, "The Structure of Sentiments," *Journal of Personality*, XV (1947), pp. 270–75.

as a "bad mother," so adults often construct more than one personification for those they know. For example, a successful career woman may conceive of herself as altruistically dedicating her life to a worthy cause and may look upon her husband as a good natured but lazy man concerned primarily with pleasure. She regards her work as being so important that his interests would naturally be secondary. She finds him useful as a servant, as someone who can help consummate her erotic impulses, and as a pleasant companion whenever she is not working. She has little respect for him, and in her daydreams of success she sees herself sharing her glory with some other man. But from time to time, in moments of serious reflection, she realizes that she is actually working for her own self-aggrandizement. On these agonizing occasions she sees her husband as a simple man who loves her, a man who cannot understand why she works so hard but accepts on faith her claim that it is important, a man who is disturbed by pangs of guilt because there is not more that he can do to help her, a man who is doing the best he can to meet a succession of difficult situations. When she realizes how much he is actually sacrificing for her, she personifies him as a loyal, lovable man. Although in most instances the various tendencies that make up a sentiment are more or less consistent, this is not necessarily the case. When conceptions of the same individual become dissociated, he may be treated periodically in ways that contrast sharply with his usual fate.

Sentiments also vary considerably in intensity, which seems to be related at least in part to the extent to which there are contradictions in one person's orientation toward another. For example, an infatuation is an intense attraction which appears to be at its height in situations in which there is a conflict between erotic impulses and the necessity of restraining oneself out of consideration for the love object. Tension presumably mounts from the fact that an organism is mobilized for acts which cannot be immediately consummated; under such circumstances one becomes so preoccupied with the love object that everything else appears dull and uninteresting. This may be contrasted to the mutual understandings between a couple who have been married for twenty years and have come to take each other for granted. Similarly, hatred seems to be more intense when there is some ambivalence, and it has been suggested that one is far more vindictive toward a traitor than he is toward an enemy. In spite of the disillusionment one is still somewhat responsive to his erstwhile comrade's views, even when he is organized to destroy him.[8] When sentiments are intense, there is a deeper sense of personal obligation, and the failure to live up to such expectations fills one with remorse. This only heightens the inner conflict even more. It has been noted frequently that there is no bitterness that is more unreasonable than that of unrequited love.

Like other meanings, sentiments, once they are formed, tend to be self-sustaining. The stability of such orientations is revealed especially by the death of someone who had been very close. Intellectually one can accept the fact that the person is dead, but he may continue to interact vicariously with the personification for some time.[9] Although the interaction of living people is highly variable, fairly stable personifications are constantly reaffirmed through selective perception. Each person constructs hypotheses that are plausible to him and becomes sensitized to those cues that tend to confirm his expectations. He is likely to give those he likes the benefit of the doubt. If he happens to see a friend doing something that appears reprehensible, he concludes either that he must have been mistaken in what he saw or that there must have been some extenuating circumstances. But the same person is not so generous with people he dislikes; he approaches them in a defensive stance, prepared for the worst. Almost any cue, including quite innocent remarks, may be interpreted as a hostile move. In these ways most people manage to retain the same evaluation of each of their associates almost independently of what they actually do. When someone constantly acts contrary to expectations, however, most people sooner or later revise their estimates. But there are remarkable personality differences in the ability to reevaluate others. Some are so rigid that they are incapable of seeing incompatible cues that flatly contradict their hypotheses. In spite of repeated rebuffs they go on as they had before—until a catastrophe forces them to make an "agonizing reappraisal" of the relationship.

Although most people believe that they are aware of all their sentiments, psychiatrists are constantly pointing out that this is not

[8] Cf. Karen Horney, "On Feeling Abused," *American Journal of Psychoanalysis*, XI (1951), 5–12; and Harold F. Searles, "The Psychodynamics of Vengefulness," *Psychiatry*, XIX (1956), 31–39.

[9] Henry H. Brewster, "Grief: A Disrupted Human Relationship," *Human Organization*, IX (1950), 19–22.

true. Usually, each person is explicitly cognizant of some of his sentiments, only intuitively aware of others, and unconscious of still others that are perfectly obvious to the people who know him. Such lack of awareness may arise either from habit or from repression. When sentiments are being formed, as in situations in which two people are just getting acquainted, there is usually a high degree of consciousness. The various characteristics of newly found friends or rivals are picked out and contemplated. Once a relationship becomes established, however, there is progressively less awareness until such matters come to be taken for granted. This does not mean that the sentiment has disappeared; there are well organized patterns of behavior, but there is no longer any awareness of them. Thus, many parents love their children dearly; they are prepared to make almost any sacrifice for them, but they rarely think about this. They simply take it for granted. Externally they may even appear a bit blasé, but in crisis situations their orientation becomes apparent; spontaneously they rush to protect their children first. The altruistic sentiment of such parents is implicit in their behavior. When such a relationship exists, constant reminders of love and various symbols of affection become superfluous. They are called forth only when something unusual happens and when the character of the relationship is temporarily in doubt. People make designations to themselves concerning the manner in which they are prepared to act toward others only when there is some uncertainty.

Whenever people are questioned about their views toward intimate associates, they generally profess those sentiments that are conventionally approved. Most mothers insist that they love their children, even though their overt conduct may betray a very different relationship. When organized dispositions to act toward particular people conflict with conventional norms to the point where a person becomes guilt stricken, sentiments may be repressed from consciousness. Sometimes the very parents who constantly make an ostentatious display of their affection—kissing, hugging, or making verbal protestations of love—are not quite so devoted to their children as others who quietly look after the interests of their offspring. In crisis situations such parents may even flee desperately to save themselves, abandoning their children to fend for themselves. Similarly, when there are serious rivalries within a family, the sentiments that develop may never be admitted. Various aggressive tendencies may be manifested through inadvertent slips of the tongue, forgetting important dates, or accidentally doing something that proves embarrassing to the others, but there is no consciousness of hostility. Not to love one's siblings is unthinkable.

What Shand apparently did not appreciate fully was the fact that sentiments develop their structure and are constantly reinforced as component parts of interpersonal relations in which the participants are interdependent. Sentiments do not exist in isolation; as elements in more inclusive relationships they are not likely to be sustained without some kind of support from other people. Jealousy, for example, is a sentiment that is not likely to last unless there is some kind of activity, actual or imagined, on the part of others. A man cannot remain jealous unless he has reason to believe that someone he cares for is interested in another party; if the others become indifferent to each other, the sentiment disappears. Even in the passionate devotion to a beautiful woman who views her lover in utter contempt the relationship is likely to be terminated unless there is some kind of responsiveness on the part of the woman. The reaction, of course, need not be reciprocating. As psychoanalysts put it, cathexis depends upon the responsiveness of the object.

Each person forms a repertoire of sentiments in the course of his associations with a limited number of people whom he comes to know as unique individuals. The responses of such people are of crucial importance for the construction and reinforcement of one's conception of himself, and those upon whom he depends for such support may be designated as his *significant others*. They constitute the audience whose judgments are most influential. Each is highly responsive to the demands of such persons because he cannot afford to lose their support; whenever there is a possibility of their not responding in the desired manner, he becomes filled with anxiety. All persons who are intimately known are significant others, but a high degree of intimacy is not necessary. A teacher or a priest, for example, may be very influential, even though little may be known of his private life. Although most significant others are real people, the audience may also include imaginary personifications—such as, popular heroes or the authors of one's favorite books. It should also be emphasized that the relationship need not be friendly. Sometimes a man who hates some of the people around him acts in ways designed to spite them, maintaining his self-respect by keeping them upset and angry. The sentiments which characterize each person, then, depend upon the attributes of the peculiar combination of people with whom he comes into close contact in the course of his career.

Once sentiments have crystallized, however, such orientations may subsequently be displaced upon a variety of other objects. Various categories of human beings may come to be evaluated as inferior, dangerous, or desirable and approached in a characteristic manner developed initially in interactions with specific individuals. One may drop a precious doll and inquire solicitously if it is hurt. One may become jealous of a dog who enjoys his sweetheart's attention; this involves imputing human experiences to the dog and directing toward it patterns of conduct developed in association with people. Indeed, in some cultures virtually all meanings are endowed with human characteristics. In contrast to the presuppositions underlying Western culture, the environment may not be divided into animate and inanimate objects. Every event—a thunderclap, a deep shadow, a stone which hurtles down the hill, a brook that bubbles— is viewed as redundant with life and with individuality. Such natural phenomena are dealt with as if they were human beings; motives are imputed, and they may be appealed to or threatened.[10] Most important of all, such orientations are directed toward oneself. Although there are a few men who can regard themselves with remarkable detachment, in most cases a man's conception of himself is a sentiment. A man may respect himself, or he may despise himself. In either case, he addresses himself in much the same manner in which he is prepared to act toward others whom he respects or despises.

Since the study of sentiments is only now getting under way, it is not surprising that only a few procedures have been set up for their observation. These techniques, on the whole, are modifications of standard procedures long in use for the assessment of personality, with the data being coded in a different manner. Thus, materials on the manner in which people are oriented toward one another are gathered through intensive interviews, through observations in prearranged contexts, and through a variety of tests.[11] Of the standard procedures the TAT (Thematic Apperception Test) appears to be especially promising, for in interpreting ambiguous pictures a sub-

[10] Cf. Henri Frankfurt et al., *The Intellectual Adventure of Ancient Man* (Chicago: University of Chicago Press, 1946).

[11] Cf. French, *op. cit.*; Leary, *op. cit.*; and Osgood et al., *op. cit.*

ject almost invariably gives away his characteristic orientations toward interpersonal roles. Once an analyst is able to ascertain which of the cast of characters with whom the subject has identified himself, he has a powerful tool for getting at that person's understanding of his place in a network of interpersonal relations. Psychoanalysts place considerable emphasis upon the importance of object relations in personality development, and psychologists are becoming more and more interested in the perception of people. Under these circumstances there is every reason to anticipate the development of more effective techniques in the near future.

The Structure of Typical Sentiments

One of the paradoxes of human life is that each sentiment is by definition idiosyncratic, and yet it is through the detection of such unique orientations that men are able to identify sympathetically with one another. Each sentiment is a meaning that develops in a succession of adjustments to the requirements of living with a particular person. Since both the subject and the object are unique, no two sentiments can be exactly the same; yet we have little difficulty in recognizing typical sentiments. Typical sentiments are component parts of recurrent patterns of interpersonal relations, and they may be regarded as ways of playing common interpersonal roles. Among men who live in association with one another certain kinds of relationships are almost unavoidable, and in them similar demands are made upon the participants. At one time or other each person finds himself at the mercy of someone else or has another in his power. Or he finds himself competing with someone for a prize. Beyond a certain age erotic interests of some sort are organically rooted, and their gratification requires soliciting the cooperation of someone else. In such contexts typical interests emerge, typical personifications are constructed, and typical evaluations of other people develop. This suggests that many sentiments are sufficiently similar to make the formulation of generalizations feasible.

The systematic study of sentiments has been rendered difficult by the intrusion of value judgments and popular beliefs. Especially in the United States, where romantic attractions are regarded as the proper basis for marriage, it is widely believed that there can be but one true love in the life of any individual. Many young people spend agonizing hours wondering whether or not this mystical experience has taken place as they contemplate the various metabolic transformations that occur as they come into contact with attractive persons of the opposite sex. Even among scholars there has been much controversy; theologians and psychiatrists have had bitter exchanges on the subject of love. The vehemence with which the argument is joined arises from the fact that such a high value is placed upon love; there is a tendency to associate it with other objects of high value—God, country, or some noble ideal.[12] Similarly, the almost universal condemnation of strife and hatred renders a candid discussion of disjunctive sentiments difficult. People who are in sustained association are not supposed to dislike one another, and these conventional norms are often confused with the facts. Hostilities which arise within intimate circles are often suppressed; if such emotional reactions become intense, they may even by repressed. Both observation and interpretation are hindered by negative value judgments, for men tend not to notice or to disavow inclinations of which they disapprove. A somewhat more objective inquiry may be initiated by considering the various *ways in which people evaluate one another* and by refusing to evaluate the sentiments themselves. Since this discussion is largely exploratory, it seems best to begin with a consideration of a limited number of the more obvious types of orientations. All that can be done is to describe the few sentiments that figure prominently in current speculation in psychiatry.

Conjunctive sentiments of all kinds are most likely to arise among those who are constantly associated in collaborative tasks. When men pursue common interests together, the attainment of their collective goal brings gratifications of some sort to each. Even when their respective interests are only reciprocating, they can be useful to each other. The participants in such contexts become interdependent, for the consummation of each person's impulses depends upon the contributions made by the others. Under such circumstances the other party is regarded as a *desirable object*. A high value is placed upon any person who is a constant source of gratification. A love object or a friend is valuable—something to be prized, coveted, and protected. One looks after its welfare and in some cases may even encourage the maximal development of its poten-

[12] Cf. Hugo G. Beigel, "Romantic Love," *American Sociological Review*, XVI (1951), 326–34.

tialities.[13] Such sentiments vary in intensity from a slight preference to a deep sense of devotion—as in the infatuation of a person completely obsessed with another, the dedication of a mother to her only child, or the love of God on the part of a devout man. Even the selfish become concerned over love objects. To the extent that one's interests cannot be satisfied without the collaboration of others, it becomes prudent to preserve a relationship that guarantees such desired responses. At times it may even become necessary to make sacrifices in order to assure the continuation of such ties. Most men are grateful for assistance, and they usually become quite fond of those who consistently contribute to their welfare.

Such sentiments may develop in a variety of conventional settings, and the designation of interpersonal roles differs somewhat by contexts. Since sex impulses require some measure of collaboration from another party, it is not surprising that many conjunctive relationships have an erotic base. The interpersonal roles in such relationships involve, of course, the lover and the love object. It should be emphasized, however, that there is no necessary connection between love and sex; people who despise one another can have frequent sex relations, and there can be deep and lasting parental or fraternal affection without erotic contacts. Sustained associations also develop in many other contexts—among boys on an athletic team, among men assigned to the same military unit, or among fellow workers in an office or factory. Among the interpersonal roles that emerge in such situations are the friend, the partner, the colleague, the helper, or the carrier of heavy burdens. Sometimes people are simply lonely. They may have anxieties about their personal worth and may seek evidence of their desirability. If so, they become responsive to almost any overture by another human being. Among the roles that may arise in such contexts are the companion and the stooge.

Even when attention is confined to the more intense attachments, in the Western intellectual tradition there is a long history of a distinction between two types of love. The Greeks referred to the love of another person who is useful as *Eros* and the love of another for his own sake as *Agape*. Using the same distinction, a number of theologians, especially in the Middle Ages, differentiated between human love, often regarded as having an erotic base, and divine

[13] Cf. Nelson Foote, "Love," *Psychiatry*, XVI (1953), 245–51.

love. Emphasis is being placed upon the difference between an orientation in which the love object is instrumental and one in which it is consummatory. A lover may be concerned primarily with his own gratifications or with those of the object. The same distinction has recently been revived in psychiatry, for it has proved useful in clarifying some of the confusion that arises when the same word is used to refer to two different sentiments.[14]

Possessive love is based upon an intuitive or explicit recognition of the fact that one's own gratifications depend upon the cooperation of another person. A high value is placed upon the personification as a *useful object*. It is nurtured, for it becomes a matter of enlightened self-interest to look after its welfare. This type of sentiment is discernible in a common pattern of behavior. A person is usually pleased at the presence of the love object and sorrowful when it is absent. If it is attacked, there is anger at the assailant; he protects it from exposure to danger, although there are limits to the extent to which he would risk himself in its defense. If the object favors others, he watches jealously. Since concern centers upon his own gratifications, however, he may not even notice frustration and pain on its part. Such love is conditional. The object continues to be valued highly only as long as it continues to render the desired services. When the lover is satiated, he may even reject the object. When it is no longer needed, it is put off or ignored—sometimes even forgotten. The goal of such behavior appears to be the complete surrender and subservience of the love object, as if it were something to be owned.

This type of sentiment can be found in many different contexts. There is an intuitive recognition of such a possibility in the initial defensive stance of those who become involved in erotic encounters. Women sometimes wonder if the men who express an interest in them actually care for them for what they are or intend only to exploit their bodies in their quest for sexual gratification. Even if they themselves feel attracted, they may refuse to cooperate. Even long frustrated spinsters may not allow themselves to be seduced until they are reasonably sure of the lover's sincerity. Some parents place their children under so much obligation that they manage to

<hr />

[14] Cf. Martin C. D'Arcy, *The Mind and Heart of Love* (New York: Meridian Books, 1956); and Pitirim A. Sorokin, ed., *Explorations in Altruistic Love and Behavior* (Boston: Beacon Press, 1950).

control them for the remainder of their lives. Those who make excessive sacrifices so that their gifted children can become great ballerinas, professional athletes, or scholars of world renown virtually enslave their beneficiaries. The latter feel so indebted that they cannot violate their parents' slightest whim without experiencing deep pangs of guilt. One frequently cited test of the manner in which one person loves another arises when there is a possibility of the love object's finding happiness away from the lover. Many a mother who professes to care for nothing but her child's happiness throws one obstacle after another in the way of his marriage. Similarly, a fatherly employer who claims to be concerned only with his secretary's future may block her marriage on quite respectable grounds; each suitor is found wanting for some reason, and she remains as a privileged clerk in his office. The love object is often treated well and may even be cherished but is never released. In common parlance it is said that people sometimes "kill with kindness."

In contrast, *disinterested love* is unconditional. A high value is placed upon the personification for what it is. As in the case of what is commonly called "maternal love" the primary concern is with the well-being of the love object. Indeed, in some cases a person cannot experience pleasure unless the object is also gratified. The pattern of behavior in terms of which this type of sentiment can be identified differs somewhat from the configuration that constitutes possessive love. There is joy at the sight of any satisfaction on the part of the love object and sorrow when it is injured or in pain. If someone should harm or threaten the love object, there is anger against the aggressor. At the sight of danger to the love object, there is great fear, and this may result in a person's exposing himself in order to conceal it. If necessary, he may even sacrifice himself to protect it. Thus, as Shand points out, the difference between possessive and disinterested love is that the latter is not self-centered; joy, sorrow, fear, and anger are aroused as the love object rather than oneself is seen in various contexts.[15] Both types of sentiments are called "love" because of the high value placed upon the object, but in this case the lover is more concerned with the object than with himself. The general tendency appears to be in the direction of identification with the object, and some psychiatrists have suggested

[15] Shand, *op. cit.*, pp. 43–50.

that the goal in this kind of relationship is complete union with the object.

Among Christians disinterested love has been idealized, and possessive love has been condemned. Altruism has been extolled as the most desirable of all human sentiments, while utilitarian love has been derogated as nothing more than an extension of selfishness. It is sometimes contended that all erotic relationships are exploitative, and they are condemned as a "lower" form of attraction which men share with other animals. Value judgments such as these make the study of sentiments difficult. When questioned about their orientations, most people insist that their love is altruistic. Because most men feel so guilty about using others for their own purposes, perceptual defenses interfere with their seeing what is rather obvious to others. This suggests that verbal claims about love cannot always be taken at face value; one can only observe what the person does in a variety of contexts to see whether his own interests or those of the love object are placed first.

Disjunctive sentiments are most likely to arise among those whose respective interests are such that the success of one person involves some kind of failure for the other. The valuation typically placed upon an opponent is negative, although there is considerable variation in intensity. Competitive situations arise when each participant, if he is to consummate his impulses, must outdo the others. In such rivalries the other party is viewed as a *frustrating object*. But frustration can range all the way from a slight inconvenience to the blocking of a man's career; hence, the desperation with which aggression is mounted varies. One may merely dislike a rival, or he may become completely preoccupied with ways of coping with him. Conflicts arise where interests are opposed, where the success of one party may require the immobilization or destruction of the other. Here the opponent is personified as a *dangerous object*, and automatic defensive reactions are elicited. It becomes necessary to protect oneself. Enemies are avoided as much as possible; and when contact is absolutely necessary, they are approached in a defensive stance—with a high degree of self-consciousness to minimize the possibilities of being exploited. The claims and obligations that make up the interpersonal roles in such relationships are twofold: aggressive action of some kind against the opponent—ranging from direct physical assault to indirect symbolic attacks—and loyalty to one's allies.

Disjunctive sentiments may develop in a number of different settings, including many in which they are forbidden. The kinds of conventional norms that emerge, the extent to which they are enforced, and the manner in which the interpersonal roles are labelled vary with these contexts. Competition of one sort or another can be found in many different situations—in the quest for the favors of an attractive woman, in the rivalry of professional colleagues, in the struggle for recognition in the eyes of the foreman, or in the factionalism found in social clubs. Competition may also arise within a family, where a mother and child may become rivals for the attention of the father. Housewives sometimes enter into seemingly friendly competition for status with their neighbors. Such contests are often not mentioned even when they are noticed, for they are generally regarded as undesirable. In most contexts some form of mild aggression is permitted, but there are stringent rules stating the limits beyond which rivals may not go. Even where the norms are not explicitly stated, there are informal understandings concerning decency and fair play. In many cases a victory won by foul means turns out to be empty, for the victor finds himself deserted, distrusted even by his former friends. Whenever competition erupts into open conflict, the opponent is transformed into an enemy. It then becomes more difficult to enforce the rules of fair play; as the popular expression goes, "All's fair in love and war." This suggests that disjunctive sentiments may arise within any group. Two sisters who fall in love with the same man or two colleagues who desire to be promoted to the same supervisory position may find themselves fighting in a manner that they had never dreamed possible.

Hatred is a commonly recognized sentiment. As Shand pointed out, it is discernible in a characteristic pattern of behavior. When one person hates another, he is sorry when the object is healthy and prosperous; he experiences anger or repugnance at its presence; he is gleeful when it suffers ill fortune; and he is filled with anxiety when it is too successful. Since these impulses are generally condemned, they are often inhibited. But such dispositions are frequently revealed through expressive movements—the quickly concealed smile when the hated person trips clumsily over himself, the grimace of disgust when he encounters a stroke of luck, or the shrug of indifference when he is in danger. When antipathies are not openly admitted, it is on the basis of such expressive movements that it becomes possible to make the inference that one person strongly dislikes another. Because men generally deny hating those with whom they are in close contact, it is frequently contended that one cannot hate someone he knows intimately. Actually, this is not the case. Relationships in which social distance is reduced have far greater potentialities for the development of intense hatred.[16] Indeed, probably the most intense form of hatred is the vindictiveness that develops when one turns against someone he had once loved and trusted.

The distribution of power among those who are interdependent need not be equal; and when the disparity is great, these sentiments take on a somewhat different character. A person may be said to have power if he can compel others to submit to his demands. *Power relationships* are bilateral. A person has power only as long as the others continue to submit; without such confirming responses the relationship is terminated—as in the case of a discharged enlisted man who confronts one of his former officers. The component interpersonal roles are readily identifiable. One person is dominant and is approached as a *superior object;* the other is submissive and is treated as an *inferior object.* Those who are dominant not only make decisions but in many cases also assume the responsibility for protecting their followers. Another attribute of such relationships is the ability of the dominant party to punish those who fail to co-operate. It is not necessary for him to mete out the punishment personally; institutional arrangements usually exist—as in the case of an employer who can discharge a recalcitrant worker and have him removed from the premises by the police. Power relationships exist, then, whenever people comply with the desires of others in fear of what might happen if they did not.[17]

Power relationships are not to be confused with legitimate authority—conventional roles that are defined by custom as dominant. The two frequently coincide. Most parents dominate their children, just as most employers dominate those who work for them.

---

[16] Cf. Henry V. Dicks, "Clinical Studies in Marriage and the Family," *British Journal of Medical Psychology*, XXVI (1953), 181–96.

[17] Cf. Harold D. Lasswell, *Power and Personality* (New York: W. W. Norton & Co., 1948), pp. 10–19.

But there are cases in which a sickly child develops considerable power over his parents by having spells and attacks whenever he is displeased. Even in a society in which men are supposed to dominate their wives a beautiful woman can rule her husband by threatening to deny him erotic favors. A worker may terrorize his employer through blackmail, should he possess knowledge that could create a scandal. A power relationship may develop in any context, then, whenever one party can enforce his ascendancy either through his own resources or by skillfully exploiting conventional arrangements.

The sentiment of a dominant person toward his cherished subordinate may be referred to as *condescension*. The object is clearly inferior as a human being but is nonetheless a source of gratification —as in the case of a loyal servant, an obedient child, or a faithful sycophant. Condescension is found in many contexts—in the attitude of many psychiatrists toward their patients, of many combat veterans toward raw recruits, and of many established professional men toward their younger colleagues. Some women speak of their husbands as a "second baby," and some husbands regard their wives in much the same manner as a lord looks upon his serf. The pattern of behavior that characterizes this orientation is paternalistic. The dominant person bestows favors upon the love object—by paying special attention to it, by teaching it to do things, by granting it gifts, by praising it for work well done, by punishing it for its "own good." It is taken for granted that he "knows best" and is actually in a position to pass judgment and to distribute rewards. The object is often personified as being childlike—not too intelligent, emotional and unstable, and not yet ready for responsibility. Like a delightful child it is to be treated with affection and consideration. But there is always a silent assumption of inferiority; the object is not treated with the respect accorded an equal, and areas of decision are often usurped. An extreme case of an inferior but desirable personification is the fool, of whom nothing serious is demanded. Since he is regarded as incompetent, he has privileges which sometimes border on licentiousness. In spite of his inferiority he is appreciated and popular.[18]

When the submissive person views his master as a desirable object, an idealized personification is constructed. In extreme cases

[18] Cf. Orrin E. Klapp, "The Fool as a Social Type," *American Journal of Sociology*, LV (1949), 157–62.

the dominant party becomes the object of *hero-worship*. "Hero" in Greek means the perfect man, the perfect expression of the group's ideals. Since different virtues are emphasized in each culture, the hero may appear in many forms; but he is usually endowed with courage, loyalty, generosity, honor, and remarkable ability. Heroes emerge in a number of conventional settings: a father, an elder brother, or a skillful athlete to a boy; an audacious leader to a band of warriors; a gangster to a group of delinquent boys; or a saint or martyr to members of a religious cult. The pattern of behavior found in hero-worship is one of admiration, deference, and respect. There is joy when one is recognized by the hero and singled out for praise; there is anger at any critic who dares to point to his weaknesses; there is a strong desire to please the hero, to do favors for him, and to pay homage; there is anxiety when the hero is in danger or when there is a possibility that one may be rejected by him. There is great curiosity about the hero, and efforts are made to find out as much as possible about him. Followers gossip avidly about their idol and attempt to emulate some of his habits. The hero is often used as a model after which one patterns his way of life.[19] This type of sentiment is found in varying degrees of intensity, but even in cases of mild admiration many of the behavior patterns found in accentuated form in hero-worship are discernible.

When there is a disparity in power among those who dislike one another, disjunctive sentiments take on somewhat different characteristics. The orientation of a dominant person toward an inferior object which is not satisfactory may be better described as *contempt*. A person who is contemptuous of another usually insists upon maintaining social distance. Should contact become necessary, a pattern of behavior develops that is marked by disparagement. There is a constant flow of criticism, cynical comment, and skepticism of the possibility of any accomplishment. Ironically, the most unabashed contempt is sometimes found among people who are themselves the objects of adoration. Overprotected children often look down upon their parents, as do the idols of "love slaves" who are ready to make

[19] Paul Meadows, "Some Notes on the Social Psychology of the Hero," *Southwestern Social Science Quarterly*, XXVI (1945), 239–47. Most sociological studies deal with popular heroes but are nonetheless suggestive. Cf. Orrin E. Klapp, "The Creation of Popular Heroes," *American Journal of Sociology*, LIV (1948), 135–41; "Hero Worship in America," *American Sociological Review*, XIV (1949), 53–62; and Gottfried Salomon, "Hero Worship," *Encyclopedia of the Social Sciences*, Vol. VII, pp. 336–38.

any sacrifice for them. They order their admirers about. They take delight in making unreasonable demands and then watching them squirm while making every effort to comply. They make invidious comparisons between them and others whose performances are deemed superior. Domination of any kind implies insufficient respect; but when the submissive party is regarded as a base object, the mistreatment sometimes becomes sadistic.

Not all persons who submit to domination believe that the arrangement is justified. Some regard the exercise of power as unfair, and they comply only because they can find no alternative. For such persons the dominant party becomes a frustrating object, and the sentiment formed is one commonly called *resentment*. The pattern of rebellion is frequently not overt. But a resentful person constructs a personification of the other party as one who is not really worthy of the deference he demands. He becomes especially sensitized to faults and complains frequently. At times, his acts may approach open defiance, if he feels he can get away with it. He is constantly alert for possibilities of disobeying orders, and he complies only when he is being watched. Once it is formed, this sentiment may persist even after the disagreeable relationship has been terminated. Children who have rebelled against parental authority sometimes grow up into adults with very little respect for authority figures of any kind.

Because of selective perception, sentiments of all kinds, once they are established, tend to be self-sustaining. A lover tends to impute ideal qualities to the love object and to overlook those features that displease him. Personifications are constructed through an imputation of motives, and only the most desirable of intentions are imputed. When an object is valued highly, it is seen as being worthy of that estimate. Once personifications have been constructed, patterns of avoidance and sensitivity become fixed. Men approach one another with hypotheses, and anything that is inconsistent with their expectations tends to be rejected. When a love object is detected doing something cheap, there is a tendency for the lover to assume that he saw the act out of context and did not understand. The extent to which personifications rest upon the hypotheses of the lover rather than the objective qualities of the love object is clearly demonstrated in the astonishment of the friends of a person who is infatuated. The lover imputes nothing but the finest of motives to his sweetheart, always gives her the benefit of the doubt, overlooks her physical blemishes, and endows her with all the other qualities he admires. Even when he is made conscious of some of her defects, he tells himself that they are insignificant when compared with all her positive features. His friends, being unable to see many of these virtues, point in vain to her obvious shortcomings.

Once disjunctive sentiments are formed, they are sustained through the construction of *contrast conceptions*. Most conflicts are visualized as contests between the good and the bad, and the adversary is often personified as the reincarnation of the devil. Combatants are selectively sensitized to those features in the behavior of their opponents which are condemned in their culture, overlooking or explaining away anything that is favorable. The most foul motives are imputed to the enemy. Since almost anything that a man does can be interpreted in a number of ways, the contrast conception is reinforced almost regardless of what the opponent actually does. If he fights courageously, he is called a fanatic; if he withdraws in the face of formidable opposition, he is called a coward. Having constructed an unfavorable personification of his foe, each combatant can conceive of himself as a fighter against evil, the defender of human virtues. Thus, the contrast is heightened even more. In all conflict situations—in rivalries within the home, in strikes, in revolutions, and in wars—the enemy is always seen as immoral, unfair, vicious, unprincipled, and inhuman.[20] The establishment of such contrasts makes possible the acceptance of a double standard of morality. Since enemies are regarded as something less than human, conventional norms do not hold when dealing with them. Treachery, trickery, bribery—anything done to gain an unfair advantage wins approval. Tactics that would never be tolerated within one's own group are praised and rewarded.[21]

From time immemorial men in conflict have committed the most incredible outrages against one another. Once peace is restored, however, they are invariably surprised to discover that their erstwhile adversaries are human and not nearly as wicked as expected. What this suggests is that opponents build up contrast conceptions of one another, impute unrealistic motives, and then react violently

[20] Eric Voegelin, "The Growth of the Race Idea," *Review of Politics*, II (1940), 283–317; and Lewis C. Copeland, "The Negro as a Contrast Conception," *Race Relations and the Race Problem*, E. T. Thompson, ed. (Durham: Duke University Press, 1939), pp. 152–79.

[21] Cf. William G. Sumner, *Folkways* (Boston: Ginn & Co., 1906), pp. 12–15.

to the personifications they themselves have constructed. Because of the kinds of motives that are characteristically imputed, rivals and foes have difficulty in grasping one another's orientations. Friendly overtures are met with suspicion, and this may unnecessarily prolong the conflict. Often opponents are characterized by imputing to them traits that one dislikes in himself. It is possible that people with a low level of self-esteem may be capable of more virulent hatred in that they are capable of projecting more vicious motives.

Since sentiments, like all other meanings, are behavioral systems that emerge in the course of interchanges between people, they may be transformed or terminated. Some sentiments, like infatuation, change relatively quickly. The patterns of response in terms of which the various sentiments are identified are predicated upon assumptions about the object. As the personification changes, the behavior pattern is also modified. Since all participants are constantly undergoing some change, with each interchange something different, however minute, is added to the relationship. But dramatic events may lead to more noticeable changes. Even disinterested love, where so little is asked of the love object, may be terminated when the latter consistently refuses to live up to reasonable expectations. The mother of a delinquent boy may at first be convinced that those who condemn her son are mistaken and unfair. But little by little she begins to wonder and finally becomes so disillusioned that she terminates the relationship. She may retain her love for a memory—an imaginary personification—but she no longer feels any special obligations to her son. Since hero-worship rests upon an idealized personification, it is not surprising that so many boys become disillusioned upon discovering that their father is only an ordinary human being. Jealousy may be terminated upon learning that the love object does not really care for the rival. Hatred has been described as a reaction to an inadequate defense against hostility; if so, once one feels secure, hatred becomes less intense and in time may be reduced to indifference. Once contact is reestablished with the foe, often through the offices of an arbiter who does not have an immediate interest in the outcome of the struggle, the combatants may tentatively redefine each other, admit the possibility of their own shortcomings, and eventually come to realize that the opponent is really not as bad as imagined.

The popular evaluation of sentiments is readily understandable.

Conjunctive sentiments are for the most part conducive to the optimal development of the participants, and most men strive to enter them. Even possessive love makes possible gratifications of many kinds, thereby providing some measure of personal security and making possible the pursuit of other objectives. Furthermore, conjunctive sentiments facilitate the carrying out of various co-operative ventures, and their general approbation is not surprising. Conversely, the development of disjunctive sentiments almost always hinders group living, and its widespread condemnation is also understandable. Continuous participation in conflict situations may lead to the development of new orientations toward people generally and to significant changes in personality. A person's sense of decency and fair play may be blunted. He may become so preoccupied with winning at all costs that he comes to evaluate everything in terms of victory. People who hate too long and too intensely continue to torture themselves by attacking contrast conceptions in their imagination. In time they may become insensitive to pity and gratitude, and sympathy becomes unimportant. Those who constantly use brute force may even become insensitive to the special conditions under which such tactics are ineffective.[22] Such possibilities have led reformers to call for the elimination of conflict, and most utopian communities have been pictured as being in perpetual harmony. Such considerations have sometimes made it difficult for sociologists to see that group solidarity is sometimes enhanced by opposition.[23]

Personality Differences in Sentiments

Individuals differ considerably in their ability to play various interpersonal roles, and each tends to become involved in networks of interpersonal relations in a characteristic way. At one time or another everyone participates in collaborative enterprises, but the manner in which he approaches his colleagues is in each case distinct. Some people are anxious to please and jump wholeheartedly into any joint undertaking. They like people, enjoy their company, and become upset when forced to work alone. Others do their share,

[22] Cf. Sidney Hook, "Violence," *Encyclopedia of the Social Sciences*, Vol. XV, pp. 264–67.
[23] Cf. Lewis Coser, *The Functions of Social Conflict* (Glencoe: Free Press, 1956), pp. 87–110.

but their contributions are conditional. As long as their partners are doing their bit, they will continue to make an effort; but they approach people with caution. Still others characteristically shirk their duties, performing only when someone else is watching or when it is clearly to their personal advantage to get something done. They believe that only a man who is stupid would work enthusiastically for someone else. Finally, there are people who characteristically fail to meet their obligations. Such performances in turn generally elicit typical reactions from other people—pity, anger, distrust, or appreciation—depending, of course, upon their respective modes of approaching their associates.

Becoming involved in conflicts of one kind or another seems to be inevitable, and each person develops a characteristic way of handling opposition. Some are straightforward; they assert their claims, challenge their opponents openly, and if necessary engage in physical combat. Others avoid an open break at all costs, concentrating upon "behind the scenes" maneuvers. The art of politics involves the manipulation of people, and some show a remarkable proclivity for the use of certain tactics: changing rules while the argument is in progress, organizing conspiracies, pressing chance advantages that arise, forming a base of operations through expedient alliances, or bargaining with opposition that cannot be overcome. Some people lose their tempers quickly; others are cold and calculating. Some people ingratiate themselves before the powerful to win their protection; others withdraw in the face of any serious challenge. Each type of maneuver tends to elicit reciprocating responses, and it is not surprising that some people are disliked everywhere.

Since a sentiment is what one individual means to another, each is by definition unique. But any given person's sentiments toward several different people may have much in common—giving his orientation toward people in general a distinctive style. Indeed, some are apparently incapable of forming certain sentiments. For example, close friendships sometimes call for giving without fully protecting oneself, leaving one open for possible exploitation. Some are so fearful of this kind of vulnerability that they refuse to enter such relationships. They prefer to be without intimate friends than to find themselves under obligation to do things that are inconvenient. Although most people have considerable difficulty in suppressing aggressive inclinations, there are some—often devoutly religious—who succeed in repressing their hostilities. They become incapable of participating in disjunctive relationships. When provoked, they "turn the other cheek" and wait patiently for their tormenters to come to their senses. Furthermore, some people are unable even to comprehend certain sentiments on the part of others. Even when they are able to see the behavioral manifestations, they cannot believe that others are *really* oriented as they are.

Sentiments are orientations predicated upon personifications, which are constructed largely through the imputation of motives. To the extent that there are personality differences in the kinds of motives that can be imputed plausibly to other people, there will be differences in the kinds of personifications that can be constructed. This is what sets limitations upon the kinds of sentiments that develop. The imputation of motives involves making inferences about the inner experiences of other people. We can only assume that others are sufficiently like ourselves and try to understand their conduct by projecting our own experiences to them. But a man cannot project experiences he has never had. If he has never had a sense of personal security, can he really appreciate the confident acts of another who has such assurance? An egotistical person cannot understand an altruistic act and begins looking for ulterior motives. Conversely, those who are convinced that all men are basically "good" have great difficulty in comprehending the acts of a man who is at war with the world. It appears, then, that the type of interpersonal relations in which a given individual may become involved is circumscribed by his personality.

People differ considerably in their sensitivity to the gestures of others. Since all perception is selective, it is not surprising that different individuals may impute diverse motives upon observing the identical movements. Those who are not sure of themselves sometimes perceive nuances in another's voice, presumably indicative of admiration or contempt, which others may not notice at all. An aggressive person is sensitive to attempts to exploit him and sometimes reacts sharply to "threats" that no one else can see. Since he himself is ready to exploit others, he is able to perceive subtle cues which may be indicative of similar intentions by others. A considerate person often notices discomfort and embarrassment on the part of others which their associates cannot see until they are told.

The attribution of motives depends upon what is perceived, which in turn depends upon one's perspective and interests.

There are some people who have unusually well developed patterns of domination and deference, who attempt to transform all contacts into power relationships. They are apparently incapable of relating themselves to others except in terms of superiority or inferiority and are constantly preoccupied with the question of relative rank. Upon being introduced to someone, their first concern is with ascertaining who is better than whom. When they are forced to accept a subordinate position, they play their part well—ingratiating themselves, currying favor, and observing all of the symbols of deference. That this syndrome is not infrequent has been shown in several studies. In a study made by Jones it was revealed that those with high scores on the California F-scale—designated as "authoritarian personalities"—tend to see their environment in terms of power, to evaluate leaders more positively, and to prefer autocratic to democratic control.[24] Men so characterized often believe that human beings are by nature aggressive and self-seeking. Scodel and Mussen showed that such persons tend to see other people, regardless of their actual attributes, as being like themselves; in contrast, those with low scores on the F-scale tend to be more flexible and to recognize a wider range of personality differences.[25] Such men apparently conceive of themselves as "realists" and see those who are unconcerned with power as "weak" or "naïve." They think of love in terms of admiration rather than affection. They fear and respect others who are similarly power-oriented and are suspicious or contemptuous of anyone who is not.

This suggests that the characteristic way in which a person approaches others depends upon his conception of human nature. If he believes that all men are basically egotistical, he can avow and impute only selfish motives. In his imaginative rehearsals he continually sees other people as ready to pounce upon him; he does not give anyone the benefit of the doubt and always anticipates the worst. If someone treats him generously, he takes it for granted that there is some ulterior motive; for it is inconceivable to him that any-

---

[24] Edward E. Jones, "Authoritarianism as a Determinant of First Impression Formation," *Journal of Personality*, XXIII (1954), 107–27.

[25] Alvin Scodel and Paul Mussen, "Social Perceptions of Authoritarians and Non-Authoritarians," *Journal of Abnormal and Social Psychology*, XLVIII (1953), 181–84.

one would do anything for him either from affection or simply for the pleasure of doing something for another human being. If a person believes that the world is a jungle, it is only natural that he should take steps to protect himself.

Since personifications are constructed by projecting one's own intentions upon others, the capacity for forming various sentiments is also limited by each man's conception of himself. Of particular importance is the evaluation that he places upon himself—his level of self-esteem. It has long been contended that the ability of a person to love someone else is related to his respect for himself. Unless one can conceive of himself as being worthy of love, he remains preoccupied with what others feel about him; his attention remains focussed upon himself. Unless he feels secure, he cannot afford to love others. But it is difficult for a man to recognize himself as someone else's love object unless he regards himself as being worthy of such affection. If he has doubts about himself, he would be suspicious of anyone who professed such a sentiment, for the claim would seem implausible. If someone treats him generously, he takes it for granted that this is being done in order to get something in return; hence, he does not lower his guard. To be able to concern oneself with the well-being of others, even when they are not sources of gratification, is a capacity that some people apparently never develop. Applying this principle to psychotherapy, Rogers contends that a patient becomes increasingly able to accept and appreciate other people as he develops the ability to accept himself.[26]

A number of clinical psychologists have attempted to put Rogers' hypothesis to an empirical test. Among the early efforts was the study by Sheerer, who developed a special scale to measure the extent to which a patient is able to regard himself as an acceptable object. She found that there is a consistent rise both in self-respect and in concern for others as therapy progresses; other investigators, using different rating scales and Rorschach tests, have reported similar findings.[27] Alexander, who used the TAT, found that teachers

[26] Carl R. Rogers, *Client-Centered Therapy* (Boston: Houghton Mifflin Co., 1951), p. 520. Cf. Erich Fromm, *Man for Himself* (New York: Rinehart & Co., 1947), pp. 118–41.

[27] Sheerer, *op. cit.* Cf. Dorothy Stock, "An Investigation into the Interrelations between the Self-Concept and Feelings Directed toward Other Persons and Groups," *Journal of Consulting Psychology*, XIII (1949), 176–80; Emanuel M. Berger, "Relation between Expressed Acceptance of Self and

with a low level of self-esteem tend to treat children with less affection.[28] McIntyre found that the relationship between acceptance of oneself and of others remains constant regardless of the popularity of the subjects.[29] Thus, in spite of the diversity of the procedures used to measure these orientations, the studies consistently show a positive correlation. Fey, who also found evidence supporting Rogers, focussed attention upon the exceptions. He found that those who profess a high level of self-esteem but have a low opinion of others tend to project their own faults upon other people.[30] His findings suggest that some of the current techniques for observing personifications miss unconscious meanings to the point where the scores become unreliable.

The hatred of some people is far more virulent and persistent than that of others; this suggests that the intensity of a sentiment may depend more upon the attributes of the person who hates than it does upon the deeds of the object. Perhaps domination and hatred come more easily to a man with a low level of self-esteem. A person who dislikes himself may unconsciously project his rejected attributes upon other people and then react aggressively against them. In the same manner a person who regards himself as deserving of exploitation and punishment may find it easier to mistreat others.

Individual differences in the ability to play various interpersonal roles also rests upon variations in empathy—the ability to identify sympathetically with other people. Some people characteristically maintain social distance; they always seem "cold" and rational. Others are immediately responsive to those around them, reacting spontaneously to their embarrassments or joys. Most people are capable of role-taking in conventional situations, but they differ considerably in their ability to detect emotional reactions in others

---

Expressed Acceptance of Others," *Journal of Abnormal and Social Psychology,* XLVII (1952), 778–82; and Fred E. La Fon, "Behavior on the Rorschach Test and a Measure of Self-Acceptance," *Psychological Monographs,* LXVIII (1954), no. 381.

[28] Theron Alexander, "Certain Characteristics of the Self as Related to Affection," *Child Development,* XXII (1951), 285–90.

[29] Charles J. McIntyre, "Acceptance by Others and Its Relations to Acceptance of Self and Others," *Journal of Abnormal and Social Psychology,* XLVII (1952), 624–25.

[30] William F. Fey, "Acceptance of Self and Others and Its Relation to Therapy-Readiness," *Journal of Clinical Psychology,* X (1954), 269–71; and "Acceptance of Others and Its Relation to Acceptance of Self and Others," *Journal of Abnormal and Social Psychology,* L (1955), 274–76.

and to respond to them by projecting their own feelings. That such variations exist is confirmed in preliminary tests by Dymond, who attempted to develop a scale for measuring empathy.[31] The manner in which some people engage in role-taking, then, precludes effective participation in relationships requiring a high or low degree of intimacy.

The distinctive qualities of a man are revealed in his behavior—among other things, in his heroic deeds, in the manner in which he dances, in his hobbies, or in his preferences for certain kinds of food. This suggests that men may be attracted to or repelled from their associates on any of a number of grounds. There has been considerable speculation concerning the bases of friendships; several studies have been made on the formation of cliques, but thus far the findings have not been impressive. It has been suggested, for example, that the development of common values, especially about matters outside the joint undertaking, would facilitate the establishment of amicable ties.[32] But another hypothesis may be proposed: that *the formation of any particular network of interpersonal relations as well as its stability depend upon the extent to which the personalities of those involved are in some way complementary.* Since people differ so much in their ability to relate themselves to one another, there are definite limitations to the kinds of ties that any given combination of individuals is likely to develop. Two aggressive and domineering men are not likely to become attached to one another; each needs his own group of sycophants. Sometimes such people find themselves bound by conventional norms—as in the case of men assigned to the same military unit or a couple whose religion does not permit divorce. If so, they develop a *modus vivendi* but continue to compete. The relationship is disjunctive, and it is terminated at the first opportunity. When a condescending person becomes the object of hero-worship by someone who is docile and dependent, however, a very satisfying relationship is

[31] Rosalind F. Dymond, "A Scale for the Measurement of Empathic Ability," *Journal of Consulting Psychology,* XIII (1949), 127–33.

[32] Cf. Paul F. Lazarsfeld and Robert K. Merton, "Friendship as Social Process," in *Freedom and Control in Modern Society,* Morroe Berger *et al.,* eds. (New York: D. Van Nostrand Co., 1954), pp. 18–66; and Joseph A. Precker, "Similarity of Values as a Factor in Selection of Peers and Near-Authority Figures," *Journal of Abnormal and Social Psychology,* XLVII (1952), 406–14.

temporarily established. Only when the hero is shown to have "clay feet" is such an arrangement jeopardized. Sometimes the most unlikely combinations of people cling desperately to each other. A very affectionate person with little insight may form a lasting attachment to a love object that is not particularly responsive—as in the case of a parent to an infant, a master to a dog, or an attendant in a mental hospital to a catatonic patient.[33] Sometimes people who despise each other remain together to preserve their self-esteem. A man who has serious doubts about his attractiveness to women may hang on to an abusive partner, for she symbolizes the fact that he is deserving of attention. Or a woman who is similarly uncertain of herself may submit to a husband who is contemptuous of her in order to retain her standing among her fellow workers in the office. In such instances the relationships are sustained through reciprocal utility.

A sentiment is not likely to persist without some kind of support from the other party, but such confirmation needs not be reciprocating. Indeed, the reciprocation of sentiments is rare. Disinterested love generally requires only that the love object realize some of its own potentialities; failure to do so leads to disappointment but not necessarily to a termination of the relationship. Indeed, some people become contemptuous of those who indulge them, but their benefactors continue to "spoil" them. In cases of possessive love, however, considerable support is required. The performance of the desired services must continue, although the relationship may be sustained for a time in spite of rebuffs. When there is uncertainty on the part of the lover, demands are made for various symbols of affection—such as, amatory declarations, gifts, the sharing of secrets, or sex relations. Such symbolic reassurances apparently assume increasing importance as the relationship is in danger of being terminated. Condescension is an orientation that can persist only as long as the love object remains subservient. Just as many people in the South "love" Negroes only as long as they know their "place" and are not "uppity," the affection of some parents is transformed into disparagement as soon as the child becomes too clever, too ambitious, or in some other way challenges their ascendancy. Although some are able to hate for a remarkably long time even without prov-

[33] Cf. Howard Rowland, "Friendship Patterns in the State Mental Hospital," *Psychiatry*, II (1939), 366.

ocation, most people are not likely to remain angry unless the other party continues to encroach upon their interests. In most cases disjunctive sentiments are reinforced by the negative reactions of the opposition. Of course, there are people who are convinced that the world is a jungle; since their defensive stance rests largely upon a projection of personal traits to others, their hatred requires very little support.

The kind of support that is required to sustain a relationship, then, varies from person to person. Although each mode of approaching others tends to provoke typical reactions, the actual response that is aroused by the personal characteristics of one individual depends upon the personality of the other. A self-effacing and shy person who offers his love may provoke arrogance on the part of some and a reciprocating love on the part of others. A person who is bitter, constantly complaining, and suspicious of everyone tends to elicit rejection on the part of most people, but there may be some who would feel sorry for him and attempt to nurture him. Aggressive action generally invites hostility, but there are some who become docile and submissive. When a man constantly takes advantage of others, most of his associates become distrustful, but there are some who permit themselves to be exploited and may even admire him for his boldness, ability, and success. Considerateness, cooperation, and agreeableness tend to elicit appreciation on the part of most people, but there are some who regard kindliness as a sign of weakness and become contemptuous.[34] Furthermore, whether the second party's reaction is sufficient to continue the relationship depends in turn upon the personality of the first. Much rests upon the peculiar gratifications each person derives from the association. Some of the most unlikely ties between people are apparently reinforced through mutual dependency.

Some sentiments, like the imaginary romances with movie idols, are unilateral. They develop their structure in fantasy, in which the dreamer can control all of the conditions of action. Such love objects are constructed by putting together all the characteristics that are desired, including the reciprocation of the other party. These idealized personifications sometimes become the object of the most intense, unselfish devotion. They are not to be dismissed lightly, for sentiments thus organized may subsequently be displaced

[34] Cf. Leary, *op. cit.*, pp. 91–131.

upon real human beings—often to their dismay. Serious difficulties may arise in such cases, for real people cannot possibly live up to the expectations conjured in a frustrated mind. There are bound to be disappointments. Some people apparently go through life looking for the ideal marriage partner, someone to match a personification built up in daydreams.

Observations of this kind led Winch to formulate his theory of mate-selection in terms of "complementary needs." It was his contention that marriage partners tend to be alike culturally, for the field of eligible partners is limited by conventional barriers. But within this field each person is attracted to those whose personality traits facilitate the consummation of their distinctive impulses. Winch is concerned, of course, only with societies in which young people are given an opportunity to choose their own mates. In a preliminary study of twenty-five couples he found considerable support for his theory. Indeed, he was able to isolate four frequently found combinations: (a) families that resemble the conventional relationship of a mother and son, where a dominant and capable woman takes care of a husband who needs someone on whom to lean, (b) families in which a strong, capable husband looks after a wife who is passive and compliant, much like a little doll that needs to be nurtured, (c) families that resemble the conventional relationship of a master and servant girl, in which a condescending husband is served by a capable wife, and (d) families in which an efficient woman dominates a frightened and frustrated husband. The degree of association revealed in the statistical analysis is low, though significant; this is not surprising, since many other considerations enter into the choice of a mate.[35] It is possible that the results might have been more satisfactory had Winch concentrated upon the marriages that last in contrast to those that fail.

The various networks of interpersonal relations that develop among people who are in sustained association take the form that they do from the manner in which the participants respond to one another as human beings. This suggests that the sentiments that make up any particular network may be unilateral, bilateral, or reciprocating. In most cases the sentiments are bilateral;

[35] Robert F. Winch, *Mate-Selection: A Study of Complementary Needs* (New York: Harper & Bros., 1958). Cf. Bela Mittelmann, "Analysis of Reciprocal Neurotic Patterns in Family Relationships," *Neurotic Interaction in Marriage*, Victor W. Eisenstein, ed. (New York: Basic Books, Inc., 1956), pp. 81–100.

each party approaches the others in a somewhat different way. For example, in a given family the mother may be altruistically oriented toward her husband and all her children; in contrast, her husband may be possessive of his daughters and may dislike his son, regarding him as a rival for his wife's attention. One daughter may love her sister, who looks upon her in contempt. The boy may view his sisters as useful tools, his mother with deep affection, and his father as a hero who is occasionally harsh. This is not an unusual portrait. The continuation of such networks apparently depends upon the arrangement's providing reciprocal gratifications of some sort for those who are involved.

Summary and Conclusion

In virtually all of the current approaches to social psychology, human conduct is explained almost exclusively in terms of the biological attributes of the human species as they are molded in a cultural matrix. The human infant is born into an organized society and learns various models of appropriate conduct in his interaction with others. What a man does is often regarded as a response to needs— some of them organically inherited and the rest acquired as a member of some group. But a serious question may be raised as to whether such conceptual schemes are adequate. Men who are in sustained association frequently become involved in a network of interpersonal relations which places them under special obligation to one another. Sentiments are behavioral systems that are neither inborn nor learned. They take shape and crystallize in the adjustments made by unique human beings to one another.

Each sentiment is unique, for it is the distinctive orientation of one human being toward another. But certain problems are unavoidable among men who are in sustained association. Typical personifications develop as each person learns to cope with those about him, and certain kinds of meanings—love, hatred, hero-worship, jealousy—are sufficiently similar to make possible a consideration of typical sentiments. Those who are involved in common activities are attracted to some of their associates and repelled from others, and an effort has been made to describe selected conjunctive and disjunctive sentiments. This pattern of attraction and repulsion sets up a network of personal obligations that greatly circumscribes the behavior of those involved. The stability of any such network of interpersonal relations depends upon the continued flow of gratifications of some sort for most of the participants.

Since those interested in the study of intimate contacts have come from diverse intellectual backgrounds, it is not surprising that the field is still marked by considerable confusion. An extensive body of literature is rapidly accumulating, but there is no agreement except that the subject matter is worthy of serious investigation. One of the major barriers to the systematic study of sentiments is the absence of an adequate set of categories in terms of which to think about them. In addition, common sense terminology, with its irrelevant and confusing associations as well as its value judgments, makes the undertaking even more difficult. To describe interpersonal relations with terms like "love," "hatred," and "jealousy" is much like a chemist's talking about "fire," "water," and "air" instead of "hydrogen," "oxygen," and the other elements. In spite of this undeveloped state of knowledge, however, the field is of such utmost importance for the understanding of what men do that some effort must be made to explore these frontiers. There is no dearth of observations, nor of theories. However premature the attempt may be, an effort must be made to organize the materials drawn from diverse sources into a reasonably coherent scheme. The study of sentiments will for some time probably remain amateurish and speculative, but even a feeble beginning may throw some light upon perplexing problems that have thus far defied even a reasoned guess.

Suggested References

BUBER, MARTIN, *I and Thou*. Ronald G. Smith, trans. New York: Charles Scribner's Sons, 1958. An eminent theologian's treatise on the differences between approaching others as human beings and as physical objects, a distinction which has become the basis for many subsequent discussions.

D'ARCY, MARTIN C., *The Mind and Heart of Love*. New York: Meridian Books, 1956. A richly documented analysis of the concepts of *Eros* and *Agape* by a Jesuit priest who contends that the two forms of love need not be irreconcilable.

HEIDER, FRITZ, *The Psychology of Interpersonal Relations*. New York:

John Wiley & Sons, 1958. An attempt to set up a conceptual scheme for the study of interpersonal relations, which differs from that presented in this chapter. Also contains a review of relevant research literature.

LEARY, TIMOTHY, *Interpersonal Diagnosis of Personality.* New York: Ronald Press Co., 1957. A thoughtful attempt to set up diagnostic procedures for the systematic study of the ways in which people consciously or unconsciously approach one another.

SHAND, ALEXANDER F., *The Foundations of Character.* London: Macmillan & Co., 1920. A pioneering effort to systematize the study of sentiments by organizing a variety of common sense observations. Although the work is dated, it is still worthy of serious study.

SMITH, ADAM, *The Theory of Moral Sentiments,* Parts I, III, V. London: George Bell & Sons, 1880. A treatise on the various passions of man and their place in the development of moral conduct, with particular emphasis upon the importance of sympathetic identification.

11

Conventional
norms
and
sentiments

Although it is frequently proclaimed that man is a rational creature, many of the things that human beings do could hardly be so characterized. Rationality generally refers to the appreciation of the relation of given means to desired ends and to the making of selections that make possible the consistent pursuit of one's avowed interests. But men sometimes act contrary to their apparent interests and are admired or even honored for doing so. An outraged employee may insult his tormentor and proudly stomp out of the plant. This may involve considerable hardship for his family, but he is admired for having the courage to stand up for his rights. Men sometimes act in accordance with their announced intentions and are greeted with disdain. If a father refuses to grant permission for his daughter to marry a handsome, fun-loving man whom he regards as unreliable, he may be condemned as unreasonable and "old fashioned." Should he place serious obstacles before the young couple, he may even be accused of being "inhuman." What is approved in each case is an act that is not utilitarian. To a man who has a family to support, losing his

temper before his employer is not the best way to realize his objective. For a father who desires the lasting happiness of his daughter to approve a marriage he is convinced will fail is self-defeating.
Yet, there are times when men expect one another to make allowances for extenuating circumstances.

Observers who approve of such non-utilitarian acts merely shrug
their shoulders knowingly and say that it is "human nature." Those
who do not approve usually condemn them as "irrational," an indication of weakness of character. Those who feel ambivalent refer to
the "frailties" of human nature. Many acts of this kind occur when
men are emotionally upset and acting impulsively. Even under more
tranquil circumstances, however, conduct is often tempered by
sentimental considerations. Although some social psychologists have
complained that human behavior would be so much easier to understand if only men were not so irrational, such conduct is what
makes them the kind of creatures that they are.

Sentimental Considerations in Conduct

Although men generally conform to conventional norms, sentiments sometimes interfere with the routine of living. The special
meanings of the various people around us may render the enactment
of a conventional role very painful or unusually delightful. Sentiments facilitate the performance of duties that are consistent with
the behavioral tendencies of which they are composed. The punishment of someone who is disliked becomes so easy that there is a
danger of being carried away to the point of unnecessary brutality.
On the other hand, sentiments inhibit acts that are inconsistent with
them. It is difficult to do a special favor for an acquaintance one
resents, and many an employer has hesitated to dismiss an inefficient
clerk whom he likes as a person. Even in casual relationships such
personal reactions make a difference. A bureaucrat may favor a
client who is attractive, while denying a similar request to someone
who strikes him as unpleasant. Although he performs within an
institutional framework, there are interstices between regulations
which enable him to exercise some judgment; and his decisions are
sometimes influenced by his personal feelings. Similarly, in a military unit, in spite of the efforts of an officer to be fair, the least

desirable duties are often assigned to men he dislikes. Furthermore, he is reluctant to send married men with children into hazardous situations, even though they may be the best qualified and the most likely to return alive. Thus, *sentimental considerations enter into the organization of conduct by facilitating some acts and inhibiting others.*

Since sentiments develop independently of cultural norms, they do not necessarily support the structure of organized groups. Jealousy and resentment often interfere with the successful completion of cooperative activities, even when the participants do their best not to reveal their inner dispositions. Colleagues are supposed to like one another and often act as if they did, externally maintaining the amenities. Actually each may be harboring grudges and resentments. Where the competition is keen, men ofter work together amicably until there is a danger that one person may outdistance the others; then, the rest may form a temporary alliance to hold him back. It should be noted that the hostilities that arise among colleagues may have nothing to do with their work. One man may resent another because the latter is handsome, affable, and apparently attractive to women—because of attainment in areas in which he himself had secretly longed for success. Or the man may resent another colleague because he works so hard, making him feel guilty about his own laziness. This suggests that some reactions are initially against one's own attributes and are subsequently displaced upon other people. Because of the negative social sanctions against vicious factionalism, internal dissension is often not apparent until matters have gotten out of hand. Then, it is conceded that all is not well. By that time many of the sentiments have been transformed into hatred, and the enterprise is confronted with the possibility of collapse.

Sentiments based upon erotic attraction are a perennial source of difficulty, especially when the relationship is proscribed by custom or law. In every society the field from which partners may be chosen is circumscribed; it is generally limited to people of the opposite sex, of the same social status, and of approximately the same age.[1] But the selection of erotic objects does not always follow customary lines. Control is difficult, for the meanings which constitute erotic

---

[1] Cf. William J. Goode, "The Theoretical Importance of Love," *American Sociological Review*, XXIV (1959), 38–47.

attraction are subtle and rarely verbalized, and the persons involved are usually unable to account for their preferences. Everywhere forbidden love affairs develop. Because of class barriers, walls between ethnic groups, incest taboos, or age differences people who are in love sometimes find themselves in impossible situations. Indeed, many of the plots in world literature deal with lovers who are forced to carry on clandestine affairs, with lovers who submit to group norms and then pine away for the rest of their lives, or with lovers who defy conventions and run off—to be ostracized or to commit suicide.

Whenever people between whom erotic attraction is thought to be unlikely marry, misunderstandings and suspicions arise. Since conjugal love is presumed to be related to erotic attraction, especially in our society, eyebrows are raised even when the arrangement is legitimate. When a beautiful woman marries a rich old man, someone in an ethnic minority, or someone of a lower class, she is suspected of having ulterior motives. Some psychiatrists may speak of an unresolved Electra complex, but few people really believe that the woman sincerely loves her husband, in spite of all her protestations. When a handsome young man marries a middle aged woman, similar suspicions arise. Such arrangements are suspected because the sentiments that are supposed to support them do not seem plausible. In some cases even the participants are not convinced. Even though she may give him no cause for concern, a rich old man may wonder whether his beautiful bride really cares for him or is merely tolerating him in order to live in comfort and to receive a generous inheritance. Whenever a younger man appears on the scene—his son by a previous marriage, his aide, or some young friend—the man becomes uncomfortable and highly sensitive to any indication of the formation of a rivalry.

The fact that erotic attraction can lead to the formation of conjunctive sentiments, however mild, and result in favorable consideration is widely recognized. Hence, its deliberate exploitation is not uncommon, even in situations in which the relationships are quite casual. For example, when a male customer walks into a restaurant, a waitress generally smiles and says "hello" rather than immediately handing him a menu. This involves an intuitive utilization of personal reactions. In theory the conventional relationship between customer and waitress is sexually neutral, but by putting the transactions partially on an interpersonal basis the waitress might conceivably exploit it to her advantage in the form of larger tips and more frequent patronage of the establishment. Some waitresses confess to developing and practicing a seductive walk. Because of this possibility, career women who take advantage of their physical assets are strongly resented, and in some corporations executives apparently make a special effort to avoid promoting them. Some business and professional women go out of their way to make themselves plain in appearance, insisting that they be judged solely on the basis of ability. Such precautionary measures on both sides imply a recognition of common dangers against which protection is deemed necessary.

In the organization of an act, sentiments enter into the imaginative rehearsals preceding overt action. When an act is delayed through indecision, a person trying to make up his mind often interacts vicariously with the various personifications involved. A girl who is trying to decide whom to marry takes into account the preferences of her parents, imagining their reaction to each of the suitors. She may also consider the reaction of each of the candidates upon learning that she has chosen another. She may spend some time arguing in her imagination with the various parties, presenting her rebuttal to the contentions she imputes to each. It is in such situations that sentiments assume great importance, for the pain or gratification imputed to such personifications constitute images that cannot be escaped. A girl who loves her mother dearly would hesitate to marry a man she knows her mother loathes. Even though she herself may find him very attractive, she would be reluctant to hurt anyone who is so dear to her. She is thus forced to consider alternative plans of action—putting off her decision until she graduates from school, reconsidering others whom she had rejected as unlikely, or finding another girl for the man in question to lighten the blow to his pride.

It has already been noted that interpersonal relations impose claims and obligations that are independent of group norms. When a person falls in love, he feels obligated not to do anything that is painful to the love object, to fulfil its expectations, and to contribute to its well-being. If he dislikes someone, he may not feel bound to honor even the conventional obligations that tie them together. Because of the sympathetic identification with those with whom such ties are established, each can usually anticipate the reactions of the other and respond to them. A person derives enjoyment from imagining the chagrin of someone he dislikes and wants to spite, the degradation and embarrassment of someone he resents, and the reassurance of someone he likes. By acting consistently with his sentiments, he experiences inner gratifications; should he fail to do so, however, he punishes himself by feeling guilty. A man who feels that he has "let down" a friend suffers, even when the friend does not feel particularly upset about it. Similarly, a person who discovers that he has inadvertently helped one of his rivals becomes disgusted with himself.

In crisis situations, when conventional norms are ineffective, such reactions take on greater significance. Where a situation is clearly defined, sentiments remain secondary. When a student falls on the border between two grades, especially at a crucial point in deciding whether or not he is to continue his education, most professors bend over backwards to give a person they dislike the benefit of the doubt, assuming that they must counteract rationally their natural inclination to mark him down. Sales clerks usually treat most of their customers alike; but when they are extremely busy or when they are fatigued at the end of the day, they may speak gruffly or be rude to someone who strikes them as unpleasant. In a catastrophe a mother who loves her son may sacrifice her life to protect him from harm, but another mother may be so concerned with saving herself that she does not even think of her child until after she has reached safety. Participants in mobs usually act in terms of sentiments. They are outraged upon learning of injury inflicted upon someone with whom they identify, or they may crush one another while adoring some popular idol. Crowd behavior, which is generally found only in unsettled situations, is impulsive and passionate.

Behavior becomes passionate when there is an inability to control the various behavioral dispositions that constitute the sentiments. When sentimental considerations become so overriding that conventional obligations recede into the background or are ignored, a man temporarily loses control of himself and acts impulsively. Examples of such behavior are commonplace. At the risk of capital punishment a betrayed husband kills his wife's lover. A soldier faces a firing squad rather than disclose the identity of his accomplices in some offense. A man infatuated with a beautiful woman gives up his wife and children just to be with her for a few years, knowing that the woman is not especially attached to him. A homely employer discharges a handsome foreman badly needed to manage his commercial enterprise simply because his wife had praised him. In many cases such passionate acts are the product of a fairly long period of brooding. There is a progressive constriction of the perceptual field and a concentration of imagery until an obsession develops. Rational considerations are brushed aside, and the advice of worried friends goes unheeded. Attention is so focussed upon a limited range of possibilities that the person lives temporarily in a private world; it is not surprising, therefore, that he may appear to be deranged. Tension mounts with each imagined event until some kind of overt action becomes imperative. Once it gets under way, such behavior is often explosive.

Passionate behavior is generally condemned because in the long run it tends to be harmful. Often it is self-defeating. It is condemned especially by those who do not understand. People who have not experienced intense infatuation, jealousy, or hatred—those who have not viewed the world from the highly circumscribed perspectives that develop under such emotional tension—are not likely to comprehend the act. But those who have had similar experiences can readily understand, even if they do not condone the deed, and are often reluctant to impose negative social sanctions. A person who has never been disappointed in love could hardly appreciate the poignancy of unrequited love. A person who has not been in danger of losing some highly valued object could hardly understand the seemingly insane jealousy of a man fighting desperately to hang on. Tolerance often comes with age. His own suffering enables one to appreciate the inner experiences of others involved in difficult situations. Of course, there are some rigid people who do not learn from experience.

People differ considerably in their ability to inhibit sentimental tendencies and to live up to conventional obligations. At one extreme is the person who is passionate about almost everyone and everything. At the other extreme is the person who is almost like the ideal model of the rational man, the person who always maintains the amenities, does the proper thing, and rarely reveals his private inclinations. Some people permit sentiments to enter into their calculations, but others steadfastly refuse to be swayed. Especially in the case of those who are rigidly conventional, the possibility of doing something improper rarely enters the imagination. Should it slip in, they are immediately assailed by intense feelings of guilt. Of course, there are also cultural differences in the extent to which such dispositions may be indulged, but within any given culture the individual variations are still quite extensive.

Although complete rationality has long been extolled by philosophers and laymen alike, it should be emphasized that any man who even approximates this ideal would be viewed as "cold" and "inhuman." What is generally called "warmth" in a person consists of his sentiments. One gets the impression that a rational man is more like a machine, human in appearance but lacking in some of the characteristics that distinguish man from other objects. Perhaps such persons can be found only among those who are psychotic. No one can deny the desirability of making most choices upon rational rather than sentimental grounds. But a judge who insists upon the enforcement of the letter of the law, refusing to take extenuating circumstances into account, seems somewhat less than human. Thus, each person has a peculiar combination of sentiments toward the various people with whom he is in constant association, and these meanings keep him from being completely utilitarian in outlook. Although sentimental considerations are often suppressed, they may color conventional acts. Through style—the enthusiasm or reluctance with which things are done—most people reveal their natural inclinations and thereby enable others to identify with them.

Variations in Social Distance

Sociologists frequently distinguish between primary and secondary relations. They designate as primary relations those intimate, face-to-face contacts that characterize the interaction in most families, in neighborhood gangs or in cliques. Secondary relations are not so well defined, but they presumably include all others. This has led to the embarrassing question of where the line is to be drawn. The difficulties encountered when attempting to make a precise distinction suggest that primary and secondary relations should not be viewed as separate categories but as polar extremes on a continuum ranging from very intimate ties to those which are highly formal. Interest centers here upon the *degree of social dis-*

tance among the participants in common transactions. It has already been noted that social distance is not the same as geographical distance; linear space is not irrelevant, but it is not directly related to degree of psychological closeness. Especially in cities, people who live near one another and who are in frequent contact remain strangers. On the other hand, it is possible for lovers to maintain intimate contact even when they are separated by several thousand miles, as long as some communication channel is available to them. In speaking of social distance, then, we are concerned with the psychological barriers which facilitate or deter easy, spontaneous interaction.

Where any particular relationship would fall on the continuum of social distance depends upon the type of knowledge the participants have of one another. Men interact in terms of the conceptions they form of one another rather than in terms of their actual attributes. Hence, social interaction is an interchange of personifications rather than one of persons. The same person may mean different things to different observers, and imaginary personifications are sometimes more important than real people. The construction of personifications rests upon what is known about the other party. All cooperative transactions are predicated upon inferences that the participants make about one another; unless one knows enough to form working conceptions of his associates he would be unable to engage in role-taking and to control his own behavior. Even in a simple economic exchange difficulties would arise unless there is some assurance that each party will return something for what he is given. On the other hand, no one, not even a psychiatrist, ever acquires complete knowledge of another human being, no matter how intimate the tie. Personifications are constructed from a variety of sensory cues—gestures and acts—from which inferences are made about inner experiences. In intimate contacts the other person sometimes confirms these hypotheses by confessing some of his secrets, but each person retains some area of privacy. Furthermore, in many relationships men deliberately hide their actual dispositions through diversionary gestures. There is a wide range of variation in what men learn about one another, and social distance can be measured along these lines.[2]

[2] Georg Simmel, *The Sociology of Georg Simmel,* Kurt H. Wolff, trans. (Glencoe: The Free Press, 1950), pp. 307–44.

In those relationships in which social distance is great, knowledge of the other party is highly specialized and categorical. In such impersonal contacts people approach one another as instances of socially defined categories. Except in very small communities in which everyone knows everyone else, men are classified, and the expectations in terms of which social interaction proceeds are derived from the presumed characteristics of each category. Most Americans, for example, are inclined to act with courtesy toward all doctors, neglecting individual differences among them. Most men driving automobiles exercise additional caution whenever they encounter a vehicle operated by a woman, even though they may admit reluctantly that some women are highly skilled drivers. This is even more obvious in the treatment of members of ethnic minorities, where all Negroes or all Jews are treated alike in spite of the vast range of variation within each category. All Jews are thought to be aggressive and to be preoccupied with money, and each individual Jew is treated as if he had these attributes. In secondary relations, then, the distinct personality of the other party is either irrelevant or of secondary importance. If a clerk has just been bereaved, his sorrow does not significantly alter the interchange in which a purchase is made. Because men live in a symbolic environment in which objects have been classified and labelled, they are able to interact effectively even with total strangers—simply by placing them in the proper category. The characterizations of other people are often inaccurate, but they nonetheless make it possible for cooperation to take place.

When the knowledge that the participants have of one another is so impersonal, concerted action can occur only in situations in which the social structure is well established. Strangers can act together only in contexts in which conventional roles are clearly delineated. Most economic transactions are of this nature. Each party becomes oriented to the other's plan of action, but successful role-taking generally occurs only within this specialized context. Cooperation involving people about whom little is known would be precarious were it not for networks of conventional norms.

Social distance is maximized in situations in which each person maintains his personal reserve. As long as one is self-conscious and confines himself to playing conventional roles, he does what others expect of him rather than what he may actually want to do. Politeness is a way of concealing one's personality. A polite man does not disclose his idiosyncrasies; all he displays is a "front" and the fact that he knows his manners. When men maintain their discretion, they conceal their joys, sorrows, and hopes behind a mask. The communication that takes place in such contexts is largely symbolic and formal; what appears to constitute expressive movements are often not spontaneous—like the practiced smile of a salesman. There are, of course, instances in which personal reserve is inadvertently relaxed, giving others unexpected glimpses into one's personality. It is difficult for a man who has just enjoyed a stroke of luck to suppress a smile, just as it is hard for a deeply embarrassed man to avoid blushing. But in general such impulses are inhibited when doing the proper thing. In her study of war-brides in Hawaii, Kimura discovered that a higher percentage of European wives of Japanese-American husbands rated their marriage as satisfactory than did wives from Japan. To account for this unexpected finding, she proposes the hypothesis that the common cultural background of the Japanese war-bride and her new relatives tended to channel their interaction into conventional patterns, thus restricting spontaneity and making it more difficult for them to appreciate one another as individuals.[3]

Since the social contexts in which people experience their greatest sense of security are characterized by primary relations, and since secondary contacts sometimes make possible the perpetuation of inequities, some sociologists have condemned the latter as undesirable. This value judgment, however, is misleading, and overlooks the fact that most secondary relations are not unfriendly. Indeed, in urban communities it is impossible for anyone to get to know each person with whom he must deal on an individual basis; categorical contacts are inevitable. Actually, all of our contacts outside of a few circles—our family, clique of friends, fellow workers, and a few others—are with relative strangers. What does one know about the friendly waiter in a restaurant he patronizes frequently? He knows that the man is an efficient waiter, that he is familiar with the preferences of his regular customers, that he gives generous portions of butter. But what does one know about the man's per-

[3] Yukiko Kimura, "War Brides in Hawaii and Their In-Laws," *American Journal of Sociology*, LXIII (1957), 70–79. Cf. Edward J. Murray and Melvin Cohen, "Mental Illness, Milieu Therapy, and Social Organization in Ward Groups," *Journal of Abnormal and Social Psychology*, LVIII (1959), 48–54.

sonal ambitions, his hopes for his children, his relations with his wife, his hobbies? And without such knowledge what does anyone know about the waiter as a human being? Yet, even without such knowledge repeated transactions occur smoothly, pleasantly, and without hostility. The vast majority of the social contacts taking place in modern mass societies are of this nature.

In relationships in which social distance is at a minimum, knowledge of the other person is highly individualized. In intimate circles each of the other parties is recognized as having a distinct personality, and his various idiosyncrasies are taken into account in dealing with him. The personifications constructed are in each instance unique. Such knowledge can be acquired only when there is a relaxation of personal reserve, and most people act more spontaneously in the company of intimate associates, often admitting some of their inner thoughts and forbidden reactions. In addition, since expressive movements are individualized, they can be read accurately only by those with whom a person is in constant association; thus, many inclinations that are ordinarily hidden from strangers are inadvertently disclosed to friends. Although this is sometimes embarrassing, it facilitates the establishment of empathy. When people who are well acquainted engage in concerted action, each makes allowances for the prejudices and weaknesses of the others. Hence, the outcome of the various transactions may rest more upon the personalities of those involved than upon conventional norms.

Furthermore, because those who are in sustained association do so many different things together their knowledge of one another becomes unspecialized. In secondary relations one's knowledge of others is limited to what is essential for carrying out a particular type of transaction—such as delivering the mail or repairing an automobile. In primary relations, however, others are observed performing a variety of tasks, and each is familiar with the views and reactions of the others in many different contexts. Close friends are generally familiar with one another's unique background of experience, and they often share one another's dreams for the future. Precisely because of the more rounded personifications of the other, each can better anticipate his moves—even in new situations.

As might be expected, increasing knowledge about others facilitates the establishment of empathy. Differences in behavior in similar contexts generally arise from differences in defining situations. For example, should a man hold a door open for a Japanese woman to pass before him, she may regard this as an indication of deep affection; an American or European woman under similar circumstances would only note that the man is polite. Their subsequent treatment of the man would differ accordingly. But as people get to know one another more intimately, they are able to speak more candidly and thereby develop a better comprehension of one another's perspectives. What this suggests is that human beings are basically alike, similar impulses being aroused in similarly defined situations. This is not immediately apparent because men so frequently conceal their inner dispositions to conform with conventional norms. A man who has suppressed erotic interests in the voluptuous wife of a friend may regard himself as depraved and peculiar until another friend, seemingly immune to her charms, confesses similar inclinations. With the relaxation of personal reserve and the disclosure of such blocked reactions, those who are close to one another come to appreciate the fact that behind their customary façade they are fundamentally alike. Although the evidence is not entirely satisfactory, in general the studies made on this topic support this contention.[4] To be sure, each person is unique and reacts somewhat differently from anyone else; yet his distinctive responses become more understandable when *his* definition of the situation becomes clear. Paradoxically, then, the more one appreciates another as a unique individual, the easier it becomes to identify with him.

It is precisely because of such identification that sentimental considerations take on such overriding importance in primary relations. Among those in intimate contact, conventional obligations are often overlooked, especially when they get in the way. When one knows someone else well, he becomes acutely aware of his unique interests, his concern over his self-esteem, and his sensitivity about matters in which there is ego-involvement. Hence, with intimacy comes mutual concern. Those who are able to identify with another person can comprehend things from his standpoint more readily, even when they do not agree with him. It is not surprising, then, that what

4 Cf. James Bieri, "Changes in Interpersonal Perceptions following Social Interaction," *Journal of Abnormal and Social Psychology*, XLVIII (1953), 61–66.

happens among those in intimate circles depends more upon their respective interpersonal roles than upon their conventional roles. Men who know one another well often act in terms of their sentiments.

In secondary contacts, people often stand in a relationship of mutual utility. Although strangers may interact politely, for all practical purposes the others are only "things" which are manipulated in the pursuit of one's own interests. If for any reason there is a temporary reduction in social distance, however, a remarkable transformation takes place. A man who happens to look directly at the eyes of a beggar suddenly experiences pangs of guilt and reluctantly makes a generous handout; a stranger who catches the ecstatic joy of an innocent child spontaneously breaks into a grin and offers him candy; a driver who notices the face of a disappointed hitchhiker remonstrates to himself for passing him by. Momentarily, the "it" becomes a "you"—a human being with whom there is sympathetic identification. Momentarily one projects himself to the standpoint of the other and responds as a human being, appreciating the plight or the joy of the other person. Momentarily, one acts sentimentally. Even in the heat of intense conflict aggression is inhibited by empathy. Although the Nazis slaughtered millions of Jews, there is evidence that some of the Germans found it extremely difficult to perform their duties whenever such identifications were established.[5]

Since there are conventional norms in most groups that persons in intimate contact should like one another or at least be considerate, it is frequently assumed that all primary relations are friendly and desirable. Even a superficial glance at the clinical materials reported by psychiatrists indicates at once that this is not true. Primary relations are not necessarily cordial. People who know one another quite well may develop intense hostilities; indeed, the most bitter hatreds of which men are capable seem to be directed against those with whom they are in intimate association. To be sure, such negative sentiments are usually suppressed or even repressed, but they manifest themselves whenever opportunities arise for jealous or resentful men to make their own decisions. Under such circumstances, some go out of their way to spite those whom they cannot otherwise

[5] Cf. Emmanuel Ringelblum, *Notes from the Warsaw Ghetto,* Jacob Sloan, trans. (New York: McGraw-Hill Book Co., 1958).

attack. It would be more accurate to state that men in sustained contact cannot remain indifferent to one another, but that the sentiments which develop may be either conjunctive or disjunctive.

In most continuing relationships there is some reduction of social distance. As people become better acquainted, they relax, revealing more of their distinct preferences. The owner of a grocery store comes to know his regular customers, and the mailman gets to know the families on his route. Except in the case of people who are rigid, personifications are periodically reconstructed after new experiences. Once a minimum identification is established, special obligations of a personal nature develop, which in turn facilitate even closer contacts. This cumulative process may also be reversed. Two friends who become disillusioned with one another are pulled apart psychologically. They become increasingly more secretive and polite to one another until in the end they are almost strangers again.

Since intimacy rests upon a mutual appreciation of one another's inner experiences, its development depends upon the relaxation of personal reserve on the part of both parties. With the reduction of social distance there is more spontaneity, less self-consciousness, and increasing ease of interchange. But there are personality differences in the capacity to enter into intimate relations with other people. Some establish rapport easily; others are guarded and defensive and unable to relax even in the presence of people they have known all their lives. Some establish intimate ties only with a few people in their entire lifetime; others join new coteries almost every month. Of course, there are cultural differences in the extent to which such relaxation is permitted. Most Americans are apparently less reserved than other people. But even in countries in which the display of inner dispositions is frowned upon, there are personality differences in candidness.

Mere physical proximity and the cheerful performance of conventional roles do not necessarily lead to the reduction of social distance. To be sure, in most cases people in constant association observe one another in a variety of contexts, occasionally give unasked assistance in time of need, and thereby begin a network of personal claims. But there are many situations in which conventional barriers make the relaxation of personal reserve beyond a certain point awkward. Master and servant in the same household learn a great deal about one another, much more than either is willing to admit. Similarly, a great artist and his disciples come to know one another quite well, but if the master prefers not to lower the barriers, polite distance is maintained, even after many years of association. In slum areas members of different ethnic minorities live side by side and engage in countless transactions. In spite of apparent pleasantness of their contacts, they generally view one another in contempt. Prisoners and guards are constantly in one another's company and are even interdependent, but there are barriers that keep them far apart; indeed, the channels of communication are completely separated, making it necessary for the guards to rely upon "stool pigeons."

Following Cooley, many sociologists have nonetheless emphasized the importance of face-to-face contacts. Such contacts probably do contribute to the reduction of social distance by facilitating the reading of expressive movements. Symbolic communication is deliberate and self-conscious; it is designed to give a desired impression, usually one that is prescribed by conventional norms. But each person inadvertently gives himself away through expressive movements that he is unable to control. Through these involuntary reactions—frequently consisting of contractions of the facial musculature—each person reveals the kind of experiences that give him great joy, the kind of frustrations that arouse anxiety, the kind of deeds that provoke awe or admiration, as well as the kind of teasing he will tolerate and how far others can go before he becomes angry.[6] Thus, physical proximity gives people access to sensory cues on the basis of which they can make reasonably accurate inferences about impulses that are inhibited and otherwise concealed.

This suggests that *the extent to which the outcome of transactions rests upon sentiments rather than upon conventional norms is inversely related to the social distance among the participants.* Sentimental considerations become foremost in those transactions in which social distance is minimized; where people know one another intimately much depends upon their reactions to each other as unique human beings. Thus, an employer who is infatuated with his secretary can more easily be persuaded to make decisions to please her. The interests of the firm as well as customary procedures

[6] Cf. Schilder, *op. cit.*, pp. 234–43.

may be flouted. On the other hand, propriety reigns in enterprises being carried on by strangers.

The Social Control of Sentiments

Since the outcome of transactions may depend more upon sentiments than upon conventional norms, in each organized group efforts of some kind are made to control interpersonal relations. There are cultural prescriptions as to the appropriate sentiments to be developed toward each of the other participants in standardized activities. Mothers are supposed to love their children and to make whatever reasonable sacrifices as are necessary to give them a decent life. Although it is well known that this is not always the case, mothers cannot neglect such norms too blatantly without incurring the displeasure of their neighbors or even of public officials. In bureaucracies there are rules against nepotism, regulations governing promotions, and codes of conduct for dealing with the clientele. Colleagues are supposed to like one another. The rivalries that may develop are expected to remain friendly, and under no circumstance should they be permitted to interfere with attaining the main objectives of the group. In war, revolution, or class conflict enemies are supposed to hate each other. Hence, when a prisoner of war and a stockade guard find that they respect and like one another more than they do many of their comrades, they feel ill at ease; should their friendship become too undisguised, they may be punished for fraternization. The members of a family are supposed to love one another and to enter into free and intimate relationships, but erotic interests are forbidden except between the married pair. In most cases it becomes obvious just from inspection that the prescribed sentiments would facilitate concerted action and that the proscribed ones would hinder cooperation; that such norms are common, then, should occasion no surprise.

Because many of these norms are so deeply inculcated, those who violate them have difficulty in admitting their failures even to themselves. A person who dislikes his neighbor or hates his parents is often haunted by guilt feelings. Since the development of sentiments occurs independently of conventional norms, however, the most embarrassing relationships may develop even when very sincere efforts are made to avoid them. In spite of the "thou shalt not" commandments, a man sometimes cannot help falling in love with his friend's wife, hating his colleague, or being jealous of one of his children. Overt manifestations of such sentiments are usually inhibited; however, inner experiences are more difficult to control. Jealous colleagues usually avoid open clashes, confining their aggression to gossip, invidious comparisons, negative judgments, or cruel jokes. When aggression cannot be expressed, the resentment may become intensified; and occasionally, especially in crisis situations, some of these blocked impulses may break through. In an extremely dangerous situation a jealous parent may not make a wholehearted effort to save his child. Such passionate outbreaks occur periodically, and it is in the areas in which recurrent difficulties arise that the most stringently enforced norms develop.

Flagrant violations of such norms apparently occur only in already disorganized groups. In a study of 203 cases of incest in Chicago, Weinberg describes the various ways in which family life is disrupted by the establishment of prohibited ties. When incongruous interpersonal relations develop, the claims and obligations that make up the conventional roles of the participants become difficult to enforce—leading to conflicts over parental prerogatives, dependency, and filial piety. If a daughter becomes the love object of her father, he may lose his authority over her, for she can threaten to withhold erotic favors. Furthermore, the daughter and her mother become rivals, and the two may compete even on matters unrelated to sex. Weinberg notes that this often occurs even when the mother does not know of the incestuous relationship. An unwilling daughter may become the protector of her younger sisters, who may resent her efforts, not understanding her intentions. Similarly, when incestuous relations are established between brother and sister, the carefree social intimacy, the frank but friendly disregard that siblings often have for one another, is lost. The brother becomes a lover; he competes with other boys, and she in turn may vie with other girls for his attention. Such developments render conventional conduct difficult if not ludicrous. Thus, the violation of incest taboos disorganizes the family even further. Family life in Hollywood is another example of what can happen where a wide range of passionate behavior is tolerated.[7] It becomes obvious, then, that some

[7] S. Kirson Weinberg, *Incest Behavior* (New York: Citadel Press, 1955), pp.

kind of conventional control is essential for the preservation of orderly group life. The formation of embarrassing conjunctive sentiments is a recurrent problem. Since sentimental considerations are foremost among those who know one another on a personal basis, attempts at control usually consist of the regulation of social distance. An effort is made to minimize the possibility of sympathetic identification. The greater the social distance, the longer behavior is likely to remain subject to social control. When people get to know one another too intimately, personal claims develop, and allowances are made which interfere with strict adherence to conventional norms. An intuitive recognition of this principle is implicit in many of the formal regulations and moral codes.

The spatial segregation of parties that might develop embarrassing ties is a common procedure. People of different classes and ethnic groups generally live in different parts of a community, making it less likely that they will meet too frequently on an informal basis. Officers and enlisted men are also billeted separately. They come together to perform their duties in situations in which the division of labor is prescribed by military regulations, but they retire to separate quarters during their off duty hours, when there is a greater likelihood of their mingling as human beings.[8] Nuns and priests are quartered apart from their parishioners, partly to minimize the temptations of secular life. In some societies boys and girls are reared and educated separately almost until the time of their marriage. Although clandestine affairs are known to occur, they are kept to a minimum by rendering the establishment of initial contacts so difficult.

When transactions require close and frequent contacts, social distance may still be maintained through deliberate formalization and ritual—through etiquette. Etiquette consists of rules of appropriate conduct for people who interact directly with one another. It is essentially a way of maintaining personal reserve in spite of proximity. Everything that is done is formal, and each person does what he is supposed to do, thereby not revealing his individuality. If he should inadvertently disclose some private inclination, the others

---

157–71. Cf. Hortense Powdermaker, *Hollywood: The Dream Factory* (Boston: Little, Brown & Co., 1950).
[8] Cf. Fred E. Fiedler, "A Note on Leadership Theory: The Effect of Social Barriers between Leaders and Followers," *Sociometry*, XX (1957), 87–94.

politely pretend not to have noticed. As long as people continue to act politely, they provide little basis for the development of intense sentiments. Especially where there are differences of status—as between master and servant, teacher and student, officer and enlisted man, executive and factory worker—the gap is constantly reinforced by a variety of rituals, such as saluting or the use of honorifics. Most teachers are in friendly contact with their students, but social distance is maintained by well-established patterns of deference. Romantic attachments are almost non-existent, but they might conceivably occur more frequently were it not for the fact that most schools have an unwritten law against them.[9]

An example of a very elaborate system of etiquette is provided by the common understandings that developed in the South during the period before the Civil War governing the relationships between master and slave. The "Jim Crow" practices that have survived until today cannot be understood apart from this background. In this rigidly stratified society there was no objection to the formation of conjunctive sentiments across the "color line," but there was great concern over preserving the disparity of power between the two ethnic groups. Many masters loved their slaves in a condescending manner, and many slaves admired their masters as superior objects. There were a number of rules concerning appellation. The slaves were always required to address anyone in the ruling group by a title—"mister," "sir," "madam." But they in turn were called "boy" or by their first name; older slaves were called "mammy" or "uncle." Slaves were never addressed by titles, and many Southerners still feel it unnatural to use them when speaking to Negroes. The slaves were required to stand, hat in hand, whenever they were addressed by anyone in the dominant group. When calling, they were required to use the side or rear entrance of the house—never the front door. Nor were the norms entirely one-sided. An owner could properly visit the slave quarters only on certain occasions—on Christmas or in some emergency. It should be noted that these rituals were enforced by both sides; the slaves themselves were contemptuous of a "Yankee" visitor who greeted them by title, for this indicated that the man did not know his manners. These rituals became status symbols. Even now, long after the abolition of slavery, many of the same symbols continue to reinforce invidious distinctions between

[9] Cf. Goffman, op. cit., pp. 481–85; and Thomas, op. cit., pp. 210–39.

the two ethnic groups.[10] One need only consider how difficult it is to retain status distinctions among intimate friends to realize the importance of etiquette in preserving a system of social stratification.

Another common procedure for preventing the development of embarrassing interpersonal relations consists of social control over the formation of personifications. Objects may be defined in such a manner that close contacts of the forbidden nature become unlikely. Most meanings are social; the ways in which we are organized to act toward various classes of objects—including categories of human beings—are developed in the course of our interaction with other people. To the extent that other people react consistently, our responses become circumscribed. That a younger brother is a valuable object is a meaning that is learned through the prohibition of aggressive acts and the encouragement of indications of affection. The notion becomes so well-established that should one unexpectedly experience hostility toward his brother, he immediately suppress it. Should he fail to do so, he feels evil and worthless—that he is not even decent enough to love his own brother.

Within the Catholic Church it is understood that a priest or a nun is addressed as an office and not as a person. In theory, the human element is missing, and a devout Catholic will live up to his obligations regardless of his personal reactions toward particular officials. There are differences among priests in their reactions to reports of minor sins, but a confession cannot be put off simply because one dislikes the priest. If a woman should fall in love with her parish priest, she must suppress her inclinations. Nor are priests and nuns themselves dispassionate. But for the effective performance of many of their duties, all parties must deny sentimental considerations.

Traditional enemies and inferior groups are frequently defined in a manner that makes intimacy seem repulsive. Social distance is preserved in inter-ethnic contacts through the construction of stereotypes. A minority group may be characterized as lazy, ignorant, dirty, immoral, and incapable of bettering themselves. Social reform is dismissed as useless because the people are born that way. Landowners often regard peasants in the same manner. Generally, such meanings are not acquired through explicit instruction. The child learns them by observing the conduct of others whenever the group is under discussion. He notes the sneer with which it is mentioned

[10] Cf. Doyle, op. cit.; and Johnson, op. cit.

and grows up feeling that such people are contemptible. He notes the hilarious laughter with which the lofty aspirations of someone in it are dismissed and concludes that they are hopelessly incompetent. He notes the aggression directed against a man who has gotten "out of place" and concludes that these people quite properly belong only at the bottom of the social scale. A Negro's personification of a "bigoted white man" and a Jew's personification of an anti-Semitic Gentile are no more complimentary; they are also contrast conceptions. Nor are ethnic stereotypes the only ones that reinforce social distance. A "hepcat" looks upon a "square" as a pathetic creature. Many Americans have a conception of a "soiled woman," perhaps developed from motion picture portrayals of prostitutes, which is so unrealistic that they could not recognize a real prostitute sitting only a few feet away.

Erotic attractions occur spontaneously, and to minimize the possibility of their leading to embarrassing interpersonal relations in situations in which contact is inevitable, potential love objects are defined as being neuter in gender. The interaction of a doctor with patients of the opposite sex provides an illustration. Medical care sometimes requires not only nakedness on the part of the patient but the exposure and even the manipulation of genital organs by a comparative stranger. But effective treatment requires rational conduct, uninfluenced by sentimental considerations. When a male doctor is treating a beautiful female patient, then, it is understood that erotic interests are non-existent. Both parties do everything they can to deny that they are human beings and constantly reacting to one another as such, and the denial is usually remarkably successful. This practice is facilitated by the fact that doctors are trained to look upon all patients as "cases." Some even prefer not to treat close friends or members of their own families; they feel that they can work effectively only when their relationship to the patient is impersonal. Some hospitals and clinics have a standing rule that whenever a male physician is to examine the genital organs of a female patient, a nurse or a relative of the patient must be present in the room. There is no fear of the woman's being exploited; it is merely a ritual to put all parties at ease. But the fact that such regulations as well as a code of professional ethics exist implies a recognition of the possibility of attraction and of ensuing dangers.

The importance as well as the precarious nature of such meanings is revealed in the embarrassment that arises when the pretense momentarily breaks down. A woman can pose in the nude for an artist with equanimity as long as she can form a self-image as a "model," and she can be examined by a male doctor as long as she visualizes herself as a "case." But if the artist or doctor should suggest by a glance or some other gesture that attention is being directed to her as an individual, she reacts with a sense of shame and becomes disposed to cover herself.[11] The transaction is temporarily interrupted until the parties involved are able to regain their composure, usually through a series of diversionary gestures.

Probably the most rigidly enforced of all circumscribed meanings are those denying erotic attractions within a family. The incest taboo is not only universal but is perhaps the strongest of all taboos.[12] When persons of the opposite sex are in close and constant association, as they are in most families, some kind of erotic interest is usually aroused. Curiosity is apparently natural, and temptations of one sort or another seem to be inevitable. Freud contended that such attractions are essential for the early socialization of a child, but that they interfere with subsequent growth. Except for the husband and wife, all persons in one's immediate family are perceived as valuable but non-erotic objects. This does not preclude recognizing that one's sister, mother, or daughter may be attractive to other men, but the thought of engaging in sexual intercourse with any of them evokes revulsion. These personifications are so constructed that they may be addressed with various symbols of affection—such as kisses or caresses—but even momentary considerations of an erotic nature lead immediately to self-condemnation.

The violation of such norms is severely punished. Even in prisons, where sex offenders in general are despised by their fellow inmates, those incarcerated for incest are placed even below the men convicted of crimes against children or the raping of elderly women. The other prisoners are utterly contemptuous of them.[13] Even if a person is not caught, he suffers severe feelings of guilt. This gives some insight into the conditions under which men become conscious of their sentiments. Consciousness occurs where there is blockage

[11] Cf. Williams, op. cit., 354–55.
[12] Cf. Talcott Parsons, "The Incest Taboo in Relation to Social Structure and the Socialization of the Child," British Journal of Sociology, V (1954), 101–17; and Thomas, op. cit., pp. 178–97.
[13] Weinberg, op. cit., pp. 153–54.

and conflict. When there is opposition between one's impulses and conventional norms, he becomes acutely aware of both. But if the inner conflict is too intense, the sentiment may be repressed. When a person cannot bear to face impulses which are the source of so much pain—in the form of guilt feelings—he becomes unable to make designations about them to himself. Then the behavioral dispositions persist without awareness.

The formation of disjunctive sentiments among those who must live and work together is just as disrupting as conjunctive sentiments between forbidden partners. People in primary groups are expected to get along amicably, but jealousies and resentments are bound to develop. Since the standing of a corporation in a community may be jeopardized by the bickering of a few men in positions of importance, regulations are often drawn up to place limitations upon the competition of the ambitious. In some professions an attempt is made to regulate rivalries through a code of ethics. Although such norms are constantly violated, they represent attempts to minimize the rending consequences of negative sentiments.[14]

There are some professions—such as nursing, psychiatry, and social work—in which service to the clientele requires not only the establishment of interpersonal relations but the manipulation of sentiments. The art of psychotherapy as it is currently practiced frequently calls for the doctor to allow the patient to displace upon him sentiments developed in relationships with significant others in the past. Additional strains arise from the revelation by cooperative patients of the most intimate details of their lives. Since psychiatrists are human beings, they also form definite orientations toward each of their patients. Practitioners in such fields are frequently plagued by personal problems and in their professional societies are continually proposing adequate procedures for dealing with them. Social workers are preoccupied with the kinds of interpersonal relations that would be desirable for the performance of various services. They appreciate the fact that personal involvement on their part can be costly; on the other hand, a completely impersonal approach is likely to be ineffective. One proposed solution consists of creating an impression of sincere interest in the client's problems without actually identifying too closely with him. Within these professions

[14] Cf. Carl F. Taeusch, *Professional and Business Ethics* (New York: Henry Holt & Co., 1926).

there are innumerable discussions of the "proper attitude" to take, but when it comes down to the actual work, many practitioners adjust to each of their clients in much the same manner that an artist approaches a new subject.

Nurses are confronted with unusually difficult problems in interpersonal relations. To do their work effectively they must come into close contact with their patients, many of them male. In addition, they sometimes care for their charges at a time when the latter are almost helpless—like infants. It is not surprising, then, that many grateful patients develop conjunctive sentiments. Within the profession there are two contradictory philosophies. One is that the nurse should get to know each of her patients as individuals so that she can speed them back to their respective careers. She can best achieve this end by taking account of idiosyncrasies and by not treating all patients alike. The other view is that the nurse should treat all patients in much the same manner, being fair to all, irrespective of their personality traits. She is cautioned against becoming too personal and is encouraged to regard her patients merely as "cases." In most hospital wards a nurse is so busy that she has little opportunity to become well acquainted with all the people placed in her care. However, a study of a chronic ward by Morimoto showed that the treatment of patients there was not unrelated to sentiments. The nurses interacted almost twice as frequently with the patients they liked and spent six times as much time with them. Routine procedural contacts were virtually the same for everyone, but whenever opportunities arose for informal interchanges, they were usually carried on only with the preferred patients.[15] Furthermore, there are informal understandings among nurses concerning male patients who propose to them. Occasionally a nurse marries one, but this generally occurs long after his recovery. The practice is generally frowned upon, and some nurses even regard it as repulsive.[16]

Prostitutes constitute another occupational group facing similar difficulties. Although they are not likely to organize a code of ethics, there is evidence that some of them are equally concerned with

[15] Françoise R. Morimoto, "Favoritism in Personnel-Patient Interaction," *Nursing Research*, III (1955), 109–12.
[16] Cf. Hildegard E. Peplau, *Interpersonal Relations in Nursing* (New York: G. P. Putnam's Sons, 1952); and Isidor Thorner, "Nursing: The Functional Significance of an Institutional Pattern," *American Sociological Review*, XX (1955), 531–38.

these problems. A prostitute must enter into considerable intimacy with her clients, and her success in establishing a stable clientele depends in part upon her ability to act as if she were responding to each man as a unique individual. At the same time she cannot afford to become too deeply involved. Procurers often develop sentimental ties with their women and exploit them. The testimony of many prostitutes indicates that their relations with their customers are in most cases highly impersonal and that their seemingly individualized reactions are merely among the tricks of the trade. Most of the women make no secret of the fact that they view their customers with contempt. The essential problem that they face is that of maintaining social distance in spite of physical proximity, of not forming conjunctive sentiments that might make them vulnerable to exploitation. Prostitutes can operate to their own advantage only by remaining self-conscious and rational.[17]

Since cooperation of some sort takes place in all groups, there are certain norms governing interpersonal relations that are found almost everywhere. Cooley referred to these as the "primary ideals," since they are usually found among men who stand in primary relations to one another. Loyalty is apparently prized everywhere. When men are loyal, they can be counted on, no matter how great the pressure to defect. Traitors are almost universally despised. Indeed, they are disdained even by the enemy who profits from the treachery. A sense of decency and fair play is also valued in most groups. This apparently rests upon the capacity to sympathize to some extent with one's foes and to be reasonable in dealing with those who are momentarily in a disadvantageous position. Sometimes this involves sacrificing immediate gains, and those who are spared appreciate the "sporting chance." There are some groups—especially those in which a high value is placed on power—in which such considerations are regarded as a sign of weakness, but such groups are relatively rare. A man who would take advantage of the helpless is condemned almost everywhere. Sincerity is another attribute that is prized, even among the cynical who are sure that there are not many sincere people left in the world. Even in circles in which hypocrites abound—as among the ambitious rivals in a highly competitive field—a premium is still placed upon sincerity. The violation of such primary ideals usually arouses aggressive tend-

[17] Cf. Rolph, op. cit.

encies. A person who steals from the blind, runs down a helpless child, or informs on his friend is usually regarded as being somewhat less than human. It is easy to see why such norms are so widespread; the survival of groups depends upon the participants' retaining some measure of faith in one another.

Human Nature and Cultural Differences

At one time or another almost everyone talks about human nature, and most of the time we seem to be able to communicate meaningfully when we do. But what is human nature? Thus far no one has been able to formulate an answer that is acceptable to social scientists. The loudest objections have come from those who have emphasized the importance of culture. The prevalent view is that men are born plastic and are molded to behave as they do through socialization. The biologically inherited tendencies may be directed in many different ways, and in each group they are channeled into conventional patterns. The comparative study of culture reveals a remarkable diversity in human conduct, and this has led some anthropologists to insist that there is no such thing as a common human nature. Yet in examining behavior in the most esoteric groups one finds much that is familiar—mothers cherishing their children, men proud of their achievements, brothers haunted by guilt as they compete for some prize. The strange customs turn out to be only cloaks, and in some respects all men appear to be alike, regardless of their cultural heritage.[18] Some anthropologists have contended that human nature itself is the product of culture, but this view fails to explain why people with different backgrounds seemingly have a common set of attributes.

The study of human nature is complicated by the fact that some working model of man underlies every social order. In one society men are thought to be rational by nature; in another, animals enslaved by passions; in another, creatures made in the image of God. Furthermore, those with vested interests have used such conceptions to support or to attack some particular social system. They have claimed that certain painful practices, like war or slavery, are neces-

[18] Robert Redfield, "The Universally Human and the Cultural Variable," *Journal of General Education*, X (1957), 150–60.

sary because they are rooted in human nature. In almost every epoch those attempting to justify the existing order have claimed that human nature is fixed, and those advocating change have insisted that man is malleable and could be transformed through education. The notion that human nature is fixed provides a powerful tool for those wishing to preserve the *status quo,* once they have persuaded people that their particular conception of man is correct. Apologists for *laissez-faire* capitalism, for example, have insisted that economic competition is inevitable because men are by nature greedy; and socialists have countered that competition is artificially induced, that men can be trained to be unselfish, and that they are inexorably caught up in a historical movement toward a utopia.[19] What hampers the systematic investigation of human nature is the fact that scholars are so often drawn into such ideological quarrels.

But it is necessary to differentiate between political ideologies and the question of whether there are certain attributes that all men have in common, over and above their biological make-up, attributes that enable them to recognize one another as being fundamentally alike. It is a matter of historical and ethnographic record that an incredible variety of social institutions have existed among men and have survived for long periods of time. Furthermore, in periods of rapid social change or widespread migration the same individuals have lived in different types of social systems during different parts of their lives. It becomes apparent, then, that the efforts to support any particular system by insisting that it rests upon human nature are only justifications by those who stand to gain by its perpetuation. Popular beliefs about human nature in each culture are a part of the world view that sanctions its practices. Like ideologies they need not be accurate to be useful. It becomes important, then, to distinguish between what men avow about themselves and what actually underlies their conduct.

If men were completely the product of culture, those with drastically different cultural backgrounds should be unable to understand one another. But the historical record of inter-ethnic contacts reveals that in spite of all the difficulties that may arise, it is only a matter of time before those in alien groups come to recognize one another as being basically alike. Anthropologists insist that there are

---

[19] John Dewey, "Human Nature," *Encyclopedia of the Social Sciences,* Vol. VII, pp. 531–36. Cf. Raymond A. Bauer, *The New Man in Soviet Psychology* (Cambridge: Harvard University Press, 1952).

no pure "races" in the world. Each ethnic group is no more than a temporarily stable type, which can maintain its physical and cultural characterictics only as long as it remains isolated. Once contact is established with another group, friendships arise, social distance is reduced, and acculturation occurs. Role-taking is progressively facilitated, and before long the cultural differences disappear. In spite of the exploitation, recriminations, and patterns of differential treatment commonly called the "color line," sooner or later assimilation and amalgamation take place. With very few exceptions, then, the contact of different ethnic groups has led to the formation of a new ethnic group. This process occurs much more quickly among literate men, who almost daily are reading books by authors who lived long before, often in strange cultures. The reading of Pliny's account of the last days of Pompeii reveals conduct that is not much different from what occurs in comparable disasters in our society. Those who see motion pictures made in India or China depicting some early period in history have little difficulty in understanding the characters and plot in spite of differences in physical appearance, dress, language, and customs. Those who read autobiographies of people in the distant past or in strange cultures find the customs odd, but the personal life of the writer is usually comprehensible. Thus, cultural differences do not constitute a barrier to role-taking and mutual understanding, even though they render initial adjustments more difficult.

This suggests that all human beings have certain properties in common, which enable strangers to identify themselves as being quite similar. This provides the basis for learning about the peculiarities of one another's customs and institutions. It is generally agreed that biologically all men are of the same species, in spite of superficial variations in appearances, a somewhat different distribution of blood types, and differential immunity to certain diseases. But is there anything else that is typical of all human beings, over and above their common biological nature? One common attribute is the high degree of flexibility in behavior, arising out of man's ability to engage in symbolic communications. Men everywhere have some kind of language and are capable of reflective thought; hence, their behavior is marked by foresight and planning. But in addition to this it was Cooley's contention that all men are characterized by certain typical sentiments. Indeed, it is through the detection of similar sentiments that role-taking across cultural boundaries is accomplished. Riezler and Scheler have taken a very similar position.[20]

The typical sentiments, according to these writers, constitute the universal basis of human society. Because of differences in conventional norms, particular acts differ from society to society, but the kinds of interpersonal relations that develop are apparently the same. The same sentiments arise under somewhat different circumstances. Men fight over different issues, but the manner in which a combatant becomes oriented toward his allies, his enemies, and toward traitors to his cause is apparently the same. Conflict makes the same demands upon the participants; hence, although the conventional roles differ, interpersonal roles are alike. Similarly, the approved procedures for love-making as well as the basis for choosing love objects differ from society to society, but the relationship between lover and love object is sufficiently alike to make it recognizable even to those not entirely familiar with the customs. Where marriages are arranged by parents and brokers rather than by the principals involved, genuine affection may not develop between some husbands and wives. But the love of a mother for her child is easy enough to see, and even romantic love is manifested in daydreams and in popular songs. In a polygamous society the wives of the same husband may not become jealous of one another, but they may become upset over other matters—such as the ownership of property or inheritance rights.

What makes detection so difficult at first is that similar sentiments are manifested in very different ways. In the United States vanity is expressed openly in various forms of exhibitionism; people who are vain allow themselves to be seen at best advantage and enjoy the attention of others. In many Oriental societies, however, where this would be regarded as being in bad taste, vain men remain aloof, deriving enjoyment by imagining the admiration of others. Outsiders sometimes believe that such people are always modest and humble; it is not until they have lived among them for some time that they realize that this is not the case. In spite of the differences in overt behavior, a vain man is unmistakably identified in terms of his outward self-assurance, his inner doubts about his worth, and his

[20] Cooley, *Human Nature and the Social Order, op. cit.;* Riezler, *Man: Mutable and Immutable, op. cit.,* pp. 111–276; and Schuetz, "Scheler's Theory of Intersubjectivity and the General Thesis of the Alter Ego," *op. cit.,* 323–25.

sensitivity to criticism. In some societies a man who falls in love with a woman makes an open declaration of his affection; in others, he gets a friend or family spokesman to speak for him; in still others, he performs various feats of valor in her behalf. But the relationship is readily discernible in the yearning for the love object's presence and sympathetic response, the desire to do something for it, the chagrin at anyone's frustrating it. If sternness in public is required by custom, it is replaced in private by tender consideration. Of course, where the cultural differences are great, it takes longer to detect such sentiments. To those who do not know that the Chinese express anger by the widening of the eyes, the fact that someone is angry may go unnoticed. But after a period of sustained contact many outsiders learn to read such conventional gestures, and thereby acquire the tools for getting at inner experiences more accurately.

In spite of the diversity of culture, typical sentiments are recognized because of the similarity in the claims and obligations that make up the various interpersonal roles. Conventional norms vary, but the various patterns of interpersonal relations are apparently universal. In all societies mothers become concerned with the careers of their offspring; rivals worry about the prowess of their opponents; lovers grieve over the loss of their love objects. Where aggressive, erotic, or domineering impulses are inhibited, they are manifested in the style of action. No matter where one looks—at tenements under elevated trains, at men crouching in foxholes on the battlefield, at people struggling for survival in concentration camps, at peasants living quietly in a village—he finds diversity in overt behavior, but performances by creatures who are remarkably alike. What all men apparently have in common are the ways in which they relate themselves to one another. As Cooley once put it, everywhere and always men seek honor and dread ridicule, defer to public opinion, admire courage and disdain cowardice.

Cooley contended further that the sentiments which enable men of diverse origins to identify with one another develop in intimate contacts with people whom each knows on a personal basis. He believed that the sentiments are universal because such intimate circles exist everywhere. Cliques, families, neighborhood groups, and juvenile gangs can be found in all societies. Regardless of the cultural matrix in which socialization takes place, the problems encountered in adjusting to other human beings are much the same. Men everywhere develop similar curiosities about one another—their emotional reactions, their secrets, their erotic preferences, peculiarities of their moral character. There are the same restraints and tensions, conflicting interests, cooperation to attain difficult ends, necessity of curbing aggressive tendencies, loyalty under conditions of duress and other tests of courage. Everyone is confronted by authority figures of one sort or other and must learn to deal with them in some way. Although he used a different vocabulary, Freud also appreciated these facts and incorporated them into his theory of socialization, which is remarkably like that of Cooley in spite of his emphasis upon different kinds of sentiments.

Even a cursory glance at the folklore and literature of the world reveals a remarkable similarity in plots, in spite of the diversity of language, costume, and setting. Indeed, the bulk of world literature seems to revolve around a handful of recurrent themes. The experiences of men, though infinitely varied, are endlessly duplicated; the stories all begin in situations that most people understand either from their own experiences or from living side by side with other human beings and noticing what it is like to endure them.[21] A beautiful girl forces an infatuated man to defile himself to demonstrate his love and then rejects him as degraded. An evil man outsmarts himself through his avarice and attains success at some terrible cost, realizing only when it is too late that he has struggled in vain. It is precisely because such events take place everywhere that novels can be translated from one language into another and be appreciated in spite of the change of literary style. The fact that *Carmen* can so easily be transposed into *Carmen Jones* is an indication of the secondary importance of the cultural setting in comparison to the plot and characterizations. Great classics in one culture are usually hailed in another; European writers credited with extraordinary insight into human nature—Balzac, Dostoyevsky, Pascal, La Rochefoucauld, Shakespeare—are appreciated elsewhere for the great "truths" that they reveal. Although the Japanese are reputed to be an unemotional people who are content to have their marriages arranged for them by parents and matchmakers, it would be difficult to find a more passionate tale of romantic love than Koyo Ozaki's ever popular

---

[21] Cf. Helen M. Hughes, *News and the Human Interest Story* (Chicago: University of Chicago Press, 1940), pp. 184–216.

Konjiki Yasha; nor do they fail to appreciate the sacrifice of Marguerite in Alexandre Dumas' *La Dame aux Camélias.* An American reading Vergil's *Aenied* discovers that human nature has not changed in 2,000 years. Thus, in spite of the innumerable divergencies in time, place, and culture, there are apparently a limited set of experiences that are universal.

Fiction writers, both serious and humorous, have long astounded their readers with imaginative productions that have taken them to strange countries, ancient times, continents like Atlantis, and even to outer space. They have populated their tales with personifications as varied as Frankenstein's monster, King Kong, and Mickey Mouse. In science fiction the powers of both the hero and the villain are extended by robots and various electronic devices. An examination of these tales reveals, however, that the sentiments of the characters are much like those of ordinary men that we know. The creatures from outer space seek ends that are readily recognizable—lust, deference, grandeur, affection. Such tales remain meaningful precisely because the imaginary personifications are endowed with the same sentiments which enable us to recognize real people as human. Animated cartoons can be translated into different languages and still be appreciated; *Pancho Tronera* is as popular in Latin America as *Joe Palooka* is in the United States. The interpersonal relations depicted are comprehensible.

From time to time situations arise in which people are accused of being "inhuman." After World War II, when the atrocities perpetrated in the German concentration camps were disclosed, it was charged that the Nazis were "beasts." The same charge is sometimes leveled against fathers who beat infants mercilessly and against managers who place the efficiency of their factory above all other considerations, treating their subordinates like cogs in a machine. Sometimes a ruthless killer is found who can supply no particular motive for his deed and admits that he gains considerable gratification from observing the agony of his victims as they die. As the man relates gruesome details without any manifestation of remorse, an observer experiences an eerie feeling and concludes that the animal before him is basically different from himself. It is similarly difficult to identify with many people who are psychotic. No one is insisting that the Germans employed in extermination centers should not be classified as *homo sapiens.* What is being charged is that some people act in ways that would be impossible once sympathetic identification is established. It is when people seem to lack sentiments that they are labelled as "inhuman."

Thus, it becomes apparent that not everything that men do is distinctively human. Kissing is a human act. What is it about a kiss that gives it its significance? A kiss can be described objectively as the propulsion of two bodies toward one another with the pursing of the lips, with a variety of internal changes—such as a rise of blood pressure and temperature—upon the establishment of contact. Such an account of the physiology of this unhygienic practice may be quite accurate, but the analysis seems cold and lifeless. What is the missing element that will bring life to a kiss? Is there some area within the totality of human behavior that can be singled out as being characteristically human? Can a distinction be made between human *behavior* and *human* behavior? A number of scholars have suggested that there is a difference and that social scientists have not paid enough attention to the latter. Generalizations about *human* behavior should be universal—not restricted to a given time, place, or culture.

Summary and Conclusion

Among men who know one another on an intimate basis, sentimental considerations temper the rational pursuit of interests as well as conformity with group norms. The better men know one another as unique individuals, the more they are inclined to make allowances. The personal obligations that they feel toward each other interfere with their carrying out their duties. It is not surprising, therefore, that in all organized groups there are special norms encouraging the establishment of some sentiments and discouraging or prohibiting others. Since sentimental considerations supersede customs and laws primarily when social distance is reduced, most attempts at social control consist of setting up polite barriers between those who might get into trouble. To the extent that such efforts are successful, behavior remains largely conventional, and people of diverse cultural heritages appear to be different.

The fact that such regulations exist everywhere, usually in the form of unwritten laws, does not mean that they are easily enforced.

Indeed, it is often the lack of success in enforcing such norms that gives group life its peculiarly "human" quality. Everywhere there are cases of forbidden love, of suppressed hatred, of refusal to act from pride or spite. When impulses emanating from sentiments are thwarted, men experience shame, embarrassment, anger, jealousy. Occasionally the pressure is too great, and a person acts passionately—sometimes even destroying himself. Although human behavior is not necessarily irrational, man can hardly be regarded as an exclusively rational creature. It is through the detection of such inner conflicts and passionate outbursts that men from different cultural backgrounds are able to recognize one another as being of a kind.

It has been argued by many scholars that human beings throughout the world are fundamentally alike. One plausible theory is that this unity of mankind arises not only from the fact that all men are biologically of the same species but also from the fact that certain recurrent patterns of interpersonal relations are inevitable. A common human nature becomes discernible in the typical sentiments that are formed as each person develops stable orientations toward his intimate associates. This important issue is by no means settled, but this theory is certainly worthy of serious consideration.

Suggested References

COOLEY, CHARLES H., *Human Nature and the Social Order*. New York: Charles Scribner's Sons, 1922. A study of socialization by a pioneer in American sociology, stressing the manner in which various attributes develop as the child comes to terms with his intimate associates.

DOYLE, BERTRAM W., *The Etiquette of Race Relations in the South*. Chicago: University of Chicago Press, 1937. A well documented account of the proper forms of greeting, salutation, conversation, and other conduct in the interaction of master and slave in the South before the Civil War.

LEA, HENRY C., *Historical Sketch of Sacredotal Celibacy in the Christian Church*. Philadelphia: J. B. Lippincott & Co., 1867. A historical study of the development of asceticism and celibacy among officials of the Catholic Church and an account of the difficulties encountered in the enforcement of these doctrines.

RIEZLER, KURT, *Man: Mutable and Immutable*, Parts IV–VII. Chicago: Henry Regnery Co., 1950. A provocative and neglected treatise on human nature, regarding the immutable in man as consisting of regularities to be found in passionate behavior.

SIMMEL, GEORG, *The Sociology of Georg Simmel*, Kurt H. Wolff, trans., pp. 40–57, 87–177, 307–329, 379–408. Glencoe: Free Press, 1950. Selections from a sociological classic: insightful essays on sociability, on dyadic and triadic relationships, and on variations in social distance as measured by the type of knowledge participants have of one another.

WEINBERG, S. KIRSON, *Incest Behavior*. New York: Citadel Press, 1955. A study of incest based upon an analysis of 203 cases reported in Chicago, containing descriptive accounts of changes in interpersonal relations as well as other transformations of family routine.

12

Personal
status
in
primary
groups

In one of Plato's dialogues
Glaucon asks Socrates whether men would not always pursue their
selfish interests whenever they were sure they could get away with
it. He recalls the tale of a shepherd who found a ring that made him
invisible, seduced his queen, killed his king, and proclaimed himself
ruler. Were it possible for other men to become similarly invisible,
he asks, could they resist similar temptations? Those who learn of a
man who had restrained himself under such circumstances would
praise him openly, but would they not secretly regard him a fool?
Glaucon's apprehensions are probably exaggerated, but one might
ask: what would happen in any American city if all men were invisible for one hour?

Taking the matter out of the realm of conjecture, under somewhat analogous circumstances the behavior patterns of some men
do undergo remarkable transformation. Some soldiers, when they
are serving on foreign soil, loot and plunder, mistreat helpless

people, collect pornographic literature, and frequent brothels in spite of repeated warnings against venereal diseases. Some businessmen, when attending conventions in large cities, do things they would not dream of doing at home, especially if there is no one else present from the same locality. Migrants who lose themselves in a huge metropolis sometimes lead lives that are markedly different from the routine they had previously followed. In such cases, the unexpected appearance of someone from the home community suddenly recalls old standards of conduct; there is a sudden sense of shame and a hurried attempt at concealment. Of course, there are many men whose conduct would not change too much under such circumstances; they may become somewhat less restrained, but they would do nothing of which they would be ashamed. But what of the people who do act differently?

A man who is lost in a city or on foreign soil, much like an invisible man, is anonymous. No one knows him, and the fact that he cannot be identified as a specific individual results in the elimination of many inhibitions. Thus, the mere presence of others who are known on a personal basis makes a difference in the conduct of many people. But why should this be? What is the difference between an audience consisting of strangers and one made up of acquaintances and friends?

Constellations of Primary Relations

Whenever the same people come together over and over—whether they be boys who live in the same neighborhood, employees of the same night club, patients thrown together in the chronic ward of a hospital, or men imprisoned together—they develop sentiments toward one another and form a distinct type of grouping. A *primary group* consists of people whose relationships with one another approach the primary pole on the continuum of social distance. It is an association of people who know one another on an individual basis. All primary groups are small, for it would not be possible for a large number of people to learn about one another's idiosyncrasies and special interests. Such associations are usually sustained over a long period of time, and it is through repeated contacts that the participants are able to build up a fund of knowledge about each other. Primary groups are also characterized by a sense of intimacy; there is often a sharing of secrets so that the members develop a set of special meanings and a distinctive outlook. Personal reserve is more relaxed, and in most cases there is a feeling of belonging together. The recognition of various mutual interests makes it easier for those associated in this manner to act more spontaneously in one another's behalf.

Among the most important characteristics of primary groups is the fact that the interaction of the participants is not specialized. People in such groups have opportunities for observing one another in many different contexts. They meet habitually in appointed places and compare their experiences. They attend one another's anniversaries, weddings, and funerals. In time they come to share their aspirations, disappointments, and sorrows. It is in this manner that each person is able to construct a unique personification of each of the others; intimate friends are not perceived as instances of categories. Being familiar with each other's foibles and virtues, they know when to joke and when to be serious. They also know what topics to avoid in the presence of a particular individual.

Although primary groups are relatively stable, in most cases their boundaries are not clear. Each grouping actually consists of a cluster of smaller cliques which overlap. For example, in a given family the mother may be a gregarious person who has a fairly extensive circle of friends. Most of these people would be known to everyone else in the family, but some of them are only nodding acquaintances. The son may be a member of a delinquent gang, only a few of whom are known to his parents. The daughter's life centers around her own circle of intimate friends, mostly girls of her age, with whom she participates in slumber parties, fan clubs, and dances. The father's co-workers, who are also his fishing and bowling companions as well as members of the same lodge, are well acquainted with the immediate family, but they do not know all of the friends of each member. Thus, surrounding most American families are several coteries of friends who are associated with them through one of the members. Once the children marry and form new friendships, the arrangements become even more complex. Therefore, it would be more accurate to speak of overlapping constellations of primary relations, although as a matter of convenience sociologists continue to use the term "primary group."

Since social distance varies on a continuum, different primary groups are characterized by different degrees of intimacy. The participants in some are very close to one another, doing all kinds of things together and sharing their innermost feelings. In others the people are friendly but remain polite and respectful. Some persons are apparently incapable of relaxing their reserve no matter whose company they are in, and the presence of one such individual may give the entire group an air of austerity. Much depends upon the personality traits of the participants and the extent to which they complement one another.

There are many kinds of primary groups, and the most spontaneous of them is the clique or coterie of friends. Such groups spring up in a variety of conventional settings among people who happen to find one another congenial. There is a selective process whereby the discordant members either leave of their own accord or are ejected. Those who are left maintain their contacts largely for the pleasure they get out of one another's company. Growth is spontaneous; other congenial people may be brought in by any of the participants. There is no formal structure; but once such groups are established, they may be quite stable, many lasting a lifetime.

Sociologists usually cite the family as an example of a primary group. It should be pointed out, however, that there are many kinds of families, and some of them are not necessarily primary groups. In societies in which mate-selection is accomplished through marriage brokers and relatives, a husband and wife may remain polite strangers for their entire lives. Most American families are primary groups, for the principals are usually able to select their own mates. Although such groups may have been formed voluntarily, they are subsequently sustained by conventional norms. Once a family is contracted, its dissolution requires legal action. It is not surprising, then, that in some families the members are very close; in others they merely recognize their conventional obligations and make no secret of the fact that their own preferences would lie elsewhere.

But there are many primary groups that are formed involuntarily. Especially in modern mass societies in which activities of all kinds are carried out in large corporate bodies, primary groups develop among those who are brought together in the various local units. Men in a work crew initially come together incidentally to the pursuit of other interests, and then form close ties. Similarly, in military organizations men share their fate with others assigned to the same squads; they are simply thrown together by the requirements of the larger organization and forced to make the best of each other's company. This is also true in the case of children who dislike their families; they did not ask to be born to their parents. Nor are prisoners who share the same cell consulted on their choice of associates. These primary groups differ from others in that the contributions expected of each individual are in part specified by the formal social structure; the goals of many of their common activities are dictated by the requirements of the larger unit of which they are a part. Whatever may be done for the personal satisfaction of the members is often subsidiary. Furthermore, authority patterns are imposed from without; sergeants and foremen are rarely selected by the men who serve under them. Since there is not much choice in the selection of one's associates, the ties in these primary groups are often less intimate than those found in the more spontaneously formed groupings. Indeed, in most cases smaller cliques arise within the groups. Nonetheless, the importance of these groups is not to be underestimated. What any person experiences of the larger organization is necessarily filtered through the eyes of those with whom he is in immediate contact. The particular ways in which he interprets new policies and events depend to a large extent upon the views of those around him. Thus, each local unit develops a perspective and a set of norms, and the particular standards that arise make a difference in the manner in which official regulations are enforced. Such primary groups, even when the participants are not too intimate, exercise considerable control over the conduct of most of their members.[1]

Each participant in a primary group evaluates and is evaluated by each of the others. Before long preferences emerge, and in time a pattern of attraction and repulsions is established. Each person chooses and rejects and at the same time is himself chosen and rejected. In each group different combinations of interpersonal roles develop in the reactions of particular personalities to one another. One person may be dominant and all the others submissive, or there may be a rivalry between two dominant individuals. Studies show that patterns of dominance do not necessarily assume a rank order,

[1] Cf. Donald Clemmer, *The Prison Community* (New York: Rinehart & Co., 1958), pp. 83–148; and Mandelbaum, *op. cit.*

as in the "pecking order" among chickens. A dominates B, who dominates C and D; but C and D dominate A.[2] The longer the period of contact the more clearly articulated such patterns become. In each case there emerges a unique network of interpersonal relations. This means that in each primary group people become involved in one another's lives in a somewhat different manner.

In every family each member develops some kind of interpersonal role, and an attempt was made by Bossard and Boll to specify some of them through a study of 100 large American families. Among the recurrent types that they found were the responsible head who supervises others, makes decisions, and commands deference; the attractive, popular, and sociable one; the socially ambitious one who is concerned with improving his lot as well as that of the family; the quiet, hardworking, and studious one who tends to withdraw; the irresponsible and self-seeking one; the hypochondriac who is plagued by a succession of ailments; the spoiled child whose demands are tolerated by the others. Other roles include the scapegoat, the perfectionist, the "black sheep," and the convenient handyman who is always doing chores for others.[3] These roles, discernible in familiar behavior patterns, can no doubt be detected in other primary groups as well.

It is apparent from the illustrations that we are concerned with a phenomenon of great complexity, and social psychologists are only beginning to devise appropriate procedures for their analysis. Moreno has pioneered the empirical investigation of networks of interpersonal relations. His procedure is relatively simple. He questions each person about everyone else in the group, asking for his preferences and dislikes and getting some indication of the intensity of the sentiment. Having obtained this information, he proceeds to make charts for each group, describing the relationship between each person and every other party. It may be one of mutual attraction or mutual repulsion; it may be one of attraction by one party and repulsion by the other; it may be one of attraction or repulsion on one side and indifference on the other; or it may be one of mutual indifference. By ascertaining the relationship of every participant to

[2] Eugenia Hanfmann, "Social Structure of a Group of Kindergarten Children," *American Journal of Orthopsychiatry*, V (1935), 407–10.

[3] James H. S. Bossard and Eleanor S. Boll, "Personality Roles in the Large Family," *Child Development*, XXVI (1955), 71–78.

each of the others, he is able to characterize the group as a whole. Some people are isolates—indifferent to others or rejected by almost all of them. Dyadic cliques within primary groups develop whenever there is reciprocal selection. Triadic cliques may emerge when three people all like one another, when one party holds together two others who do not particularly care for each other, or when two people are dependent upon a third who exploits them. Moreno also speaks of the formation of a star, consisting of a natural leader and his circle of followers. The numerous charts drawn by Moreno and his associates are sometimes extremely complex, but they have proved very useful in a number of studies.[4]

Moreno concerns himself only with attraction and repulsion, variations in the intensity of each, and degree of reciprocity. This is a gross oversimplification, for there are many other ways in which people become involved in one another's lives. For example, the distinction between disinterested and possessive love is not made, nor is resentment distinguished from jealousy. Transformations in the network of interpersonal relations can be described only in terms of new preferences or rejections, and changing nuances in the quality of various sentiments cannot be recorded. Since the charts are already quite intricate, the addition of more dimensions would so complicate the picture that complex mathematical tools may become necessary. Indeed, the kind of multi-dimensional analysis that appears necessary is even difficult to visualize, for it would probably require the use of some form of non-Euclidean geometry. Moreno's sociometric scales constitute only a beginning, but his work points to the difficulties involved and gives us some appreciation of what still remains to be done.

How a person feels and what he does often depend upon the web of interpersonal relations in which he is involved. In each primary group there is a prevailing "emotional atmosphere," which develops in the interaction of the distinct combination of personalities. The atmosphere may be congenial, somber, serious, or hateful—depending upon the sustained reactions of the participants to one another. Such persistent moods color behavior, for acts that are consistent with them are facilitated and those which are not are inhibited. The

[4] Jacob L. Moreno, Who Shall Survive? (New York: Beacon House, 1953). Cf. Helen H. Jennings, Leadership and Isolation (New York: Green & Co., 1950).

same enterprises carried out by different primary groups vary considerably in style and sometimes even in organization. Networks of interpersonal relations, then, are agencies of social control in that they provide a matrix within which life goes on.

Each community may be viewed as a galaxy of primary groups. Each person participates in different combinations of sometimes overlapping constellations of primary relations, and each is constrained by the personal obligations which develop in them. He plays a somewhat different interpersonal role in each circle, depending upon his reaction to the others. These intimate circles are important because they consist of significant others, people whose judgments are crucial in the formation of each person's evaluation of himself. One's level of self-esteem depends largely upon the responses of people he knows on a personal basis, and he cannot afford to let them down.

The Culture of Primary Groups

Culture is the product of communication, and the ease with which members of primary groups communicate with one another in contrast to their reticence before strangers leads to the development of a special culture. A number of meanings emerge which are shared only within the circle. Many of these norms deal with the idiosyncrasies of the members; everyone yells at grandmother, knowing that she is a bit deaf. Special occasions, ways of celebrating them, mementoes, peculiar appellations, touchy subjects to be avoided—all these are matters of concern only to those within the group. There are peculiar expressions and bodily gestures, and public symbols are used in special ways. Unusual words are sometimes used to refer to objects of disdain or to private matters. Role-taking is greatly facilitated within such groups because of the private universe of discourse in which only those who belong can partake. Since each primary group consists of a unique combination of personalities, it is not strange that the culture of each primary group is distinct, although not so different from that of neighboring groups as to be beyond comprehension.

Each primary group develops an internal organization, consisting of a set of shared beliefs, standards of conduct, and means of enforcing conformity. Such norms are often referred to as *informal social structure*, for the codes prescribe correct forms of behavior on matters not covered in the formal organization of the community. Such unwritten codes are rarely stated explicitly and in most cases are only intuitively felt. Laws and formal regulations indicate what people are supposed to do, but everywhere people make exceptions for their friends and improvise when the rules appear unreasonable. These informal understandings are not necessarily in conflict with conventional norms or laws, but there may be significant differences. Many customs are observed only in public and not at home. Official ideologies are not always popular. For example, Americans generally avow an egalitarian philosophy, but the fact that class and ethnic stratification persists is a matter of record. Many laws are difficult to enforce, and even in a totalitarian dictatorship popular beliefs develop independently of official views. People are often unimpressed by formal announcements, laugh contemptuously at them among their trusted friends, and rely more on the "grapevine" for their information. There is little enthusiasm for elections that will make no difference.[5] This suggests that spontaneous perspectives develop which may differ considerably from the position that is supported by legitimate authority.

Although most families living in a homogeneous community share a more or less similar outlook, each has a culture that is unique. There are shared memories of happy events, of tragedies, and of unusual hardships which give various conventional meanings a special quality. Roberts made a comparative study of three contiguous households in a Navaho village, linked not only by proximity but by marriage as well. His item analysis shows a marked difference, not only in the material objects owned but also in the accepted procedures for performing various tasks. Although each household shares many items and practices with its neighbors, the particular configuration is in each case distinct.[6]

Considerable attention has been directed by sociologists toward the informal codes that develop in the local units of large organizations. Each corporate body—commercial, educational, governmental,

[5] Cf. Bauer and Gleicher, *op. cit.*; Eugene Lyons, "Stifled Laughter," *Harper's Mazagine*, CLXX (1935), 557–67; and Saville R. Davis, "Morale in Fascist Italy in Wartime," *American Journal of Sociology*, XLVII (1941), 434–38.

[6] J. M. Roberts, "Three Navaho Households: A Comparative Study in Small Group Culture," *Papers of the Peabody Museum of American Archeology and Ethnology*, XL (1951), No. 3. Cf. Robert D. Hess and Gerald Handel, *Family Worlds* (Chicago: University of Chicago Press, 1959).

industrial, or military—is divided into a number of smaller units, each of them with a distinct culture. These unwritten codes emerge in the spontaneous interaction of the participants, and they are usually not sanctioned by the officials. It has been pointed out that such *informal norms develop at those points where the formal social structure proves inadequate,* usually in the interstices between regulations. They develop when unexpected situations not covered by the rules arise, when the formal regulations are so rigid that special circumstances cannot be met effectively, or when the peculiarities of the local situation make the application of otherwise acceptable norms difficult. Such codes are not necessarily unethical or illegal, but they sometimes deviate from the official position.

Following the pioneering studies at a Western Electric Company plant in Chicago, numerous inquiries have been made in a variety of large organizations. It has been found that informal norms concerning the performance of duties, and not coinciding with official policy, develop in each local unit. If men work for money, being paid on a piecework basis should provide the incentive to produce at maximum capacity. But it was found in the Western Electric study that most men do not exert themselves to their utmost, even when offered special rewards. Common understandings emerge in each department as to what constitutes the proper output for a day, and those who produce too much are condemned as "rate busters" or "speed kings," while shirkers are penalized for not keeping up. The men work hard until the completion of the day's quota is in sight and then relax.[7] Similar findings have come from studies of military units in World War II. There are tacit understandings among soldiers, especially when assigned to routine tasks, that they should not do their work exceptionally well. On the other hand, in situations in which human lives or special privileges for the group are at stake, each is expected to exert himself. Men who conduct themselves according to regulations sometimes win the commendation of their officers but are accused by their fellows of "bucking."[8] Universities ostensibly exist for the development and dissemination of knowledge,

[7] Fritz Roethlisberger and William J. Dickson, *Management and the Worker* (Cambridge: Harvard University Press, 1939), pp. 379–548. Cf. Donald Roy, "Quota Restriction and Goldbricking in a Machine Shop," *American Journal of Sociology,* LVII (1952), 427–42.

[8] Cf. Samuel Stouffer et al., *The American Soldier* (Princeton: Princeton University Press, 1949), Vol. I, pp. 410–29.

but there are many student groups in which this is regarded as a somewhat outmoded ideal. Unless one shows reasonable interest in "dates," athletic events, and other extracurricular activities, he is looked upon as being "queer." Many are even prevented from studying as hard as they would like from the necessity of being a "good fellow" in the eyes of those with whom they live.

Professional men are often faced with common problems and tend to get together for mutual assistance. In the informal contacts among those in each profession, special codes of conduct are sustained and reinforced. In the medical profession, for example, the efficiency with which clients can be served is sometimes circumscribed by considerations that have nothing to do with the technical skills of the doctor. The kinds of services that a doctor can render are often limited by the hospital facilities available to him, but the appointment of interns, residents, and senior staff members of the better hospitals rests on grounds other than ability. It is not enough that a young doctor has the appropriate class and ethnic background. He must also show proper deference for his elders, never question a diagnosis before a patient, nor treat another doctor's patient without his consent. Part of the working code of any profession is discretion; there are frequent exchanges of confidences—expressions of cynicism about the "mission" of the profession and gossip of the foibles of practitioners and typical patients—which could not be betrayed to outsiders. Some doctors depend heavily upon referrals, and these go only to those who cooperate and fit into the accepted pattern. Thus, the type of medical care available in a given community depends not only upon the competence of the doctors practicing there, but also upon the informal understandings that develop among them.[9]

Studies have also been made of the informal social structure of adolescent gangs. Although the slum areas in which gangs flourish are sometimes called "jungles," presumably because there is comparatively little law and order in the conventional sense, there is evidence that, within each gang, codes of conduct are strictly enforced. The culture of many gangs includes values that are condemned elsewhere. There is emphasis upon "toughness" and virility, and many boys feel that they must live dangerously to maintain the

[9] Cf. Oswald Hall, "The Stages in a Medical Career," *American Journal of Sociology*, LIII (1948), 327–36; Eliot Freidson, "Client Control and Medical Practice, *ibid.*, LXV (1960), 374–82; and E. C. Hughes, *op. cit.*, pp. 102–15.

respect of their friends. Policemen, called "bulls" or less complimentary epithets, are objects of scorn and distrust. In each area a special language develops, one that is strange to outsiders, even to gang members of another generation, and this results in the creation of a special universe of discourse. To those who can comprehend the perspective that is shared in such groups, the vicious beatings that sometimes come to public attention do not appear as "senseless" as charged. Since so many boys apparently feel that they need one another's support and protection to survive against the encroachment of rival gangs, their strong sense of solidarity is understandable. That a boy might commit an illegal act to conform to group expectations is also understandable, for nothing is regarded as worse than being "chicken" or "punking out."[10]

In recent years there has been accumulating evidence that primary group norms sometimes interfere with the accomplishment of formal objectives and under some circumstances may even supersede institutional norms. Military units are equipped and organized alike, but variations in morale are notorious. Some companies are daring and brilliant; others are steady and reliable; still others are completely unreliable. Such differences in performance can hardly be accounted for in terms of formal social structure; they apparently arise from differences in primary group norms and the extent to which they are enforced among the men. In some units the ultimate objectives of the war are taken seriously; in others only lip service is paid to them. In some units there is absolute confidence in the leadership, and in others there is no confidence at all. In some instances the men expect one another to make the supreme sacrifice; in others, only a token performance; in still others, not to take any unnecessary risks. Some platoons consist of closely cooperating circles of friends; others are made up of men who reluctantly tolerate each other. The combat situation may be defined in many different ways, and shared expectations develop in each primary group as to the best way to cope with it.[11]

[10] Cf. Albert K. Cohen, *Delinquent Boys* (Glencoe: Free Press, 1955); Frederick M. Thrasher, *The Gang* (Chicago: University of Chicago Press, 1927); and William F. Whyte, *Street Corner Society* (Chicago: University of Chicago Press, 1943).

[11] Cf. Roy R. Grinker and John P. Spiegel, *Men Under Stress* (Philadelphia: Blakiston Co., 1945), pp. 21–49; Mandelbaum, *op. cit.*; and Stouffer *et al.*, *op. cit.*, Vol. II, pp. 105–91.

There are cases in which the local representatives of competing organizations cooperate informally in order to accomplish their respective aims. Contrary to the expectations of the executive officers of both union and management, there are many departures from the provisions of the negotiated contract at the local level, especially when there are special conditions that impose unreasonable hardships. In some cases the local representatives of the union and the plant superintendent evade the formal labor agreement by making private arrangements that are mutually advantageous. The workers are thereby able to get better wages, to take vacations at desired times, and receive other benefits; the superintendent in turn is assured of more efficient production. Sometimes the negotiators may even trade personal favors to make things easier for one another, and there have been instances in which a local union has offered to go out on a "wildcat" strike in support of a superintendent having difficulties with his superiors. In the local elections the men who show shrewdness in making such agreements are continually reelected to the grievance committees, indicating that the rank and file of workers, while certainly not opposing union policies, are often concerned more with immediate advantages than they are with details of the contract.[12] In much the same manner criminal lawyers often work closely with the very officials they must oppose in court, for the successful practice of criminal law requires the cooperation of various governmental agencies. Seeing his client in jail, obtaining information pertinent to the case, setting bail, bargaining for an informal settlement, scheduling the time and place for trial— all these transactions require decisions on the part of some official, and a lawyer must maintain friendly contacts to serve his clients more effectively. Since the opposing attorneys usually wish to avoid a court battle, they sometimes cooperate in establishing an equitable settlement, especially when the client is obviously guilty.[13] Informal norms frequently arise among men who are constantly working together, even when their major interests are in conflict.

Recognizing the enormous potential influence of the media of mass communication, many political observers have been haunted by

12 Melville Dalton, "Unofficial Union-Management Relations," *American Sociological Review*, XV (1950), 611–19.

13 Arthur L. Wood, "Informal Relations in the Practice of Criminal Law," *American Journal of Sociology*, LXII (1956), 48–55.

the specter of millions of people being duped and manipulated by unscrupulous men in control of the channels. Whereas publicists had once been under the impression that the people could be swayed merely by manipulating communication content, they are now discovering that there are remarkable variations in response from one local setting to another to what is presented in a given radio or television program. Studies of voting show that the manner in which political appeals are interpreted depends largely upon the interaction that occurs among those in the audience; the appeals are reconstructed by influential people in each locality.[14] Even the reactions of children to cartoons depend upon the group setting in which they are seen, and a study of preferences in popular music among Chicago adolescents reveals a remarkable degree of overlapping in the choices of songs and disc jockeys among those who are members of the same club.[15] While not minimizing the importance of the media of mass communication, it must be remembered that all perception is selective and that many of the hypotheses that men project when reading newspapers or watching television are derived from the people with whom they are in immediate contact.

Although most primary group norms reinforce those of the larger community, there are some arrangements that constitute outright violations of customs and laws. When laws are unpopular, they are secretly violated. If divorce laws are too harsh, people get together to circumvent the requirements that they regard as unreasonable. If monetary regulations result in severe hardships, a "black market" arises spontaneously in which money can be exchanged and goods sold at prices that are more commensurate with supply and demand. Stringent regulations against the illegal sale of drugs have not halted the flow of opium and marihuana; the punitive laws have only raised prices to fantastic levels to compensate for the risks taken, thereby forcing some addicts to turn to crime to finance their "habit." Profes-

[14] Paul F. Lazarsfeld, Bernard Berelson, and Hazel Gaudet, *The People's Choice* (New York: Columbia University Press, 1948), pp. 150–58; and Berelson, Lazarsfeld, and McPhee, *loc. cit.*

[15] John Johnstone and Elihu Katz, "Youth and Popular Music," *American Journal of Sociology*, LXII (1957), 563–68. Cf. Matilda W. Riley and Samuel H. Flowerman, "Group Relations as a Variable in Communications Research," *American Sociological Review*, XVI (1951), 174–80.

sional athletes are well aware of the rules of their game. There are many infractions that pass undetected by the officials; but the players have their own conception of what is unacceptable, and special arrangements are made among themselves to deal with "dirty" players on the opposing team. In this way, transactions that are unchartered, unconventional, and sometimes illegal are carried on through the cooperation of men with personal claims upon one another.

Even among police officers, whose duty it is to enforce the laws, there are informal understandings that are illegal. For example, there is an unwritten code that a policeman is not to testify against a fellow officer. In a study of the police force of a midwestern city, officers were asked if they would report a partner who had stolen $500 from a drunken prisoner. They were also asked if they would testify against the partner if the prisoner subsequently brought formal charges that he had been robbed. Only one man answered "yes" to both questions, and he was a "rookie." All of these men were aware of the fact that perjury was illegal and punishable by suspension or dismissal. But they also realized that anyone labelled as a "stool pigeon" would be ostracized, even by those who would not condone stealing. Police work requires close cooperation, for there are many dangerous assignments, and no officer can accomplish much alone. Furthermore, any officer may become vulnerable to prosecution; in line of duty many of them must maintain contacts with the underworld and occasionally resort to the illegal use of violence. Under these circumstances, the men must protect one another against the charges of people who are constantly accusing them of corruption and dishonesty.[16]

There is increasing evidence that the recovery or deterioration of patients in mental hospitals depends not only upon planned therapeutic measures, but also upon the interpersonal relations developing spontaneously in the wards. Stanton and Schwartz discovered that increased agitation and dissociation on the part of a patient can often be related to disagreements among staff members over the manner in which the case should be handled. The excitement of the patient is especially noticeable when neither the people in authority

[16] William A. Westley, "Secrecy and the Police," *Social Forces*, XXXIV (1956), 254–57.

nor the patient is conscious of the disagreement. The emotional reactions of all parties are betrayed in their expressive movements, and the patient is adversely affected in each encounter. They also found that when such disagreements among staff members are brought into the open and resolved, the patient quickly recovers.[17]

Those who are confined in mental hospitals do not escape society; they are only placed in a different one. In spite of difficulties in communication, the patients in each ward develop their own culture. In most cases, a status ladder is formed, giving greater prestige to those closer to being released. Caudill describes some of the values that develop among patient groups. There is considerable pressure for each to acknowledge that he is mentally ill and not to accept other explanations of his confinement. The patients also expect one another to give up their "defenses," to support their fellow patients and to help them whenever assistance is requested, to have faith in the competence of the doctor and to cooperate with him, and to try to be thoughtful and pleasant to the staff. Although there is much gossip about one another's peculiarities, it is understood that the positive qualities of each person should be emphasized. Should someone violate a hospital regulation, it is understood that the others should not inform on him. Repeaters and old patients who "know the ropes" help the newcomers. Only those who conform to the code are tolerated and helped. Those who continue to violate these informal norms are eventually isolated. The patients, by helping each other to define themselves and their place in the hospital, also cooperate in their efforts to recover. Of course, there are some who become "institutional cures"; their original problems are resolved, but they become so habituated to the hospital routine that they cannot leave.[18] Especially in overcrowded state asylums, the recovery rate can hardly be credited to psychotherapy, for there are not enough psychiatrists on the staff to care for even a small percentage of the patients.

The recognition that the social milieu in which the patients spend their time has so much to do with their mental health has led to attempts to manipulate this context and to provide, through ad-

[17] Alfred H. Stanton and Morris S. Schwartz, The Mental Hospital (New York: Basic Books, 1954), pp. 342–65.
[18] William Caudill et al., "Social Structure and Interaction Processes on a Psychiatric Ward," American Journal of Orthopsychiatry, XXII (1952), 314–34; and Rowland, op. cit.

ministrative procedures, the kind of therapeutic setting most conducive to recovery. Pioneering work along this line has been done by Jones and his associates in England, who began experimenting with such techniques while treating British casualties in World War II. A variety of collective transactions are planned in which the patients have an opportunity to see themselves as others do, come to see their symptoms more objectively, and thereby participate in their own treatment.[19]

The informal codes that develop in different conventional settings show a remarkable similarity. Therefore, it is possible to formulate generalizations about the manner in which they emerge, their relation to formal social structure, and the conditions under which they are most effective. It should be emphasized, however, that the particular culture that emerges in each primary group is different. The common understandings that arise depend in each instance upon the unique historical background of the group and the peculiar network of interpersonal relations that develops.

The Preservation of Personal Status

Informal codes are as effective as they are because most men act to preserve or enchance their *personal status* in the primary groups in which they participate. Maintaining status involves saving "face," keeping up one's reputation for integrity, and preserving the same relationships with the people he knows. Most men are highly responsive to the demands of those whom they know as individuals, and they undergo considerable sacrifice, occasionally risking the wrath of public officials and even death in order to keep faith with them.

Personal status differs from social status, and the difference coincides with the distinction made by the Chinese between two ways of saving "face." Social status refers to a person's position in a community, where his prestige and the deference he commands rest upon the manner in which he is classified and the evaluation of his category in the prevailing system of social stratification. A person maintains social status by living up to the conventional norms gov-

---

[19] Cf. Maxwell Jones *et al.*, *The Therapeutic Community* (New York: Basic Books, 1953); and William Caudill, *The Psychiatric Hospital as a Small Society* (Cambridge: Harvard University Press, 1958).

erning the conduct of people of his category. When the Chinese speak of saving *mien,* they are referring to the protection of the reputation that one has from success or high birth. The higher one's position in the community and the more he is in the public eye, the more essential it becomes for him to comply with customary expectations. A successful merchant is expected to provide his daughter with a handsome dowry befitting his station in life, although he may have to go into debt in order to do so. A poor man in a similar situation would not lose "face" if he failed his daughter, for not so much is expected of him. Both impoverished ex-aristocrats and the *nouveau riche* encounter special difficulties, for both are driven toward ostentation to bolster their uncertain prestige. But those who do not enjoy high social status need not concern themselves with losing *mien.*

The Chinese are also concerned with saving *lien;* each individual must protect his reputation for personal integrity. *Lien* is more important than *mien,* for it involves one's reputation as a man who will fulfil his obligations regardless of the hardships this may entail. *Lien* can be lost if a frand is detected, a crime exposed, faithlessness revealed, cheating discovered, or if subsequent events betray inexcusably poor judgment. Losing "face" in this sense is far more serious than the loss of social position. The latter is something that can be borrowed, struggled for, added to, or padded; *lien* is something to be maintained or lost as a whole. One cannot live without it, for he will be isolated. In order to retain the confidence of his fellow men even the poorest laborer or bandit, who have no *mien,* will struggle and sacrifice. Of course, *lien* is not unrelated to social status; the higher one's standing the more dignity and control is expected of him, and the more vulnerable he is. But the two are distinct. A man of great importance can be viewed in contempt by his close associates and family, just as an ordinary citizen may be prized by his friends.[20] Personal status is the position that one enjoys in primary groups because of the way in which he is evaluated as a human being.

Personal status, like one's standing in a community, is a social process. The manner in which a man is accepted in each of the primary groups in which he participates can be defined only in terms of the stable relationships he establishes with the other mem-

[20] Hsien Chin Hu, "The Chinese Concepts of 'Face,'" *American Anthropologist,* XLVI (1944), 45–64. Cf. Clemmer, *op. cit.,* pp. 149–80.

bers. The personal status of a husband in relation to his wife can be ascertained only in terms of their expectations of one another. He can take certain liberties with her that others may not; he can work late into the night with his secretary without having to provide excuses; he may not gamble with his co-workers without incurring her wrath. Her approach rests upon a unique personification, and he would be quite upset if he found her treating other men in the same manner. Personal status consists, then, of the network of relationships that exist between a particular individual and the various people with whom he is in sustained contact. He can swear at his brother and joke with his father, and he can do these things because he is a particular human being. The preservation of personal status, then, consists of acting in ways that will insure the perpetuation of these relationships. One cannot do anything to damage the personification others have constructed of him, for any change will alter these ties.

Each man's conception of himself is buttressed and reinforced primarily by the responses of people he knows personally. The manner in which one evaluates himself—his sense of pride, humility, or inferiority—depends in part upon social status but more upon the estimates he can impute to significant others. Especially in closely knit primary groups, all members are interdependent and immediately affected by one another's actions. Every major experience one has had in some way involves some of the other members, and his self-conception is bound up in this web of relationships. Some couples do not realize how much they depend upon one another until after they are divorced. The sense of obligation to those with whom one is bound by affectionate ties is very strong. Anyone who catches a friend cheating is deeply hurt, and he can readily imagine how others would feel if they caught him doing something similarly disdainful. Some measure of mutual trust exists among people who know one another well, and the violation of such trust sets off emotional reactions. Generally, there are one or two people whose judgments are more important than those of others—perhaps one's mother, older brother, wife, or favorite teacher. The views attributed to such individuals often set the standards of conduct in terms of which a person lives.[21]

Personal status is important because these relationships provide

[21] Cf. Trigant Burrow, "Social Images versus Reality," *Journal of Abnormal and Social Psychology*, XIX (1924), 230–35.

the stable basis for the pursuit of other interests. Being able to fore-tell with reasonable accuracy what other people are about to do enables each person to channel his own conduct more effectively, and such anticipation is easiest in primary groups. Psychiatrists have long been pointing out that a person experiences his greatest sense of security in intimate circles, especially if the sentiments are pre-dominantly conjunctive. He can count on the support of the others, even when they are not entirely agreed with him. For most people, there is some primary group that provides assurance of support, affection, and an appreciation of him as an individual. A secure position in such a group often becomes more important than success in the wider world. If a man is not satisfactorily anchored in some primary group, he can remain lonely and alienated, despite great public acclaim and high social status.

Each individual has a personal reputation and often struggles to maintain it. Much of our conscious and voluntary conduct is marked by restraint; impulses are checked to live up to the expectations im-puted to the people we know. A gangster may serve many years in a penitentiary rather than reveal the identity of his accomplices. It is not only a fear of vengeance but a matter of personal honor. When his sentence is over, he will return to his friends in the underworld, where a "squealer" is viewed contemptuously. Studies of fear and panic reveal that some men would rather die than disappoint those they know. Whether a man faces danger with courage or flees hys-terically seems to hinge upon his pride. Studies of combat reveal that military units characterized by conjunctive interpersonal rela-tions are not as likely to crack under fire, for each soldier prefers to risk death than to appear cowardly in the eyes of his comrades. Kelland, a writer who was trapped in a theater fire, provides an instructive account of the manner in which the presence of his son inhibited his impulses to flee. He kept repeating to himself that for the rest of his life his little boy would remember his father as a coward, and this thought was enough to prevent him from joining the wild scramble for the exit.[22] There are, of course, cultural dif-ferences in the emphasis placed upon "honor," but almost every-

[22] Clarence B. Kelland, "Panic: How Men and Women Act When Facing Terror," *American Magazine,* CIX (March, 1930), 44–45, 92–95. Cf. Samuel L. A. Marshall, *Men Against Fire* (New York: William Morrow & Co., 1947); and Edward A. Shils and Morris Janowitz, "Cohesion and Disintegration in the *Wehrmacht* in World War II," *Public Opinion Quarterly,* XII (1948), 280–315.

where those who do not defend it are viewed with disdain. However humble a man's social status, he struggles to uphold his personal status, his reputation among his friends. In this respect all men, big or little, have the same concern.

The extent to which some people sacrifice their personal interests to conform with primary group expectations is revealed in the problem of mate-selection among older bachelors and spinsters, so tellingly portrayed in the memorable motion picture *Marty*. Most unmarried people over the age of 25 are under constant pressure from their well-meaning parents and friends to marry, and in some cases would be delighted to do so. Whenever a man selects a potential bride, however, she is evaluated critically by his close friends, and unless they approve of her it becomes difficult for him to continue his romance. Erotic attraction being what it is, some men are able to ignore the taunts and go on, but there are many cases in which a man gives up a girl he actually cares for rather than put up with the disparagement of his friends.

Many college students, especially those who are enrolled in the larger centers of learning, are disappointed in the low quality of teaching in comparison to the instruction they had received in preparatory schools. They should remember, however, that a good teacher is appreciated primarily by his students and rarely by his colleagues. Among his peers, a professor is evaluated in terms of his contributions to the world of scholarship and science, through research reported in publications, or in terms of other activities not necessarily related to teaching. In some intellectual circles concern with pedagogical procedures is openly disdained, and there are some professors who even take pride in the fact that they are unconcerned with the techniques of instruction. Most professors, especially at the beginning of their careers, are far more conscientious about their teaching than their students suspect. If they seem to be giving less than their best efforts to instruction, their conduct must be seen in the light of the pressures which they face from their colleagues. In some cases a professor who spends too much time and effort working with his students is resented, and treated in much the same manner as a "rate-buster" in a factory.[23]

[23] Cf. Theodore Caplow and Reece J. McGee, *The Academic Marketplace* (New York: Basic Books, 1958), pp. 81–93, 158–63; Lewis A. Coser, "Georg

Most men are constantly concerned with personal status. In primary relations there is a continual, though slight, modification of personifications. With each new transaction conceptions and evaluations are somewhat altered. Some people work desperately to improve their personal desirability—their physical attractiveness, their personality traits, their social standing in the community. Why? One reasonable hypothesis is that they want to enhance their value in the eyes of the people whom they themselves love. If they become attractive enough, they may presumably assure themselves of other gratifications. Men are interdependent, and those who become love objects are much more likely to receive cooperation.

In a study of moral judgment, Turner asked 120 college students to imagine themselves as being involved in the theft of $500, to estimate the probable reaction of their friends to such misconduct, and to indicate the probable fate of their associations. Those who expected to be rejected or relegated to second class friendship indicated that they would terminate the relationship, even before their friends found out what had happened. Those who thought their friends would stand by them but would disapprove of what they had done indicated that they would confess, make amends, and give other proof of good character. Those who believed that their friends would not allow the crime to affect their personal ties indicated that they would continue their association as before. The reactions of persons involved in the hypothetical crime differed considerably, varying with the expectations imputed to others in their primary groups. These findings suggest that many people would rather withdraw from a group than face the stigma of losing personal status.[24]

There are instances in which men voluntarily give up their lives rather than risk losing personal status. Soldiers are known to hurl themselves upon live grenades to protect their comrades. It is reported that more and more was demanded by the bull-fighting public of the great matador Manolete, even though he complained that he had no more to give. Finally, in a superb performance, he gave his life. As he was dying, he was pleased to learn that the

Simmel's Style of Work: A Contribution to the Sociology of the Sociologist," American Journal of Sociology, LXIII (1958), 635–41; and Logan Wilson, The Academic Man (London: Oxford University Press, 1942), pp. 175–214.

[24] Ralph H. Turner, "Self and Other in Moral Judgment," American Sociological Review, XIX (1954), 249–59.

crowd had voted him two ears and a tail. There are cases, that sometimes baffle doctors, of people who get into trouble of which they are deeply ashamed, and just wither away and die. Certain that their friends will reject them, they apparently no longer care to live. For most people, one of the highest values is the maintenance of one's reputation before an audience consisting of his closest associates.

Of course, there is considerable variation in the extent to which people are willing to sacrifice in response to primary group expectations, especially when the informal codes conflict with customary procedures or laws. Some people compulsively do the "correct" thing; others completely ignore the formal regulations. Most people suffer pangs of conscience and somehow blunder through. Differences in concern over personal status are apparently related, at least in part, to empathy. Some persons, in spite of their friendly and congenial exterior, are less sensitive to the views of people immediately around them; they are not so likely to risk arrest or other punishment. But there are other people who are so dependent upon their intimate associates that they would not dream of violating their personal trust. The extent to which primary group norms are felt to be binding apparently depends also upon one's position in the network of interpersonal relations. A person who is a recognized leader not only fights to uphold the standards of the circle, but often applies them even more rigidly to himself.[25] Since he bears the major responsibility for their enforcement, he can hardly flout these codes without losing some of the respect that he commands. To some extent almost everyone is in some way responsive to the demands of his friends, but some feel additional pressures by virtue of the sentiments they form toward the others and toward themselves.

Informal Sanctions in Primary Groups

Those who desire acceptance in a primary group must conform to local demands, and this sometimes requires their violating the norms of the larger community. Sometimes newcomers innocently violate informal codes and are shocked at the anger of their fellows. Fresh

[25] Jennings, *op. cit.*, p. 200.

recruits in military units, "rookie" police officers, or men imprisoned for the first time often abide strictly with official regulations and get into trouble. Immigrant workers in industrial plants often please their employers by their diligence and willingness to work for low wages, but their co-workers are rarely so appreciative. Newcomers in a profession sometimes encounter difficulty in getting cooperation, and may even find themselves the object of intrigues; it is not until much later that they realize that they had been violating an un-written rule. In most cases someone who is "in the know" takes the neophyte aside and explains the "facts of life" to him. Primary group norms are also violated by misfits who occasionally go out of their way to express their resentment.

When informal codes are violated, appeal to legitimate authority is not always possible. Offenses like incest may be reported to the police, but a juvenile gang can hardly expect the police to enforce their territorial rights or to incarcerate a "squealer." Those who work in a factory cannot expect the management to enforce their limited production quotas by dismissing a conscientious "rate-buster." Hence, primary groups must enforce their own norms. *Informal social sanctions* consist of the techniques whereby people who know one another on a personal basis accord praise to those who comply with their expectations and show displeasure to those who do not. Since the praise or punishment thought to be appropriate is decided within each primary group, there is no uniformity in the rewards and deprivations that are meted out.

The most common of the informal sanctions involves communica-tive activity. The offender is harassed through taunts, name-calling, and disparagement. Winks, glares, laughter, sneers, and "coldness" are gestures for showing disapproval. Ridicule is especially effective, for it undermines a person's level of self-esteem. A consistently mocking attitude on the part of others almost forces a redefinition of oneself. Furthermore, it is very difficult to fight back. Further argu-ment evokes additional laughter and makes one look even more ridiculous.

Another effective negative sanction is the redefinition of the offender through gossip. Gossip is usually about private and intimate details of the conduct of specific individuals, and the items that arouse the most interest deal with the violation of moral codes. The personal status of an individual is threatened, for the obligations that had previously bound him to others may be transformed. While such talk may seem trivial to an outsider, it plays an important part in the reconstitution of interpersonal relations within a primary group.[26]

Informal social sanctions sometimes involve the use of violence, including forms that are not approved in the larger community. The spanking of a child is condoned, but the stabbing of a prisoner who had cooperated with the guards is certainly illegal. In a military unit a man who consistently ignores informal codes may find some of his equipment missing; he may be challenged to a fight during off duty hours; or in serious cases he may sustain an unaccountable injury while out on a patrol. Should a "rate-buster" pay no heed to warnings, someone may trip him as he walks past. His tools may become "lost," or the people preceding him on the assembly line may make extra work for him by feeding him defective parts. Should he persist in the face of such warnings, a crate may "accidentally" fall upon him. In the professions the sanctions are not so violent, but those who fail to conform suffer a variety of inconveniences. In crisis situations they may be denied help; well deserved promotions are delayed, and funds needed to carry on their work may be diverted elsewhere.

In extreme cases an offender may be ostracized from the primary group. Ostracism is a form of isolation. As the offender is more and more condemned, increasing social distance is maintained from him. He receives no more confidences, and those who do communicate with him find themselves under suspicion. Pressure is placed upon those who had been closest to him to keep their contacts to a minimum. Ostracism is the equivalent to expulsion from a primary group. A person may be physically present, but he is no longer a participant. The claims he once had upon the other members are no longer honored. He becomes lonely and anxiety ridden and may suffer some disintegration, for all meanings are sustained in social interaction.

Informal social sanctions are effective because the primary group is one place where personal identity is never in doubt. There may be arguments over whether a given act constitutes a transgression, over

[26] Cf. Albert Blumenthal, "The Nature of Gossip," *Sociology and Social Research*, XXII (1937), 31–37; and William I. Thomas, *The Unadjusted Girl* (Boston: Little, Brown & Co., 1923), pp. 41–69.

extenuating circumstances, or over the worthiness of motives. If a person is observed performing the act, however, evasion of responsibility is difficult, if not impossible.

One of the characteristics of informal codes is the manner in which enforcement is individualized. Unlike laws, which presumably apply equally to everyone and are therefore impersonal, primary group norms are applied differently to each person. Allowances are made for special abilities, idiosyncrasies, and sentiments. Those who are believed to be weak and unable to withstand pain or frustration are excused more readily than others. If a man is known to have a violent temper, it is taken for granted that he will explode periodically at slight provocation. If a person is known to be infatuated, he is not expected to exercise the judgment that he might under other circumstances. Similarly, in meting out punishment a weak child is not beaten in the same way as one who is healthy and strong. An intelligent child is not rewarded for his superior performances with the same enthusiasm as one who has to struggle. Where people know one another on a personal basis, they can readily take each other's roles, identify sympathetically, and thereby qualify their judgments. Informal social sanctions are usually tempered by such special considerations.

Where the primary group norms clash with those of the larger community, it is understood that outsiders, especially officials, expect the formal regulations to be enforced. Therefore, in the presence of strangers most people abide by the rules; it is assumed that there is no alternative. In situations in which an infraction might be detected, demands for conformity to informal codes are qualified. However, in situations in which there appears to be no possibility of detection, a "decent fellow" is expected to violate the formal regulations. Should someone be caught by officials in the midst of an illicit act, it is generally understood that the culprit will not implicate anyone else, and that his friends will do whatever they can to make things easier for him and, if it is possible, to compensate him for his loss. Giving assistance to the prosecution is prohibited, and when it is necessary, members of a primary group may even perjure themselves to help the victim.

The effectiveness with which informal codes can be enforced depends upon the manner in which the primary group is evaluated by its members. If a person places a high value upon the group, he identifies closely with it and takes pride in being a part of it; his sense of obligation is likely to be very strong. He is also likely to react sharply to the transgressions of others. But if he has a low estimate of the group, as in the case of many intellectuals drafted into the armed forces, he is not so likely to become concerned with its norms. A number of studies made by specialists in small groups tend to confirm the hypothesis that the stronger the attraction of the group to its participants, the stronger will be the pressure toward uniformity in performance and opinions.[27]

Each primary group develops a special, circumscribed perspective through which situations may be defined. Most people see their world from the standpoint they share with those immediately around them. The outlook and standards of the primary group are felt to be more binding as the social distance among the participants is reduced by conjunctive sentiments. It is difficult to violate the expectations of those with whom one can identify easily, for an appreciation of their feelings arouses feelings of guilt. The extent to which informal codes can be enforced also depends, then, upon the kinds of sentiments formed by the participants toward each other.

Summary and Conclusion

Since people in primary groups associate with one another in ways that they do not with strangers, through differential communication there develops in each circle a distinct culture. Although such informal understandings are generally consistent with the culture of the larger community, this is not necessarily the case. When there are differences, it becomes necessary for each primary group to enforce its own norms—through informal social sanctions. Informal social control is characterized by the uniqueness of the norms enforced, the low degree of formalization of the sanctions, and the making of allowances for the idiosyncrasies of the various persons involved. Informal sanctions are effective because each man's personal identity and responsibility are clearly fixed and because failure to live up to the codes can result in a reduction of personal status.

[27] Cf. Leon Festinger *et al.*, "The Influence Process in the Presence of Extreme Deviates," *Human Relations*, V (1952), 327–46; and James E. Dittes, "Attractiveness of Group as Function of Self-Esteem and Acceptance by Group," *Journal of Abnormal and Social Psychology*, LIX (1959), 77–82.

Violations often lead to transformations in interpersonal relations, the reevaluation of individuals, and in some instances expulsion from the group. A man has difficulty in maintaining an adequate level of self-esteem unless he has some support from significant others, and most people undergo considerable sacrifice to maintain their position. Thus, no matter how encompassing the formal regulations may be—as in a totalitarian dictatorship or in military organizations—there are a number of practices which arise spontaneously to circumvent the official procedures.

As Cooley insisted, everywhere and always men live in primary groups of some kind, and participation in such intimate associations enables them to develop the qualities that make them human. In the special kind of continued and unspecialized contacts that occur in such circles they learn to appreciate one another as distinct personalities and to adjust to each other's characteristics on an individual basis. What makes such groupings so important is that the sentiments which emerge in them often supersede conventional expectations in the development of conduct. The claims and obligations that make up one's interpersonal roles are often more binding than those which constitute his conventional role. Therefore, the course of events sometimes depends more upon the network of interpersonal relations than it does upon customs and laws.

Many of the decisions that men make appear "senseless" to observers who do not know them intimately. Informal social control sometimes assumes disproportionate importance because efforts to preserve personal status may have consequences far beyond the range of the primary group. For example, many of the acts of labor leaders and of the representatives of management in collective bargaining sessions cannot be understood exclusively in terms of the economic interests of their respective organizations. The negotiators on each side are participants in different primary groups, and they sometimes cannot afford to make concessions that would result in their losing "face" before their peers, even though they may be tactically wise. Many decisions in international politics are made by officials whose personal ties are limited to a small circle of men with definite ideological commitments. Hence, an official responding to the views of a personal friend may qualify a decision that is to the national interest and thereby inadvertently affect the lives of millions of other men who are complete strangers to him. In the controversies raging over the control of atomic energy one must remember that the scientists, generals, congressmen, and businessmen involved are all participants in primary groups in which different values prevail. If a tycoon would rather face war than a depression, he is not necessarily greedy. All his friends are similarly located in the economic system, and all of them would lose prestige if their corporations showed a loss. These men do not need money for themselves, but they are concerned with maintaining one another's respect. Unless one realizes that the perspective shared in each primary group constitutes a filter through which situations are defined, much of human conduct will remain a source of wonderment.

Suggested References

BARNARD, CHESTER I., *The Functions of the Executive*. Cambridge: Harvard University Press, 1938. A brilliant analysis by a business executive of the formal and informal structure of large corporations, revealing how many decisions rest upon considerations other than the announced objectives.

BLUMENTHAL, ALBERT, *Small Town Stuff*. Chicago: University of Chicago Press, 1932. A neglected study of the organization of a small American community, containing a thoughtful treatment of the manner in which gossip reconstitutes interpersonal relations.

HOMANS, GEORGE C., *The Human Group*. New York: Harcourt, Brace & Co., 1950. A comparative analysis of five case studies of small groups as a basis for the construction of a theory of human behavior in such contexts.

MANDELBAUM, DAVID G., *Soldier Groups and Negro Soldiers*. Berkeley: University of California Press, 1952. A review of the literature on the importance of primary groups in military organizations, with emphasis on the special problems of units containing soldiers of different ethnic categories.

ROETHLISBERGER, FRITZ J. and WILLIAM J. DICKSON, *Management and the Worker*, Part IV. Cambridge: Harvard University Press, 1939. A pioneering investigation of the social structure of a factory, revealing the importance of informal codes in the establishment of production norms.

STANTON, ALFRED H. and MORRIS S. SCHWARTZ, *The Mental Hospital*. New York: Basic Books, 1954. An intensive study of a ward in a psychiatric hospital, depicting its formal and informal structure, and showing that the recovery of patients does not rest solely upon planned therapy.

13

Self-esteem
and
social
control

At the turn of the century Alfred Adler, deviating somewhat from the teachings of Freud, attempted to account for personality development and for some mental disorders in terms of compensatory reactions to feelings of inadequacy. His writings aroused widespread interest among scholars and laymen alike, and it was not long before an oversimplified version of his views became popular, making the expression "inferiority complex" a household term. In the controversies that followed, Adler was attacked viciously by psychiatrists holding competing views; but as the heat of opposition died down, many admitted that he had pointed to something of importance, even though his views were incomplete and one-sided. Today most people concede that a person plagued by a sense of inferiority may feel driven to engage in a variety of activities, some of which may indeed constitute neurotic symptoms. Attention is again being directed toward this question, especially by psychiatrists influenced by Horney and Sullivan. Investigations of schizophrenia reveal that many patients are convinced that they are unworthy, despicable human beings. An increasing number of doctors are beginning to wonder whether a sense of personal inadequacy does not in fact underlie most personality disorders.

Even superficial observation reveals that a man who despises himself will act differently from one who has considerable pride. Self-contempt and pride are both sentiments that a person may develop toward himself. Just as men form personifications and estimates of others, they form self-conceptions and evaluations of themselves. Although McDougall long ago pointed to the importance of what he called the "self-regarding sentiment," his work has been largely ignored in the United States.[1] This chapter represents an attempt to organize diverse observations about the manner in which men evaluate themselves, the characteristic techniques that they use to make up for inadequacies, and some of the personality disorders that may develop among those who are unable to accept themselves.

The Preservation of Self-Esteem

Each person places some kind of estimate upon himself as an object of value. A value is a preference. To place a value upon oneself is to locate whatever one conceives himself to be within a hierarchical order. People vary considerably in their sense of self-esteem, and many of these differences are recognized in daily discourse. When a man declines to do something that he desires on the grounds that it would be inconsistent with his moral worth, he is said to have pride. When a man goes out of his way to impress others with his importance, he is accused of vanity. When a man refuses to place as high an estimate upon himself as others feel he deserves, he is regarded as modest. If one's personality is an organization of his values, the nucleus of this functional unit is his evaluation of himself.[2]

Much of what a person does or refuses to do depends upon his level of self-esteem. Those who do not regard themselves as particularly talented do not aspire to lofty goals, nor are they overly disturbed when they fail to perform well. People who regard themselves as unable to resist temptation avoid situations in which they might be enticed. Those who are convinced that they are wicked

[1] McDougall, *op. cit.*, pp. 125–214.
[2] Cf. Lecky, *op. cit.*, pp. 152–55.

sometimes set up harsh standards of conduct, holding themselves rigidly to a code. A man who thinks of himself as a worthless object is often reluctant to take the trouble to improve his lot. A man without any pride often surrenders to self-indulgence, pursuing his animal joys from day to day. On the other hand, those who place a high value upon themselves are often willing to work very hard. They consider it beneath their dignity not to do their very best. Each individual has some kind of self-conception which he seeks to maintain and enhance, but there is considerable variation in the extent to which he is willing to sacrifice in his own behalf.

Psychiatrists often speak of a man's sense of self-esteem as being adequate or inadequate, but the question invariably arises as to where the line is to be drawn. Level of self-esteem is also treated as varying on a continuum, on a unidimensional scale from high to low. Actually, the matter is far more complicated, for a man's sense of personal worth consists of the sentiments that he develops toward himself. Any orientation that may be directed toward other people can be displaced upon oneself. Just as another person may be the object of disinterested love, one may approach himself as an object of intrinsic value. He addresses himself with respect, just as a seasoned athlete will not make unreasonable demands upon his body. Just as someone else may be the object of possessive love, a person may approach himself as an object of utility. Psychoanalysts frequently speak of "narcissism"; in extreme cases people may even dissipate themselves seeking pleasure. Just as others may be resented or hated, one may regard himself as a dangerous object. Sir Thomas Browne once wrote, "There is a man within me, a man who hates me," describing a person alienated from himself. Vanity may be regarded as a form of hero-worship—with oneself as the hero. Just as other people can be approached with condescension, a person may be humble—an inferior object to be treated with consideration. People with little confidence in their ability often seek out submissive roles and avoid situations that require their assuming responsibility. Each man approaches himself in a somewhat different manner. Our knowledge of this phenomenon is so rudimentary, however, that we can barely differentiate between conjunctive and disjunctive sentiments. Under the circumstances, the oversimplified unidimensional procedure seems justified.

Like other meanings, sentiments toward oneself are formed and reinforced in the regularized responses of other people. Through role-taking a proud man is able to visualize himself as an object toward which others have feelings of respect, admiration, or even awe. If others consistently address him with deference, he comes to take it for granted that he deserves such treatment. On the other hand, if someone is consistently mistreated or ridiculed, he cannot help but conclude that others despise him. If a person is always ignored, especially in situations in which others like himself are given attention, he may become convinced that he is a comparatively worthless object. Once such estimates have crystallized, they become more independent of the responses of other people. A man who has an "inferiority complex" is not easily assuaged by the assurances of his friends. Similarly, a proud man dismisses as inconsequential any person who does not address him with proper deference. Like other sentiments, once one's level of self-esteem has been established, it tends to be self-sustaining.

To some extent one's sense of personal worth depends upon his social status; the manner in which he is treated depends upon his rank in the community. In an industrial society, where social status depends largely upon one's job rather than his personal qualities, men categorize and judge one another in terms of their occupations. Those in occupations without prestige—such as junk dealers, custodians, and garbage collectors—are sometimes ashamed of themselves, even though they have done nothing immoral. Prostitutes, as one might expect of people in pariah groups, are often characterized by a low level of self-esteem. Studies show that many of them have a highly moralistic attitude toward sex, feel disgusted with their work, and are contemptuous of their clients and co-workers. They share the popular evaluation of their occupation, and they judge themselves accordingly.[3] In our society, then, a person's level of self-esteem is to some extent tied to what he does to earn a living.

But, quite apart from social status, most people also evaluate themselves as distinct human beings. Social status is something that can be changed, especially in a society like ours in which social mobility is possible, but what one is as a human being remains relatively constant. Each person has a unique set of physical character-

[3] Cf. Frank J. Curran and Matthew Levine, "A Body Image Study of Prostitutes," *Journal of Criminal Psychopathology*, IV (1942), 93–116; and Muzafer Sherif and Hadley Cantril, *The Psychology of Ego-Involvements* (New York: John Wiley & Sons, 1947), pp. 387–89.

istics, which he may find attractive or unattractive. He is also marked by a distinctive set of behavior patterns—his personality—which he may find admirable or deplorable. These are the features by which he is evaluated, both by others and himself. It is possible for a man to achieve high social status and still have a low level of self-esteem. He may be aware of the prestige that he commands, but he may still look upon himself as a despicable human being, unworthy of the respect and affection of others. He may suffer chronic pangs of inferiority because he is not handsome; he may feel badly that he is physically weak and a coward; or he may regard himself as innately doomed because of his ethnic identity. Just as interpersonal relations vary independently of conventional norms, sentiments toward oneself are, for the most part, also independent of cultural definitions of achievement. Particularly important to most people is the affection of significant others, especially those whom they themselves love and respect. The personal status that one enjoys in his primary groups, then, is in most cases more important than his social position in the community.

Since men are socialized creatures whose perspectives develop through communication, the criteria by which they evaluate themselves are cultural. Standards differ from one reference group to another. In the social worlds that make up American society there are an amazing variety of attributes of which people are proud or ashamed: their speaking voices, the straightness of their teeth, their ancestry, their muscular strength, their ability to fight, the number of books they have read, the number of prominent people they know, their honesty, their ability to withstand pain, their memory, their ability to earn money, their manners, their ability to manipulate other people, the accessories on their automobiles, or their acquaintance with exotic foods. Each person sees himself from the standpoint of the groups in which he participates, and whatever he believes will impress his audience becomes a source of pride. These criteria of judgment are also excuses for already established levels of self-esteem. They reinforce and justify evaluations that have already been made, and a person comes to believe that his interpersonal relations are what they are because of the presence or absence of such traits.

Although such standards are learned by participating in reference groups, each person emphasizes different criteria in evaluating himself. A man who is poor or is a member of an ethnic minority may feel sorry for himself because he is sometimes treated as a second class citizen, not realizing how he is envied for his healthy limbs by a neighbor crippled by paralytic poliomyelitis. Another person may feel inferior because his teeth are crooked, because he has a poor complexion, and because he is a poor student; he does not appreciate how much his full head of hair is coveted by his handsome and brilliant friend who is becoming prematurely bald. A woman may feel inadequate because she has a poor figure, but she may be admired by those who are beautiful for her intelligence and good humor. In spite of many exhortations, men often do not "count their blessings." Sometimes a person feels badly about things that no one else even notices—like a barely visible scar. Each man rationalizes his fate in different terms.

Among the more common standards of self-judgment is one's capacity for erotic attraction. Ideals of masculinity and femininity differ from culture to culture, but whatever they may be, men and women feel inadequate when they believe that they do not measure up to them.[4] Women often judge themselves and one another in terms of their ability to attract and hold desirable men. Highly successful career women sometimes suffer a tragic sense of incompleteness from a conviction that they are failures as women. They may even reject suitors on the assumption that they will only be exploited for their influence. Some regard the bearing of children as the ultimate criterion of femininity and insist upon having offsprings they do not actually want—to prove to themselves that they are women. The same is true of the various measures of masculinity. Some men emphasize brute strength; others point with pride to their sexual prowess. In spite of successes elsewhere, men who have doubts about their potency are frequently afflicted with personality disorders. Their demands upon themselves may be unreasonable, but they nonetheless feel inadequate. In each culture there are a number of symbolic performances in which masculinity and femininity are tested. Some people are afraid of such challenges, being inwardly persuaded that they will fail.

Although men generally use the same criteria in evaluating themselves and others, they are often more severe on themselves. In

[4] Cf. Sidney M. Jourard and Paul F. Secord, "Body-Cathexis and the Ideal Female Figure," *Journal of Abnormal and Social Psychology*, L (1955), 243–46.

forming an estimate of himself, each person takes into account inner experiences that are inaccessible to others. Whether he regards him-self as a good person or bad, courageous or cowardly, honest or dis-honest depends more upon what he knows about himself than upon his prestige in the community. Men sometimes condemn themselves viciously for their inhibited impulses. A person may experience ag-gressive tendencies, indulge in erotic fantasies, practice what he regards as a perversion, or have childish desires that he is too ashamed to reveal even to his most intimate friends. Since others do not reveal their inner dispositions either, each gets the impres-sion that only he and a few other maladjusted individuals are guilty of such reprehensible thoughts and deeds, not realizing that such impulses are actually quite commonplace.

A distinction must be made between a person's level of self-esteem and his consciously avowed estimate of himself, for the two may contrast rather sharply. In moments of sober self-examination, most people can look at themselves with reasonable honesty, but conscious estimates are often misleading. Each man forms a fairly stable personification of himself, but he is often unaware of many of the component behavioral tendencies, especially those of which he is ashamed. All too often he is conscious only of what he would like to see. Furthermore, some people make a serious effort to live up to these ideals and may believe that they are more successful than is actually the case. Conscious estimates are often rationaliza-tions to justify compensatory reactions to deep-seated feelings of inadequacy. This suggests that many of the differences between conscious estimates—what a man says to himself—and level of self-esteem—the presuppositions that actually underlie his conduct— are defensive reactions.[5]

One's sense of personal adequacy may be threatened in a number of ways. People are sensitive about different things, and they also vary in the extent to which they can tolerate challenging cues. In general, however, anything that is interpreted as a threat to the esteem in which one is held evokes sharp reactions. Whenever a person detects anything in the gestures of others that indicates that their feelings are not quite what he thinks they ought to be, he becomes upset. Painstaking efforts are usually made toward a

[5] Cf. Ezra Stotland and Alvin Zander, "Effects of Public and Private Failure on Self-Evaluation," *ibid.* LVI (1958), 223–29.

restoration of proper respect. When such deliberate efforts fail, a number of typical behavior patterns are automatically activated. Because they are believed to serve as protective devices, they are designated as *mechanisms of defense*. Although psychoanalysts have popularized this notion, not all of them have recognized that what is being defended is not so much the biological organism as the person's conception of himself. Such mechanisms are often elicited by anticipated deprivation, not so much of physical pain as the loss of the support of other people. All defense mechanisms have self-reference; they are adjustments to anxieties and feelings of guilt. They enable a man to maintain his sense of personal worth in his own eyes.[6]

Defense mechanisms consist for the most part of perceptual and symbolic processes. The hypothesis was put explicitly by Sullivan, who insisted that *the limits of conscious awareness—what a man is capable of communicating to himself—are set by security operations.* If a person cannot face his glaring faults and still maintain his self-respect, the painful experiences are repressed; life goes on as if the events did not occur. All perception is selective, and what Sullivan called "selective inattention" is only an accentuation of the direction of sensitivity.[7] Since self-conceptions are reflections of the treatment received from others, those who feel insecure are often preoccupied with the kind of impression they are making. Perceptual defenses therefore include selective responsiveness to the gestures of other people. We often overlook glances of disapproval, or interpret them as manifestations of a generally disagreeable temperament. Perceptual defenses are apparently spontaneous reactions which protect each person from recognizing certain facts about himself which are obvious to almost everyone else.

Most psychiatrists have accepted the theory of defense mechanisms and by now take the matter for granted, but many psychologists have insisted upon experimental evidence. Some interesting facts have been uncovered, but there is a controversy over their interpretation. Bruner and Postman ascertained the reaction time of their subjects to various words by administering a word-association test.

---

[6] Cf. Anna Freud, *The Ego and the Mechanisms of Defense,* Cecil Baines, trans. (New York: International Universities Press, 1946); and Ernest R. Hilgard, "Human Motives and the Concept of the Self," *American Psychologist,* IV (1949), 374–82.

[7] Sullivan, *Clinical Studies in Psychiatry, op. cit.,* pp. 38–76.

Then, eighteen words were chosen for each subject, including six for which reaction was fast and six for which it was slow—the latter presumably representing disturbing meanings. Two weeks later these words were shown in random order in a tachistoscope, an instrument on which exposure time can be controlled by the experimenter. Each word was presented for increasingly greater time intervals until the subject was able to recognize it correctly. In most instances there was a high correlation between slower reaction time and increased exposure necessary for recognition. This finding was interpreted as a defensive process; the threshold of recognition is raised when there is anxiety. But some subjects recognized words for which they had long reaction times at exposures considerably below their average recognition threshold. These instances were interpreted as cases of special alertness to danger. The conclusion was that for some persons there is a critical degree of emotional reaction beyond which perceptual defenses no longer operate.[8] Whittaker and her associates repeated the study on Negro subjects, including words that would be particularly painful for those in minority groups. They also found that threatening words have a higher recognition threshold, but they argued that when disagreeable words were shown, their subjects suppressed their responses until they were certain, being less willing to guess while the sensory cues were still ambiguous.[9] The theory of perceptual defense has also been criticized by Howie on the grounds that it makes perception both a process of knowing and of avoiding knowledge. He argued that the findings from these and similar experiments could be explained in terms of the relative dominance of meanings. If one is organized to approach his world in a particular way, incongruent responses are inhibited, but such inhibitions are not necessarily defensive.[10] Although the findings in such studies have been consistent, doubts are still being expressed over their significance.

A person with a low level of self-esteem may not only be unable to see his weaknesses, but may also form an idealized self-concep-

[8] Jerome S. Bruner and Leo Postman, "Emotional Selectivity in Perception and Reaction," *Journal of Personality*, XVI (1947), 69–77.

[9] Edna Whittaker, J. C. Gilchrist, and Jean W. Fischer, "Perceptual Defense or Response Suppression?" *Journal of Abnormal and Social Psychology*, XLVII (1952), 732–33.

[10] Duncan Howie, "Perceptual Defense," *Psychological Review*, LIX (1952), 308–15. Cf. Beckner, *op. cit.*, pp. 119–28.

tion, regarding himself as perfect or nearly perfect. The construction of such a personification is facilitated by the fact that the attributes of any man can be selected and interpreted in several ways. Passive compliance can be viewed as considerateness; aggressiveness can be seen as strength; and aloofness can be regarded as self-sufficiency. Freud noted that insecure people sometimes attempt to cultivate traits which are the opposite of their natural inclinations and referred to this process as "reaction formation." A man who is power-oriented may act as if he were indifferent to social status. A petty man may insist that he is generous; a stingy man, that he is extravagant; and a suspicious man, that he is open. Some people manage to block their faults out of their conscious life so completely and rigidly that even the most conclusive negative evidence is cast aside as irrelevant. Idealized personifications may also be reinforced by fantasies of achievement and of acclaim from others. Sometimes a serious attempt is made to live up to these ideals, and difficulties arise as the person overtaxes his capacity. Especially when demands are made upon other people on the basis of these inflated self-conceptions, disruptions occur in interpersonal relations.[11]

Sometimes people who adopt such personifications realize secretly that they are false, and in sober moments recognize their limitations. For example, a man who had been a weak and cowardly child and actually has little confidence in himself may spend considerable time enjoying fantasies of himself as a powerful figure. As he daydreams of a succession of impressive victories, he may begin to approach others more boldly. As an adult he may find himself in social worlds in which physical violence is not tolerated, and be amazed to find that other people actually back down in the face of his aggressive gestures. This provides confirmation for his idealized self-conception. In time he may consistently act with seeming self-confidence. He is safe as long as he is not caught in a crisis situation, where his "front" may suddenly collapse.

In a revealing study along this line, Frenkel-Brunswik asked each of her subjects to describe their own personality traits and to indicate the guiding principles of their lives. She compared their replies with the ratings of a group of judges who knew each of them well and found amazing discrepancies. The data showed clearly that

[11] Cf. Karen Horney, *Neurosis and Human Growth* (New York: W. W. Norton & Co., 1950).

these people were unaware of many of their shortcomings, defects that were so apparent that there was a high degree of consensus among the judges. Among the regularities noted was the frequent insistence of the subject that he had traits exactly opposite from those that impressed the observers. A person consistently rated as "insincere" by his associates would claim that he was very sincere. Or an undesirable trait would be entirely omitted from the self-portrait. In some cases a person would acknowledge the behavior observed by others but would describe it in such a way that it would appear in a different light; for example, a man who was rated as "aggressive" indicated that he did not allow himself to be intimidated by other people. Another common tendency was the use of descriptive terms that belittled recognized shortcomings by shifting emphasis; a person generally regarded as "shiftless" referred to himself as "playful." There was also a shifting of the order of importance of various attributes; what would be recognized as a prominent trait by others would appear as a minor one in the eyes of the subject. A statistical analysis of the estimates of the observers and the self-ratings on guiding principles of life revealed striking contrasts; on "sincerity" the coefficient of correlation was −.58.[12] This strongly suggests that assertions concerning one's guiding principles may in many cases constitute reactions against a self-conception he cannot bear to face.

Another common mechanism of defense is *projection*, the confusion of the boundary between one's self-conception and other personifications. The concept is used by psychiatrists to refer to the attribution to other people of one's own undesirable traits or motives. For example, a very angry man represses his own homicidal impulses and accuses his opponent of wanting to kill him. Since all the experiences that a person has are necessarily his own, the imputation of malicious motives to others involves being mobilized to act in a certain way and then ascribing this orientation to another. Projection is a form of role-taking, in which there is a selective imputation to others of those features that one cannot stand in himself. It should be noted also that the unconscious projection of one's dangerous dispositions provides a suitable justification for his own defensive stance and aggression. Sullivan accounted for the formation of paranoid disorders in these terms. Whatever a man despises

[12] Else Frenkel-Brunswik, "Mechanisms of Self-Deception," *Journal of Social Psychology*, X (1939), 409–20.

in himself—especially the hostile tendencies he has difficulty in controlling—become split off into a separate personification—a "not-me." This personification then becomes the object of intense hatred. As it is subsequently displaced upon real people, the man becomes frightened, for he believes himself to be surrounded by villains characterized by all of the most dreadful dispositions he has ever experienced. It is not strange, then, that he feels persecuted and becomes suspicious of everyone.[13]

To test the hypothesis that traits that are judged reprehensible are projected upon other people, Sears had members of three fraternity houses rate themselves and one another on stinginess, obstinacy, and disorderliness. He found that there was considerable variability in the degree of self-insight displayed by his subjects and that those who had less discernment tended to show greater distaste for the very traits that were attributed to them by the others. The coefficients of association were disappointingly low, but they were consistent. This study provides some support for the contention of psychoanalysts that people who are unable to recognize their own faults tend to impute them to others.[14]

The use of various defense mechanisms is simplified by the ability of men to rationalize, to redefine otherwise incongruent or embarrassing activities in such a manner that they appear sensible. In a study of embezzlers, Cressey found that the men looked upon their violation of financial trust as a form of "borrowing." He found that embezzlers had a special vocabulary of motives that enabled them to see themselves in an acceptable light, in spite of the fact that their act was clearly illegal.[15] Torrance asked students who were taking a college entrance examination to rate their own ability, and found that sixty-two per cent of those in the bottom quartile of the class insisted they belonged in the top fourth. When they were asked afterward why they had done so poorly in the examination, seventy-five per cent said they had been "nervous," and ninety per cent claimed they had been bothered by a "headache."[16] Men are capable of rationalizing to the point of constructing an elaborate

[13] Sullivan, *Clinical Studies in Psychiatry, op. cit.*, pp. 86–90, 145–65; and *The Interpersonal Theory of Psychiatry, op. cit.*, pp. 344–63.

[14] Robert R. Sears, "Experimental Studies of Projection," *Journal of Social Psychology*, VII (1936), 151–63.

[15] Donald R. Cressey, *Other People's Money* (Glencoe: Free Press, 1953).

[16] Paul Torrance, "Rationalizations about Test Performance as a Function of Self-Concepts," *Journal of Social Psychology*, XXXIX (1954), 211–17.

intellectual system to justify their activities. Philosophers and religious leaders, whose cosmological schemes may prove to be of great benefit to mankind, sometimes hit upon their beliefs while attempting to meet personal problems. Patients who are psychotic also build up special conceptions of the universe, often with themselves in lofty positions, and they become upset when others fail to acknowledge their importance. What characterizes such conceptual schemes, in contrast with those of scientists, is the lack of interest in contradictory evidence. A scientist will dismiss even his pet theory if it cannot stand the test of evidence, but a person who is using his intellectual device to justify his way of life attempts to explain away negative evidence or rigidly refuses to see demonstrated facts.

Quite apart from what a man may declare publicly or what he may sincerely believe about himself in his conscious life, in behavioristic terms his level of self-esteem is discernible in the manner in which he consistently acts toward himself as an object of value. If a man is highly sensitive to slights, if he avoids with desperation situations in which his weaknesses might be exposed, if he daydreams so much that his efficiency is impaired, there is reason to suspect that he has some doubts about himself, regardless of what he may say or believe. Some people are so completely preoccupied with the pursuit of their own interests that they hardly seem to notice others. Is a person who is really secure in his own eyes likely to become obsessed with taking full advantage of every opportunity that falls his way? Even among laymen there are criteria for recognizing a person whose level of self-esteem is adequate, even though he may be quite modest: he uses his own standards as guides for his conduct, while making allowances to avoid hurting others; he does not become upset when other people disagree with him; when he fails, he makes no excuses and engages in no extended self-condemnation; he treats other people respectfully as equals, regardless of their social status; he has no doubts of his ability to contribute to the welfare of others and attempts to do so; he does not approach other people with the expectation that they will automatically reject him; he is neither shy nor excessively self-conscious; he does not reject praise that he clearly deserves.[17] He approaches himself on the assumption that he is worthy of being appreciated and respected.

There are some people who openly admit their shortcomings.

17 Cf. Sheerer, op. cit., 170–71.

They state candidly that they cannot hope to achieve lofty goals because they do not have the ability. What is significant about such people is that they have enough confidence in themselves to be able to face their limitations. It has long been suspected that those who are very conceited and overbearing are compensating for deep-seated feelings of inferiority. If a man speaks confidently but withdraws from any situation in which his skills will be put to a fair test, one begins to wonder about him. Some women who claim to be proud of their femininity refuse to compete with other women on equal terms. They deliberately emulate men; they dress sloppily, while making disparaging remarks about the "conformity" of the middle classes; they are often obsessed with the danger of being exploited sexually without love. Such tendencies strongly suggest that they have serious doubts about their capacity as women. A person who dislikes himself often puts on masks. Why should a man who is satisfied with what he is pretend to be different? When a man cannot admit that he might be less than perfect, it seems probable that his conscious estimate of himself is a defensive armor, a way of preventing him from looking too carefully at what he is.

The hypothesis has been advanced that rigidity and lack of self-insight are directly related to a low level of self-esteem. When a person can no longer accept himself, much effort is expended in defending rather than in exploring; it was Freud's opinion that so much effort goes into being sure he does not see his faults that he becomes too tired to do anything constructive. In an effort to test this contention, Taylor and Combs assessed 205 sixth grade children, using a standard personality test. The subjects were divided into the better adjusted and the poorly adjusted on the basis of test scores. Then, each child was presented with twenty statements of a derogatory nature, probably true of all children, and asked which of the items applied to them. Those in the better adjusted category admitted a larger number of defects, and the boy with the highest adjustment score marked every item but one.[18] Those who have a low level of self-esteem also tend to become rigid; they are so alienated from themselves that they cling desperately to their idealized self-conceptions.

The characteristic ways in which a person defends himself is an

[18] Charles Taylor and Arthur W. Combs, "Self-Acceptance and Adjustment," *Journal of Consulting Psychology*, XVI (1952), 89–91.

important part of his personality. Such response patterns are residues, the products of past experience. Since each person has a unique background of experience, each develops a different way of protecting himself. Some people accept their limitations and do the best they can; others compensate for them through special effort; others are unable to notice obvious things in themselves. Psychiatrists are especially interested in such defensive techniques; some of them appear repeatedly as integral parts of neurotic and psychotic patterns. Boss gives a case history of a sadist who would begin his seductions with insults. If a woman tolerated this indignity, he would turn to physical mistreatment, tying her up and torturing her. It was only then that he could experience sexual excitement. He even had a collection of whips and took pleasure in selecting the proper one for each partner. He was deeply grateful whenever a woman submitted to this torture, for it enabled him to drop his façade. Apparently his objective was not so much to injure the woman but to get her to yield. He could not conceive of himself as the kind of man to whom an attractive woman would voluntarily surrender; she had to prove her willingness before he could relax.[19] Many symptoms of various mental disorders are apparently manifestations of special meanings that develop in the person's efforts to come to terms with himself.

The estimate a person places upon himself becomes an important part of his personality, for many of his characteristic ways of acting depend upon it. This leads to the question of how such sentiments may be studied empirically, and the discussion thus far suggests that direct inquiries about self-esteem are not likely to yield satisfactory results. Studies that have been made on the accuracy of self-ratings reveal that the subjects consistently overrate themselves on desirable traits and tend to overlook undesirable attributes. This has led some psychologists to wonder whether self-rating scales are of any value at all.[20] It appears, then, that a person's level of self-esteem can be measured only through procedures in which the intention of the investigator is concealed, giving the subjects little occasion for defense. Another possibility is to make observations of behavior in a wide variety of contexts. Men intuitively make such

[19] Boss, *op. cit.*, pp. 79–114.
[20] E. B. Hurlock, "A Study of Self-Ratings by Children," *Journal of Applied Psychology*, XI (1927), 490–502; cf. Kurt Lewin *et al.*, "Level of Aspiration," in Hunt, *op. cit.*, Vol. I, pp. 333–78.

judgments about one another, and the task confronting the social psychologist is that of making this common procedure explicit and repeatable. The development of more adequate techniques for the assessment of self-esteem is a task of considerable importance, for there are a number of generalizations that cannot be tested without some reliable method of measurement.

The Struggle for Recognition and Power

There are a number of ways in which people attempt to counter-balance a low level of self-esteem. With varying degrees of success each person tries to disown or to cast off those traits that he regards as alien to a desirable self-conception. Some become convinced that inadequate social status lies at the root of their difficulties, and they become preoccupied with *social mobility*. They devote a substantial portion of their lives to improving their standing in the community. They strive for a position in which they can command respect; they want the admiration of other people, to be assured that they count for something, to feel that their presence and activities make a difference in the lives of those with whom they come into contact. In a changing society, especially in a democratic one in which upward social mobility is accepted as natural and desirable, there are a number of sanctioned avenues through which the dissatisfied can help themselves. Those who conclude that there is not much hope for themselves may drive their children. In the United States, many strive for advancement simply because it is the expected thing to do. These people are not to be confused with the inordinately ambitious, whose dedicated pursuit of success is often at the expense of family, friends, moral principles, and perhaps even freedom. Not all successful people are driven by a sense of inadequacy, but all too often those who are characterized by extreme determination have a long history of disturbances in interpersonal relations.

Even among those who are insecure, there is considerable variation in the extent of preoccupation with upward mobility; for some extremists it becomes a naked struggle for power. The frequency with which such people appear in a wide variety of cultural settings has led political scientists and psychiatrists to refer to them as "power-oriented." Of course, each person is ambitious in his own way, but there are a number of characteristics found with amazing frequency among those obsessed with advancement. There is often a persistent aggressiveness toward others, almost as if approval had to be wrenched from them by force. At the same time social distance is generally maintained, perhaps to curb some of the more violent hostilities. Power-oriented people usually have idealized self-conceptions; they want to excel in everything, becoming upset whenever their talents prove wanting. They seem to be unable to accept other people as equals, tending to judge them in terms of relative status. They attempt to dominate others; whenever they are forced into a subordinate position, they become acutely sensitized to the mistakes of their superiors and derive great pleasure from them. They are sensitive to slights. There is great interest in status symbols, the external marks of success, and a constant preoccupation with the impression they are making upon those around them. It has also been noted that such persons generally suffer from a variety of psychosomatic disorders.

Power-oriented men often appear strong, independent, and self-confident. It has long been suspected, however, by laymen as well as psychiatrists, that *excessive ambition is a way of compensating for a low level of self-esteem.* Power is sought as insurance against an underlying feeling of worthlessness. In a study of levels of aspiration and self-acceptance, as measured by the Rorschach test, Cohen found that the setting of both very high and very low goals was directly related to self-rejection.[21] Seemingly resolute men are often plagued by doubts about the affection of others. They are often highly susceptible to flattery. They cling tenaciously to anything symbolic of their sense of worth, and they assiduously avoid activities in which they might be reminded of their shortcomings. The fact that they form idealized self-conceptions indicates their inability to accept themselves as they are. It is widely believed that the sense of inadequacy develops early in life during a childhood lacking in warmth and affection, and to test this hypothesis Ellis studied sixty unmarried career women in Montgomery, Alabama, comparing the successful with those who were not. Attachment to parents was

[21] Louis D. Cohen, "Level of Aspiration Behavior and Feelings of Adequacy and Self-Acceptance," *Journal of Abnormal and Social Psychology*, XLIX (1954), 84–86. An explicit statement of the theory can be found in Lasswell, *op. cit.*, pp. 39–58. Cf. Adorno *et al., op. cit.*; and Horney, *Neurosis and Human Growth, op. cit.*

rated as "less than average" by thirty-six per cent of the successful and only six per cent of the unsuccessful; it was rated as "more than average" by thirty-six per cent of the successful and sixty-one per cent of the unsuccessful. The most successful women indicated that they felt rejected both by their parents and their community.[22]

Power-oriented people are very egocentric. Those with a low level of self-esteem do not respect themselves (disinterested love); they are narcissistic (possessive love). They tend to see things almost exclusively in terms of their own interests. There is so much ego-involvement that they do not see their environment as other people do. They are often blind to relationships that are obvious to others, for all their meanings are formed from a highly individualized standpoint. If others are useful for their purposes, they are treated well; when they are of no further use, they are dropped. Expediency is the keynote in interpersonal relations. Power-oriented people are usually regarded as "selfish," because they are so preoccupied with themselves that they are often oblivious to the interests of others. The more adequate one's level of self-esteem, the more he can afford to be concerned with others; indeed, studies show that natural leaders are usually people with sufficient freedom from self-concern to enable them to deal with matters affecting others.[23]

Men differ considerably in the desperation with which they seek recognition and power. Some make overt efforts in that direction only when opportunities arise; their advancement, therefore, is uneven. But there are others who are so desperate for eminence that they become insensitive to everything else. They pay any price in their effort to reach the top. The hypothesis may be proposed that the degree of desperation with which men seek power is directly related to the extent of the deprivation suffered earlier in life.

In many cases the struggle for recognition is sublimated. Instead of a bald quest for glory, a man may identify himself with a worthy cause and devote his life to it. Many programs of social reform have been advanced through the dedicated efforts of men who had suffered humiliation, hardship, and injustice. Many religious move-

---

[22] Evelyn Ellis, "Social Psychological Correlates of Upward Social Mobility among Unmarried Career Women," *American Sociological Review*, XVII (1952), 558–63.

[23] Jennings, *op. cit.* Cf. Robert R. Holt, "Effects of Ego-Involvement upon Levels of Aspiration," *Psychiatry*, VIII (1945), 299–317; Max Wertheimer, *Productive Thinking* (New York: Harper & Bros., 1945), pp. 136–147.

ments have been initiated by men torn by feelings of guilt. Once they hit upon a satisfactory solution for their own problems, they try to persuade others to embrace the new outlook and to save themselves from similar difficulties. Not all of the participants in social movements are as dedicated as the founders, but support generally comes from the dissatisfied, who see in the enterprise opportunities for themselves. The appeal of the three great social movements among the American Indians after their subjugation by the settlers—the Iroquois Great Message in the Northeast, Shakerism in the Pacific Northwest, and Peyotism in the Plains—appears to have been the possibility of regaining self-respect. Originally the Indians could enhance their personal and social status through hunting and warfare, but these channels had been shut off by the conquest. None of these movements attempted to recapture the past; they emphasized mutual helpfulness and provided new avenues for attaining status.[24]

People who make up the "hard core" of protest movements fight with incredible determination, making sacrifices far beyond the call of duty. Religious movements have numerous martyrs who die in their behalf, and political movements also have heroes who spend a large part of their lives in jail, only to emerge unbroken and more grimly determined than ever. Such men are rigid in their commitment. This has led Hoffer to suggest that fanatics are people who are alienated from themselves. The "true believers," as he calls them, are able to conceive of themselves as worthwhile only when they can identify with a great cause. Then fighting for it becomes a way to achieve self-respect.[25] They develop a blind faith and cling on even under conditions of great adversity. If a movement succeeds, its leaders are personified as righteous men who gave their lives for others. It is of interest to note, however, that many of these heroes are people who are thoroughly disliked and distrusted by their intimate associates. It is paradoxical that a fanatic dedication to a humanitarian cause is so often accompanied by a callous lack of concern for those who are close to them, such as the members of their own family. It is now believed that the roots of such fanaticism are planted in childhood. Those who have had a happy childhood

[24] Fred W. Voget, "The American Indian in Transition," *American Journal of Sociology*, LXII (1957), 369–78.
[25] Eric Hoffer, *The True Believer* (New York: Harper & Bros., 1951). Cf. Burke, *Permanence and Change, op. cit.*, pp. 69–163.

often support worthwhile enterprises, but they are not reliable when public opposition becomes intense; defections occur as soon as the circumstances become difficult. Without a "hard core" that can always be counted on, most social movements that challenge the legitimate order would probably not survive.

Sublimation may take other forms, such as attempting to make great contributions in art, literature, science, or even athletics. In virtually all fields of endeavor there are men who are so completely devoted to their work that they do not allow anything else to interfere with it. Their remarkable achievements are often the result of their willingness to drive themselves so much harder than their competitors. Many adolescent boys daydream of becoming professional athletes, but only a few are out of bed at the crack of dawn on their own initiative for several hours of road-work. There are actors who have no life apart from their work, no other interest, no other source of pleasure, and no other love. Once their careers are terminated, they die. Many artists and scientists of stature are rigidly dedicated, and sacrifice themselves and everyone with whom they come into contact to pursue the objectives that give meaning to their lives. Although their avowed ends are often humanitarian, such men are uncommonly concerned with the extent to which their accomplishments win the plaudits of others.

The endeavor of power-oriented men is compulsive. There is no spontaneity or flexibility. There is a disregard for what would appear to be in their best interests, even their own health. They do not permit themselves to be sidetracked by the possibility of hurting other people. They justify what they do by pointing to the value of the activity itself. When they are frustrated in their efforts, they work even harder than before. Such people are often "perfectionists"; they generally set their own standards and drive themselves mercilessly to meet them. They are also insensitive to the negative appraisals of critics, dismissing them as incompetent fools. They set up an ideal and pursue it, disregarding all extenuating circumstances—even insufficient ability. They make such excessive and unreasonable demands upon themselves that many of them fail to produce anything. The few who have unusual talent and good fortune do great work; the rest are perpetually disgruntled.

Nor is their inordinate ambition mollified by success. Elite groups made up of the successful—in high government circles, among corporation executives, among labor leaders, among outstanding specialists in a profession, or among scientists in great universities—are usually plagued by clashes between stubborn, power-oriented men. The participants themselves refer to the constant struggle for power as a "rat race," and express their disgust. Successful revolutionaries often weaken their cause through internal strife; after working together for many years to overthrow the old order, they frequently fall out among themselves after victory has been achieved. The intelligentsia is made up of gifted men who make substantial contributions to culture, but such circles are usually characterized by the petty bickering of jealous rivals. Since power-oriented people are continually manipulating others, they are constantly on guard against such exploitation. Each thinks himself more adroit than all the others, but mutual suspicion is common. These difficulties are usually tolerated on the grounds that talented and creative people are temperamental and must be left alone if they are to make further contributions.

The zeal of power-oriented men is often fed by the goal of vindictive triumph. They spend considerable time daydreaming of their hour of victory and especially of the disappointed surprise of their vanquished foes—people who had opposed them, those who had ridiculed them, their rivals in the field, and members of their primary group who had argued that their ambitions were too lofty. Imagination plays an important part in sustaining the endeavor of a person who does not enjoy the support of those immediately around him. He buttresses his ambitions with fantasies of humiliating others and of being regarded in awe. This is demanded as vengeance for the deprivations of their earlier years.

Among the most pathetic features of compulsive endeavor is the lack of satisfaction even for those who succeed in achieving their lofty objectives. A financier who had promised himself that he would retire to enjoy life after making ten million dollars finds himself bored. Furthermore, he does not know whether those around him actually admire him for what he is or because of the convenience of his wealth. Power-oriented people are always dissatisfied with their fate, no matter how fortunate they may be. The demand for power appears to be insatiable. The fact that high social status does not placate them suggests that they were actually dissatisfied with themselves as human beings. Although they may attain cminence, their personal status and level of self-esteem often remain much as they had been. Outwardly they may become more poised, but most upwardly mobile people are still tormented by a sense of inadequacy. In the previously cited study of career women in Montgomery, Alabama, Ellis found that successful women seemed to lack the capacity for making friends. They had to hunt for pleasures to overcome their loneliness, and many had pets as outlets for their affection. A number suffered from psychosomatic disorders, and many of them openly admitted their unhappiness.[26]

Thus, men with a low level of self-esteem, especially if they have talent in any area, attempt to raise their social status through excessive zeal. It is not until they have succeeded that they realize that the sense of inadequacy which had haunted them throughout their lives has not been eliminated. If anything, they may be even more insecure, since they alienated almost everyone with whom they came into contact in their desperate struggle for the top. These observations underscore the position of psychoanalysts, who have stressed the importance of satisfactory personal status in primary groups.

Disorders Involving Personal Identity

Other ways of coming to terms with a low level of self-esteem include escaping from oneself. Such withdrawals may consist of nothing more than the refusal to look at something threatening; a person may deliberately ignore gossip about himself. Or he may substitute some distracting activity. A professor who fears that he cannot make an important contribution to knowledge may find himself mired in administrative duties. He may complain about this, insisting that he really wants to do research, but he gives himself away by the desperation with which he looks for new excuses when he is relieved of his burden. Or one may withdraw from situations that tend to accentuate his sense of inadequacy. A student who feels deficient in the social graces may become so engrossed in his work that his friends no longer invite him out, making it unnecessary for him to commit himself in an area in which he does not perform well. Some people isolate themselves, cynically laughing at others who

26 E. Ellis, *op. cit.*

continue to struggle. Others become addicted to alcohol or to drugs, finding temporary refuge in intoxication. Those who are more rebellious may withdraw into a deviant group. This provides a way of escaping conventional standards, as well as enjoying the camaraderie and support of others who suffer a similar fate.

In severe cases a person may retreat to the point of taking refuge in psychosis, remaining alive biologically but refusing to participate in society, thus absolving themselves of responsibility. These disorders often involve a partial or complete withdrawal from the "reality" over which there is consensus, making communication with other people difficult, if not impossible. In spite of the attention that mental disorders have received in recent years, there is a remarkable lack of agreement among psychiatrists. Since there is so much speculation and so little established knowledge, the proposing of sociological hypotheses seems justified, even though the substantiating evidence for them is no more satisfactory than what is offered in support of other positions.

From the sociological standpoint one of the most instructive of the various mental disorders is *depersonalization*, the loss of personal identity. The individual feels that he is not himself; there is a sense of estrangement—that he is more an observer than a participant in what his body is doing. The condition may be transitory or chronic; it may be a component in a psychotic syndrome, or it may occur by itself. Mild depersonalization occurs at some time to most people when they have some unusual or traumatic experience. A person who is being robbed wonders momentarily if this is "really happening to me." A prostitute who was ashamed of her work reported that she felt as though intercourse with clients was taking place in a body only vaguely connected with herself.[27] In severe cases a person may experience a visual hallucination of his own body, as if he were looking at his "double" in a mirror. Unlike other hallucinations, he feels himself somehow connected with the image, since it speaks, thinks, and acts much like himself.[28] In an account of his experiences under mescalin intoxication, Huxley describes a similar separation of his body from his conception of himself. He had difficulty in

[27] Sherif and Cantril, *op. cit.*, pp. 387–88.
[28] Jean Lhermitte, "Visual Hallucinations of the Self," *British Medical Journal*, No. 4704 (March 3, 1951), 431–35.

identifying with himself the arms and legs that he experienced as being "out there." During a meal he observed that "somebody" was eating ravenously, as he looked on from a distance without much interest.[29] These illustrations reveal that a person may become detached from his self-conception under a variety of circumstances.

Chronic depersonalization, or amnesia, is of particular interest, for personal identity is one's only tie with society. His personal and social status are defined in terms of reciprocating relationships with people who recognize him as a specific individual. The loss of personal identity is therefore a terrifying experience. In most cases of amnesia there is a partial and selective loss of memory. The victim may not be able to recognize his own parents, but he usually maintains an adequate orientation to impersonal things. Beck reports a case in which the victim gradually regained all of his memory but for one gap, which subsequently turned out to be the period in his life of which he was most ashamed; and Abeles and Schilder contend that most cases of amnesia are initiated by a traumatic experience, an event that is reminiscent of some severe conflict in the past, one involving deep feelings of guilt.[30] One possible hypothesis is that amnesia is a form of adaptation, a way of coming to terms with oneself by blotting out memories that are too painful. A person who can no longer form an acceptable conception of himself becomes someone else, and lives a new life.

It has been suggested, most explicitly by Federn, that depersonalization occurs when a person is unable to form a sentiment toward himself. In psychoanalytic terminology, there is a withdrawal of cathexis from oneself. Sentiments rest upon empathy. They are meanings which take on their distinctive characteristics through identification with the object and an imputation to it of various emotional reactions. Empathy is inversely related to social distance; strangers are usually perceived as things. Similarly, the more one withdraws from himself, the less he is able to perceive himself in terms of human qualities. Since each individual is an organic unit, he cannot escape his inner experiences entirely, but they may be set apart as belonging to someone else. It has been observed that patents suffering of depersonalization often do not develop the

[29] Huxley, op. cit., pp. 35–60.
[30] Abeles and Schilder, op. cit.; and Beck, op. cit. Cf. Hilgard, op. cit.

ordinarily expected sentiments toward other objects. For example, they may perceive their own children as material objects.[31]

Another mental disorder involving self-conceptions is the multiple personality, in which two or more organized systems of behavior, each integrated as a distinct unit, develop in a single organism. In some cases there is complete amnesia for the personality that is not active; in others, one may be aware of the other's conduct. Robert Louis Stevenson popularized this type of illness in his fascinating novel *Dr. Jekyll and Mr. Hyde*, and Morton Prince's study of the numerous personalities of Miss Beauchamps aroused considerable interest at the turn of the century. Because of the comparative rarity of the disorder, however, many psychiatrists expressed doubts about Prince's observations. Interest has recently been revived by the careful study reported by Thigpen and Cleckley in *The Three Faces of Eve*. The authors not only provide insightful descriptions of the three personalities of the woman, but also furnish scores from projective tests, the semantic differential test, and even electroencephalograms. The victim apparently has two or more self-conceptions and tries in turn to live up to the obligations assumed by each. Each personality consists of a somewhat different set of meanings; hence, dominant interests, knowledge, and standards of conduct shift dramatically. Cases have been reported in which there is even a change in erotic interests— from homosexual to heterosexual.[32]

Several attempts have been made to reproduce this phenomenon experimentally through hypnosis, and the results have largely confirmed clinical observations. In one study, reported by Leavitt, three personalities emerged when a shell-shocked soldier named Dick was being treated through hypnoanalysis. Through hypnotic suggestion, the therapist was able to produce a secondary personality, called Frank, and a tertiary personality, called Leo. The contrast among the three was amazing. As Frank, the soldier was polite, attentive, and eager to please. As Leo, he slouched back in

[31] Cf. Sidney Bockner, "The Depersonalization Syndrome," *Journal of Mental Science*, XCV (1949), 968–71; and Paul Federn, *Ego Psychology and the Psychoses* (New York: Basic Books, 1952).

[32] Cf. Morton Prince, *The Dissociation of a Personality* (New York: Longmans, Green & Co., 1906); W. S. Taylor and Mabel F. Martin, "Multiple Personality," *Journal of Abnormal and Social Psychology*, XXXIX (1944), 281–300; and Thigpen and Cleckley, *op. cit.*

his seat with a bored expression; he was impatient and in general uncooperative. Even his language was different. When the soldier was asked, as each of his three personalities, identical questions concerning his willingness to commit murder, rape, and theft, he indicated each time that he would refuse. However, Frank objected on moral grounds, regarding such acts as outrageous. Leo objected on pragmatic grounds; he did not feel that the gain would be worth the risk of incarceration. Dick's reaction was a combination of the two. The scores on projective tests—Rorschach and TAT—also showed consistent differences among the three.[33]

There is no generally accepted theory accounting for the development of such alternating personalities. One hypothesis that has been entertained, however, is that the secondary and succeeding personalities constitute the mobilization, organization, and eventual emergence as a unit of meanings that have been repressed from conscious life. As Pierre Janet emphasized long ago, dissociation is not a random matter; it is a separation of systems which have already been integrated. This suggests that, for each person, there are sets of meanings which are organized into different roles; to some extent everyone's life is compartmentalized. When driving an automobile, delivering a speech, engaging in sexual activity, or defending oneself in a dangerous situation a person may act quite differently from his usual style. Such fragmentation becomes more readily discernible in people who play incongruent roles. A businessman who is so reliable in his financial transactions that his associates never question his integrity may maintain a mistress and lie constantly to his wife. In the case of the shell-shocked soldier, Leavitt provides a psychoanalytic interpretation; however, his data reveal that Dick played contrasting roles in different reference groups. The puritannical standards stressed by his mother clashed with those of a delinquent gang in which he was an active participant.

Previous discussions of the integration of meanings into roles and of consciousness as inner communication provide a possible way of accounting both for the phenomenon of multiple personalities and the relative ease with which it can be induced through hypnosis. In a study already cited on the formation of secondary personalities under hypnosis, Harriman found that his subjects usu-

[33] Harry C. Leavitt, "A Case of Hypnotically Produced Secondary and Tertiary Personalities," *Psychoanalytic Review*, XXXIV (1947), 274–95.

ally played an already familiar role—that of a miler in a track meet, of a famous criminal lawyer, or of a particular person they knew. Each person has an appreciation of the roles performed by his associates; this makes it possible for him to anticipate their activities and to participate successfully in concerted action. These roles constitute neuromuscular sets within ourselves, experiences that are attributed to others. This conceptual structure can apparently be disrupted by intense personal conflict. When there is a suppression of the subject's self-conception in a hypnotic trance, it becomes possible for the hypnotist to bring out the other roles through symbolic manipulation.[34]

Since the term "schizophrenia" is used to refer to so many different disorders, generalizations are difficult. However, it seems probable that some forms of schizophrenia are reactions to a low level of self-esteem. Many of the victims are described as being "out of contact with reality." It is through symbolic manipulation that a person constructs his orientation toward his environment; he can destroy it in the same manner. He may even deny his own existence. If a person finds himself immersed in a hostile setting in which he cannot find satisfaction, he may create a substitute world in which his lot is better. Such a scheme may become his only guarantee of security; if so, its preservation becomes a value in itself.

Since "reality" is a social process, loss of contact with it means that there has been a breakdown in communication. The isolation of those who are psychotic is not physical. Furthermore, in most cases the inability to communicate is not complete, for nurses and attendants are usually able to solicit cooperation. The hypothesis has been proposed that the crucial break in social contacts results from an impairment in the ability to form sentiments toward others and toward oneself. The development of schizophrenia has been viewed by some psychiatrists as a cumulative process in which the inability to recognize people as being "human" constitutes a decisive step. Initially there is a withdrawal of attention and interest from the environment, especially from people; autistic fantasy then replaces the environment, and personality disorganization follows;

[34] Harriman, *op. cit.* Cf. Robert W. White and Benjamin J. Shevach, "Hypnosis and the Concept of Dissociation," *Journal of Abnormal and Social Psychology*, XXXVII (1942), 309–28.

finally, there is a psychotic reorganization, an integration of private meanings, often bizarre or morbid, into a coherent scheme. The patient loses his capacity for empathy; in the language of Buber, another human being is not perceived as a "you" but as an "it."[35] Psychiatrists of different persuasions have noted this phenomenon, and have made numerous references to "emotional incongruity," "flatness of affect," and "lack of affect." Empirical studies comparing the empathy of patients classified as schizophrenic with that of "normal" people have thus far been inconclusive. Much of the difficulty arises from the operational definition of empathy as the ability to predict accurately what someone else will do; in this respect some patients score much better than those who make up the control group.[36]

A further hypothesis may be entertained that the loss of empathy is related to an extremely low level of self-esteem. Psychiatrists have noted repeatedly that many of their patients regard themselves as utterly worthless. Self-depreciation and self-reproach are common symptoms, and many of the delusions are of persecution or of self-punishment. The remarks made by the patients about themselves, their dreams, and their compulsive acts also imply low estimates of themselves. Furthermore, accounts of successful psychotherapy reveal the extent to which the doctor has to emphasize his love for the patient. After countless compliments, favors, gifts—all symbolic demonstrations of his worthiness—some patients gradually develop respect and affection for themselves.[37]

In social contact there is always some kind of emotional interchange, and other people "come to life" only when we can project certain familiar capacities and experiences to them. With the impairment of empathy, all meanings become devoid of life; as psychoanalysts would put it, objects do not feel "real" without

[35] Cf. Leslie H. Farber, "Martin Buber and Psychiatry," *Psychiatry*, XIX (1956), 109–20; Richard L. Jenkins, "The Schizophrenic Sequence: Withdrawal, Disorganization, Psychotic Reorganization," *American Journal of Orthopsychiatry*, XXII (1952), 738–48; and Lyman C. Wynne *et al.*, "Pseudo-Mutuality in the Family Relations of Schizophrenics," *Psychiatry*, XXI (1958), 205–20.

[36] Cf. William Jackson and Arthur C. Carr, "Empathic Ability in Normals and Schizophrenics," *Journal of Abnormal and Social Psychology*, LI (1955), 79–82.

[37] Cf. Marguerite Sechehaye, *Symbolic Realization*, B. and H. Würsten, trans. (New York: International Universities Press, 1951), pp. 78–82.

cathexis. Victims of schizophrenia recognize and interact with people, but all personifications become things. Intellectually they may be aware of the fact that they are dealing with human beings, but the objects lack human attributes. One patient, for example, referred to people only by their occupations. She recognized social status and conventional roles, but she had no contact with any of them as human beings. For her these people did not have distinct personalities. If part of her underclothing became unfastened while she was on the street, she would fix it there as though there were no one else present.[38]

When a person is unable to accept himself, many of his behavioral tendencies are projected elsewhere. Patients sometimes insist that they are being controlled by external forces; their own inclinations are apparently attributed to outside agencies. Complaints of tactile and kinesthetic sensations, sometimes called "somatic delusions," also appear to be the result of depersonalization.[39] To test the hypothesis that hallucinations are linguistic acts projected to an outside source, Gould set up instruments to measure incipient muscular movements in the speech organs of patients known to hallucinate. Of those who reported hallucinations eighty-three per cent showed increased action potential. Since he measured only the total increase of action potential, he had no way of ascertaining whether any particular increase in muscular activity coincided with a given hallucination. Roberts therefore developed a more effective technique of measurement. His findings, however, were less conclusive; of forty-three reports of hallucinations, there were only four in which there was a coincidental rise in muscular activity. Gould also collected data on the distinctive speech habits of his subjects and tried to match them with the vocal patterns of their hallucinations.[40] The hypothesis has sufficient substantiation

[38] *Ibid.*, pp. 31–32.

[39] Cf. Andrus Angyal, "The Perceptual Basis of Somatic Delusions in a Case of Schizophrenia," *Archives of Neurology and Psychiatry*, XXXIV (1935), 270–79; and "The Experience of the Body Self in Schizophrenia," *ibid.*, XXXV (1936), 1029–53.

[40] Lewis N. Gould, "Verbal Hallucinations and Activity of Vocal Musculature," *American Journal of Psychiatry*, CV (1948), 367–72; and "Verbal Hallucinations as Automatic Speech," *ibid.*, CVII (1950), 110–19. Cf. Bertram Roberts *et al.*, "Movements of the Vocal Apparatus during Auditory Hallucinations," *ibid.*, CVIII (1952), 912–14; and Jerome M. Schneck, "An Experimental Study of Hypnotically Induced Auditory Hallucinations," *Journal of Clinical and Experimental Hypnosis*, II (1954), 163–70.

to merit further inquiry, but it cannot be accepted without qualifications.

Many psychiatrists have referred to schizophrenia as a form of regression; upon encountering inimical conditions a person retreats to modes of adjustment that he had found acceptable earlier in life. But schizophrenia may also be regarded as a form of adaptation, a way of surviving in an unbearable world in which powerful impulses cannot be consummated. Mental disorders are revealing in that they indicate the extent to which men may be driven to come to terms with themselves. They also point to the importance of symbolic processes. When a man cannot form a satisfactory conception of himself, he can deny or forget the things that are humiliating through symbolic manipulation. In extreme cases he may even deny the existence of the world or of himself.

Human Society as a Moral Order

Human society exists in concerted action, which rests upon the self-control exercised by those who share a common perspective. Although the participants are physically separate and capable of some measure of independent action, they are able to coordinate their activities because each is able to inhibit his impulses and to redirect his conduct in accordance with group expectations.

Human beings tend to recognize as an obligation what others expect them to do. Most norms are easy to fulfil, but situations occasionally arise in which compliance would entail considerable sacrifice or pain. What happens under such circumstances? It appears that *the extent to which obligations are honored depends upon the sentiments that have been formed.* It is difficult to go against the known wishes of a person one loves. By reading expressive movements, men live vicariously in each other's minds, and the reproachful glance of a love object, even when nothing is said, may hurt far more than physical deprivation. On the other hand, violating the expectations of those toward whom one has formed disjunctive sentiments is easy; one may even derive pleasure from imagining the frustration of the other party. The persistence of social structures of all kinds rests upon the willingness of the participants to live up to their responsibilities. In the last analysis, human society rests upon the personal obligations that people feel toward one another.

In every group there are social sanctions, both formal and informal, to enforce conformity. But no person can be watched all the time; each finds himself in situations in which he can violate norms with only the slightest risk of being caught. Group patterns persist because most men are moral. *Moral conduct* consists of behavior that has no sanction other than the actor's own sense of right and wrong. Of course, not all men live up to their obligations each time they are free to choose. Some consistently pursue their selfish interests as long as they feel they can safely get away with it. On the other hand, some are compulsively correct, rigidly resisting all temptation. It has long been suspected that such people are reacting against their own impulses; those who condemn sexual laxity most vigorously are often the very people who secretly enjoy vice. In spite of such personality differences, however, most men are moral to a greater extent than even they themselves suspect.

Each person sometimes acts expediently, sometimes compulsively, and sometimes morally. But what is significant is that those who consistently fail to meet personal obligations form disjunctive sentiments toward themselves. Everyone performs for some kind of audience. Significant others need not be physically present, nor do they even have to know about the offense. A person who succeeds in deceiving others can still judge himself in terms of standards attributed to them, and can readily imagine their reactions should they learn the truth. A man who fails to live up to his moral obligations condemns and punishes himself, even when other people do not. Even those who are unscrupulous apparently feel that it is necessary for them to explain their conduct. To whom are such justifications really addressed? Each person's level of self-esteem depends upon what he knows about himself.

Of course, a conscious sense of guilt may be repressed. If so, punitive measures of an indirect nature often manifest themselves. Some unscrupulous people rationalize their conduct by declaring that only "suckers" are honest, but their very defensiveness betrays a low level of self-esteem. Although they may be successful in improving their social status, they cannot convince themselves that they really deserve their good fortune. They are often filled with anxiety lest someone discover their secrets. Many are plagued by psychosomatic disorders, and some become so depressed that they suddenly commit suicide. Disapproval of oneself, even when it is transitory, is manifested somehow. For example, Katz gave thirty-five students a simulated intelligence test and then informed them all that they had failed. Some of the students denied that they were frustrated, but others admitted feeling badly. All of the subjects were then asked to make drawings of faces. The judges agreed that the drawings of those who believed they had failed, whether or not they admitted their chagrin, were significantly different from those of a control group. Some of the faces were covered with masks; some appeared dehumanized, inanimate and statue-like; some were drawn with a blank stare; and some were distorted by the omission of various features.[41] This suggests that even people who appear blasé and cynical are constantly responding to themselves. Most men are moral; they have incorporated the standards and ideals of their reference groups and judge themselves in these terms, even though the sentences they pass upon themselves are sometimes blotted out of their conscious life.

The boundaries of any society are set by the range within which the participants feel constrained to live up to their obligations. This in turn depends upon the extent to which they can identify with one another as being of a kind. This is shown clearly in the relationships among people in different segments of a stratified community—in inter-ethnic or inter-class contacts. Historical accounts of the British settlement of Tasmania, the Dutch settlement of South Africa, and the westward expansion of the American frontier reveal that the natives were sometimes hunted like wild animals. But once individuals in the opposing groups got to know one another as human beings, the violence was tempered, and in time suppressed. Even in communities that are rigidly stratified, there is no "color line" among personal friends. Similarly, some aristocrats treated their serfs with far less consideration than they had for their horses or household pets. A common saying in Eastern Europe was that the only difference between a pig and a peasant was that the latter had a passport. The Nazis taught that the Jews

<hr/>

[41] Irwin Katz, "Emotional Expression in Failure," *Journal of Abnormal and Social Psychology*, XLV (1950), 329–49. Cf. Karl Menninger, *Man Against Himself* (New York: Harcourt, Brace & Co., 1938); and Elwin H. Powell, "Occupation, Status, and Suicide," *American Sociological Review*, XXIII (1958), 131–39.

were a race apart, biologically different from themselves. Men have committed some of the most incredible outrages against one another, but the violence can go on only as long as they are unable to establish a sense of identity.

Outsiders are initially perceived as instances of categories, but with the reduction of social distance they come to be seen as unique individuals basically like oneself. Once such identification is established, role-taking assumes a different form, and mistreatment becomes unlikely. Once someone else is recognized as being like oneself, his inner experiences can be appreciated, and it is difficult to torment someone whose painful reactions can be felt. The development of empathy, then, is a matter of decisive importance.

The importance of moral conduct is revealed by the instability of groups in which it is kept to a minimum. In some sophisticated circles, especially among those who claim to be experts on human nature, there are people who become amoral, although not necessarily immoral. They rationalize their behavior by declaring that only the weak must depend upon moral codes and that the strong and the intelligent should not be hampered by such limitations. They sneer at ideals as indications of immaturity and often contend that all men are basically selfish and only hypocrites will not admit it. They may even regard it as their duty to live a purely rational life, in pursuit of their own interests. In groups in which such views are tolerated, the participants are constantly on guard against one another. They seldom accept at face value the remarks of their associates, always searching beneath the surface for hidden meanings. They impute selfish motives to themselves and one another, and their ties rest largely upon reciprocal utility. La Rochefoucauld once wrote, "The true way to be deceived is to think oneself more clever than others," and in a group in which everyone thinks himself the most adroit, each is able to detect the diversionary gestures of his associates, but believes that he alone is successful in hiding his motives. Such groups usually collapse when confronted with adversity, since men who do not trust one another can hardly be expected to work together in a dangerous situation.

The moral codes and religious creeds of diverse peoples, in spite of their differences in other respects, emphasize with remarkable consistency values such as loyalty and personal integrity. It is

conceivable that these values are cherished in so many groups because they have passed a pragmatic test; folk wisdom develops
through the selective preservation of the ideas that have proved
worthwhile. It is possible that the accumulated experience of countless generations shows that a group cannot long survive unless these
values, although difficult to implement, are recognized and enforced.
If this be the case, morality is not the exclusive property of the
self-righteous and the respectable. It becomes an essential ingre-
dient of human life.

Summary and Conclusion

Each person places some kind of estimate upon himself as a
human being and consciously or unconsciously struggles to maintain an adequate level of self-esteem. Whenever it is threatened,
a number of defense mechanisms are activated. This accounts for
the fact that the evaluation that is actually presupposed in acts
having self-reference may differ considerably from one's conscious
appraisal. Men often do not see in themselves attributes that they
find painful, nor do they always notice the negative gestures of
other people that would confirm their apprehensions. Some people
are deeply hurt during childhood and devote a lifetime to improving their lot; it is not until after they have succeeded that
they realize that their pangs of guilt and inferiority are still with
them. In unusual cases of very low self-esteem a person may even
deny his own existence, insisting that he is someone else.

Self-preservation is said to be the basic law of life, and this is
certainly true of human beings. Among men, however, self-preservation includes considerably more than the survival of the organism. What is protected by each person is his conception of himself.
Since self-conceptions emerge in and are sustained by social interaction, self-preservation involves being assured of the desired responses of other people, especially of those toward whom one has
formed conjunctive sentiments. Much of what a man does can
be explained in terms of the adjustive tendencies found in all living
creatures, except that many things are done to maintain a desirable
personification. Men struggle for social status, to be assured of

being treated with reasonable respect in their community; they struggle for personal status, to keep up their reputation for integrity; they also struggle for self-respect. In some cases, then, a suicide may constitute self-preservation, the destruction of the organism to maintain one's reputation or self-respect. It is in this manner, in effect, that Socrates eventually answers Glaucon's queries about injustices that go unpunished. Man's deepest gratifications come from living well according to his own standards, which in most cases are the standards of the society in which he lives. A person must do those things that make him acceptable to himself. It is the fact that most men are moral and live up to the expectations that they impose upon themselves that makes possible the continuation of an orderly social life.

Of course, not all men succeed in coming to terms with themselves, and there are some who lead pathetic lives. It is easy for those who are more fortunate to scorn the maladjusted. Most of them die forsaken and unknown, but it should be remembered that some of the greatest contributions to art, knowledge, and justice have been made by disorganized men. Many of the great religious and political movements of the world have been led by men fighting fanatically for humanitarian ideals with which they identified themselves while in the throes of self-contempt. Of course, not all geniuses suffer from mental disorders, but the kind of dedication that results in great work is often defensive and rigid. Great achievement in any field requires hard work, and those who have lived too easily are often unwilling to make the sacrifices. Signal contributions are made by men who are relatively independent of prevailing opinions and are willing to develop their proficiency through sustained effort. Independence is found often among those who disdain authority figures and are not easily swayed; dedication may develop in a number of ways, but it is most marked among those who are compensating for a low level of self-esteem. Geniuses are often immature, immoral, and unhappy; many of them are described as "queer" by the people who know them as individuals. Some have even been regarded as psychotic. Through their incredible sacrifices, obstinacy, and perfectionism such people bring much into the lives of others, even though they themselves live in misery.

Suggested References

ADLER, ALFRED, *The Individual Psychology of Alfred Adler,* Heinz and Rowena Ansbacher, trans. and ed. New York: Basic Books, 1956. An orderly presentation of Adler's position through selections from his numerous writings, showing how various styles of life develop as each individual copes with a sense of personal inadequacy.

FREUD, ANNA, *The Ego and the Mechanisms of Defense,* Cecil Baines, trans. New York: International Universities Press, 1946. A classic in psychoanalytic literature, describing the manner in which the various mechanisms of defense protect self-conceptions rather than organisms.

HORNEY, KAREN, *Neurosis and Human Growth.* New York: W. W. Norton & Co., 1950. An insightful discussion of the neurotic quest for glory, contrasting the characteristics of ordinary endeavor with the dedicated struggles of those who are reacting against themselves.

LASSWELL, HAROLD D., *Power and Personality.* New York: W. W. Norton & Co., 1948. A treatise by an eminent political scientist on the genesis of power-oriented people in certain types of interpersonal relations.

THIGPEN, CORBETT H. and HERVEY M. CLECKLEY, *The Three Faces of Eve.* New York: McGraw-Hill Book Co., 1957. A case study of a woman who developed alternating personalities while undergoing psychotherapy, containing insightful observations, test scores, and a review of the literature in the light of these data.

WEST, RANYARD, *Conscience and Society.* London: Methuen & Co., 1942. A critique of the view that human nature is repressed in society, showing that much of the orderliness of human life rests upon self-control and that laws become necessary only to reinforce conscience.

Part Four

Socialization

14

The
social
matrix
of
personal
growth

Among the incomparable studies of insect life by J. Henri Fabre is a fascinating account of the surgery performed by the solitary wasp upon certain grasshoppers, whose eggs provide nourishment for its grubs. After digging a burrow, the wasp hunts for a female victim of the proper species and partially paralyzes her with a poison sting. Should the victim resist too viciously while being dragged to the burrow, she is further immobilized by the manipulation of the main center of innervation control. For this task the wasp resorts to compression rather than stinging. No external wound is inflicted; instead, the wasp probes under the skull for the proper place and pinches it until resistance ceases. After observing this technique, Fabre repeated the surgery with apparent success; but all of his grasshoppers died within four or five days, whereas those operated on by the wasps recovered in a few hours and remained fresh for days, providing a continuous supply of food for the larvae. The second operation, a very delicate one, is accomplished by the wasp as if it had mastered the mysteries of neurology as well as the principles of surgery. But these complicated procedures are executed by the insect without ever having been taught, indeed, without even having seen it practiced by others. This is but one of the countless miracles of nature, the remarkable ability of various creatures to follow highly complex life cycles without instructions of any kind from their elders.

What makes all this seem so incredible is the comparative helplessness of the human infant. Man cannot even survive, let alone go through his life cycle, without the sustained care of his elders. Human beings develop their various attributes—their sentiments, their capacity for linguistic communication and thinking, their ability to play diverse social roles—not by biological maturation but in the course of social interaction. The metamorphosis of man from birth to adulthood is far more extensive than it is for most creatures, for each human being is transformed from a helpless animal into a more or less independent person who pursues values in a symbolic environment. In the study of socialization we are concerned with the general principles of development, the regularities found in this fantastic transformation.

The Problem of Socialization

With the exception of those suffering severe personality disorders, virtually all adults are capable of participating in a wide variety of collective transactions. Each person is able to anticipate the reactions of his associates and to control his own activities in accordance with the expectations he imputes to them. But infants are not capable of doing this; they are creatures of impulse. Indeed, at the time of their birth human infants have little capacity for integrated activity of any kind. Human beings are born physiologically undeveloped, the myelination of the nerve cells complete only in the oral area, making possible the coordination of sucking movements. The ability to control muscular movements in other parts of the body develops very slowly.

These observations provide the basis for the problem of socialization. How does an infant develop into a value-seeking person
who, though different from all others, is capable of acting in con-
cert with them? *Socialization* refers to those processes whereby
newcomers learn to participate effectively in social groups. Since
this kind of learning is most extensive during childhood, most studies
of socialization are confined to the development of behavior patterns in the early years. Even in daily discourse the acquisition
of such skills is associated with childhood. An adult who does
not conduct himself in the expected manner is sometimes regarded
as "immature"; a person is considered "grown up" not when he
matures biologically but when he is able to assume responsibilities
and can control himself. A person is socialized, then, when he is
able to engage in concerted action on the basis of conventional
norms.

Human beings are equipped with numerous reflexes which enable them to maintain life under varied conditions. Vegetative
processes—such as digestion, absorption, respiration, and circula-
tion—are automatic and ordinarily require neither attention nor
training. But virtually all other behavior patterns are learned.
There are many theories of learning; perhaps the most sophisticated of them is the work of Clark Hull, based largely upon a
series of careful experiments on rats. Attempts have been made
to adapt his concepts to human learning, but psychologists are
by no means agreed over the adequacy of this scheme. There
seems to be little doubt that a great many motor skills are learned
in the manner described by Hull, but the question has been raised
as to whether the formation of those attributes that are regarded
as distinctly human can be explained in these terms. Some psychologists contend that the principles apply best to infants, im-
beciles, and other animals.[1]

Learning is often thought to consist of a gradual accretion of
small increments. New behavior patterns are formed as an or-

[1] Applications of Hull's principles to human beings include Neal E. Miller
and John Dollard, *Social Learning and Imitation* (New Haven: Yale University
Press, 1941); and John W. M. Whiting, *Becoming a Kwoma* (New Haven: Yale
University Press, 1941). Critiques include Gordon W. Allport, "Effect: A
Secondary Principle of Learning," *Psychological Review*, LIII (1946), 335–47;
and Alfred R. Lindesmith and Anselm Strauss, "Comparative Psychology and
Social Psychology," *American Journal of Sociology*, LVIII (1952), 272–79.

ganism adjusts to the requirements of the situation, and the new habit is then regarded as being added to the previously learned repertoire. It may be more fruitful, however, not to think of socialization as a series of separate adjustments, but as a process of development that continues throughout each person's life span. The acquisition of a new skill is more than the addition of an element; it involves a reorganization of the entire organism. Achievement in any particular situation is a phase of the continual development of new, unified orientations.

Since both the organism and its environment are continually undergoing change, some kind of transformation is always taking place. However, noticeable changes occur when previously established behavior patterns turn out to be inadequate; men are most likely to learn in situations in which they are confronted with problems. This may explain why consciousness is usually heightened while learning is going on; other emergency reactions, like increased excitement, are also an integral part of learning. Once a new pattern for meeting such circumstances has become established, attention is relaxed, emotional reactions subside, and performance takes place with less effort. Once an act becomes cystallized into a habit, it can usually be set off like an innate reflex. Well-established behavior patterns, then, are solutions of past problems. Since each person meets a unique set of problems and solves them in his own way, each forms a distinct personality. Personality development may therefore be regarded as the progressive transformation of a given organism to cope with the disturbing situations it encounters.[2]

In any perplexing situation there are usually a number of alternative solutions, and *new behavior patterns develop through a process of natural selection*. One solution is chosen, repeated, and eventually becomes fixed in habit. Selection is apparently on the basis of expediency; men continue to do those things that work and are in some way gratifying. Although it is customary in sophisticated circles to eschew such crude hedonism as being outmoded, actually all current theories of socialization in some way depend upon it. Learning consists of the persistence of behavior patterns that bring pleasure and the extinction of those that result in pain. The substitution of words like "gratification" and "deprivation"

[2] Cf. Lecky, *op. cit.*, pp. 114–43.

or "euphoria" and "disphoria" does not alter the basic argument.[3] Thus, habits of all kinds—particular ways of consummating impulses—emerge through successful adjustments and become fixed through repetition. As the acts are repeated, they are executed with greater speed, accuracy, and nicety of coordination; useless movements are eliminated. As behavior patterns become well established, they become more abbreviated, automatic, and unconscious; socialization is a form of adaptation.

Experimental studies of learning are often set up as if the organism acquired its habits in social isolation. But among the most important of the life conditions to which all human beings must adjust is the presence of other people, who become involved in socialization as agents of instruction, as models to be imitated, and as sources of reinforcement. By inflicting punishment and providing rewards, they place limitations upon the avenues along which personal growth can take place. The manner in which each individual is oriented toward his world is set by the necessity of coming to terms with the demands of other people. For human beings, learning is not the accretion of discrete skills by an isolated organism; it is a continuous communicative process in which men meet their difficulties together and in adjusting to one another evolve new ways of approaching various aspects of their environment.

The important role played by other people in socialization is underscored by the fate of children who somehow manage to survive in spite of their isolation. There have been numerous reports of abandoned or lost children being reared by wild animals, but most of them are hoaxes. Fortunately, there are a few accounts that stand up reasonably well under careful scrutiny, and they are remarkably consistent. The most carefully documented and detailed record is the case of two girls found in India—Kamala, whose age was estimated at eight, and Amala, whose age was estimated as a year and a half. They were captured by a missionary in a den of wolves and brought back to his orphanage, where daily records were kept of their behavior.[4] Among other authenticated accounts is the case reported by Davis of Anna, a five year old girl found

[3] Cf. Allport, op. cit.; and Dorrian Apple, "Learning Theory and Socialization," American Sociological Review, XVI (1951), 23–27.

[4] J. A. L. Singh and Robert M. Zingg, Wolf-Children and Feral Men (New York: Harper & Bros., 1939), pp. 3–113.

in 1938 on a Pennsylvania farm. Anna was the illegitimate child of a frightened mother, who kept her alive but otherwise avoided all contacts with her.[5] All three of these girls were maturing biologically, but there was no socialization. In spite of their organic development these creatures were incapable of participating in concerted action.

Although the use of such materials has been severely criticized, the objections do not justify ignoring these valuable data. Since Anna had failed to acquire social skills even with the most tender care, Davis concluded that a child who is deprived of intimate social contacts during the early years of infancy is incapable of later socialization. In a thoughtful critique, Dennis objected to the use of such data for the testing of this particular hypothesis, pointing to the possibility that the isolated children might have been mentally defective and therefore incapable of learning. After having an opportunity to study another girl who had been found under similar circumstances but had subsequently developed satisfactorily, Davis repudiated his earlier hypothesis.[6] Perhaps the most extreme of the critiques is that of Bettelheim. Pointing to the remarkable similarity of the attributes of isolated children and those with certain mental disorders, he contended that *all* accounts of feral children must be false. He went so far as to insist that the Indian missionary, whose integrity he does not question, must have been mistaken when he thought he saw the children with a pack of wolves.[7] Since Bettelheim's own hypothesis has not yet been demonstrated, he is hardly in a position to challenge the accuracy of an eyewitness account that does not happen to be in accord with it. No one questions the contention that children deprived of contacts with other human beings are incapable of participating in collective transactions. Although many social psychologists have been reluctant to use such data, a brief examination of the report by Singh and Zingg is in order.

[5] Kingsley Davis, "Extreme Social Isolation of a Child," *American Journal of Sociology,* XLV (1940), 554–65.

[6] Wayne Dennis, "The Significance of Feral Men," *American Journal of Psychology,* LIV (1941), 425–32; and Kingsley Davis, "Final Note on a Case of Extreme Isolation," *American Journal of Sociology,* LII (1947), 432–37.

[7] Bruno Bettelheim, "Feral Children and Autistic Children," *ibid.,* LXIV (1959), 455–67.

In 1920, at the time of their capture, the two girls had the physical characteristics of human beings, but they behaved much like the wolves with whom they had been living. They crawled and ran on all fours, and their bodies indicated long adaptation to quadruped locomotion. They would eat only milk and meat, and smelled their food before taking it into their mouths. When they were thirsty, they licked their lips. Their sensory organs were unusually well developed; they could apparently see quite well in the dark and could smell fresh meat at a distance of seventy-five yards. The children showed great fear of fire; furthermore, they disliked the sunlight and ran for cover whenever they were exposed. There was no fear of darkness, however, and they frequently had to be restrained from going outside during the night.

As might be expected, the children were unable to communicate through conventional gestures, and the ability for using linguistic symbols developed very slowly under captivity. At the time of their capture, the only sounds the children made were loud howls. They never laughed. Kamala had a smiling face, but the smile was apparently not a gesture indicative of joy. When they were through eating, there were other manifestations of satisfaction, such as romping about and jumping upon each other. In 1921, when Amala died, Kamala was seen to have shed a few tears, but there was no noticeable change in her facial expression. The inference that she was upset was based upon her refusal to eat or drink for the next few days. In 1922 Kamala began saying "bhoo" for water; in 1923, "hoo" for cold. In 1924 she observed an injured child yelling "na," and the next time she was hurt she uttered the same sound. She also said "na" when the water for her bath was too hot, and in time the gesture came to stand for "no." By 1926 there was evidence that Kamala could understand simple commands, and she could indicate "yes" or "no." Furthermore, she knew the other children by name and could point out each of them upon request. At this time, when her estimated age was fourteen, she had a vocabulary of about thirty words. It increased steadily until her death in 1929.

Kamala's ability to participate in cooperative transactions was very limited, even after several years of captivity. During the first few years at the orphanage she permitted only Mrs. Singh to nurse her, and she and Amala went to her whenever they were frightened.

The two girls had little to do with the other children; they played with each other, some puppies, a baby hyena, and the chickens. By 1927, however, Kamala mixed freely, and she even insisted upon being dressed like the others. One incident, which occurred in December, 1927, was quite noteworthy. Kamala entered the dining room while the ladies were setting the table for their afternoon tea, and was given a biscuit. When she noticed that the other children did not have any, she returned the biscuit to the table. Later on, at tea, when each child was given two biscuits, Kamala accepted only one and then retrieved the one she had placed on the table. This incident, which occurred after seven years at the orphanage, was such a rare instance of conduct obviously oriented toward group norms that a detailed record was made of it. Kamala was forced to fit into the routine at the orphanage, but she apparently did so uncomprehendingly, much as a pet dog becomes adjusted to the routine of family life. Yet with increasing social contacts she developed the techniques necessary for taking a more active part.[8]

As the critics have insisted, these children may have been mentally retarded, so that socialization would not have occurred even under ideal circumstances. But the data point to the remarkable flexibility of the human organism—the ability to meet the requirements of living with men or with other creatures. They also point to the crucial part played by the others in the construction of behavior patterns.

Although learning is explained largely in terms of a crude hedonism, it must be remembered that pleasure and pain for human beings includes much more than physical punishment and the gratification of animal impulses. Anxiety over the possibility of losing affection, feelings of guilt, and a wide variety of symbolic gratifications complicate the picture. Men struggle to achieve social position, a reputation for personal integrity, and self-respect, and the loss of any of these goals is usually far more difficult to bear than physical pain. The formation of behavior patterns is to be seen in terms of what a person has to do to get along with the particular human beings with whom he shares his fate. Human sentiments play a crucial part in socialization.

The secondary importance of physical deprivation in socialization

[8] Singh and Zingg, *loc. cit.*

is shown dramatically by cases of people who are congenitally incapable of experiencing pain. McMurray reported the case of a twenty-two year old woman who had to inspect her feet carefully after a day at the beach to be sure that she had no cuts. She had a long record of hospitalization, for tissue damage had often gone unnoticed and had become infected. She regarded her insensitivity as a defect and was reticent about it; she was curious about the sensations that led to the pain reactions she had observed in others. As she grew older, she developed increasing sensitivity to danger through other sensory channels, but tests revealed a complete lack of the usual physiological responses to noxious stimuli. She could recognize a pin prick, but there was no withdrawal, wincing, or crying; she showed no changes in blood pressure, in pulse, or in respiration. Mental tests showed that she was of superior intelligence, and various projective tests showed no personality disturbances. In a survey of the medical literature on similar cases, McMurray noted that such persons usually show a long history of broken bones, cuts, burns, and tongue biting.[9] But in spite of their insensitivity to pain, these people are successfully socialized; they are capable of participating in concerted action. They even learn to feign pain reactions so that others will not be shocked. This suggests that physical pain is but one of the numerous selective factors involved in socialization.

Most studies of socialization concentrate upon childhood training, when learning is admittedly most impressive. The early years are important because almost everything is new and problematic; a child learns so much in a short period of time. These are the years in which a style of life is established, and this provides a basis for selection in all subsequent socialization. But the learning of new skills goes on throughout each person's life. New patterns of conduct develop when a person joins a religious sect, migrates to another community, attends a college away from home, joins an *avant-garde* circle, participates in a juvenile gang, or gets a new job. Like all other living creatures, men are continually coming to terms with ever-changing life conditions. Each person must keep pace, developing modes of conduct better suited to the new circumstances.

[9] Gordon A. McMurray, "Experimental Study of a Case of Insensitivity to Pain," *Archives of Neurology and Psychiatry*, LXIV (1950), 650–67; and "Congenital Insensitivity to Pain and Its Implications for Motivational Theory," *Canadian Journal of Psychology*, IX (1955), 121–31.

The Formation of Conventional Meanings

Each person's outlook toward his environment consists of meanings. Meanings are orientations toward objects and classes of objects, and concerted action is facilitated when the participants share common meanings. But since each person's background of experience is necessarily unique, how is it possible for different people to share meanings?

The formation of common meanings is possible partly because all human beings have similar biological characteristics. The physical world is known to us primarily through manipulation, and there is agreement concerning the properties of physical objects because all men have similar experiences in handling them. Everyone agrees that a table top is hard, for no one is able to press his hand through it. Not long after World War II, the Veterans' Administration announced successful experiments with an artificial hand which resembled the human hand in appearance, but not in prehensile strength. Even a very strong man can maintain a grip with a pressure of thirty pounds for only a few seconds, but the wearer of this artificial limb could exert pressure of forty-three pounds for an indefinite period. This would enable him to crush most table tops with the ease of a steel vise. Because of his memory, an amputee would continue to regard table tops as hard objects, but anyone born with such strength would encounter difficulty in understanding the orientations of others. In spite of variations in size and strength, human beings are constructed remarkably alike; hence, agreements concerning the attributes of physical objects are relatively easy to reach.

Shared conceptions of reality rest in part upon the proper functioning of the sensory organs. Recently a group of Canadian psychologists conducted a series of experiments in which they cut off sensory cues for long periods of time. Volunteer subjects lay for days on a comfortable bed in a chamber in which sound was limited to the hum of the air conditioner. Their eyes were covered by translucent visors which permitted no vision, and they wore cotton gloves with cardboard cuffs to prevent their touching anything. The subjects took time out only for their meals and toilets, and were interviewed and tested at regular intervals. Hallucinations were reported by all subjects, many of them resembling those occurring in mescalin intoxication.[10] Although these and similar experiments have been hailed as studies of social isolation, the subjects were actually not alone. Since they interacted with the experimenters, a crucial variable was left uncontrolled. They are actually studies of prolonged sensory deprivation, and what they show is that meanings are stable relationships between organisms and various phases of their environment. Any interference with these sensory processes renders the experiences of each person more idiosyncratic, and the possibilities of achieving consensus are reduced.

When dealing with the meaning of anything that cannot be directly perceived or manipulated, however, similarity of biological characteristics is hardly enough to account for the development of consensus. Most conventional meanings are formed by the standardized ways in which other people respond to the behavior of a newcomer. For example, how does a child learn the significance of a cross? Initially he does not even differentiate it from other forms, but he learns to discriminate after being punished each time he does something regarded as disrespectful. Even before he has any appreciation of the ideology justifying the reverence with which a cross is approached, he learns many of the rituals. He notices others kneeling and praying before it. Even if he never becomes a Christian, somehow blasphemy before a cross remains incongruous and improper. The meanings of most categories become clearly established because the responses of other people are institutionalized. While participating in organized groups, each person's adjustments become fixed in habit and are reinforced through social sanctions.[11]

The acquisition of conventional meanings consists of learning the appropriate ways of identifying and classifying objects and developing the accepted ways of acting toward them. Because the classifications in our own universe of discourse are so well established, we tend to think of them as natural; only after noting mistakes made by children and contemplating some of their embarrassing questions do

[10] W. H. Bexton, Woodburn Heron, and T. H. Scott, "Effects of Decreased Variation in the Sensory Environment," *Canadian Journal of Psychology*, VIII (1954), 70–76; W. Heron, B. K. Doane, and T. H. Scott, "Visual Disturbances after Prolonged Perceptual Isolation," *ibid.*, X (1956), 13–18; and Philip Solomon *et al.*, "Sensory Deprivation," *American Journal of Psychiatry*, CXIV (1957), 357–63.

[11] Cf. Mead, *The Philosophy of the Present, op. cit.*, pp. 106–39, 161–75.

we realize how arbitrary many of the categories are. Among the
Ojibwa Indians of Canada, for example, the word *kinebikominin*
means "snake berries." The term is applied to berries that botanists
would classify in a number of different species; their common
feature is that they are considered inedible. Although the fruits are
actually not poisonous, most Indians never have an opportunity to
test the belief. As a child is about to reach for any of these berries,
his hand is slapped by his mother who shouts, *"kinebikominin!"* In
this manner the child learns to identify this heterogeneous category
as a unit and develops a definite orientation toward it, not only as
something to be shunned as food but also as something forbidden.[12]

Even after the categories of the group have been learned, the
criteria used for differentiation may for a time remain superficial. In
a study of the ability of children to make distinctions between the
sexes, Conn and Kanner interviewed, in the context of playing with
dolls, 200 subjects ranging in age from four to twelve. They found
that the youngest children tended to distinguish between boys and
girls in terms of tonsorial differences; five-year old children also
noted differences in clothing; eight-year old children pointed to
differences in strength and body build; and those who were a bit
older pointed to differences in gait. Of the 200 children studied, 116
were aware of genital differences, but this was not the criterion
initially cited.[13]

Once objects are classified, the newcomer must learn the proper
ways of acting toward them. In some cases there is deliberate training, but many conventional meanings are learned as by-products of
other activities, as in the ways in which children learn to locate
themselves within stratified communities. In a study of how white
children in the South learn to make ethnic distinctions, Quinn found
that direct instruction is relatively infrequent. It occurs only after
some incident in which a child has violated the "color line"—inviting
a Negro friend to a birthday party and eating side by side at the
same table or referring to a Negro woman as a "lady." Justifications
are not always given in ethnic terms; often the children are asked
simply to trust their elders. Indirect techniques of training are sometimes used; children are permitted to eavesdrop on adult conversations about the immoral conduct of some Negro, when similar

[12] A. Irving Hallowell, "Cultural Factors in the Structuralization of Perception," in Rohrer and Sherif, *op. cit.*, pp. 164–95.

[13] Jacob H. Conn and Leo Kanner, "Children's Awareness of Sex Differences," *Journal of Child Psychology*, I (1947), 3–57.

conduct by others is not discussed so candidly in their presence. The Negroes themselves help stabilize meanings by conforming to the expectations that prevail in the community. Negro nurses and servants address their young charges with deference, and may even teach them the proper ways to act toward those of lower status.[14]

Values of all kinds are sometimes learned through instruction, but more often they are formed through the consistent emotional reactions of other people. Children in our society are told repeatedly that they will have bad luck if their path is crossed by a black cat, but the significance of this superstition is communicated by the desperation with which stray animals are assaulted. The meaning of a four-leaf clover, which extends far beyond any direct utility of this plant, is shaped in the shrieks of delight of those who find them. Angyal cited the case of a schizophrenic boy for whom excreta and erotic objects had the same meaning; the boy was oriented to act toward both in identical ways. He suggested that such similarities in behavior patterns develop not so much because of the close anatomical relations between excretory and genital organs, but more because they are socially forbidden in the same manner, in similar situations, by the same people. Their meaning as disgusting objects which are to be avoided thereby becomes fixed.[15] The occupation of undertaker, although highly lucrative and certainly essential to any community, fails to attract many young men, not on the basis of rational considerations but from the vague sense of discomfort evoked by images of handling dead bodies. Such meanings are seldom transmitted with conscious intent. A large part of each person's education, then, is informal.

As a newcomer is incorporated into a group, there is a successive approximation of the accepted standards of conduct, beginning with rough imitations and gradually developing into the conventional procedures. Blake and Dennis asked a group of white students in Charlottesville, Virginia, ranging from the fourth to the eleventh grades, to compare their own group with Negroes on sixty traits. Among the younger students there was considerably less consensus in the characterization of either category, but the conceptions became more alike with increasing age. The younger students, in general, were unwilling to attribute any good traits to Negroes, but

[14] Olive W. Quinn, "The Transmission of Racial Attitudes Among White Southerners," *Social Forces*, XXXIII (1954), 41–47. Cf. Mary E. Goodman, *Race Awareness in Young Children* (Cambridge: Addison-Wesley Press, 1952).
[15] Angyal, "Disgust and Related Aversions," *op. cit.*

the older ones used the adult stereotype, which is not entirely unfavorable. Traits such as being cheerful, easygoing, and religious were attributed more often to Negroes by the older subjects.[16] In a study of sixty-six subjects, ranging in age from four to eleven, Strauss traced the manner in which children learn the meaning of money and its proper use. Although the youngest children could distinguish between money and other objects, they were rather vague in the use of coins. Most children of five knew that money was something to be spent, and had some comprehension of primitive rules of exchange. Those who were somewhat older knew that money was good for payments of all kinds. Still older subjects were aware of the mathematical character of the transaction, and had begun to grasp the concept of receiving "change." Most of the older children understood more complex concepts, such as credit, profit making, and money as a way of acquiring more money.[17]

Once the appropriate orientations are established, they are repeatedly reinforced in social interaction. The reaffirmation of ethnic categories provides a good example. The mistaken belief that Negroes are inferior objects is inadvertently strengthened in jokes in which the point rests on the assumption that they are ignorant and superstitious, and in expressions like "the last one there is a nigger baby," even when they are used in contexts in which ethnic identity is irrelevant. The stereotype of the penurious Jew is reinforced in the same manner—in jokes in which the point rests on the premise that all Jews are preoccupied with money, and in the use of expressions like "Jew the man down." In a study of nearly 200 stories appearing in popular American magazines in 1937 and 1943 Berelson and Salter found that the various ethnic minorities were represented largely by stereotyped personifications. Of the nearly 900 characters in these stories, eighty-four per cent were "American." Virtually all of the nine per cent from the unpopular minorities were in minor roles; their occupation was always menial, and none appeared as a hero or heroine.[18] This does not mean that there was a conspiracy

---

[16] Robert Blake and Wayne Dennis, "The Development of Stereotypes Concerning the Negro," *Journal of Abnormal and Social Psychology*, XXXVIII (1943), 525–31.

[17] Anselm L. Strauss, "The Development and Transformation of Monetary Meanings in the Child," *American Sociological Review*, XVII (1952), 275–86.

[18] Bernard Berelson and Patricia J. Salter, "Majority and Minority Americans," *Public Opinion Quarterly*, X (1946), 168–90.

among the authors and editors to disparage certain minority groups; most of the writers probably thought of ethnic categories in these terms or else assumed that their readers would not find more favorable characterizations plausible. Since the study was made, there has been a deliberate effort within the mass communications industry to correct some of these beliefs. Ethnic stereotypes are reaffirmed for the most part by people who harbor no ill will; they are unintentionally perpetuated as by-products of other activities. This is also true of other conventional meanings.

Children acquire the meanings that are shared in the groups in which they are reared. Since the same objects are characterized differently in each group, this can lead to misunderstandings. To a child growing up in a middle class suburb a policeman is an official to be respected and obeyed; he is accepted as an authority figure, and his integrity is not questioned. But to a child growing up in a slum area a "cop" is viewed as a hypocrite who demands bribes while parading in public under the cloak of respectability. Reporting any infractions to the police, therefore, becomes a reprehensible offense. Differences in the meanings of the most familiar objects were shown in a study by Dennis comparing American, Lebanese, and Sudanese children. A dog was regarded by forty-nine per cent of the Americans as a pet, but to sixty-six per cent of the Lebanese and to sixty-two per cent of the Sudanese it was a guard. Sand was a plaything for forty-one per cent of the Americans, but fifty-eight per cent of the Lebanese saw it as material for building.[19] Many Americans think of Communists as horrible creatures, and it is incomprehensible to them that in other parts of the world, especially where people live in great privation, they may be hailed as the only ray of hope in an otherwise forlorn existence. The manner in which each person is oriented toward his world depends upon the groups in which he participates.

Adaptation is a characteristic of all living organisms, but in the case of human beings it occurs within a social context. Men develop their ability to participate in organized groups through participation, at first in a clumsy manner but eventually in ways that resemble the accepted patterns. Socialization is basically a selective process; one repeats those acts which prove expedient and rejects those which

[19] Wayne Dennis, "Uses of Common Objects as Indicators of Cultural Orientations," *Journal of Abnormal and Social Psychology*, LV (1957), 21–28.

result in pain or the loss of the support of others. Although each person solves his problems in his unique way, limitations are placed upon him by other people who have already developed fixed ways of meeting recurrent situations. Conventional meanings are behavioral systems shaped in the course of the successive adjustments of each person to the requirements of group life.

Induction into Symbolic Environments

Since concerted action is so much easier when there is consensus, learning to participate effectively in an organized group requires gaining some appreciation of its symbolic environment. It becomes necessary for a newcomer to learn not only the accepted categories and their symbols, but also the unstated assumptions about the ways in which these units are interrelated. Only then can people with diverse backgrounds of experience anticipate things together and make the necessary adjustments to one another.

A newcomer usually enters a group which already has an established universe of discourse. The comprehension of this perspective requires learning the language; after that, conventional meanings can be shaped through linguistic communication. This is true not only of children but of any neophyte. When a first offender encounters the underworld in prison or when a thrill seeker becomes a drug addict, he must learn the argot of the new group. Since symbols are easily formed substitutes for complex meanings, the manipulation of meanings as well as their elaboration is simplified. Role-taking is also made easier as one learns the vocabulary of motives taken for granted in the group. Since so many conventional meanings are acquired through communication, ascertaining how a newcomer learns to use symbols is an important problem.

In every universe of discourse there are norms on how words are to be articulated and the order in which this is to be done. The correct construction of vocal gestures is learned through natural selection, and the responses of other people play a crucial part in this process. According to students of language, children throughout the world between the ages of about three months to a year are able to utter an extensive range of sounds—far more than are used in any of the languages spoken by their parents. This period is sometimes referred to as the "babbling stage." In each language there are certain sounds that are never used, and adults who have become accustomed to this are usually unable to utter them. Most Americans, for example, have difficulty in pronouncing a German "ü," nor can they trill or roll their "r's" in Latin style. In both Chinese and Japanese there are sounds that fall somewhere between the English "l" and "r," and most natives of both cultures are unable to pronounce either English letter clearly. Such limitations account for much of what is called a "foreign accent." But infants in the babbling stage are apparently able to make all of these sounds; hence, some students of linguistics have referred to this period as the "vocal stone quarry" of all languages. This amazing repertoire of sounds is progressively restricted as a child grows older until, in time, each person's enunciation resembles that of the other people in his group. This occurs partly through the imitation of their vocalizations, sometimes in games in which adults repeat the desired sounds until a child learns to coordinate his vocal musculature in the correct manner. Even more important, unless the child can form gestures that resemble the conventional symbols, others are not likely to respond, for they have no basis for recognizing what he is attempting to say. There is a successive correction of vocal activity, then, until it becomes understandable.[20] Conventional bodily gestures are built up in much the same manner.

The crucial importance of the responses of other people in the shaping of gestures into conventional patterns is shown by cases of blind or deaf children who are cut off from one of the channels of testing and correction. Hearing one's own vocalizations is an essential part of learning to speak, and only a very small percentage of children who are born deaf can be taught to speak like other people, even though their vocal organs and intelligence are normal. The fact that they can read, write, and lip read proves that they have the ability to learn a language, but they cannot articulate sounds in the accepted manner. Their speaking voice is flat; articulation is labored; and nuances of meaning are not conveyed by inflections of the voice. Those who have never heard the speech of others have no models for the construction of their own gestures.[21]

[20] Cf. Morris M. Lewis, Infant Speech (New York: Harcourt, Brace & Co., 1936), pp. 55–102.

[21] Clarence V. Hudgins, "Problems of Speech Comprehension in Deaf

Similarly, the facial expressions of blind children differ considerably from those who can see. Their instinctive responses—such as smiling in joy or crying in pain or in fear—are identical with those of other people. However, they are unable to construct the conventional gestures. Since they cannot see the facial expressions of other people nor see themselves in a mirror, they do not have an adequate conception of the configuration to be formed by their facial musculature.[22]

Gestures are used as symbols for conventional meanings. While learning to form gestures properly, one must also learn which meanings are represented by each of them. In his study of the development of consensus, Latif contended that it is the responses of older people to the various gestures of the infant that provide the basis for shared meanings. A child who is hungry wriggles and moves his whole body in the direction of the nursing bottle. Others who happen to be present make inferences on the basis of these movements about the child's intentions, and cooperate by handing him the bottle. As this procedure is repeated, the consistent cooperation of the adults reduces the various movements to a simple gesture—pointing to the bottle, uttering a sound, or some other phase of the total movement. Whenever this gesture is produced, it comes to stand for the entire act that had once been necessary. The gesture becomes a symbol for the entire movement. Similarly, to the extent that the adults are able to impute a desire for the bottle whenever they perceive this gesture, it has the same meaning for them. It is important to note that the gesture is being used as an instrument, as one of the means of consummating an impulse. This objective is being sought in a cooperative context in which other people are assisting the infant in his efforts. The closer the gesture approximates the conventional symbol, the more likely it is to elicit the desired responses with minimum delay. Even at this very rudimentary level, meanings emerge in a social matrix; living and acting together are prerequisites for the development of symbolic communication.[23]

Children," *The Nervous Child*, IX (1951), 57–63; and Helton McAndrew, "Rigidity and Isolation: A Study of the Deaf and the Blind," *Journal of Abnormal and Social Psychology*, XLIII (1948), 476–94.

[22] John S. Fulcher, " 'Voluntary' Facial Expression in Blind and Seeing Children," *Archives of Psychology*, XXXVIII (1942), no. 272; and Jane Thompson, "Development of Facial Expression of Emotion in Blind and Seeing Children," *ibid.*, XXVII (1941), no. 264.

[23] Israil Latif, "The Physiological Basis of Linguistic Development and of

In one of his early studies, Piaget showed that much of a child's early vocalizations does not constitute speech directed toward other people. He pointed out that in "egocentric speech" children often repeat remarks for the sheer pleasure of talking, that children often talk to themselves as if they were thinking aloud, not addressing anyone in particular, and that children in groups often engage in a collective monologue in which each talks and pays no attention to what the others are saying. He showed that many of the difficulties in communication between children arise from the fact that the speaker does not bother to tell the others what he himself already knows; this implies that his perspective is entirely personal. In time, the child comes to differentiate himself more clearly from other people and to develop some appreciation of the fact that the perspectives of others are different from his own. Then he is able to assume the roles of others and to adapt his remarks to the end of eliciting their cooperation. This type of vocal activity Piaget called "socialized speech," speech articulated for the benefits of others. It was his contention that the ratio of egocentric to socialized speech diminishes as children grow older; with increasing age a larger proportion of their total vocal activity is addressed to other people.[24] Since gestures are used in social contexts as instruments, it is not long before children restrict themselves to the symbols to which others respond. Those gestures which prove expedient are used repeatedly and become fixed in habit.

As the child's capacity for participating in concerted action develops, he becomes increasingly sensitive to the views of others, and his egocentric speech is checked. Vigotsky has suggested the provocative hypothesis that it does not actually disappear but is internalized to become thinking—subvocal communication with oneself. Taking Piaget's study as his point of departure, Vigotsky noted that the distinctive characteristic of inner speech is its abbreviated character. When we are thinking, it is not necessary for us to define familiar terms or to cover each logical step in an argument, as we might in presenting a case to someone else. In his experiments he showed that egocentric speech also has this abbreviated character, and that it becomes more abbreviated with increasing

the Ontogeny of Meaning," *Psychological Review*, XLI (1934), 55–85, 153–76, 246–64. Cf. Lindesmith and Strauss, *Social Psychology, op. cit.*, pp. 159–96.
    [24] Jean Piaget, *The Language and Thought of the Child*, Marjorie Gabain, trans. (New York: Harcourt, Brace & Co., 1926).

age. Although egocentric speech decreases with age and finally seems to disappear, it merely becomes inaudible to other people. While his demonstration was not conclusive, his argument is plausible.[25]

By learning to think in conventional terms, one becomes a participant in the symbolic environment of the group. He orients himself in time and space in terms of the coordinates used in the group; he locates himself in its history, and he projects his career into the future—a conception that is organized through its symbols. He thinks in the same terms that he uses to speak and others use in speaking to him. This makes it possible to compare experiences, to sharpen meanings that are inadequate, and to receive instruction about matters that are not clear.

Students of socialization sometimes underestimate the extent to which meanings are learned or clarified through symbolic communication. The natural history of our orientation toward any object begins with a period when we are doubtful and confused, progresses toward the stage when our expectations become fairly well-defined, and then proceeds to the point where action is automatic and unconscious. Throughout this process we constantly rely upon reports from others about what we are supposed to experience. Our reliance upon other people is shown in our attempts to clarify meanings that are vague. Most Americans expect to "fall in love," but many are not quite sure of how they are supposed to feel when it happens. This results in persistent and anxious queries, which usually elicit such unsatisfactory replies as "you'll know when it happens." An illustration may be drawn from Becker's study of marihuana addiction.

A novice rarely gets "high" on his first smoke, for marihuana cannot be smoked like tobacco if one is to become intoxicated. He must learn the proper smoking technique through observation and imitation. Even after learning the technique some people do not notice any difference, although experienced addicts can recognize their symptoms. The organic transformations occur, but the smoker is often unable to identify the experience as the condition of being "high." It is through discussions with other users of the drug that the newcomer becomes sensitive to particular sensations, such as the rubbery feeling in his legs. He must first learn how to identify those sensations which constitute the desired effect and then attribute

[25] Vigotsky, "Thought and Speech," op. cit.

them to the drug. It was Becker's contention that a person does not become addicted to marihuana unless he learns to identify the sensations, associates them with the drug, acquires the techniques for producing them, and learns to enjoy them.[26] Many meanings are clarified, then, when other people can block out and define for us what it is that we are supposed to experience.

Most adults take their symbolic environment so much for granted that they have difficulty in imagining their experiences prior to induction. There is reason to believe that the pre-linguistic world of the child is drastically different from any of his later experiences. In a thoughtful study, Schachtel contended that memories of events that take place early in life are necessarily vague because an infant has no linguistic symbols with which to hold and manipulate units of experience. Adult memory is couched in categories that are conventional and logic that is utilitarian, but childhood experiences are not so organized. The child lives in the immediate present. Lacking a symbolic framework, he has no way of measuring the passage of time. Only after he learns a language can he form a conception of himself and locate it within some kind of temporal scheme. It is for this reason that adults so often misunderstand children, and find their own infancy a mystery. Since many of the experiences of children do not fit into a conventional mold, they seem to be amorphous and meaningless.[27]

In the course of their development most children participate in a variety of groups, many of them made up of others their own age. The perspectives shared in such peer groups, while they are not entirely alien, are somewhat different from the symbolic environment of adults. When Hartley and his associates asked children in a lower class neighborhood in New York to identify, in ethnic terms, themselves and others in the area, they found that a different frame of reference was used. Categories that most adults would regard as mutually exclusive were apparently not incompatible for the children.[28] In their study of how children learn to use money, Strauss

[26] Howard S. Becker, "Becoming a Marihuana User," *American Journal of Sociology,* LIX (1953), 235–42.
[27] Cf. Ernest G. Schachtel, *Metamorphosis* (New York: Basic Books, 1959), pp. 279–322.
[28] Eugene L. Hartley, Max Rosenbaum, and Shepard Schwartz, "Children's Use of Ethnic Frames of Reference," *Journal of Psychology,* XXVI (1948), 367–86.

and Schuessler pointed out that many of the common errors made by youngsters do not arise from their being illogical. Until they grasp the various concepts involved in the use of money, their perception is undifferentiated; they appear to be blind to things that are readily understood by adults.[29] In his study of the changing preferences of children for offerings on the media of mass communication, Freidson found a regular transformation in tastes. Kindergarten children generally prefer humorous stories with animal or puppet characters; second graders like westerns; fourth graders like comedy and adventure, and sixth graders prefer comedy, adventure, and horror stories. Why should this consistent change in taste occur? He contended that as the children grow older, their conception of the world progressively approximates that of adults. Standards of judgment change, and drama that had once seemed plausible appears contrived. They may accept ghosts as real and become frightened, but when the hero with a six-shooter fires ten rounds without reloading, that is obviously "phoney."[30] To the extent that children at various age levels participate in different communication channels, their environment will differ from the world of adults. Their experiences are organized in terms of somewhat different categories, and there are bound to be some misunderstandings.

For most people, changes in outlook after reaching adulthood are so gradual that they are hardly noticed. But those who become involved in crisis situations sometimes gain access to new communication channels, and this may result in a drastic transformation. A citizen who is conscripted for military duty usually acquires a somewhat different perspective. In the beginning he is only vaguely familiar with his new roles, and he feels awkward and uncomfortable. He listens carefully as non-commissioned officers explain his duties; his mistakes are corrected through ridicule and sometimes through extra duty; he imitates those who have more experience. He learns a new vocabulary, not only of military terms but of special words used by soldiers to refer to familiar objects. Gradually he begins to talk, think, and act like other soldiers. The contrast between military and civilian perspectives is sharpened especially in time of

[29] Anselm Strauss and Karl Schuessler, "Socialization, Logical Reasoning, and Concept Development in the Child," *American Sociological Review,* XVI (1951), 514-23.

[30] Eliot Freidson, "Adult Discount: An Aspect of Children's Changing Taste," *Child Development,* XXIV (1953), 39-49.

war, but a recruit does not realize how much he has changed until he receives a well-meaning but useless gift from home, or leaves camp on furlough. The same kind of transformation occurs in the outlook of those hospitalized for chronic diseases. In his study of convalescence from paralytic poliomyelitis, Davis showed how different conceptions of time develop as patients become assimilated to the hospital world. The treatment procedure provides a new set of criteria for measuring one's progress—hydrotherapy, moving one's leg while lying in a prone position, standing while being held, taking one's first step. Patients and staff members alike think in these terms rather than of the number of months in confinement.[31]

The development of perspectives is apparently irreversible. Once an adult outlook is established, retrospection is necessarily from this standpoint. The difficulty of recapturing the past as it was originally experienced is shown in studies of hypnotic age regression. Prodigious feats of memory have been performed by people while in a hypnotic trance; minute details of events that took place on one's fourth or fifth birthday can sometimes be remembered. Since so much of current psychotherapy depends upon recalling such long lost experiences, there has been much interest in this phenomenon. Some subjects have even claimed to remember events that occurred long before learning a language.[32] To throw light on such contentions, Sarbin compared the performances of nine adult subjects on (a) tests administered when their age had been reduced by hypnotic suggestions to eight or nine, (b) the same tests taken when they were consciously pretending to be at that age level, and (c) the records of the same tests taken when the subjects were children. The results showed that there was no authentic age regression; all scores made by adults were higher than what each had made as a child. But what was done under hypnosis was found to resemble childhood performances more closely than the simulated attempts.[33] In another study Orne hypnotized ten subjects, ranging in age from seventeen to twenty-six, and reduced their ages to six; he then gave them a Rorschach test and asked for drawings and handwriting

[31] Fred Davis, "Definitions of Time and Recovery in Paralytic Polio Convalescence," *American Journal of Sociology*, LXI (1956), 582–87.

[32] Cf. Robert M. Lindner, *Rebel Without a Cause* (New York: Grune & Stratton, 1944).

[33] Theodore R. Sarbin, "Mental Age Changes in Experimental Regression," *Journal of Personality*, XIX (1950), 221–28.

samples. He was fortunate in having drawings made by one subject when he was six and the results of a Rorschach test taken by another subject at that age. He concluded that, while the drawings under hypnosis were childlike in conception and form, they were adult in execution. The performances on the projective test were also different, although he could not detect any consistent pattern.[34] These studies reveal that many otherwise forgotten events can be recalled under hypnosis, but they are seen from an adult perspective.

These observations support the view that socialization does not consist of the addition of elements to a total from which some could then be subtracted. Studies of regression in schizophrenia also point in this direction. Since behavior patterns integrated during infancy—sucking, biting, playing with feces, and masturbating—are found among adults suffering serious personality disorders, many psychiatrists contend that the victims have slipped back to an earlier stage of development. Those with severe psychoses are viewed as becoming desocialized. But Cameron asked whether the deterioration found in these patients actually constitutes a peeling off of previously acquired habits, or reorganization of a different sort. In a study already cited, he compared the reasoning of the patients with that of children and found some amazing differences. Over eighty per cent of the explanations of events given by children were in terms of motives, but almost half of the explanations given by the patients were in terms of "cause" and "effect"—the customary mode of reasoning for adults in our society. To be sure, the patients may use many childish tools, but not necessarily in a childish manner. Once an adult perspective has been attained, items are not merely subtracted and forgotten.[35] This suggests that the development of a psychosis constitutes an adaptation to an intolerable situation in which some of the behavior patterns well-established in early years are incorporated into a new outlook.

Socialization is a continuous process of communication in which a newcomer selectively incorporates into his behavioral sets those patterns of conduct that are sanctioned in the group. Once he learns the conventional meanings and symbols, he can participate with

---

[34] Martin T. Orne, "The Mechanism of Hypnotic Age Regression," *Journal of Abnormal and Social Psychology*, XLVI (1951), 213–25.

[35] Cameron, "Reasoning, Regression, and Communication in Schizophrenics," *op. cit.*; see also his "Deterioration and Regression in Schizophrenic Thinking," *Journal of Abnormal and Social Psychology*, XXXIV (1939), 265–70.

greater ease in a variety of collective enterprises. He learns to make more refined distinctions, and this in turn makes it possible for him to partake in even more complex forms of cooperation. With each communication channel that becomes accessible to him, he is introduced to a somewhat different symbolic environment.

The Formation of Defensive Fixations

Meanings vary considerably in stability. Most of them are flexible, in that the behavior patterns are altered with experience. But for each person there are some meanings that are rigid. Many of these compulsive orientations are private meanings of little consequence—a sense of disquietude upon perceiving a certain facial expression or exaltation upon hearing a particular combination of sounds. There are others, however, that interfere with successful participation in groups, and pressures are often brought to bear upon the person to transform his outlook. In many cases one learns to comply externally, but has difficulty in suppressing impulses. He may feel guilty or become convinced that he is abnormal. Each person has certain areas in which he is apparently unable to profit from experience, either because he does not notice contradictory cues or because he consistently misinterprets what he sees to support his original orientation.

The variation in the flexibility of meanings suggests that there may be at least two different kinds of behavioral systems, and a fruitful distinction has emerged from experimental psychology. As a result of his studies on learning among rats, Maier concluded that there are two ways in which stable behavior patterns develop. One is the formation of a *habit,* in which rats learn to act in a particular way by receiving rewards; the second is the development of a *fixation,* using the term somewhat differently from Freud, in which behavior patterns are established as *ad hoc* defenses against frustrating situations. Fixations are defensive tactics to avoid pain, hit upon accidentally while trying to cope with a difficult situation and thereafter repeated automatically with each similar threat. Maier was able to demonstrate experimentally that habits can be modified by altering the reward pattern; fixations, however, remain the same no matter what is rewarded. He also found that habits can be reinforced by additional gratifications but that fixations are not affected by further rewards. When rats are systematically punished for performing in a habitual manner, habits disappear; but punishment only increases the strength of fixations. Working on the development of relatively simple behavior patterns on the basis of physical pleasure (food) and pain (electric shock), Maier demonstrated that there are two clearly discernible modes of learning. He went on to argue that fixations constitute activities that are not goal-oriented.[36]

Although Maier has been very cautious about applying his findings, to human beings, psychiatrists have long assumed a similar position. Although they have been concerned with more complex meanings and with pain that is not necessarily physical, they have explained the formation of neurotic symptoms in much the same manner. When goal-oriented activity is blocked, some measure of satisfaction is derived from compensatory adjustments; when these reactions are repeated, they develop into rigid meanings. Psychiatrists have discussed a wide variety of phobias, tics, and obsessions that are apparently compulsive; they have shown that even conventionally accepted forms of activity can become compulsive. Some men work constantly, even when it is not necessary and they dislike it intensely. It is now widely believed that such behavior patterns are the products of frustration. They are defensive reactions, protective devices set off in threatening situations. Studies show that such patterns cannot be eliminated through punishment. Children who are scolded too severely for toilet accidents continue their bed wetting; those chastized for aggression become more aggressive; and those punished for dependency remain dependent.[37]

Although Maier's empirical findings have not been questioned, there has been some controversy among psychologists over his interpretation. Several critics have insisted that he was not justified in claiming that fixations are not goal-oriented, for even a protective ritual results in some kind of tension reduction.[38] For our purposes it

[36] Norman R. F. Maier, *Frustration: The Study of Behavior Without a Goal* (New York: McGraw-Hill Book Co., 1949).

[37] Robert R. Sears, Eleanor E. Maccoby, and Harry Levin, *Patterns of Child Rearing* (Evanston: Row Peterson & Co., 1957), pp. 484–86. Cf. Aubrey J. Yates, "The Application of Learning Theory to the Treatment of Tics," *Journal of Abnormal and Social Psychology,* LVI (1958), 75–82.

[38] Cf. F. Knöpfelmacher, "Fixations, Position Stereotypes, and their Relation to the Degree and Pattern of Stress," *Quarterly Journal of Experimental Psy-*

is important that behavior patterns may be established as defensive maneuvers as well as in the quest for gratification.

There is an extensive body of clinical evidence of fixations among human beings. In many cases a man is unconscious of these compulsive meanings, but there are instances in which he experiences an urgent impulse to do something that is proscribed and finds himself breaking out in a sweat. Sullivan pointed to excessive chattering as a defensive measure, a way of keeping people at a safe distance. The compulsive talker may have to gasp for air and repeat himself when he no longer has anything to say, but when his self-esteem is threatened, he talks on in desperation. A person may experience aggressive impulses whenever he feels compelled to do something against his will, or even when he observes someone else under coercion. He reacts negatively to all authority figures, however benevolent they may appear. Whenever he finds himself under orders, however trivial the matter, his reaction of rage is far out of proportion to what might otherwise be expected. In extreme cases, a person may even experience homicidal impulses in situations in which he is aware that his response is irrational.

The pursuit of pleasures can become compulsive for some people. There is increasing recognition in medical circles that obesity, if it is not glandular, is a psychiatric problem. As many people advised to diet by their doctor can testify, excessive eating is often compulsive. Intelligent people who know that they need only a small proportion of the food they consume have difficulty in checking their appetite. Sometimes, especially when dejected, they eat even when they are not hungry. The excessive consumption of alcohol is also compulsive for some people. Although many derive considerable pleasure from alcoholic beverages, there are some who drink to excess and enjoy neither the flavor nor the effects. They realize they are jeopardizing their own future as well as injuring others close to them, but they cannot stop drinking. Similarly, there are many smokers who dislike the flavor of tobacco, who get headaches from being in rooms filled with smoke, who are aware of the stench it leaves in hair and clothing, and who are familiar with the alarming correlation between cigarette smoking and lung cancer. It has been suggested that addic-

chology, V (1953), 150–58; Norman R. F. Maier and Paul Ellen, "Can the Anxiety-Reduction Theory Explain Abnormal Fixations?" *Psychological Review*, LVIII (1951), 435–45; and Joseph Wolpe, "Learning Theory and Abnormal Fixations," *ibid.*, LX (1953), 111–16.

tion to various narcotics, to gambling, and to various disapproved sex practices may also be of the same defensive character. The complexity of the phenomenon under consideration is suggested by the contention of psychoanalysts that many of these activities are not only defensive, but symbolic as well. Just as excessive eating may represent an effort to fill a psychological void, compulsive handwashing may constitute symbolic atonement.

These meanings are not only compulsive, but in most cases they are also rigid. The behavior pattern remains much the same whether or not it is appropriate in a given situation. One may be conscious of the fact that what he is doing is senseless and even dangerous, but such awareness does not enable him to exercise control. Nor are these meanings easy to transform through conscious effort. Since compulsive meanings do not arise through rewards, they cannot be altered by changing gratification patterns. This may be the reason why an addict cannot be bribed out of his addiction.

In tracing the development of fixations, psychoanalysts have focussed their attention upon the traumatic experience, a single terrifying event against which the behavior pattern presumably emerged as a defense. Some rigid meanings probably are formed in this manner. The blindness of a man whose eyes are not injured may be traced to the shock of witnessing his parents engaging in sexual intercourse, or a compulsive stutterer may find that his difficulties began upon being forced to kiss a dead relative at a funeral. Memories of frightful experiences are often repressed, and psychoanalytic therapy has been devoted largely to their recovery, the revaluation of such events from an adult perspective, and an attempt to institute conscious control. It seems unlikely, however, that all fixations are reactions to single events. Such meanings may be formed in response to anxieties that are sustained over a long period of time. An unreasonable resentment of all authority figures may develop in the course of many years of harassment by an ill tempered parent, and a morbid dread of confinement may be the product of repeated torture in the hands of an older brother who took delight in tying up his victims.

Some compulsive behavior patterns become established only after a conscious recognition of the source of pain. In his study of opiate addiction, Lindesmith found that the mere fact that one has taken drugs does not result in addiction; many hospital patients are given opiates over a long period of time to ease pain. Even the knowledge of having been drugged does not lead to addiction. Addiction occurs only when the victim is able to identify and define withdrawal symptoms. Once a body has become accustomed to the drug, a number of reactions occur when the supply is cut off. It starts with yawning, sniffles, and restlessness. It then builds up in intensity with severe stomach cramps, chills, fever, muscular spasms, nausea, vomiting, and diarrhea. Realizing that this horrible experience constitutes the readjustment of his body to the absence of the drug and that the discomfort can be relieved with an additional dosage is a necessary condition to becoming an addict.[39] Many victims want to "kick the habit," but their fear of the withdrawal symptoms forces them to continue.

Although the evidence is not conclusive, the hypothesis that fixations develop in a manner different from other meanings seems to be reasonable. Rigid meanings of all kinds, including stereotyped conceptions of people that do not change with experience, may be products of frustration. Many stereotypes are not merely careless generalizations; in some cases the individual has an important stake in maintaining them. It should be emphasized, however, that not all private meanings are defensive, nor are all defensive stances necessarily as inflexible as the cases cited. There are "bad habits" that can be terminated through conscious effort. Furthermore, there are many idiosyncratic meanings manifested in unorthodox impulses which rarely eventuate into overt conduct. They are inhibited out of consideration for the anticipated reactions of other people.

Summary and Conclusion

Successful participation in common life is possible for those who share conventional meanings, and the problem of socialization consists of accounting for their genesis. Socialization is essentially a communicative process. Each person gradually develops the ability to participate in organized groups through participation, having his efforts successively corrected until he is able to anticipate the reactions of others and to conform. The initially unorganized tend-

[39] Alfred R. Lindesmith, *Opiate Addiction* (Bloomington: Principia Press, 1947).

encies gradually attain coordination and refinement, and through repetition they become automatic. It is the recurrent and uniform reactions of other people that shape and fix behavior patterns. Meanings develop in each individual through a process of natural selection. The modes of conduct that enable a person to adjust successfully to the extant conditions of life are perpetuated to become a part of his orientation toward the world.

Although socialization is often regarded as the piece by piece accretion of habits, it is more fruitful to see it as the continuous adaptation of a living organism to its environment. All creatures struggle to survive and to reproduce in the life conditions in which they find themselves. But in the case of human beings the environment is larely conceptualized; objects are classified and labelled, often in an arbitrary manner. Furthermore, it includes other human beings, each one unique and making distinctive demands. Men adjust to the situations in which they find themselves and repeat those performances that appear to be successful. In measuring success, however, it is very important not to restrict it to mere physical survival. Men are concerned with status—personal and social—as well as a variety of symbolic gratifications. Most important of all, human beings are concerned with self-respect and the sentiments of those about them. Coming to terms with this human environment may include assuming defensive postures in situations that cannot be handled in any other way. Socialization, like motivation, can be explained in terms of the adjustive tendencies inherent in living organisms.

What this suggests is that the organization of functional units of all kinds—social structures, their component social roles, meanings (physical objects, personifications, and self-conceptions), and each one's personality—are the *products* of activity. Living organisms struggle to cope with life conditions, and the modes of response that are found useful are perpetuated and reinforced through continued use. Activity comes first, and structures emerge as the crystallization of successful attempts to live. Since each individual is unique and must cope with a distinct historical context, the structures that develop are in each instance different. But the processes of development are regular, and they can be described in a set of general principles.

Suggested References

HERRIGEL, EUGEN, *Zen in the Art of Archery*, R. F. C. Hull, trans. New York: Pantheon Books, 1953. A German professor's account of his experiences while learning archery from a Zen master, with a revealing discussion of the kind of social context in which the skill was developed.

KOFFKA, KURT, *The Growth of the Mind*, Robert M. Ogden, trans. New York: Harcourt, Brace & Co., 1928. A classic in the field of child development, written from the standpoint of Gestalt psychology and showing that socialization consists of the solution of a succession of problems.

LEWIS, MORRIS M., *Infant Speech*. New York: Harcourt, Brace & Co., 1936. A study of the manner in which a child learns a language, from the early cries of infancy to the mastery of conventional symbols, with particular attention to the contributions made by other people.

LINDESMITH, ALFRED R., *Opiate Addiction*. Bloomington: Principia Press, 1947. A neglected study of the conditions under which opiate addiction takes place—through the identification of withdrawal symptoms and the conscious attribution of these discomforts to the absence of the drug.

PIAGET, JEAN, *Play, Dreams, and Imitation in Childhood*, C. Gattegno and F. M. Hodgson, trans. New York: W. W. Norton & Co., 1951. An intensive study of the early development of three children, focusing on the beginnings of symbolic behavior in the context of play, when already organized neuromuscular systems come to be represented by conventional gestures.

SCHACHTEL, ERNEST G., *Metamorphosis*. New York: Basic Books, 1959. A psychoanalytic study of socialization, treating personal growth in terms of the realization of potentialities, in contrast to the tension-reduction approach of Freud and of this chapter.

15

The
development
of
self-control

Students of the history of
religion have often been embarrassed by the fact that some of the
most staid and respectable of our present day denominations had
their origin in orgiastic revivals, much like the more recent "holy
roller" meetings. In their ecstasy the worshippers gave way to rolling
on the ground, dancing and leaping, uttering short guttural sounds
like the barking of a dog, sobbing, singing, and shouting. Some
had convulsions; others had visions while in a trance. Some were
struck motionless and stood rigidly like statues for many hours. After
a few days the meetings would become so disorderly that the more
responsible leaders had to post guards, especially to discourage
sexual licentiousness.[1] Nor are religious revivals the only context in
which impulsive behavior is found. Celebrations and festivals sometimes get out of hand, and there are some cults in which this state of
frenzy is deliberately fostered. In the heat of intense excitement self-
control breaks down, and people who are otherwise quite ordinary

[1] Cf. Catherine C. Cleveland, *The Great Revival in the West, 1797-1805*
(Chicago: University of Chicago Press, 1916).

behave in ways that contrast sharply with their customary conduct.

Among human beings, unlike the social insects, the continuation of orderly group life is possible only when each participant is able to control himself. With few exceptions each person identifies himself as an individual of a particular sort, assumes certain responsibilities, and inhibits his impulses to maintain his conception of himself. Although most adults exercise some measure of autonomy, they cooperate voluntarily.

Infants are creatures of impulse, but most adults are not. Older people who have difficulty controlling themselves are called "childish," and a person who is carried away and acts impulsively later condemns his own behavior as "infantile." The mentally deficient or psychotic also have difficulty in disciplining themselves, and they are usually approached condescendingly as overgrown children. Something happens to most people between infancy and adulthood. Living up to one's responsibilities is a very complex form of behavior. How does this remarkable ability develop? A definitive answer cannot be given, but there are a number of hypotheses worthy of serious consideration.

The Dialectic of Personal Growth

Self-control by those who partake in concerted action depends upon their ability to respond to themselves. Before a man can inhibit and redirect impulses that are likely to be troublesome, he must get outside of himself, imagine his plan of action as others are likely to see it, and respond to this perceptual object. He must be able to experience and identify himself as a unit. He must also construct personifications of others and impute motives and expectations to them. All this calls for the ability to manipulate symbols. How does a child develop these complex skills?

Since most adults assume that they are organic units capable of independent action, it is difficult for them to realize that human beings are not born with self-conceptions. Although there is no conclusive proof, most child psychologists agree that a newly born infant is unable to differentiate between himself and his surrounding world. A baby covers his thumb and then cries over not being able to suck on it. He tugs on his toes and then screams in pain, refusing to let go when others try to relieve his distress. The infant merely has experiences; his outlook is necessarily egocentric, for he has as yet no frame of reference for identifying himself as an entity. Freud believed this period to be a euphoric one, for the infant presumably feels omnipotent. This sense of boundlessness he called the "oceanic feeling," and he was convinced that there always remains in each person a longing to return to this state of bliss.[2]

Self-awareness develops gradually, and it apparently begins with the definition of the boundaries of the body. Koffka suggested that this bipolarization of experience arises from the fact that the sensations emanating from one's body are reasonably consistent, in contrast to those from other sources. The experiences a person has with the parts of his body that he cannot see are sufficiently similar to those with the parts that he can see that he can set off the whole body as a separate entity.[3] But this process usually takes several years, and there is a period characterized by confusion between what is to be attributed to oneself and what belongs to the outside world. External events sometimes coincide with a child's desires, and he assumes that there is a necessary connection. It is not strange that children tend to form an animistic orientation toward their world. It is not until the child can conceive of himself as a separate unit that some measure of objectivity develops.[4]

But a self-conception consists of more than the mere delimitation of the body. It is a personification that places an individual within a social system, it involves recognizing a set of claims and obligations. Even after the boundaries of the organism are clearly established, there is a period during which a child does not fully understand his responsibilities. The sense of exercising control over one's conduct and being held accountable for it is something that develops gradually.

Cooley and Mead contended that a child learns to conceive of himself as an object by taking the roles of other people. In speaking

[2] Sigmund Freud, Civilization and Its Discontents, Joan Riviere, trans. (London: Hogarth Press, 1930), pp. 7–22. For a critical appraisal of this view see Schachtel, op. cit., pp. 3–77.

[3] Koffka, op. cit., pp. 319–24.

[4] Cf. Jean Piaget, The Child's Conception of the World, Joan and Andrew Tomlinson, trans. (New York: Harcourt, Brace & Co., 1929), pp. 123–68; and Gordon W. Allport, Personality: A Psychological Interpretation (New York: Henry Holt & Co., 1937), pp. 159–65.

of a "looking-glass self," Cooley meant that each person's orientation toward himself is a reflection of the manner in which he is treated. He imagines how he appears to someone else, imputes a judgment to the observer, and reacts with pride or mortification to the imputed judgment. Cooley pointed out that a child experiences himself as a recipient of action before he views himself as an actor. A child recognizes other people as objects before he sees himself as one, and he uses the names of others before learning his own. These observations have been confirmed by Bain.[5] By noting the manner in which other people treat him, especially the allowances made for him that are not made for others, a child begins to identify himself as a distinct object, and to locate himself within the interpersonal and cultural matrices into which he is cast.

This leads to the question of how the capacity for role-taking develops. Role-taking consists of constructing personifications and imputing motives to them. It involves the ability to recognize other human beings as objects capable of independent action, to appreciate the range of responses that are possible in a given situation, and to estimate the likelihood of one of these alternatives being chosen in dealing with the personification one identifies as himself. These are all difficult skills, and not all children develop them with equal ease. Indeed, there are extensive differences among adults in their ability to take the roles of others.

Baldwin pointed out that the first step consists of distinguishing people from things; after that, the child learns to recognize differences between individuals. One of the characteristics of human beings, in contrast to physical objects, is that their conduct appears more irregular and is therefore more difficult to anticipate. The same person may not only behave quite differently under different circumstances, but may even contradict himself. This comparative lack of uniformity in behavior gives the impression of autonomy, the capacity to act in terms of whims and caprices. Although there is a period during which children impute human desires and responses to inanimate objects, they eventually learn to approach this class of objects differently from the others. To face human beings with the

[5] Cooley, *Human Nature and the Social Order*, op. cit., pp. 183–85; and Read Bain, "The Self-and-Other Words of a Child," *American Journal of Sociology*, XLI (1936), 767–75. Cf. George H. Mead, "Cooley's Contribution to American Social Thought," *ibid.*, XXXV (1930), 693–706.

same monotonous expectations with which one handles a doorknob would be disastrous.[6]

Quite early in life the child learns the importance of responding to intentions. A number of psychologists have observed that children can perceive and respond to physiognomic gestures long before they understand conventional symbols. When a mother is very angry, the child seems to sense that it is time to go elsewhere, even though she has said nothing to that effect. The flashing of her eyes as well as other expressive movements are enough. Emotional reactions are goal-oriented. The person who is upset has an urgent disposition to attack, to flee, to vomit; those who do not take such inclinations into account may suffer mishaps. Sullivan contended that many personality disorders can be traced to early infancy, when the anxieties of the mother are communicated to the child through such expressive movements.[7]

In the intimacy of primary group life, each child is able to watch other people in a wide range of contexts. He develops a better appreciation of the kind of creatures human beings are by observing their reactions to various events. He learns the significance of humiliation by noting the kinds of situations in which people are mortified, their attempts to hide their feelings, and the manner in which they strike back at those deemed responsible. He learns the meaning of desire by noting how differently people act when they covet something—be it a toy, a shiny new automobile, or a team championship. The focussing of attention upon the object, the manifestations of anxiety at the possibility of losing it, the willingness to sacrifice other things for it, and the manner in which self-respect is compromised—these are soon recognized as indices of lust. As he develops an increasing appreciation of the properties that make people different from other classes of objects, he begins to attribute many of these traits to himself.

It is not long before most children realize that there is a discrepancy between overt behavior and inner dispositions. They increase their insight into the subjective experiences of others by examining their own reactions in similar situations. For example, at

[6] Cf. James M. Baldwin, *Mental Development in the Child and the Race* (New York: Macmillan & Co., 1906), pp. 318–22.

[7] Cf. Arnheim, *op. cit.;* and Sullivan, *The Interprersonal Theory of Psychiatry, op. cit.,* pp. 41–45.

some time everyone finds himself at the mercy of someone else. If the other party does not press his advantage and tries to make things easy for him, he is relieved and very grateful. Having undergone the anguish generated in such situations, it is easy to impute similar experiences to others. He then learns the meaning of mercy, and this may constitute the basis for considerations of decency and fair play. He learns that although almost everyone, under certain circumstances, feels aggressive impulses, most people learn to inhibit them, and some do not give any external indications of their anger. Each person uses his own experiences to illuminate the conduct of others.

Role-taking is largely intuitive until the child learns to use a language and acquires a vocabulary of motives. In each culture, recurrent behavior patterns are explained in terms of intentions, both approved and condemned, which are regarded as plausible grounds. Impulses and their accompanying images are often vague and amorphous; they are difficult to describe accurately. When such dispositions are classified and labelled as anger, erotic attraction, hunger, or hypertension, it becomes easier for each person to understand himself. Seeing someone else in a situation likely to elicit a given reaction within himself, one person can plausibly impute a similar experience to the other—regardless of the latter's overt moves and verbal protestations to the contrary.

Since role-taking involves the projection of one's own experiences to other people, limitations are set by the background of each individual. A person who has never been beaten to the point of losing consciousness can hardly be expected to understand the fear that haunts many boys who grow up in slum areas. The fortunate individual who has always been treated with affection in his family has great difficulty in comprehending the hatred that some people have for their parents. He feels that this is a violation of group norms on filial piety. In the same way, a child who grew up in a family torn with bitter conflicts suspects that most demonstrations of filial devotion are hypocritical.

The capacity for role-taking develops in a cumulative process in which human qualities come to be attributed to personifications of others and of oneself. The child initially learns to differentiate between himself and the rest of the world; then he learns to distinguish human beings from other objects. He forms an appreciation of the characteristics of human beings partly by observing others in a variety of situations and partly by examining his own experiences in similar contexts. As he masters the language of his group, he learns to classify his experiences and to impute motives to explain the things that men do. This process of going back and forth from one's own experiences to the characterizations of others Baldwin designated as the "dialectic of personal growth." He insisted that "the ego and the alter are born together."[8] Needless to say, this process continues throughout each person's life. Much of the wisdom attributed to elders is of this nature; it is an intuitive knowledge of human nature that accumulates from studying one's own reactions and observing the fate of others.

Adjustments to Significant Others

Everyone grows up in some kind of primary group, and his conception of himself gains its initial structure in doing what he must to acquire and maintain a satisfactory personal status. Since each primary group has a different culture, the standards in terms of which newcomers are judged vary considerably. In some circles size, virility, and strength are emphasized in judging men; in others, intellectual attainment is regarded as paramount, the other criteria being regarded as a survival of the barbaric past. In some groups honesty is the supreme value; in others, success is idolized. What would bring praise in one primary group would only invite scorn or severe punishment in another. Each person must meet the demands that are made in the circles in which he participates. There have been a number of attempts to account for the early development of children within such contexts, and several plausible generalizations may be drawn from psychoanalytic theory.

Since an infant is unable to exercise self-control, he attempts to consummate his impulses immediately. There is no ability to delay gratification, to accept frustration, or to cope with limiting or dangerous circumstances. These adjustments are made for the child by his mother or someone else who is responsible for his care. Each child is egocentric, but not autonomous. He is highly dependent upon someone else for survival, for the accomplishment of essential

[8] Baldwin, loc. cit. Cf. Wayne Dennis, "A Note on the Circular Response Hypothesis," Psychological Review, LXI (1954), 334–38.

adjustments which he subsequently controls for himself, and compliance with the demands of others arises initially from this dependency. Tenderness and provision for one's needs are gratifying, and a child cannot afford to alienate the source. Direction is introduced into his life from the outside. Psychiatrists have contended that the initial relationships formed by the child are of crucial importance in the development of his personality, for the manner in which such tasks are performed for him establishes orientations that cannot easily be altered. The manner in which a mother acts toward her child depends upon her sentiment toward him; if for any reason she feels resentful or ambivalent, this will be reflected in her treatment of the child, even though she may repress such inclinations from consciousness. Many meanings, including neurotic tendencies, become fixed early in life as a parent or parent surrogate inadvertently manifests repressed impulses.

Although a child is confronted from the beginning with demands that he curb his impulses, he continues to strive for immediate gratification. Long before his sense of personal identity is established, he struggles for autonomy. Initially he resists parental control in an attempt to realize his biological impulses. Later he learns to temper his outbursts, but he still strives to reserve an area in which he can make his own decisions. At this point there is no self-control as such, only compliance with the demands of people recognized as capable of enforcing them. Parents are not equal partners in the process of socialization; the norms that they impose constitute external conditions to which the child must adjust.

For most children, the voluntary inhibition of impulses begins with attempts to please those whom they admire. Within primary groups older people are often perceived as omnipotent. They are bigger, stronger, faster, and better coordinated; they have countless skills that are far beyond the reach of any child. It is not unusual for a child to set up one or more of his elders—his father, older brother, or an uncle—as an object of hero-worship. Nor is hero-worship confined to the family. In peer groups the gang leader may command considerable respect. Those who idolize temporarily surrender their independence in recognition of the hero's superior judgments and skills and permit crucial decisions to be made for them. They also derive satisfaction from identifying with him. Boys in gangs take great pride in the toughness of their leader and in the deference with which he is addressed by outsiders. Some people, often designated as "passive-dependent," apparently never outgrow this phase of their life.

Many meanings take shape during the unconscious imitation of heroes. Freud contended that a child identifies vicariously with those whom he admires and unconsciously copies their behavior patterns. The personification of his hero represents what he would like to be; it becomes a model, an ideal. Mannerisms, dialect, personal habits, as well as ways of playing interpersonal roles may be imitated from his father, gang leader, or someone else who is greatly admired. In adulthood many a man is amazed to be told by an old family friend or relative that whenever he is irritated with his wife, he treats her just as his father had treated his mother in similar situations. Members of the same family often develop similar postural sets and gestures. A wife may scold her children in the same manner as her husband chastises her—by grimacing, screaming, or maintaining stony silence. Thus, voluntary conduct is initially patterned in making adjustments to specific people.[9]

The unconscious imitation of significant others is important in that it provides the basis for an appreciation of the roles of other people. In imitating his teacher, a child performs in situations in which she plays a conventional role. He thereby begins to get some inkling of her responsibilities—toward himself as well as toward his fellow students. Studies of children ranging in age from three to seven show that they begin to differentiate parental roles quite early; the father is seen as a provider and the mother as a housekeeper.[10] In coming to terms with the authority figures by whom he is surrounded, the child learns to act first in terms of one party and then another. By observing and imitating each of these people, he comes to appreciate their interests and expectations. This is the beginning

[9] Sigmund Freud, "The Passing of the Oedipus Complex," *Collected Papers, op. cit.,* Vol. II, pp. 269–76. Cf. David P. Ausubel, *Ego Development and the Personality Disorders* (New York: Grune & Stratton, 1952), pp. 41–473; David Beres, "The Person and the Group: Object Relationships," in *Psychoanalysis and Social Work,* Marcel Heiman, ed. (New York: International Universities Press, 1953), pp. 53–75; and Talcott Parsons, "Social Structure and the Development of Personality," *Psychiatry,* XXI (1958), 321–40.

[10] Helen M. Finch, "Young Children's Concepts of Parent Roles," *Journal of Home Economics,* XLVII (1955), 99–103; and Sina M. Mott, "Concept of Mother," *Child Development,* XXV (1954), 99–106.

of vicarious participation in the lives of others.[11]

Another context in which children get practice in role-taking is spontaneous play. They often play games in which they enact in turn the roles of all the parties involved; vicariously they identify not only with familiar people but also with inanimate objects, feared objects, and animals. A child who is playing house by himself may do something he has been told is naughty; he then scolds himself from the standpoint of his mother. He is taking her role, only he is acting it out overtly rather than in his imagination. In such activities we see the beginnings of the process of getting outside of oneself and seeing different roles in relation to one another. To be sure, the role-taking is still rudimentary; but play is very important in socialization, for it is in such transactions that behavior patterns begin to crystallize into well-organized meanings and roles.

Initially a child forms a number of specific self-images. He is one kind of person to the grocer, another to his father, another to the postman, and still another to each of his neighbors. He forms a different perceptual object as he addresses himself from the standpoint of each of the parties with whom he interacts, and at first there is apparently no integration of these diverse experiences.[12]

The disparate images gradually become integrated as a child is approached in a consistent manner. The scion of a wealthy family is always addressed with deference and consideration, even by older people. An attractive child with a friendly smile is everywhere greeted with reciprocating smiles and affection, just as a sadistic child with a surly, defiant countenance is repeatedly rebuffed. If a boy is told over and over by his parents that he is "naughty," if the neighbors refuse to permit their children to play with him, if the local merchants become apprehensive whenever he appears on the scene, if his teacher reminds him constantly that he is hopeless, it is not long before he sees himself as a "bad" boy. He certainly will not go out of his way to be "good," since such conduct is not expected of him. When an object so consistently treated is simultaneously ad-

[11] Cf. Faris, *op. cit.*, pp. 73–83; and Louisa P. Howe, "Some Sociological Aspects of Identification," *Psychoanalysis and the Social Sciences*, IV (1955), 61–79.

[12] Mead, *Mind, Self, and Society, op. cit.*, pp. 149–54. Cf. Lawrence K. Frank, "Play in Personality Development," *American Journal of Orthopsychiatry*, XXV (1955), 576–90.

dressed by the same symbol, the task of integrating diverse experiences is simplified. As a child learns to identify himself by a particular name, the most commonly used symbol for himself, he develops a clearer conception of the unit, its attributes, and its responsibilities.

Self-control involves a person's responding to the anticipated reactions of other people with whom he is participating in a common transaction, thereby enabling him to inhibit impulses that are likely to cut off their cooperation. This complex process is readily observable in children who have not yet learned to think inaudibly, for they argue aloud with the supposed responses of significant others. A child may want to play with a goldfish and begins to reach into the bowl, but he reproaches himself from the standpoint of his mother: "No! No! Bad boy! Don't do that!" Upon saying this, he draws back. He then tells himself, "But I just want to pet it," and approaches the bowl again. In young children, the inner opposition of conflicting impulses through which self-control occurs is manifested overtly in linguistic activity. The proscriptions are often put in the very words used by specific people. This suggests that social responsibilities are initially obligations felt to particular people and only later generalized into moral principles.

The perceptual object that a person forms of himself is shaped largely by the consistent responses of significant others. Self-conceptions emerge in a social process in which the anticipated responses of these people become incorporated into one's acts. By observing the people with whom he is in constant association, a child learns how to do many things; without deliberate effort he adopts many of their beliefs as his own. In a study of fifty high school freshmen and their parents, Helper asked each student to describe himself, the person he would like to be, what he rejects in himself, and his mother. He also asked each of the parents to characterize in comparable terms himself, his spouse, his child, the person he would like to be, and his conception of an ideal child. It was expected that the self-conception of each student would resemble the model of an ideal child described by his parents, since his behavior patterns would develop along the lines most rewarded by them. The data did not confirm the hypothesis tested, but they did suggest that more satisfactory results might be achieved with a few changes in the study design.[13]

[13] Malcolm M. Helper, "Learning Theory and the Self Concept," *Journal of Abnormal and Social Psychology*, LI (1955), 184–94; and "Parental Evaluations

The particular manner in which his significant others enact their conventional and interpersonal roles has much to do with the manner in which an individual learns to control himself.

The harshness with which a person punishes himself for deviant behavior is related to the manner in which he had been punished by others. Freud believed that, since a child learns to check himself by identifying with authority figures, he develops an unreasonably severe conscience if such persons are excessively punitive. If significant others are very insistent upon conformity, not relaxing even when extenuating circumstances may warrant it, the child may subsequently set the same rigid standards for himself. On the other hand, a child brought up in an overly permissive atmosphere may simply assume that everything exists for his personal benefit and not feel badly even when he injures or inconveniences others.

Of particular interest are the imaginary companions that many children construct—phantom siblings, make-believe friends, fairies and elves, anthropomorphized animals, dolls, and other objects. Most studies of such personifications have been made by psychiatrists, who assume that they are symptoms of mental disorders, created to compensate for the lack of warmth in real life. In one study of 210 children of pre-school age, forty-five were found to have imaginary companions; of this number twenty-one were the only child in the family, and twenty-one others had but one sibling each. The observers noted that although the forty-five had many opportunities for playing with other children, they did not.[14] But another fascinating question arises. In taking the roles of real people a child can organize his conduct in response to the demands that are actually made upon him. But an imaginary companion is a creation of the child himself, who can endow it with whatever attributes he wishes and have the personification address him in any way he desires. Whence the organization of the demands made upon the child from this standpoint? It has been noted that play involving such companions sometimes reflects parental attitudes, and Bender and Vogel have reported the case of a girl who had two imaginary associates—one endowed with all the virtues as she understood them, and the other with all the defects that she recognized in herself.[15]

of Children and Children's Self-Evaluations," *ibid.*, LVI (1958), 190–94.

[14] Louise Ames and Janet Learned, "Imaginary Companions and Related Phenomena," *Journal of Genetic Psychology*, LXIX (1946), 147–67.

[15] Lauretta Bender and Frank B. Vogel, "Imaginary Companions of Children," *American Journal of Orthopsychiatry*, XI (1941), 56–65.

But the mystery still remains. Imaginary companions are apparently agents of socialization created by those who are being socialized.

All children are assertive at birth but are forced to conform to the minimum requirements set forth by their elders because of their dependence upon them. The growing child meets his obligations by learning conventional roles, first by imitating those around him and gradually by gaining a clearer grasp of the expectations of others. It is through vicarious identification with other people that a child is transformed into an effective participant of his group. As he develops some measure of independence, he voluntarily does his share in collective transactions. But *the manner in which each person controls himself* is in each case unique, for it *develops in response to the specific demands made upon him by the particular people with whom he is in sustained contact.*

Participation in Concerted Action

But a person restricted by the demands of his immediate associates is not independent. *He achieves the freedom to choose, even when his preferences happen to be contrary to the interests of significant others, to the extent that he develops a more comprehensive perspective, one that transcends that of any particular primary group.*[16] Sooner or later each child ventures beyond the confines of intimate circles to interact with strangers who will not make exceptions for his idiosyncrasies. At first, not too much is expected of a newcomer, but he learns before long that the conduct of those playing well-defined roles is highly circumscribed. He learns the component claims and obligations that make up various roles, some through actual participation and others through observation. In this way his repertoire grows, and most adults have some understanding of a variety of conventional roles, including many that they themselves never enact. Each person broadens his outlook as he engages in new forms of activity, especially in organized groups with different cultures.

Many children are socialized in peer groups even when their parents fail to meet their responsibilities. In every community the children in each age level have a language and culture of their own,

[16] Mead, *Mind, Self, and Society, op. cit.,* pp. 152–64.

one that is remarkably persistent, which develops independently of the adult world.[17] Except for the overprotected, each child must struggle for status in a succession of such social worlds. Especially when participating in organized games—whether it be marbles, baseball, soccer, tag, or hide-and-go-seek—he faces the necessity of taking a number of different roles simultaneously. For example, a second-baseman must be able to anticipate the movements of the batter, the base-runners, and his teammates playing first-base and shortstop if he is to execute a double-play. Successful participation in any game rests upon the ability to take the roles of any or all of the other participants on the field. Games are important in socialization in that the roles of the participants are specified; what each player may or may not do is clearly delineated, the goals of the transaction are defined, and the area of personal choice is limited. It has been noted that many children learn of discipline and responsibility in juvenile gangs, even delinquent gangs, to an extent not matched at home.

This is not to suggest that a child must participate in sports to learn conventional roles. Social psychologists are only pointing to the organized game as an example of the kind of setting in which self-control develops—concerted action carried out in terms of group norms. Other organized activities that are almost unavoidable include going to school, attending parties, and performing chores for spending money. In each context a child must learn to comply with group expectations. It has been pointed out, however, that overprotected children who are held back from games—an only child or one who is sickly or clumsy—often encounter difficulties in interpersonal relations later in life. It is possible that lack of experience in the free give and take of peer groups, where mistakes are rudely corrected, blunts one's sensitivity to the interests of other people.

What is significant about participating in organized groups is that the roles that a newcomer is asked to play are standardized and *impersonal*. Second-baseman is a conventional role. Regardless of who plays the position, he is expected to perform in certain ways in recurrent situations. The differences in the skills of various players are recognized, of course, but any individual who plays the role is expected to do his best to approximate the ideal performance.

[17] Cf. Iona and Peter Opie, *The Lore and Language of Schoolchildren* (London: Clarendon Press, 1959).

Through such participation each child learns how the various component roles fit together for the accomplishment of the collective goal—scoring points, winning sets, or whatever else it may be. After having played football, one appreciates the importance of blockers; he learns that even the most skillful runners cannot get far without their aid. In this way each newcomer begins to appreciate the reciprocating claims and obligations that make up the various interrelated roles.

Well-established activities proceed according to rules. There are conventional norms which apply to everyone. This is the mark of an organized group; its procedures enjoy a high degree of formalization and are not subject to the whims of those who happen to be present. When special allowances are made, it is by common consent. For example, if one of the participants happens to be crippled, some of the rules may be abrogated in order to make the contest more fair; but everyone knows that an exception is being made because of unusual circumstances. The standards of judgment in terms of which the participants evaluate themselves and one another are also impersonal. Skills are defined socially, and those who most closely approximate the accepted ideals win esteem. Those who wish to excel must cultivate the skills that are valued in the group.

In organized groups, failure to comply with norms results in the invocation of negative social sanctions. Those who refuse to conform are punished or ejected. The special considerations that one receives in primary groups are no longer forthcoming. One must earn his way in the larger world, and the manner in which he is treated depends to a large extent upon his willingness to do his part. In his study of moral judgments, Piaget noted that an appreciation of group norms develops slowly. At first a child merely imitates his seniors and does not actually understand the rules he may be following. Then he sees rules from an egocentric standpoint, using them to his personal advantage. But, as other psychologists have also observed, the child begins to make grudging concessions once he realizes that in a state of anarchy only the strongest has his way but that each gets something when everyone follows the rules. When a child has learned this, he places considerable emphasis upon rules, mostly in self-defense. Mutual understanding emerges in the course of participating in cooperative enterprises. Once they have mastered the code, children apparently derive pleasure from juridical discussions in which rules are considered for their own sake.[18]

In forming an object of himself as a participant in concerted action, the child begins to assume a broader perspective. He evaluates his own performance, not only from the standpoint of the individuals present, but also from the outlook which constitutes the social world of people who engage in such activities. In the words of Mead, he constructs a self-image by taking the role of a "generalized other" rather than that of specific individuals. In each reference group there are generally accepted standards of conduct against which each person can measure himself, and those who are enacting a conventional role are judged in comparison with their predecessors. An athlete cannot become a star merely by pleasing a few friends, nor can a student body president be evaluated as an official except in comparison with other presidents. In his study of how children learn to use money, Strauss showed that a child finally succeeds when he can assume an abstract perspective, appreciate the roles of seller and customer, and discount some of his own unique interests.[19] It is in this manner that men learn to play conventional roles. Each person uses a perspective shared by all of the participants in the transaction and controls himself to comply with their expectations.

The capacity for moral conduct develops as an individual learns to exercise upon himself the controls previously wielded by others. An infant is subject to surveillance and direct intervention, for he does as he pleases until someone stops him. This is followed by a period of self-control based upon fear of punishment or anticipation of reward, merely an extension of external control. But once a person has assimilated a group perspective, he becomes a society in miniature and automatically perceives himself from this standpoint. Should he violate a norm, he punishes himself. Even though his misdeed has not been detected by someone else, he is stricken by feelings of guilt. Most adults voluntarily do what they themselves regard as right and decent, and since the outlook of each person coincides with that of his associates, they can participate together in a moral order.

[18] Jean Piaget, *The Moral Judgment of the Child,* Marjorie Gabain, trans. (Glencoe: Free Press, 1948), pp. 1–69. Cf. Susan Isaacs, *Social Development in Young Children* (London: George Routledge & Sons, 1933).

[19] Anselm L. Strauss, "The Development of Conceptions of Rules in Children," *Child Development,* XXV (1954), 193–208.

As a child goes out beyond his primary groups, he learns that human beings are classified and that many rules apply differently to people in different categories. Each child must place himself in terms of social status. Once he has located himself within a community, he recognizes certain expectations on the part of others as well as his own responsibilities, obligations he assumes by virtue of being a particular kind of human being. His overt behavior becomes more consistent as he controls himself to preserve his conception of himself.

In all known societies the lines of social differentiation in some way coincide with the distinction between the sexes. Since the roles of men and women are in most cases so clearly delineated, we tend to regard them as inherent in nature. To some extent this is true; men cannot bear children. But there is considerable evidence that sex roles are more arbitrary and learned. Each child is classified as male or female and is then taught the proper modes of conduct for that category; this classification becomes an integral part of each person's self-conception. In an already cited study, Ellis showed that in most cases the traits and interests developed by hermaphrodites and pseudohermaphrodites are those regarded as typical of the sex in which they had been reared. Those who had been brought up as boys developed masculine interests, including an erotic attraction toward women, regardless of their actual biological classification.[20] Masculine and feminine roles are remarkably similar in many different societies, strengthening the impression that they are organically rooted. In a comparative study of child rearing practices in 110 cultures, Barry and his associates discovered that the same kinds of traits are frequently encouraged for each sex in otherwise dissimilar cultures. In the training of boys, emphasis is often placed upon developing self-reliance and achievement; in the training of girls emphasis is more frequently placed upon duty, nurturance, and obedience. But there are societies in which the educational pattern is different, and in these men and women behave quite differently.[21] Training is more important than organic

---

[20] A. Ellis, *op. cit.* Cf. Hurxthal and Musulin, *op. cit.*, Vol. II, pp. 1089–91.

[21] Herbert Barry, Margaret K. Bacon, and Irvin L. Child, "A Cross-Cultural Survey of Some Sex Differences in Socialization," *Journal of Abnormal and Social Psychology*, LV (1957), 327–32. Cf. Mirra Komarovsky, "Functional Analysis of Sex Roles," *American Sociological Review*, XV (1950), 508–16; and Margaret Mead, *Male and Female* (New York: William Morrow & Co., 1949).

differences, underscoring the hypothesis that self-conceptions are the product of consistent treatment on the part of other people. Particularly instructive is the manner in which children born into various strata learn of their respective stations in life. Some are given explicit instructions; those who are of the privileged classes are reminded repeatedly, "Remember, son, who you are." Those who are born into pariah groups learn sooner or later that they will not be accorded the same rights as other people. How do members of American minorities learn that they are different? Weaver asked 100 Negro children in the South when they first discovered their ethnic identity. Several mentioned differential treatment in a store, a restaurant, a train, a circus, or a neighbor's home. Some realized that they were different when they were sent to a separate school, taunted by other children, or denied something while playing. Some learned from their parents, when being admonished not to hurt white children or observing their submissive behavior. Such recognized differences were often reinforced by tales of slave ancestors and mistreatment.[22] In a series of studies, Clark showed that the concept of race differences as indicated by skin color develops from year to year and becomes fixed for most Negroes by the age of seven. At first many of the children showed a preference for light skin, but this changed with increasing age. When they were shown drawings which differed in skin color and asked which was more like themselves, children who were darker in complexion consistently made more accurate choices.[23] Radke and Trager studied the conceptions of 242 children in six Philadelphia schools—one without any Negroes, three in which Negroes constituted a minority, and two which were predominantly Negro. Inferior roles were consistently ascribed to Negroes by sixteen per cent of the Negroes and thirty-eight per cent of the others. The majority in both ethnic groups selected inferior housing for Negroes, regardless of where they themselves lived.

[22] Edward K. Weaver, "How Do Children Discover They Are Negroes?" *Understanding the Child,* XXIV (1955), 108–12. Cf. Eugene A. Weinstein, "Development of the Concept of Flag and the Sense of National Identity," *Child Development,* XXVIII (1957), 167–74.

[23] Kenneth B. and Mamie P. Clark, "The Development of Consciousness of Self and the Emergence of Racial Identification in Negro Pre-School Children," *Journal of Social Psychology,* X (1939), 591–99; "Skin Color as a Factor in Racial Identification of Negro Pre-School Children," *ibid.,* XI (1940), 159–69; and "Emotional Factors in Racial Identification and Preference in Negro Children," *Journal of Negro Education,* XIX (1950), 341–50.

When shown two dolls differing in color and asked which they preferred, fifty-seven per cent of the Negroes chose the darker doll, and eighty-nine per cent of the others chose the lighter one.[24] By placing themselves in their community and forming some appreciation of the manner in which various categories of people are evaluated, children incorporate customary patterns into their way of approaching the world.

From the manner in which they are treated, those who are in any way unusual learn to recognize themselves as being different. In a study of how a child with cerebral palsy comes to realize that he is not like other children, Bice observed that at first the victim does not recognize any difference and demands the same privileges and gifts as others, such as skates and bicycles he cannot use. Even after some of the differences are recognized, there is initially little ego-involvement; a child may say without much concern, "This arm is no good; I'm going to get a new one." There is considerable variation in the age at which the victim realizes fully that he is handicapped, and the behavior of others plays a crucial part. Many parents unintentionally overstress the importance of developing substitute capacities to compensate for the deficiencies. Taunts by other children as well as having to stay home when others go to school provide convincing proof of being different. In time each becomes reconciled to the fact that in many situations he must be content just to watch.[25] Those who are committed to an insane asylum usually deny belonging there, but most of them learn before long to conceive of themselves as being "sick." Everyone, including their fellow inmates, treats them as if they were incapacitated.[26] Previously cited studies of plastic surgery also show the extent to which differential responses on the part of other people fix personifications of oneself as unusual.

In the course of his life each person makes his way through a dis-

[24] Marion J. Radke and Helen G. Trager, "Children's Perceptions of the Social Roles of Negroes and Whites," Journal of Psychology, XXIX (1950), 3–33.

[25] Harry V. Bice, "Some Factors that Contribute to the Concept of Self in the Child with Cerebral Palsy," Mental Hygiene, XXXVIII (1954), 120–31. Cf. Ednita P. Bernabeu, "The Effects of Severe Crippling on the Development of a Group of Children," Psychiatry, XXI (1958), 169–94; and E. Jane Watson and Adelaide M. Johnson, "The Emotional Significance of Acquired Physical Disfigurement in Children," American Journal of Orthopsychiatry, XXVIII (1958), 85–97.

[26] Cf. Erving Goffman, "The Moral Career of the Mental Patient," Psychiatry, XXII (1959), 123–42.

tinct combination of social worlds. Since many reference groups are already organized, most people follow along well-defined career lines. Whether one wishes to become a doctor, a diplomat, an airline pilot, a socialite, a ballerina, or a professional killer, the paths of advancement are largely circumscribed. Most organizations have procedures for recruitment and training, apprenticeships, and standards that must be met before one is fully accepted. A young man studying medicine must advance up a ladder, learning new meanings as he goes along. He must complete a prescribed undergraduate curriculum, gain admission to an acceptable medical school, have himself placed as an interne, obtain access to the facilities of a hospital, acquire and retain a clientele, develop informal relations with his professional colleagues, and eventually arrange to transfer his practice to a successor. As Hall showed in his studies, what is actually required of a doctor is not quite what an outsider would expect, nor does it comply with the official pronouncements of various medical organizations. One must work his way through the informal social structure of the medical profession.[27] When career lines are thus institutionalized, a candidate can organize his aspirations and anticipate what needs to be done. He learns many roles by watching those who are ahead of him. Furthermore, when career lines are well defined, each candidate has criteria for evaluating his own progress.

In our society, social status depends largely upon the occupation of the provider of the family, and one's sense of personal identity is shaped by his position in the economic system. In their study of the manner in which people in the professions develop similar values and behavior patterns, Becker and Carper compared graduate students in physiology, engineering, and philosophy. They wanted to see how the formative years after making a commitment are spent. They found that physiologists conceive of themselves primarily as "scientists," develop pride in their technical skills, and aspire to make some discovery that will be of benefit to mankind. Such an ideology develops in the informal contacts with co-workers and professors that take place in the years that they must work together in laboratories. Engineers are primarily concerned with "opportunities for

[27] Hall, op. cit., Cf. Howard S. Becker and Anselm Strauss, "Careers, Personality, and Adult Socialization," American Journal of Sociology, LXII (1956), 253-63; and Strauss, Mirrors and Masks: The Search for Identity (Glencoe: Free Press, 1959), pp. 89-176.

advancement." They see their future in the industrial system, and are in school to acquire specific skills or make contacts that will help them in the future. They take pride not only in their technical competence but in their ability to solve problems rationally. Philosophers conceive of themselves as "intellectuals" and are proud of their broad, unspecialized learning, encompassing the arts, sciences, and literature. Since most of their primary relations are with students in a number of different fields of specialization, they feel no pressure toward depth; they look to teaching as a way to subsidize the continuation of their intellectual pursuits. It is in informal contacts that those preparing in these fields acquire a new vocabulary of motives which enables them to explain what they are doing. The labels used to designate their respective callings are important, for they symbolize the characteristics of those who identify with them. Since they rationalize their lives in terms of the new vocabulary, everything makes sense.[28]

Regardless of the social status he achieves, everyone ages, and with advancing years each person is forced to assume a number of new roles. There is an increased likelihood of illness and death. An elderly person retires from work and withdraws from various community organizations. The death of his mate and the loss of an independent household, with his concomitant dependence upon others, also reminds him of his new position. He must relinquish many of the activities he had once enjoyed, and he cannot plausibly set up goals that will require many years to reach. But alterations in self-conception that occur at this time rest largely upon the changed responses of other people. In the already cited study by Blau, it was shown that the manner in which an elderly person classifies himself depends in part upon the comparative age and the outlook of his associates.[29] But if they live long enough, sooner or later most people acknowledge that they are old. They are treated gently even by strangers, who defer to their presumed weakness and wisdom. As they are stripped of their responsibilities, they accept the fact that their contributions to society are about over.

In response to regularities in the behavior of others, each person

[28] Howard S. Becker and James Carper, "Development of Identification with Occupations," *American Journal of Sociology,* LXI (1956), 289–98; and "The Elements of Identification with an Occupation," *American Sociological Review,* XXI (1956), 341–48.

[29] Blau, *op. cit.* Cf. Bernard S. Phillips, "A Role Theory Approach to Adjustment in Old Age," *American Sociological Review,* XXII (1957), 212–17.

places himself into a category in terms of criteria such as sex, ethnic identity, occupation, and age. Knowing what is generally expected of various kinds of people, he places limitations upon his own conduct. Each person develops a sense of autonomy to the extent that he assumes a generalized, pervasive outlook that transcends that of all the local units of which he is a part. But the conduct of such autonomous units is voluntarily restricted, as each person tries to live up to the obligations he assumes by virtue of the manner in which he identifies himself.

Each person participates in many kinds of enterprises. As his interests become extended, his self-conception becomes more generalized. A boy may initially conceive of himself as a proficient second-baseman, then as a good baseball player, and eventually as a skilful athlete. He may also be a reasonably obedient son who manages to keep up with the others in school. Each person's conception of himself is shaped in what he does in cooperative contexts. To the extent that similar norms and values are shared in the groups of which he is a part, he can make consistent demands upon himself. But the norms of different groups may clash, resulting in severe inner conflicts. This suggests that the extent to which one's conception of himself can be integrated depends upon the consistency of the demands that are made upon him by other people.

Transformations of Personal Identity

Once his conception of himself is established, a person acts consistently in a variety of situations. Drastic transformations in behavior patterns are quite rare, but there are cases in which a person acts so differently that his friends and relatives have difficulty in recognizing him. When such changes do occur, they are accompanied by a psychological reorientation in which the person sees his world and himself in a different light. He retains many of his idiosyncrasies, but develops a new set of values and different criteria of judgment. The study of such transformations, called "conversions" when they are extensive, is especially rewarding, for they throw light upon the manner in which behavior patterns, self-conceptions, reference groups, and significant others are related.

Some people change after a dramatic experience, especially if it is traumatic. The impact of death and brutality in infantry combat is so great that some soldiers come to perceive their world in a different light; some develop severe psychoses from which they never recover. Serious failures sometimes lead to despondency, collapse, and then a new life. The sudden loss of one's fortune, especially for a person who has always been wealthy, can be a shattering experience. But one hears occasionally of the man who "finds himself" for the first time after losing all his money. Crisis rites sometimes result in remarkable changes. A carefree girl may become "another woman" after her marriage, voluntarily assuming duties of which her parents and friends had believed her incapable. Sometimes even more amazing changes occur to one or both parents after the birth of their first child and the sudden realization of their responsibilities. In all such cases, changes in interpersonal relations and in self-conceptions are apparent.

Changes may also occur when a person finds himself in a different social setting, giving him opportunities for releasing previously suppressed impulses. Although the proverbial transformation of the sweet and cooperative fiancee into the domineering wife does not occur as frequently as cartoonists are wont to suggest, such radical changes do sometimes take place. A young man who had never distinguished himself in civilian life sometimes becomes an outstanding war hero. Being reticent, he had never before asserted himself; but on the battlefield, where few men have the courage to do voluntarily what must be done, he may find it necessary to carry an increasing share of the burden. His comrades begin to look to him for leadership, and he is left with no alternative to assuming command. In bureaucratic organizations of all kinds a man who had been regarded as dependable, honorable, and not excessively ambitious may be elected to a foremanship, a chairmanship, or some other position of authority. Once in office he becomes a domineering and vengeful tyrant, and much to everyone's dismay becomes completely preoccupied with enhancing his personal power. In such cases it is extremely unlikely that the new tendencies develop overnight; it is more probable that they are latent dispositions that had never been manifested in overt conduct. As a previously established balance is upset with the assumption of a new role, long hidden interests move to the forefront. Especially where different interpersonal roles are assumed, the changes can be quite extensive. The common belief that success and power change men is apparently based upon observations of cases of this kind.

Conversions occur in a variety of contexts. The term is most widely used to refer to religious conversions, in which previously indifferent men embrace a faith and pursue a new way of life with fanatic zeal. Such converts are sometimes referred to as being "twice born" in recognition of the comprehensive changes in their conduct. When political conversions occur, angry people become dedicated workers in illegitimate cults, underground resistance movements, or revolutionary organizations of all kinds. Among the most spectacular of conversions are those that take place in Alcoholics Anonymous, a volunteer group in which men and women given up by psychiatrists, clergymen, and their families as hopelessly addicted to alcohol acquire a new perspective which enables them to stop drinking and to reconstruct their lives. In spite of the diversity of the contexts in which they occur, conversions reveal a characteristic natural history.

What kind of people are attracted to esoteric cults? In his classic study of religious movements, Niebuhr called them the "disinherited," and many others have contended that the disgruntled, maladjusted, and frustrated are the people who are most receptive to new ideas. An examination of autobiographies reveals that the sense of frustration usually arises from a succession of disturbances in interpersonal relations; the initial phase of conversion is the gradual alienation from significant others. Converts sometimes reject their families and forsake their former friends. Many testify that they felt unappreciated; they were not enjoying the personal status they felt they deserved. Outward appearances are sometimes deceptive, for members of a family often feel obligated to suppress their hostilities. They may therefore become anxiety ridden and not be aware of the source of their discomfort. Generally, however, the difficulties are readily discernible. Rapoport's study of Mormon missions in Rimrock showed that the Indians who were attracted were those who did not fit into Navaho life. Many were women who were unhappy over their subordinate roles. There were also young people who wanted to identify with the larger American community; some were so assimilated that they were almost completely ignorant of Navaho culture.[30] It is the people who feel unfulfilled who become sensitive to new possibilities. For them, the rejection of the past is relatively easy.

[30] Robert N. Rapoport, "Changing Navaho Religious Values," *Papers of the Peabody Museum of American Archeology and Ethnology*, XLI (1954), No. 2. Cf. H. Richard Niebuhr, *The Social Sources of Denominationalism* (New York: Henry Holt & Co., 1929), pp. 26–76.

Almost invariably the period preceding conversion is one of torment and self-examination. There are intense feelings of guilt. The person's level of self-esteem is lowered to the point where suicide may be seriously contemplated. Those who become alcoholic are sometimes so disgusted with themselves that they cannot bear to remain sober. Being unable to control their drinking, they become even more disgusted and seek perpetual anaesthetization. Tiebout contended that there is a remarkable similarity in the personalities of those addicted to alcohol; they are often narcissistic, dominated by a sense of omnipotence, and intent upon maintaining their autonomy at all costs. Such persons cannot be helped by anyone until they surrender their defiant individuality; then they become utterly humble and turn to God, to a psychiatrist, or to anyone who can help for guidance and control from the outside.[31] The period of acute crisis, when self-rejection is at its peak, is generally brought about by some unusual event. Because of selective perception the entire world looks depressing; everything appears hopeless. Under such circumstances people become responsive to possibilities of forming new self-images.

The "lost soul" is introduced to a new communication channel, often by accident, and he becomes aware of another way of looking at life and at himself. The revelation may take place in a single dramatic event; it may occur suddenly from a chance reading of the Bible, a hallucination, the shock of a beating, or meeting a person who strikes him as being exceptional. On the other hand, many conversions take considerable time. Figures released by Alcoholics Anonymous after the first ten years of operation reveal that the majority of its members were cured only after six or seven years of participation. When a person partakes in a new communication channel, suddenly or gradually, he enters a new social world. Experiences are classified differently; many old objects become unfamiliar, and others take on a new significance. The convert becomes responsive to a new audience, which uses different standards in placing an estimate upon him. Each sectarian group has a unique perspective, and a person who had been a misfit adjusts, not by

[31] Harry M. Tiebout, "Therapeutic Mechanisms of Alcoholics Anonymous," *American Journal of Psychiatry*, C (1944), 468–73. Cf. Stanley Rosenman, "The Skid Row Alcoholic and the Negative Ego Image," *Quarterly Journal of Studies on Alcohol*, XVI (1955), 447–73.

altering any part of the world, but by altering his outlook.[32]

The adoption of a new perspective makes possible a reexamination and redefinition of oneself. New self-images need not be favorable from the first. In the case reported by Tiebout, the man saw himself as a selfish fraud. He was able to penetrate beyond the façade of perceptual defenses and rationalizations for the first time. Whereas he had hitherto been unaware of other people except as they affected him, it suddenly occurred to him that they too might have separate existences, different from his own and yet similar to it. Once he had this insight, he began to feel closer to people; he no longer felt the necessity of fighting and dominating them. Acceptance in a new group also helps to restore one's level of self-esteem. He becomes convinced that someone cares, and this implies that he is worthy of care. Doing something worthwhile also provides avenues for enhancing his self-esteem. This may account for the crusading zeal found in so many converts. One of the rules of Alcoholics Anonymous is that each participant should help others who are less fortunate than himself. Since former alcohol addicts can understand the agonies of their fellows in a manner that the sober could not, effective role-taking becomes possible. One of the co-founders of Alcoholics Anonymous declared that from the very beginning working with other victims helped him to fight temptations; but his friend, who took little interest in others, would occasionally backslide into drink.[33] An intense belief in the new and an intolerance of deviation is another mark of converts. There is total rejection, even contempt toward all old beliefs. Sometimes converts even change their names, ridding themselves of the symbol for their old self-conception.[34] Another frequently observed feature of conversions is the clarity of life goals; the person redefines himself and locates the new object unequivocally within the stable new order.

The new meanings and self-conceptions are reinforced by a new set of significant others with whom more cordial interpersonal relations are established. Since any conception of reality is a social process, a new way of approaching one's surroundings is likely to be

[32] Cf. Faris, op. cit., pp. 46–60; and William James, The Varieties of Religious Experience (New York: Random House, Inc., 1936), pp. 77–253.

[33] William Wilson, "The Society of Alcoholics Anonymous," American Journal of Psychiatry, CVI (1949), 370–75.

[34] Cf. Erdmann D. Beynon, "The Voodoo Cult among Negro Migrants in Detroit," American Journal of Sociology, XLIII (1938), 894–907.

transitory unless it wins the support of others whom one respects. It is through the constant comparison of experiences that consensus emerges and is reaffirmed. The sympathetic support of other people is a crucial part of all conversions. The founder of a new religion goes forth to report on his conversations with God; were it not for the acceptance of his associates, anyone claiming such experiences would be incarcerated as insane. In cults of all kinds new converts are warmly welcomed. The sincerity and genuine concern of the members give the newcomer a sense of belonging, perhaps for the first time in his life. In Alcoholics Anonymous informal face-to-face work with people in similar predicaments is emphasized. Those who had been blamed, shamed, and rejected suddenly find themselves being treated with respect as human beings. Converts are often able to withstand the severe discipline required in their way of life because of the sense of personal loyalty toward their new associates.[35]

In conversions a person who is alienated from himself and his significant others acquires a new perspective, which enables him to reappraise himself and to form new patterns of behavior. If the new standpoint provides some measure of relief, a lasting change may occur. It is of interest to note that the onset of psychosis, one of the most drastic transformations a person can undergo, presents a similar natural history. It is often detected when unusual, sometimes grotesque, forms of behavior develop. There is also a change of perspectives; one is generally designated as psychotic when he can no longer partake in the "reality" over which there is consensus. As the patient's outlook becomes more and more private, previously familiar objects assume new meanings, and gestures are interpreted in idiosyncratic ways. No one knows just how a person becomes psychotic. Psychiatrists often make a distinction between precipitating factors and predispositions. The dramatic event that often precedes the onset of illness—being divorced, being ejected from home, losing a job, failing in school, and similar difficulties—is generally regarded only as the "straw that broke the camel's back." Emphasis is placed upon the condition of the victim that rendered him so vulnerable to frustration. Psychiatrists are turning their attention toward the disturbances in interpersonal relations almost invariably found in the

---

[35] Cf. Oscar W. Ritchie, "A Sociohistorical Survey of Alcoholics Anonymous," *Quarterly Journal of Studies on Alcohol,* IX (1948), 119-56; and Herrigel, *op. cit.,* pp. 53-93.

background of those who suffer from severe mental disorders. Recovery from mental disorders also has many features that resemble conversions. Indeed, Burke once referred to successful psychoanalytic therapy as a "secular conversion" in that the patient is persuaded to redefine himself from a new standpoint. He contended that the psychoanalysts have built up their own symbolic environment, with a special vocabulary of motives, which enables a patient to reduce his distress by renaming his faults. He referred to this technique as "exorcism by misnomer."[36] Although some psychiatrists have been outraged by this seemingly flippant characterization of their conscientious work, there is some basis for Burke's position. While undergoing analysis, a patient does learn a new language and orientation. He begins to speak of becoming "hostile" instead of "getting mad." He cannot do something over and over merely because he enjoys it; it becomes an "obsession." If he is tidy, he refers to himself as "compulsive." If he is happy, he says he is "euphoric"; if he becomes worried or nervous, he expresses concern over his "anxieties." If he believes that someone has insulted him, he describes his reaction as "paranoid." If he agrees with someone else, he acknowledges that he is "submissive"; and if he disagrees, he is "defensive." As he masters the new vocabulary and becomes a more effective participant in the symbolic environment, he begins to see human nature in a different light, and this enables him to redefine himself in a manner that no longer calls for guilt feelings. He is then able to accept many of the inner experiences which had been the source of considerable torment. Among other things, successful psychotherapy involves a transformation of self-conceptions. Rogers put the matter explicitly by contending that, as therapy progresses, the patient becomes more able to accept himself as a person worthy of respect. This hypothesis has been tested repeatedly, and although there have been some negative findings, most of the evidence supports Rogers.[37]

Before a patient can be persuaded to accept the new perspective, the therapist must establish a particular kind of interpersonal tie between them. Freud referred to this relationship as "transference."

[36] Burke, Permanence and Change, op. cit., pp. 125–47.
[37] Rogers, op. cit., pp. 77–88, 135–72. Cf. Bernard Chodorkoff, "Adjustment and the Discrepancy between the Perceived and Ideal Self," Journal of Clinical Psychology, X (1954), 266–68.

The doctor becomes a significant other who teaches the new outlook and then supports it. This enables the patient to relive his past life vicariously in the company of a more sympathetic and understanding substitute parent, who also provides explanations. Many patients fall in love with their analysts; psychiatrists continually find themselves the objects of hero-worship. Some patients are able to make painful sacrifices only because of personal loyalty to their therapists. Freud was quite explicit, insisting that a person becomes accessible to influence only to the extent that he can form sentiments.[38] The analyst does not actually cure the patient; he produces a situation in which the patient can cure himself. In many cases a patient who had recovered reverts to his old behavior patterns soon after his treatment is terminated; without the interpersonal support, the new meanings sometimes do not persist. Since psychiatrists trained in many different schools of thought apparently have approximately the same rate of success, special techniques based upon doctrines probably have little to do with recovery. The one common feature seems to be the establishment of warm personal ties.

Since most mental hospitals are so inadequately staffed, it is possible to provide psychiatric treatment for only a small proportion of the patients. All that can be done for the others is to make them as comfortable as possible and restrain them from injuring themselves and others. Even without therapy, however, a surprisingly large number of patients get well. One case of such a "spontaneous recovery" illustrates the importance of the support of sympathetic individuals. The patient, who was so completely withdrawn that he became weak from malnutrition and infection, unaccountably improved and was eventually discharged. According to his subsequent testimony, he had believed himself the object of attack by an organization headed by his former employer. The organization had placed him in a novel kind of jail and was taking movies of his strange behavior in order to expose him to the public. He was convinced that everyone at the hospital—staff members, visitors, and other patients—were a part of the organization; they were all highly trained and dedicated actors. During a period when he was so withdrawn that the staff members thought he was completely out of contact with reality, he noticed that one of the attendants, a Negro

[38] Sigmund Freud, *A General Introduction to Psychoanalysis*, Joan Riviere, trans. (New York: Garden City Publishing Co., 1938), p. 387.

woman, took a special interest in him. She spoke of him by name and asked about his condition each day before starting her work. At first he thought that she too had been placed in the ward by the organization, as a representative of Negroes to place him a level below ethnic minorities. Although she tended him in much the same manner as she cared for the others, he sensed vaguely that her interest in him was kindly. Before long, much of his thinking centered upon her. He felt comfortable whenever she was on the ward and eagerly waited for her to come to work. During her days off he prayed for strength to endure the pain while she was away. In time he began to feel that she exemplified goodness, affection, loyalty, and sacrifice—the qualities that enabled a Negro to get along in a hostile world. It was at this time that the patient began to improve. Long afterward, when he was well on his way to recovery and she had been transferred to another ward, he arranged a meeting with her and was surprised to find that she was actually quite different from the idealized personification he had constructed. But there was little doubt that she had taken a special interest in him. Her husband had been hospitalized for tuberculosis, and she had been working in a hospital to help the ill. She had detected the great pain of this particular patient and wanted to do whatever she could to help relieve it. She had accepted him without disdain for what he was; she expected nothing in return from him, not even the joy of a "therapeutic triumph." Her sincerity, humility, and dignity had apparently evoked his response.[39]

An examination of drastic changes in behavior patterns in a number of different contexts shows that a displacement of perspectives is usually involved. Since any human being can be personified in a number of different ways, depending upon his sensitivities and frame of reference, it is possible for a man to alter his self-conception simply by noticing things that he had previously overlooked. When he conceives of himself as a different person, he tries to live up to a new set of standards. This suggests that a conversion is a form of adaptation. In many cases it represents the last desperate effort of a man with a low level of self-esteem to come to terms with himself. The rigidity, fanaticism, and dedication that characterize so many converts may constitute a way of atoning for a sense of guilt.

The displacement of perspectives is both preceded and followed

[39] Boverman, *op. cit.*

by changes in interpersonal relations, usually with different individuals as significant others. Each person forms a conception of himself by acquiring the perspective of the various groups of which he is a part, but such participation is always in the company of specific people. A person is not likely to redefine himself without a change in perspectives, and a displacement of reference groups is not likely to occur unless the significant others representing the points of view are also replaced. A convert not only develops a new self-conception, but may also assume new interpersonal roles more congenial to his personality. As he wins acceptance and becomes the object of conjunctive sentiments, he experiences a warmth and serenity that contrasts sharply with his past. Those who are psychotic are often supported by imaginary personifications. Being accepted within some primary group is a matter of crucial importance for all men. Personal stability rests upon reasonable satisfaction with oneself, and it is difficult for anyone to accept himself without the affection and respect of significant others.

Summary and Conclusion

All human beings begin as egocentric creatures but gradually learn to restrain themselves and to participate in the give and take of group life. The structure of personal identity is introduced from the outside. At first the child is restrained through reward and punishment, in much the same fashion as other animals. In time, however, he learns to address himself from the standpoint of other people and to inhibit troublesome impulses. He begins by assuming specific roles, imitating the behavior of significant others, and carrying on conversations with himself. As he grows older, he begins to participate in a variety of organized transactions. These enterprises are directed toward understood objectives; the component roles are already related to each other, and the appropriate responses are already organized into rules. While performing in groups, the child learns to visualize his contributions from a standpoint over which there is consensus. Once such perspectives become incorporated, they are used to define situations even when the person is all alone; individual behavior becomes subject to social control. Each person achieves some degree of autonomy, but he acts voluntarily in ways

THE DEVELOPMENT OF SELF-CONTROL 533

that perpetuate the structure of organized groups. Perspectives, once they are established, continue to be supported by significant others; they are not likely to change unless the ties to these people are also altered.

Voluntary conduct is possible only if a man has a reasonably well-developed self-conception. He has to know who he is, what is expected of him, and what constitutes his distinct interests in relation to those of others. Self-conceptions reflect group patterns, but a person is not a mere counterpart of society. To be sure, each individual controls himself in terms of group standards, but he is capable of some measure of independent action. Each person is the product of a unique background of experience. The pattern that emerges is the product of natural selection, and much depends upon the particular demands made upon him by those with whom he associates as well as upon his inborn sensitivities.

As paradoxical as it may seem, the autonomy of the individual is a product of participating in organized groups. Before one can control himself he must be able to think, and this presupposes the ability to manipulate linguistic symbols, a skill that one cannot learn alone. Self-control is also predicated upon a sense of right and wrong, which does not develop through biological maturation. Finally, before one can control himself he must be able to respond to a self-image. Anyone who cannot form a perceptual object of himself remains a creature of impulse, for he cannot check himself effectively without being able to anticipate what he is about to do. There would be no point in anyone's directing his activities unless he has some understanding of where he is going and of what obstacles he is likely to encounter. The ability to respond to oneself from the standpoint of others develops through active participation in cooperative transactions. Freedom is the product of society; men have rights only if they share common perspectives. Each individual can have rights only insofar as people are willing to live up to their responsibilities.

Suggested References

AUSUBEL, DAVID P., *Ego Development and the Personality Disorders,* Parts II–III. New York: Grune & Stratton, 1952. A reformulation of the psychoanalytic theory of personality development, documented with materials drawn from current research in child psychology.

BOISEN, ANTON T., *The Exploration of the Inner World.* New York: Harper & Bros., 1936. A searching study by a clergyman, viewing psychoses and religious conversions as attempts at reorganization on the part of men suffering of a sense of personal failure.

BURKE, KENNETH, *Permanence and Change.* Los Altos: Hermes Publications, 1955. A brilliant treatise on the manner in which a meaningful orientation toward one's surroundings is formed, sustained, and then transformed, with particular emphasis on the importance of linguistic symbols.

CLAYTON, ALFRED S., *Emergent Mind and Education.* New York: Columbia University Press, 1943. A critical review of George H. Mead's theory of the development of individuality and self-control and a discussion of its implications for education in a democratic society.

PIAGET, JEAN, *The Moral Judgment of the Child,* Marjorie Gabain, trans. Glencoe: Free Press, 1948. A classic study of the manner in which group norms are learned, beginning with rules in children's games and going on to the moral precepts taught by adults.

SULLIVAN, HARRY S., *The Interpersonal Theory of Psychiatry,* H. S. Perry and M. L. Gawel, eds. New York: W. W. Norton & Co., 1953. The posthumously published lectures of a famed psychiatrist on the development of self-control, pointing to the sources of serious personality disorders.

16

The
development
of
personal
idiom

A listener who has some familiarity with music can often identify a piece heard for the first time as the work of a particular composer. Each creative artist has a distinct style, and from style alone the music of Chopin, the painting of van Gogh, the sculpture of Rodin, or the writing of Shakespeare can often be recognized. Before the recent development of more precise techniques of measuring age, many disputes over the authenticity of art treasures were settled largely on this basis. The same distinctiveness is found in the work of actors, athletes, cooks, and dentists. Indeed, a dentist is sometimes called in by the police to identify an otherwise unrecognizable corpse on the basis of the bridgework. Most activities are largely circumscribed by conventional norms; even artists who claim to be unconventional receive similar training and conceive of themselves within some historical tradition. Yet each person does his work in a unique manner. Style is often regarded as the personal idiom of conduct; as the French proverb puts it: "the style is the man himself."

In some respects human beings all over the world are alike; in other respects those who share the same cultural heritage are more or less alike; and in still other respects each human being is different. All men fall in love, become jealous, resent domination, and indulge in hero worship. But the gestures that are symbolic of love in one society may be regarded as insulting in another. Although love is found everywhere, each individual has different preferences and reveals them in different ways. Each person talks, walks, plays, attacks, or defends in characteristic ways that enable his associates to recognize him; each individual seems to be suited for some conventional roles and hopelessly unfit for others. Men all over the world share a common human nature, but within each culture it is manifested in a somewhat different manner, and each person is human in his own distinct way.

A man's personality consists of the system of meanings that make up his unique orientation toward his world. One of the central problems in the study of socialization consists of ascertaining how personal idiom develops. A number of social scientists have emphasized the importance of culture, insisting that the behavior patterns typical of each individual emerge as he learns conventional meanings. Since the participants in organized groups do share a common symbolic environment, there is much that is similar in their conduct, yet each individual performs his roles in his own way. Personality development, therefore, cannot be explained exclusively in terms of the acquisition of culture, and this complex question has not yet been settled.

Culture and Personality Development

Largely as a reaction against the biological explanations that have long prevailed among psychologists and psychiatrists, anthropologists have stressed the importance of the cultural matrix in which personality development takes place. They have objected that many of the generalizations formulated by psychologists apply only to Western culture and, calling attention to the amazing variety of meanings in esoteric cultures throughout the world, have asked for a theory of socialization that will take these variations into account.

Some have advocated the study of the cultural "determinants" of personality; others have written of the cultural "conditioning" of personality; still others have gone so far as to contend that personality is only the individual counterpart of culture. Such claims, while providing a much needed corrective to blind biological determinism, are quite misleading. The relationship between culture and personality is a matter over which there is still considerable controversy. Unfortunately, the issue, with its vitriolic polemics, has been kept alive by ambiguous terminology.

If personality is the product of culture, there should be a differential distribution of personality types. In each culture certain behavior patterns are favored, and others are proscribed. If personality is the product of childhood experiences, there should be a corresponding diversity in the personalities of people in different societies, for each has a different way of treating children. Prominent in this type of approach is the effort to depict the "modal personality structure" for each culture. The people in one society are said to be predominantly friendly and indulgent, while those in another are predominantly suspicious and hostile, or industrious and materialistic. Similar attempts have been made to characterize the typical person found in certain classes and ethnic groups. It is not always clear whether the modal personality is the type that is found with the greatest frequency in a society, the type that is essential for the preservation of the culture, or the type that is most congenial to the prevailing institutions and ethos.[1] Some anthropologists now go forth in their field work armed with a variety of projective and psychometric tests.

There have also been a number of studies by sociologists and political scientists of "national character," in which the same approach has been used to study complex industrial societies. Attempts have been made to account for the emergence of certain political institutions among Americans, British, Germans, Japanese, and Russians in terms of proclivities arising from the typical childhood experiences of these peoples. The rise of anti-Semitism, Nazism, and other social movements has been explained in terms of the typical

[1] Cf. Abram Kardiner, *The Individual and His Society* (New York: Columbia University Press, 1939), pp. 237–38; Ralph Linton, *The Cultural Background of Personality* (New York: D. Appleton-Century Co., 1945); and S. S. Sargent and M. W. Smith, eds., *Culture and Personality* (New York: The Viking Fund, 1949).

patterns of motivation which presumably characterize a large proportion of certain populations.[2] Numerous objections have been raised to this type of study, and the controversy still rages.

Since psychotic syndromes are presumably easier to identify than other personality types, attempts have been made to isolate class and culture differentials in the incidence of various mental disorders. In some societies, because of the permissive manner in which the children are reared, personality disorders are presumably less likely to develop; in other societies, because of the harsh discipline imposed on the children, problems are more likely to arise. Such assertions have been difficult to test because the observations have not always been made by trained psychiatrists, and the data are therefore not comparable.[3]

Since people with different cultural backgrounds classify their experiences differently and have different conceptions of causality, of man's place in the universe, and of themselves, there are bound to be some differences in symptoms. But there is no real evidence that any clinical syndrome is found in different proportions in different societies. Delusions vary in content. Menimoni Indians who are paranoid fear witches or snakes, in contrast to those in our society who may fear a radio station or F.B.I. agents. But the imputation of malevolent motives to imaginary personifications and the taking of defensive measures against them are similar patterns. In his study of paranoid psychosis, Lambo compared ten cases of Yoruba tribesmen from a rural background, ten cases of Yoruba who had had considerable contact with Europeans, and ten Nigerian students in England. He found delusions of persecution in all three categories, but delusions of grandeur were less frequent among the patients from rural areas. The delusions of all Yoruba patients reflected beliefs in the supernatural, but those who were familiar with European culture tended to be more like the Europeans.[4] Lin studied three Chinese communities in Formosa—a rural area, a small town, and a section of a large city—and examined 19,931 people. He

[2] Cf. Erich Fromm, *Escape from Freedom* (New York: Farrar & Rinehart, 1941); and Alex Inkeles and Daniel J. Levinson, "National Character," in Lindzey, *op. cit.*, Vol. II, pp. 977–1020.

[3] Paul E. Benedict and Irving Jacks, "Mental Illness in Primitive Societies," *Psychiatry,* XVII (1954), 377–89.

[4] T. Adeoye Lambo, "The Role of Cultural Factors in Paranoid Psychosis among the Yoruba Tribe," *Journal of Mental Science,* CI (1955), 239–66.

found 214 cases of aberrations, both active and partially recovered. There was no significant difference in the incidence of various syndromes in the three areas. His data do not support the contention of an eminent anthropologist that manic-depressive psychosis is more prevalent than schizophrenia among the Chinese. In fact, the incidence of the various disorders did not differ appreciably from what it is known to be in other parts of the world.[5] Symptoms differ from culture to culture, but the structure of the psychoses, and perhaps their etiology, appear to be much the same. If this were not the case, they would not be recognizable.[6]

Some critics of modern industrial societies have pointed to their complexity and internal contradictions as sources of strain. They contend that the incidence of schizophrenia is higher in mass societies than it is in the simpler, more stable primitive societies, in which the social status of each individual is more clearly defined. To test this contention, Eaton and Weil studied several communities of Hutterites, a religious sect inhabiting rural regions in the Dakotas, Montana, and the adjacent Canadian provinces. This closed, almost autonomous group has maintained its isolation for more than 100 years and has a well-ordered way of life that contrasts sharply with the rest of the American scene. The investigators found 199 persons who were ill or had at one time suffered some mental aberration; of these, fifty-three were classified as psychotic, sixty-nine as neurotic, fifty-one as mentally deficient, twenty as epileptic, and six in other categories. The strict taboo against overt aggression was kept even by victims of schizophrenia, and depressive moods and severe feelings of guilt were common both in psychotic and neurotic patients. In contrast to many other communities, the sick had been treated permissively and had not lost their status. But the figures reveal that a simple and uncomplicated way of life does not necessarily provide immunity from mental disturbances. Although cohesion, consistency, and clearly defined expectations and career lines existed, presumably ideal from a psychiatric standpoint, the incidence of mental illness did not differ appreciably from that in other parts of

[5] Tsung-yi Lin, "A Study of the Incidence of Mental Disorder in Chinese and Other Cultures," *Psychiatry*, XVI (1953), 313–36.

[6] Cf. A. Irving Hallowell, "Psychic Stresses and Cultural Patterns," *American Journal of Psychiatry*, XCII (1936), 1291–1310; and James S. Slotkin, "Culture and Psychopathology," *Journal of Abnormal and Social Psychology*, LI (1955), 269–75.

the country. The Hutterites were somewhat lower in all categories except psychosis, where they were quite high.[7]

Since people in different classes utilize somewhat different communication channels, they differ to some extent in their cultural backgrounds. To check the relationship between class position and mental illness, Hollingshead and Redlich conducted a large scale study in New Haven, covering about ninety-eight per cent of those receiving treatment at the time of the investigation. Using an index of class position—based on occupation, education, and area of residence—the authors found marked differences in the proportion of people being treated for mental disturbances. The more privileged classes made up 11.4 per cent of the population, but contributed only eight per cent of the patients; the lowest class made up 18.4 per cent of the population and contributed 38.2 per cent of the patients. They also found differences in the incidence of different types of disorders. In the upper classes more patients were classified as neurotic than psychotic, but in the lowest class 91.6 per cent of the patients were diagnosed as psychotic. Of course, among the poor many who are plagued with neurotic symptoms cannot afford psychiatric care.[8] On the basis of an intensive study of fifty patients in the same investigation, Myers and Roberts found that the background of patients from different classes contrasted sharply. Lower class victims of schizophrenia came from families marked by disorganization, parental neglect, and lack of guidance; but patients from middle class families suffered more from anxieties over their inability to realize the high goals set by their mothers and by the lack of respect for their fathers.[9] These data point to significant class differences in personality development, but contradictory evidence comes from other studies. In an investigation involving 1,462 rural Wisconsin children, Sewell and Haller found no impressive relationship between social status and personality.[10]

[7] Joseph W. Eaton and Robert J. Weil, *Culture and Mental Disorders* (Glencoe: Free Press, 1955).

[8] August B. Hollingshead and Frederick C. Redlich, *Social Class and Mental Illness* (New York: John Wiley & Sons, 1958), pp. 194–250.

[9] Jerome K. Myers and Bertram H. Roberts, *Family and Class Dynamics in Mental Illness* (New York: John Wiley & Sons, 1959), pp. 57–126.

[10] William H. Sewell and Archie O. Haller, "Social Status and the Personality Adjustment of the Child," *Sociometry*, XIX (1956), 114–25; and "Factors in the Relationship between Social Status and the Personality Adjustment of the Child," *American Sociological Review*, XXIV (1959), 511–20.

As part of an attempt to explain alleged differences in the distribution of personality types, there has been an increasing interest in the comparative study of child-rearing practices. Anthropologists now investigate the training of the young in considerably more detail than they had in the past.[11] A number of studies have also been made on class differences in child-training. In 1943, Davis and Havighurst questioned 200 lower and middle class mothers in Chicago on breast-feeding, bottle-feeding, and toilet training. They found that middle class parents were more rigorous in disciplining their offsprings for cleanliness and regularity in feeding, and expected their children to assume various responsibilities at an earlier age. In general, Negroes tended to be more permissive, but the same class differences were found among Negroes.[12] In 1952, Sears and his associates launched a comprehensive study of 379 mothers in the suburbs of Boston. They found that working class mothers were consistently more punitive and restrictive, tended to give tangible rewards as incentives, and inclined to discipline their children through physical punishment rather than the withdrawal of affection.[13] Since both studies have been repeated with similar results, it has been suggested that the seemingly contradictory findings may be due to changes in the ideology of child-rearing during the intervening decade.[14] Taking account of the changes in the American economic system since the turn of the century, Miller and Swanson introduced a distinction between two types of families—the "entrepreneurial," consisting of people who operate or work in small enterprises with a relatively simple division of labor, and the "bureaucratic," consisting of people employed in large corporations. In a survey in Detroit, they found that entrepreneurial middle class mothers tended to emphasize an active, manipulative approach toward life, teaching their children self-reliance. In entrepreneurial families, lower class mothers were more permissive than middle class

[11] Cf. Abram Kardiner, et al., The Psychological Frontiers of Society (New York: Columbia University Press, 1945); and Dorothea Leighton and Clyde Kluckhohn, Children of the People (Cambridge: Harvard University Press, 1948).

[12] Allison Davis and Robert J. Havighurst, "Social Class and Color Differences in Child-Rearing," American Sociological Review, XI (1946), 698–710.

[13] Sears, et al., op. cit., pp. 427–33. Cf. Martha S. White, "Social Class, Child Rearing Practices, and Child Behavior," American Sociological Review, XXII (1957), 704–12.

[14] Richard A. Littman, et al., "Social Class Differences in Child Rearing," ibid., XXII (1957), 694–704.

mothers; in bureaucratic families, however, no significant class differences could be found.[15] Kohn asked 400 mothers in Washington, D.C., what qualities they would most like to see in their children at various age levels, and found that working class parents were oriented toward qualities that assure repsectablity, while middle class parents stressed internalized standards of conduct.[16] Most investigators agree that there are class differences in child training practices, but they disagree on the nature of these differences.

Evidence that child-rearing practices are related to personality development is still inconclusive. Sewell and his associates studied 162 children from rural Wisconsin communities with a barrage of personality tests, inventories, and rating scales, and also questioned their parents about their training. They found that the personality adjustment scores and the traits of children who had undergone a variety of training procedures were not significantly different. Items such as the length of breast-feeding, the age of toilet training, and the handling of masturbation were then divided into practices approved and disapproved in psychoanalysis. There were no impressive correlations between permissive upbringing and favorable personality development; in fact, some of the coefficients were negative.[17] This suggests that training procedures as such may not be as important as the sentiments directed toward the child. Virtually all of these studies focus upon what the parents do rather than the way they do it. The style of parental conduct toward the child is often mentioned, but it has not been studied effectively.

Although the question of the differential distribution of personality types is not settled, it appears that all kinds of personalities are to be found in all societies. It is true that those who share a common culture are characterized by similar behavior patterns, but a distinction must be made between the façade of conventional conduct and what an individual is actually disposed to do. Personality is to be identified in terms of one's potentialities for action, not in terms of his overt conduct. It is revealed in his spontaneous inclinations to

[15] Daniel R. Miller and Guy E. Swanson, *The Changing American Parent* (New York: John Wiley & Sons, 1958).

[16] Melvin L. Kohn, "Social Class and Parental Values," *American Journal of Sociology*, LXIV (1959), 337–51.

[17] William H. Sewell, "Infant Training and the Personality of the Child," *ibid.*, LVIII (1952), 150–59; and Sewell, Paul H. Mussen, and Chester W. Harris, "Relationships among Child Training Practices," *American Sociological Review*, XX (1955), 137–48.

act, which are so often inhibited. To be sure, many impulses are responses to conventional meanings, but many others are unique. What is remarkable is that these dispositions are so often found together in recognizable syndromes. Authoritarian personalities are found in all cultural settings. In societies in which the overt domination of others is not tolerated, all kinds of indirect procedures are developed for accomplishing the same ends. Similarly, passive-dependent personalities, masochistic personalities, and paranoid personalities can be found everywhere. If this were not the case, novels translated from one language to another would be incomprehensible.

There are many conceptions of personality, but most psychiatrists and psychologists use the term to refer to the distinct style of behavior that marks off a given individual, best exemplified in his characteristic ways of handling people. The concept refers to something that is unique. Although most meanings are learned through participation in organized groups, they appear in a unique combination in each individual. It is difficult to see how one can account for the formation of a unique object in terms of culture patterns—conventional patterns presumably held in common by everyone in a group. If personality is the product of culture, everyone sharing a common cultural heritage should be alike. What needs to be explained is the fact that each person is different.

The widespread acceptance of culture and personality studies is quite amazing in view of the questionable evidence upon which they rest. In many of the studies of child-rearing practices, the coefficients of association are very low, and the data presented in different studies are contradictory. Of course, the empirical testing of ideas is always difficult, but acceptance must await proof. Perhaps all that can be said is that some types of persons are more likely to find fulfilment in one culture and failure in another. If so, a somewhat different incidence of personality disorders may be found. Many of the claims that have been made about various groups are plausible only when the people are viewed at a great distance. Literate members of the primitive tribes studied have been shocked at what has been said about them; many Americans were amazed at Gorer's account of their national character, just as Japanese scholars were unimpressed by the studies of Benedict and of Gorer.[18] Since

[18] Alfred R. Lindesmith and Anselm Strauss, "A Critique of Culture-Per-

the concepts of "modal personality" and "national character" are so tenuous in their reference, generalizations based upon them are dangerous. A political theorist who contends that the people in some country are more susceptible to Communism because they have been toilet trained in a particular manner is treading on very thin ice, if indeed there is any ice under him at all. National character, in spite of the allegedly scientific nature of its study, is much like a respectable ethnic stereotype—plausible primarily to those who do not have a sufficiently intimate familiarity with the people in question.

Individual Differences in Temperament

Any mother who has had more than one child can testify that no two children are alike. From the moment of their birth there are remarkable differences in patterns of sensitivity and reaction. Even identical twins and other offsprings of multiple birth show differences in temperament.[19] Although such observations are commonplace, social scientists tend to ignore constitutional differences, and imply that everything significant about human conduct can be accounted for in terms of environmental influences. But it is not necessary to take such an extreme stand to defend the integrity of the social sciences. Since social psychologists are concerned with the regularities in human behavior arising from associative living, they are interested in biological differences only to the extent that they affect one's capacity to participate in collective transactions. Although the matter is not yet settled, there is evidence of innate dispositions that cannot be ignored. The term *temperament* will be used to refer to those behavioral tendencies that are presumably inborn, although there is still some argument over which patterns are inherited and which are learned.

The aversion of many social scientists to discussions of temperament is often a reaction against the excessive claims of biological determinists. In popular discourse various crimes, personality dis-

sonality Writings," *ibid.*, XV (1950), 587–600. Cf. Reinhard Bendix, "Compliant Behavior and Individual Personality," *American Journal of Sociology,* LVIII (1952), 292–303.

[19] Cf. William E. Blatz, *The Five Sisters* (New York: William Morrow & Co., 1938).

orders, and undesirable traits are sometimes explained in terms of inheritance. The matter assumes greater significance when political parties or colonial settlers justify their ascendancy in terms of racial superiority. What social scientists oppose is the view that everything is determined by our genes, as if one's destiny were settled at the time of his conception, and that nothing that happens after his birth makes any difference. No competent biologist would take such an absurd position.

The recognition of constitutional differences does not require the rejection of the hypothesis that human infants are plastic and that most of their behavior patterns are learned in association with other people. It merely involves acknowledging that adjustment may be selective. Each human being is born with some patterns of receptivity already organized. For example, there is considerable variation among people in the extent to which they can tolerate frustration, the ease with which they become angry, and the intensity of their aggression if the frustration persists. Physiologists declare that epinephrine is injected into the blood stream when we are emotionally aroused, and they have been able to produce imagery and overt behavior patterns resembling those in psychosis by the artificial injection of this hormone. Since each person is born with a different endocrine balance, would it not be strange if there were no differences in the ease with which such chemical changes occur? Whether a person becomes a rebel or remains submissive may depend upon his threshold of frustration. All behavior is an organic process, and it would be strange if inherited variations in capacity did not make some difference.

A number of the behavior patterns that play an important part in daily life appear to be instinctive. Anyone who has observed the remarkable similarity between the stance of a cowardly dog and that of a faint-hearted human being cannot help but wonder of the extent to which such configurations are organically rooted. A dastardly dog barks menacingly when safely behind a barrier but flees in panic when exposed to the possibility of retaliation. The more primitive patterns of behavior, which are observable in children or in adults under conditions of intense excitement, are similar among human beings the world over. *All* human behavior certainly cannot be explained in terms of instincts, for such reactions are usually inhibited and redirected along conventional channels. But it would be a serious mistake to deny the existence of inborn dispositions.

Biologically inherited equipment does not determine what a man will do, but it sets definite limitations upon what he can do. Some children are weak and lack muscular coordination. Their inability to participate effectively in group games may lead to the formation of compensatory interests. Some children are very keen and can detect abstract relationships more readily than others; the ease with which they can handle intellectual problems opens many avenues for them that are closed to others. One obviously cannot hope to become a prima donna, a prizefighter, a research biochemist, or a professional gambler without special talents. Many skills can be cultivated through training, but even the most expertly managed program cannot produce a ballerina from a woman without the requisite physique and aptitude. Even more important, of course, are the conventional definitions of inherited characteristics, such as skin color, which in each society circumscribe the career lines that an individual might follow.

Sheldon made an extensive investigation of temperament, examining 200 college men over a period of five years. He was concerned with the spontaneous dispositions, presumably innate, which characterize each individual, and the frequency with which they occur together. After many preliminary studies he developed through factor analysis three scales for measuring such patterns, and devised a scheme whereby any human being could be conveniently described by a mathematical statement. His work has been maligned by a number of social scientists, some of whom have apparently not bothered to familiarize themselves with it.

Since extreme cases are more readily discernible, Sheldon devoted much of his attention to the types of people who would register very high scores on each of the scales. The type of individual characterized by general relaxation, love of comfort, and gluttony for food he referred to as "viscerotonic." They are people who are also marked by warmth, earthiness, indiscriminate good will, some slowness of reaction, and practicality in outlook; they enjoy the physical proximity of others and become anxious when isolated. The type of person marked by the predominance of muscular activity and bodily assertiveness he referred to as "somatotonic." They have physical drive and endurance and do not require too much sleep or food. But they do need exercise and show a strong preference for a vigorous life. A

third type he called "cerebrotonic." These individuals are characterized by restraint, tenseness, and a tendency to conceal. They shrink
away from conviviality; they repress their somatic and visceral expressions and are prone to digestive disturbances; and in critical
situations they have poor voice control. They also have difficulty in
tolerating excessive heat or cold, show good resistance to contagious
diseases other than colds, and are acutely sensitive to pain. In many
respects the third type resembles what Jung called an "introvert." It
should be emphasized that these are polar types, and Sheldon did
not claim that all men fall into one of these categories.

Nor did he claim that all of the behavioral tendencies he studied
were innate; he was quite cautious about drawing conclusions. But
the coefficient of correlation between temperament, as measured
on his scales, and the body types measured in a preceding study,
which are undeniably inherited, was about .8! This suggests that
many of the traits mentioned may be more closely related to one's
physical constitution than had previously been supposed.[20] Actually,
this has been recognized intuitively. In their portrayals of various
personifications, writers and artists rarely put the temperament of a
Falstaff into a lean and wiry body, nor is the disposition of a Scrooge
ever placed in an apple-cheeked and rotund man. No definite conclusions can be reached about such traits being inborn, but the
evidence is too compelling to be dismissed lightly.

Kallmann's study of the incidence of schizophrenia among those
genetically related to one another also points to the possible importance of temperament in personality development. His study centered upon the 691 patients admitted to twenty mental hospitals in
New York over a period of nine years who had a twin brother or
sister available for examination. He computed the incidence of
schizophrenia among these twins and other members of their immediate family and found that 1.8 per cent of their step-siblings, 2.1
per cent of their marriage partners, seven per cent of their half-
siblings, 9.2 per cent of their parents, 14.3 per cent of their full
siblings, 14.7 per cent of their two-egg co-twins, and 85.8 per cent
of their one-egg co-twins were also ill. The farther away the genetic
relationship, the lower the incidence of schizophrenia. Of course,
many of these cases can be explained in terms of a disturbed family

[20] William H. Sheldon, *The Varieties of Temperament* (New York: Harper
& Bros., 1942).

atmosphere, but a number of the siblings who were ill had been brought up separately in foster homes.[21] Some psychiatrists have contended that susceptibility to schizophrenia is inherited. This has never been demonstrated, but it is possible that some innate attribute does make a person more likely to meet stress in ways that tend to cut him off from other people.

There is some evidence that various patterns of sensitivity and response that are probably innate circumscribe the directions in which a person is likely to develop. This makes the formation of personal idiom easier to explain. No two people are born biologically alike, and no two people have identical backgrounds of experience. The meanings which make up each individual's orientation toward his surroundings are bound to be different. Although the study of constitutional differences lies beyond the range of social psychology, social psychologists cannot afford to remain indifferent to the findings in this field.

The Development of Sentiments

Since human beings make up an important part of the environment of any person, the manner in which he approaches them is a prominent part of his personality. Personal idiom becomes discernible in one's consistent orientation toward a distinct set of values, and his sentiments represent the manner in which he evaluates human beings. In our dealings with those with whom we are in sustained contact, we have to learn to do certain things and to avoid other things; some tactics work and others do not. We are then able to construct a fairly stable personification of each of these people and to know what to do in adjusting to them in a variety of circumstances. *Sentiments are behavioral systems that are formed in the course of learning to cope with significant others.*

The sentiments of different people are sufficiently alike to be recognizable, yet their variation is almost infinite. What is typical in each sentiment is organized through participation in recurrent networks of interpersonal relations, and what is idiosyncratic emerges from differential participation in such networks and from the distinctive demands made by the people with whom one as-

[21] Franz J. Kallmann, "The Genetic Theory of Schizophrenia," *American Journal of Psychiatry*, CIII (1946), 309-22.

sociates. Regardless of the cultural setting, many of the problems of adjusting to other human beings are alike. Each person must deal with authority figures, satisfy his curiosity about human beings, learn to handle differences of opinion, undergo crises in the company of others. Each individual learns to enact interpersonal roles by imitating or reacting to models. He may learn through direct participation in transactions or through vicarious participation, by observing the relationships between other people. The manner in which a given individual learns to handle himself in such contexts depends upon the demands that are made upon him by the people he meets in them. Each significant other has a unique personality, and there are certain ways of handling him that prove more expedient than others.

One should not confuse interpersonal roles with conventional roles, as Freud did in his otherwise insightful discussion of the formation of sentiments. In his theory of the Oedipus complex, for example, he wrote of the boy's attraction to his mother and his inability to compete successfully against his powerful father. But networks of interpersonal relations emerge in the reactions of unique individuals to one another; in one family the father is dominant, and in another the mother, the older brother, the maiden aunt, or the governess may exercise control. Furthermore, erotic attraction may in some cases be homosexual. To be sure, psychoanalysts do speak of "father-figures" and "mother-surrogates," but much of their research is still predicated upon ethnocentric assumptions. Malinowski pointed out long ago that Freud's principles would have much wider applicability if adjustments were made to take account of the variability of kinship systems.[22] It would be desirable to go even further to take account of the variability of interpersonal relations within the family.

Since all children are dependent upon others, collaboration of some sort is unavoidable. In cooperative transactions, a person learns to evaluate his partners as desirable objects, as sources of gratification. Typical experiences in such situations include resentment against those who fail to do their part, concern over those who are preoccupied only with personal gain, and gratitude toward those who contribute beyond their conventional obligations. Freud be-

[22] Bronislaw Malinowski, *Sex and Repression in Savage Society* (London: Routledge & Kegan Paul, 1927).

lieved that all children are at first egocentric, and learn to love other people only to the extent that they are useful as a means to their own pleasures. Such narcissism may subsequently develop into disinterested love, or "genuine object cathexis." This is probably true in many cases. The manner in which a child learns to love other people depends upon his peculiar experiences in collaborative activities. An overprotective mother, while pursuing her own interests, may smother her child with gestures of affection, perhaps to compensate for the loneliness of her own life. The child who is faced with the necessity of coping with selfish demands from a source of pleasure may develop a conditional and defensive orientation toward all love objects.

Since conflicting interests are bound to arise among those who are in constant association, opposition is also unavoidable. It is in contests of all kinds that children learn to evaluate other people as frustrating or even dangerous objects, and to develop ways of approaching rivals and enemies. Typical experiences include disappointment in defeat, elation at victory, respect for the ability of a foe who puts up a sturdy fight, appreciation of the importance of fair play. Freud not only recognized the inevitability of rivalries within each family, but placed great stress upon them. There are many other competitive contexts, and the manner in which each person forms disjunctive sentiments depends upon his fate in them—the frequency of his success or the intensity of his deprivations. In sibling rivalries it is far more difficult to have to compete with an attractive sister who can get anything she wants than it is to deal with an obstinate brother who is always in trouble. Aggression rests upon contrast conceptions, and individuals differ in their ability to impute vile motives to other people. The capacity for hating with great intensity is probably established quite early in life. The extent to which hostilities exist among very young children was dramatically revealed in a study of sibling rivalries by Levy. Some of the children who had been given dolls representing various members of their family smashed them into small bits, while they were professing their love.[23]

Since the egocentric impulses of children must be curbed, the imposition of some kind of external control becomes necessary. In

[23] David M. Levy, *Studies in Sibling Rivalry* (New York: American Orthopsychiatric Association, 1937).

each group someone assumes responsibility for coordinating activities. Most parents approach their offspring with condescension, viewing them as lovable but incompetent and feeling that important decisions must be made for them. At the same time the children themselves come into contact with personifications they can dominate—younger and weaker children, dolls, pets, and other toys. Very early in life each child develops ways of approaching powerful as well as subordinate figures, and it is in such contexts that he learns to evaluate people as superior or inferior objects. Authority figures may be addressed with awe, with respect, or with resentment. Subordinates may be treated with condescension, contempt, or with the appearance of equality. The sentiment formed depends upon the personality of his father, elder sister, gang leader, scoutmaster, teacher, or anyone else who plays a prominent part in providing guidance. A father with paranoid tendencies, though overtly agreeable, is rigid and quite demanding, and his child may find that submission is the only way to get along with him.

Although the transactions just described are unavoidable, there are considerable differences among people in the frequency with which they are called upon to assume various interpersonal roles. Part of the uniqueness in the sentiments of various individuals arises from differential participation. Even though most men are able to comprehend the gamut of human sentiments, there are differences in their sensitivities, in the kinds of personifications they characteristically construct, and in their ability to perform interpersonal roles effectively. Those who have rarely been the object of disinterested love find it difficult to believe that anyone could be more concerned with the welfare of another human being than with his own interests. When a child is thoroughly "spoiled," he remains egocentric; he takes it for granted that everything exists for his personal benefit. In psychoanalytic terminology, in the absence of adequate authority figures the superego does not develop, and the child's object relations remain at the narcissistic level. Such individuals encounter difficulties in cooperating with others on equal terms and tend to withdraw from the kinds of contacts in which they might learn to appreciate altruistic orientations.

An important feature of each individual's orientation toward other people is the characteristic social distance that he maintains from them. Some are immediately responsive to others. Others tend to remain aloof; although they are courteous and considerate, they always hold themselves off at a polite distance. No one actually knows how these differences emerge, but the hypothesis may be advanced that the characteristic social distance that any person maintains constitutes an adaptation to the demands of the people with whom he has had to deal in his primary groups. If significant others are warm and affectionate, a child learns to reciprocate in kind, for this is the easiest path to gratifications of all kinds. On the other hand, if a child is constantly rebuffed or reproached for his spontaneous exuberance, he soon learns to protect himself. Traumatic experiences following candid revelations of inner feelings may result in greater caution in dealing with people. Some children rarely have an opportunity to get very close to anyone. The ability to establish intimate ties with people is apparently related to one's conception of human nature—whether he regards human beings as dangerous or as sources of pleasure. Empathy is apparently established quite early in life.

The sentiments that are formed early in life are subsequently displaced upon other objects, giving each person a distinct style of approaching people in general. Some men respond affectionately to all older women; others are repelled by fat men or dislike shaggy eyebrows. To test the hypothesis that people are attracted to personifications similar to those which had provided satisfactions in the past, Strauss studied 373 engaged or recently married subjects to see whether or not there were any similarities between their mate and their parent of the opposite sex. There was not much resemblance in physical type nor in political opinions, but a significant relationship appeared in personal traits. Those who loved their parent tended to choose the same type of person for a mate, and those who did not tended to select the opposite type. Although the statistics are not impressive, some of the interview materials cited are revealing.[24] Some psychiatrists have contended that the succession of people with whom one falls in love are only so many transformations of a single love object formed early in life. Some people respond to all authority figures—teachers, police officers, foremen, sergeants—in much the same way that they once reacted to their parents. Innovators in the political, religious, or intellectual

[24] Anselm Strauss, "The Influence of Parent-Images upon Marital Choice," *American Sociological Review*, XI (1946), 554–59.

world are sometimes rebels; they are contemptuous of the prevailing tendencies and go out of their way to assert their independence. Some people apparently go through life displacing upon others their hatred for their parents. Although clinical reports frequently support this contention, the evidence is not entirely consistent.[25] The manner in which interpersonal roles are handled early in life apparently leaves marks upon each person. He develops a limited vocabulary of motives and a working conception of human nature. It is no accident that Burgess and Cottrell found that happy marriages are more frequent among children of happily married parents. The affectional patterns established in childhood tend to carry over into adult life.[26]

Most important of all, sentiments are displaced upon oneself. Each person forms a self-conception within a social matrix, and the way in which he evaluates himself depends upon the manner in which he has been treated by significant others. His level of self-esteem is adequate if he is able to direct conjunctive sentiments toward himself. But if he regards himself as an inferior or a dangerous object, he is likely to encounter difficulties. Each person's level of self-esteem is apparently set quite early in life, and subsequent transformations occur only under rather unusual circumstances.

There appears to be increasing consensus among psychiatrists that *the development of an adequate level of self-esteem depends upon one's being the object of disinterested love.* Self-respect does not rest upon success, for successful people sometimes despise themselves. Nor does pride automatically follow from ability or beauty, for there are competent and attractive men and women who are known to suffer from an inferiority complex. A sense of personal worth apparently develops from the spontaneous and unsolicited affection and respect of those with whom one identifies himself. If there is evidence of being missed when he is gone, a person feels that he is needed. If his word is not questioned, his ability not belittled, and his judgments, immature as they may be, taken

[25] Cf. Leroy S. Burwen and Donald T. Campbell, "The Generality of Attitudes toward Authority and Nonauthority Figures," *Journal of Abnormal and Social Psychology*, LIV (1957), 24–31.

[26] Ernest W. Burgess and Leonard S. Cottrell, *Predicting Success and Failure in Marriage* (New York: Prentice-Hall, Inc., 1939), pp. 90–113. Cf. Donald L. Burnham, "Misperception of Other Persons in Schizophrenia," *Psychiatry*, XIX (1956), 283–303; and Nelson N. Foote and L. S. Cottrell, *Identity and Interpersonal Competence* (Chicago: University of Chicago Press, 1955).

seriously and corrected without embarrassment, he is able to feel respected and trusted. If he is envied by his rivals for the attention the he receives, he can feel that he is desired; the jealousy of siblings often confirms the affection imputed to parents. The love must be unconditional. Then the child can conceive of himself as a worthwhile object because of what he is, not because he happens to be obedient for the moment.

Conversely, a person develops a low level of self-esteem if as a child he becomes the object of disjunctive sentiments or of possessive love. One way a child may learn to conceive of himself as undesirable is by being the object of constant disparagement. An insecure parent often asserts his ascendancy over the comparatively helpless child. If the latter refuses to submit, their relationship becomes competitive. The parent laughs at the child's aspirations, belittles his efforts, gloats triumphantly at his failures, and overlooks his successes as inconsequential. Another way a child may learn to question his worth is to be told over and over that he is "bad." As he is continually punished, he accepts this estimate and at times may even feel obliged to comply with it. A low level of self-esteem may also arise when a child is approached as a useful object. Some parents shower their children with affection only when they are "good," when they comply with demands. Many children are used merely as tools for gratification. Some parents see in their children the possibility of realizing their own thwarted ambitions, and begin to groom them from a tender age for a career in which the youngsters may have no interest. Such children are presented with many advantages, but they are placed under heavy pressure to succeed. Should they fail to attain the parental goal, they are struck with remorse and become convinced that they are worthless.

Sometimes parents of mental patients are outraged at the suggestion that they do not love their children enough, and tend to blame the difficulties upon heredity or upon some childhood accident. They often point to the material advantages they had provided, perhaps at considerable sacrifice, and to their constant protestations of love. But many sentiments are unconscious. The lack of awareness on the part of the parent places many of his dispositions beyond control, and the child is consistently treated as a source of deprivations. A child brought up by an unkempt grandfather who is too busy supporting the family for ostentatious displays of affection may develop considerable self-confidence, if he can see that sacrifices are made for him. What is apparently decisive are the premises upon which a long succession of overt acts rest. If the diverse acts directed toward a child, including punishment, are all predicated upon concern for his well-being, he will probably be able to see himself as an object of value.

Sentiments toward oneself, once formed, tend to be self-sustaining. Behavior patterns are altered somewhat each time a person learns a new conventional role, but his characteristic ways of approaching people usually remain fairly stable. Each individual tends to construct personifications in terms of motives that are plausible to him and to perceive in other people what he is already prepared to see. Each person's level of self-esteem is established when he is still quite young, and it is not too likely to be transformed by subsequent experiences of success or failure. Feelings of inadequacy usually impair ones' capacity to change; a person who is convinced that he is unlovable often surrounds himself with a protective shell and becomes so anxiety ridden that he cannot get close enough to other people to find out what their sentiments are. The feeling of being unloved also impairs one's ability to love others. A man with a low level of self-esteem needs respect and affection from someone that he loves, but he is so preoccupied with defending himself that he is unable to love anyone except as a useful object.[27] This suggests that the difficulties may go on for several generations, as egocentric parents mete out only conditional affection.

Although characteristic ways of approaching people crystallize early in life, they are not necessarily fixed for all time. Sentiments are emergent orientations, and as life conditions change, they are also altered. Since sentiments are built up in primary groups, any drastic change in the network of interpersonal relations in which one is involved should lead to some alteration. Each time a new person comes into his life, each time a stranger becomes an intimate friend, each time a friend proves to be a disappointment, one learns something new about human nature. Erotic attraction sometimes results in remarkable transformations. Initially the appeal of the love object may be primarily physical, but sustained interaction with a person very different from those previously encountered may lead

[27] Cf. Andrus Angyal, "A Theoretical Model for Personality Studies," *Journal of Personality*, XX (1951), 131–42.

to a new outlook on life. The relationship between a husband and wife may change when a child is born. Both may vie for its affection and find themselves rivals rather than lovers. Those who had previously been incapable of disinterested love may be moved by the completely helpless and dependent infant with whom they are so closely identified. As children grow older, parent-child relationships also change. Growing children often resent their inferior status. The "psychological weaning" that occurs during adolescence often consists of breaking off dependence upon one's parents, acquiring a somewhat different perspective, and asserting autonomy. Similar changes in interpersonal relations can occur in many other conventional settings.[28]

Each person's orientation toward his human environment is formed and sustained in social interaction. His sentiments, toward himself as well as toward other people, are organized while he is learning to cope with specific people. With the establishment of new interpersonal relationships, especially with the appearance of new significant others at critical moments, one may alter his perspective and perceive himself and his fellows in a different light. Psychoanalysts should be the last to contend that sentiments do not change. If this were true, there would be little point to psychotherapy. But as Freud pointed out, the transformations can take place only after the establishment of "transference," an intimate tie between the patient and the therapist.

Significant Others and Personality

The distinctive demands made upon each person by the individuals among whom he grows up are of crucial importance in the formation of his personality, for the manner in which he becomes oriented toward his surroundings takes shape in the course of dealing with them. Meanings are shaped in a social matrix. Orientations toward various objects are learned in response to the expectations of other people, each of whom has a distinct personality. The meanings that are built up in childhood contain the longings, the contradictions, and the ambivalences of their origin; incorporated in them are the responses to the ministrations and frustrations of significant others.

[28] Cf. French, op. cit., 276–77.

Each person develops a special way of approaching his world, and this style is related to the personalities of his intimate associates.

This suggests that specific child-rearing practices are not related to personality development except insofar as they constitute manifestations of the mother's sentiment toward the child. In her study of thirty-two mothers, Brody concentrated upon feeding procedures, since they are central in a mother's interaction with her child. Collecting data through extended interviews, motion pictures, and a variety of questionnaires, she found that there are different modes of approaching the infant. Some mothers are able to adjust readily to the needs of the child; others are consciously willing to accommodate but are more distant and insensitive; others tend to be efficient but are detached and lacking in spontaneity; and still others are erratic and unaware of the consequences of their activities for the child. Breast-feeding or staying on a schedule, for example, can be accomplished in many different ways. As far as the personal adjustment of the child is concerned, the *style* of the mother's care appeared to be more important than the particular technique used.[29] Behrens studied twenty-five mothers of maladjusted children through interviews, projective tests, group therapy sessions, and home visits. An analysis of their child-training practices revealed no common pattern; indeed, it showed a wide range of variation. However, there was a high correlation between the mother's general orientation toward her offspring and the personality adjustment score of the child.[30] It is possible that the current interest in child-rearing techniques, although valuable for other purposes, is likely to yield little that is relevant for an understanding of personality development.

Among the earlier attempts to examine the importance of networks of interpersonal relations in the formation of personal idiom were the studies of order of birth in the family. Several psychiatrists, Adler in particular, had suggested that the first child is likely to be treated differently from his successors, and therefore more likely to develop along certain lines. Taking all of the admissions to Elgin State Hospital, Illinois, for a period of six months, Wahl studied the

[29] Sylvia Brody, *Patterns of Mothering* (New York: International Universities Press, 1956), pp. 319–21.

[30] Marjorie C. Behrens, "Child Rearing and the Character Structure of the Mother," *Child Development*, XXV (1954), 225–38. Cf. Sewell, Mussen, and Harris, *op. cit.*

ordinal position of 392 patients in their respective families. Approximately twenty-four per cent of the cases were the oldest, but twenty-three per cent were the youngest. There was ample evidence of disturbances in interpersonal relations, rejection, overprotection, separation from parents, and other childhood tragedies; however, he was forced to conclude that order of birth is unrelated to mental illness.[31] On the other hand, McArthur studied the families of eighty-six Harvard alumni, each of whom had two or more children. Of the fathers, twenty-five were first-born, and thirteen were second-born. He found that the eldest child in a family tends to be adult-oriented —serious, easily hurt, obedient, fond of adult company, and self-reliant. The second child is likely to be more placid, friendly, cheerful, stubborn, and rebellious; he is easier to look after, although he makes no special effort to please. In spite of the striking differences in the child-rearing practices of the two generations, the personalities of the first-born and second-born bear striking resemblances. This suggests that parents handle the second child more permissively, and sixty-five per cent of those interviewed admitted that they became more relaxed by the time the second child came along.[32] Being the oldest or the youngest child may bring certain typical privileges or responsibilities. However, there are many significant others besides parents—siblings, friends, and teachers, as well as imaginary personifications—and they are met in a variety of contexts.

Since many behavioral dispositions are manifested in exaggerated form among those who are psychotic, special attention has been directed toward the past interpersonal relations of those suffering of mental disorders. Since the patients are classified according to their symptoms, something is known about their personality traits. Unfortunately, there is considerable disagreement among psychiatrists over nosology, but these rough categories provide some basis for the formulation of generalizations.

Levy's exploratory study of maternal overprotection points to the relationship between the compulsive behavior of mothers and the

[31] C. W. Wahl, "Some Antecedent Factors in the Family Histories of 392 Schizophrenics," *American Journal of Psychiatry*, CX (1954), 668–76.

[32] Charles McArthur, "Personalities of First and Second Children," *Psychiatry*, XIX (1956), 47–54. Cf. Robert R. Sears, "Ordinal Position in the Family as a Psychological Variable," *American Sociological Review*, XV (1950), 397–401; and Sears, Maccoby, and Levin, *op. cit.*, pp. 394–419.

development of disturbances among their children. He defined "overprotection" in terms of excessive physical contacts, treating a growing child like a helpless infant, and oversolicitous prevention of risks. Some overprotective mothers dominate their children; their credo seems to be: this is my child, and he must do as I wish. Other mothers indulge them; their credo appears to be: I am his mother, and I will do whatever he wants. But the second type of woman tends to dominate other people, such as her husband. To these parents a child is something owned, not another human being with rights of his own. Another characteristic of such mothers is that they constantly remind the child of the enormous sacrifices that devoted parents are forced to make. Although Levy's study is based upon a limited number of cases, it points to the remarkable similarity in the interpersonal relations of those with similar problems.[33]

The relationship between female patients and their mothers has also been investigated. Especially revealing is the report by Abrahams and Varon of group therapy sessions held at St. Elizabeth's Hospital, Washington, D.C., of seven pairs of schizophrenic women and their mothers. The account showed that the mothers depended upon the sickness of their daughters, almost as if they had so little self-confidence that they could not feel adequate unless their children remained completely dependent. The sessions revealed the extremely condescending, destructive superiority on the part of the mothers and the cold rejection by the daughters. The mothers exhibited unabashed seduction, vindictive domineering, distant and pained non-intervention toward their daughters. The daughters usually presented a blank face, broken occasionally by a mocking smile or laugh. Despite the seemingly close attachment between each mother and her daughter, an observer formed the impression that there were two groups meeting simultaneously—one of neurotic women and another of psychotic women. The two groups were hardly on speaking terms. The mothers occasionally got together in general discussions of their problems, and the daughters on occasion joined in laughing at some mother who had been made to feel uncomfortable. The patients did not say very much, but they did

[33] David M. Levy, *Maternal Overprotection* (New York: Columbia University Press, 1943). Cf. Jacob Kasanin *et al.*, "The Parent-Child Relationship in Schizophrenia," *Journal of Nervous and Mental Disease*, LXXIX (1934), 249–63.

interject curiously appropriate comments—mostly sarcastic or contradictory. After more than forty sessions some of the mothers recognized the life-long opposition between their daughters and themselves. After more than eighty sessions some of the mothers confessed their resentment toward their daughters, but others continued to deny any disjunctive sentiment. Although there were no dramatic cures, the relationship between each mother and her child was somewhat improved. The data presented are unusual in that the therapy sessions provided a setting in which each parent and her child could live out before the eyes of a psychiatrist the relationships that are usually recited retrospectively from a defensive standpoint.[34]

Considerable attention has been devoted to identifying the type of parent who makes unreasonable demands upon his offsprings, and the personality of the mothers of those confined for schizophrenia has come in for special scrutiny. Of the twenty-five mothers studied by Tietze, thirteen admitted that their marriage was unhappy, and nine claimed that it was "perfect," even in the face of alcoholism, suicide, and other contradictory evidence. In each family the mother played the dominant role, even if the father was the provider. The mothers were found to be sexually unresponsive, and they punished their children severely for showing an interest in sex. Some of the patients claimed that they could "feel" the hostility of their mother even when they were treated well.[35] Using 139 statements on the proper manner in which a child should be reared, Mark asked 100 mothers of male mental patients and a control group of 100 mothers of other patients to indicate the extent to which they agreed with each item. There were some remarkable similarities in the answers given by the mothers of mental patients, and their position was significantly different from that of the other mothers. Among the items on which they showed a high degree of consensus were: children should be escorted to and from school until they are eight years old; a mother should know everything her child is thinking; if a child is quiet, the mother should go to see what he is doing; a child should not annoy his parents with unimportant problems; a devoted mother has no time for social life; a watchful mother can

[34] Joseph Abrahams and Edith Varon, *Maternal Dependency and Schizophrenia* (New York: International Universities Press, 1953).

[35] Trude Tietze, "A Study of Mothers of Schizophrenic Patients," *Psychiatry*, XII (1949), 55–65.

keep her child from having accidents; playing too much with a child will "spoil" him; parents must never make mistakes before a child; parents should sacrifice everything for their child; when a father punishes a child for no good reason, the mother should side with the child; a mother has to suffer much and can say little; most children are toilet trained by the time they are fifteen months old; children who take part in sex play become sex criminals; a child should not enter an occupation of which his parents do not approve; too much affection will turn a child into a "softie." These mothers seemed to agree upon restrictive and coercive measures.[36] Rather than interview parents, Kohn and Clausen questioned forty-five patients and compared their replies with a control group of people matched with the patients except for their mental health. A larger proportion of those with schizophrenia perceived their mother as having played a major role in family decision-making; saw their mother as having been strict, sure of herself, dominating, and restrictive; and saw their father as having wielded relatively little authority over them. However, the male patients indicated that they preferred their mother, and the women said that they preferred their father.[37] There is a remarkable similarity in the overall pattern revealed. Study after study shows that an understanding of the feelings of the child is conspicuously lacking among parents of mental patients; the data point to domineering women and parents who are horrified at sex.

Although the evidence is not entirely consistent, it tends to support the hypothesis that there is a relationship between the compulsive tendencies of the parent and the personality disorders of the child. Although investigators have concentrated largely upon the mother, the same patterns of domination may be enacted by whoever is given the responsibility of caring for the child—an older sister, a cousin, a nurse, a governess, a maiden aunt, a grandmother, or the father.[38] Each child becomes attached to someone upon whom he is dependent, identifies himself with that person, and uses him as a

[36] Joseph C. Mark, "The Attitudes of the Mothers of Male Schizophrenics toward Child Behavior," *Journal of Abnormal and Social Psychology*, XLVIII (1953), 185–89.

[37] Melvin L. Kohn and John A. Clausen, "Parental Authority Behavior and Schizophrenia," *American Journal of Orthopsychiatry*, XXVI (1956), 297–313.

[38] Cf. Theodore Lidz et al., "The Intrafamilial Environment of the Schizophrenic Patient: The Father," *Psychiatry*, XX (1957), 329–42; and Suzanne Reichard and Carl Tillman, "Patterns of Parent-Child Relationships in Schizophrenia," *ibid.*, XIII (1950), 247–57.

model in role-playing. It might be more economical to formulate generalizations about an interpersonal role. Then the personality of the child can be seen as being related to the manner in which this role is played, regardless of the conventional designation of the person who plays it.

Other theories have been advanced by psychiatrists which emphasize the important part played by significant others in the development of schizophrenia. Bateson and his associates have contended that schizophrenia is a form of adaptation, a way of dealing with a "double-bind" situation. The orientation of the patient is marked by helplessness, fear, exasperation, and rage. But the person whose behavior elicits such reactions has no understanding of the process, because what he does is necessary for his own defense. Difficulties arise when an individual is involved in an intense relationship with a person from whom he receives simultaneously two messages that contradict each other. For example, his mother may say something through conventional symbols which is flatly contradicted by her expressive movements. She may profess her love for him, then stiffen when he reaches out to kiss her. The constant reception of such contradictory messages leads the patient to see his world in these confused terms. The disorder is much like any self-correcting system that has lost its governor; it spirals on in a never ending distortion.[39]

It is difficult to generalize about schizophrenia because the term does not refer to a homogeneous category. Bonner's study of the antecedents of paranoid disorders is confined to a more narrowly defined set of syndromes. A person who is paranoid is marked by boundless ambition and drives himself toward goals that are often beyond his ability. He conceives of himself as being mistreated; if he fails, he does not retreat but attacks. Other characteristics include the formation of persistent, systematized delusion, the relative infrequency of hallucinations, and the development of intense hatred and suspicion. On the surface his conduct does not appear disturbed, and he is socially acceptable, but inwardly the person is rigid and unable to form reasonable judgments in the areas covered by his delusions. In a study of 250 patients classified as paranoid, Bonner found that very few came from happy homes. The parents

[39] Gregory Bateson, D. D. Jackson, Jay Haley, and John Weakland, "Toward a Theory of Schizophrenia," *Behavioral Science*, I (1956), 251–64; and Jay Haley, "An Interactional Description of Schizophrenia," *Psychiatry*, XXII (1959), 321–32.

often set up perfectionist standards that produced a "well brought up" child with a low level of self-esteem. A person who is paranoid probably hates his parents because they hate him, and this sentiment becomes his permanent way of approaching people.[40]

If parents unconsciously make compulsive demands upon their children, there should be a succession of mental aberrations from generation to generation. According to Horney, neurotic symptoms develop when a child experiences his environment as unreliable, unappreciative, unfair, or merciless. When parental behavior is inconsistent, the child feels harassed and is forced to build defensive strategies which will enable him to cope with this world.[41] The neurotic symptoms of children often complement those of the parents. Fisher and Mendell studied six families for three generations with projective tests and interviews. In each family they found a consistent preoccupation with certain themes, such as death, exhibitionism, or fear over the loss of self-control. There were similarities between grandparents and grandchildren who had had only limited contacts with one another.[42] Freud contended that no generation could conceal its more important psychic processes from the next, and data from various sources support his belief.

If personality is formed and sustained in an interpersonal matrix, any change in the behavior patterns of a single participant should result in the disturbance of the network, and studies of the family ties of people undergoing psychotherapy show that this is the case. The recovery of a mental patient—the termination of his inappropriate acts—upsets the previously established equilibrium, and new problems emerge. In a study of the husbands of women undergoing intensive psychotherapy with male therapists, Moran found that at first the husband feels allied with the therapist and participates sympathetically. As the therapy gets under way, however, he is disappointed at being left out and becomes apprehensive. When transference is established, he becomes envious or jealous, depending upon his sentiment toward the doctor. In one case the woman,

[40] Hubert Bonner, "Sociological Aspects of Paranoia," *American Journal of Sociology*, LVI (1950), 255–62; and "The Problem of Diagnosis in Paranoic Disorder," *American Journal of Psychiatry*, CVII (1951), 677–83.

[41] Karen Horney, *Our Inner Conflicts* (New York: W. W. Norton & Co., 1945).

[42] Seymour Fisher and David Mendell, "The Communication of Neurotic Patterns over Two and Three Generations," *Psychiatry*, XIX (1956), 41–46. Cf. Levy, *Maternal Overprotection, op. cit.*, pp. 148–49; and Winch, *op. cit.*

during sexual intercourse, called her husband by the therapist's first name, and he became so upset that he sought sterilization. As treatment progresses, the husband becomes more and more concerned. Some of his wife's symptoms had gratified him, and as they change, he finds himself with unexpected difficulties. At the termination of therapy many husbands are ambivalent. Some even claim that the psychiatrist is responsible for "wrecking my home." Of course, successful psychotherapy often results in favorable changes in the experiences of those involved with the patient.[43]

Since most of the studies cited have been made by psychiatrists or clinical psychologists concerned with the etiology of mental disorders, emphasis has been placed upon the emergence of traits regarded as undesirable. This sometimes results in the erroneous inference that children who are treated in the opposite ways will develop desirable attributes. This error arises from the tendency to divide people into the "normal" and the "abnormal," as if the two categories were diametrically opposed. There is no agreement as to what constitutes a "normal" person; certainly he cannot be an individual without faults, for *everyone* has some compulsion that would be defined as neurotic. Those who are the object of affection tend to show greater spontaneity and are able to relate themselves more readily to others. But they may also become so preoccupied with having a good time that they are somewhat lax about their responsibilities. A child brought up indulgently may develop a horror of any kind of pain and avoid it with desperation. He may also become extremely dependent. It has been observed that those who have had a happy childhood are unable to keep up in a highly competitive field, for they are reluctant to exert themselves. Whether special effort is needed to lose weight, save a marriage, or work for a promotion, a person who has never had to struggle may be unable to act with intense determination. He tends to acquiesce to practices of which he disapproves rather than insist upon improvements. Many of the people who are blessed with the traits approved by psychiatrists are also marked by dispositions that are condemned. Avoiding the contexts in which serious illnesses develop does not produce the perfect man—only one that is different.

[43] Marion L. Moran, "Some Emotional Responses of Patients' Husbands to the Psychotherapeutic Course," *American Journal of Orthopsychiatry*, XXIV (1954), 317–25. Cf. Erika Chance, *Families in Treatment* (New York: Basic Books, Inc., 1959).

Although it is not conclusive, there is considerable evidence to support the view that characteristic modes of approaching the world arc crystallized while coming to terms with specific people encountered relatively early in life. Some anthropologists have suggested that there are cultural differences in interpersonal relations. In their study of Truk Island, for example, Gladwin and Sarason contended that the Trukese child, being dependent upon adults who are highly egocentric, develops into an adult who is incapable of deep, lasting personal ties.[44] This may prove to be true. But astute observers of human nature, including Cooley and Freud, are inclined to disagree. Cooley wrote primarily of conjunctive sentiments, and Freud concentrated upon disjunctive sentiments, but in their theories of the formation of personal idiom both stressed the importance of adjusting to particular people. What is unique in the personality of a significant other is manifested in those dispositions that are *not* organized along conventional lines.

Summary and Conclusion

Social psychologists generally conceive of socialization in terms of learning—the acquisition of the conventional meanings that constitute the culture of the group. But this does not account for individual differences. The variation found among those sharing a common cultural heritage is often explained in terms of innate differences in temperament. But this does not account for the remarkable similarities found in personality types among those who are not likely to have had common ancestors. Considerations such as these lead to the hypothesis, increasingly entertained by psychiatrists, that one's personality is shaped while coping with the demands of significant others in recurrent networks of interpersonal relations. Interpersonal relations vary independently of culture, and similar sentiments are found everywhere. Since each significant other has a unique personality, each individual becomes human in his own unique way.

Personal idiom arises in part from constitutional differences, for no one is born quite like anyone else. These differences are further accentuated by the fact that each person has a unique background of experience; even identical twins cannot possibly approach the world

[44] Thomas Gladwin and Seymour B. Sarason, *Truk: Man in Paradise* (New York: The Viking Fund, 1953).

from the same standpoint. The diversity is even more accentuated by the necessity of coming to terms with a unique combination of significant others. Each personality begins to take shape during the early years and is most affected by the sentiments with which a child is approached. Once a style of life has developed, it becomes the basis for selection in later development. Each person is handicapped or assisted by the tools found expedient in dealing with the people encountered during the formative years. Each functional unit is emergent, and the attributes of each person may be regarded as adaptations to extant conditions of life.

Suggested References

EATON, JOSEPH W. and ROBERT J. WEIL, *Culture and Mental Disorders.* Glencoe: Free Press, 1955. A study of mental disorders in selected Hutterite communities, revealing differences in symptoms and in treatment but an incidence of psychosis similar to that in unstable communities.

ERIKSON, ERIK H., *Childhood and Society.* New York: W. W. Norton & Co., 1950. An attempt to integrate anthropological data into the psychoanalytic theory of personal growth, pointing to the irrational dispositions inadvertently shaped in each society as by-products of efforts to produce a desired type of adult.

HORNEY, KAREN, *Our Inner Conflicts.* New York: W. W. Norton & Co., 1945. The development of neurotic personalities viewed as a reaction to disturbances in interpersonal relations, with a preliminary classification of ways of coping with situations that provoke anxiety.

LEVY, DAVID M., *Maternal Overprotection.* New York: Columbia University Press, 1943. An investigation of extreme cases of maternal overprotection, with accounts of the typical patterns of domination and of the characteristic difficulties encountered by sheltered children.

PARSONS, TALCOTT and ROBERT F. BALES, *Family, Socialization, and Interaction Process.* Glencoe: Free Press, 1955. A proposed scheme for the systematic study of personality development, drawing upon psychoanalysis, group dynamics, and the comparative study of kinship systems.

SHELDON, WILLIAM H., *Varieties of Human Temperament.* New York: Harper & Bros., 1942. An extensive study of the measurement of temperamental differences, with accounts of the three types of men who register extreme scores on the scales.

17

Social
change
and
personal
growth

The popularity of social psychology may be increasing because so many people in modern mass societies are plagued by personal problems. In any rapidly changing society, there are apparently fewer people who feel fulfilled. Many are tense, irritable, and restless, dissatisfied no matter what they do. They experience amorphous impulses. Their behavior becomes erratic; they try one thing after another without being sure of just what it is that they want to do. With no particular goal in sight, sometimes life itself seems pointless. Their imagination also wanders; they often find themselves immersed in daydreams that are remote from probabilities. Some people are confronted with more specific difficulties—marital discord, violations of the law, inability to hold a job, addiction to proscribed practices, or chronic psychosomatic disorders.

Some observers have contended that a sick individual is the product of a sick society, as if personal problems were the individual counterpart of social disorganization. But the person and the group are separate functional units, and changes in the two do not necessarily coincide. There are people who live through a revolution and retain their personalities intact, and there are others who live in relatively stable societies and still develop neurotic or psychotic symptoms. But there are characteristic problems which confront those who live in a changing society and typical ways in which men attempt to cope with environmental changes. From the standpoint of the participant, the cultural matrix may be altered in two ways— through transformations in social structure or through social mobility. In either case the person must deal with new demands.

Socialization is a lifelong process of adapting to new conditions, and living in a changing society only adds to the usual problems. Groups of which one had been a part may dissolve, and he finds himself with new associates. His status in the community may rise or fall, and he may find himself in organizations quite different from those he had encountered in the past. Although the study of social change is only beginning, striking similarities have already been noted in the experiences of people caught in such circumstances. A closer study of these adjustments will not only give us a better appreciation of some of our own difficulties, but will also enable us to understand the sustaining processes that make most societies appear stable.

Social Change and Deviant Behavior

Since the common sense view of the world is replete with value judgments, it is not surprising that we tend to look upon crime, pecuniary dependency, suicide, or the high incidence of neurosis as "evils" that should be eliminated. Such phenomena are often explained in terms of the inheritance of undesirable traits, lack of moral fortitude, or the inadequacy of educational facilities. One of the most valuable theories in sociology is the view of Thomas and Znaniecki that *social disorganization is an incidental part of the process of social change.* They pointed out that most of the phenomena condemned by those who are well-established occur when there is a decreasing influence of group norms upon the conduct of individuals. *Social change,* the transformation of social structures, is not likely to occur without a temporary breakdown of consensus.[1]

Social structure consists of patterns of concerted action. These patterns remain intact and are discernible as long as each participant conforms to conventional norms. When life conditions are fairly stable, men continue to act in a habitual manner; the "cake of custom" is not easily broken, for social sanctions discourage those who are tempted to defect. But in crisis situations, a number of people find it difficult to continue living under their old obligations. Understandings that had once been shared are called into question. Social change almost invariably involves some breakdown in social control.

When life conditions change, new needs arise, and a collective effort is made to adjust to the situation. New procedures are suggested and tried, and some old meanings are abandoned. It is not often that all of the people involved will do this simultaneously, although new collective patterns are sometimes instituted by common consent.[2] There is usually a period of transition marked by disagreement over the appropriate modes of conduct. This is a period of misunderstandings; people who act in good faith find themselves rebuffed. Concerted action breaks down. Moral conduct results in coordination only in a stable setting. When consensus breaks down, individuals who continue to live in accordance with old principles are often ridiculed; sometimes they are viciously condemned, especially by those who feel guilty about violating the norms they had once accepted. During this period, starts are made toward new patterns of coordination.

When life conditions change, old groups dissolve, and new ones are formed. Difficulties in attaining reasonable gratifications lead to alienation from old meanings and an increasing sensitivity to new possibilities. Those defending the traditional ways view the innovations with alarm, but others see the old patterns as barriers to the quest of reasonable aspirations, barriers perpetuated by selfish old men who want to exercise authority that is no longer legitimate. Networks of interpersonal relations also undergo transformation. A man who had once commanded unquestioned authority in his primary group may find his views challenged by younger associates. The greatest strain falls upon those whose position has been rendered

---

[1] Thomas and Znaniecki, *op. cit.*, Vol. II, pp. 1117–1264, 1647–1827. Cf. Wirth, *Community Life and Social Policy, op. cit.*, pp. 192–205.

[2] Cf. Margaret Mead, *New Lives for Old* (New York: William Morrow & Co.. 1956).

obsolete. A man once secure in his position may suddenly find himself the victim of technological unemployment, or a once honored profession may be reevaluated—as in the case of the European knight and the Japanese *samurai* with the invention of firearms.

In a changing society, the perspectives of the people are undergoing transformation, but to minimize conflict many of them may for a time continue to act overtly as if they were supporting the traditional values. Should someone else violate the old norms, however, they would not become too upset. Ritualism and the sanctioned evasion of norms are frequently found in periods of transition. A set of informal understandings arises among people who know one another as they cooperate surreptitiously to attain their ends. Graft and corruption in the politics of large cities is known to all but those who refuse to look. In a study of moral standards, Smigel interviewed 212 people in Bloomington, Indiana, on hypothetical situations involving theft. There was a general disapproval of stealing, but there were variations in the intensity of condemnation. The condemnation of stealing from large corporations was not as strong as the disapproval of theft from the government, and stealing from small firms was most strongly opposed. This variation in the application of moral codes was justified in terms of the size of corporations, their anonymity, and the inefficiency of their bureaucracies.[3] Many of the difficulties in intercollegiate athletics in the United States arise from the attempt of schools to profess codes of amateurism that they privately violate. In a study demonstrating the use of refined procedures for the study of choices, Stouffer questioned students on what they would do if they saw a fellow student cheat. His data revealed that some even failed to see any incongruence between cheating and their moral standards. But a majority of those who did regard such conduct as wrong assumed a position sympathetic to the cheaters.[4] It is not uncommon for people who live in such societies to complain of widespread hypocrisy and to look upon "sincerity" as a prime value—an ideal that is almost impossible to attain.

When group norms are not clear, conflicting, or not taken seri-

[3] Erwin O. Smigel, "Public Attitudes toward Stealing as Related to the Size of the Victim Organization," *American Sociological Review*, XXI (1956), 320–27.

[4] Samuel A. Stouffer, "An Analysis of Conflicting Social Norms," *ibid.*, XIV (1949), 707–17.

ously, individualism becomes widespread. Released from constraints they had long regarded as frustrating, people feel more free to pursue their own interests. When others do not live up to their obligations, each begins to wonder if there is any point in doing his part, especially where it involves sacrifice. In the absence of clearly defined career lines, life becomes more uncertain, and expediency becomes a key consideration. Periods of transition are marked by greater variation in behavior. Not only are innovations introduced, but people are under less restraint. Of course, there are individual differences in the reluctance with which one gives up group standards.

This conception of social disorganization points to complications in the definition of *deviant behavior.* Deviant by whose standards? Crime and delinquency are usually defined legally, but in some segments of the community laws are not taken seriously. There are distinctions that must be made. Acts that are alike in appearance may actually develop in very different ways. Phenomenally similar acts may be generically different—depending upon who is performing the deed, its meaning from his perspective, and the audience for whom it is performed. The reference group of the actor must always be taken into account. This suggests that there are at least three different types of deviant behavior.

In a pluralistic society, a number of groups emerge whose perspectives differ from the standpoint of people in positions of prestige and power. Conformity to the norms of such groups makes one a law-breaker. Much of what is called "juvenile delinquency" constitutes conformity to the demands of a special reference group. Many of the activities of juvenile gangs are not regarded as wrong by the participants. A gang fight over territorial prerogatives is a matter of honor. Robbing "drunks" and stealing minor items from stores are not regarded as immoral; often a younger member exposes himself to the risk of arrest to demonstrate his courage. Many delinquent deeds are enacted by boys in a slum area who are trying to achieve or enhance their status in the eyes of their fellows.[5] An "incorrigible" boy often has many qualities which win him respect in his primary

---

[5] Cf. Ernest W. Burgess, "The Study of the Delinquent as a Person," *American Journal of Sociology,* XXVIII (1923), 657–80; A. K. Cohen, *op. cit.;* Daniel Glaser, "Criminality Theories and Behavioral Images," *American Journal of Sociology,* LXI (1956), 433–44; and Edwin H. Sutherland, *Principles of Criminology* (Chicago: J. B. Lippincott Co., 1939), pp. 4–9.

group—courage, loyalty, personal integrity, and a sense of decency and fair play. Such boys do not necessarily suffer from personality disorders; indeed, they are quite well adjusted to their world. Their conduct is judged deviant by those who are not a part of the same reference group.

A similar variation in the standards of conduct approved in different reference groups is illustrated by the "white collar crimes" of respectable businessmen, who violate laws, are consciously aware of what they are doing, but nonetheless do not conceive of themselves as criminals. Many businessmen who avoid paying all of the income tax required by law regard themselves as very clever; they are often acclaimed by their friends for the illegal maneuvers. Sutherland pointed out that wealthy people are rarely punished for cheating in taxes even when they are caught, although a poor man charged with the same offense may go to jail.[6] The abandonment of dependents by a husband who is capable of supporting them is an offense in many states, and Negroes have often been condemned by social workers for their disproportionately high incidence of desertion. In some of the poorer segments of Negro society, however, the matriarchal family has long been the accepted pattern of life. While the departure of the father is roundly condemned by middle class Negroes, it is not regarded as desertion by those who have only recently emigrated from the rural South.[7]

The fact that these people conform to the expectations shared in their respective reference groups does not mean that they are unaware of the law or customs of the community in which they reside. Many delinquent boys are well versed in giving verbal analyses of situations in terms of middle class values. Some boys even show shame and remorse when they are arrested, although many visualize themselves as martyrs. It is difficult to see how anyone can fail to gain some understanding of the formal regulations of the community, since exposure to its communication channels is almost unavoidable.[8]

[6] Edwin H. Sutherland, *White Collar Crime* (New York: Dryden Press, 1949).

[7] E. Franklin Frazier, *The Negro Family in the United States* (Chicago: University of Chicago Press, 1939), pp. 3–181.

[8] Cf. Dale B. Harris, "The Socialization of the Delinquent," *Child Development*, XIX (1948), 143–53; and Gresham M. Sykes and David Matza, "Techniques of Neutralization: A Theory of Delinquency," *American Sociological Review*, XXII (1957), 664–70.

Another type of deviant behavior arises from the temporary breakdown of self-control, especially under conditions of intense excitement. There are many cases of desertion, stealing, or violence in which the performer violates his own standards of conduct, often in an impulsive act. A man may steal food to feed a starving family. Later on, he may be overcome with remorse over what he has done, and turn himself in to the police. Sometimes a person violates conventional norms in a rebellion against "society" or against a particular person that he resents. He gets "even" with a significant other by embarrassing or hurting him.

The third type of deviant behavior is compulsive. Offenses such as drug addiction, violent assaults at slight provocation, and alcoholism are often fixations. Although the person sometimes tries to conform to middle class norms, he cannot help himself. Some delinquent boys are aggressive, bitter, and without guilt feelings. They make no secret of their hostility toward almost everyone, and some of them are even feared by members of their own gang. Because they participate in stealing, truancy, and other illegal activities, they are classified with the loyal gang members, but they are different. They engage in malicious mischief against their friends; they start fights without reason; and they are unnecessarily cruel in the treatment of their victims.[9] Many of these compulsive patterns apparently rest upon basically defensive private meanings. A person who is sadistic may be infuriated by the personification he constructs, which is vicious because of the motives that he himself imputes to it.

Psychiatrists sometimes look upon all juvenile delinquents and criminals as psychopathic, but this approach is much too narrow. Law-enforcement officers, social workers, judges, and social reformers often come from middle class backgrounds. They tend to judge everyone by their own class standards, and some offenses become incomprehensible. One explanation of deviant behavior that has gained widespread acceptance is the theory of the "psychopathic personality," the deranged individual who is insensitive to the expectations of other people. Although there are some people who are incredibly autonomous, many offenders *are* conforming to norms— norms of a different reference group. They are socialized and act as they do in order to maintain their self-respect. Indeed, in many slum

[9] Richard L. Jenkins, "Motivation and Frustration in Delinquency," *American Journal of Orthopsychiatry*, XXVII (1957), 528–37.

areas it is the "good" boy who is out of tune with the prevailing codes of conduct.[10] Only the third type of deviant behavior can be traced to personal maladjustments. The recommendation that all law-breakers be subjected to psychiatric treatment is not only impracticable, but rests upon false premises.

Prison guards and the prisoners themselves intuitively make a distinction between "habitual criminals," those who made a mistake, and the "sick." A "hardened" criminal is an offender whose contacts are confined largely to the underworld, who has accepted the values of this reference group, and for whom crime is a career. Stated more accurately, his way of life is one that is likely to keep him constantly in trouble with the police. He does not feel ashamed of what he has done; he may even be proud of his record. Those who are experienced in prison work can often tell which men are likely to be rehabilitated if given an opportunity and which are likely to go on until they are given a life sentence or are executed.

If social disorganization is an aspect of social change, it follows that social reorganization sometimes involves the eventual acceptance of some of the behavior patterns once condemned as deviant. This is especially true of radical political views and innovations in the arts and letters. Offenses involving violence are much less likely to win approval. The period of transition varies considerably in length, but sooner or later communication is restored, and misunderstandings are corrected. The old people become more accustomed to the new ways of doing things. New behavior patterns become fixed in habit, and a new social order is established.

Marginal Status and Inner Conflicts

Among the problems facing people in a changing society is being caught on the boundary of two or more cultures. As people move about, mingle, fight, and trade, the horizons of their respective worlds cross, overlap, and interpenetrate. Each new group in which a person participates circumscribes his conduct; to the extent that he incorporates its norms into his outlook, his behavior is inhibited in terms of them. Changing societies are likely to be pluralistic, and

[10] Walter C. Reckless, Simon Dinitz, and Ellen Murray, "The Good Boy in a High Delinquency Area," *ibid.*, XLVIII (1957), 18–25.

a person finds himself confronted by several reference groups. He imputes different expectations to each audience, and some of the norms contradict each other. When perspectives are incongruent, it is difficult for a person to define situations consistently or to form a well integrated self-conception.

In mass societies all but the most isolated people participate in more than one social world. Overlapping group affiliations need not lead to any difficulty, for the reference groups of most people are mutually sustaining. But incongruent demands may be made upon a man from different standpoints. A person becomes acutely aware of the differences between his social worlds when he is caught in a situation in which he faces conflicting demands—both of which cannot possibly be satisfied. Although several Protestant denominations still frown upon the consumption of alcoholic beverages, there are more and more fields in which success depends in part upon one's performance at cocktail parties. Such conflicts represent alternative ways of defining the same situation.

For most people, conflicts of this kind arise only on infrequent occasions. The difficulties are confined to specific situations. A sophisticated Catholic who is too poor to support any more children must choose between birth control and the consequences of a larger family. In all other matters, however, there are no dilemmas. Even if one's behavior is inconsistent, it is not noticed as long as the reference groups are far apart and their purposes unconnected. A soldier kills on the battlefield, but such behavior patterns do not carry over into his civilian life. A sedate attorney may scream himself hoarse at a boxing match, in contrast to his decorous conduct in the courtroom. For many people, the alternative perspectives become compartments; in each setting a somewhat different outlook is used to define situations. Many individuals who play incongruent roles are saved from dilemmas by the segregation of their audiences.

But there are people who occupy ambiguous positions and embody within their careers the inconsistencies of the pluralistic society in which they live. They are called upon to play roles which consist of contradictory claims and obligations, and they face difficulties in one situation after another. A foreman is often identified as a representative of management, although he has little to do with making decisions. He only transmits orders, trains new workers, checks the flow of work, and keeps records. But he does have authority over the other workers. In labor conflicts, he is often criticized from both sides.[11] A military chaplain also occupies a contradictory position. He serves an organization avowedly set up for the destruction of some of the values that he, as a man of religion, is expected to uphold. Of the seventy-one chaplains and ex-chaplains interviewed by Burchard after World War II, only a few reported serious inner conflicts. But they pointed to several difficult situations. For example, should they drink with their fellow officers? Most of the respondents did not voluntarily raise the question of the morality of killing, but when asked, several went to some length to prove that war was different from murder.[12] A Pentecostal minister is in a similarly difficult position. He is a sectarian leader, but as his position becomes better established, his group becomes more and more like the respectable denominations against which the sect had previously rebelled.[13] Doctors who are on the margin of the medical profession also face difficulties. Psychiatrists receive a medical education which they rarely use, but they identify themselves with other doctors. In their work many of them rely heavily upon psychology and the social sciences, which are disdained by other medical men. A chiropractor's status is even more ambiguous, because what is expected of him has not yet been established.[14] Nor do we have to go to such unusual contexts to encounter such dilemmas. The status of an American housewife, especially if she is well educated, also contains contradictions. An educated woman is confronted with mutually exclusive goals; assets for the pursuit of a professional career are liabilities for the roles she must play as a woman who appeals to men.[15]

To investigate such inner conflicts, sociologists have used the concept of the "marginal man." It was first developed by Park in the study of inter-ethnic contacts. Some men are marginal in that they

[11] Donald E. Wray, "Marginal Men of Industry: The Foremen," *American Journal of Sociology*, LIV (1949), 298–301.

[12] Waldo Burchard, "Role Conflicts of Military Chaplains," *American Sociological Review*, XIX (1954), 528–35.

[13] Bryan R. Wilson, "The Pentecostal Minister: Role Conflicts and Status Contradictions," *American Journal of Sociology*, LXIV (1959), 494–504.

[14] Harvey L. Smith, "Psychiatry in Medicine," *ibid.*, LXIII (1957), 285–89; and Walter I. Wardwell, "A Marginal Professional Role: The Chiropractor," *Social Forces*, XXX (1952), 339–48.

[15] Mirra Komarovsky, "Cultural Contradictions and Sex Roles," *American Journal of Sociology*, LII (1946), 184–89.

stand on the border between two or more social worlds but are not accepted as full participants in either. Negro intellectuals, because of their sophisticated interests, often encounter difficulties in getting along with other Negroes, but they are not fully accepted among other intellectuals because of their ethnic identity. Sociologists have long contended that the seemingly high incidence of delinquency and neurosis among the children of immigrants arises from their living in two incongruous worlds—learning the values of the old country at home and American values at school. Detribalized natives in colonial areas and children of mixed parentage may also face similar problems. Like many other innovators, Park overstated his case, contending that such persons developed characteristic personality disorders. Among the attributes of marginal men that he listed were: serious doubts about their personal worth, uncertainty of their ties with friends and a constant fear of rejection, the tendency to avoid uncertain situations rather than risk humiliation, painful self-consciousness in the presence of other people, loneliness and extensive daydreaming, excessive worry about the future and apprehension of any new venture, inability to enjoy themselves, and a conviction that they are being treated unjustly.[16]

But not all people who occupy a *marginal status* exhibit such traits, and critics have pointed out that Park's description applies only to a limited number. The vast majority of the children of immigrants do not suffer such maladjustments. Often they form a society of their own, as do the offsprings of mixed ancestry. They develop their own distinctive culture and live for their own values.[17] Some resolve their conflicts by becoming specialists who use their unusual position to advantage. A Negro sociologist can become an expert on inter-ethnic contacts; women engineers can concentrate upon designing household appliances; and chiropractors can restrict their practice to "safe" illnesses that do not interest doctors.[18] It appears that the only people who do develop neurotic symptoms are those who

[16] Robert E. Park, *Race and Culture*, E. C. Hughes *et al.*, ed. (Glencoe: Free Press, 1950), pp. 345–92. Cf. Everett V. Stonequist, *The Marginal Man* (New York: Charles Scribner's Sons, 1937).

[17] Cf. Milton M. Goldberg, "A Qualification of the Marginal Man Theory," *American Sociological Review*, VI (1941), 52–58.

[18] E. C. Hughes, *op. cit.*, pp. 102–15. Cf. Gross, Mason, and McEachern, *op. cit.*, pp. 244–318; and Walter I. Wardwell, "Reduction of Strain in Marginal Social Role," *American Journal of Sociology*, LXI (1955). 16–25.

attempt to improve their lot by identifying with the higher stratum and rebel when they are rejected. In their study of eighty-four Chippewa children, Kerckhoff and McCormick measured the degree of identification of each child with modern American culture through questions on their self-conceptions and their acceptance of Indian ideas; they also collected data with personality inventories and judged the extent to which each child resembled in appearance the stereotype of the Indian. The personality traits attributed to marginal men were most evident among those who identified closely with the main stream of American life but were most likely to be rejected because of their "Indian" appearance.[19]

There is no necessary relationship, then, between marginal status and personality disorders. But a study of the few who do develop maladjustments is instructive, for they reveal in exaggerated form the inner conflicts experienced with less intensity by others who occupy marginal positions.

People who occupy a marginal status are continually confronted with the necessity of forming moral judgments. Situations that would be routine for other people call for choice, often a choice between different conceptions of what is right. For example, when the crisis over school integration arose in 1957 in Little Rock, Arkansas, most clergymen outside of the South took a strong stand against the segregationists. But the ministers in Little Rock were placed in an awkward position. If they spoke up as Christians, they knew they would lose at least a part of their congregations. Campbell and Pettigrew found that most of the clergymen were personally in favor of integration. However, they realized that within their respective church hierarchies each minister is judged in terms of how his church prospers, and they could not succeed within their profession without the support of their congregations. Hence, they were unable to state their views too openly.[20]

The dilemma confronting a person in a marginal position is that, no matter what he does, someone will be displeased. If the child of

[19] Alan C. Kerckhoff and Thomas C. McCormick, "Marginal Status and Marginal Personality," Social Forces, XXXIV (1955), 48–55. Cf. Arnold W. Green, "A Re-examination of the Marginal Man Concept," ibid., XXVI (1947), 167–71.

[20] Ernest Q. Campbell and Thomas F. Pettigrew, "Racial and Moral Crisis: The Role of Little Rock Ministers," American Journal of Sociology, LXIV (1959), 509–16.

an immigrant marries the girl chosen for him by his parents, he hurts his sweetheart and disappoints his friends; if he marries the girl he loves, he injures his parents. Interpersonal relations are sometimes altered drastically from the bitterness aroused by such choices. The person also has trouble in coming to terms with himself, finding it difficult to maintain an adequate level of self-esteem. Because he identifies so closely with significant others, he can readily appreciate their sorrow. He tries to defend and justify his action, but he is stricken with guilt.

There are individual differences in the manner in which such situations are handled. Some people, especially if they are otherwise satisfied with themselves, try to put aside their troubles and go on to other things. But for those who are already alienated from themselves, such crises can lead to the formation of neurotic symptoms. Men who are guilt ridden often accuse themselves mercilessly, thereby making their lives even more miserable. Alienation from oneself may develop to the point where there is depersonalization. Self-images may become impersonal, as if one were a spectator looking at himself from the outside. In this way a person can detach himself from some of the responsibility for what he has done.

In severe cases, punitive action may become compulsive. When a person regards himself as evil or as an object of contempt, he often reacts aggressively against himself. In periods of depression he becomes selectively sensitive to his negative attributes; through the accumulation of such cues he may construct a personification so horrible that he may try to destroy it. That suicide may be related to marginal status has been recognized by several investigators. In his famous study, Durkheim pointed to "anomie"—a condition in which norms do not enjoy consensus—as one of the circumstances under which the incidence of suicide rises.[21]

Studies on the assimilation of American Indians reveal that personal maladjustments are more common among those who are in close contact with other Americans. In his study of Navaho veterans of World War II, Vogt found a positive correlation between the degree of acculturation and the extent to which a person's life is marked by insecurity and conflict.[22] Thompson and Joseph made a

[21] Emile Durkheim, *Suicide: A Study in Sociology*, J. A. Spaulding and G. Simpson, trans. (Glencoe: Free Press, 1951), pp. 241–360.
[22] Evon Z. Vogt, "Navaho Veterans," *Papers of the Peabody Museum of American Archeology and Ethnology*, XLI (1951), No. 1, pp. 105–6.

comparative study of two Hopi villages, which differed in the extent of their contacts with the outside world. One of them, founded by Mennonites in 1910, was the only Hopi community with a village constitution. Many of the people there wanted to abandon the old Indian ways and go into business for themselves. Personal problems as well as marital discord were more common than they were in the traditional village. Psychological tests showed that the more acculturated Hopi were less spontaneous, less outgoing, and more troubled by various anxieties.[23] But there are also contradictory findings. Hallowell studied two groups of the Ojibwa, one of them living in a remote area and retaining much of the old culture. Rorschach tests showed that the acculturated Indians were not only more like other Americans but were less disturbed.[24]

It is of interest to note that inconsistent cues can result in behavior patterns in other animals that resemble neuroses in human beings. Pavlov discovered this accidentally in the course of one of his experiments with dogs. Since that time it has been shown in a number of experiments that disturbed reactions can be developed by demanding increasingly finer discriminations between stimuli, by establishing progressively more delayed conditioned reflexes, or by the sudden reversal of long familiar conditioned stimuli. When the stimuli which had previously been followed by some kind of gratification are followed by deprivation, or vice versa, the animals develop chronic emotional disturbances.[25] This suggests that some of the reaction patterns frequently observed in neurosis may be organically rooted.

There are many people who are not marginal who develop neurotic tendencies. Neurosis is apparently the product of a succession of disturbances in interpersonal relations, and this can occur even in a very stable setting. But in a changing society, those who occupy marginal status are repeatedly confronted with situations that maximize the probability of conflicts with significant others. Therefore, the possibilities of alienation from oneself are proportionately greater.

[23] Laura Thompson and Alice Joseph, "White Pressures on Indian Personality and Culture," *American Journal of Sociology*, LIII (1947), 17–22. Cf. Benedict and Jacks, *op. cit.*

[24] A. Irving Hallowell, "Acculturation Processes and Personality Changes as Indicated by the Rorschach Technique," *Rorschach Research Exchange*, VI (1942), 42–48. Cf. his *Culture and Experience, op. cit.*, pp. 307–66.

[25] H. S. Liddell, "Conditioned Reflex Method and Experimental Neurosis," in Hunt, *op. cit.*, Vol. I, pp. 389–412.

Park contended that marginal men also tend to be more creative than others. People who are happily immersed within a single culture are not so likely to make innovations; they take too many things for granted. Those who participate in two or more social worlds are less attached to a particular way of defining situations and are accustomed to considering alternatives. Simmel also emphasized the freedom and uniqueness of a person who partakes in a variety of groups. The larger the number of perspectives appreciated, the less an individual is monopolized by any single way of life.[26] The major advances in any culture usually come during periods of rapid social change, and many of the great contributions are made by marginal men.

Personal Loyalty and Group Solidarity

Among the perennial interests of sociologists is the problem of group solidarity, the study of the conditions under which groups persist and the conditions under which they collapse. A group can be identified by its recurrent patterns of cooperative action. As long as the participants continue to comply with one another's expectations, the action pattern persists. Since each person is capable of independent action, group structures can continue only as long as the participants are willing to honor their obligations. The collective pattern collapses when a sufficient proportion of individuals, especially those who play the key roles, defect. Even social sanctions are effective only when they enjoy consensus. In the last analysis, our interest is narrowed to a single problem: what are the conditions under which men continue to comply with conventional norms, even when such conformity involves considerable sacrifice and pain?

Individual defections are relatively easy to study in periods of transition, especially among the people who acquire new meanings before the others. Many people resist changes, and some do not accept new patterns even when they are no longer controversial. But there are people who are extremely sensitive to novel ideas and eagerly pursue new possibilities. Members of the same family sometimes split on this issue, one favoring a revolutionary proposal and another insisting upon upholding the traditional values.

[26] Cf. Park, *Race and Culture, loc. cit.;* and Simmel, *Conflict and the Web of Group-Affiliations, op. cit.* pp. 150–54, 162–63, 185–91.

Superficial observations indicate that one of the essential differences between those who defend the traditional values and those who are eager for innovations lies in their sentiments toward significant others. An individual who violates norms to which he had once adhered is generally a person who is not bound by loyalties to people who are known to support the existing order. This suggests two hypotheses. *If a person forms disjunctive sentiments toward significant others who support the status quo or conjunctive sentiments toward those who are opposed to it, he will be receptive to changes and will defect when the occasion arises.* Case records of adolescents who go "wild" often reveal a long history of disrupted interpersonal relations, especially with parents who have a conventional outlook. Conversely, *if a person forms conjunctive sentiments toward significant others who support the status quo or disjunctive sentiments toward those who seek changes, he will find the violations of conventional norms painful and will resist change.* A person who is closely attached to his mother is not likely to do anything that will pain her. Reckless and his associates found in their study of a slum area that the children who are not delinquent are satisfied with the affection they receive at home and do not feel themselves overly supervised. They conform to parental expectations, even if it involves difficulties with some of their classmates.[27] The study of defection becomes focussed upon two variables: (a) the extent to which group norms are supported by significant others, and (b) the sentiments of the person toward these personifications.

One context in which group solidarity can be studied is in a stratified community in which there are possibilities of upward social mobility. Since a high value is placed upon upward mobility in American society, we rarely realize that it involves the desertion of the subordinate stratum and its way of life. If enough people in an ethnic minority become assimilated, for example, the minority group itself will become extinct. Social mobility involves a change in perspectives—a displacement of reference groups. Especially for those in an ethnic minority, upward mobility means gaining advantages at the cost of losing a part of one's former sense of identity.

[27] Reckless, Dinitz, and Murray, "Self Concept as an Insulator against Delinquency," *op. cit.* Cf. William McCord, Joan McCord and Irving Zola, *Origins of Crime* (New York: Columbia University Press, 1959), pp. 73–123; and F. Ivan Nye, *Family Relationships and Delinquent Behavior* (New York: John Wiley & Sons, 1958).

Many upwardly mobile people become assimilated; they acquire a new way of looking at their world. Assimilation is a slow, gradual process in which the perspective of a newcomer—an immigrant, a recruit, a *parvenue*—is transformed until he shares the outlook of his new associates. In the beginning the newcomer still lives in his old social world and sees other people through ethnocentric eyes. The strangers appear odd and are seen essentially in terms of their utility. Although the contacts need not be unfriendly, the deeds of others are often misinterpreted and at times seem bizarre. In time the newcomer realizes that the other people are placing an estimate upon him. He becomes concerned with the manner in which he is evaluated, for the respect with which he is treated depends upon it. In spite of himself he begins to struggle for some sort of recognition in the new setting. The quest for a more acceptable position in the new community requires role-taking. One must learn something of the values accepted there to understand how the others judge him. As the years pass, especially if his new contacts prove satisfactory, the person organizes his experiences in terms of the newly acquired perspective. If contacts with his former friends are limited, he begins to see his former group from the standpoint of an outsider, and he notices its many faults. Once a person has incorporated the standards of the more privileged stratum into his outlook, unless there are definite barriers against mobility, he becomes an active participant in the new social world. Some people even disown all connections with the past, pretending that they had never been part of it. Of course, not all of the people who succeed in improving their lot become fully assimilated. Some enjoy the material gains, but do not alter their standards of conduct.[28]

In the United States this drama has occurred countless times, and one immigrant colony after another has disappeared into the mainstream of American life. During the period of transition three types of orientations are commonly found. Those who become assimilated earlier are more sensitive to the views of outsiders; their reference group is made up of other Americans. They realize why their group is despised. They become ardent critics, harping constantly upon the characteristics that lead others to look down upon it. They adopt American standards and attempt to "improve" themselves by imitating American ways, sometimes ostentatiously. There are others, how-

28 Cf. Young, *op. cit.*, pp. 98–276.

ever, who reject American values; they emphasize their ethnic identity and look back to the land of their ancestors. They condemn those who are assimilating, and do what they can to reaffirm their own values and symbols. They often point to glorious chapters in the history of the old country and emphasize the superiority of its culture to the materialism of the young land. The reference group of these people consists of those with whom they identify on an ethnic basis; they seek status in the eyes of their own "kind." Most people in minority groups, however, stand between these extremists. The children of immigrants, especially where they are concentrated in one area, form their own colony and develop their own hybrid culture. Their reference group consists of others in the minority group; they are not overly concerned with their ancestors or with other Americans. In his study of Italian-Americans in New Haven, Child found such differences, and Emery and Katz found similar cleavages among the Jews in Australia. The Gentile community constituted the reference group for most of the Jews born in Australia. Those who had migrated from Eastern Europe looked to Jews as their audience and attempted to strengthen ties among all Jews, while those from Western Europe were not in either extreme. The Eastern Europeans detected considerably more anti-Semitism than the Western Europeans. Those who had always been in Australia tended to blame the Jews as well as the Gentiles for the anti-Semitism, and to improve the situation they proposed instituting reforms among the Jews.[29]

The autobiographies of those who have risen from subordinate groups to achieve recognition in American society show that the first to become assimilated are often repelled from the minority group by disjunctive sentiments toward the people seen as its representatives. There is a history of conflicts with parents who attempted unsuccessfully to assert their authority according to the norms of the old country. Sometimes they are attracted by conjunctive sentiments toward a sympathetic outsider—a teacher, a Y.M.C.A. secretary, or a playground director who becomes a confessor for a child who feels misunderstood. Those who are among the first to intermarry are frequently people who have been unhappy in the ethnic colony. They know that their parents will be heartbroken, but this does not

[29] Irvin L. Child, *Italian or American?* (New Haven, Yale University Press, 1943); and F. E. Emery and F. M. Katz, "Social Theory and Minority Group Behaviour," *Australian Journal of Psychology*, III (1951), 22–35.

stop them. It is the dissatisfied who form the vanguard of social change. Nothing but external barriers hold them back; they defect as soon as they see an opportunity.[30]

The defenders of the old traditions in a minority group are usually people whose conjunctive sentiments are limited to people with whom they identify on an ethnic basis. Since their contacts with outsiders are usually limited, they often form disjunctive sentiments toward them without even having had unfavorable experiences. In all minority groups there are numerous tales of discrimination and mistreatment. When one has established warm and affectionate ties within an ethnic colony, he is reluctant to move out, even when possibilities for upward mobility present themselves. In the previously cited study of Navaho veterans, Vogt found that those who retained Nahavo values had warm personal ties with other Indians, just as those who were becoming assimilated reported a lack of satisfying ties within the group.[31]

Another context in which group solidarity can be studied is in the variations of morale in military units. Morale refers to the quality of performance, the degree of enthusiasm and dedication with which activities are carried out. The ultimate test of adequate morale is persistence even in the most unfavorable circumstances. The resolute facing of almost certain death in the charge of the light brigade in Crimea, immortalized in Tennyson's verse, has been repeated countless times by military units throughout the world. But other units in the same armies have broken and fled when faced with only slight danger. These differences in morale cannot be explained in terms of social structure, for all units in a given army are organized along similar lines.

The persistence of collective enterprises under duress has been explained in terms of the faith that men have in their cause, the attributes of the leaders, and even innate qualities. The hypothesis that has attracted considerable support in recent years, however, places emphasis upon the faith that men have in one another. Many students have pointed to the importance of informal social structure, the understandings that develop among men who make up the various primary groups concerning how much each is to contribute.

[30] Cf. Peter M. Blau, "Social Mobility and Interpersonal Relations," *American Sociological Review*, XXI (1956), 290–95; and Myers and Roberts, *op. cit.*, pp. 129–71.

[31] Vogt, *op. cit.*, pp. 105–6.

Marshall declares that, on the battlefield, social control is on a man-to-man basis. Courage is contagious; to a man who is terrified and on the verge of panic, nothing provides a more stabilizing influence than the observation of others around him who retain their composure and go on doing their work. A terrified man may become even more afraid of running away, fearing what his comrades would think of him.[32] This recalls George Bernard Shaw's observation that there is no courage, only pride. But such sacrifices are made only for comrades who are liked, whose opinions really matter. Further evidence of the importance of personal ties comes from the already cited study by Stein showing that the American soldiers who were absent without leave during World War II differed from the others only in one respect: they were isolated, not identified with any primary group in their platoon. They were the men who were not sensitive to the views of those around them.[33]

Conversely, demoralization is the product of disjunctive sentiments. The disintegration of a group is usually a gradual process, involving the redefinition of significant others, the formation of factions, and egocentric action. Once a group begins to deteriorate, there is a transitional period marked by bickering, misunderstanding, and ill will. People conform overtly, often in a ritualistic fashion. Reluctance is initially revealed primarily in expressive movements. The individuals become suspicious of one another's motives and sincerity. Men with diverse interests break into cliques; they share their suspicions, and before long factional interests begin to supersede group interests. Then, individualism becomes more prevalent. People begin to think and plan primarily in terms of personal interests. The unit may be preserved temporarily by a system of checks and balances, but the establishment of this type of accommodation is a tact admission that the participants really do not trust one another. Some of the people dislike members of the opposing factions more than their avowed enemies. If there is no unusual strain, such groups may persist for some time, but in a crisis situation coordinated effort is difficult to organize. Each person tries to save himself. A military unit in this condition is unreliable; a political movement in this state collapses under fire; a football team thus de-

---

[32] Marshall, op. cit., p. 148. Cf. Grinker and Spiegel, op. cit.; and Stouffer et al., The American Soldier, op. cit., Vol. II, pp. 105–241.

[33] Stein, op. cit.

moralized cannot win against a foe of approximately equal strength. When the men become convinced that they cannot count on their comrades, they have no alternative to looking after themselves. This suggests that group solidarity depends upon the kinds of sentiments that prevail among those who are in intimate contact.

With the recognition of the importance of ideological warfare, dramatic cases of defections to the enemy in time of war have aroused considerable interest. Susceptibility to "brainwashing" has become a problem of major concern to the armed forces. A survey by a journalist of the backgrounds of the twenty-one American soldiers who refused repatriation after the Korean War revealed that the one characteristic they all had in common was a long history of difficulties in interpersonal relations.[34] Although there were no doubt a large number of other American prisoners with equally unhappy backgrounds who elected to return home, this report is not without interest.

There are other studies pointing to the connection between the persistence of groups and interpersonal relations. Angell studied fifty families that lost more than twenty-five per cent of their income during the depression, and found that some of them showed greater solidarity than before, while others collapsed. A closer examination of the data revealed that, where the interpersonal relations were predominantly conjunctive, there was a tendency to close ranks and to face the crisis together, but where the prevailing sentiments were disjunctive, the participants could no longer stand one another and eventually separated.[35] When sentiments are only apparently friendly and actually disjunctive, duress adds to the strain, for the possibilities of misunderstanding are maximized. Previously unnoticed traits, such as cowardice or obstinacy, loom to the center of attention. Foul or selfish motives are imputed as people who are already wary of one another find their suspicions confirmed.

Social solidarity rests upon the willingness of participants to conform to group norms even when this involves a great sacrifice, and most men willingly make sacrifices only when the alternative is even more painful. Conformity to conventional or informal norms under conditions of adversity rests upon loyalty to the individuals regarded

[34] Virginia Pasley, *Twenty-One Stayed* (New York: Farrar, Straus & Cudahy, 1955).

[35] Robert C. Angell, *The Family Encounters the Depression* (New York: Charles Scribner's Sons, 1936).

as representatives of the group. This sense of loyalty is strongest when the sentiment is conjunctive and weakest when it is disjunctive. Men act in a manner designed to maintain their personal status, especially in the eyes of those for whom they care. If they hate someone, however, they may deliberately attempt to annoy him. The push of disjunctive sentiments can be just as important as the pull of conjunctive sentiments.

Consensus and Interpersonal Relations

The "reality" to which men are continually adjusting consists of conventional meanings, modes of approaching various categories of objects over which there is consensus. The comparative study of cultures reveals that this "reality" is not just "out there"; it is an interpretation of sensory cues. These interpretations emerge in and are sustained in communication—interaction with particular people who are approached with empathy. Empathy involves much more than role-taking. Other people are recognized as specific personalities, and attributes are projected to them that facilitate sympathetic identification. A sense of closeness develops in anticipating, desiring, or fearing things together. Although the exact character of the connection is not clear, there is some kind of relationship between one person's sentiment toward another and the extent to which they share a common outlook. It is apparently not possible to accept another person and at the same time reject his values. As unlikely as it may sound, the manner in which a person experiences "reality" is somehow related to his intimate ties with other people.

Recent investigations reveal that what is perceived depends upon interpersonal relations to a far greater extent than had been suspected. To carry out experiments on perception, Ames constructed a special room with a sloping floor, a rear wall receding from right to left, and windows of various sizes and shapes. From a given point an observer using only one eye would see the room as if it were normal, with a level floor and walls at right angles; otherwise it would appear grotesquely distorted. A human being standing in the room would ordinarily be seen as startlingly large or small, and at times parts of his body would seem to be out of proportion. In 1949, a woman saw her husband and another man together in the room. The other man changed in size and shape as expected, but her husband did not! He was a distinguished man for whom she had great admiration. After this unexpected turn of events, an experiment was conducted with ten married couples in which each person was asked to observe the spouse and a stranger in the room. The results confirmed the experience of the woman; in each case the spouse was perceived as being less distorted than the stranger.[36] This suggests that a person to whom one is especially devoted becomes a standard in terms of which other objects are measured.

When there is disagreement, effective persuasion rests as much upon personal considerations as it does upon the merits of the argument. Studies reveal that the acceptance of the views of others depends not only upon the appeal and plausibility of the content, but also upon the evaluation of the source. When the speaker is regarded highly, both for credibility and as an object of affection or admiration, significantly greater changes in views occur. When a recipient who has other grounds for judging the message cannot accept it in spite of his conjunctive orientation toward the source, there is a tendency to dissociate the source from the content.[37] Even presentations over the media of mass communication are experienced in personal terms; Merton found that the marathon sale of war bonds by Kate Smith was successful because of the manner in which the star was personified by the audience.[38] When Newcomb studied transformations in the political views of girls at Bennington College, he found a general tendency for a change from conservative positions during the freshman year to liberal or radical views during the senior year. On the campus, considerable prestige was associated with the entertainment of extreme views, but some of the girls were not even aware of this fact. A reexamination of the data showed that those who were more isolated from the campus community managed to get through school relatively unscathed in politics, while those who were active on the campus tended to alter their views, at least temporarily, toward the left.[39] Pearlin studied beliefs about Negroes in a college for women in the South, where the prevailing views were more favorable toward Negroes than they were likely to be at

[36] Warren J. Wittreich, "The Honi Phenomenon: A Case of Selective Perceptual Distortion," *Journal of Abnormal and Social Psychology,* XLVII (1952), 705–12. Cf. Hadley Cantril, "Perception and Interpersonal Relations," *American Journal of Psychiatry,* CXIV (1957), 119–26.

[37] Hovland, Janis, and Kelley, *op. cit.,* pp. 19–55.

[38] Robert K. Merton, *Mass Persuasion* (New York: Harper & Bros., 1946).

[39] Theodore M. Newcomb, "Attitude Development as a Function of Reference Groups: The Bennington Study," in Maccoby *et al., op. cit.,* pp. 265–75.

the students' home. Of the 383 interviewed, those who accepted liberal views were found to consist largely of students who had drifted away from home and had even clashed with their parents; on the other hand, about half of those who rejected the campus views reported that they were still quite close to home. When they were asked with whom they discussed their personal problems, it was found that 80.4 per cent of those who accepted the liberal views talked things over with their fellow students, but 45.4 per cent of those who rejected them still took their troubles home.[40] These findings suggest that the first person point of view is quite different from the abstract third person standpoint of science.

Other data already cited also support this view. The formation of a new perspective and the concomitant transformation of behavior patterns—in conversions, in social mobility, in deviant conduct, and in the quest for independence among adolescents—are facilitated when there are conjunctive sentiments toward those who represent the new standpoint. The same relationship is disclosed by studies of group solidarity. Conjunctive sentiments facilitate role-taking and the development of sympathetic concern with the other person, rendering the violation of trust difficult. Disjunctive sentiments lead to greater social distance and a lack of concern.

Conventional meanings are learned in contexts in which significant others are involved. From the very beginning our orientations toward objects are formed while interacting with specific people, and these intimate interchanges continue as the welding and assimilating matrix through which we are able to understand the place of various things in the universe.

There are some people who claim to live in terms of abstract principles, unconcerned with the views of other people. The ideal of moral conduct for some is the person who is autonomous, who acts in accordance with his sense of right or wrong, regardless of the expectations of others. To be sure, there are people who are relatively insensitive to the views imputed to their immediate associates, but they are often supported by others who are not physically present—a spouse who is temporarily away, a parent who is dead, or a former teacher with whom regular correspondence is carried on. In crisis situations, especially where moral conduct could prove very

[40] Leonard I. Pearlin, "Shifting Group Attachments and Attitudes toward Negroes," *Social Forces*, XXXIII (1954), 47–50.

costly, most men fall back upon the support of significant others. At moments of indecision, when in doubt and confusion, certain personifications appear in imagery. The person in a quandary argues with them, explains his alternative to them, imputes telling counterarguments to them, and imagines their chagrin or applause. In some cases the support comes from imaginary personifications—the author of an inspiring book, a character once seen in a motion picture, or some deity.

"Reality" as human beings usually experience it is invested with a quality called "life." This is not to suggest that all objects are regarded as being alive, but without the kind of orientation that men develop toward living objects even the physical world seems "unreal." Each person develops his orientations toward the world, other people, and himself in the context of intimate ties in primary groups. If he withdraws from such participation, he progressively loses his capacity for projecting this quality upon objects. Scientists must train themselves to perceive from an impersonal standpoint, and scientific knowledge is often described as being "lifeless." It is matter of fact and unsentimental. Because scientific concepts are neutral, the meanings are deprived of empathy. The objects to which they refer do not have the capacity for tempering their conduct from sentimental considerations.

Accounts of the experiences of those who are psychotic—human beings who do not partake in the "reality" over which there is consensus—underscore the importance of intimate ties for the maintenance of the human environment. Remarkable documentation of this process can be found in the study by Sechehaye, containing both the patient's retrospective account of her inner experiences and the record of the therapist. When Renee, the patient, felt herself loved by the therapist, "normal" perception replaced morbid distortion. Instead of seeing things and people as isolated and unrelated, she could see them in their usual proportions and places. But whenever Renee felt that her analyst was irritated or disappointed, she lost contact and relapsed into the world of "unreality." Even human beings appeared metallic, like automatons without life. She snapped in and out of the world of "reality," depending upon her shifting relationships with her doctor.[41] Human beings are interdependent in

[41] Sechehaye, *Autobiography of a Schizophrenic Girl, op. cit.*, pp. 85–106. Cf. Otto A. Will, "Human Relatedness and the Schizophrenic Reaction," *Psychiatry*, XXII (1959), 205–23.

a far more profound sense than is generally supposed. Through their sentiments they support one another's conception of the environment. There is an intuitive recognition of this in mental hospitals. When a patient shows some interest in his personal appearance, this is usually welcomed as an indication that he is on his way to recovery. When he becomes concerned over the opinions of other people, he is engaging in role-taking—the first step on his way back to "reality."

Although their views have been all but lost in this materialistic era, it appears that Cooley and his predecessors, the Scottish moralists, were correct in their insistence that human society rests upon a particular kind of communication, interchanges among those who identify sympathetically with one another. The kinds of meanings that are formed in our intimate associations, the sentiments, are subsequently displaced upon other objects. The key to understanding a man's conduct appears to lie in his relationships with other people. No man who lives psychologically alone retains for long the attributes that make him human. Lives are inextricably intertwined, and personalities are formed, reaffirmed, and transformed in a succession of reciprocal exchanges marked by empathy. This does not mean that the scientific study of human nature is impossible, but such inquiries must take into account the fact that human beings are related to their world in this manner.

Summary and Conclusion

Human society may best be viewed as a communicative process; it is a system of mutual, reciprocal responses. Each person is formed and transformed in the succession of transactions in which he participates. As a social product he acts back and modifies the organization of the transactions themselves. But when life conditions change, the contributions of different people no longer fit together. Previously accepted patterns are disrupted, and special adjustments become necessary. There is a period of transition during which misunderstandings and conflicts arise. Those who are caught in such circumstances often experience discomfort, embarrassment, and pain.

Everyone living in a changing society encounters some difficulties, but for most people the conflicts are mild and intermittent.

However, some find themselves in marginal status, a position that incorporates within it the contradictions of the structure of the community. Compliance with everyone's expectations becomes impossible, and marginal men find it difficult to maintain an adequate level of self-esteem. In moves to maintain their acceptability, some of them search for special tasks which enable them to exploit their anomalous situations, some withdraw into a special group of marginal people, and some even withdraw into psychosis or destroy themselves. Rebellious individuals sometimes try to wrest respect from others through neurotic endeavor, a compulsive dedication to some objective they regard as worthwhile.

Social change consists of a change in the outlook of men, and such transformations apparently depend upon interpersonal relations. The close tie between perspectives and sentiments poses a serious problem for education, where the acquisition of knowledge is presumed to rest upon the merits of the material. The differential responsiveness of students to teachers is readily noticeable. Some students learn well from one teacher and react against another. Some are alienated from an entire field of learning if they happen to dislike the teacher who introduces them to it. Even among graduate students, ideas are often evaluated in terms of sentiments toward the professor who proposes them. Since the accuracy of a proposition is independent of the motives and personality of those who sponsor it, eventually some kind of reality testing is likely to occur. But for a long time one may be blinded by the biases of a favorite teacher, which had not been examined with sufficient care. Since sentiments toward teachers generally rest upon grounds other than their professional competence, there are grave dangers of choices resting upon irrelevant criteria. In forming rational judgments, every effort is made to suppress sentiments, but these orientations probably have more to do with what a person learns than most educators are willing to admit.

Suggested References

ANGELL, ROBERT C., *The Family Encounters the Depression.* New York: Charles Scribner's Sons, 1936. A study of fifty Michigan families facing adversity in the depression, revealing the differences between the groups that became more closely integrated and those which collapsed.

DURKHEIM, EMILE, *Suicide: A Study in Sociology,* J. A. Spaulding and

G. Simpson, trans. Glencoe: Free Press, 1951. A classic investigation of the social matrix in which acts of self-destruction take place, showing the relationship between the incidence of suicide and the extent to which a group is integrated.

FREUD, SIGMUND, *Group Psychology and the Analysis of the Ego*, James Strachey, trans. New York: Liveright Publishing Co., 1949. A provocative study of the conditions of group solidarity, with particular emphasis upon the manner in which the participants identify with one another.

GRINKER, ROY R. and JOHN P. SPIEGEL, *Men under Stress*, Chapters I–III. Philadelphia: Blakiston Co., 1945. A study of the variations in morale found among different combat crews in the U. S. Army Air Corps during World War II, pointing to the importance of interpersonal relations and of the characteristics of the leaders.

PARK, ROBERT E., *Race and Culture*, E. C. Hughes, *et al.*, eds., pp. 3–52, 204–20, 331–42. Glencoe: Free Press, 1950. Selected essays on interethnic contacts with special emphasis upon the typical experiences of those caught on the borders of two or more cultures.

THOMAS, WILLIAM I. and FLORIAN ZNANIECKI, *The Polish Peasant in Europe and America*, Vol. II, pp. 1117–1264, 1303–6, 1647–1827 New York: Alfred A. Knopf, 1927. A pioneering investigation of the breakdown of traditional norms in an immigrant colony in the United States and their replacement by new models of conduct.

Conclusion

18

Social
psychology
and
social
control

One of the paradoxes of our age is the increasing control over our material environment and the continuing inability to understand ourselves. Among the most remarkable achievements of man is the development of the physical sciences, which has made possible a standard of living beyond the dreams of the utopian philosophers of the past. Advances in the biological sciences have resulted in the conquest of one disease after another, reducing the mortality rate to the point where the world is threatened with overpopulation. But the inability to develop an adequate understanding of human conduct renders difficult the optimum use of this great power for human welfare. Presumably intelligent men are stockpiling weapons of mass destruction, even when it is widely recognized that a nuclear war may result in the extermination of the species. Technological unemployment is expected to result from the increasing use of automation, but many employers refuse to cut working hours, throwing part of their labor force out of work and reducing overall purchasing power. Many religious groups, presumably the guardians of moral standards, seem to be more concerned with rituals and other matters that are only remotely related to daily life. In the midst of this confusion, men are asking once again the question that has been raised in other eras: what is the meaning of human existence?

In each society the intellectuals are expected to interpret what is happening and to provide some guidance for others. But so many of the artists, writers, and philosophers of our era appear to be preoccupied with other matters. They hardly notice the magnificent achievements of a species courageous enough to push back the frontiers of the unknown to the point where serious plans are being made for space explorations. They appear to be concerned largely with the abnormal, the sordid, the unusual. Many of them find man a despicable creature, and this can be debilitating. Since human beings act in terms of their self-conceptions, those who despise themselves may condone acts that are intolerable to people who live by higher standards. And what have social scientists contributed at a time when an understanding of man is so sorely needed? Serious studies are being made throughout the world, but little is being contributed at the moment that can play a substantial part in meeting the challenge.

Of all the social sciences, the field that comes closest to the subject matter of the humanities is social psychology. It represents an attempt to study systematically, using methods similar to those of the other sciences, the same topic on which intellectual curiosity has centered throughout the ages: man as a participant in society. The field of social psychology is still in an embryonic stage. In view of the seriousness of the crisis we face, why do these men not forget their differences and join forces in a concerted effort? We must remember that social psychologists are human beings and are subject to social control. If some of them appear to be more concerned with impressing one another than they are in finding solutions to pressing problems, it means only that they are like other people.

Some Characteristics of Mass Societies

A comparison of modern mass societies with other forms of community life—frontier outposts, peasant communities, nomadic settlements, medieval towns, or plantations—reveals that they are marked by several distinctive features. Successive developments in technology—in communication, production, and transportation—have transformed the organization of group life, necessitating social relationships less frequently found in other types of communities. What is the character of social control in mass societies? We must know something of the peculiarities of our kind of society in order to understand many of the problems that arise in it. One characteristic of mass societies is that so many transactions occur on a large scale, bringing together thousands of people whose contacts with one another are necessarily secondary.

Most modern societies are highly industrialized, and those that are not are adopting this mode of production and distribution. Industrialization is a particular way of organizing sustenance activities. The requirements of efficient production are transforming more and more enterprises into large corporate units. There is a division of labor, and each person performs a highly technical task; what comes out at the end of the assembly line is a collective product. The principle of mass production is not confined to the manufacturing of automobiles; it is found in many other spheres of activity. The modern hospital, with its array of clinics manned by specialists, provides a sharp contrast to the "horse and buggy" doctor of the past. Large universities are also organized along these lines, and students are constantly complaining about the impersonality of their contacts with their teachers. We live in a society of large productive units, operated by professional managers, highly skilled technicians, and a large labor force—all of them employees divorced from the ownership. Industrialization is rapidly transforming the entire civilized world into a series of gigantic, interdependent units.

This has led to a redefinition of work and a change in its significance for personal identity. Since each individual goes through life participating in one large organization after another, he tends to identify himself and other people in terms of the corporate units of which they are a part. One of the consequences of this type of social organization is the separation of the worker both from the product and the means of production. Unlike the artisans of past eras, no factory worker can make the product by himself. Most workers are merely replaceable cogs in a huge, impersonal machine. He amounts to something only as long as he is employed. The pride of the artist or craftsman in his work cannot develop except among those who hold unusual positions. The social status of a person in an industrial society depends not so much upon the *work* he does as upon his *job*. His prestige depends not so much upon the importance of what he does as upon his position in a respectable organization. Unemployment becomes a serious problem even among those who are adequately clothed and fed, for an unemployed man is somewhat like an outcast from society.[1]

The development of industries has led to the concentration of population in cities. The increasing density of population in urban centers means that we cannot possibly establish primary relations with all the people with whom we come into contact and upon whom we are dependent. Urban dwellers associate with many more people than those who live in other kinds of communities, but in most of these contacts they maintain their personal reserve. Strangers are perceived as instances of some category and are judged by the uniform they wear—their clothing, skin color, taste, or cleanliness. We may greet our acquaintances cheerfully, but we get to know only a small proportion of them as unique individuals.

When population density rises to the point where it becomes impossible for anyone to know everyone else, many social relationships are based upon reciprocal utility. The pecuniary nexus replaces personal preference as a basis for association. The clerk in a store facilitates the acquisition of needed objects, and his customers contribute to his livelihood. This results in freedom from the sentimental considerations that are so binding in small communities, but the participants also lose the sense of belonging together that is found in most primary groups. The close and frequent contact of individuals unrestrained by sentiments can lead to exploitation. Most city people learn to protect themselves; sophistication and rationality are common in urban communities. City people usually approach one another with caution, often assuming that others are only looking after their selfish interests. Increasing reliance is placed upon formal social sanctions. City people depend upon law enforcement agencies to maintain order and to adjudicate differences.[2]

Another characteristic of mass societies is the development of the media of mass communication and the consequent enlargement of perspectives. The remarkable growth of the print media, radio, tele-

[1] Cf. Peter F. Drucker, *The New Society* (New York: Harper & Bros., 1949), pp. 1–98.
[2] Cf. Simmel, *The Sociology of Georg Simmel, op. cit.*, pp. 402–24; and Wirth, *Community Life and Social Policy, op. cit.*, pp. 110–32.

vision, and motion pictures has made accessible all kinds of experiences that one could not have hoped for in the past. Perspectives have been extended to the point where the entire civilized world has become a potential universe of discourse. Prior to the development of these media, the lives of men were confined largely to the local community. Occasionally they heard vague reports from travellers, but their meaningful world was circumscribed by the range of their direct contacts. The accessibility of communication channels now widens the horizon of each person; we not only know about events that take place thousands of miles away, but often take them into account in making our decisions.

Extensive studies have been conducted on the manner in which audiences respond to various mass media programs. One of the significant findings is that most people experience the programs as a succession of transactions with personifications. People who read a human interest story in the newspaper or a novel participate vicariously in the plot that is being described. They tend to see international affairs as contests between key political figures—prime ministers, presidents, and dictators. The extent to which people identify with such personifications is indicated by the spontaneous response to the troubles faced by characters in daytime serials; radio and television stations are swamped with suggested solutions from sympathetic listeners. When Joe Palooka was married, many people sent wedding gifts to the cartoonist; in the winter of 1956, when Charlie Brown complained that he had not received a single Christmas card, newspapers carrying the comic strip were inundated with messages of cheer. General Mills has long had a fictional home economist named "Betty Crocker" giving advice to housewives. Most people who write to her apparently do not realize that she is the product of the imagination of one of the corporation's executives. One of the essential features of primary relations is empathy, and in modern societies millions of people participate vicariously in the lives of the characters they encounter on the media of mass communication and react to them in much the same manner as they react to real people. Actors are often stopped in the street by strangers who call them by their first name and act as if they were old friends.[3]

[3] Cf. Donald Horton and Richard Wohl, "Mass Communication and Para-Social Interaction," *Psychiatry*, XIX (1956), 215-29; W. Lloyd Warner and

There are indications that tastes and standards of conduct are formed through vicarious participation in such transactions. Most Americans have a remarkable faith in romantic love as the only important basis for a happy marriage. Similarity of interests or of background is regarded as being of secondary significance. In spite of the high divorce rate, Americans continue to believe in "love at first sight," and the content of American motion pictures may help account for the persistence of this belief. Wolfenstein and Leites made a comparative study of "chance encounters" in American and French movies and discovered that in approximately two-thirds of the American films the boy meets the girl by accident. Indeed, one-third of the cases are "pickups," but there is no loss of status for either party. The two introduce themselves and go merrily through their adventures. The dangers of sexual exploitation are denied, and in spite of the questionable circumstances in which the action often takes place, both characters turn out to be people of remarkable integrity. In the end they come together to live happily ever after. In contrast to this familiar pattern, such casual meetings are not only rare in French films but almost invariably lead to danger, disgrace, or death. In most films with happy endings, the boy meets the girl in some conventional setting, often through mutual friends. The authors point out that these films reflect and reinforce the accepted values of American and French life.[4] At the same time, constant participation in such imagery reaffirms conceptions and crystallizes dispositions that would otherwise remain vague. Studies such as these suggest that the one-sided primary relations play a far more important part in socialization than had been supposed.

One of the consequences of the extension of perspectives and the pluralism of mass societies is the declining influence of local groups as exclusive agencies of social control. Each person is able to develop some measure of detachment from those with whom he is in direct contact. Those who are concerned with "keeping up with the times" may even defy the people with whom they live. This does not mean that there are fewer primary groups, nor that such inti-

William E. Henry, "The Radio Daytime Serial: A Symbolic Analysis," *Genetic Psychology Monographs*, XXXVII (1948), 3–71.

[4] Martha Wolfenstein and Nathan Leites, "Analysis of Themes and Plots," *Annals of the American Academy of Political and Social Science*, CCLIV (November, 1947), 41–48.

mate circles are no longer important. But a person whose interests clash with those of his immediate associates can turn elsewhere for support.

Men in mass societies often find themselves involuntary participants in gigantic transactions in which personal choice is minimized. People are swept along in patriotic fervor, in war, in inflation, or in fashion movements. There is little that a dissenting individual can do. During the height of "McCarthyism," for example, anyone who questioned the tactics of the senator was suspected of being a Communist and thereby immobilized. Choices are often limited. In politics the issues and candidates on which an individual can express himself are already preselected; in many instances he can vote only for what he considers the lesser of evils. When war is declared, it does not matter whether a citizen feels that his country's cause is just or unjust; he is expected to do his share. Even in a more stable setting, those who are employed in large corporations must follow standard procedures, even when they are personally convinced that some of them are idiotic.

A good example of the type of social control that characterizes mass societies is the fashion movement. Fashions are by no means limited to women's clothing but can be found in art, architecture, literature, philosophy, and even in the social sciences. These movements apparently take shape through the convergence of selections made by large numbers of people. Thousands of women individually try to make themselves attractive, and the convergence of their purchases creates a movement. Similarly, a large number of people find some currently available song enjoyable, and the convergence of their record purchases and requests to "disc jockeys" makes the tune popular. As many women who have resisted new styles have discovered, it is almost useless to fight. In a political revolution there is someone representing the government who can be identified as the foe, but in a fashion movement there is no one to attack. Dissenters are left with a sense of impotence, for resistance is futile. Whereas the violation of conventional norms leads to indignation and punishment, the violation of fashion trends elicits amusement and pity. The dissenter is made to feel ridiculous; by refusing to comply she hurts herself but not the fashion. Once the trend is set, women make necessary additions to their wardrobes. This has led to the widespread suspicion that there must be a gigantic conspiracy in the garment industry, but there is considerable evidence that this is not the case.[5] Each person is free not to conform, but only a few defy the trends. By conforming, each person inadvertently contributes to the movement.

Generals, key government officials, those who actually control political parties, corporation executives, and labor leaders wield enormous power. Their whims, predilections, or personal defenses can affect the lives of millions or the destiny of nations. They wield such power only because they exercise legitimate authority, which rests upon consensus. Democratization is another characteristic of mass societies. As Mannheim pointed out, ours is a society in which very large numbers of ordinary people intervene in the political process in a manner that was unheard of in other societies. Politics is no longer the exclusive domain of elite groups. Legitimate authority requires the support or at least the acquiescence of large numbers of people. Even dictators are limited by what people will tolerate. This means that the men who control communication channels are in an especially advantageous position.[6]

Basically, social control in a mass society is much like social control in smaller communities. The key difference is that the audience before which men seek status is considerably larger and somewhat more impersonal. For example, many keep up with changes in fashions because they do not want "people" to laugh at them. But who are these "people"? Most of them are strangers. Men are to some extent released from the control of their primary groups, but they are still confronted by group expectations. Many of these reference groups, however, are large, amorphous, and constantly undergoing change.

As in all other societies, men still form and reaffirm their perspectives and self-conceptions through communication. One difference is that the ease and range of communication has made it possible for people to participate vicariously in the lives of many they do not meet directly. The importance of personifications encountered in the media of mass communication is not to be underestimated. One's

[5] Cf. Blumer, "Collective Behavior," *op. cit.*, pp. 185–89, 216–18; Neil H. Borden, *The Economic Effects of Advertising* (Chicago: Richard D. Irwin, 1947); and Paul Nystrom, *The Economics of Fashion* (New York: Ronald Press Co., 1928).

[6] Karl Mannheim, *Man and Society in an Age of Reconstruction*, E. Shils, trans. (New York: Harcourt, Brace & Co., 1940), pp. 44–49.

choice of career lines, taste in clothing, or preference for companions may rest upon values imputed to popular heroes. As in primary groups, people impute expectations to personifications and then try to live up to them. The social world of modern man is larger, but the process of self-control remains the same.

Although the vast majority of the contacts among men who live in urban communities are categorical, human beings are fundamentally the same. Primary groups still flourish everywhere, and the sentiments have not changed. Men still love and hate; they are jealous and resentful. This is revealed in the spontaneous responses of ordinary people to the various personal crises reported in human interest stories. When some unfortunate family is unjustly deprived of housing, strangers by the hundreds volunteer to help. Anyone who has followed a blind beggar can testify to the sympathy of people, even in an impersonal metropolis. Contacts are not readily established in large cities; most people keep up their guards. But once the outer shell is penetrated by some dramatic event, the apparent callousness disappears, and people respond sentimentally. The average man may be bewildered and misinformed, but he fights for what he thinks is worthwhile. Of course, there are some people who are so egocentric that they do not care about anyone but themselves, but such individuals can be found anywhere. Even a mass society is a moral order; men still judge themselves and one another in terms of the standards of conduct learned in primary groups. Social control is complicated by the life conditions encountered in mass societies, but the basic processes are not altered.

Social Control of Intellectual Activity

It appears that, in the future, social psychologists will continue to be confronted by demands for more reliable knowledge. Social workers, psychiatrists, penologists, and even statesmen are making increasing use of the social sciences, although they must still rely primarily upon intuitive "rule of thumb" judgments. Administrators are beginning to realize that large organizations, in spite of their generally impersonal atmosphere, run more smoothly when the employees are recognized as human beings. Since their clientele and public also consist of people, increasing knowledge about human behavior could greatly facilitate all operations. Every changing society has its reformers; many of them are visionary, but they nonetheless wrestle with very real problems. They also need more reliable knowledge to plan their strategies. In these activities there is an obvious discrepancy between what might be done and what is actually accomplished, and this leaves the practitioners with a gnawing sense of incompleteness. Their very receptivity to the inferior materials provided them thus far is an indication of their desperation. All of the social sciences will be tapped, and social psychology will no doubt play an important part. These disciplines will continue to develop because of the increasing need for such knowledge in our complex and ever changing society.

Students of human behavior are expected to respond to this challenge as scientists. The model of ideal conduct for the scientist is fairly well defined; there is a long tradition of selfless dedication to the quest of knowledge for the welfare of humanity. But the spirit in which most social psychologists are working today is an embarrassing contrast to that of Pasteur, who struggled against the famous medical men of his time, of Fabre, who lived in poverty while relentlessly pursuing his research, or of the Curies, who worked without laboratory assistants under incredibly primitive conditions. Many idealistic students entering the field are quickly disillusioned. Some reorient themselves to pursue one of the conventional career lines; others drop out to pursue their humanitarian interests elsewhere. This is true not only of social psychology but of the other social sciences as well. Before condemning these men too severely, it should be remembered that they are human beings and subject to social control. To the extent that the generalizations developed in this book are true, they apply to social psychologists as well as to other people. The ideal of the dedicated scientist is learned as a participant in society. The fact that research is carried on by men who are subject to the kind of social control prevailing in our society both aids and hampers their efforts to develop reliable knowledge.

Especially in the United States, research in social psychology is being carried out increasingly in corporate settings. Social psychologists are employed in organizations with large staffs that are supported by large grants—universities, government research institutes, industrial firms, and hospitals. Each organization has a bureaucratic structure, and the participants are bound by its norms. The advantages should not be minimized. Large-scale research makes possible the use of superior facilities, expensive equipment, a high degree of specialization, and freedom from financial worries. Many complex problems cannot be pursued effectively by the solitary scholar. On the other hand, there are many disadvantages. The most important is that creative minds are forced to operate within a bureaucratic framework, and the interests of corporations do not always foster the advancement of knowledge. The reputation of an organization in the community is important for raising funds, and administrators tend to emphasize interests that are likely to improve public relations—the hiring of a staff with a high percentage of doctorates, the production of a large number of publications, and the execution of spectacular studies easily appreciated by the uninitiated. Sometimes high standards of performance are compromised in the interests of harmony. The most competent men in each field tend to be promoted to administrative posts, where they are tempted to spend many of their most productive years doing routine work. Career lines are defined with increasing clarity, and promotions are based upon many considerations other than the quality of one's work. However competent he may be, an individualist who does not "get along" with others is often left behind.[7] This does not mean that the majority of scholars and scientists are any less sincere in their quest for knowledge, but they are handicapped by the pressures under which they work. Under the circumstances it is remarkable that so much work of high quality is produced.

The world of social psychologists is held together by fairly efficient communication channels—specialized journals, meetings of professional societies, and personal contacts. Social psychologists strive to preserve or enhance their status before an audience made up largely of their fellow specialists and professional colleagues in adjacent fields. Among them the greatest prestige usually goes to those who are employed in large and famous organizations. Mature scholars and ambitious young men alike move from one position to another as they struggle upward in the status hierarchy. Especially in large universities, promotions are based primarily upon one's publication record; all too often the stress is upon quantity rather than quality. It is not strange that so many young scholars become preoccupied

[7] Cf. William H. Whyte, Jr., *The Organization Man* (New York: Doubleday & Co., 1957), pp. 225-65.

with publishing their material, whether or not it adds anything to knowledge.[8] But specialists also evaluate one another in terms of the caliber of their work. Men who achieve high rank in a well known organization—a dean of a university or a director of a government institute—are sometimes disdained by their colleagues. Often the men most respected by their peers are unknown to outsiders.

The theoretical schemes and investigative procedures that become widely accepted are those advocated by the men with the greatest prestige. Research funds are often allocated by cliques of men from the staffs of well known organizations who serve as consultants to various grant-dispensing agencies. It is not strange, then, that various fields of study are periodically upset by a struggle for power among those who represent divergent approaches. What begins as an attempt to defend a particular intellectual orientation sometimes degenerates into a personal brawl in which the intellectual objectives are all but forgotten. In universities, graduate students are sometimes immunized against the literature of rival schools of thought and then sent out to smaller colleges to preach a particular standpoint. Since untested newcomers in a profession are usually placed in their first position through the sponsorship of professors, the student is in their debt. The younger men in turn send their best students to their old professors for advanced training. An ambitious man's influence may be extended even further when he gains control over publication outlets—by becoming the editor of a key journal or a consultant for a publisher. Those who occupy key positions in highly esteemed organizations exercise disproportionate influence over the development of their field, and some of them have built intellectual empires. Sometimes this can result in considerable damage. If the convictions of an influential scholar should turn out to be badly mistaken, it is conceivable that his engaging personality and political skill may set back his field for fifty years.

As in many other circles made up of ambitious men, the various intellectual worlds are often split into factions. Sometimes the differences are debated openly in a series of dignified critiques, but consideration of alternative hypotheses, especially where the evidence is not clear, often degenerates into vindictive personal quarrels. Sometimes these spectacles constitute nothing more than

[8] Cf. Caplow and McGee, *op. cit.,* pp. 81–93; and L. Wilson, *op. cit.,* pp. 175–214.

struggles for personal power. The famous physiologist Cannon, writing in retrospect of his life work, pointed to the carping criticism his theories encountered. He did not mind the fact that other scientists disagreed with him as much as the highly personal manner in which the attacks were made. Often the critiques were delivered with an air of contempt, suggesting that the opponent was stupid.[9] The sadistic criticism of views that differ from those which prevail among the leaders of a field often results in widespread conformity, especially among younger academicians. Those who advocate unorthodox theories are subjected to negative social sanctions, much like heretics in the religious world. Since many of the revolutionary discoveries are made by men whose views are unorthodox, this conduct is harmful. But innovators are deviants, and like deviants anywhere they face the opposition of those who have a vested interest in the *status quo*. They find it difficult to publish their works, to get funds for their research, or to place their students and assistants in desirable positions. All this merely signifies that social psychologists are human, but a wider recognition of the dangers of such practices may result in their eventually being brought under better control—perhaps through a code of professional ethics.

Among the many controversies among social psychologists today the question of measurement stands out as a central issue. The quest for recognition has resulted in the uncritical imitation of procedures that enjoy prestige in other fields, even though they have not proved especially productive in the study of human behavior. Some place great emphasis upon accurate measurement, even to the point of insisting that whatever cannot be measured should not be studied. No one can argue with the desirability of accurate observation, but where the concepts are so inadequate, precise measuring devices can be applied only to very limited aspects of human experience, such as differential responses to colors. In many universities there is a bifurcation of academic departments into theorists and empiricists, who not only disagree but in many cases cannot even understand one another. Theory, when unrestrained by the sobering influence of facts, tends to run wild. It becomes esoteric, refined, and so complex that it cannot be tested through available techniques. Empirical research, when unrelated to theory, tends to be addressed to trivial

[9] Walter B. Cannon, *The Way of an Investigator* (New York: W. W. Norton & Co., 1945), pp. 97–107.

problems. Technically refined investigations based upon common sense assumptions and popular concepts produce results that are unrelated to the more speculative inquiries. In the heat of argument, both parties often forget that, in a field as new as social psychology, no one can know with certainty the road to salvation.

Many social psychologists feel that more exploratory research is needed, but this type of study has been discouraged. This difficulty is one that all of the social sciences have in common. Reichenbach has pointed to the difference between the "context of discovery" and the "context of justification," and has noted that what is commonly called "scientific method" is used only in the latter setting, to test hypotheses that have already been formulated.[10] Many social scientists seem to be unaware of this distinction. Those who are intent upon copying the physical sciences overlook the fact that physicists can rely so heavily upon experimental designs today because of the foundations established by the patient, ground-breaking observations of past centuries. As Francis Bacon pointed out so long ago, during the early phases of any discipline it is necessary for an investigator to concern himself with classifications and natural histories.[11] Some social psychologists are contemptuous of such work, but can this step actually be skipped? For example, attempts have been made to do experimental studies on anti-Semitism, but "anti-Semitism" is a popular category formed on the basis of superficial similarities. It includes any hostility against Jews, and such acts may take many different forms. Furthermore, the same type of acts may be directed against other categories of people. To inquire into the "causes" of anti-Semitism is to ask a meaningless question. Hostility against Jews may develop in many different kinds of transactions, and until these are more adequately classified, useful generalizations can neither be formulated nor tested. The intensive analysis of case studies, small-scale experiments to test hunches, and the successive refinement of concepts are all essential steps in the development of reliable knowledge. Such studies are rarely conducted, for they are not rewarded. Sociologists who have suggested such inductive procedures have been ignored.[12]

[10] Hans Reichenbach, *The Rise of Scientific Philosophy* (Berkeley: University of California Press, 1951), pp. 229–33.

[11] Filmer S. C. Northrop, *The Logic of the Sciences and the Humanities* (New York: Macmillan Co., 1947), pp. 35–58.

[12] Cf. Angell, *op. cit.*, pp. 265–307; and Florian Znaniecki, *The Method of Sociology* (New York: Farrar & Rinehart, 1934), pp. 249–319.

It would seem reasonable to suppose that the social psychologist with an intimate familiarity with human life is most likely to formulate useful hypotheses. It is amazing, therefore, that the acquisition of this type of knowledge is often opposed, although it is painstakingly cultivated by artists and writers. Some have charged that the humanities are a part of the "unscientific" past that is to be escaped, presumably because many judgments are necessarily intuitive and inexact. But because so many social psychologists are not acquainted with the life patterns of a wide variety of people, they sometimes display incredible naïveté and ethnocentrism in their experimental studies, going to considerable trouble to control variables that are irrelevant. Psychiatrists are especially guilty of using their personal values, usually the standards of the American middle class, as absolute criteria, and condemning those who fail to conform as defective, evil, or maladjusted. One of the most economical ways of acquiring such knowledge is through the extensive reading of *personal documents*—autobiographies, diaries, letters, and confessions—in which individuals reveal their inner experiences. These materials not only reveal the similarities in the thought processes and emotional reactions of men throughout the world, but also the fantastic diversity of conventional meanings. Many difficulties arise when such documents are used in systematic research, but in spite of these limitations clinical psychologists have found them indispensable. These accounts may also be useful in giving students some familiarity with the inner experiences of many different types of people, thereby providing them with a sounder foundation for the countless judgments they will have to make as they move on to more exact research procedures.[13] Although experimental psychologists have objected to such materials on the grounds that they are subjective, what is needed is not so much the elimination of subjectivity as the development of intersubjectivity.

These controversies, sometimes carried on with great bitterness, actually settle nothing and tend to impede progress. Since knowledge is used as an instrument in adjustment, the products of intellec-

[13] Cf. Gordon W. Allport, *The Use of Personal Documents in Psychological Science* (New York: Social Science Research Council, 1942); Bernard Berelson, "The Quantitative Analysis of Case Records," *Psychiatry*, X (1947), 395–403; Louis Gottschalk, Clyde Kluckhohn, and Robert Angell, *The Use of Personal Documents in History, Anthropology, and Sociology* (New York: Social Science Research Council, 1945); and Siegfried Kracauer, "The Challenge of Qualitative Content Analysis," *Public Opinion Quarterly*, XVI (1952), 631–42.

tual activity are subject to reality testing. Whatever does not pass the acid test of utility is eventually discarded. Various schools of psychiatrists frequently battle among themselves over minor points of doctrine, but if the number of hospitalized mental patients does not begin to drop in the near future, impatient demands for a drastically different approach will probably arise. Many approaches to social psychology have survived up to this point primarily because no occasions have arisen for a clear-cut test of their key propositions. Scholars who become involved in struggles for power seem to forget that *the truth or falsity of generalizations rests upon evidence, not upon the prestige of those who sponsor them*. It is obvious that the existing knowledge of human behavior is hardly adequate for handling the numerous problems that we face; much of the work that is currently accepted will eventually be replaced with something better.

Like most scholars and scientists of our day, social psychologists are hampered by the bureaucratic setting in which they work, but the long range outlook for the discipline is optimistic. There are temptations and pressures that are distracting; too many acts are directed through motives other than the advancement of knowledge. Factional quarrels are disconcerting. But other fields have also been plagued by such difficulties, especially during their formative years, when it was still difficult to put the competing views to a decisive test. Various national academies have been dominated by strong men who managed to suppress rival approaches. But one by one the mistaken hypotheses have been exposed and dismissed. Scientific knowledge develops through a process of natural selection, and utility is the key selective factor. Although some superstitions are remarkably tenacious, in the long run a generalization cannot survive unless it can stand the test of evidence.

Knowledge and Social Engineering

Scientific knowledge enjoys an esteemed position in our society because of the many benefits that have been derived from it. The social sciences are receiving encouragement on the assumption that its products can be used for the construction of a better world, one with less strife and frustration and greater possibilities of fulfilment. Most scientists and educators take it for granted that scientific research is desirable. The more adequate the knowledge, the more effective it becomes as a tool for the betterment of mankind. This belief is accepted on faith, and many are shaken to discover that it is not necessarily true.

Knowledge is a source of power, for knowledge facilitates control. A person who understands how something works can manipulate some of the conditions so that the course of events can be redirected to his benefit. Knowledge is generally used to implement the values accepted in a society. Even the meager findings of the social sciences have been used to reduce graft and corruption in government, to improve health through preventive medicine, to increase the productive capacity of factories, to improve morale in the armed forces, to educate citizens to new areas of knowledge, and to develop more reliable procedures for processing prisoners for parole.

In pluralistic societies, however, arguments sometimes arise over whose values are to be implemented. Social reform proves inconvenient for those who had been profiting from the old arrangements, and social scientists have been attacked by those with vested interests. Unfortunately, the social sciences are especially vulnerable. Almost everyone is against disease, but not everyone is in favor of social change. Attempts are made from time to time to suppress "dangerous thoughts."

All knowledge is ethically neutral. In itself it is neither good nor bad, for it can be used in many ways. Just as the development of nuclear physics has led to the production of devastating bombs as well as new sources of energy, knowledge about human behavior could be used to facilitate exploitation as well as to further the welfare of mankind. An understanding of human behavior can be used by management to exploit its labor force or by a dictator to eliminate resistance to his policies. Some colonial governments have used the latest developments in political science to suppress recalcitrant natives, and some social scientists have used their learning to advance their personal interests within the university community. Precisely because of the possibilities of exploitation, the problem of the development of knowledge cannot be separated from considerations of political power and moral standards.

To some extent the issue has already arisen. Since success in politics or business in a mass society rests upon widespread public support, many attempts have been made to manipulate people through appeals over the media of mass communication. There has been much concern over the possibility that the exploitation of people through advertising and propaganda might be rendered more effective if too much is known about human nature. It is contended that people are being deceived into purchasing objects they do not need through subliminal suggestion and other tricks based upon recent research. Many of the charges are exaggerated. It is to the advantage of the advertising industry to create the impression that it possesses "scientifiic" knowledge which enables it to manipulate behavior. If advertisers can persuade their clients that this is the case, they can certainly increase their own profits, if not those of their customers. There is little doubt that many advertising campaigns have been very successful, but whether the success resulted from verified knowledge or from the intuitive hunches of a clever executive is a matter of conjecture. Some of the claims that have been made presuppose systematic knowledge that does not even exist! Many skillful propagandists have developed their techniques through trial and error; frequently, what they do is effective for reasons they do not understand. But the potentialities for exploitation are ever present. We cannot ignore the possibility that with the development of reliable knowledge some of the wild claims of today may eventually become true. Publicists are apparently far more alert to new developments in social psychology than are reformers or government officials.

Although there appears to be no immediate danger, further progress in social psychology may render imperative the institution of safeguards against domination by ambitious individuals, elite groups, or tyrannical majorities. The more adequate the knowledge, the more dangerous it can become as a weapon. The continued development of all the social sciences, unless accompanied by concern for moral standards, can conceivably result in disaster.

But can there be consensus in a pluralistic society on moral standards? Most Americans share certain basic values to a greater extent than they realize. For example, people in other countries are periodically amazed to learn that the U.S. Navy had sent a plane to remove a critically injured crewman from a ship at sea to a base hospital. Such operations not only involve considerable expense to the American taxpayers, but risks to the lives of aviators and medical personnel. Other people can understand doing this for an admiral, but they are puzzled that it is done to save the life of an ordinary seaman who can easily be replaced. In the United States, disclosure that the Navy had failed to do this for a sailor could result in mass protests, and possibly a Congressional investigation. What is implicit in such an operation is the principle that each individual, regardless of his social status, is an object of value. When stated as an abstract principle many Americans find it "corny," but they live from day to day on the basis of this principle. A poor housewife whose dress had been splashed by a passing limousine does not hesitate to protest loudly against the wealthy owner, nor does the average citizen hesitate to demand his rights when he feels that he has been arrested unfairly. This moral principle is taken so much for granted in American life that we are not even aware of it.

Many have asked whether superior moral values can be established through the scientific study of human conduct. This is an issue over which philosophers have long disagreed. Standards of conduct are products of collective adjustments. But can rational controls be instituted by those who are familiar with the process? Social psychologists can show that all societies are moral orders; anthropologists can describe the values shared in a given society; sociologists can show what happens when consensus breaks down; and psychiatrists can show what happens to people who are immoral or amoral. But can such knowledge tell us what men *ought* to do? A better comprehension of human life can narrow down the area of uncertainty by revealing what kinds of acts are harmful in the long run, but even deciding what is "harmful" and what is not implies an external standard. There are many ramifications, and the question remains unanswered.

Although the continuing development of social psychology may conceivably place powerful weapons in the hands of the unscrupulous, we cannot afford to declare a moratorium upon research until absolute safeguards are established. There is little doubt that many personal and social problems with which we are currently troubled will be eliminated with increasing understanding. Ways may be found for curing or preventing serious mental aberrations. There is even the possibility that more equitable ways of settling disputes can be developed. The potential utility of a reliable social psychology is too great. We continue on the faith that with an increasing understanding of themselves, men will learn to live more intelligently and in peace.

Summary and Conclusion

Although the structure of organized groups has been altered considerably in the efforts of men to adapt to recent technological advances, human nature apparently has not changed. Men still grow up in primary groups, form the same sentiments, and control themselves as they always have. One significant change in modern times, however, is the development of mass societies in which people participate in gigantic transactions. This provides unprecedented opportunities for manipulation and exploitation. At the same time, developments in the physical sciences have made weapons so destructive that finding more equitable ways of settling disputes is becoming imperative. Ironically, the development of the kind of knowledge that makes possible more intelligent social engineering also increases the possibilities of exploitation. The growth of social psychology is both facilitated and hampered by the fact that social psychologists are subject to the type of social control prevailing in mass societies. In the last analysis, the major issues that men will face are moral, and perhaps a better understanding of human nature will facilitate a more rational solution to such difficulties.

Social psychology is still in its infancy, and it will be a long time before knowledge comparable to the physical and biological sciences today will become available. Whatever is developed should prove to be of immense value even in the age of atomic power and space travel. Should men succeed in escaping the gravitation of the earth, they will no doubt move forward in the same daring and courage of the pioneers of the past. Should they fight for the various planets, it will probably be for the same senseless reasons for which wars have been fought on earth for thousands of years. The human spirit, so well depicted by Balzac, da Cunha, Euripides, and Lady Murasaki, will probably be easy to recognize. Perhaps even after the conquest of outer space men will still be wondering about themselves and the many strange things that they do, confirming the ancient adage that to man the greatest mystery of mysteries is man.

Suggested References

BARBER, BERNARD, *Science and the Social Order.* Glencoe: Free Press, 1952. A study of scientific research, especially in the United States, with emphasis upon the social structure of the organizations in which it takes place.

MANNHEIM, KARL, *Man and Society in an Age of Reconstruction,* Edward Shils, trans. New York: Harcourt, Brace & Co., 1940. An insightful analysis of the characteristics of modern mass societies and of the place of intellectuals in them.

MILLS, C. WRIGHT, *The Sociological Imagination.* New York: Oxford University Press, 1959. A harsh critique of American sociology, pointing to the failure of sociologists to study problems related to the practical difficulties now confronting mankind.

WHYTE, WILLIAM H., JR., *The Organization Man.* New York: Doubleday & Co., 1957. A study of the social structure of large corporations and of the type of person who is likely to survive and prosper in them, with an account of the fate of scientists in such settings.

WILSON, LOGAN, *The Academic Man.* London: Oxford University Press, 1942. A sociological study of the academic world, describing the status hierarchy and the channels of upward social mobility.

WIRTH, LOUIS, *Community Life and Social Policy,* E. W. Marvick and A. J. Reiss, eds. Chicago: University of Chicago Press, 1956. Selected essays on the characteristics of mass societies, the typical problems that emerge in them, and the difficulties confronting those who plan for a better future.

APPENDIX List of personal documents

ABRAHAMS, PETER, *Tell Freedom: Memories of Africa.* New York: Alfred A. Knopf, 1956. A Cape-Coloured novelist's account of his childhood in the slums of Johannesburg.

ADLER, POLLY, *A House Is Not a Home.* New York: Rinehart & Co., 1953. Autobiography of a brothel-keeper.

BARRY, HENRY M., *I'll Be Seeing You.* New York: Alfred A. Knopf, 1952. Adjustment to life without sight by a soldier blinded in combat.

BEERS, CLIFFORD W., *A Mind that Found Itself.* New York: Doubleday, Doran & Co., 1921. Retrospective account of mental illness.

BELMONTE, JUAN, *Juan Belmonte: Killer of Bulls,* Manuel C. Nogales and Leslie Charteris, ed. New York: Doubleday & Co., 1937. Autobiography of a matador.

BENNEY, MARK, *Angels in Undress.* New York: Random House, Inc., 1937. An educator's account of his childhood in the slums of London.

BERLIOZ, HECTOR, *Memoirs of Hector Berlioz from 1803 to 1865,* Rachel and Eleanor Holmes and Ernest Newman, trans. New York: Alfred A. Knopf, 1932. Autobiography of a tempestuous composer.

BOTTOME, PHYLLIS, *Search for a Soul.* New York: Harcourt, Brace & Co., 1948. Childhood memories of a novelist and student of psychoanalysis.

BYRD, RICHARD E., *Alone.* New York: G. P. Putnam's Sons, 1938. Account of five months of isolation at the South Pole.

CATHARINE II, *The Memoirs of Catharine the Great,* Dominique Maroger, ed., and Moura Budberg, trans. London: H. Hamilton, 1955. Autobiography of an 18th century empress of Russia.

CELLINI, BENVENUTO, *The Autobiography of Benvenuto Cellini,* John A. Symonds, trans. New York: Garden City Publishing Co., 1927. Adventures of a Renaissance sculptor.

CHAPLIN, RALPH, *Wobbly.* Chicago: University of Chicago Press, 1948. Autobiography of an early American labor leader.

CHAUDHURI, NIRAD C., *The Autobiography of an Unknown Indian.* New York: The Macmillan Co., 1951. Village and city life in modern India.

CLEMENS, SAMUEL, *The Autobiography of Mark Twain,* Charles Neider, ed. New York: Harper & Bros., 1959.

CUSTANCE, JOHN, *Wisdom, Madness, and Folly.* New York: Pellegrini & Cudahy, 1952. Retrospective account of manic-depressive psychosis.

DUROCHER, LEO, *The Dodgers and Me.* Chicago: Ziff-Davis Publishing Co., 1948. A colorful manager's account of major league baseball.

DYK, WALTER, ed., *Son of Old Man Hat: A Navaho Autobiography.* New York: Harcourt, Brace & Co., 1938.

FINK, HAROLD K., ed., *Long Journey.* New York: The Julian Press, 1954. Verbatim report on the psychoanalysis of a Mexican-American.

FORD, CLELLAN S., ed., *Smoke from Their Fires: The Life of a Kwakiutl Chief.* New Haven: Yale University Press, 1941.

FOREL, AUGUSTE H., *Out of My Life and Work,* Bernard Miall, trans. New York: W. W. Norton & Co., 1937. Autobiography of a Swiss biologist.

FRANK, ANNE, *The Diary of a Young Girl,* B. M. Mooyaart-Doubleday, trans. New York: Doubleday & Co., 1952. Moving account of a Jewish family hiding from Nazi persecution.

FREDERICS, DIANA, *Diana: A Strange Autobiography.* New York: The Citadel Press, 1954. Self-revelations of a homosexual.

FREUD, SIGMUND, *The Origins of Psychoanalysis: Letters to Wilhelm Fliess,* Marie Bonaparte, Anna Freud, and Ernst Kris, eds. New York: Basic Books, Inc., 1954. Freud's letters during the period of his most important discoveries.

GLASGOW, ELLEN A. G., *The Woman Within.* New York: Harcourt, Brace & Co., 1954. Autobiography of a novelist.

GOGH, VINCENT VAN, *Dear Theo: The Autobiography of Vincent van Gogh,* Irving and Jean Stone, eds. New York: Doubleday & Co., 1946. Letters from a tormented artist to his brother.

GUNTEKIN, RESAT N., *The Autobiography of a Turkish Girl,* Wyndham Deedes, trans. London: G. Allen & Unwin, 1949.

HAVOC, JUNE, *Early Havoc.* New York: Simon & Schuster, 1959. Autobiography of an actress.

HITTI, PHILIP K., ed., *An Arab-Syrian Gentleman and Warrior in the Period of the Crusades.* New York: Columbia University Press, 1929. A Moslem view of the crusades.

HSIEH, PINGYING, *Girl Rebel,* Adet and Anor Lin, trans. New York: John Day Co., 1940. Autobiography of a Chinese girl.

KELLER, HELEN, *The Story of My Life.* New York: Doubleday, Page & Co., 1915. Adjustment to a life of deafness and blindness.

KNIGHT, JOHN, *The Story of My Psychoanalysis.* New York: McGraw-Hill Book Co., 1950. Retrospective account of an American Jewish scientist.

KOESTLER, ARTHUR, *The Invisible Writing.* New York: The Macmillan Co., 1954. Autobiography of a disillusioned ex-Communist writer.

LAYE, CAMARA, *The Dark Child,* James Kirkup, Ernest Jones, Elaine Gottlieb, trans. New York: Noonday Press, 1954. Memories of childhood in French Guinea.

LINDNER, ROBERT M., *Rebel without a Cause: The Hypnoanalysis of a Criminal Psychopath.* New York: Grune & Stratton, 1944.

MARBLE, ALICE, *The Road to Wimbledon.* New York: Charles Scribner's Sons, 1946. Autobiography of a tennis star.

MARTIN, JOHN B., ed., *My Life in Crime: The Autobiography of a Professional Criminal.* New York: Harper & Bros., 1952.

PANUNZIO, CONSTANTINE M., *The Soul of an Immigrant.* New York: The Macmillan Co., 1921. Autobiography of a sociology professor.

QUINCY, THOMAS DE, *The Confessions of an English Opium-Eater.* New York: Three Sirens Press, 1932.

RADIN, PAUL, ed., *Crashing Thunder: Autobiography of an American Indian.* New York: Appleton & Co., 1926.

REYHER, REBECCA H., ed., *Zulu Woman.* New York: Columbia University Press, 1948. Autobiography of a Zulu housewife.

ROTH, LILLIAN, MIKE CONNOLLY, AND GEROLD FRANK, *I'll Cry Tomorrow.*

New York: Frederick Fell, Inc., 1954. A famous singer's account of her alcoholism and recovery.

ROUSSEAU, JEAN-JACQUES, *Confessions,* J. M. Cohen, trans. London: Penguin Books, 1953. Memoirs of a famous 18th century philosopher.

RUSS, MARTIN, *The Last Parallel: A Marine's War Journal.* New York: Rinehart & Co., 1957. Account of the Korean War.

SACHS, WULF, *Black Anger.* Boston: Little, Brown & Co., 1947. Autobiography of a South African witch doctor.

SANGER, MARGARET, *Margaret Sanger: An Autobiography.* New York: W. W. Norton & Co., 1938. Memoirs of one of the founders of the birth control movement.

SECHEHAYE, MARGUERITE, ed., *Autobiography of a Schizophrenic Girl,* Grace Rubin-Rabson, trans. New York: Grune & Stratton, 1951.

SLADE, CAROLINE, ed., *Sterile Sun.* New York Vanguard Press, 1936. Autobiography of a prostitute.

STERN, KARL, *The Pillar of Fire.* New York: Harcourt, Brace & Co., 1951. Conversion of a psychiatrist from Judaism to Catholicism.

SUGIMOTO, ETSU I., *A Daughter of the Samurai.* New York: Doubleday, Page & Co., 1927. Autobiography of a Japanese girl.

TALAYESVA, DON C., *Sun Chief: The Autobiography of a Hopi Indian,* Leo W. Simmons, ed. New Haven: Yale University Press, 1942.

TENZING, NORGAY AND JAMES R. ULLMAN, *Tiger of the Snows.* New York: G. P. Putnam's Sons, 1955. Memoirs of one of the conquerors of Mt. Everest.

TETTEMER, JOHN M., *I Was a Monk,* Janet Mabie, ed. New York: Alfred A. Knopf, 1951. Record of 25 years as a Catholic monk followed by defection.

WAKSMAN, SELMAN A., *My Life with the Microbes.* New York: Simon & Schuster, 1954. Autobiography of the discoverer of streptomycin.

WATERS, ETHEL AND CHARLES SAMUELS, *His Eye Is on the Sparrow.* New York: Doubleday & Co., 1951. Autobiography of a Negro actress and singer.

WOLFE, THOMAS, *The Letters of Thomas Wolfe,* Elizabeth Nowell, ed. New York: Charles Scribner's Sons, 1956. A novelist's letters to those who played a significant part in his life.

WONG, SU-LING AND EARL HERBERT CRESSY, *Daughter of Confucius: A Personal History.* New York: Farrar, Strauss, & Young, 1952. Life among the Chinese gentry before the Communist revolution.

WRIGHT, FRANK LLOYD, *An Autobiography.* New York: Duell, Sloan & Pearce, 1943. Memoirs of an innovator in American architecture.

WRIGHT, RICHARD, *Black Boy: A Record of Childhood and Youth.* New York: Harper & Bros., 1945. Recollections of an American Negro novelist.

YANG, TWAN, *Houseboy in India.* New York: John Day Co., 1945. A servant's view of various households in modern Indian.

YEN, LIANG, *Daughter of the Khans.* New York: W. W. Norton & Co., 1954. Autobiography of a Mongolian immigrant to the United States.

Subject Index

Name Index